Java™

software solutions

foundations of program design | 3rd edition

Java™
software solutions

foundations of program design | 3rd edition

JOHN LEWIS
Villanova University

WILLIAM LOFTUS
Gestalt, LLC

Addison
Wesley

Boston San Francisco New York
London Toronto Sydney Tokyo Singapore Madrid
Mexico City Munich Paris Cape Town Hong Kong Montreal

Executive Editor	Susan Hartman Sullivan
Project Editor	Emily Genaway
Executive Marketing Manager	Michael Hirsch
Associate Managing Editor	Pat Mahtani
Production Supervisor	Kim Ellwood
Project Management	Argosy Publishing
Copyeditor	Shannon Leuma
Proofreader	Kim Cofer
Composition and Art	Argosy Publishing
Interior and Cover Design	Joyce Cosentino Wells
Prepress and Manufacturing	Caroline Fell

Access the latest information about Addison-Wesley titles from our World Wide Web site: http://www.aw.com/computing

Many of the designations used by manufacturers and sellers to distinguish their products are claimed as trademarks. Where those designations appear in this book, and Addison-Wesley was aware of a trademark claim, the designations have been printed in initial caps or all caps.

The programs and applications presented in this book have been included for their instructional value. They have been tested with care, but are not guaranteed for any particular purpose. The publisher does not offer any warranties or representations, nor does it accept any liabilities with respect to the programs or applications.

Library of Congress Cataloging-in-Publication Data

Lewis, John, Ph.D.

Java Software Solutions: Foundations of Program Design / by John Lewis and William Loftus. – 3rd ed.

p. cm.

ISBN 0-201-78129-8

1. Java (Computer program language) 3. Object-oriented programming (Computer science). I. Loftus, William.
III. Title

QA76.73.J38 L49 2003

005.13'3—dc21

2002071697

CIP

ISBN 0-321-19719-4

12345678910-QWT-06050403

This book is dedicated to our families.
Sharon, Justin, and Kayla Lewis
and
Veena, Isaac, and Dévi Loftus

Welcome to the Third Edition of Java Software Solutions, Foundations of Program Design. We are pleased that this book has served the needs of so many students and faculty over the years. This edition is designed to further enhance the pedagogy of introductory computing.

what's new in the third edition

The overall flow of the book has not changed significantly from that of the second edition. We embraced the feedback we've gotten from you over the years and specifically adopted a policy of "Don't fix it if it's not broke." Topics are covered in generally the same order and the emphasis remains on underlying core concepts. The Graphics Track sections in each chapter still segregate the coverage of graphics and graphical user interfaces. The casual writing style and entertaining examples still rule the day.

The changes made for this edition are designed to permeate and reinforce the pedagogy of the material. Specifically:

- The discussions and examples fully embrace the Java 2 Version 1.4 Standard Edition, and are backward compatible with previous versions.

- We now use a full color design, making it easier to distinguish between various elements in code and diagrams. Full color screen shots make the discussions of graphical user interfaces more insightful and realistic.

- Programming examples have been added and improved. These include both code fragments and full program listings.

- The coverage of specific topics such as object serialization and graphical user interfaces is enhanced.

- The Self-Review Questions, Exercises, and Programming Projects found at the end of the chapters have been greatly improved. Over 50% more of this material is included.

- We use the Unified Modeling Language to present and illustrate program designs throughout the book.

- The details of "real" Java keyboard I/O are covered earlier in the book, though we still rely on the helpful abstraction of the Keyboard class to simplify the process.

- The reference material in the appendices (particularly the Class Library reference in Appendix M) has been updated.

- A whole suite of new and improved supplements is available with this edition. The supplements are discussed in detail later in the preface.

cornerstones of the text

This text is based on the following basic ideas that we believe make for a sound introductory text.

▸ **True object-orientation.** A text that really teaches a solid object-oriented approach must use what we call object-speak. That is, all processing should be discussed in object-oriented terms. That does not mean, however, that the first program a student sees must discuss the writing of multiple classes and methods. A student should learn to use objects before learning to write them. This text uses a natural progression that culminates in the ability to design real object-oriented solutions.

▸ **Sound programming practices.** Students should not be taught how to program; they should be taught how to write good software. There's a difference. Writing software is not a set of cookbook actions, and a good program is more than a collection of statements. This text integrates practices that serve as the foundation of good programming skills. These practices are used in all examples and are reinforced in the discussions. Students learn how to solve problems as well as how to implement solutions. We introduce and integrate basic software engineering techniques throughout the text and devote a chapter to some more advanced software development activities.

▸ **Examples.** Students learn by example. This text is filled with fully-implemented examples that demonstrate specific concepts. We have intertwined small, readily understandable examples with larger, more realistic ones. There is a balance between graphics and nongraphical programs and between applets and applications. Additional examples can be found on the book's Web site.

▸ **Graphics and GUIs.** Graphics can be a great motivator for students, and their use can serve as excellent examples of object-orientation. As such, we use them throughout the text in a well-defined set of sections that we call the Graphics Track. This coverage includes the use of event processing and graphical user interfaces (GUIs). Students learn to build GUIs in the appropriate way by using a natural progression of topics. The Graphics Track can be avoided entirely for those who do not choose to use graphics.

paths through the text

This book is designed to be flexible, so that instructors can tailor its presentation to the needs of their students. Instructors can take a variety of paths through the text. The dependencies that exist between particular sections of the book are shown in the following figure. Other than these dependencies, an instructor can vary the coverage as needed. Graphics can be emphasized or deemphasized as desired.

chapter breakdown

Chapter 1 (Computer Systems) introduces computer systems in general, including basic architecture and hardware, networking, programming, and language translation. Java is introduced in this chapter, and the basics of program development are discussed. This chapter contains broad introductory material that can be covered while students become familiar with their development environment.

Chapter 2 (Objects and Primitive Data) establishes the concept of objects and how they can be used. Many predefined classes from the Java standard library are explored and used, as well as the Keyboard class provided by the textbook authors. Primitive types, operators, and expressions are also explored.

Chapter 3 (Program Statements) covers most of the fundamental statements including conditionals and loops. Some additional operators are introduced at this point as well. Establishing key statements at this point allows the classes of the next chapter to be fully functional and realistic.

Chapter 4 (Writing Classes) explores issues related to writing classes and methods. Topics include instance data, visibility, scope, method parameters, and return types. Method overloading is covered as well. Some of the more involved topics are deferred to or revisited in Chapter 5. The key to Chapter 4 is the many fully implemented, realistic classes that are presented as examples of class design.

Chapter 5 (Enhancing Classes) covers additional issues related to class design and revisits topics that need further exploration. Object references are revisited and carefully explored, and their impact on parameter passing is discussed. The underlying processing of the Keyboard class is now introduced here. Nested classes, interfaces, and their effect on design are also covered.

Chapter 6 (Arrays) contains extensive coverage of arrays and array processing. Topics include multidimensional arrays and sorting. The ArrayList class is explored as well.

Chapter 7 (Inheritance) covers class derivations and associated concepts such as class hierarchies, overriding, and polymorphism. Emphasis is put on the proper use of inheritance and its role in software design.

Chapter 8 (Exceptions and I/O Streams) covers the related topics of exception handling and Java I/O. The inner processing of the Keyboard class is further

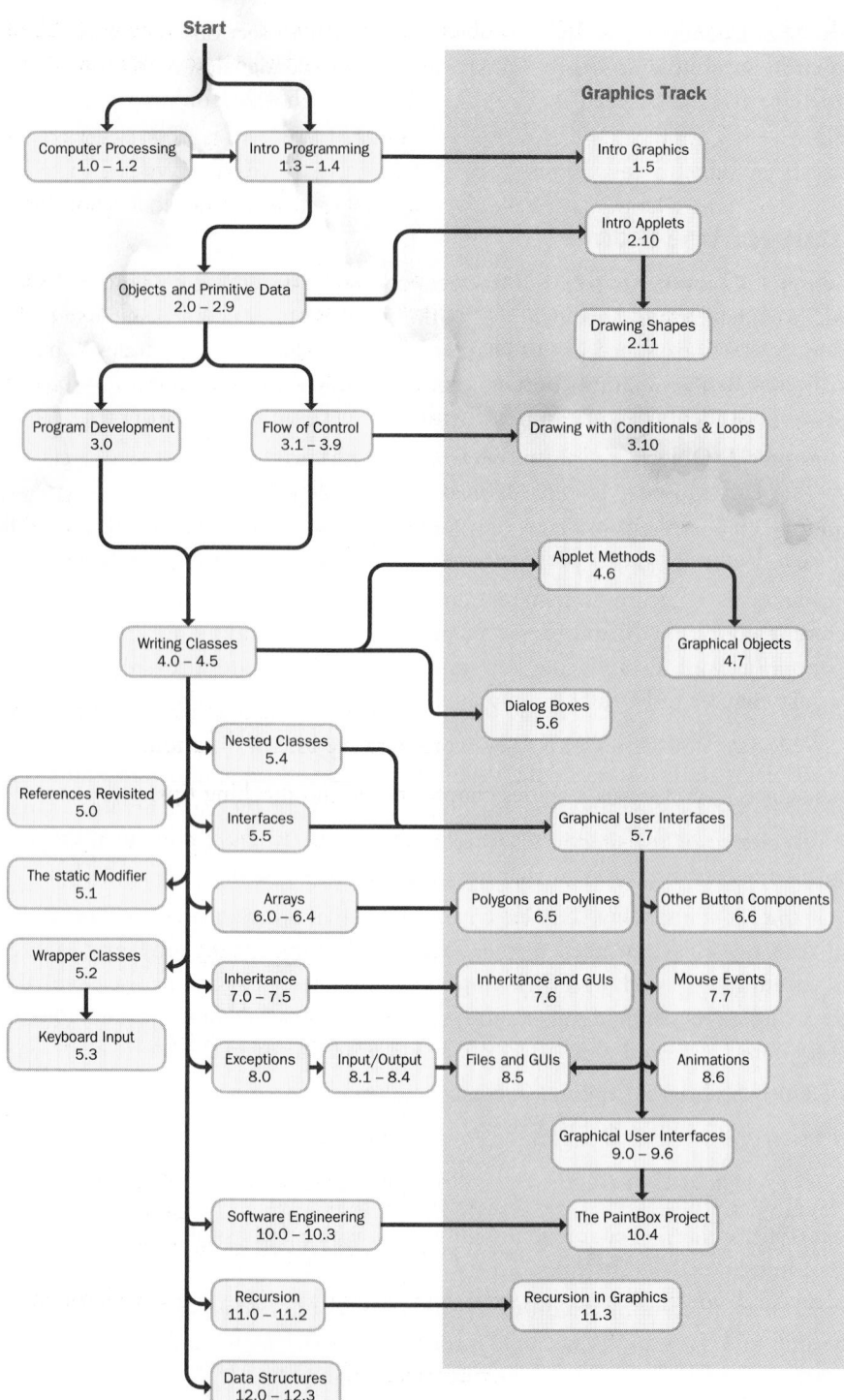

explored at this point. File I/O and object serialization are covered as well. All of the classes used in this chapter are clearly categorized to make sense out of the maze of Java I/O.

Chapter 9 (Graphical User Interfaces) builds on the Graphics Track sections of previous chapters to fully explore the development of GUIs. Coverage includes GUI design tenets, layout managers, special features, and additional containers and components.

Chapter 10 (Software Engineering) presents key issues related to the software development process. A truly object-oriented process model is presented, and then followed using a large example.

Chapter 11 (Recursion) covers the concept, implementation, and proper use of recursion. Several examples from various domains are used to demonstrate how recursive techniques make certain types of processing elegant.

Chapter 12 (Data Structures) introduces the idea of a collection and its underlying data structure. Abstraction is revisited in this context and the classic data structures are explored. This chapter serves as a introduction to a CS2 course.

supplements

The following supplements are available on-line for qualified instructors only. Please contact your Addison-Wesley representative for information.

- **Instructor's Manual**—includes chapter notes and teaching tips.

- **Solutions**—includes solutions to all exercises and programming projects.

- **Test Bank** in powerful test generator software – includes a wealth of free response, multiple choice, and true/false type questions.

- **Lab Manual**—lab exercises are designed to accompany the topic progression in the text.

Students are welcome to visit www.aw.com/cssupport for the following resources.

- **Source Code** to all program examples in the text.

- **PowerPoint** slides which include art from the text.

- **CD**—includes Java Development Environments—Java^{TM} 2 Platform, Standard Edition version 1.4 and jGRASP^{TM} compliments of Auburn University, and source code to all program examples in the text.

Students and faculty are encouraged to visit the author's Web site as well for additional materials:

jss.villanova.edu

acknowledgments

We are most grateful to the faculty and students from around the world who have provided their feedback on previous editions of this book. We are pleased to see the depth of the faculty's concern for their students and the students' thirst for knowledge. Your comments and questions are always welcome.

Susan Hartman Sullivan and Emily Genaway, our editors at Addison-Wesley, went above and beyond the call of duty to ensure that the book met the highest quality standards. Their support and enthusiasm are greatly appreciated. We are also grateful to Michael Hirsch and his assistant Lesly Hershman for making sure that instructors understand the pedagogical advantages of this text. The devotion that the Addison-Wesley folks show to their books is evident in the high-quality results.

The production team for the third edition is a group of gifted and hard-working people—miracle workers all. Thanks go to Patty Mahtani, Joyce Wells (for the wonderful cover), Daniel Rausch, and Sally Boylan. The quality of the book is due largely to their personal attention, and it is greatly appreciated.

Special thanks go to Robert Burton of Brigham Young University, who served as a special and dedicated technical reviewer of the evolving content for the third edition. His insight was invaluable, as was his patience, professionalism, energy, speed, and thoroughness.

The reviewers of previous editions of this text, as well as many other instructors and friends, have provided valuable feedback. They include:

Lewis Barnett	University of Richmond
Tom Bennet	Mississippi College
Gian Mario Besana	DePaul University
Hans-Peter Bischof	Rochester Institute of Technology
Robert Burton	Brigham Young University
James Cross	Auburn University
Eman El-Sheikh	University of West Florida
John Gauch	University of Kansas
Chris Haynes	Indiana University
Laurie Hendren	McGill University
Mike Higgs	Austin College
Karen Kluge	Dartmouth College
Jason Levy	University of Hawaii
Peter MacKenzie	McGill University

Blayne Mayfield	Oklahoma State University
Lawrence Osborne	Lamar University
Barry Pollack	City College of San Francisco
B. Ravikumar	University of Rhode Island
David Riley	University of Wisconsin (La Crosse)
Jerry Ross	Lane Community College
Carolyn Schauble	Colorado State University
Arjit Sengupta	Georgia State University
Vijay Srinivasan	JavaSoft, Sun Microsystems, Inc.
Katherine St. John	Lehman College, CUNY
Ed Timmerman	University of Maryland, University College
Shengru Tu	University of New Orleans
Paul Tymann	Rochester Institute of Technology
John J. Wegis	JavaSoft, Sun Microsystems, Inc.
Linda Wilson	Dartmouth College
David Wittenberg	Brandeis University
Wang-Chan Wong	California State University (Dominguez Hills)

Thanks also go to my colleagues at Villanova University who have provided so much wonderful feedback. They include Bob Beck, Paul Gormley, Cathy Helwig, Dan Joyce, Najib Nadi, Beth Taddei, and Barbara Zimmerman.

Special thanks go to Pete DePasquale, currently working on his doctorate at Virginia Tech, for the design and evolution of the PaintBox project, as well as the original Java Class Library appendix. His interest in pedagogy is a joy to see. Pete will soon be a member of the faculty at some college or university; that school, and their students, will be lucky to have him.

Many other people have helped in various ways. They include Ken Arnold, Kevin Henry, John Loftus, and Sammy Perugini. Our apologies to anyone we may have forgotten.

The ACM Special Interest Group on Computer Science Education (SIGCSE) is a tremendous resource. Their conferences provide an opportunity for educators from all levels and all types of schools to share ideas and materials. If you are an educator in any area of computing and are not involved with SIGCSE, you're missing out.

Most importantly, we thank our wives and families for their support and patience. They put up with more than they should have to during the busy process of writing, not to mention the other times.

feature walkthrough

Key Concepts. Throughout the text, the Key Concept boxes highlight fundamental ideas and important guidelines. These concepts are summarized at the end of each chapter.

9.1 layout managers

In addition to the components, events, and listeners that comprise the backbone of a GUI, the most important activity in GUI design is the use of layout managers. A *layout manager* is an object that governs how components are arranged in a container. It determines the size and position of each component and may take many factors into account to do so. Every container has a default layout manager, although we can replace it if we prefer another one.

> **key concept**
> The layout manager of a container determines how components are visually presented.

A container's layout manager is consulted whenever a change to the visual appearance of its contents might be needed. When the size of a container is adjusted, for example, the layout manager is consulted to determine how all of the components in the container should appear in the resized container. Every time a component is added to a container, the layout manager determines how the addition affects all of the existing components.

> **key concept**
> When changes occur, the components in a container reorganize themselves according to the layout manager's policy.

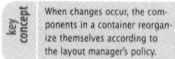

```
 listing
   4.4

//********************************************************************
//  Banking.java          Author: Lewis/Loftus
//
//  Driver to exercise the use of multiple Account objects.
//********************************************************************

public class Banking
{
   //-----------------------------------------------------------------
   //  Creates some bank accounts and requests various services.
   //-----------------------------------------------------------------
   public static void main (String[] args)
   {
      Account acct1 = new Account ("Ted Murphy", 72354, 102.56);
      Account acct2 = new Account ("Jane Smith", 69713, 40.00);
      Account acct3 = new Account ("Edward Demsey", 93757, 759.32);

      acct1.deposit (25.85);

      double smithBalance = acct2.deposit (500.00);
      System.out.println ("Smith balance after deposit: " +
                          smithBalance);

      System.out.println ("Smith balance after withdrawal: " +
                          acct2.withdraw (430.75, 1.50));

      acct3.withdraw (800.00, 0.0);  // exceeds balance

      acct1.addInterest();
      acct2.addInterest();
      acct3.addInterest();

      System.out.println ();
      System.out.println (acct1);
      System.out.println (acct2);
      System.out.println (acct3);
   }
}
```

Listings. All programming examples are presented in clearly labeled listings, followed by the program output, a sample run, or screen shot display as appropriate. The code is colored to visually distinguish comments and reserved words.

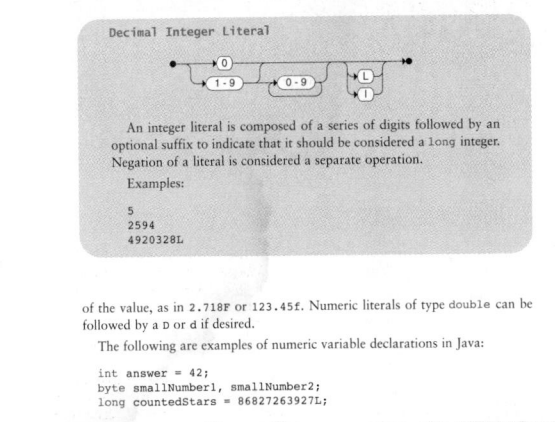

```
Decimal Integer Literal
```

An integer literal is composed of a series of digits followed by an optional suffix to indicate that it should be considered a `long` integer. Negation of a literal is considered a separate operation.

Examples:

```
5
2594
4920328L
```

of the value, as in `2.718F` or `123.45f`. Numeric literals of type `double` can be followed by a `D` or `d` if desired.

The following are examples of numeric variable declarations in Java:

```
int answer = 42;
byte smallNumber1, smallNumber2;
long countedStars = 86827263927L;
```

Syntax Diagrams. At appropriate points in the text, syntactic elements of the Java language are discussed in special highlighted sections with diagrams that clearly identify the valid forms for a statement or construct. Syntax diagrams for the entire Java language are presented in Appendix L.

Graphics Track. All processing that involves graphics and graphical user interfaces is discussed in one or two sections at the end of each chapter that we collectively refer to as the Graphics Track. This material can be skipped without loss of continuity, or focused on specifically as desired. The material in any Graphics Track section relates to the main topics of the chapter in which it is found. Graphics Track sections are indicated by a patterned border on the edge of the page.

Enumeration interface does not have a remove method. Generally, the `Iterator` interface is the preferred choice between the two.

We explore an example that uses the `Iterator` interface later in this text.

5.6 dialog boxes

A *dialog box* is a graphical window that pops up on top of any currently active window so that the user can interact with it. A dialog box can serve a variety of purposes, such as conveying some information, confirming an action, or allowing the user to enter some information. Usually a dialog box has a solitary purpose, and the user's interaction with it is brief.

The Swing package (`javax.swing`) of the Java class library contains a class called `JOptionPane` that simplifies the creation and use of basic dialog boxes. Figure 5.7 lists some of the methods of `JOptionPane`.

The basic formats for a `JOptionPane` dialog box fall into three categories. A *message dialog* simply displays an output string. An *input dialog* presents a prompt and a single input text field into which the user can enter one string of data. A *confirm dialog* presents the user with a simple yes-or-no question.

> `JOptionPane` is a Swing class that facilitates the creation of dialog boxes.
>
> key concept

Let's look at a program that uses each of these types of dialog boxes. Listing 5.12 shows a program that first presents the user with an input dialog box requesting that an integer be entered. After the user presses the OK button on the

```
static String showInputDialog (Object msg)
    Displays a dialog box containing the specified message and an input text
    field. The contents of the text field are returned.
```

Web Bonus. The authors' Web site contains additional examples and discussions. These are noted throughout the text as web bonuses.

---

in the list. That is, although the selection and insertion sorts are equivalent (generally) in the number of comparisons made, selection sort makes fewer swaps.

6.3 two-dimensional arrays

The arrays we've examined so far have all been *one-dimensional arrays* in the sense that they represent a simple list of values. As the name implies, a *two-dimensional array* has values in two dimensions, which are often thought of as the rows and columns of a table. Figure 6.6 graphically compares a one-dimensional array with a two-dimensional array. We must use two indexes to refer to a value in a two-dimensional array, one specifying the row and another the column.

Brackets are used to represent each dimension in the array. Therefore the type of a two-dimensional array that stores integers is `int[][]`. Technically, Java represents two-dimensional arrays as an array of arrays. A two-dimensional integer array is really a one-dimensional array of references to one-dimensional integer arrays.

The `TwoDArray` program shown in Listing 6.14 instantiates a two-dimensional array of integers. As with one-dimensional arrays, the size of the dimensions is specified when the array is created. The size of the dimensions can be different.

---

summary of
key concepts

- An object reference variable stores the address of an object.
- The reserved word `null` represents a reference that does not point to a valid object.
- The `this` reference always refers to the currently executing object.
- Several references can refer to the same object. These references are aliases of each other.
- The `==` operator compares object references for equality, returning true if the references are aliases of each other.
- The `equals` method can be defined to determine equality between objects in any way we consider appropriate.
- If an object has no references to it, a program cannot use it. Java performs automatic garbage collection by periodically reclaiming the memory space occupied by these objects.
- When an object is passed to a method, the actual and formal parameters become aliases of each other.
- A static variable is shared among all instances of a class.
- A method is made static by using the `static` modifier in the method declaration.
- A wrapper class represents a primitive value so that it can be treated as an object.
- If designed properly, inner classes preserve encapsulation while simplifying the implementation of related classes.
- An interface is a collection of abstract methods. It cannot be instantiated.
- A class implements an interface, which formally defines a set of methods

Summary of Key Concepts. The Key Concepts presented throughout a chapter are summarized at the end of the chapter.

Self-Review Questions and Answers. These short-answer questions review the fundamental ideas and terms established in the chapter. They are designed to allow students to assess their own basic grasp of the material. The answers to these questions can be found at the end of the problem sets.

Exercises. These intermediate problems require computations, the analysis or writing of code fragments, and probing questions about the chapter content. While the exercises may deal with code, they generally do not require any online activity.

Programming Projects. These problems require the design and implementation of Java programs. They vary widely in level of difficulty.

contents

This book is about writing well-designed software. To understand software, we must first have a fundamental understanding of its role in a computer system. Hardware and software cooperate in a computer system to accomplish complex tasks. The nature of that cooperation and the purpose of various hardware components are important prerequisites to the study of software development. Furthermore, computer networks have revolutionized the manner in which computers are used, and they now play a key role in even basic software development. This chapter explores a broad range of computing issues, laying the foundation for the study of software development.

chapter objectives

▶ Describe the relationship between hardware and software.

▶ Define various types of software and how they are used.

▶ Identify the core hardware components of a computer and explain their purposes.

▶ Explain how the hardware components interact to execute programs and manage data.

▶ Describe how computers are connected together into networks to share information.

▶ Explain the impact and significance of the Internet and the World Wide Web.

▶ Introduce the Java programming language.

▶ Describe the steps involved in program compilation and execution.

▶ Introduce graphics and their representations.

1.0   introduction

We begin our exploration of computer systems with an overview of computer processing, defining some fundamental terminology and showing how the key pieces of a computer system interact.

basic computer processing

A computer system is made up of hardware and software. The *hardware* components of a computer system are the physical, tangible pieces that support the computing effort. They include chips, boxes, wires, keyboards, speakers, disks, cables, plugs, printers, mice, monitors, and so on. If you can physically touch it and it can be considered part of a computer system, then it is computer hardware.

> **key concept**
>
> A computer system consists of hardware and software that work in concert to help us solve problems.

The hardware components of a computer are essentially useless without instructions to tell them what to do. A *program* is a series of instructions that the hardware executes one after another. *Software* consists of programs and the data those programs use. Software is the intangible counterpart to the physical hardware components. Together they form a tool that we can use to solve problems.

The key hardware components in a computer system are:

- central processing unit (CPU)
- input/output (I/O) devices
- main memory
- secondary memory devices

Each of these hardware components is described in detail in the next section. For now, let's simply examine their basic roles. The *central processing unit* (CPU) is the device that executes the individual commands of a program. *Input/output (I/O) devices*, such as the keyboard, mouse, and monitor, allow a human being to interact with the computer.

Programs and data are held in storage devices called memory, which fall into two categories: main memory and secondary memory. *Main memory* is the storage device that holds the software while it is being processed by the CPU. *Secondary memory* devices store software in a relatively permanent manner. The most important secondary memory device of a typical computer system is the hard disk that resides inside the main computer box. A floppy disk is similar to a hard disk, but it cannot store nearly as much information as a hard disk. Floppy disks have the advantage of portability; they can be removed temporarily or moved from computer to computer as needed. Other portable secondary memory devices include zip disks and compact discs (CDs).

Figure 1.1 shows how information moves among the basic hardware components of a computer. Suppose you have an executable program you wish to run. The program is stored on some secondary memory device, such as a hard disk. When you instruct the computer to execute your program, a copy of the program is brought in from secondary memory and stored in main memory. The CPU reads the individual program instructions from main memory. The CPU then executes the instructions one at a time until the program ends. The data that the instructions use, such as two numbers that will be added together, are also stored in main memory. They are either brought in from secondary memory or read from an input device such as the keyboard. During execution, the program may display information to an output device such as a monitor.

> **key concept**
>
> To execute a program, the computer first copies the program from secondary memory to main memory. The CPU then reads the program instructions from main memory, executing them one at a time until the program ends.

The process of executing a program is fundamental to the operation of a computer. All computer systems basically work in the same way.

software categories

Software can be classified into many categories using various criteria. At this point we will simply differentiate between system programs and application programs.

The *operating system* is the core software of a computer. It performs two important functions. First, it provides a *user interface* that allows the user to

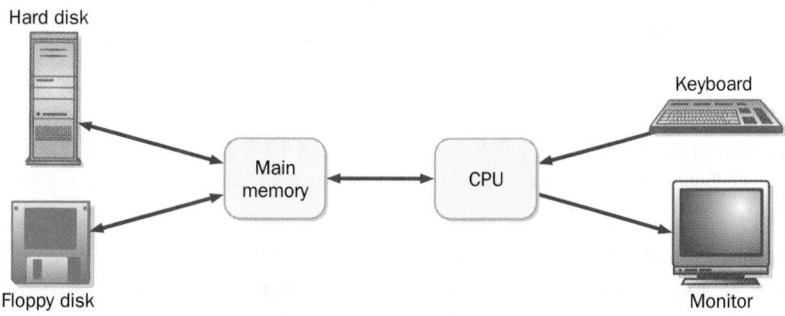

figure 1.1   A simplified view of a computer system

key concept

The operating system provides a user interface and manages computer resources.

interact with the machine. Second, the operating system manages computer resources such as the CPU and main memory. It determines when programs are allowed to run, where they are loaded into memory, and how hardware devices communicate. It is the operating system's job to make the computer easy to use and to ensure that it runs efficiently.

Several popular operating systems are in use today. Windows 98, Windows NT, Windows 2000, and Windows XP are several versions of the operating system developed by Microsoft for personal computers. Various versions of the Unix operating system are also quite popular, especially in larger computer systems. A version of Unix called Linux was developed as an open source project, which means that many people contributed to its development and its code is freely available. Because of that, Linux has become a particular favorite among some users. Mac OS is the operating system used for computing systems developed by Apple Computers.

An *application* is a generic term for just about any software other than the operating system. Word processors, missile control systems, database managers, Web browsers, and games can all be considered application programs. Each application program has its own user interface that allows the user to interact with that particular program.

The user interface for most modern operating systems and applications is a *graphical user interface* (GUI), which, as the name implies, make use of graphical screen elements. These elements include:

- *windows,* which are used to separate the screen into distinct work areas
- *icons,* which are small images that represent computer resources, such as a file
- *pull-down menus,* which provide the user with lists of options
- *scroll bars,* which allow the user to move up and down in a particular window
- *buttons,* which can be "pushed" with a mouse click to indicate a user selection

The mouse is the primary input device used with GUIs; thus, GUIs are sometimes called *point-and-click interfaces*. The screen shot in Fig. 1.2 shows an example of a GUI.

The interface to an application or operating system is an important part of the software because it is the only part of the program with which the user directly interacts. To the user, the interface *is* the program. Chapter 9 discusses the creation of graphical user interfaces.

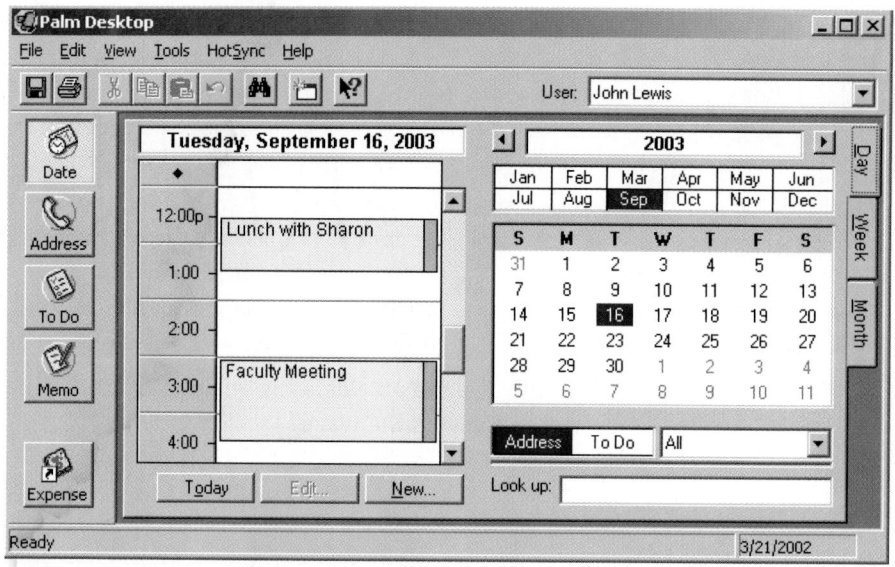

figure 1.2   An example of a graphical user interface (GUI) (Palm Desktop™
courtesy of 3COM Corporation)

The focus of this book is the development of high-quality application programs. We explore how to design and write software that will
perform calculations, make decisions, and control graphics. We use the
Java programming language throughout the text to demonstrate various computing concepts.

As far as the user is concerned, the interface *is* the
program.

key
concept

digital computers

Two fundamental techniques are used to store and manage information: analog
and digital. *Analog* information is continuous, in direct proportion to the source
of the information. For example, a mercury thermometer is an analog device for
measuring temperature. The mercury rises in a tube in direct proportion to the
temperature outside the tube. Another example of analog information is an electronic signal used to represent the vibrations of a sound wave. The signal's voltage varies in direct proportion to the original sound wave. A stereo amplifier
sends this kind of electronic signal to its speakers, which vibrate to reproduce the
sound. We use the term analog because the signal is directly analogous to the
information it represents. Figure 1.3 graphically depicts a sound wave captured
by a microphone and represented as an electronic signal.

Sound wave   Analog signal of the sound wave

figure 1.3   A sound wave and an electronic analog signal
that represents the wave

Digital technology breaks information into discrete pieces and represents those pieces as numbers. The music on a compact disc is stored digitally, as a series of numbers. Each number represents the voltage level of one specific instance of the recording. Many of these measurements are taken in a short period of time, perhaps 40,000 measurements every second. The number of measurements per second is called the *sampling rate*. If samples are taken often enough, the discrete voltage measurements can be used to generate a continuous analog signal that is "close enough" to the original. In most cases, the goal is to create a reproduction of the original signal that is good enough to satisfy the human ear.

Figure 1.4 shows the sampling of an analog signal. When analog information is converted to a digital format by breaking it into pieces, we say it has been *digitized*. Because the changes that occur in a signal between samples are lost, the sampling rate must be sufficiently fast.

Sampling is only one way to digitize information. For example, a sentence of text is stored on a computer as a series of numbers, where each number represents a single character in the sentence. Every letter, digit, and punctuation symbol has been assigned a number. Even the space character is assigned a number. Consider the following sentence:

Hi, Heather.

key concept

Digital computers store information by breaking it into pieces and representing each piece as a number.

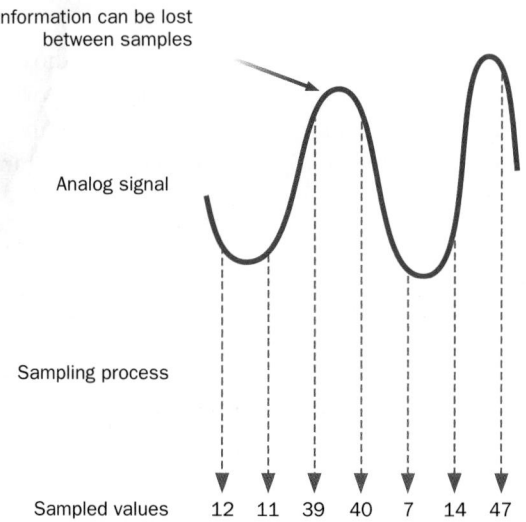

Information can be lost between samples

Analog signal

Sampling process

Sampled values   12 11 39 40 7 14 47

figure 1.4   Digitizing an analog signal by sampling

The characters of the sentence are represented as a series of 12 numbers, as shown in Fig. 1.5. When a character is repeated, such as the uppercase 'H', the same representation number is used. Note that the uppercase version of a letter is stored as a different number from the lowercase version, such as the 'H' and 'h' in the word Heather. They are considered separate and distinct characters.

Modern electronic computers are digital. Every kind of information, including text, images, numbers, audio, video, and even program instructions, is broken into pieces. Each piece is represented as a number. The information is stored by storing those numbers.

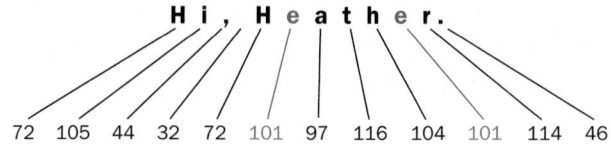

Hi, Heather.

72 105 44 32 72 101 97 116 104 101 114 46

figure 1.5   Text is stored by mapping each character to a number

binary numbers

A digital computer stores information as numbers, but those numbers are not stored as *decimal* values. All information in a computer is stored and managed as *binary* values. Unlike the decimal system, which has 10 digits (0 through 9), the binary number system has only two digits (0 and 1). A single binary digit is called a *bit*.

All number systems work according to the same rules. The *base value* of a number system dictates how many digits we have to work with and indicates the place value of each digit in a number. The decimal number system is base 10, whereas the binary number system is base 2. Appendix B contains a detailed discussion of number systems.

key concept

Binary values are used to store all information in a computer because the devices that store and manipulate binary information are inexpensive and reliable.

Modern computers use binary numbers because the devices that store and move information are less expensive and more reliable if they have to represent only one of two possible values. Other than this characteristic, there is nothing special about the binary number system. Computers have been created that use other number systems to store information, but they aren't as convenient.

Some computer memory devices, such as hard drives, are magnetic in nature. Magnetic material can be polarized easily to one extreme or the other, but intermediate levels are difficult to distinguish. Therefore magnetic devices can be used to represent binary values quite efficiently—a magnetized area represents a binary 1 and a demagnetized area represents a binary 0. Other computer memory devices are made up of tiny electrical circuits. These devices are easier to create and are less likely to fail if they have to switch between only two states. We're better off reproducing millions of these simple devices than creating fewer, more complicated ones.

Binary values and digital electronic signals go hand in hand. They improve our ability to transmit information reliably along a wire. As we've seen, analog signal has continuously varying voltage, but a digital signal is *discrete*, which means the voltage changes dramatically between one extreme (such as +5 volts) and the other (such as –5 volts). At any point, the voltage of a digital signal is considered to be either "high," which represents a binary 1, or "low," which represents a binary 0. Figure 1.6 compares these two types of signals.

As a signal moves down a wire, it gets weaker and degrades due to environmental conditions. That is, the voltage levels of the original signal change slightly. The trouble with an analog signal is that as it fluctuates, it loses its original information. Since the information is directly analogous to the signal, any change in the signal changes the information. The changes in an analog signal cannot be

Analog signal   Digital signal

figure 1.6 An analog signal vs. a digital signal

recovered because the degraded signal is just as valid as the original. A digital signal degrades just as an analog signal does, but because the digital signal is originally at one of two extremes, it can be reinforced before any information is lost. The voltage may change slightly from its original value, but it still can be interpreted as either high or low.

The number of bits we use in any given situation determines the number of unique items we can represent. A single bit has two possible values, 0 and 1, and therefore can represent two possible items or situations. If we want to represent the state of a light bulb (off or on), one bit will suffice, because we can interpret 0 as the light bulb being off and 1 as the light bulb being on. If we want to represent more than two things, we need more than one bit.

Two bits, taken together, can represent four possible items because there are exactly four permutations of two bits: 00, 01, 10, and 11. Suppose we want to represent the gear that a car is in (park, drive, reverse, or neutral). We would need only two bits, and could set up a mapping between the bit permutations and the gears. For instance, we could say that 00 represents park, 01 represents drive, 10 represents reverse, and 11 represents neutral. In this case, it wouldn't matter if we switched that mapping around, though in some cases the relationships between the bit permutations and what they represent is important.

> **key concept**
> There are exactly 2^N permutations of N bits. Therefore N bits can represent up to 2^N unique items.

Three bits can represent eight unique items, because there are eight permutations of three bits. Similarly, four bits can represent 16 items, five bits can represent 32 items, and so on. Figure 1.7 shows the relationship between the number of bits used and the number of items they can represent. In general, N bits can represent 2^N unique items. For every bit added, the number of items that can be represented doubles.

1 bit 2 items	2 bits 4 items	3 bits 8 items	4 bits 16 items	5 bits 32 items	
0	00	000	0000	00000	10000
1	01	001	0001	00001	10001
	10	010	0010	00010	10010
	11	011	0011	00011	10011
		100	0100	00100	10100
		101	0101	00101	10101
		110	0110	00110	10110
		111	0111	00111	10111
			1000	01000	11000
			1001	01001	11001
			1010	01010	11010
			1011	01011	11011
			1100	01100	11100
			1101	01101	11101
			1110	01110	11110
			1111	01111	11111

figure 1.7   The number of bits used determines the number of items that can be represented

We've seen how a sentence of text is stored on a computer by mapping characters to numeric values. Those numeric values are stored as binary numbers. Suppose we want to represent character strings in a language that contains 256 characters and symbols. We would need to use eight bits to store each character because there are 256 unique permutations of eight bits (2^8 equals 256). Each bit permutation, or binary value, is mapped to a specific character.

Ultimately, representing information on a computer boils down to the number of items there are to represent and determining the way those items are mapped to binary values.

1.1 hardware components

Let's examine the hardware components of a computer system in more detail. Consider the computer described in Fig. 1.8. What does it all mean? Is the system capable of running the software you want it to? How does it compare to other systems? These terms are explained throughout this section.

- 950 MHz Intel Pentium 4 processor
- 512 MB RAM
- 30 GB Hard Disk
- CD-RW 24x/10x/40x
- 17" Video Display with 1280 x 1024 resolution
- 56 Kb/s modem

figure 1.8   The hardware specification of a particular computer

computer architecture

The architecture of a house defines its structure. Similarly, we use the term *computer architecture* to describe how the hardware components of a computer are put together. Figure 1.9 illustrates the basic architecture of a generic computer system. Information travels between components across a group of wires called a *bus*.

The CPU and the main memory make up the core of a computer. As we mentioned earlier, main memory stores programs and data that are in active use, and the CPU methodically executes program instructions one at a time.

Suppose we have a program that computes the average of a list of numbers. The program and the numbers must reside in main memory while the program runs. The CPU reads one program instruction from main memory and executes it. If an instruction needs data, such as a number in the list, to perform its task, the CPU reads that information as well. This process repeats until the program ends. The average, when computed, is stored in main memory to await further processing or long-term storage in secondary memory.

> **key concept**
> The core of a computer is made up of the CPU and the main memory. Main memory is used to store programs and data. The CPU executes a program's instructions one at a time.

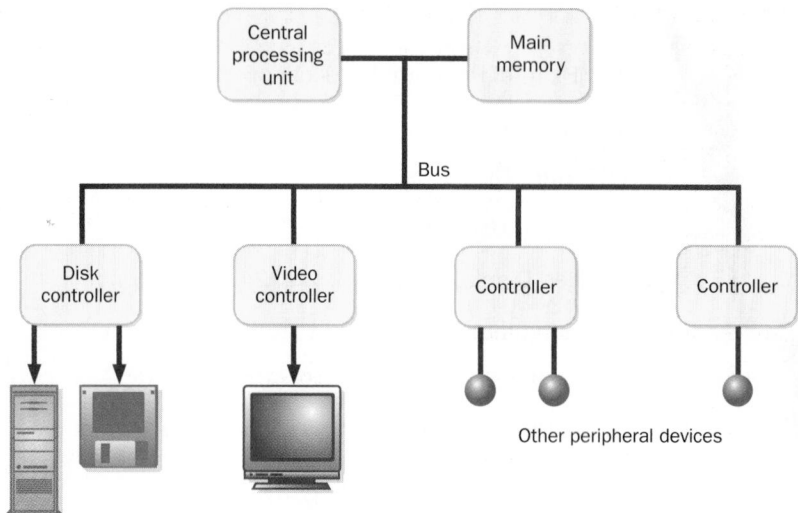

figure 1.9   Basic computer architecture

Almost all devices in a computer system other than the CPU and main memory are called *peripherals*; they operate at the periphery, or outer edges, of the system (although they may be in the same box). Users don't interact directly with the CPU or main memory. Although they form the essence of the machine, the CPU and main memory would not be useful without peripheral devices.

Controllers are devices that coordinate the activities of specific peripherals. Every device has its own particular way of formatting and communicating data, and part of the controller's role is to handle these idiosyncrasies and isolate them from the rest of the computer hardware. Furthermore, the controller often handles much of the actual transmission of information, allowing the CPU to focus on other activities.

Input/output (I/O) devices and secondary memory devices are considered peripherals. Another category of peripherals includes *data transfer devices,* which allow information to be sent and received between computers. The computer specified in Fig. 1.8 includes a data transfer device called a *modem*, which allows information to be sent across a telephone line. The modem in the example can transfer data at a maximum rate of 56 *kilobits* (Kb) per second, or approximately 56,000 *bits per second* (bps).

In some ways, secondary memory devices and data transfer devices can be thought of as I/O devices because they represent a source of information (input) and a place to send information (output). For our discussion, however, we define I/O devices as those devices that allow the user to interact with the computer.

input/output devices

Let's examine some I/O devices in more detail. The most common input devices are the keyboard and the mouse. Others include:

- *bar code readers,* such as the ones used at a grocery store checkout
- *joysticks,* often used for games and advanced graphical applications
- *microphones,* used by voice recognition systems that interpret simple voice commands
- *virtual reality devices,* such as gloves that interpret the movement of the user's hand
- *scanners,* which convert text, photographs, and graphics into machine-readable form

Monitors and printers are the most common output devices. Others include:

- *plotters,* which move pens across large sheets of paper (or vice versa)
- *speakers,* for audio output
- *goggles,* for virtual reality display

Some devices can provide both input and output capabilities. A touch screen system can detect the user touching the screen at a particular place. Software can then use the screen to display text and graphics in response to the user's touch. Touch screens are particularly useful in situations where the interface to the machine must be simple, such as at an information booth.

The computer described in Fig. 1.8 includes a monitor with a 17-inch diagonal display area. A picture is created by breaking it up into small pieces called *pixels,* a term that stands for "picture elements." The monitor can display a grid of 1280 by 1024 pixels. The last section of this chapter explores the representation of graphics in more detail.

main memory and secondary memory

Main memory is made up of a series of small, consecutive *memory locations,* as shown in Fig. 1.10. Associated with each memory location is a unique number called an *address.*

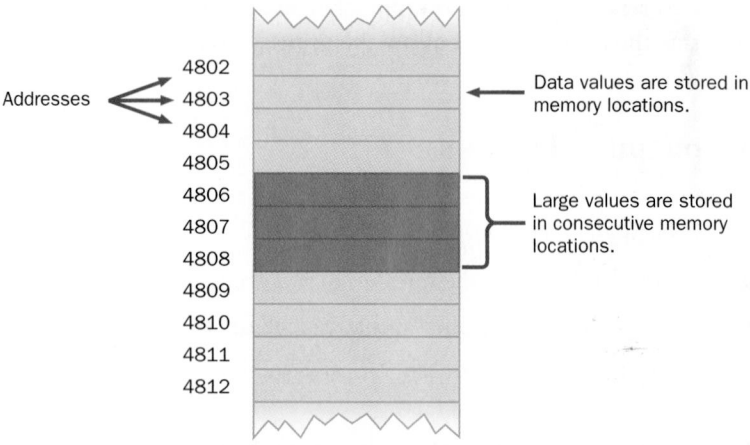

figure 1.10   Memory locations

An address is a unique number associated with each memory location. It is used when storing and retrieving data from memory.

When data is stored in a memory location, it overwrites and destroys any information that was previously stored at that location. However, data is read from a memory location without affecting it.

On many computers, each memory location consists of eight bits, or one *byte*, of information. If we need to store a value that cannot be represented in a single byte, such as a large number, then multiple, consecutive bytes are used to store the data.

The *storage capacity* of a device such as main memory is the total number of bytes it can hold. Devices can store thousands or millions of bytes, so you should become familiar with larger units of measure. Because computer memory is based on the binary number system, all units of storage are powers of two. A *kilobyte* (KB) is 1,024, or 2^{10}, bytes. Some larger units of storage are a *megabyte* (MB), a *gigabyte* (GB), and a *terabyte* (TB), as listed in Fig. 1.11. It's usually easier to think about these capacities by rounding them off. For example, most computer users think of a kilobyte as approximately one thousand bytes, a megabyte as approximately one million bytes, and so forth.

Data *written* to a memory location overwrites and destroys any information that was previously stored at that location. Data *read* from a memory location leaves the value in memory unaffected.

Many personal computers have 128, 256, or 512 megabytes of main memory, or RAM, such as the system described in Fig. 1.8 (we discuss RAM in more detail later in the chapter). A large main memory allows large programs, or multiple programs, to run efficiently because they don't have to retrieve information from secondary memory as often.

Unit	Symbol	Number of Bytes
byte		$2^0 = 1$
kilobyte	KB	$2^{10} = 1024$
megabyte	MB	$2^{20} = 1,048,576$
gigabyte	GB	$2^{30} = 1,073,741,824$
terabyte	TB	$2^{40} = 1,099,511,627,776$

figure 1.11   Units of binary storage

Main memory is usually *volatile,* meaning that the information stored in it will be lost if its electric power supply is turned off. When you are working on a computer, you should often save your work onto a secondary memory device such as a disk in case the power is lost. Secondary memory devices are usually *nonvolatile;* the information is retained even if the power supply is turned off.

The most common secondary storage devices are hard disks and floppy disks. A high-density floppy disk can store 1.44 MB of information. The storage capacities of hard drives vary, but on personal computers, capacities typically range between 10 and 40 GB, such as in the system described in Fig. 1.8.

A disk is a magnetic medium on which bits are represented as magnetized particles. A read/write head passes over the spinning disk, reading or writing information as appropriate. A hard disk drive might actually contain several disks in a vertical column with several read/write heads, such as the one shown in Fig. 1.12.

To get an intuitive feel for how much information these devices can store, consider that all the information in this book, including pictures and formatting, requires about 6 MB of storage.

Magnetic tapes are also used as secondary storage but are considerably slower than disks because of the way information is accessed. A disk is a *direct access device* since the read/write head can move, in general, directly to the information needed. The terms direct access and *random access* are often used interchangeably. However, information on a tape can be accessed only after first getting past the intervening data. A tape must be rewound or fast-forwarded to get to the appropriate position. A tape is therefore considered a *sequential access device.*

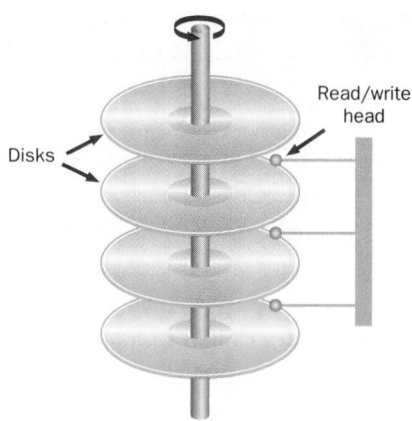

figure 1.12   A hard disk drive with multiple disks and read/write heads

Tapes are usually used only to store information when it is no longer used frequently, or to provide a backup copy of the information on a disk.

Two other terms are used to describe memory devices: *random access memory* (RAM) and *read-only memory* (ROM). It's important to understand these terms because they are used often, and their names can be misleading. The terms RAM and main memory are basically interchangeable. When contrasted with ROM, however, the term RAM seems to imply something it shouldn't. Both RAM and ROM are direct (or random) access devices. RAM should probably be called read-write memory, since data can be both written to it and read from it. This feature distinguishes it from ROM. After information is stored on ROM, it cannot be altered (as the term "read-only" implies). ROM chips are often embedded into the main circuit board of a computer and used to provide the preliminary instructions needed when the computer is initially turned on.

A *CD-ROM* is a portable secondary memory device. CD stands for compact disc. It is accurately called ROM because information is stored permanently when the CD is created and cannot be changed. Like its musical CD counterpart, a CD-ROM stores information in binary format. When the CD is initially created, a microscopic pit is pressed into the disc to represent a binary 1, and the disc is left smooth to represent a binary 0. The bits are read by shining a low-intensity laser beam onto the spinning disc. The laser beam reflects strongly from a smooth area on the disc

key concept

The surface of a CD has both smooth areas and small pits. A pit represents a binary 1 and a smooth area represents a binary 0.

but weakly from a pitted area. A sensor receiving the reflection determines whether each bit is a 1 or a 0 accordingly. A typical CD-ROM's storage capacity is approximately 650 MB.

Variations on basic CD technology have emerged quickly. It is now common for a home computer to be equipped with a *CD-Recordable* (CD-R) drive. A CD-R can be used to create a CD for music or for general computer storage. Once created, you can use a CD-R disc in a standard CD player, but you can't change the information on a CD-R disc once it has been "burned." Music CDs that you buy in a store are pressed from a mold, whereas CD-Rs are burned with a laser.

A *CD-Rewritable* (CD-RW) disc can be erased and reused. They can be reused because the pits and flat surfaces of a normal CD are simulated on a CD-RW by coating the surface of the disc with a material that, when heated to one temperature becomes amorphous (and therefore non-reflective) and when heated to a different temperature becomes crystalline (and therefore reflective). The CD-RW media doesn't work in all players, but CD-Rewritable drives can create both CD-R and CD-RW discs.

> **key concept**
> A rewritable CD simulates the pits and smooth areas of a regular CD using a coating that can be made amorphous or crystalline as needed.

CDs were initially a popular format for music; they later evolved to be used as a general computer storage device. Similarly, the *DVD* format was originally created for video and is now making headway as a general format for computer data. DVD once stood for digital video disc or digital versatile disc, but now the acronym generally stands on its own. A DVD has a tighter format (more bits per square inch) than a CD and can therefore store much more information. It is likely that DVD-ROMs eventually will replace CD-ROMs completely because there is a compatible migration path, meaning that a DVD drive can read a CD-ROM. There are currently six different formats for recordable DVDs; some of these are essentially in competition with each other. The market will decide which formats will dominate.

The speed of a CD drive is expressed in multiples of x, which represents a data transfer speed of 153,600 bytes of data per second. The CD-RW drive described in Fig. 1.8 is characterized as having 24x/10x/40x maximum speed, which means it can write data onto CD-R discs at 24x, it can write data onto CD-RW discs at 10x, and it reads data from a disc at 40x.

The capacity of storage devices changes continually as technology improves. A general rule in the computer industry suggests that storage capacity approximately doubles every 18 months. However, this progress eventually will slow down as capacities approach absolute physical limits.

the central processing unit

The central processing unit (CPU) interacts with main memory to perform all fundamental processing in a computer. The CPU interprets and executes instructions, one after another, in a continuous cycle. It is made up of three important components, as shown in Fig. 1.13. The *control unit* coordinates the processing steps, the *registers* provide a small amount of storage space in the CPU itself, and the *arithmetic/logic unit* performs calculations and makes decisions.

The control unit coordinates the transfer of data and instructions between main memory and the registers in the CPU. It also coordinates the execution of the circuitry in the arithmetic/logic unit to perform operations on data stored in particular registers.

In most CPUs, some registers are reserved for special purposes. For example, the *instruction register* holds the current instruction being executed. The *program counter* is a register that holds the address of the next instruction to be executed. In addition to these and other special-purpose registers, the CPU also contains a set of general-purpose registers that are used for temporary storage of values as needed.

The concept of storing both program instructions and data together in main memory is the underlying principle of the *von Neumann architecture* of computer design, named after John von Neumann, who first advanced this programming concept in 1945. These computers continually follow the *fetch-decode-execute* cycle depicted in Fig. 1.14. An instruction is fetched from main memory at the address stored in the program counter and is put into the instruction register. The

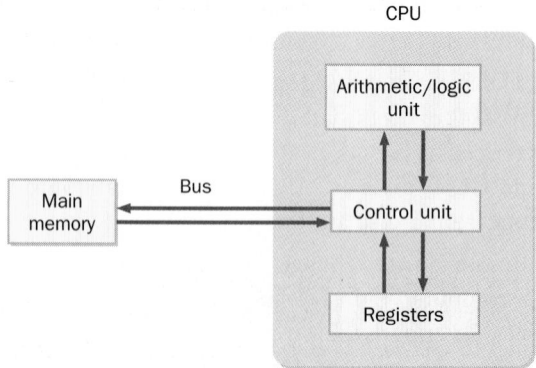

figure 1.13   CPU components and main memory

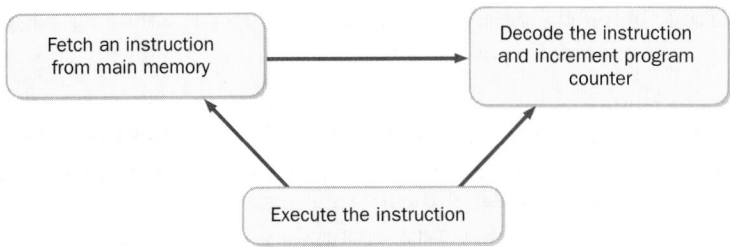

figure 1.14   The continuous fetch-decode-execute cycle

program counter is incremented at this point to prepare for the next cycle. Then the instruction is decoded electronically to determine which operation to carry out. Finally, the control unit activates the correct circuitry to carry out the instruction, which may load a data value into a register or add two values together, for example.

> **key concept**
> The von Neumann architecture and the fetch-decode-execute cycle form the foundation of computer processing.

The CPU is constructed on a chip called a *microprocessor*, a device that is part of the main circuit board of the computer. This board also contains ROM chips and communication sockets to which device controllers, such as the controller that manages the video display, can be connected.

Another crucial component of the main circuit board is the *system clock*. The clock generates an electronic pulse at regular intervals, which synchronizes the events of the CPU. The rate at which the pulses occur is called the *clock speed*, and it varies depending on the processor. The computer described in Fig. 1.8 includes a Pentium 4 processor that runs at a clock speed of 950 megahertz (MHz), or approximately 950 million pulses per second. The speed of the system clock provides a rough measure of how fast the CPU executes instructions. Similar to storage capacities, the speed of processors is constantly increasing with advances in technology, approximately doubling every 18 months.

> **key concept**
> The speed of the system clock indicates how fast the CPU executes instructions.

1.2 networks

A single computer can accomplish a great deal, but connecting several computers together into networks can dramatically increase productivity and facilitate the sharing of information. A *network* is two or more computers connected together so they can exchange information. Using networks has become the normal mode of commercial computer operation. New technologies are emerging every day to capitalize on the connected environments of modern computer systems.

Figure 1.15 shows a simple computer network. One of the devices on the network is a printer, which allows any computer connected to the network to print a document on that printer. One of the computers on the network is designated as a *file server,* which is dedicated to storing programs and data that are needed by many network users. A file server usually has a large amount of secondary memory. When a network has a file server, each individual computer doesn't need its own copy of a program.

network connections

If two computers are directly connected, they can communicate in basically the same way that information moves across wires inside a single machine. When connecting two geographically close computers, this solution works well and is called a *point-to-point connection.* However, consider the task of connecting many computers together across large distances. If point-to-point connections are used, every computer is directly connected by a wire to every other computer in the network. A separate wire for each connection is not a workable solution because every time a new computer is added to the network, a new communication line will have to be installed for each computer already in the network. Furthermore, a single computer can handle only a small number of direct connections.

> **key concept**
>
> A network consists of two or more computers connected together so they can exchange information.

Figure 1.16 shows multiple point-to-point connections. Consider the number of communication lines that would be needed if two or three additional computers were added to the network.

Contrast the diagrams in Fig. 1.15 and Fig. 1.16. All of the computers shown in Fig. 1.15 share a single communication line. Each computer on the network

figure 1.15   A simple computer network

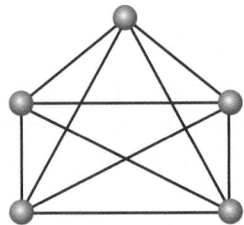

figure 1.16   Point-to-point connections

has its own *network address*, which uniquely identifies it. These addresses are similar in concept to the addresses in main memory except that they identify individual computers on a network instead of individual memory locations inside a single computer. A message is sent across the line from one computer to another by specifying the network address of the computer for which it is intended.

Sharing a communication line is cost effective and makes adding new computers to the network relatively easy. However, a shared line introduces delays. The computers on the network cannot use the communication line at the same time. They have to take turns sending information, which means they have to wait when the line is busy.

> **key concept**
> Sharing a communication line creates delays, but it is cost effective and simplifies adding new computers to the network.

One technique to improve network delays is to divide large messages into segments, called *packets,* and then send the individual packets across the network intermixed with pieces of other messages sent by other users. The packets are collected at the destination and reassembled into the original message. This situation is similar to a group of people using a conveyor belt to move a set of boxes from one place to another. If only one person were allowed to use the conveyor belt at a time, and that person had a large number of boxes to move, the others would be waiting a long time before they could use it. By taking turns, each person can put one box on at a time, and they all can get their work done. It's not as fast as having a conveyor belt of your own, but it's not as slow as having to wait until everyone else is finished.

local-area networks and wide-area networks

A *local-area network* (LAN) is designed to span short distances and connect a relatively small number of computers. Usually a LAN connects the machines in only one building or in a single room. LANs are convenient to install and manage and are highly reliable. As computers became increasingly small and versatile, LANs became an inexpensive way to share information throughout an organization. However, having a LAN is like having a telephone system that allows you to call only the people in your own town. We need to be able to share information across longer distances.

A *wide-area network* (WAN) connects two or more LANs, often across long distances. Usually one computer on each LAN is dedicated to handling the communication across a WAN. This technique relieves the other computers in a LAN from having to perform the details of long-distance communication. Figure 1.17 shows several LANs connected into a WAN. The LANs connected by a WAN are often owned by different companies or organizations, and might even be located in different countries.

The impact of networks on computer systems has been dramatic. Computing resources can now be shared among many users, and computer-based communication across the entire world is now possible. In fact, the use of networks is now so pervasive that some computers require network resources in order to operate.

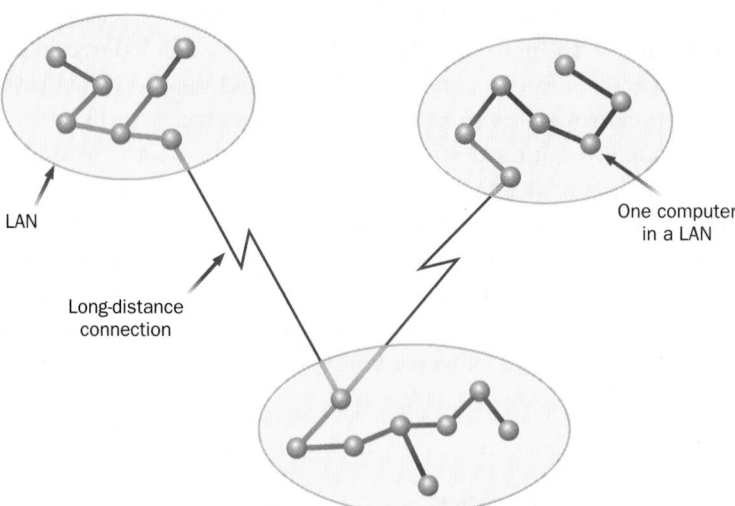

LAN

One computer
in a LAN

Long-distance
connection

figure 1.17   LANs connected into a WAN

the Internet

Throughout the 1970s, a United States government organization called the Advanced Research Projects Agency (ARPA) funded several projects to explore network technology. One result of these efforts was the ARPANET, a WAN that eventually became known as the Internet. The *Internet* is a network of networks. The term Internet comes from the WAN concept of *internetworking*—connecting many smaller networks together.

> **key concept**
> The Internet is a wide-area network (WAN) that spans the globe.

From the mid 1980s through the present day, the Internet has grown incredibly. In 1983, there were fewer than 600 computers connected to the Internet. By the year 2000, that number had reached over 10 million. As more and more computers connect to the Internet, the task of keeping up with the larger number of users and heavier traffic has been difficult. New technologies have replaced the ARPANET several times since the initial development, each time providing more capacity and faster processing.

A *protocol* is a set of rules that governs how two things communicate. The software that controls the movement of messages across the Internet must conform to a set of protocols called TCP/IP (pronounced by spelling out the letters, T-C-P-I-P). TCP stands for *Transmission Control Protocol*, and IP stands for *Internet Protocol*. The IP software defines how information is formatted and transferred from the source to the destination. The TCP software handles problems such as pieces of information arriving out of their original order or information getting lost, which can happen if too much information converges at one location at the same time.

> **key concept**
> TCP/IP is the set of software protocols that govern the movement of messages across the Internet.

Every computer connected to the Internet has an *IP address* that uniquely identifies it among all other computers on the Internet. An example of an IP address is 204.192.116.2. Fortunately, the users of the Internet rarely have to deal with IP addresses. The Internet allows each computer to be given a name. Like IP addresses, the names must be unique. The Internet name of a computer is often referred to as its *Internet address*. Two examples of Internet addresses are spencer.villanova.edu and kant.gestalt-llc.com.

The first part of an Internet address is the local name of a specific computer. The rest of the address is the *domain name,* which indicates the organization to which the computer belongs. For example, villanova.edu is the domain name for the network of computers at Villanova University, and spencer is the name of a particular computer on that campus. Because the domain names are unique, many organizations can have a computer

> **key concept**
> Every computer connected to the Internet has an IP address that uniquely identifies it.

named spencer without confusion. Individual departments might be assigned *sub-domains* that are added to the basic domain name to uniquely distinguish their set of computers within the larger organization. For example, the csc.villanova.edu subdomain is devoted to the Department of Computing Sciences at Villanova University.

The last part of each domain name, called a *top-level domain* (TLD), usually indicates the type of organization to which the computer belongs. The TLD edu indicates an educational institution. The TLD com refers to a commercial business. For example, gestalt-llc.com refers to Gestalt, LLC, a company specializing in software technologies. Another common TLD is org, used by nonprofit organizations. Many computers, especially those outside of the United States, use a TLD that denotes the country of origin, such as uk for the United Kingdom. Recently, in response to a diminishing supply of domain names, some new top-level domain names have been created, such as biz, info, and name.

When an Internet address is referenced, it gets translated to its corresponding IP address, which is used from that point on. The software that does this translation is called the *Domain Name System* (DNS). Each organization connected to the Internet operates a *domain server* that maintains a list of all computers at that organization and their IP addresses. It works somewhat like telephone directory assistance in that you provide the name, and the domain server gives back a number. If the local domain server does not have the IP address for the name, it contacts another domain server that does.

The Internet has revolutionized computer processing. Initially, the primary use of interconnected computers was to send electronic mail, but Internet capabilities continue to improve. One of the most significant uses of the Internet is the World Wide Web.

the World Wide Web

The Internet gives us the capability to exchange information. The *World Wide Web* (also known as WWW or simply the Web) makes the exchange of information easy. Web software provides a common user interface through which many different types of information can be accessed with the click of a mouse.

key concept

The World Wide Web is software that makes sharing information across a network easy.

The Web is based on the concepts of hypertext and hypermedia. The term *hypertext* was first used in 1965 to describe a way to organize information so that the flow of ideas was not constrained to a linear progression. In fact, that concept was entertained as a way to manage large amounts of information as early as the 1940s. Researchers on the Manhattan Project, who were developing the first atomic bomb, envisioned such an approach. The underlying idea is that documents can be linked at various points according to natural relationships so that the reader can jump from one document to another, following the appropriate path for that reader's needs. When other media components are incorporated, such as graphics, sound, animations, and video, the resulting organization is called *hypermedia*.

A *browser* is a software tool that loads and formats Web documents for viewing. *Mosaic,* the first graphical interface browser for the Web, was released in 1993. The designer of a Web document defines *links* to other Web information that might be anywhere on the Internet. Some of the people who developed Mosaic went on to found the Netscape Communications Corp. and create the Netscape Navigator browser, which is shown in Fig. 1.18. It is currently one of the most popular systems for accessing information on the Web. Microsoft's Internet Explorer is another popular browser.

A computer dedicated to providing access to Web documents is called a *Web server*. Browsers load and interpret documents provided by a Web server. Many such documents are formatted using the *HyperText Markup Language* (HTML). Appendix J gives an overview of Web publishing using HTML. The Java programming language has an intimate relationship with Web processing because links to Java programs can be embedded in HTML documents and executed through Web browsers. We explore this relationship in more detail in Chapter 2.

> **key concept**
> A browser is a software tool that loads and formats Web documents for viewing. These documents are often written using the HyperText Markup Language (HTML).

Uniform Resource Locators

Information on the Web is found by identifying a *Uniform Resource Locator* (URL). A URL uniquely specifies documents and other information for a browser to obtain and display. An example URL is:

http://www.yahoo.com

The Web site at this particular URL enables you to search the Web for information using particular words or phrases.

A URL contains several pieces of information. The first piece is a protocol, which determines the way the browser should communicate. The second piece is the Internet address of the machine on which the document is stored. The third piece of information is the file name of

> **key concept**
> A URL uniquely specifies documents and other information found on the Web for a browser to obtain and display.

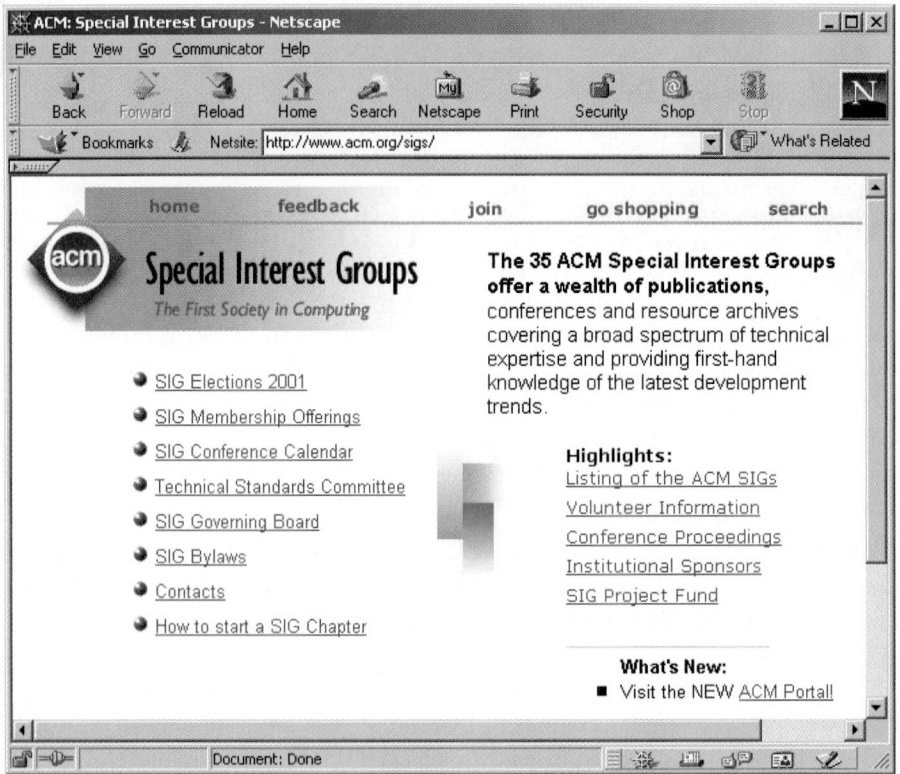

figure 1.18   Netscape Navigator browsing an HTML document
(used with permission of ACM)

interest. If no file name is given, as is the case with the Yahoo URL, the web server often provides a default page (such as index.html).

Let's look at another example URL:

http://www.gestalt-llc.com/vision.html

In this URL, the protocol is http, which stands for *HyperText Transfer Protocol*. The machine referenced is www (a typical reference to a Web server), found at domain gestalt-llc.com. Finally, vision.html is a file to be transferred to the browser for viewing. Many other forms for URLs exist, but this form is the most common.

the Internet vs. the World Wide Web

The terms Internet and World Wide Web are sometimes used interchangeably, but there are important differences between the two. The Internet makes it possible to communicate via computers around the world. The Web makes that communication a straightforward and enjoyable activity.

The Web is essentially a distributed information service and is based on a set of software applications. It is not a network. Although it is used effectively with the Internet, it is not inherently bound to it. The Web can be used on a LAN that is not connected to any other network or even on a single machine to display HTML documents.

1.3 programming

The Java programming language was another important evolutionary step that allowed software to be easily exchanged and executed via the Web. The rest of this book explores the process of creating programs using Java. This section discusses the purpose of programming in general and introduces the Java programming language.

problem solving

The purpose of writing a program is to solve a problem. Problem solving, in general, consists of multiple steps:

1. Understanding the problem.
2. Breaking the problem into manageable pieces.
3. Designing a solution.
4. Considering alternatives to the solution and refining the solution.
5. Implementing the solution.
6. Testing the solution and fixing any problems that exist.

Although this approach applies to any kind of problem solving, it works particularly well when developing software. We refine this series

> **key concept**
> The purpose of writing a program is to solve a problem.

of activities and apply it to writing programs at various points throughout this text.

The first step, understanding the problem, may sound obvious, but a lack of attention to this step has been the cause of many misguided efforts. If we attempt to solve a problem we don't completely understand, we often end up solving the wrong problem or at least going off on improper tangents. We must understand the needs of the people who will use the solution. These needs often include subtle nuances that will affect our overall approach to the solution.

After we thoroughly understand the problem, we then break the problem into manageable pieces and design a solution. These steps go hand in hand. A solution to any problem can rarely be expressed as one big activity. Instead, it is a series of small cooperating tasks that interact to perform a larger task. When developing software, we don't write one big program. We design separate pieces that are responsible for certain parts of the solution, subsequently integrating them with the other parts.

key concept

The first solution we design to solve a problem may not be the best one.

Our first inclination toward a solution may not be the best one. We must always consider alternatives and refine the solution as necessary. The earlier we consider alternatives, the easier it is to modify our approach.

Implementing the solution is the act of taking the design and putting it in a usable form. When developing a software solution to a problem, the implementation stage is the process of actually writing the program. Too often programming is thought of as writing code. But in most cases, the final implementation of the solution is one of the last and easiest steps. The act of designing the program should be more interesting and creative than the process of implementing the design in a particular programming language.

Finally, we test our solution to find any errors that exist so that we can fix them and improve the quality of the software. Testing efforts attempt to verify that the program correctly represents the design, which in turn provides a solution to the problem.

Throughout this text we explore programming techniques that allow us to elegantly design and implement solutions to problems. Although we will often delve into these specific techniques in detail, we should not forget that they are just tools to help us solve problems.

the Java programming language

A program is written in a particular *programming language* that uses specific words and symbols to express the problem solution. A programming language defines a set of rules that determine exactly how a programmer can combine the words and symbols of the language into *programming statements,* which are the instructions that are carried out when the program is executed.

Since the inception of computers, many programming languages have been created. We use the Java language in this book to demonstrate various programming concepts and techniques. Although our main goal is to learn these underlying software development concepts, an important side-effect will be to become proficient in the development of Java programs.

Java is a relatively new programming language compared to others. It was developed in the early 1990s by James Gosling at Sun Microsystems. Java was introduced to the public in 1995 and has gained tremendous popularity since.

One reason Java got some initial attention was because it was the first programming language to deliberately embrace the concept of writing programs that can be executed using the Web. The original hype about Java's Web capabilities initially obscured the far more important features that make it a useful general-purpose programming language.

Java is an *object-oriented programming language.* The principles of object-oriented software development are the cornerstone of this book, and we discuss them throughout the text. Objects are the fundamental pieces that make up a program. Other programming languages, such as C++, allow a programmer to use objects but don't reinforce that approach, which can lead to confusing program designs.

> **key concept**
>
> This book focuses on the principles of object-oriented programming.

Most importantly, Java is a good language to use to learn programming concepts. It is fairly elegant in that it doesn't get bogged down in unnecessary issues as some other languages do. Using Java, we are able to focus on important issues and not on superfluous details.

The Java language is accompanied by a library of extra software that we can use when developing programs. This library provides the ability to create graphics, communicate over networks, and interact with databases, among many other features. Although we won't be able to cover all aspects of the libraries, we will explore many of them. The set of supporting libraries is huge, and quite versatile.

Java is used in commercial environments all over the world. It is one of the fastest growing programming technologies of all time. So not only is it a good language in which to learn programming concepts, it is also a practical language that will serve you well in the future.

a Java program

Let's look at a simple but complete Java program. The program in Listing 1.1 prints two sentences to the screen. This particular program prints a quote by Abraham Lincoln. The output is shown below the program listing.

listing
1.1

```java
//********************************************************************
//  Lincoln.java        Author: Lewis/Loftus
//
//  Demonstrates the basic structure of a Java application.
//********************************************************************

public class Lincoln
{
   //-----------------------------------------------------------------
   //  Prints a presidential quote.
   //-----------------------------------------------------------------
   public static void main (String[] args)
   {
      System.out.println ("A quote by Abraham Lincoln:");

      System.out.println ("Whatever you are, be a good one.");
   }
}
```

output

```
A quote by Abraham Lincoln:
Whatever you are, be a good one.
```

All Java applications have a similar basic structure. Despite its small size and simple purpose, this program contains several important features. Let's carefully dissect it and examine its pieces.

The first few lines of the program are comments, which start with the `//` symbols and continue to the end of the line. Comments don't affect what the program does but are included to make the program easier to understand by humans. Programmers can and should include comments as needed throughout a program to clearly identify the purpose of the program and describe any special processing. Any written comments or documents, including a user's guide and technical references, are called *documentation*. Comments included in a program are called *inline documentation*.

> **key concept**
> Comments do not affect a program's processing; instead, they serve to facilitate human comprehension.

The rest of the program is a *class definition*. This class is called `Lincoln`, though we could have named it just about anything we wished. The class definition runs from the first opening brace (`{`) to the final closing brace (`}`) on the last line of the program. All Java programs are defined using class definitions.

Inside the class definition are some more comments describing the purpose of the `main` method, which is defined directly below the comments. A *method* is a group of programming statements that are given a name. In this case, the name of the method is `main` and it contains only two programming statements. Like a class definition, a method is also delimited by braces.

All Java applications have a `main` method, which is where processing begins. Each programming statement in the `main` method is executed, one at a time in order, until the end of the method is reached. Then the program ends, or *terminates*. The `main` method definition in a Java program is always preceded by the words `public`, `static`, and `void`, which we examine later in the text. The use of `String` and `args` does not come into play in this particular program. We describe these later also.

> **key concept**
> The `main` method must always be defined using the words `public`, `static`, and `void`.

The two lines of code in the `main` method invoke another method called `println` (pronounced print line). We *invoke*, or *call*, a method when we want it to execute. The `println` method prints the specified characters to the screen. The characters to be printed are represented as a *character string*, enclosed in double quote characters (`"`). When the program is executed, it calls the `println` method to print the first statement, calls it again to print the second statement, and then, because that is the last line in the program, the program terminates.

The code executed when the `println` method is invoked is not defined in this program. The `println` method is part of the `System.out` object, which we explore in more detail in Chapter 2.

`comments`

Let's examine comments in more detail. Comments are the only language feature that allow programmers to compose and communicate their thoughts independent of the code. Comments should provide insight into the programmer's original intent. A program is often used for many years, and often many modifications are made to it over time. The original programmer often will not remember the details of a particular program when, at some point in the future, modifications are required. Furthermore, the original programmer is not always available to make the changes; thus, someone completely unfamiliar with the program will need to understand it. Good documentation is therefore essential.

As far as the Java programming language is concerned, comments can be written using any content whatsoever. Comments are ignored by the computer; they do not affect how the program executes.

The comments in the `Lincoln` program represent one of two types of comments allowed in Java. The comments in `Lincoln` take the following form:

```
// This is a comment.
```

This type of comment begins with a double slash (`//`) and continues to the end of the line. You cannot have any characters between the two slashes. The computer ignores any text after the double slash and to the end of the line. A comment can follow code on the same line to document that particular line, as in the following example:

```
System.out.println ("Monthly Report"); // always use this title
```

The second form a Java comment may have is:

```
/*  This is another comment.  */
```

This comment type does not use the end of a line to indicate the end of the comment. Anything between the initiating slash-asterisk (`/*`) and the terminating asterisk-slash (`*/`) is part of the comment, including the invisible *newline* character that represents the end of a line. Therefore, this type of comment can extend over multiple lines. No space can be between the slash and the asterisk.

If there is a second asterisk following the `/*` at the beginning of a comment, the content of the comment can be used to automatically generate external documentation about your program using a tool called *javadoc*. (We do not discuss this feature in this book, but we do include a description and examples of this process on the book's Web site. Throughout the book, we highlight additional information and examples that you can find on the Web site.)

web bonus

The Web site supporting this text describes how you can generate automatic program documentation using a special form of Java comments and a software tool called *javadoc*.

The two basic comment types can be used to create various documentation styles, such as:

```
// This is a comment on a single line.

//------------------------------------------------------------
// Some comments such as those above methods or classes
// deserve to be blocked off to focus special
// attention on a particular aspect of your code.  Note
// that each of these lines is technically a separate comment.
//------------------------------------------------------------

/*
   This is one comment
   that spans several lines.
*/
```

Programmers often concentrate so much on writing code that they focus too little on documentation. You should develop good commenting practices and follow them habitually. Comments should be well written, often in complete sentences. They should not belabor the obvious but should provide appropriate insight into the intent of the code. The following examples are *not* good comments:

```
System.out.println ("hello");  // prints hello
System.out.println ("test");   // change this later
```

The first comment paraphrases the obvious purpose of the line and does not add any value to the statement. It is better to have no comment than a useless one. The second comment is ambiguous. What should be changed later? When is later? Why should it be changed?

It is considered good programming style to use comments in a consistent way throughout an entire program. Appendix G presents guidelines for good programming practices and includes specific techniques for documenting programs.

> **key concept**
>
> Inline documentation should provide insight into your code. It should not be ambiguous or belabor the obvious.

identifiers and reserved words

The various words used when writing programs are called *identifiers*. The identifiers in the Lincoln program are class, Lincoln, public, static, void, main, String, args, System, out, and println. These fall into three categories:

- words that we make up (Lincoln and args)
- words that another programmer chose (String, System, out, println, and main)
- words that are reserved for special purposes in the language (class, public, static, and void)

While writing the program, we simply chose to name the class Lincoln, but we could have used one of many other possibilities. For example, we could have called it Quote, or Abe, or GoodOne. The identifier args (which is short for arguments) is often used in the way we use it in Lincoln, but we could have used just about any identifier in its place.

The identifiers String, System, out, and println were chosen by other programmers. These words are not part of the Java language. They are part of a huge library of predefined code, a set of classes and methods that someone has already written for us. The authors of that code chose the identifiers—we're just making use of them. We discuss this library of predefined code in more detail in Chapter 2.

Reserved words are identifiers that have a special meaning in a programming language and can only be used in predefined ways. In the Lincoln program, the reserved words used are class, public, static, and void. Throughout the book, we show Java reserved words in blue type. Figure 1.19 lists all of the Java reserved words in alphabetical order. The words marked with an asterisk are reserved for possible future use in later versions of the language but currently have no meaning in Java. A reserved word cannot be used for any other purpose, such as naming a class or method.

An identifier that we make up for use in a program can be composed of any combination of letters, digits, the underscore character (_), and the dollar sign ($), but it cannot begin with a digit. Identifiers may be of any length. Therefore total, label7, nextStockItem, NUM_BOXES, and $amount are all valid identifiers, but 4th_word and coin#value are not valid.

Both uppercase and lowercase letters can be used in an identifier, and the difference is important. Java is *case sensitive*, which means that two identifier names that differ only in the case of their letters are considered to be different

abstract	do	implements	protected	throws
boolean	double	import	public	transient
break	else	instanceof	return	true
byte	extends	int	short	try
case	false	interface	static	void
catch	final	long	strictfp	volatile
char	finally	native	super	while
class	float	new	switch	
const*	for	null	synchronized	
continue	goto*	package	this	
default	if	private	throw	

figure 1.19   Java reserved words

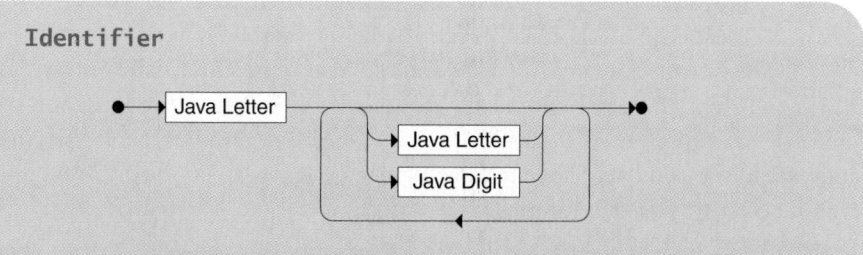

Identifier

An identifier is a letter followed by zero or more letters and digits. A Java Letter includes the 26 English alphabetic characters in both uppercase and lowercase, the $ and _ (underscore) characters, as well as alphabetic characters from other languages. A Java Digit includes the digits 0 though 9.

Examples:

```
total
MAX_HEIGHT
num1
Keyboard
```

identifiers. Therefore `total`, `Total`, `ToTaL`, and `TOTAL` are all different identifiers. As you can imagine, it is not a good idea to use multiple identifiers that differ only in their case because they can be easily confused.

Although the Java language doesn't require it, using a consistent case format for each kind of identifier makes your identifiers easier to understand. For example, we use *title case* (uppercase for the first letter of each word) for class names. That is a Java convention, although it does not technically have to be followed. Throughout the text, we describe the preferred case style for each type of identifier as they are encountered. Appendix G presents various guidelines for naming identifiers.

> **key concept**
> Java is case sensitive. The uppercase and lowercase versions of a letter are distinct. You should use a consistent case convention for different types of identifiers.

While an identifier can be of any length, you should choose your names carefully. They should be descriptive but not verbose. You should avoid meaningless names such as `a` or `x`. An exception to this rule can be made if the short name is actually descriptive, such as using x and y to represent (x, y) coordinates on a two-dimensional grid. Likewise, you should not use unnecessarily long names, such as the identifier `theCurrentItemBeingProcessed`. The name `currentItem` would serve just as well.

As you might imagine, the use of identifiers that are verbose is a much less prevalent problem than the use of names that are not descriptive. If you must err, you should err on the side of readability, but a reasonable balance can almost always be found. Also, you should always be careful when abbreviating words. You might think `curStVal` is a good name to represent the current stock value, but another person trying to understand the code may have trouble figuring out what you meant. It might not even be clear to you two months after writing it.

> **key concept**
> Identifier names should be descriptive and readable.

A *name* in Java is a series of identifiers separated by the dot (period) character. The name `System.out` is the way we designate the object through which we invoked the `println` method. Names appear quite regularly in Java programs.

white space

All Java programs use *white space* to separate the words and symbols used in a program. White space consists of blanks, tabs, and newline characters. The phrase white space refers to the fact that, on a white sheet of paper with black printing, the space between the words and symbols is white. The way a programmer uses white space is important because it can be used to emphasize parts of the code and can make a program easier to read.

> **key concept**
> Appropriate use of white space makes a program easier to read and understand.

Except when it's used to separate words, the computer ignores white space. It does not affect the execution of a program. This fact gives programmers a great deal of flexibility in how they format a program. The lines of a program should be divided in logical places and certain lines should be indented and aligned so that the program's underlying structure is clear.

Because white space is ignored, we can write a program in many different ways. For example, taking white space to one extreme, we could put as many words as possible on each line. The code in Listing 1.2, the Lincoln2 program, is formatted quite differently from Lincoln but prints the same message.

**listing
   1.2**

```
//************************************************************************
//   Lincoln2.java         Author: Lewis/Loftus
//
//   Demonstrates a poorly formatted, though valid, program.
//************************************************************************

public class Lincoln2{public static void main(String[]args){
System.out.println("A quote by Abraham Lincoln:");
System.out.println("Whatever you are, be a good one.");}}
```

output

```
A quote by Abraham Lincoln:
Whatever you are, be a good one.
```

Taking white space to the other extreme, we could write almost every word and symbol on a different line, such as Lincoln3, shown in Listing 1.3.

All three versions of Lincoln are technically valid and will execute in the same way, but they are radically different from a reader's point of view. Both of the latter examples show poor style and make the program difficult to understand. The guidelines for writing Java programs presented in Appendix G include the appropriate use of white space. You may be asked to adhere to these or similar guidelines when you write your programs. In any case, you should adopt and consistently use a set of style guidelines that increase the readability of your code.

> **key concept**
> You should always adhere to a set of guidelines that establish the way you format and document your programs.

**listing
    1.3**

```
//***************************************************************
//  Lincoln3.java        Author: Lewis/Loftus
//
//  Demonstrates another valid program that is poorly formatted.
//***************************************************************

          public          class
      Lincoln3
   {
                   public
     static
         void
   main
         (
String
             []
     args                       )
   {
   System.out.println          (
"A quote by Abraham Lincoln:"             )
     ;           System.out.println
               (
       "Whatever you are, be a good one."
         )
     ;
}
           }
```

output

```
A quote by Abraham Lincoln:
Whatever you are, be a good one.
```

1.4 programming languages

Suppose a particular person is giving travel directions to a friend. That person might explain those directions in any one of several languages, such as English, French, or Italian. The directions are the same no matter which language is used to explain them, but the manner in which the directions are expressed is different. Furthermore, the friend must be able understand the language being used in order to follow the directions.

Similarly, a problem can be solved by writing a program in one of many programming languages, such as Java, Ada, C, C++, Pascal, and Smalltalk. The purpose of the program is essentially the same no matter which language is used, but the particular statements used to express the instructions, and the overall organization of those instructions, vary with each language. Furthermore, a computer must be able to understand the instructions in order to carry them out.

This section explores various categories of programming languages and describes the special programs used to prepare and execute them.

programming language levels

Programming languages are often categorized into the following four groups. These groups basically reflect the historical development of computer languages:

- machine language
- assembly language
- high-level languages
- fourth-generation languages

In order for a program to run on a computer, it must be expressed in that computer's *machine language*. Each type of CPU has its own language. For that reason, we can't run a program specifically written for a Sun Workstation, with its Sparc processor, on an IBM PC, with its Intel processor.

Each machine language instruction can accomplish only a simple task. For example, a single machine language instruction might copy a value into a register or compare a value to zero. It might take four separate machine language instructions to add two numbers together and to store the result. However, a computer can do millions of these instructions in a second, and therefore many simple commands can be quickly executed to accomplish complex tasks.

> All programs must be translated to a particular CPU's machine language in order to be executed.
>
> **key concept**

Machine language code is expressed as a series of binary digits and is extremely difficult for humans to read and write. Originally, programs were entered into the computer using switches or some similarly tedious method. Early programmers found these techniques to be time consuming and error prone.

These problems gave rise to the use of *assembly language,* which replaced binary digits with *mnemonics,* short English-like words that represent commands or data. It is much easier for programmers to deal with words than with binary digits. However, an assembly language program cannot be executed directly on a computer. It must first be translated into machine language.

Generally, each assembly language instruction corresponds to an equivalent machine language instruction. Therefore, similar to machine language, each assembly language instruction accomplishes only a simple operation. Although assembly language is an improvement over machine code from a programmer's perspective, it is still tedious to use. Both assembly language and machine language are considered *low-level languages*.

Today, most programmers use a *high-level language* to write software. A high-level language is expressed in English-like phrases, and thus is easier for programmers to read and write. A single high-level language programming statement can accomplish the equivalent of many—perhaps hundreds—of machine language instructions. The term high-level refers to the fact that the programming statements are expressed in a form approaching natural language, far removed from the machine language that is ultimately executed. Java is a high-level language, as are Ada, C, C++, and Smalltalk.

Figure 1.20 shows equivalent expressions in a high-level language, assembly language, and machine language. The expressions add two numbers together. The assembly language and machine language in this example are specific to a Sparc processor.

The high-level language expression in Fig. 1.20 is readable and intuitive for programmers. It is similar to an algebraic expression. The equivalent assembly language code is somewhat readable, but it is more verbose and less intuitive. The machine language is basically unreadable and much longer. In fact, only a small portion of the binary machine code to add two numbers together is shown in Fig. 1.20. The complete machine language code for this particular expression is over 400 bits long.

High-level language code must be translated into machine language in order to be executed. A high-level language insulates programmers from needing to know the underlying machine language for the processor on which they are working.

key concept Working with high-level languages allows the programmer to ignore the underlying details of machine language.

Some programming languages are considered to operate at an even higher level than high-level languages. They might include special facilities for automatic report generation or interaction with a database. These languages are called *fourth-generation languages,* or simply 4GLs, because they followed the first three generations of computer programming: machine, assembly, and high-level.

High-Level Language	Assembly Language	Machine Language
a + b	ld [%fp-20], %o0	. . .
	ld [%fp-24], %o1	1101 0000 0000 0111
	add %o0, %o1, %o0	1011 1111 1110 1000
		1101 0010 0000 0111
		1011 1111 1110 1000
		1001 0000 0000 0000
		. . .

figure 1.20   A high-level expression and its assembly language and machine language equivalent

compilers and interpreters

Several special-purpose programs are needed to help with the process of developing new programs. They are sometimes called software tools because they are used to build programs. Examples of basic software tools include an editor, a compiler, and an interpreter.

Initially, you use an *editor* as you type a program into a computer and store it in a file. There are many different editors with many different features. You should become familiar with the editor you will use regularly because it can dramatically affect the speed at which you enter and modify your programs.

Each time you need to make a change to the code of your program, you open it in an editor. Figure 1.21 shows a very basic view of the program development process. After editing and saving your program, you attempt to translate it from high-level code into a form that can be executed. That translation may result in errors, in which case you return to the editor to make changes to the code to fix the problems. Once the translation occurs successfully, you can execute the program and evaluate the results. If the results are not what you want (or if you want to enhance your existing program), you again return to the editor to make changes.

The translation of source code into (ultimately) machine language for a particular type of CPU can occur in a variety of ways. A *compiler* is a program that translates code in one language to equivalent code in another language. The original code is called *source code*, and the language into which it is translated is

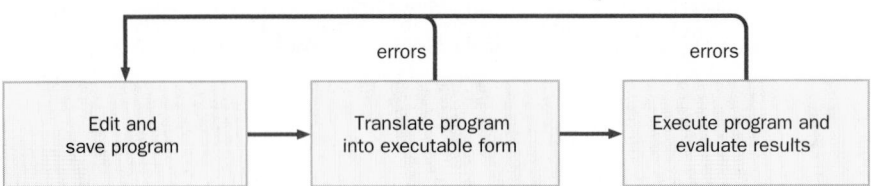

figure 1.21   Editing and running a program

called the *target language*. For many traditional compilers, the source code is translated directly into a particular machine language. In that case, the translation process occurs once (for a given version of the program), and the resulting executable program can be run whenever needed.

An *interpreter* is similar to a compiler but has an important difference. An interpreter interweaves the translation and execution activities. A small part of the source code, such as one statement, is translated and executed. Then another statement is translated and executed, and so on. One advantage of this technique is that it eliminates the need for a separate compilation phase. However, the program generally runs more slowly because the translation process occurs during each execution.

The process often used to translate and execute Java programs combines the use of a compiler and an interpreter. This process is pictured in Fig. 1.22. The Java compiler translates Java source code into Java *bytecode,* which is a representation of the program in a low-level form similar to machine language code. The Java interpreter reads Java bytecode and executes it on a specific machine. Another compiler could translate the bytecode into a particular machine language for efficient execution on that machine.

> **key concept**
>
> A Java compiler translates Java source code into Java bytecode. A Java interpreter translates and executes the bytecode.

The difference between Java bytecode and true machine language code is that Java bytecode is not tied to any particular processor type. This approach has the distinct advantage of making Java *architecture neutral,* and therefore easily portable from one machine type to another. The only restriction is that there must be a Java interpreter or a bytecode compiler for each processor type on which the Java bytecode is to be executed.

Since the compilation process translates the high-level Java source code into a low-level representation, the interpretation process is more efficient than

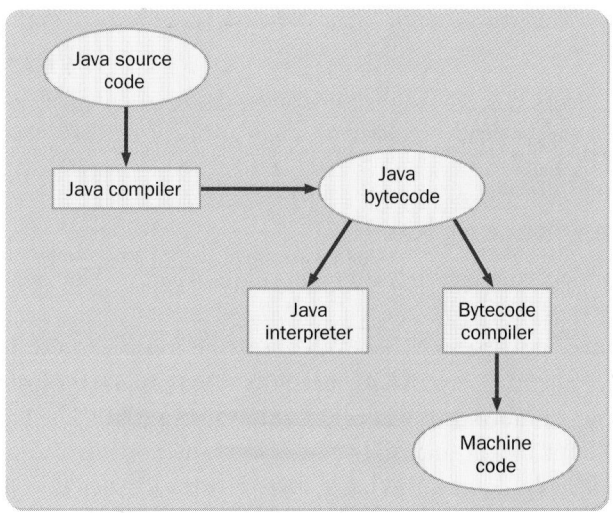

figure 1.22   The Java translation and execution process

interpreting high-level code directly. Executing a program by interpreting its bytecode is still slower than executing machine code directly, but it is fast enough for most applications. Note that for efficiency, Java bytecode could be compiled into machine code.

> Java is architecture neutral because Java bytecode is not associated with any particular hardware platform.
>
> **key concept**

The Java compiler and interpreter are part of the Java *Software Development Kit* (SDK), which is sometimes referred to simply as the *Java Development Kit* (JDK). This kit also contains several other software tools that may be useful to a programmer. The JDK can be downloaded for free from the Sun Microsystem Web site (java.sun.com) or from this book's Web site. Note that the standard JDK tools are executed on the command line. That is, they are not graphical programs with menus and buttons. The standard JDK tools also do not include an editor, although any editor that can save a document as simple text can be used.

Other programs, called *Integrated Development Environments* (IDEs), have been created to support the development of Java programs. IDEs combine an editor, compiler, and other Java support tools into a single application. The specific tools you will use to develop your programs depend on your environment.

web bonus

This book's Web site contains information about several specific Java development environments.

syntax and semantics

Each programming language has its own unique *syntax*. The syntax rules of a language dictate exactly how the vocabulary elements of the language can be combined to form statements. These rules must be followed in order to create a program. We've already discussed several Java syntax rules (for instance, the fact that an identifier cannot begin with a digit is a syntax rule). The fact that braces are used to delimit (begin and end) classes and methods is also a syntax rule. Appendix L formally defines the basic syntax rules for the Java programming language.

During compilation, all syntax rules are checked. If a program is not syntactically correct, the compiler will issue error messages and will not produce bytecode. Java has a similar syntax to the programming languages C and C++, and therefore the look and feel of the code is familiar to people with a background in those languages. Because of these similarities, some people tend to think of Java as a variant of C and C++. However, beyond the basic syntax issues, there are many important differences between Java and these other languages. Appendix I contains a summary of the differences between Java and C++.

The *semantics* of a statement in a programming language define what will happen when that statement is executed. Programming languages are generally unambiguous, which means the semantics of a program are well defined. That is, there is one and only one interpretation for each statement. On the other hand, the natural languages that humans use to communicate, such as English and French, are full of ambiguities. A sentence can often have two or more different meanings. For example, consider the following sentence:

Time flies like an arrow.

The average human is likely to interpret this sentence as a general observation: that time moves quickly in the same way that an arrow moves quickly. However, if we interpret the word *time* as a verb (as in "run the 50-yard dash and I'll time you") and the word *flies* as a noun (the plural of fly), the interpretation changes completely. We know that arrows don't time things, so we wouldn't normally interpret the sentence that way, but it is a valid interpretation of the words in the sentence. A computer would have a difficult time trying to determine which meaning is intended. Moreover, this statement could describe the preferences of an unusual insect known as a "time fly," which might be found near an archery range. After all, fruit flies like a banana.

> The syntax rules of a programming language dictate the form of a program. The semantics dictate the meaning of the program statements.
>
> *key concept*

The point is that the same exact English sentence can have multiple valid meanings. A computer language cannot allow such ambiguities to exist. If a programming language instruction could have two different meanings, a computer would not be able to determine which one to follow.

errors

Several different kinds of problems can occur in software, particularly during program development. The term computer error is often misused and varies in meaning depending on the person using it. From a user's point of view, anything that goes awry when interacting with a machine is often called a computer error. For example, suppose you charged a $23 item to your credit card, but when you received the bill, the item was listed at $230. After you have the problem fixed, the credit card company apologizes for the "computer error." Did the computer arbitrarily add a zero to the end of the number, or did it perhaps multiply the value by 10? Of course not. A computer follows the commands we give it and operates on the data we provide. If our programs are wrong or our data inaccurate, then we cannot expect the results to be correct. A common phrase used to describe this situation is "garbage in, garbage out."

> A computer follows our instructions exactly. The programmer is responsible for the accuracy and reliability of a program.
>
> *key concept*

You will encounter three kinds of errors as you develop programs:

▸ compile-time error

▸ runtime error

▸ logical error

The compiler checks to make sure you are using the correct syntax. If you have any statements that do not conform to the syntactic rules of the language, the compiler will produce a *syntax error*. The compiler also tries to find other problems, such as the use of incompatible types of data. The syntax might be technically correct, but you are still attempting to do something that the language doesn't semantically allow. Any error identified by the compiler is called a *compile-time error*. If a compile-time error occurs, an executable version of the program is not created.

The second kind of problem occurs during program execution. It is called a *runtime error,* and it causes the program to terminate abnormally. For example, if we attempt to divide by zero, the program will "crash" and halt execution at that point. Because the requested operation is undefined, the system simply abandons its attempt to continue processing your program. The best programs are *robust;* that is, they avoid as many run time errors as possible. For example, the program code could guard against the possibility of dividing by zero and handle the situation appropriately if it arises. In Java, many runtime errors are represented as *exceptions* that can be caught and dealt with accordingly. We discuss exceptions in Chapter 8.

The third kind of software problem is a *logical error.* In this case, the software compiles and executes without complaint, but it produces incorrect results. For example, a logical error occurs when a value is calculated incorrectly or when a graphical button does not appear in the correct place. A programmer must test the program thoroughly, comparing the expected results to those that actually occur. When defects are found, they must be traced back to the source of the problem in the code and corrected. The process of finding and correcting defects in a program is called *debugging.* Logical errors can manifest themselves in many ways, and the actual root cause might be quite difficult to discover.

language evolution

As computer technology evolves, so must the languages we use to program them. The Java programming language has undergone various changes since its creation. This text uses the most recent Java technology. Specifically, this book uses the *Java 2 Platform,* which simply refers to the most advanced collection of Java language features, software libraries, and tools. Several important advances have been made since the previous version. The Java 2 Platform is organized into three major groups:

- Java 2 Platform, Standard Edition (J2SE)
- Java 2 Platform, Enterprise Edition (J2EE)
- Java 2 Platform, Micro Edition (J2ME)

This book focuses on the Standard Edition, which, as the name implies, is the mainstream version of the language and associated tools.

As we discussed earlier in this chapter, the Java Development Kit (JDK) is the set of software tools provided by Sun Microsystems that can be used for creating

Java software. These tools include a compiler and an interpreter, among others. The most recent version of the JDK (at the time of this printing), which corresponds to the latest version of the Standard Edition of the Java 2 Platform, is JDK 1.4. You might use the JDK to develop your programs, or you might use some other development environment.

Some parts of early Java technologies have been *deprecated,* which means they are considered old-fashioned and should not be used. When it is important, we point out deprecated elements and discuss their state-of-the-art alternatives.

One particular area in which Java has evolved is in the software libraries that support the development of graphical user interfaces (GUIs). Specifically, earlier releases of Java used the *Abstract Windowing Toolkit* (AWT). Included with the Java 2 Platform is a software library called *Swing,* which builds on the AWT and extends its capabilities. The Swing library contains many elements that replace older, less useful AWT elements. Whenever appropriate, we use Swing technology in this text.

1.5 graphics

Graphics play a crucial role in computer systems. Throughout this book we explore various aspects of graphics and discuss how they are accomplished. In fact, the last one or two sections of each chapter are devoted to graphics topics. (These sections can be skipped without losing continuity through the rest of the text.) In this section, we explore the basic concepts of representing a picture in a computer and displaying it on a screen.

A picture, like all other information stored on a computer, must be digitized by breaking the information into pieces and representing those pieces as numbers. In the case of pictures, we break the picture into *pixels* (picture elements), as we mentioned earlier in this chapter. A pixel is a tiny region that represents a very small piece of the picture. The complete picture is stored by storing the color of each individual pixel.

A black and white picture can be stored by representing each pixel using a single bit. If the bit is zero, that pixel is white; if the bit is 1, it is black. The picture can be reproduced when needed by reassembling its pixels. The more pixels used to represent a picture, the more realistic it looks when it is reproduced. Figure 1.23 shows a black and white picture that has been stored digitally and an enlargement of a portion of that picture, which shows the individual pixels.

> **key concept**
>
> The pixels of a black and white picture can be represented using a single bit each, mapping 0 to white and 1 to black.

 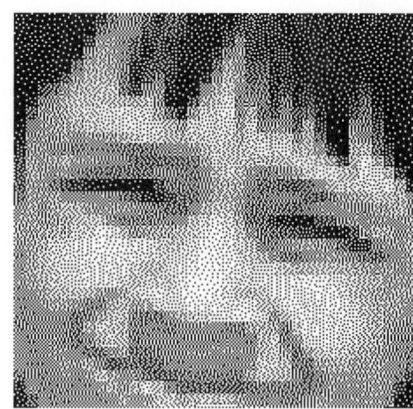

figure 1.23   A digitized picture with a small portion magnified

coordinate systems

When drawn, each pixel of a picture is mapped to a pixel on the screen. Each computer system and programming language defines a coordinate system so that we can refer to particular pixels.

A traditional two-dimensional Cartesian coordinate system has two axes that meet at the origin. Values on either axis can be negative or positive. The Java programming language has a relatively simple coordinate system in which all of the visible coordinates are positive. Figure 1.24 shows a traditional coordinate system and the Java coordinate system.

Each point in the Java coordinate system is represented using an (x, y) pair of values. The top-left corner of any Java drawing area has coordinates $(0, 0)$. The x-axis coordinates get larger as you move to the right, and the y-axis coordinates get larger as you move down.

A Java program does not have to be graphical in nature. However, if it is, each graphical component in the program has its own coordinate system, with the origin $(0, 0)$ in the top-left corner. This consistent approach makes it relatively easy to manage various graphical elements.

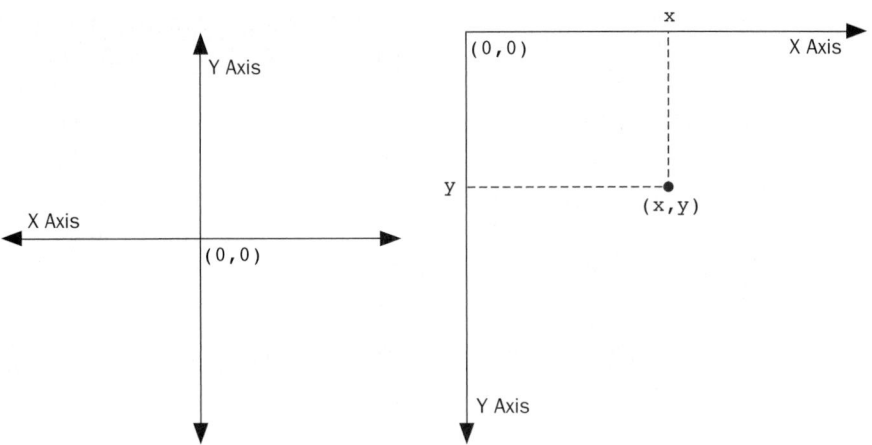

figure 1.24 A traditional coordinate system and the Java coordinate system

representing color

Color pictures are divided into pixels, just as black and white pictures are. However, because each pixel can be one of many possible colors, it is not sufficient to represent each pixel using only one bit. There are various ways to represent the color of a pixel. This section explores one popular technique.

Every color can be represented as a mix of three *primary colors*: red, green, and blue. In Java, as in many other computer languages, colors are specified by three numbers that are collectively referred to as an *RGB value*. RGB stands for Red-Green-Blue. Each number represents the contribution of a primary color. Using one byte (8 bits) to store each of the three numbers, the numbers can range from 0 to 255. The level of each primary color determines the overall color. For example, high values of red and green combined with a low level of blue results in a shade of yellow.

> **key concept**
>
> The pixels of a color picture can be represented using three numbers, collectively called the RGB value, which represent the relative contributions of three primary colors: red, green, and blue.

In the graphics sections of other chapters we explore the use of color and how to control it in a Java program.

summary of
key concepts

- A computer system consists of hardware and software that work in concert to help us solve problems.

- To execute a program, the computer first copies the program from secondary memory to main memory. The CPU then reads the program instructions from main memory, executing them one at a time until the program ends.

- The operating system provides a user interface and manages computer resources.

- As far as the user is concerned, the interface *is* the program.

- Digital computers store information by breaking it into pieces and representing each piece as a number.

- Binary values are used to store all information in a computer because the devices that store and manipulate binary information are inexpensive and reliable.

- There are exactly 2^N permutations of N bits. Therefore N bits can represent up to 2^N unique items.

- The core of a computer is made up of the CPU and the main memory. Main memory is used to store programs and data. The CPU executes a program's instructions one at a time.

- An address is a unique number associated with each memory location. It is used when storing and retrieving data from memory.

- Data *written* to a memory location overwrites and destroys any information that was previously stored at that location. Data *read* from a memory location leaves the value in memory unaffected.

- Main memory is volatile, meaning the stored information is maintained only as long as electric power is supplied. Secondary memory devices are usually nonvolatile.

- The surface of a CD has both smooth areas and small pits. A pit represents a binary 1 and a smooth area represents a binary 0.

- A rewritable CD simulates the pits and smooth areas of a regular CD using a coating that can be made amorphous or crystalline as needed.

- The von Neumann architecture and the fetch-decode-execute cycle form the foundation of computer processing.

- The speed of the system clock indicates how fast the CPU executes instructions.

- A network consists of two or more computers connected together so they can exchange information.

- Sharing a communication line creates delays, but it is cost effective and simplifies adding new computers to the network.

- A local-area network (LAN) is an inexpensive way to share information and resources throughout an organization.

- The Internet is a wide-area network (WAN) that spans the globe.

- TCP/IP is the set of software protocols that govern the movement of messages across the Internet.

- Every computer connected to the Internet has an IP address that uniquely identifies it.

- The World Wide Web is software that makes sharing information across a network easy.

- A browser is a software tool that loads and formats Web documents for viewing. These documents are often written using the HyperText Markup Language (HTML).

- A URL uniquely specifies documents and other information found on the Web for a browser to obtain and display.

- The purpose of writing a program is to solve a problem.

- The first solution we design to solve a problem may not be the best one.

- This book focuses on the principles of object-oriented programming.

- Comments do not affect a program's processing; instead, they serve to facilitate human comprehension.

- The `main` method must always be defined using the words `public`, `static`, and `void`.

- Inline documentation should provide insight into your code. It should not be ambiguous or belabor the obvious.

- Java is case sensitive. The uppercase and lowercase versions of a letter are distinct. You should use a consistent case convention for different types of identifiers.

- Identifier names should be descriptive and readable.

- Appropriate use of white space makes a program easier to read and understand.

- You should always adhere to a set of guidelines that establish the way you format and document your programs.

- All programs must be translated to a particular CPU's machine language in order to be executed.

- Working with high-level languages allows the programmer to ignore the underlying details of machine language.

- A Java compiler translates Java source code into Java bytecode. A Java interpreter translates and executes the bytecode.

- Java is architecture neutral because Java bytecode is not associated with any particular hardware platform.

- The syntax rules of a programming language dictate the form of a program. The semantics dictate the meaning of the program statements.

- A computer follows our instructions exactly. The programmer is responsible for the accuracy and reliability of a program.

- A Java program must be syntactically correct or the compiler will not produce bytecode.

- The pixels of a black and white picture can be represented using a single bit each, mapping 0 to white and 1 to black.

- The pixels of a color picture can be represented using three numbers, collectively called the RGB value, which represent the relative contributions of three primary colors: red, green, and blue.

self-review questions

1.1   What is hardware? What is software?

1.2   What are the two primary functions of an operating system?

1.3   What happens to information when it is stored digitally?

1.4   How many unique items can be represented with the following?

    a. 2 bits

    b. 4 bits

    c. 5 bits

    d. 7 bits

1.5 How many bits are there in each of the following?

a. 8 bytes

b. 2 KB

c. 4 MB

1.6 What are the two primary hardware components in a computer? How do they interact?

1.7 What is a memory address?

1.8 What does volatile mean? Which memory devices are volatile and which are nonvolatile?

1.9 What is a file server?

1.10 What is the total number of communication lines needed for a fully connected point-to-point network of five computers? Six computers?

1.11 What is the origin of the word Internet?

1.12 Explain the parts of the following URLs:

a. duke.csc.villanova.edu/jss/examples.html

b. java.sun.com/products/index.html

1.13 What is the relationship between a high-level language and machine language?

1.14 What is Java bytecode?

1.15 What is white space? How does it affect program execution? How does it affect program readability?

1.16 Which of the following are not valid Java identifiers? Why?

a. `RESULT`

b. `result`

c. `12345`

d. `x12345y`

e. `black&white`

f. `answer_7`

1.17 What do we mean by the syntax and semantics of a programming language?

1.18 How can a black and white picture be represented using 1s and 0s?

exercises

1.1   Describe the hardware components of your personal computer or of a computer in a lab to which you have access. Include the processor type and speed, storage capacities of main and secondary memory, and types of I/O devices. Explain how you determined your answers.

1.2   Why do we use the binary number system to store information on a computer?

1.3   How many unique items can be represented with each of the following?

a. 1 bit

b. 3 bits

c. 6 bits

d. 8 bits

e. 10 bits

f. 16 bits

1.4   If a picture is made up of 128 possible colors, how many bits would be needed to store each pixel of the picture? Why?

1.5   If a language uses 240 unique letters and symbols, how many bits would be needed to store each character of a document? Why?

1.6   How many bits are there in each of the following? How many bytes are there in each?

a. 12 KB

b. 5 MB

c. 3 GB

d. 2 TB

1.7   Explain the difference between random access memory (RAM) and read-only memory (ROM).

1.8   A disk is a random-access device but it is not RAM (random access memory). Explain.

1.9   Determine how your computer, or a computer in a lab to which you have access, is connected to others across a network. Is it linked to the Internet? Draw a diagram to show the basic connections in your environment.

1.10 Explain the differences between a local-area network (LAN) and a wide-area network (WAN). What is the relationship between them?

1.11 What is the total number of communication lines needed for a fully connected point-to-point network of eight computers? Nine computers? Ten computers? What is a general formula for determining this result?

1.12 Explain the difference between the Internet and the World Wide Web.

1.13 List and explain the parts of the URLs for:

a. your school

b. the Computer Science department of your school

c. your instructor's Web page

1.14 Use a Web browser to access information through the Web about the following topics. For each one, explain the process you used to find the information and record the specific URLs you found.

a. the Philadelphia Phillies baseball team

b. wine production in California

c. the subway systems in two major cities

d. vacation opportunities in the Caribbean

1.15 Give examples of the two types of Java comments and explain the differences between them.

1.16 Which of the following are not valid Java identifiers? Why?

a. `Factorial`

b. `anExtremelyLongIdentifierIfYouAskMe`

c. `2ndLevel`

d. `level2`

e. `MAX_SIZE`

f. `highest$`

g. `hook&ladder`

1.17 Why are the following valid Java identifiers not considered good identifiers?

a. `q`

b. `totVal`

c. `theNextValueInTheList`

1.18 Java is case sensitive. What does that mean?

1.19 What do we mean when we say that the English language is ambiguous? Give two examples of English ambiguity (other than the example used in this chapter) and explain the ambiguity. Why is ambiguity a problem for programming languages?

1.20 Categorize each of the following situations as a compile-time error, runtime error, or logical error.

a. multiplying two numbers when you meant to add them

b. dividing by zero

c. forgetting a semicolon at the end of a programming statement

d. spelling a word wrong in the output

e. producing inaccurate results

f. typing a { when you should have typed (

1.21 Compare and contrast a traditional coordinate system and the coordinate system used by Java graphical components.

1.22 How many bits are needed to store a color picture that is 400 pixels wide and 250 pixels high? Assume color is represented using the RGB technique described in this chapter and that no special compression is done.

programming projects

1.1 Enter, compile, and run the following application:

```java
public class Test
{
    public static void main (String[] args)
    {
        System.out.println ("An Emergency Broadcast");
    }
}
```

1.2 Introduce the following errors, one at a time, to the program from the programming project 1.1. Record any error messages that the compiler produces. Fix the previous error each time before you introduce a new one. If no error messages are produced, explain why. Try to predict what will happen before you make each change.

a. change `Test` to `test`

b. change `Emergency` to `emergency`

c. remove the first quotation mark in the string

d. remove the last quotation mark in the string

e. change `main` to `man`

f. change `println` to `bogus`

g. remove the semicolon at the end of the `println` statement

h. remove the last brace in the program

1.3 Write an application that prints, on separate lines, your name, your birthday, your hobbies, your favorite book, and your favorite movie. Label each piece of information in the output.

1.4 Write an application that prints the phrase `Knowledge is Power`:

a. on one line

b. on three lines, one word per line, with the words centered relative to each other

c. inside a box made up of the characters = and |

1.5 Write an application that prints the following diamond shape. Don't print any unneeded characters. (That is, don't make any character string longer than it has to be.)

```
       *
      ***
     *****
    *******
********
    *******
     *****
      ***
       *
```

1.6   Write an application that displays your initials in large block letters. Make each large letter out of the corresponding regular character. For example:

```
JJJJJJJJJJJJJJJ    AAAAAAAAA      LLLL
JJJJJJJJJJJJJJJ    AAAAAAAAAAA    LLLL
         JJJJ      AAA     AAA    LLLL
         JJJJ      AAA     AAA    LLLL
         JJJJ      AAAAAAAAAAA    LLLL
J        JJJJ      AAAAAAAAAAA    LLLL
JJ       JJJJ      AAA     AAA    LLLL
  JJJJJJJJJJJ      AAA     AAA    LLLLLLLLLLLLLL
    JJJJJJJJJ      AAA     AAA    LLLLLLLLLLLLLL
```

answers to self-review questions

1.1   The hardware of a computer system consists of its physical components such as a circuit board, monitor, or keyboard. Computer software are the programs that are executed by the hardware and the data that those programs use. Hardware is tangible, whereas software is intangible. In order to be useful, hardware requires software and software requires hardware.

1.2   The operating system provides a user interface and efficiently coordinates the use of resources such as main memory and the CPU.

1.3   The information is broken into pieces, and those pieces are represented as numbers.

1.4   In general, N bits can represent 2^N unique items. Therefore:

   a. 2 bits can represent 4 items because $2^2 = 4$.

   b. 4 bits can represent 16 items because $2^4 = 16$.

   c. 5 bits can represent 32 items because $2^5 = 32$.

   d. 7 bits can represent 128 items because $2^7 = 128$.

1.5   There are eight bits in a byte. Therefore:

   a. 8 bytes = 8 * 8 bits = 64 bits

   b. 2 KB = 2 * 1,024 bytes = 2,048 bytes = 2,048 * 8 bits = 16,384 bits

   c. 4 MB = 4 * 1,048,576 bytes = 4,194,304 bytes = 4,194,304 * 8 bits = 33,554,432 bits

1.6   The two primary hardware components are main memory and the CPU. Main memory holds the currently active programs and data. The CPU retrieves individual program instructions from main memory, one at a time, and executes them.

1.7   A memory address is a number that uniquely identifies a particular memory location in which a value is stored.

1.8   Main memory is volatile, which means the information that is stored in it will be lost if the power supply to the computer is turned off. Secondary memory devices are nonvolatile; therefore the information that is stored on them is retained even if the power goes off.

1.9   A file server is a network computer that is dedicated to storing and providing programs and data that are needed by many network users.

1.10 Counting the number of unique connections in Fig. 1.16, there are 10 communication lines needed to fully connect a point-to-point network of five computers. Adding a sixth computer to the network will require that it be connected to the original five, bringing the total to 15 communication lines.

1.11 The word Internet comes from the word internetworking, a concept related to wide-area networks (WANs). An internetwork connects one network to another. The Internet is a WAN.

1.12 Breaking down the parts of each URL:

   a. `duke` is the name of a computer within the `csc` subdomain (the Department of Computing Sciences) of the `villanova.edu` domain, which represents Villanova University. The `edu` top-level domain indicates that it is an educational organization. This URL is requesting a file called `examples.html` from within a subdirectory called `jss`.

   b. `java` is the name of a computer (Web server) at the `sun.com` domain, which represents Sun Microsystems, Inc. The `com` top-level domain indicates that it is a commercial business. This URL is requesting a file called `index.html` from within a subdirectory called `products`.

1.13 High-level languages allow a programmer to express a series of program instructions in English-like terms that are relatively easy to read and use. However, in order to execute, a program must be expressed in a particular computer's machine language, which consists of a series of bits that are basically unreadable by humans. A high-level language program must be translated into machine language before it can be run.

1.14 Java bytecode is a low-level representation of a Java source code program. The Java compiler translates the source code into bytecode, which can then be executed using the Java interpreter. The bytecode might be transported across the Web before being executed by a Java interpreter that is part of a Web browser.

1.15 White space is a term that refers to the spaces, tabs, and newline characters that separate words and symbols in a program. The compiler ignores extra white space; therefore, it doesn't affect execution. However, it is crucial to use white space appropriately to make a program readable to humans.

1.16 All of the identifiers shown are valid except 12345 (since an identifier cannot begin with a digit) and black&white (since an identifier cannot contain the character &). The identifiers RESULT and result are both valid, but should not be used together in a program because they differ only by case. The underscore character (as in answer_7) is a valid part of an identifier.

1.17 Syntax rules define how the symbols and words of a programming language can be put together. The semantics of a programming language instruction determine what will happen when that instruction is executed.

1.18 A black and white picture can be drawn using a series of dots, called pixels. Pixels that correspond to a value of 0 are displayed in white and pixels that correspond to a value of 1 are displayed in black. By using thousands of pixels, a realistic black and white photo can be produced on a computer screen.

This chapter explores the key elements that we use in a program: objects and primitive data. We develop the ability to create and use objects for the services they provide. This ability is fundamental to the process of writing any program in an object-oriented language such as Java. We use objects to manipulate character strings, obtain information from the user, perform complex calculations, and format output. In the Graphics Track of this chapter, we explore the relationship between Java and the Web, and delve into Java's abilities to manipulate color and draw shapes.

chapter
objectives

- Establish the difference between primitive data and objects.

- Declare and use variables.

- Perform mathematical computations.

- Create objects and use them for the services they provide.

- Explore the difference between a Java application and a Java applet.

- Create graphical programs that draw shapes.

2.0 an introduction to objects

As we stated in Chapter 1, Java is an object-oriented language. As the name implies, an *object* is a fundamental entity in a Java program. This book is centered on the idea of developing software by defining objects with which we can interact and that interact with each other.

In addition to objects, a Java program also manages primitive data. *Primitive data* include common, fundamental values such as numbers and characters. An object usually represents something more specialized or complex, such as a bank account. An object often contains primitive values and is in part defined by them. For example, an object that represents a bank account might contain the account balance, which is stored as a primitive numeric value.

A *data type* defines a set of values and the operations that can be performed on those values. We perform operations on primitive types using *operators* that are built into the programming language. For example, the addition operator + is used to add two numbers together. We discuss Java's primitive data types and their operators later in this chapter.

An object is defined by a *class*, which can be thought of as the data type of the object. The operations that can be performed on the object are defined by the methods in the class. As we discussed in Chapter 1, a method is a collection of programming statements that is given a specific name so that we can invoke the method as needed.

Once a class has been defined, multiple objects can be created from that class. For example, once we define a class to represent the concept of a bank account, we can create multiple objects that represent specific, individual bank accounts. Each bank account object would keep track of its own balance. This is an example of *encapsulation*, meaning that each object protects and manages its own information. The methods defined in the bank account class would allow us to perform operations on individual bank account objects. For instance, we might withdraw money from a particular account. We can think of these operations as services that the object performs. The act of invoking a method on an object sometimes is referred to as sending a *message* to the object, requesting that the service be performed.

Classes can be created from other classes using *inheritance*. That is, the definition of one class can be based on another class that already exists. Inheritance is a form of software *reuse*, capitalizing on the similarities between various kinds of classes that we may want to create. One class can be used to derive several new classes. Derived classes can then be used to derive even more classes. This creates a hierarchy of classes, where characteristics defined in one class are inherited by its children, which in turn pass them on to their children, and so on. For example, we might create a hierarchy of classes that represent various types of accounts. Common characteristics are defined in high-level classes, and specific differences are defined in derived classes.

Classes, objects, encapsulation, and inheritance are the primary ideas that make up the world of object-oriented software. They are depicted in Fig. 2.1.

This chapter focuses on how to use objects and primitive data. In Chapter 4, we explore how to define our own objects by writing our own classes and methods. In Chapter 7, we explore inheritance.

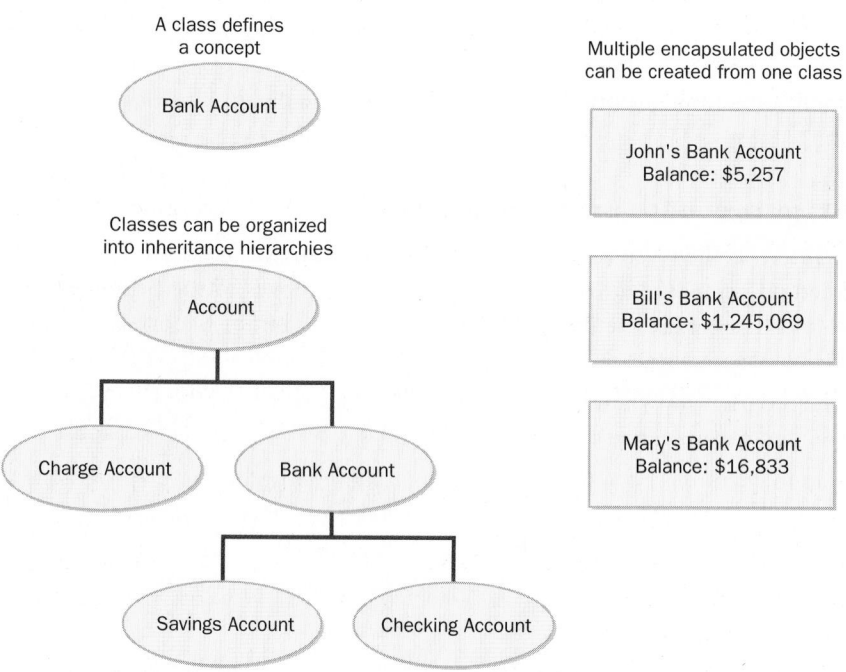

figure 2.1   Various aspects of object-oriented software

2.1 using objects

In the `Lincoln` program in Chapter 1, we invoked a method through an object as follows:

```
System.out.println ("Whatever you are, be a good one.");
```

The `System.out` object represents an output device or file, which by default is the monitor screen. To be more precise, the object's name is `out` and it is stored in the `System` class. We explore that relationship in more detail at the appropriate point in the text.

The `println` method represents a service that the `System.out` object performs for us. Whenever we request it, the object will print a string of characters to the screen. We can say that we send the `println` message to the `System.out` object to request that some text be printed.

Each piece of data that we send to a method is called a *parameter*. In this case, the `println` method takes only one parameter: the string of characters to be printed.

The `System.out` object also provides another service we can use: the `print` method. Let's look at both of these services in more detail.

the `print` and `println` methods

The difference between `print` and `println` is small but important. The `println` method prints the information sent to it, then moves to the beginning of the next line. The `print` method is similar to `println`, but does not advance to the next line when completed.

The program shown in Listing 2.1 is called `Countdown`, and it invokes both the `print` and `println` methods.

Carefully compare the output of the `Countdown` program to the program code. Note that the word `Liftoff` is printed on the same line as the first few words, even though it is printed using the `println` method. Remember that the `println` method moves to the beginning of the next line *after* the information passed to it is printed.

Often it is helpful to use graphics to show objects and their interaction. Figure 2.2 shows part of the situation that occurs in the `Countdown` program. The `Countdown` class, with its `main` method, is shown invoking the `println` method of the `System.out` object.

listing
    2.1

```java
//********************************************************************
//  Countdown.java        Author: Lewis/Loftus
//
//  Demonstrates the difference between print and println.
//********************************************************************

public class Countdown
{
   //-----------------------------------------------------------------
   //  Prints two lines of output representing a rocket countdown.
   //-----------------------------------------------------------------
   public static void main (String[] args)
   {
      System.out.print ("Three... ");
      System.out.print ("Two... ");
      System.out.print ("One... ");
      System.out.print ("Zero... ");

      System.out.println ("Liftoff!"); // appears on first output line
      System.out.println ("Houston, we have a problem.");
   }
}
```

output

```
Three . . . Two . . . One . . . Zero . . . Liftoff!
Houston, we have a problem.
```

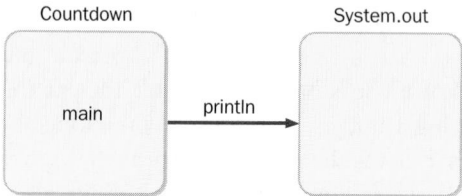

figure 2.2   Sending a message

We mentioned in the previous section that the act of invoking a method is referred to, in object-oriented terms, as sending a message. The diagram in Figure 2.2 supports this interpretation by showing the method name—the message—on the arrow. We could also have shown the information that makes up the rest of the message: the parameters to the methods.

As we explore objects and classes in more detail throughout this book, we will formalize the types of diagrams we use to represent various aspects of an object-oriented program. The more complex our programs get, the more helpful such diagrams become.

abstraction

An object is an *abstraction,* meaning that the precise details of how it works are irrelevant from the point of view of the user of the object. We don't really need to know how the `println` method prints characters to the screen as long as we can count on it to do its job. Of course, it is sometimes helpful to understand such information, but it is not necessary in order to *use* the object.

Sometimes it is important to hide or ignore certain details. Humans are capable of mentally managing around seven (plus or minus two) pieces of information in short-term memory. Beyond that, we start to lose track of some of the pieces. However, if we group pieces of information together, those pieces can be managed as one "chunk" in our minds. We don't actively deal with all of the details in the chunk, but we can still manage it as a single entity. Therefore, we can deal with large quantities of information by organizing them into chunks. An object is a construct that organizes information and allows us to hide the details inside. An object is therefore a wonderful abstraction.

We use abstractions every day. Think about a car for a moment. You don't necessarily need to know how a four-cycle combustion engine works in order to drive a car. You just need to know some basic operations: how to turn it on, how to put it in gear, how to make it move with the pedals and steering wheel, and how to stop it. These operations define the way a person interacts with the car. They mask the details of what is happening inside the car that allow it to function. When you're driving a car, you're not usually thinking about the spark plugs igniting the gasoline that drives the piston that turns the crankshaft that turns the axle that turns the wheels. If you had to worry about all of these underlying details, you'd probably never be able to operate something as complicated as a car.

Initially, all cars had manual transmissions. The driver had to understand and deal with the details of changing gears with the stick shift. Eventually, automatic transmissions were developed, and the driver no longer had to worry about shifting gears. Those details were hidden by raising the *level of abstraction*.

> **key concept**
>
> An abstraction hides details. A good abstraction hides the right details at the right time so that we can manage complexity.

Of course, someone has to deal with the details. The car manufacturer has to know the details in order to design and build the car in the first place. A car mechanic relies on the fact that most people don't have the expertise or tools necessary to fix a car when it breaks.

Thus, the level of abstraction must be appropriate for each situation. Some people prefer to drive a manual transmission car. A race car driver, for instance, needs to control the shifting manually for optimum performance.

Likewise, someone has to create the code for the objects we use. Soon we will define our own objects by defining classes and their methods. For now, we can make use of objects that have been defined for us already. Abstraction makes that possible.

2.2 string literals

A character string is an object in Java, defined by the class `String`. Because strings are so fundamental to computer programming, Java provides the ability to use a *string literal*, delimited by double quotation characters, as we've seen in previous examples. We explore the `String` class and its methods in more detail later in this chapter. For now, let's explore two other useful details about strings: concatenation and escape sequences.

string concatenation

The program called `Facts` shown in Listing 2.2 contains several `println` statements. The first one prints a sentence that is somewhat long and will not fit on one line of the program. A character string, delimited by the double quotation character, cannot be split between two lines of code. One way to get around this problem is to use the *string concatenation* operator, the plus sign (+). String concatenation produces one string in which the second string is appended to the first. The string concatenation operation in the first `println` statement results in one large string that is passed to the method and printed.

listing
  2.2

```
//********************************************************************
//  Facts.java        Author: Lewis/Loftus
//
//  Demonstrates the use of the string concatenation operator and the
//  automatic conversion of an integer to a string.
//********************************************************************

public class Facts
{
   //-----------------------------------------------------------------
   //  Prints various facts.
   //-----------------------------------------------------------------
   public static void main (String[] args)
   {
      // Strings can be concatenated into one long string
      System.out.println ("We present the following facts for your "
                          + "extracurricular edification:");

      System.out.println ();

      // A string can contain numeric digits
      System.out.println ("Letters in the Hawaiian alphabet: 12");

      // A numeric value can be concatenated to a string
      System.out.println ("Dialing code for Antarctica: " + 672);

      System.out.println ("Year in which Leonardo da Vinci invented "
                          + "the parachute: " + 1515);

      System.out.println ("Speed of ketchup: " + 40 + " km per year");
   }
}
```

output

```
We present the following facts for your extracurricular edification:

Letters in the Hawaiian alphabet: 12
Dialing code for Antarctica: 672
Year in which Leonardo da Vinci invented the parachute: 1515
Speed of ketchup: 40 km per year
```

Note that we don't have to pass any information to the println method, as
shown in the second line of the Facts program. This call does not print any vis-

ible characters, but it does move to the next line of output. In this case, the call to `println` passing in no parameters has the effect of printing a blank line.

The rest of the calls to `println` in the `Facts` program demonstrate another interesting thing about string concatenation: Strings can be concatenated with numbers. Note that the numbers in those lines are not enclosed in double quotes and are therefore not character strings. In these cases, the number is automatically converted to a string, and then the two strings are concatenated.

Because we are printing particular values, we simply could have included the numeric value as part of the string literal, such as:

```
"Speed of ketchup: 40 km per year"
```

Digits are characters and can be included in strings as needed. We separate them in the `Facts` program to demonstrate the ability to concatenate a string and a number. This technique will be useful in upcoming examples.

As we've mentioned, the + operator is also used for arithmetic addition. Therefore, what the + operator does depends on the types of data on which it operates. If either or both of the operands of the + operator are strings, then string concatenation is performed.

The `Addition` program shown in Listing 2.3 demonstrates the distinction between string concatenation and arithmetic addition. The `Addition` program uses the + operator four times. In the first call to `println`, both + operations perform string concatenation. This is because the operators execute left to right. The first operator concatenates the string with the first number (24), creating a larger string. Then that string is concatenated with the second number (45), creating an even larger string, which gets printed.

In the second call to `println`, parentheses are used to group the + operation with the two numbers. This forces that operation to happen first. Because both operands are numbers, the numbers are added in the arithmetic sense, producing the result 69. That number is then concatenated with the string, producing a larger string that gets printed.

We revisit this type of situation later in this chapter when we formalize the rules that define the order in which operators get evaluated.

escape sequences

Because the double quotation character (") is used in the Java language to indicate the beginning and end of a string, we must use a special technique to print the quotation character. If we simply put it in a string (""""), the compiler gets

listing
2.3

```
//********************************************************************
//  Addition.java        Author: Lewis/Loftus
//
//  Demonstrates the difference between the addition and string
//  concatenation operators.
//********************************************************************

public class Addition
{
   //-----------------------------------------------------------------
   //  Concatenates and adds two numbers and prints the results.
   //-----------------------------------------------------------------
   public static void main (String[] args)
   {
      System.out.println ("24 and 45 concatenated: " + 24 + 45);

      System.out.println ("24 and 45 added: " + (24 + 45));
   }
}
```

output

```
24 and 45 concatenated: 2445
24 and 45 added: 69
```

confused because it thinks the second quotation character is the end of the string and doesn't know what to do with the third one. This results in a compile-time error.

To overcome this problem, Java defines several *escape sequences* to represent special characters. An escape sequence begins with the backslash character (\), and indicates that the character or characters that follow should be interpreted in a special way. Figure 2.3 lists the Java escape sequences.

The program in Listing 2.4, called Roses, prints some text resembling a poem. It uses only one println statement to do so, despite the fact that the poem is several lines long. Note the escape sequences used throughout the string. The \n escape sequence forces the output to a new line, and the \t escape sequence represents a tab character. The \" escape sequence ensures that the quote character is treated as part of the string, not the termination of it, which enables it to be printed as part of the output.

Escape Sequence	Meaning
\b	backspace
\t	tab
\n	newline
\r	carriage return
\"	double quote
\'	single quote
\\	backslash

figure 2.3   Java escape sequences

listing
2.4

```java
//********************************************************************
//  Roses.java        Author: Lewis/Loftus
//
//  Demonstrates the use of escape sequences.
//********************************************************************

public class Roses
{
   //-----------------------------------------------------------------
   //  Prints a poem (of sorts) on multiple lines.
   //-----------------------------------------------------------------
   public static void main (String[] args)
   {
      System.out.println ("Roses are red,\n\tViolets are blue,\n" +
         "Sugar is sweet,\n\tBut I have \"commitment issues\",\n\t" +
         "So I'd rather just be friends\n\tAt this point in our " +
         "relationship.");
   }
}
```

output

```
Roses are red,
        Violets are blue,
Sugar is sweet,
        But I have "commitment issues",
        So I'd rather just be friends
        At this point in our relationship.
```

2.3 **variables and assignment**

Most of the information we manage in a program is represented by variables. Let's examine how we declare and use them in a program.

variables

A *variable* is a name for a location in memory used to hold a data value. A variable declaration instructs the compiler to reserve a portion of main memory space large enough to hold a particular type of value and indicates the name by which we refer to that location.

Consider the program PianoKeys, shown in Listing 2.5. The first line of the main method is the declaration of a variable named keys that holds an integer (int) value. The declaration also gives keys an initial value of 88. If an initial value is not specified for a variable, the value is undefined. Most Java compilers give errors or warnings if you attempt to use a variable before you've explicitly given it a value.

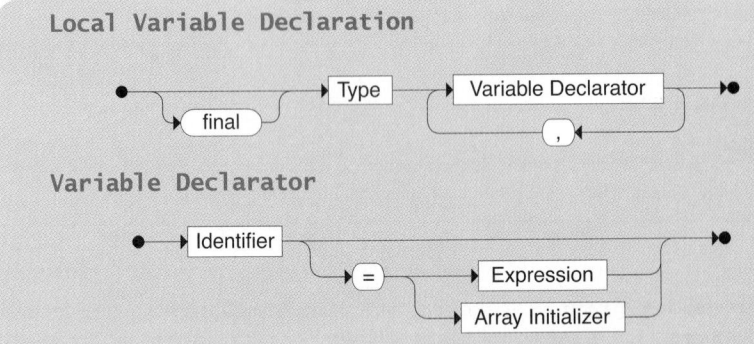

A variable declaration consists of a Type followed by a list of variables. Each variable can be initialized in the declaration to the value of the specified Expression. If the final modifier precedes the declaration, the identifiers are declared as named constants whose values cannot be changed once set.

Examples:

```
int total;
double num1, num2 = 4.356, num3;
char letter = 'A', digit = '7';
final int MAX = 45;
```

listing
   2.5

```
//********************************************************************
//   PianoKeys.java        Author: Lewis/Loftus
//
//   Demonstrates the declaration, initialization, and use of an
//   integer variable.
//********************************************************************

public class PianoKeys
{
   //-----------------------------------------------------------------
   //   Prints the number of keys on a piano.
   //-----------------------------------------------------------------
   public static void main (String[] args)
   {
      int keys = 88;

      System.out.println ("A piano has " + keys + " keys.");
   }
}
```

output

```
A piano has 88 keys.
```

In the `PianoKeys` program, two pieces of information are provided in the call to the `println` method. The first is a string, and the second is the variable `keys`. When a variable is referenced, the value currently stored in it is used. Therefore when the call to `println` is executed, the value of `keys` is obtained. Because that value is an integer, it is automatically converted to a string so it can be concatenated with the initial string. The concatenated string is passed to `println` and printed.

Note that a variable declaration can have multiple variables of the same type declared on one line. Each variable on the line can be declared with or without an initializing value.

the assignment statement

Let's examine a program that changes the value of a variable. Listing 2.6 shows a program called `Geometry`. This program first declares an integer variable called `sides` and initializes it to 7. It then prints out the current value of `sides`.

listing
  2.6

```
//********************************************************************
//  Geometry.java        Author: Lewis/Loftus
//
//  Demonstrates the use of an assignment statement to change the
//  value stored in a variable.
//********************************************************************

public class Geometry
{
   //----------------------------------------------------------------
   //  Prints the number of sides of several geometric shapes.
   //----------------------------------------------------------------
   public static void main (String[] args)
   {
      int sides = 7;   // declaration with initialization
      System.out.println ("A heptagon has " + sides + " sides.");

      sides = 10;   // assignment statement
      System.out.println ("A decagon has " + sides + " sides.");

      sides = 12;
      System.out.println ("A dodecagon has " + sides + " sides.");
   }
}
```

output

```
A heptagon has 7 sides.
A decagon has 10 sides.
A dodecagon has 12 sides.
```

The next line in main changes the value stored in the variable sides:

```
sides = 10;
```

This is called an *assignment statement* because it assigns a value to a variable. When executed, the expression on the right-hand side of the assignment operator (=) is evaluated, and the result is stored in the memory location indicated by the variable on the left-hand side. In this example, the expression is simply a number, 10. We discuss expressions that are more involved than this in the next section.

> **Basic Assignment**
>
> ●──→ Identifier ──→ = ──→ Expression ──→ ; ──→●
>
> The basic assignment statement uses the assignment operator (=) to store the result of the Expression into the specified Identifier, usually a variable.
>
> Examples:
>
> ```
> total = 57;
> count = count + 1;
> value = (min / 2) * lastValue;
> ```

A variable can store only one value of its declared type. A new value overwrites the old one. In this case, when the value 10 is assigned to sides, the original value 7 is overwritten and lost forever. However, when a reference is made to a variable, such as when it is printed, the value of the variable is not changed.

> **key concept**
>
> A variable can store only one value of its declared type.

The Java language is *strongly typed*, meaning that we are not allowed to assign a value to a variable that is inconsistent with its declared type. Trying to combine incompatible types will generate an error when you attempt to compile the program. Therefore, the expression on the right-hand side of an assignment statement must evaluate to a value compatible with the type of the variable on the left-hand side.

> **key concept**
>
> Java is a strongly typed language. Each variable is associated with a specific type for the duration of its existence, and we cannot assign a value of one type to a variable of an incompatible type.

constants

Sometimes we use data that is constant throughout a program. For instance, we might write a program that deals with a theater that can hold no more than 427 people. It is often helpful to give a constant value a name, such as MAX_OCCUPANCY, instead of using a literal value, such as 427, throughout the code. Literal values such as 427 are sometimes referred to as "magic" numbers because their meaning in a program is mystifying.

Constants are identifiers and are similar to variables except that they hold a particular value for the duration of their existence. In Java, if you precede a declaration with the reserved word final, the identifier is made a constant. By convention, uppercase letters are used when naming constants to distinguish them from regular variables, and individual words are separated using the underscore character. For example, the constant describing the maximum occupancy of a theater could be declared as follows:

```
final int MAX_OCCUPANCY = 427;
```

The compiler will produce an error message if you attempt to change the value of a constant once it has been given its initial value. This is another good reason to use them. Constants prevent inadvertent coding errors because the only valid place to change their value is in the initial assignment.

There is a third good reason to use constants. If a constant is used throughout a program and its value needs to be modified, then you have to change it in only one place. For example, if the capacity of the theater changes (because of a renovation) from 427 to 535, then you have to change only one declaration, and all uses of MAX_OCCUPANCY automatically reflect the change. If the literal 427 had been used throughout the code, each use would have to be found and changed. If you were to miss one or two, problems would surely arise.

2.4   primitive data types

There are eight primitive data types in Java: four subsets of integers, two subsets of floating point numbers, a character data type, and a boolean data type. Everything else is represented using objects. Let's examine these eight primitive data types in some detail.

integers and floating points

Java has two basic kinds of numeric values: integers, which have no fractional part, and floating points, which do. There are four integer data types (byte, short, int, and long) and two floating point data types (float and double). All of the numeric types differ by the amount of memory space used to store a value of that type, which determines the range of values that can be represented. The size of each data type is the same for all hardware platforms. All numeric types are *signed,* meaning that both positive and negative values can be stored in them. Figure 2.4 summarizes the numeric primitive types.

Remember from our discussion in Chapter 1 that a bit can be either a 1 or a 0. Because each bit can represent two different states, a string of n bits can be

Type	Storage	Min Value	Max Value
byte	8 bits	–128	127
short	16 bits	–32,768	32,767
int	32 bits	–2,147,483,648	2,147,483,647
long	64 bits	–9,223,372,036,854,775,808	9,223,372,036,854,775,807
float	32 bits	Approximately –3.4E+38 with 7 significant digits	Approximately 3.4E+38 with 7 significant digits
double	64 bits	Approximately –1.7E+308 with 15 significant digits	Approximately 1.7E+308 with 15 significant digits

figure 2.4   The Java numeric primitive types

used to represent 2^n different values. Appendix B describes number systems and these kinds of relationships in more detail.

web bonus

The book's Web site includes a description of the internal storage representation of primitive data types.

When designing a program, we sometimes need to be careful about picking variables of appropriate size so that memory space is not wasted. For example, if a value will not vary outside of a range of 1 to 1000, then a two-byte integer (short) is large enough to accommodate it. On the other hand, when it's not clear what the range of a particular variable will be, we should provide a reasonable, even generous, amount of space. In most situations memory space is not a serious restriction, and we can usually afford generous assumptions.

Note that even though a float value supports very large (and very small) numbers, it only has seven significant digits. Therefore if it is important to accurately maintain a value such as 50341.2077, we need to use a double.

A *literal* is an explicit data value used in a program. The various numbers used in programs such as Facts and Addition and PianoKeys are all *integer literals*. Java assumes all integer literals are of type int, unless an L or l is appended to the end of the value to indicate that it should be considered a literal of type long, such as 45L.

Likewise, Java assumes that all *floating point literals* are of type double. If we need to treat a floating point literal as a float, we append an F or f to the end

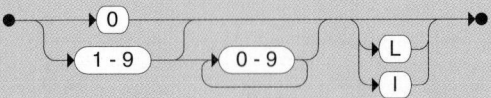

Decimal Integer Literal

An integer literal is composed of a series of digits followed by an optional suffix to indicate that it should be considered a `long` integer. Negation of a literal is considered a separate operation.

Examples:

```
5
2594
4920328L
```

of the value, as in `2.718F` or `123.45f`. Numeric literals of type `double` can be followed by a `D` or `d` if desired.

The following are examples of numeric variable declarations in Java:

```
int answer = 42;
byte smallNumber1, smallNumber2;
long countedStars = 86827263927L;
float ratio = 0.2363F;
double delta = 453.523311903;
```

characters

Characters are another fundamental type of data used and managed on a computer. Individual characters can be treated as separate data items, and as we've seen in several example programs, they can be combined to form character strings.

A *character literal* is expressed in a Java program with single quotes, such as 'b' or 'J' or ';'. You will recall that *string literals* are delineated using double quotation marks, and that the `String` type is not a primitive data type in Java, it is a class name. We discuss the `String` class in detail later in this chapter.

Note the difference between a digit as a character (or part of a string) and a digit as a number (or part of a larger number). The number `602` is a numeric value that can be used in an arithmetic calculation. But in the string `"602 Greenbriar Court"` the 6, 0, and 2 are characters, just like the rest of the characters that make up the string.

The characters we can manage are defined by a *character set*, which is simply a list of characters in a particular order. Each programming language supports a particular character set that defines the valid values for a character variable in that language. Several character sets have been proposed, but only a few have been used regularly over the years. The *ASCII character set* is a popular choice. ASCII stands for the American Standard Code for Information Interchange. The basic ASCII set uses seven bits per character, providing room to support 128 different characters, including:

- uppercase letters, such as `'A'`, `'B'`, and `'C'`
- lowercase letters, such as `'a'`, `'b'`, and `'c'`
- punctuation, such as the period (`'.'`), semicolon (`';'`), and comma (`','`)
- the digits `'0'` through `'9'`
- the space character, `' '`
- special symbols, such as the ampersand (`'&'`), vertical bar (`'|'`), and back-slash (`'\'`)
- control characters, such as the carriage return, null, and end-of-text marks

The *control characters* are sometimes called nonprinting or invisible characters because they do not have a specific symbol that represents them. Yet they are as valid as any other character and can be stored and used in the same ways. Many control characters have special meaning to certain software applications.

As computing became a worldwide endeavor, users demanded a more flexible character set containing other language alphabets. ASCII was extended to use eight bits per character, and the number of characters in the set doubled to 256. The extended ASCII contains many accented and diacritical characters not used in English.

However, even with 256 characters, the ASCII character set cannot represent the world's alphabets, especially given the various Asian alphabets and their many thousands of ideograms. Therefore the developers of the Java programming language chose the *Unicode character set,* which uses 16 bits per character, supporting 65,536 unique characters. The characters and symbols from many languages are included in the Unicode definition. ASCII is a subset of the Unicode character set. Appendix C discusses the Unicode character set in more detail.

In Java, the data type `char` represents a single character. The following are some examples of character variable declarations in Java:

```
char topGrade = 'A';
char symbol1, symbol2, symbol3;
char terminator = ';', separator = ' ';
```

booleans

A boolean value, defined in Java using the reserved word `boolean`, has only two valid values: `true` and `false`. A boolean variable is usually used to indicate whether a particular condition is true, but it can also be used to represent any situation that has two states, such as a light bulb being on or off.

A boolean value cannot be converted to any other data type, nor can any other data type be converted to a boolean value. The words `true` and `false` are reserved in Java as *boolean literals* and cannot be used outside of this context.

The following are some examples of boolean variable declarations in Java:

```
boolean flag = true;
boolean tooHigh, tooSmall, tooRough;
boolean done = false;
```

2.5   arithmetic expressions

An *expression* is a combination of one or more operators and operands. Expressions usually perform a calculation. The value calculated does not have to be a number, but it often is. The operands used in the operations might be literals, constants, variables, or other sources of data. The manner in which expressions are evaluated and used is fundamental to programming.

> **key concept**
>
> Many programming statements involve expressions. Expressions are combinations of one or more operands and the operators used to perform a calculation.

For now we will focus on arithmetic expressions that use numeric operands and produce numeric results. The usual arithmetic operations are defined for both integer and floating point numeric types, including addition (+), subtraction (–), multiplication (*), and division (/). Java also has another arithmetic operation: The *remainder operator* (%) returns the remainder after dividing the second operand into the first. The sign of the result of a remainder operation is the sign of the numerator. Therefore, 17%4 equals 1, –20%3 equals –2, 10%–5 equals 0, and 3%8 equals 3.

As you might expect, if either or both operands to any numeric operator are floating point values, the result is a floating point value. However, the division operator produces results that are less intuitive, depending on the types of the operands. If both operands are integers, the / operator performs *integer division,* meaning that any fractional part of the result is discarded. If one or the other or both operands are floating point values, the / operator performs *floating point division,* and the fractional part of the result is kept. For example, the result of 10/4 is 2, but the results of `10.0/4` and `10/4.0` and `10.0/4.0` are all 2.5.

operator precedence

Operators can be combined to create more complex expressions. For example, consider the following assignment statement:

```
result = 14 + 8 / 2;
```

The entire right-hand side of the assignment is evaluated, and then the result is stored in the variable. But what is the result? It is 11 if the addition is performed first, or it is 18 if the division is performed first. The order of operator evaluation makes a big difference. In this case, the division is performed before the addition, yielding a result of 18. You should note that in this and subsequent examples we have used literal values rather than variables to simplify the expression. The order of operator evaluation is the same if the operands are variables or any other source of data.

All expressions are evaluated according to an *operator precedence hierarchy* that establishes the rules that govern the order in which operations are evaluated. In the case of arithmetic operators, multiplication, division, and the remainder operator all have equal precedence and are performed before addition and subtraction. Any arithmetic operators at the same level of precedence are performed left to right. Therefore we say the arithmetic operators have a *left-to-right association.*

> **key concept**
>
> Java follows a well-defined set of rules that govern the order in which operators will be evaluated in an expression. These rules form an operator precedence hierarchy.

Precedence, however, can be forced in an expression by using parentheses. For instance, if we really wanted the addition to be performed first in the previous example, we could write the expression as follows:

```
result = (14 + 8) / 2;
```

Any expression in parentheses is evaluated first. In complicated expressions, it is good practice to use parentheses even when it is not strictly necessary in order to make it clear how the expression is evaluated.

Parentheses can be nested, and the innermost nested expressions are evaluated first. Consider the following expression:

```
result = 3 * ((18 - 4) / 2);
```

In this example, the result is 21. First, the subtraction is performed, forced by the inner parentheses. Then, even though multiplication and division are at the same level of precedence and usually would be evaluated left to right, the division is performed first because of the outer parentheses. Finally, the multiplication is performed.

After the arithmetic operations are complete, the computed result is stored in the variable on the left-hand side of the assignment operator (=). In other words, the assignment operator has a lower precedence than any of the arithmetic operators.

Figure 2.5 shows a precedence table with the relationships between the arithmetic operators, parentheses, and the assignment operator. Appendix D includes a full precedence table showing all Java operators.

A *unary operator* has only one operand, while a *binary operator* has two. The + and − arithmetic operators can be either unary or binary. The binary versions accomplish addition and subtraction, and the unary versions represent positive and negative numbers. For example, −1 is an example of using the unary negation operator to make the value negative.

Precedence Level	Operator	Operation	Associates
1	+	unary plus	R to L
	−	unary minus	
2	*	multiplication	L to R
	/	division	
	%	remainder	
3	+	addition	L to R
	−	subtraction	
	+	string concatenation	
4	=	assignment	R to L

figure 2.5   Precedence among some of the Java operators

For an expression to be syntactically correct, the number of left parentheses must match the number of right parentheses and they must be properly nested. The following examples are *not* valid expressions:

```
result = ((19 + 8) % 3) − 4);    // not valid
result = (19 (+ 8 %) 3 − 4);     // not valid
```

The program in Listing 2.7, called `TempConverter`, converts a Celsius temperature value to its equivalent Fahrenheit value. Note that the operands to the division operation are double to ensure that the fractional part of the number

listing
2.7

```
//********************************************************************
//   TempConverter.java        Author: Lewis/Loftus
//
//   Demonstrates the use of primitive data types and arithmetic
//   expressions.
//********************************************************************

public class TempConverter
{
   //-----------------------------------------------------------------
   //   Computes the Fahrenheit equivalent of a specific Celsius
   //   value using the formula F = (9/5)C + 32.
   //-----------------------------------------------------------------
   public static void main (String[] args)
   {
      final int BASE = 32;
      final double CONVERSION_FACTOR = 9.0 / 5.0;

      int celsiusTemp = 24;   // value to convert
      double fahrenheitTemp;

      fahrenheitTemp = celsiusTemp * CONVERSION_FACTOR + BASE;

      System.out.println ("Celsius Temperature: " + celsiusTemp);
      System.out.println ("Fahrenheit Equivalent: " + fahrenheitTemp);
   }
}
```

output

```
Celsius Temperature: 24
Fahrenheit Equivalent: 75.2
```

is kept. The precedence rules dictate that the multiplication happens before the addition in the final conversion computation, which is what we want.

data conversion

Because Java is a strongly typed language, each data value is associated with a particular type. It is sometimes helpful or necessary to convert a data value of one type to another type, but we must be careful that we don't lose important information in the process. For example, suppose a `short` variable that holds the number 1000 is converted to a `byte` value. Because a `byte` does not have enough bits to represent the value 1000, some bits would be lost in the conversion, and the number represented in the `byte` would not keep its original value.

A conversion between one primitive type and another falls into one of two categories: widening conversions and narrowing conversions. *Widening conversions* are the safest because they usually do not lose information. They are called widening conversions because they go from one data type to another type that uses an equal or greater amount of space to store the value. Figure 2.6 lists the Java widening conversions.

For example, it is safe to convert from a `byte` to a `short` because a `byte` is stored in 8 bits and a `short` is stored in 16 bits. There is no loss of information. All widening conversions that go from an integer type to another integer type, or from a floating point type to another floating point type, preserve the numeric value exactly.

Although widening conversions do not lose any information about the magnitude of a value, the widening conversions that result in a floating point value can lose precision. When converting from an `int` or a `long` to a `float`, or from

From	To
byte	short, int, long, float, or double
short	int, long, float, or double
char	int, long, float, or double
int	long, float, or double
long	float or double
float	double

figure 2.6 Java widening conversions

a `long` to a `double`, some of the least significant digits may be lost. In this case, the resulting floating point value will be a rounded version of the integer value, following the rounding techniques defined in the IEEE 754 floating point standard.

Narrowing conversions are more likely to lose information than widening conversions are. They often go from one type to a type that uses less space to store a value, and therefore some of the information may be compromised. Narrowing conversions can lose both numeric magnitude and precision. Therefore, in general, they should be avoided. Figure 2.7 lists the Java narrowing conversions.

An exception to the space-shrinking situation in narrowing conversions is when we convert a `byte` (8 bits) or `short` (16 bits) to a `char` (16 bits). These are still considered narrowing conversions because the sign bit is incorporated into the new character value. Since a character value is unsigned, a negative integer will be converted into a character that has no particular relationship to the numeric value of the original integer.

Note that `boolean` values are not mentioned in either widening or narrowing conversions. A `boolean` value cannot be converted to any other primitive type and vice versa.

In Java, conversions can occur in three ways:

▶ assignment conversion

▶ arithmetic promotion

▶ casting

From	To
byte	char
short	byte or char
char	byte or short
int	byte, short, or char
long	byte, short, char, or int
float	byte, short, char, int, or long
double	byte, short, char, int, long, or float

figure 2.7   Java narrowing conversions

Assignment conversion occurs when a value of one type is assigned to a variable of another type during which the value is converted to the new type. Only widening conversions can be accomplished through assignment. For example, if `money` is a `float` variable and `dollars` is an `int` variable, then the following assignment statement automatically converts the value in `dollars` to a `float`:

```
money = dollars;
```

Therefore, if `dollars` contains the value 25, after the assignment, `money` contains the value 25.0. However, if we attempt to assign `money` to `dollars`, the compiler will issue an error message alerting us to the fact that we are attempting a narrowing conversion that could lose information. If we really want to do this assignment, we have to make the conversion explicit using a cast.

Arithmetic promotion occurs automatically when certain arithmetic operators need to modify their operands in order to perform the operation. For example, when a floating point value called `sum` is divided by an integer value called `count`, the value of `count` is promoted to a floating point value automatically, before the division takes place, producing a floating point result:

```
result = sum / count;
```

Casting is the most general form of conversion in Java. If a conversion can be accomplished at all in a Java program, it can be accomplished using a cast. A cast is a Java operator that is specified by a type name in parentheses. It is placed in front of the value to be converted. For example, to convert `money` to an integer value, we could put a cast in front of it:

```
dollars = (int) money;
```

The cast returns the value in `money`, truncating any fractional part. If `money` contained the value 84.69, then after the assignment, `dollars` would contain the value 84. Note, however, that the cast does not change the value in `money`. After the assignment operation is complete, `money` still contains the value 84.69.

Casts are helpful in many situations where we need to treat a value temporarily as another type. For example, if we want to divide the integer value `total` by the integer value `count` and get a floating point result, we could do it as follows:

```
result = (float) total / count;
```

First, the cast operator returns a floating point version of the value in `total`. This operation does not change the value in `total`. Then, `count` is treated as a floating point value via arithmetic promotion. Now the division operator will perform floating point division and produce the intended result. If the cast had not been included, the operation would have performed integer division and truncated the answer before assigning it to `result`. Also note that because the cast operator has a higher precedence than the division operator, the cast operates on the value of `total`, not on the result of the division.

2.6   creating objects

A variable can hold either a primitive value or a *reference to an object*. Like variables that hold primitive types, a variable that serves as an object reference must be declared. A class is used to define an object, and the class name can be thought of as the type of an object. The declarations of object references have a similar structure to the declarations of primitive variables.

The following declaration creates a reference to a `String` object:

```
String name;
```

That declaration is like the declaration of an integer, in that the type is followed by the variable name we want to use. However, no string object actually exists yet. To create an object, we use the `new` operator:

```
name = new String ("James Gosling");
```

The act of creating an object using the `new` operator is called *instantiation*. An object is said to be an *instance* of a particular class. After the `new` operator creates the object, a *constructor* is invoked to help set it up initially. A constructor has the same name as the class and is similar to a method. In this example, the parameter to the constructor is a string literal that specifies the characters that the string object will hold.

> The `new` operator returns a reference to a newly created object.
>
> key concept

The act of declaring the object reference variable and creating the object itself can be combined into one step by initializing the variable in the declaration, just as we do with primitive types:

```
String name = new String ("James Gosling");
```

After an object has been instantiated, we use the *dot operator* to access its methods. We've used the dot operator many times in previous programs, such as in calls to `System.out.println`. The dot operator is appended directly after the object reference, followed by the method being invoked. For example, to invoke the `length` method defined in the `String` class, we use the dot operator on the name reference variable:

```
count = name.length()
```

The `length` method does not take any parameters, but the parentheses are still necessary to indicate that a method is being invoked. Some methods produce a value that is *returned* when the method completes. The purpose of the `length` method of the `String` class is to determine and return the length of the string (the number of characters it contains). In this example, the returned value is assigned to the variable `count`. For the string `"James  Gosling"`, the `length` method returns 13 (this includes the space between the first and last names). Some methods do not return a value.

An object reference variable (such as `name`) actually stores the address where the object is stored in memory. We explore the nuances of object references, instantiation, and constructors in later chapters.

the `String` class

Let's examine the `String` class in more detail. Strings in Java are objects represented by the `String` class. Figure 2.8 lists some of the more useful methods of the `String` class. The method headers are listed, and they indicate the type of information that must be passed to the method. The type shown in front of the method name is called the *return type* of the method and indicates the type of information that will be returned, if anything. A return type of `void` indicates that the method does not return a value. The returned value can be used in the calling method as needed.

Once a `String` object is created, its value cannot be lengthened, shortened, nor can any of its characters change. Thus we say that a `String` object is *immutable*. However, several methods in the `String` class return new `String` objects that are often the result of modifying the original string's value.

Note also that some of the `String` methods refer to the *index* of a particular character. A character in a string can be specified by its position, or index, in the string. The index of the first character in a string is zero, the index of the next character is one, and so on. Therefore in the string `"Hello"`, the index of the character `'H'` is zero and the character at index four is `'o'`.

Several `String` methods are exercised in the program called `StringMutation`, shown in Listing 2.8.

```
String (String str)
    Constructor: creates a new string object with the same characters as str.
char charAt (int index)
    Returns the character at the specified index.
int compareTo (String str)
    Returns an integer indicating if this string is lexically before (a negative return
    value), equal to (a zero return value), or lexically after (a positive return value),
    the string str.
String concat (String str)
    Returns a new string consisting of this string concatenated with str.
boolean equals (String str)
    Returns true if this string contains the same characters as str (including
    case) and false otherwise.
boolean equalsIgnoreCase (String str)
    Returns true if this string contains the same characters as str (without
    regard to case) and false otherwise.
int length ()
    Returns the number of characters in this string.
String replace (char oldChar, char newChar)
    Returns a new string that is identical with this string except that every
    occurrence of oldChar is replaced by newChar.
String substring (int offset, int endIndex)
    Returns a new string that is a subset of this string starting at index offset
    and extending through endIndex-1.
String toLowerCase ()
    Returns a new string identical to this string except all uppercase letters are
    converted to their lowercase equivalent.
String toUpperCase ()
    Returns a new string identical to this string except all lowercase letters are
    converted to their uppercase equivalent.
```

figure 2.8   Some methods of the String class

Figure 2.9 shows the String objects that are created in the StringMutation program. Compare this diagram to the program code and the output. Keep in mind that this is not a single String object that changes its data; this program creates five separate String objects using various methods of the String class.

listing
    2.8

```
//********************************************************************
//  StringMutation.java        Author: Lewis/Loftus
//
//  Demonstrates the use of the String class and its methods.
//********************************************************************

public class StringMutation
{
   //----------------------------------------------------------------
   //  Prints a string and various mutations of it.
   //----------------------------------------------------------------
   public static void main (String[] args)
   {
      String phrase = new String ("Change is inevitable");
      String mutation1, mutation2, mutation3, mutation4;

      System.out.println ("Original string: \"" + phrase + "\"");
      System.out.println ("Length of string: " + phrase.length());

      mutation1 = phrase.concat (", except from vending machines.");
      mutation2 = mutation1.toUpperCase();
      mutation3 = mutation2.replace ('E', 'X');
      mutation4 = mutation3.substring (3, 30);

      // Print each mutated string
      System.out.println ("Mutation #1: " + mutation1);
      System.out.println ("Mutation #2: " + mutation2);
      System.out.println ("Mutation #3: " + mutation3);
      System.out.println ("Mutation #4: " + mutation4);

      System.out.println ("Mutated length: " + mutation4.length());
   }
}
```

output

```
Original string: "Change is inevitable"
Length of string: 20
Mutation #1: Change is inevitable, except from vending machines.
Mutation #2: CHANGE IS INEVITABLE, EXCEPT FROM VENDING MACHINES.
Mutation #3: CHANGX IS INXVITABLX, XXCXPT FROM VXNDING MACHINXS.
Mutation #4: NGX IS INXVITABLX, XXCXPT F
Mutated length: 27
```

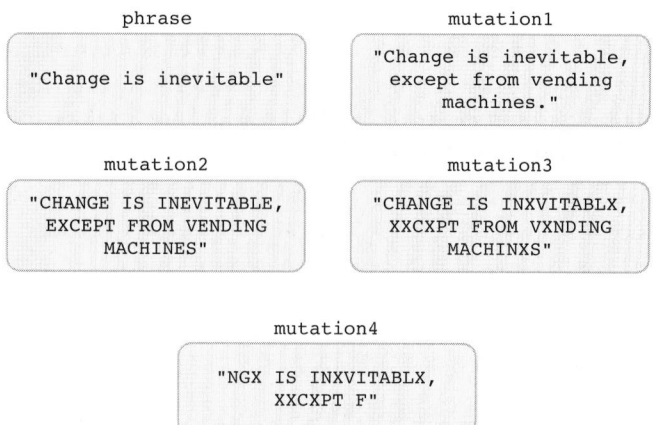

figure 2.9   The String objects created in the StringMutation program

Even though they are not primitive types, strings are so fundamental and so often used that Java defines string literals delimited by double quotation marks, as we've seen in various examples. This is a shortcut notation. Whenever a string literal appears, a String object is created. Therefore the following declaration is valid:

```
String name = "James Gosling";
```

That is, for String objects, the explicit use of the new operator and the call to the constructor can be eliminated. In most cases, we will use this simplified syntax.

2.7   class libraries and packages

A *class library* is a set of classes that supports the development of programs. A compiler often comes with a class library. Class libraries can also be obtained separately through third-party vendors. The classes in a class library contain methods that are often valuable to a programmer because of the special functionality they offer. In fact, programmers often become dependent on the methods in a class library and begin to think of them as part of the language. However, technically, they are not in the language definition.

The String class, for instance, is not an inherent part of the Java language. It is part of the Java *standard class library* that can be found in any Java development environment. The classes that make up the library were created by employees at Sun Microsystems, the people who created the Java language.

The class library is made up of several clusters of related classes, which are sometimes called Java APIs, or *Application Programmer Interface*. For example, we may refer to the Java Database API when we're talking about the set of classes that help us write programs that interact with a database. Another example of an API is the Java Swing API, which refers to a set of classes that define special graphical components used in a graphical user interface (GUI). Sometimes the entire standard library is referred to generically as the Java API, though we generally avoid that use.

The classes of the Java standard class library are also grouped into *packages*, which, like the APIs, let us group related classes by one name. Each class is part of a particular package. The String class, for example, is part of the java.lang package. The System class is part of the java.lang package as well. Figure 2.10 shows the organizations of packages in the overall library.

The package organization is more fundamental and language based than the API names. Though there is a general correspondence between package and API names, the groups of classes that make up a given API might cross packages. We primarily refer to classes in terms of their package organization in this text.

Figure 2.11 describes some of the packages that are part of the Java standard class library. These packages are available on any platform that supports Java software development. Many of these packages support highly specific programming techniques and will not come into play in the development of basic programs.

Various classes of the Java standard class library are discussed throughout this book. Appendix M serves as a general reference for many of the classes in the Java class library.

the import declaration

The classes of the package java.lang are automatically available for use when writing a program. To use classes from any other package, however, we must either *fully qualify* the reference, or use an *import declaration*.

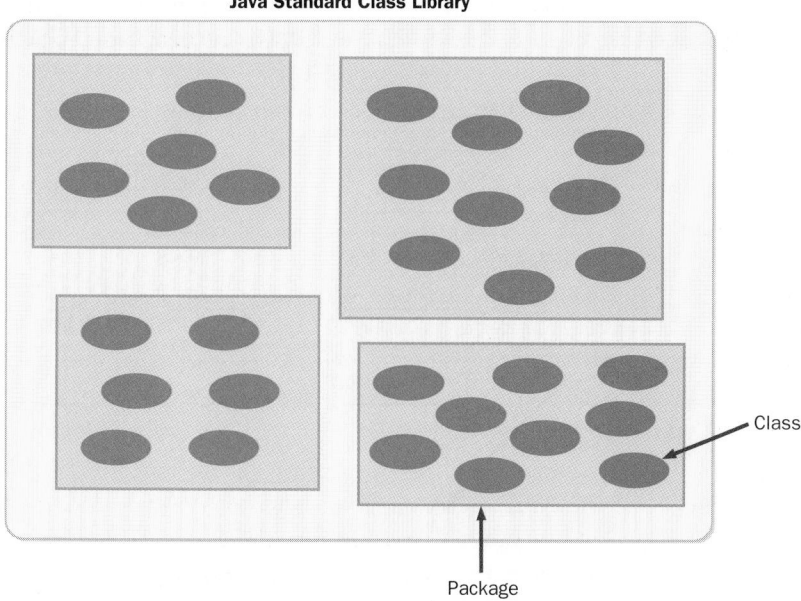

Java Standard Class Library

Class

Package

figure 2.10   Classes organized into packages in the
Java standard class library

When you want to use a class from a class library in a program, you could use its fully qualified name, including the package name, every time it is referenced. For example, every time you want to refer to the Random class that is defined in the java.util package, you can write java.util.Random. However, completely specifying the package and class name every time it is needed quickly becomes tiring. Java provides the import declaration to simplify these references.

The import declaration identifies the packages and classes that will be used in a program so that the fully qualified name is not necessary with each reference. The following is an example of an import declaration:

```
import java.util.Random;
```

This declaration asserts that the Random class of the java.util package may be used in the program. Once this import declaration is made, it is sufficient to use the simple name Random when referring to that class in the program.

Another form of the import declaration uses an asterisk (*) to indicate that any class inside the package might be used in the program. Therefore, the following

Package	Provides support to
`java.applet`	Create programs (applets) that are easily transported across the Web.
`java.awt`	Draw graphics and create graphical user interfaces; AWT stands for Abstract Windowing Toolkit.
`java.beans`	Define software components that can be easily combined into applications.
`java.io`	Perform a wide variety of input and output functions.
`java.lang`	General support; it is automatically imported into all Java programs.
`java.math`	Perform calculations with arbitrarily high precision.
`java.net`	Communicate across a network.
`java.rmi`	Create programs that can be distributed across multiple computers; RMI stands for Remote Method Invocation.
`java.security`	Enforce security restrictions.
`java.sql`	Interact with databases; SQL stands for Structured Query Language.
`java.text`	Format text for output.
`java.util`	General utilities.
`javax.swing`	Create graphical user interfaces with components that extend the AWT capabilities.
`javax.xml.parsers`	Process XML documents; XML stands for eXtensible Markup Language.

figure 2.11   Some packages in the Java standard class library

declaration allows all classes in the `java.util` package to be referenced in the program without the explicit package name:

```
import java.util.*;
```

If only one class of a particular package will be used in a program, it is usually better to name the class specifically in the `import` statement. However, if two or more will be used, the * notation is fine. Once a class is imported, it is as if its code has been brought into the program. The code is not actually moved, but that is the effect.

The classes of the `java.lang` package are automatically imported because they are fundamental and can be thought of as basic extensions to the language.

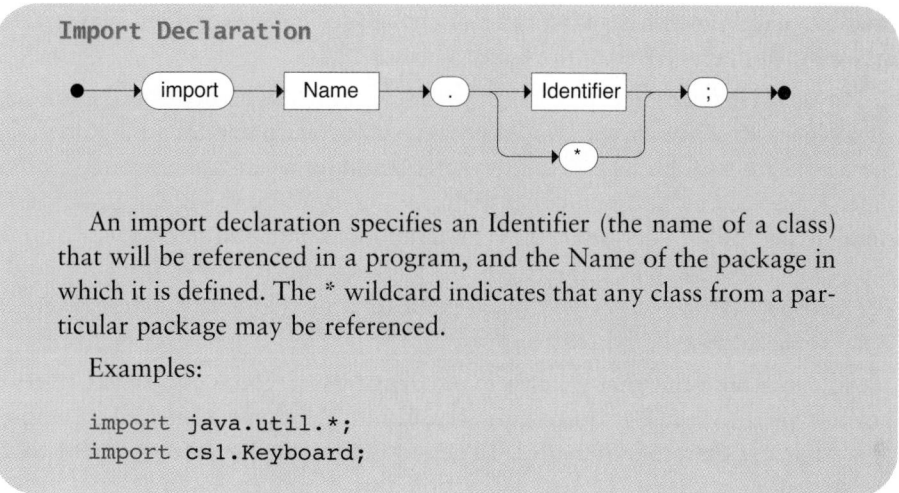

Import Declaration

An import declaration specifies an Identifier (the name of a class) that will be referenced in a program, and the Name of the package in which it is defined. The * wildcard indicates that any class from a particular package may be referenced.

Examples:

```
import java.util.*;
import cs1.Keyboard;
```

Therefore, any class in the `java.lang` package, such as `String`, can be used without an explicit `import` statement. It is as if all programs automatically contain the following statement:

```
import java.lang.*;
```

the Random class

The need for random numbers occurs frequently when writing software. Games often use a random number to represent the roll of a die or the shuffle of a deck of cards. A flight simulator may use random numbers to determine how often a simulated flight has engine trouble. A program designed to help high school students prepare for the SATs may use random numbers to choose the next question to ask.

The `Random` class implements a *pseudorandom number generator.* A random number generator picks a number at random out of a range of values. A program that serves this role is technically pseudorandom, because a program has no means to actually pick a number randomly. A pseudorandom number generator might perform a series of complicated calculations, starting with an initial *seed value,* and produces a number. Though they are technically not random (because they are calculated), the values produced by a pseudorandom number generator usually appear random, at least random enough for most situations. Figure 2.12 lists some of the methods of the Random class.

The nextInt method can be called with no parameters, or we can pass it a single integer value. The version that takes no parameters generates a random number across the entire range of int values, including negative numbers. Usually, though, we need a random number within a more specific range. For instance, to simulate the roll of a die we might want a random number in the range of 1 to 6. If we pass a value, say N, to nextInt, the method returns a value from 0 to N–1. For example, if we pass in 100, we'll get a return value that is greater than or equal to 0 and less than or equal to 99.

Note that the value that we pass to the nextInt method is also the number of possible values we can get in return. We can shift the range as needed by adding or subtracting the proper amount. To get a random number in the range 1 to 6, we can call nextInt(6) to get a value from 0 to 5, and then add 1.

The nextFloat method of the Random class returns a float value that is greater than or equal to 0.0 and less than 1.0. If desired, we can use multiplication to scale the result, cast it into an int value to truncate the fractional part, then shift the range as we do with integers.

The program shown in Listing 2.9 produces several random numbers in various ranges.

Random ()
    Constructor: creates a new pseudorandom number generator.

float nextFloat ()
    Returns a random number between 0.0 (inclusive) and 1.0 (exclusive).

int nextInt ()
    Returns a random number that ranges over all possible int values (positive and negative).

int nextInt (int num)
    Returns a random number in the range 0 to num–1.

---

figure 2.12   Some methods of the Random class

listing
   2.9

```java
//************************************************************************
//   RandomNumbers.java        Author: Lewis/Loftus
//
//   Demonstrates the import statement, and the creation of pseudo-
//   random numbers using the Random class.
//************************************************************************

import java.util.Random;

public class RandomNumbers
{
   //-----------------------------------------------------------------
   //   Generates random numbers in various ranges.
   //-----------------------------------------------------------------
   public static void main (String[] args)
   {
      Random generator = new Random();
      int num1;
      float num2;

      num1 = generator.nextInt();
      System.out.println ("A random integer: " + num1);

      num1 = generator.nextInt(10);
      System.out.println ("From 0 to 9: " + num1);

      num1 = generator.nextInt(10) + 1;
      System.out.println ("From 1 to 10: " + num1);

      num1 = generator.nextInt(15) + 20;
      System.out.println ("From 20 to 34: " + num1);

      num1 = generator.nextInt(20) - 10;
      System.out.println ("From -10 to 9: " + num1);

      num2 = generator.nextFloat();
      System.out.println ("A random float [between 0-1]: " + num2);

      num2 = generator.nextFloat() * 6;   // 0.0 to 5.999999
      num1 = (int) num2 + 1;
      System.out.println ("From 1 to 6: " + num1);
   }
}
```

listing
2.9   continued

output

```
A random integer: -2038016157
From 0 to 9: 6
From 1 to 10: 4
From 20 to 34: 30
From -10 to 9: 7
A random float [between 0-1] : 0.052495003
From 1 to 6: 6
```

2.8   invoking class methods

Some methods can be invoked through the class name in which they are defined, without having to instantiate an object of the class first. These are called *class methods* or *static methods*. Let's look at some examples.

the Math class

The Math class provides a large number of basic mathematical functions. The Math class is part of the Java standard class library and is defined in the java.lang package. Figure 2.13 lists several of its methods.

The reserved word static indicates that the method can be invoked through the name of the class. For example, a call to Math.abs(total) will return the absolute value of the number stored in total. A call to Math.pow(7, 4) will return 7 raised to the fourth power. Note that you can pass integer values to a method that accepts a double parameter. This is a form of assignment conversion, which we discussed earlier in this chapter.

We'll make use of some Math methods in examples after examining the Keyboard class.

the Keyboard class

The Keyboard class contains methods that help us obtain input data that the user types on the keyboard. The methods of the Keyboard class are static and are therefore invoked through the Keyboard class name.

```
static int abs (int num)
    Returns the absolute value of num.

static double acos (double num)

static double asin (double num)

static double atan (double num)
    Returns the arc cosine, arc sine, or arc tangent of num.

static double cos (double angle)

static double sin (double angle)

static double tan (double angle)
    Returns the angle cosine, sine, or tangent of angle, which is measured
    in radians.

static double ceil (double num)
    Returns the ceiling of num, which is the smallest whole number greater
    than or equal to num.

static double exp (double power)
    Returns the value e raised to the specified power.

static double floor (double num)
    Returns the floor of num, which is the largest whole number less than
    or equal to num.

static double pow (double num, double power)
    Returns the value num raised to the specified power.

static double random ()
    Returns a random number between 0.0 (inclusive) and 1.0 (exclusive).

static double sqrt (double num)
    Returns the square root of num, which must be positive.
```

figure 2.13   Some methods of the Math class

One very important characteristic of the Keyboard class must be made clear: The Keyboard class is *not* part of the Java standard class library. It has been written by the authors of this book to help you read user input. It is defined as part of a package called cs1 (that's cs-one, not cs-el). Because it is not part of the Java standard class library, it will not be found on generic Java development environments.

You may have to configure your environment so that it knows where to find the Keyboard class.

The process of reading input from the user in Java can get somewhat involved. The Keyboard class allows you to ignore those details for now. We explore these issues later in the book, at which point we fully explain the details currently hidden by the Keyboard class.

For now we will use the Keyboard class for the services it provides, just as we do any other class. In that sense, the Keyboard class is a good example of object abstraction. We rely on classes and objects for the services they provide. It doesn't matter if they are part of a library, if a third party writes them, or if we write them ourselves. We use and interact with them in the same way. Figure 2.14 lists the input methods of the Keyboard class.

web bonus

For each example in this book that uses the Keyboard class, the Web site contains a version of the program that does not use it (for comparison purposes).

Let's look at some examples that use the Keyboard class. The program shown in Listing 2.10, called Echo, simply reads a string that is typed by the user and echoes it back to the screen.

```
static boolean readBoolean ()

static byte readByte ()

static char readChar ()

static double readDouble ()

static float readFloat ()

static int readInt ()

static long readLong ()

static short readShort ()

static String readString ()
    Returns a value of the indicated type obtained from user keyboard input.
```

figure 2.14 Some methods of the Keyboard class

listing
   2.10

```java
//**********************************************************************
//   Echo.java          Author: Lewis/Loftus
//
//   Demonstrates the use of the readString method of the Keyboard
//   class.
//**********************************************************************

import cs1.Keyboard;

public class Echo
{
   //----------------------------------------------------------------
   //   Reads a character string from the user and prints it.
   //----------------------------------------------------------------
   public static void main (String[] args)
   {
      String message;

      System.out.println ("Enter a line of text:");

      message = Keyboard.readString();

      System.out.println ("You entered: \"" + message + "\"");
   }
}
```

output

```
Enter a line of text:
Set your laser printer on stun!
You entered: "Set your laser printer on stun!"
```

The Quadratic program, shown in Listing 2.11 uses the Keyboard and Math classes. Recall that a quadratic equation has the following general form:

$ax^2 + bx + c$

The Quadratic program reads values that represent the coefficients in a quadratic equation (a, b, and c), and then evaluates the quadratic formula to determine the roots of the equation. The quadratic formula is:

$$\text{roots} = \frac{-b \pm \sqrt{b^2 - 4ac}}{2a}$$

listing
    2.11

```
//********************************************************************
//  Quadratic.java       Author: Lewis/Loftus
//
//  Demonstrates a calculation based on user input.
//********************************************************************

import cs1.Keyboard;

public class Quadratic
{
   //-----------------------------------------------------------------
   //  Determines the roots of a quadratic equation.
   //-----------------------------------------------------------------
   public static void main (String[] args)
   {
      int a, b, c;  // ax^2 + bx + c

      System.out.print ("Enter the coefficient of x squared: ");
      a = Keyboard.readInt();

      System.out.print ("Enter the coefficient of x: ");
      b = Keyboard.readInt();

      System.out.print ("Enter the constant: ");
      c = Keyboard.readInt();

      // Use the quadratic formula to compute the roots.
      // Assumes a positive discriminant.

      double discriminant = Math.pow(b, 2) - (4 * a * c);
      double root1 = ((-1 * b) + Math.sqrt(discriminant)) / (2 * a);
      double root2 = ((-1 * b) - Math.sqrt(discriminant)) / (2 * a);
```

```
listing
   2.11     continued


      System.out.println ("Root #1: " + root1);
      System.out.println ("Root #2: " + root2);
   }
}
```

output

```
Enter the coefficient of x squared: 3
Enter the coefficient of x: 8
Enter the constant: 4
Root #1: -0.6666666666666666
Root #2: -2.0
```

2.9 formatting output

The NumberFormat class and the DecimalFormat class are used to format information so that it looks appropriate when printed or displayed. They are both part of the Java standard class library and are defined in the java.text package.

the NumberFormat class

The NumberFormat class provides generic formatting capabilities for numbers. You don't instantiate a NumberFormat object using the new operator. Instead, you request an object from one of the methods that you can invoke through the class itself. The reasons for this approach involve issues that we haven't covered yet, but we explain them in due course. Figure 2.15 lists some of the methods of the NumberFormat class.

Two of the methods in the NumberFormat class, getCurrencyInstance and getPercentInstance, return an object that is used to format numbers. The getCurrencyInstance method returns a formatter for monetary values whereas the getPercentInstance method returns an object that formats a percentage. The format method is invoked through a formatter object and returns a String that contains the number formatted in the appropriate manner.

The Price program shown in Listing 2.12 uses both types of formatters. It reads in a sales transaction and computes the final price, including tax.

```
String format (double number)
    Returns a string containing the specified number formatted according to
    this object's pattern.

static NumberFormat getCurrencyInstance()
    Returns a NumberFormat object that represents a currency format for the
    current locale.

static NumberFormat getPercentInstance()
    Returns a NumberFormat object that represents a percentage format for
    the current locale.
```

figure 2.15   Some methods of the NumberFormat class

listing
  2.12

```java
//********************************************************************
//  Price.java        Author: Lewis/Loftus
//
//  Demonstrates the use of various Keyboard and NumberFormat
//  methods.
//********************************************************************

import cs1.Keyboard;
import java.text.NumberFormat;

public class Price
{
   //-----------------------------------------------------------------
   //  Calculates the final price of a purchased item using values
   //  entered by the user.
   //-----------------------------------------------------------------
   public static void main (String[] args)
   {
      final double TAX_RATE = 0.06;  // 6% sales tax

      int quantity;
      double subtotal, tax, totalCost, unitPrice;

      System.out.print ("Enter the quantity: ");
      quantity = Keyboard.readInt();
```

listing
    2.12   continued

```
    System.out.print ("Enter the unit price: ");
    unitPrice = Keyboard.readDouble();

    subtotal = quantity * unitPrice;
    tax = subtotal * TAX_RATE;
    totalCost = subtotal + tax;

    // Print output with appropriate formatting
    NumberFormat money = NumberFormat.getCurrencyInstance();
    NumberFormat percent = NumberFormat.getPercentInstance();

    System.out.println ("Subtotal: " + money.format(subtotal));
    System.out.println ("Tax: " + money.format(tax) + " at "
                        + percent.format(TAX_RATE));
    System.out.println ("Total: " + money.format(totalCost));
  }
}
```

output

```
Enter the quantity: 5
Enter the unit price: 3.87
Subtotal: $19.35
Tax: $1.16 at 6%
Total: $20.51
```

the DecimalFormat class

Unlike the NumberFormat class, the DecimalFormat class is instantiated in the traditional way using the new operator. Its constructor takes a string that represents the pattern that will guide the formatting process. We can then use the format method to format a particular value. At a later point, if we want to change the pattern that the formatter object uses, we can invoke the applyPattern method. Figure 2.16 describes these methods.

The pattern defined by the string that is passed to the DecimalFormat constructor gets fairly elaborate. Various symbols are used to represent particular formatting guidelines.

```
DecimalFormat (String pattern)
  Constructor:  creates a new DecimalFormat object with the specified pattern.

void applyPattern (String pattern)
  Applies the specified pattern to this DecimalFormat object.

String format (double number)
  Returns a string containing the specified number formatted according to the
  current pattern.
```

figure 2.16   Some methods of the `DecimalFormat` class

The pattern defined by the string `"0.###"`, for example, indicates that at least one digit should be printed to the left of the decimal point and should be a zero if the integer portion of the value is zero. It also indicates that the fractional portion of the value should be rounded to three digits. This pattern is used in the `CircleStats` program shown in Listing 2.13, which reads the radius of a circle from the user and computes its area and circumference. Trailing zeros, such as in the circle's area of 78.540, are not printed.

2.10 an introduction to applets

key concept

Applets are Java programs that are usually transported across a network and executed using a Web browser. Java applications are stand-alone programs that can be executed using the Java interpreter.

There are two kinds of Java programs: Java applets and Java applications. A Java *applet* is a Java program that is intended to be embedded into an HTML document, transported across a network, and executed using a Web browser. A Java *application* is a stand-alone program that can be executed using the Java interpreter. All programs presented thus far in this book have been Java applications.

**listing
    2.13**

```java
//********************************************************************
//  CircleStats.java        Author: Lewis/Loftus
//
//  Demonstrates the formatting of decimal values using the
//  DecimalFormat class.
//********************************************************************

import cs1.Keyboard;
import java.text.DecimalFormat;

public class CircleStats
{
    //-----------------------------------------------------------------
    //  Calculates the area and circumference of a circle given its
    //  radius.
    //-----------------------------------------------------------------
    public static void main (String[] args)
    {
        int radius;
        double area, circumference;

        System.out.print ("Enter the circle's radius: ");
        radius = Keyboard.readInt();

        area = Math.PI * Math.pow(radius, 2);
        circumference = 2 * Math.PI * radius;

        // Round the output to three decimal places
        DecimalFormat fmt = new DecimalFormat ("0.###");

        System.out.println ("The circle's area: " + fmt.format(area));
        System.out.println ("The circle's circumference: "
                             + fmt.format(circumference));
    }
}
```

output

```
Enter the circle's radius: 5
The circle's area: 78.54
The circle's circumference: 31.416
```

The Web enables users to send and receive various types of media, such as text, graphics, and sound, using a point-and-click interface that is extremely convenient and easy to use. A Java applet was the first kind of executable program that could be retrieved using Web software. Java applets are considered just another type of media that can be exchanged across the Web.

Though Java applets are generally intended to be transported across a network, they don't have to be. They can be viewed locally using a Web browser. For that matter, they don't even have to be executed through a Web browser at all. A tool in Sun's Java Software Development Kit called appletviewer can be used to interpret and execute an applet. We use appletviewer to display most of the applets in the book. However, usually the point of making a Java applet is to provide a link to it on a Web page and allow it to be retrieved and executed by Web users anywhere in the world.

Java bytecode (not Java source code) is linked to an HTML document and sent across the Web. A version of the Java interpreter embedded in a Web browser is used to execute the applet once it reaches its destination. A Java applet must be compiled into bytecode format before it can be used with the Web.

There are some important differences between the structure of a Java applet and the structure of a Java application. Because the Web browser that executes an applet is already running, applets can be thought of as a part of a larger program. As such they do not have a `main` method where execution starts. The `paint` method in an applet is automatically invoked by the applet. Consider the program in Listing 2.14, in which the `paint` method is used to draw a few shapes and write a quotation by Albert Einstein to the screen.

The two import statements at the beginning of the program explicitly indicate the packages that are used in the program. In this example, we need the `Applet` class, which is part of the `java.applet` package, and various graphics capabilities defined in the `java.awt` package.

A class that defines an applet extends the `Applet` class, as indicated in the header line of the class declaration. This process is making use of the object-oriented concept of inheritance, which we explore in more detail in Chapter 7. Applet classes must also be declared as `public`.

The `paint` method is one of several applet methods that have particular significance. It is invoked automatically whenever the graphic elements of the applet need to be painted to the screen, such as when the applet is first run or when another window that was covering it is moved.

listing
   2.14

```
//********************************************************************
//   Einstein.java        Author: Lewis/Loftus
//
//   Demonstrates a basic applet.
//********************************************************************

import java.applet.Applet;
import java.awt.*;

public class Einstein extends Applet
{
   //-----------------------------------------------------------------
   //  Draws a quotation by Albert Einstein among some shapes.
   //-----------------------------------------------------------------
   public void paint (Graphics page)
   {
      page.drawRect (50, 50, 40, 40);      // square
      page.drawRect (60, 80, 225, 30);     // rectangle
      page.drawOval (75, 65, 20, 20);      // circle
      page.drawLine (35, 60, 100, 120);    // line

      page.drawString ("Out of clutter, find simplicity.", 110, 70);
      page.drawString ("-- Albert Einstein", 130, 100);
   }
}
```

display

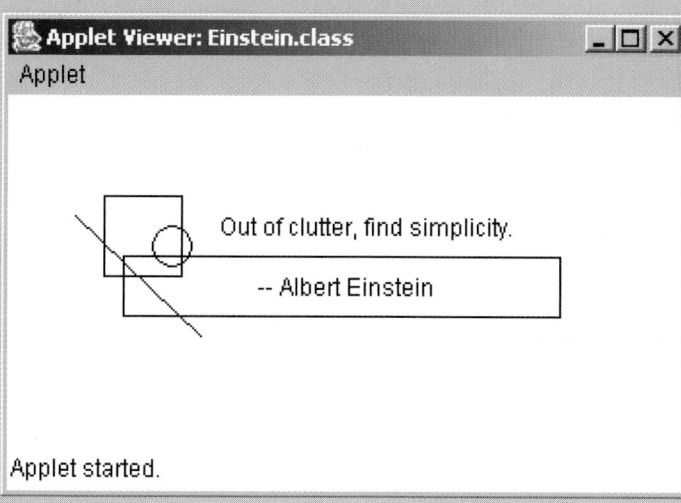

Note that the `paint` method accepts a `Graphics` object as a parameter. A `Graphics` object defines a particular *graphics context* with which we can interact. The graphics context passed into an applet's `paint` method represents the entire applet window. Each graphics context has its own coordinate system. In later examples, we will have multiple components, each with its own graphic context.

A `Graphics` object allows us to draw various shapes using methods such as `drawRect`, `drawOval`, `drawLine`, and `drawString`. The parameters passed to the drawing methods specify the coordinates and sizes of the shapes to be drawn. We explore these and other methods that draw shapes in the next section.

executing applets using the Web

In order for the applet to be transmitted over the Web and executed by a browser, it must be referenced in a HyperText Markup Language (HTML) document. An HTML document contains *tags* that specify formatting instructions and identify the special types of media that are to be included in a document. A Java program is considered a specific media type, just as text, graphics, and sound are.

An HTML tag is enclosed in angle brackets. Appendix J contains a tutorial on HTML that explores various tag types. The following is an example of an applet tag:

```
<applet code="Einstein.class" width=350 height=175>
</applet>
```

This tag dictates that the bytecode stored in the file `Einstein.class` should be transported over the network and executed on the machine that wants to view this particular HTML document. The applet tag also indicates the width and height of the applet.

Note that the applet tag refers to the bytecode file of the `Einstein` applet, not to the source code file. Before an applet can be transported using the Web, it must be compiled into its bytecode format. Then, as shown in Fig. 2.17, the document can be loaded using a Web browser, which will automatically interpret and execute the applet.

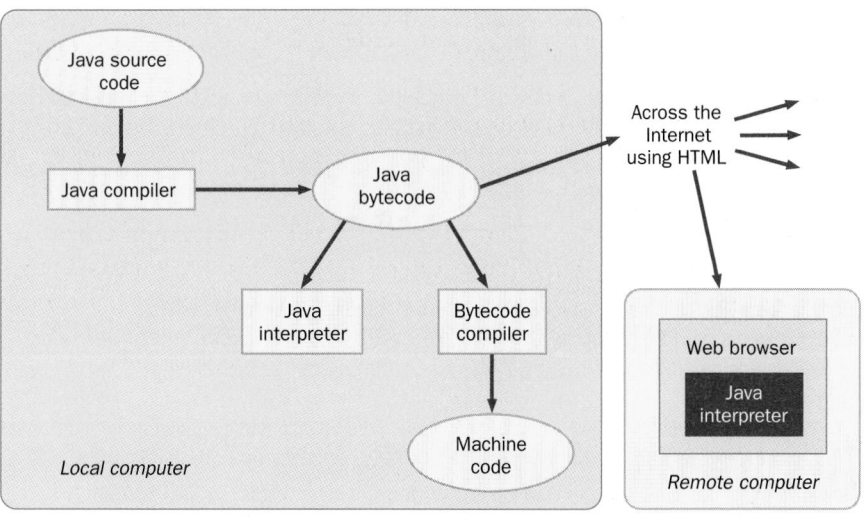

figure 2.17 The Java translation and execution process, including applets

2.11 drawing shapes

The Java standard class library provides many classes that let us present and manipulate graphical information. The `Graphics` class is fundamental to all such processing.

the `Graphics` class

The `Graphics` class is defined in the `java.awt` package. It contains various methods that allow us to draw shapes, including lines, rectangles, and ovals. Figure 2.18 lists some of the fundamental drawing methods of the `Graphics` class. Note that these methods also let us draw circles and squares, which are just specific types of ovals and rectangles, respectively. We discuss additional drawing methods of the `Graphics` class later in the book at appropriate points.

The methods of the `Graphics` class allow us to specify whether we want a shape filled or unfilled. An unfilled shape shows only the outline of the shape and is otherwise transparent (you can see any underlying graphics). A filled shape is solid between its boundaries and covers any underlying graphics.

> **key concept**
> Most shapes can be drawn filled (opaque) or unfilled (as an outline).

```
void drawArc (int x, int y, int width, int height, int
startAngle, int arcAngle)
    Paints an arc along the oval bounded by the rectangle defined by x, y, width,
    and height. The arc starts at startAngle and extends for a distance defined by
    arcAngle.

void drawLine (int x1, int y1, int x2, int y2)
    Paints a line from point (x1, y1) to point (x2, y2).

void drawOval (int x, int y, int width, int height)
    Paints an oval bounded by the rectangle with an upper left corner of (x, y) and
    dimensions width and height.

void drawRect (int x, int y, int width, int height)
    Paints a rectangle with upper left corner (x, y) and dimensions width and
    height.

void drawString (String str, int x, int y)
    Paints the character string str at point (x, y), extending to the right.

void fillArc (int x, int y, int width, int height,
int startAngle, int arcAngle)

void fillOval (int x, int y, int width, int height)

void fillRect (int x, int  y, int width, int height)
    Same as their draw counterparts, but filled with the current foreground color.

Color getColor ()
    Returns this graphics context's foreground color.

void setColor (Color color)
    Sets this graphics context's foreground color to the specified color.
```

figure 2.18   Some methods of the Graphics class

All of these methods rely on the Java coordinate system, which we discussed in Chapter 1. Recall that point (0,0) is in the upper-left corner, such that *x* values get larger as we move to the right, and *y* values get larger as we move down. Any shapes drawn at coordinates that are outside the visible area will not be seen.

Many of the Graphics drawing methods are self-explanatory, but some require a little more discussion. Note, for instance, that an oval drawn by the

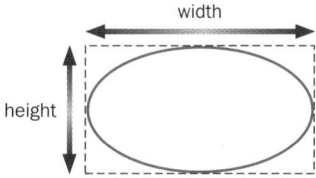

figure 2.19   An oval and its bounding rectangle

drawOval method is defined by the coordinate of the upper-left corner and dimensions that specify the width and height of a *bounding rectangle*. Shapes with curves such as ovals are often defined by a rectangle that encompasses their perimeters. Figure 2.19 depicts a bounding rectangle for an oval.

> **key concept**
> A bounding rectangle is often used to define the position and size of curved shapes such as ovals.

An arc can be thought of as a segment of an oval. To draw an arc, we specify the oval of which the arc is a part and the portion of the oval in which we're interested. The starting point of the arc is defined by the *start angle* and the ending point of the arc is defined by the *arc angle*. The arc angle does not indicate where the arc ends, but rather its

> **key concept**
> An arc is a segment of an oval; the segment begins at a specific start angle and extends for a distance specified by the arc angle.

range. The start angle and the arc angle are measured in degrees. The origin for the start angle is an imaginary horizontal line passing through the center of the oval and can be referred to as 0°; as shown in Fig. 2.20.

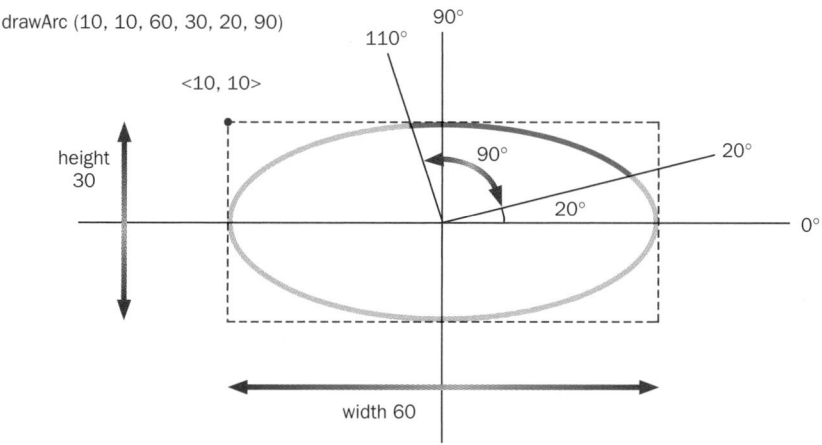

figure 2.20   An arc defined by an oval, a start angle, and an arc angle

the `Color` class

In Java, a programmer uses the `Color` class, which is part of the `java.awt` package, to define and manage colors. Each object of the `Color` class represents a single color. The class contains several instances of itself to provide a basic set of predefined colors. Figure 2.21 lists the predefined colors of the `Color` class.

The `Color` class also contains methods to define and manage many other colors. Recall from Chapter 1 that colors can be defined using the RGB technique for specifying the contributions of three additive primary colors: red, green, and blue.

Color	Object	RGB Value
black	`Color.black`	0, 0, 0
blue	`Color.blue`	0, 0, 255
cyan	`Color.cyan`	0, 255, 255
gray	`Color.gray`	128, 128, 128
dark gray	`Color.darkGray`	64, 64, 64
light gray	`Color.lightGray`	192, 192, 192
green	`Color.green`	0, 255, 0
magenta	`Color.magenta`	255, 0, 255
orange	`Color.orange`	255, 200, 0
pink	`Color.pink`	255, 175, 175
red	`Color.red`	255, 0, 0
white	`Color.white`	255, 255, 255
yellow	`Color.yellow`	255, 255, 0

figure 2.21   Predefined colors in the `Color` class

Every graphics context has a current *foreground color* that is used whenever shapes or strings are drawn. Every surface that can be drawn on has a *background color*. The foreground color is set using the `setColor` method of the `Graphics` class, and the background color is set using the `setBackground` method of the component on which we are drawing, such as the applet.

Listing 2.15 shows an applet called `Snowman`. It uses various drawing and color methods to draw a winter scene featuring a snowman. Review the code carefully to note how each shape is drawn to create the overall picture.

listing
2.15

```
//************************************************************************
//   Snowman.java        Author: Lewis/Loftus
//
//   Demonstrates basic drawing methods and the use of color.
//************************************************************************

import java.applet.Applet;
import java.awt.*;

public class Snowman extends Applet
{
   //-----------------------------------------------------------------
   //  Draws a snowman.
   //-----------------------------------------------------------------
   public void paint (Graphics page)
   {
      final int MID = 150;
      final int TOP = 50;

      setBackground (Color.cyan);

      page.setColor (Color.blue);
      page.fillRect (0, 175, 300, 50);   // ground

      page.setColor (Color.yellow);
      page.fillOval (-40, -40, 80, 80);   // sun

      page.setColor (Color.white);
```

listing
2.15   **continued**

```
        page.fillOval (MID-20, TOP, 40, 40);        // head
        page.fillOval (MID-35, TOP+35, 70, 50);     // upper torso
        page.fillOval (MID-50, TOP+80, 100, 60);    // lower torso

        page.setColor (Color.black);
        page.fillOval (MID-10, TOP+10, 5, 5);       // left eye
        page.fillOval (MID+5, TOP+10, 5, 5);        // right eye

        page.drawArc (MID-10, TOP+20, 20, 10, 190, 160);    // smile

        page.drawLine (MID-25, TOP+60, MID-50, TOP+40);    // left arm
        page.drawLine (MID+25, TOP+60, MID+55, TOP+60);    // right arm

        page.drawLine (MID-20, TOP+5, MID+20, TOP+5);    // brim of hat
        page.fillRect (MID-15, TOP-20, 30, 25);          // top of hat
    }
}
```

display

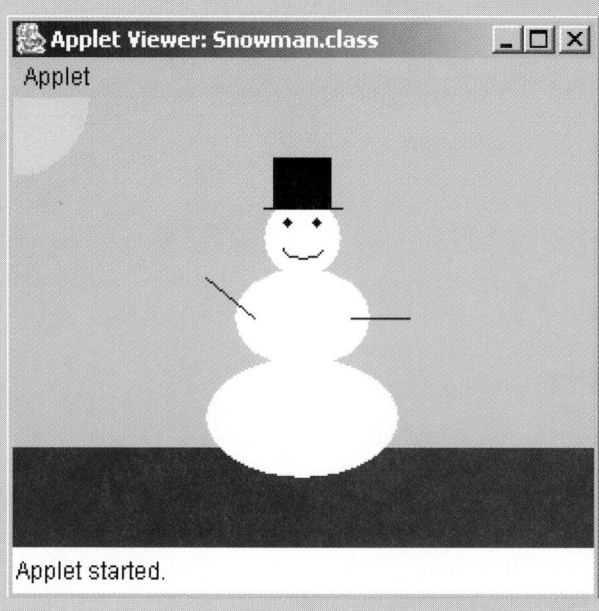

Note that the snowman figure is based on two constant values called MID and TOP, which define the midpoint of the snowman (left to right) and the top of the snowman's head. The entire snowman figure is drawn relative to these values. Using constants like these makes it easier to create the snowman and to make modifications later. For example, to shift the snowman to the right or left in our picture, only one constant declaration would have to change.

summary of
key concepts

- The information we manage in a Java program is either represented as primitive data or as objects.

- An abstraction hides details. A good abstraction hides the right details at the right time so that we can manage complexity.

- A variable is a name for a memory location used to hold a value of a particular data type.

- A variable can store only one value of its declared type.

- Java is a strongly typed language. Each variable is associated with a specific type for the duration of its existence, and we cannot assign a value of one type to a variable of an incompatible type.

- Constants are similar to variables, but they hold a particular value for the duration of their existence.

- Java has two kinds of numeric values: integers and floating point. There are four integer data types (`byte`, `short`, `int`, and `long`) and two floating point data types (`float` and `double`).

- Many programming statements involve expressions. Expressions are combinations of one or more operands and the operators used to perform a calculation.

- Java follows a well-defined set of rules that govern the order in which operators will be evaluated in an expression. These rules form an operator precedence hierarchy.

- Avoid narrowing conversions because they can lose information.

- The `new` operator returns a reference to a newly created object.

- The Java standard class library is a useful set of classes that anyone can use when writing Java programs.

- A package is a Java language element used to group related classes under a common name.

- The `Keyboard` class is not part of the Java standard library. It is therefore not available on all Java development platforms.

- Applets are Java programs that are usually transported across a network and executed using a Web browser. Java applications are stand-alone programs that can be executed using the Java interpreter.

- Most shapes can be drawn filled (opaque) or unfilled (as an outline).

- A bounding rectangle is often used to define the position and size of curved shapes such as ovals.

- An arc is a segment of an oval; the segment begins at a specific start angle and extends for a distance specified by the arc angle.

- The `Color` class contains several common predefined colors.

self-review questions

2.1 What are the primary concepts that support object-oriented programming?

2.2 Why is an object an example of abstraction?

2.3 What is primitive data? How are primitive data types different from objects?

2.4 What is a string literal?

2.5 What is the difference between the `print` and `println` methods?

2.6 What is a parameter?

2.7 What is an escape sequence? Give some examples.

2.8 What is a variable declaration?

2.9 How many values can be stored in an integer variable?

2.10 What are the four integer data types in Java? How are they different?

2.11 What is a character set?

2.12 What is operator precedence?

2.13 What is the result of `19%5` when evaluated in a Java expression? Explain.

2.14 What is the result of `13/4` when evaluated in a Java expression? Explain.

2.15 Why are widening conversions safer than narrowing conversions?

2.16 What does the `new` operator accomplish?

2.17 What is a Java package?

2.18 Why doesn't the `string` class have to be specifically imported into our programs?

2.19 What is a class method (also called a static method)?

2.20 What is the difference between a Java application and a Java applet?

exercises

2.1   Explain the following programming statement in terms of objects and the services they provide:

```
System.out.println ("I gotta be me!");
```

2.2   What output is produced by the following code fragment? Explain.

```
System.out.print ("Here we go!");
System.out.println ("12345");
System.out.print ("Test this if you are not sure.");
System.out.print ("Another.");
System.out.println ();
System.out.println ("All done.");
```

2.3   What is wrong with the following program statement? How can it be fixed?

```
System.out.println ("To be or not to be, that
is the question.");
```

2.4   What output is produced by the following statement? Explain.

```
System.out.println ("50 plus 25 is " + 50 + 25);
```

2.5   What is the output produced by the following statement? Explain.

```
System.out.println ("He thrusts his fists\n\tagainst" +
" the post\nand still insists\n\the sees the \"ghost\"");
```

2.6   Given the following declarations, what result is stored in each of the listed assignment statements?

```
int iResult, num1 = 25, num2 = 40, num3 = 17, num4 = 5;
double fResult, val1 = 17.0, val2 = 12.78;
```

a. iResult = num1 / num4;

b. fResult = num1 / num4;

c. iResult = num3 / num4;

d.   fResult = num3 / num4;

e. fResult = val1 / num4;

f. fResult = val1 / val2;

g. iResult = num1 / num2;

h. fResult = (double) num1 / num2;

i. fResult = num1 / (double) num2;

```
j. fResult = (double) (num1 / num2);
k. iResult = (int) (val1 / num4);
l. fResult = (int) (val1 / num4);
m. fResult = (int) ((double) num1 / num2);
n. iResult = num3 % num4;
o. iResult = num 2 % num3;
p. iResult = num3 % num2;
q. iResult = num2 % num4;
```

2.7 For each of the following expressions, indicate the order in which the operators will be evaluated by writing a number beneath each operator.

```
a. a − b − c − d
b. a − b + c − d
c. a + b / c / d
d. a + b / c * d
e. a / b * c * d
f. a % b / c * d
g. a % b % c % d
h. a − (b − c) − d
i. (a − (b − c)) − d
j. a − ((b − c) − d)
k. a % (b % c) * d * e
l. a + (b − c) * d − e
m. (a + b) * c + d * e
n. (a + b) * (c / d) % e
```

2.8 What output is produced by the following code fragment?

```
String m1, m2, m3;
m1 = "Quest for the Holy Grail";
m2 = m1.toLowerCase();
m3 = m1 + " " + m2;
System.out.println (m3.replace('h', 'z'));
```

2.9 Write an assignment statement that computes the square root of the sum of num1 and num2 and assigns the result to num3.

2.10 Write a single statement that computes and prints the absolute value of total.

2.11 What is the effect of the following import statement?

```
import java.awt.*;
```

2.12 Assuming that a Random object has been created called generator, what is the range of the result of each of the following expressions?

a. generator.nextInt(20)

b. generator.nextInt(8) + 1

c. generator.nextInt(45) + 10

d. generator.nextInt(100) − 50

2.13 Write code to declare and instantiate an object of the Random class (call the object reference variable rand). Then write a list of expressions using the nextInt method that generates random numbers in the following specified ranges, including the endpoints. Use the version of the nextInt method that accepts a single integer parameter.

a. 0 to 10

b. 0 to 500

c. 1 to 10

d. 1 to 500

e. 25 to 50

f. −10 to 15

2.14 Write code statements to create a DecimalFormat object that will round a formatted value to 4 decimal places. Then write a statement that uses that object to print the value of result, properly formatted.

2.15 Explain the role played by the Web in the translation and execution of some Java programs.

2.16 Assuming you have a Graphics object called page, write a statement that will draw a line from point (20, 30) to point (50, 60).

2.17 Assuming you have a Graphics object called page, write a statement that will draw a rectangle with height 70 and width 35, such that its upper-left corner is at point (10, 15).

2.18 Assuming you have a Graphics object called page, write a statement that will draw a circle *centered* on point (50, 50) with a radius of 20 pixels.

2.19 The following lines of code draw the eyes of the snowman in the Snowman applet. The eyes seem centered on the face when drawn, but the first parameters of each call are not equally offset from the midpoint. Explain.

```
page.fillOval (MID-10, TOP+10, 5, 5);
page.fillOval (MID+5, TOP+10, 5, 5);
```

programming projects

2.1 Create a revised version of the Lincoln application from Chapter 1 such that quotes appear around the quotation.

2.2 Write an application that reads three integers and prints their average.

2.3 Write an application that reads two floating point numbers and prints their sum, difference, and product.

2.4 Create a revised version of the TempConverter application to convert from Fahrenheit to Celsius. Read the Fahrenheit temperature from the user.

2.5 Write an application that converts miles to kilometers. (One mile equals 1.60935 kilometers.) Read the miles value from the user as a floating point value.

2.6 Write an application that reads values representing a time duration in hours, minutes, and seconds, and then prints the equivalent total number of seconds. (For example, 1 hour, 28 minutes, and 42 seconds is equivalent to 5322 seconds.)

2.7 Create a revised version of the previous project that reverses the computation. That is, read a value representing a number of seconds, then print the equivalent amount of time as a combination of hours, minutes, and seconds. (For example, 9999 seconds is equivalent to 2 hours, 46 minutes, and 39 seconds.)

2.8 Write an application that reads the (x,y) coordinates for two points. Compute the distance between the two points using the following formula:

$$\text{Distance} = \sqrt{(x_2 - x_1)^2 + (y_2 + y_1)^2}$$

2.9　Write an application that reads the radius of a sphere and prints its volume and surface area. Use the following formulas. Print the output to four decimal places. r represents the radius.

$$\text{Volume} = \tfrac{4}{3}\pi r^3$$

$$\text{Surface area} = 4\pi r^2$$

2.10　Write an application that reads the lengths of the sides of a triangle from the user. Compute the area of the triangle using Heron's formula (below), in which s represents half of the perimeter of the triangle, and a, b, and c represent the lengths of the three sides. Print the area to three decimal places.

$$\text{Area} = \sqrt{s(s-a)(s-b)(s-c)}$$

2.11　Write an application that computes the number of miles per gallon (MPG) of gas for a trip. Accept as input a floating point number that represents the total amount of gas used. Also accept two integers representing the odometer readings at the start and end of the trip. Compute the number of kilometers per liter if you prefer.

2.12　Write an application that determines the value of the coins in a jar and prints the total in dollars and cents. Read integer values that represent the number of quarters, dimes, nickels, and pennies. Use a currency formatter to print the output.

2.13　Write an application that creates and prints a random phone number of the form xxx-xxx-xxxx. Include the dashes in the output. Do not let the first three digits contain an 8 or 9 (but don't be more restrictive than that), and make sure that the second set of three digits is not greater than 742. *Hint:* Think through the easiest way to construct the phone number. Each digit does not have to be determined separately.

2.14　Create a personal Web page using HTML (see Appendix J).

2.15　Create a revised version of the Snowman applet with the following modifications:

- Add two red buttons to the upper torso.
- Make the snowman frown instead of smile.
- Move the sun to the upper-right corner of the picture.
- Display your name in the upper-left corner of the picture.
- Shift the entire snowman 20 pixels to the right.

2.16 Write an applet that writes your name using the `drawString` method. Embed a link to your applet in an HTML document and view it using a Web browser.

2.17 Write an applet that draws a smiling face. Give the face a nose, ears, a mouth, and eyes with pupils.

2.18 Write an applet that draws the Big Dipper. Add some extra stars in the night sky.

2.19 Write an applet that draws some balloons tied to strings. Make the balloons various colors.

2.20 Write an applet that draws the Olympic logo. The circles in the logo should be colored, from left to right, blue, yellow, black, green, and red.

2.21 Write an applet that draws a house with a door (and doorknob), windows, and a chimney. Add some smoke coming out of the chimney and some clouds in the sky.

2.22 Write an applet that displays a business card of your own design. Include both graphics and text.

2.23 Write an applet that displays your name in shadow text by drawing your name in black, then drawing it again slightly offset in a lighter color.

2.24 Write an applet the shows a pie chart with eight equal slices, all colored differently.

answers to self-review questions

2.1 The primary elements that support object-oriented programming are objects, classes, encapsulation, and inheritance. An object is defined by a class, which contains methods that define the operations on those objects (the services that they perform). Objects are encapsulated such that they store and manage their own data. Inheritance is a reuse technique in which one class can be derived from another.

2.2 An object is considered to be abstract because the details of the object are hidden from, and largely irrelevant to, the user of the object. Hidden details help us manage the complexity of software.

2.3   Primitive data are basic values such as numbers or characters. Objects are more complex entities that usually contain primitive data that help define them.

2.4   A string literal is a sequence of characters delimited by double quotes.

2.5   Both the `print` and `println` methods of the `System.out` object write a string of characters to the monitor screen. The difference is that, after printing the characters, the `println` performs a carriage return so that whatever's printed next appears on the next line. The `print` method allows subsequent output to appear on the same line.

2.6   A parameter is data that is passed into a method when it is invoked. The method usually uses that data to accomplish the service that it provides. For example, the parameter to the `println` method indicate what characters should be printed. The two numeric operands to the `Math.pow` method are the operands to the power function that is computed and returned.

2.7   An escape sequence is a series of characters that begins with the backslash (\) and that implies that the following characters should be treated in some special way. Examples: \n represents the newline character, \t represents the tab character, and \" represents the quotation character (as opposed to using it to terminate a string).

2.8   A variable declaration establishes the name of a variable and the type of data that it can contain. A declaration may also have an optional initialization, which gives the variable an initial value.

2.9   An integer variable can store only one value at a time. When a new value is assigned to it, the old one is overwritten and lost.

2.10   The four integer data types in Java are `byte`, `short`, `int`, and `long`. They differ in how much memory space is allocated for each and therefore how large a number they can hold.

2.11   A character set is a list of characters in a particular order. A character set defines the valid characters that a particular type of computer or programming language will support. Java uses the Unicode character set.

2.12   Operator precedence is the set of rules that dictates the order in which operators are evaluated in an expression.

2.13 The result of 19%5 in a Java expression is 4. The remainder operator % returns the remainder after dividing the second operand into the first. Five goes into 19 three times, with 4 left over.

2.14 The result of 13/4 in a Java expression is 3 (not 3.25). The result is an integer because both operands are integers. Therefore the / operator performs integer division, and the fractional part of the result is truncated.

2.15 A widening conversion tends to go from a small data value, in terms of the amount of space used to store it, to a larger one. A narrowing conversion does the opposite. Information is more likely to be lost in a narrowing conversion, which is why narrowing conversions are considered to be less safe than widening ones.

2.16 The new operator creates a new instance (an object) of the specified class. The constructor of the class is then invoked to help set up the newly created object.

2.17 A Java package is a collection of related classes. The Java standard class library is a group of packages that support common programming tasks.

2.18 The String class is part of the java.lang package, which is automatically imported into any Java program. Therefore, no separate import declaration is needed.

2.19 A class or static method can be invoked through the name of the class that contains it, such as Math.abs. If a method is not static, it can be executed only through an instance (an object) of the class.

2.20 A Java applet is a Java program that can be executed using a Web browser. Usually, the bytecode form of the Java applet is pulled across the Internet from another computer and executed locally. A Java application is a Java program that can stand on its own. It does not require a Web browser in order to execute.

All programming languages have specific statements that allow you to perform basic operations. These statements accomplish all programmed activity, including our interaction with objects and the definition of the services those objects provide. This chapter examines several of these programming statements as well as some additional operators. It begins by exploring the basic activities that a programmer goes through when developing software. These activities form the cornerstone of high-quality software development and represent the first step toward a disciplined development process. Finally, we use the statements we examine in this chapter to augment our ability to produce graphical output.

3.0   program development

Creating software involves much more than just writing code. As you learn more about the programming language statements that you can use in your problem solutions, it is also important to develop good habits in the way you develop and validate those solutions. This section introduces some of the basic programming activities necessary for developing software.

Any proper software development effort consists of four basic *development activities*:

▸ establishing the requirements

▸ creating a design

▸ implementing the code

▸ testing the implementation

It would be nice if these activities, in this order, defined a step-by-step approach for developing software. However, although they may seem to be sequential, they are almost never completely linear in reality. They overlap and interact. Let's discuss each development stage briefly.

Software requirements specify *what* a program must accomplish. They indicate the tasks that a program should perform, not how to perform them. You may recall from Chapter 1 that programming is really about problem solving; we create a program to solve a particular problem. Requirements are the clear expression of that problem. Until we truly know what problem we are trying to solve, we can't actually solve it.

The person or group who wants a software product developed (the *client*) will often provide an initial set of requirements. However, these initial requirements are often incomplete, ambiguous, or even contradictory. The software developer must work with the client to refine the requirements until all key decisions about what the system will do have been addressed.

Requirements often address user interface issues such as output format, screen layouts, and graphical interface components. Essentially, the requirements establish the characteristics that make the program useful for the end user. They may also apply constraints to your program, such as how fast a task must be performed. They may also impose restrictions on the developer such as deadlines.

A *software design* indicates *how* a program will accomplish its requirements. The design specifies the classes and objects needed in a program and defines how they interact. A detailed design might even specify the individual steps that parts of the code will follow.

> A software design specifies *how* a program will accomplish its requirements.
>
> key concept

A civil engineer would never consider building a bridge without designing it first. The design of software is no less essential. Many problems that occur in software are directly attributable to a lack of good design effort. Alternatives need to be considered and explored. Often, the first attempt at a design is not the best solution. Fortunately, changes are relatively easy to make during the design stage.

One of the most fundamental design issues is defining the *algorithms* to be used in the program. An algorithm is a step-by-step process for solving a problem. A recipe is like an algorithm. Travel directions are like an algorithm. Every program implements one or more algorithms. Every software developer should spend time thinking about the algorithms involved before writing any code.

An algorithm is often described using *pseudocode,* which is a mixture of code statements and English phrases. Pseudocode provides enough structure to show how the code will operate without getting bogged down in the syntactic details of a particular programming language and without being prematurely constrained by the characteristics of particular programming constructs.

> An algorithm is a step-by-step process for solving a problem, often expressed in pseudocode.
>
> key concept

When developing an algorithm, it's important to analyze all of the requirements involved with that part of the problem. This ensures that the algorithm takes into account all aspects of the problem. The design of a program is often revised many times before it is finalized.

Implementation is the process of writing the source code that will solve the problem. More precisely, implementation is the act of translating the design into a particular programming language. Too many programmers focus on implementation exclusively when actually it should be the least creative of all development activities. The important decisions should be made when establishing the requirements and creating the design.

Testing a program includes running it multiple times with various inputs and carefully scrutinizing the results. Testing might also include hand-tracing program code, in which the developer mentally plays the role of the computer to see where the program logic goes awry.

> Implementation should be the least creative of all development activities.
>
> key concept

The goal of testing is to find errors. By finding errors and fixing them, we improve the quality of our program. It's likely that later on someone else will find errors that remained hidden during development, when the cost of that error is much higher. Taking the time to uncover problems as early as possible is always worth the effort.

Running a program with specific input and producing the correct results establishes only that the program works for that particular input. As more and more test cases execute without revealing errors, our confidence in the program rises, but we can never really be sure that all errors have been eliminated. There could always be another error still undiscovered. Because of that, it is important to thoroughly test a program with various kinds of input. When one problem is fixed, we should run previous tests again to make sure that while fixing the problem we didn't create another. This technique is called *regression testing*.

> **key concept**
>
> The goal of testing is to find errors. We can never really be sure that all errors have been found.

Various models have been proposed that describe the specific way in which requirements analysis, design, implementation, and testing should be accomplished. For now we will simply keep these general activities in mind as we learn to develop programs.

3.1   control flow

The order in which statements are executed in a running program is called the *flow of control*. Unless otherwise specified, the execution of a program proceeds in a linear fashion. That is, a running program starts at the first programming statement and moves down one statement at a time until the program is complete. A Java application begins executing with the first line of the main method and proceeds step by step until it gets to the end of the main method.

Invoking a method alters the flow of control. When a method is called, control jumps to the code defined for that method. When the method completes, control returns to the place in the calling method where the invocation was made and processing continues from there. In our examples thus far, we've invoked methods in classes and objects using the Java libraries, and we haven't been concerned about the code that defines those methods. We discuss how to write our own separate classes and methods in Chapter 4.

> **key concept**
>
> Conditionals and loops allow us to control the flow of execution through a method.

Within a given method, we can alter the flow of control through the code by using certain types of programming statements. In particular, statements that control the flow of execution through a method fall into two categories: conditionals and loops.

A *conditional statement* is sometimes called a *selection statement* because it allows us to choose which statement will be executed next. The conditional statements in Java are the `if` statement, the `if-else` statement, and the `switch` statement. These statements allow us to decide which statement to execute next. Each decision is based on a *boolean expression* (also called a *condition*), which is an expression that evaluates to either true or false. The result of the expression determines which statement is executed next.

For example, the cost of life insurance might be dependent on whether the insured person is a smoker. If the person smokes, we calculate the cost using a particular formula; if not, we calculate it using another. The role of a conditional statement is to evaluate a boolean condition (whether the person smokes) and then to execute the proper calculation accordingly.

A *loop*, or *repetition statement,* allows us to execute a programming statement over and over again. Like a conditional, a loop is based on a boolean expression that determines how many times the statement is executed.

For example, suppose we wanted to calculate the grade point average of every student in a class. The calculation is the same for each student; it is just performed on different data. We would set up a loop that repeats the calculation for each student until there are no more students to process.

Java has three types of loop statements: the `while` statement, the `do` statement, and the `for` statement. Each type of loop statement has unique characteristics that distinguish it from the others.

Conditionals and loops are fundamental to controlling the flow through a method and are necessary in many situations. This chapter explores conditional and loop statements as well as some additional operators.

3.2 the if statement

The *if statement* is a conditional statement found in many programming languages, including Java. The following is an example of an `if` statement:

```
if (total > amount)
    total = total + (amount + 1);
```

An `if` statement consists of the reserved word `if` followed by a boolean expression, or condition. The condition is enclosed in parentheses and must evaluate to true or false. If the condition is true, the statement is executed and processing continues with the next statement. If the condition is false, the statement is skipped and processing continues immediately with the next statement. In this example, if the value in total is greater than the value in amount, the assignment statement is executed; otherwise, the assignment statement is skipped. Figure 3.1 shows this processing.

Note that the assignment statement in this example is indented under the header line of the if statement. This communicates that the assignment statement is part of the if statement; it implies that the if statement governs whether the assignment statement will be executed. This indentation is extremely important for the human reader.

The example in Listing 3.1 reads the age of the user and then makes a decision as to whether to print a particular sentence based on the age that is entered.

The Age program echoes the age value that is entered in all cases. If the age is less than the value of the constant MINOR, the statement about youth is printed. If the age is equal to or greater than the value of MINOR, the println statement is skipped. In either case, the final sentence about age being a state of mind is printed.

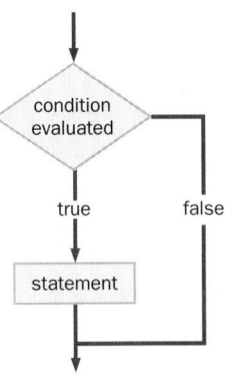

figure 3.1 The logic of an if statement

listing
   3.1

```
//***************************************************************
//   Age.java          Author: Lewis/Loftus
//
//   Demonstrates the use of an if statement.
//***************************************************************

import cs1.Keyboard;

public class Age
{
   //-----------------------------------------------------------
   //   Reads the user's age and prints comments accordingly.
   //-----------------------------------------------------------
   public static void main (String[] args)
   {
      final int MINOR = 21;

      System.out.print ("Enter your age: ");
      int age = Keyboard.readInt();

      System.out.println ("You entered: " + age);

      if (age < MINOR)
         System.out.println ("Youth is a wonderful thing. Enjoy.");

      System.out.println ("Age is a state of mind.");
   }
}
```

output
```
Enter your age: 35
You entered: 35
Age is a state of mind.
```

equality and relational operators

Boolean expressions evaluate to either true or false and are fundamental to our ability to make decisions. Java has several operators that produce a true or false result. The == and != operators are called *equality operators;* they test if two values are equal or not equal, respectively. Note that the equality operator consists of two equal signs side by side and should not be mistaken for the assignment operator that uses only one equal sign.

The following if statement prints a sentence only if the variables total and sum contain the same value:

```
if (total == sum)
    System.out.println ("total equals sum");
```

Likewise, the following if statement prints a sentence only if the variables total and sum do *not* contain the same value:

```
if (total != sum)
    System.out.println ("total does NOT equal sum");
```

In the Age program we used the < operator to decide whether one value was less than another. The less than operator is one of several *relational operators* that let us decide the relationships between values. Figure 3.2 lists the Java equality and relational operators.

The equality and relational operators have precedence lower than the arithmetic operators. Therefore, arithmetic operations are evaluated first, followed by equality and relational operations. As always, parentheses can be used to explicitly specify the order of evaluation.

Operator	Meaning
==	equal to
!=	not equal to
<	less than
<=	less than or equal to
>	greater than
>=	greater than or equal to

figure 3.2   Java equality and relational operators

Let's look at a few more examples of basic `if` statements.

```
if (size >= MAX)
    size = 0;
```

This `if` statement causes the variable `size` to be set to zero if its current value is greater than or equal to the value in the constant `MAX`.

The condition of the following `if` statement first adds three values together, then compares the result to the value stored in `numBooks`.

```
if (numBooks < stackCount + inventoryCount + duplicateCount)
    reorder = true;
```

If `numBooks` is less than the other three values combined, the boolean variable `reorder` is set to `true`. The addition operations are performed before the less than operator because the arithmetic operators have a higher precedence than the relational operators.

The following `if` statement compares the value returned from a call to `nextInt` to the calculated result of dividing the constant `HIGH` by 5. The odds of this code picking a winner are approximately 1 in 5.

```
if (generator.nextInt(HIGH) < HIGH / 5)
    System.out.println ("You are a randomly selected winner!");
```

the if-else statement

Sometimes we want to do one thing if a condition is true and another thing if that condition is false. We can add an *else clause* to an `if` statement, making it an *if-else statement*, to handle this kind of situation. The following is an example of an `if-else` statement:

```
if (height <= MAX)
    adjustment = 0;
else
    adjustment = MAX - height;
```

If the condition is true, the first assignment statement is executed; if the condition is false, the second assignment statement is executed. Only one or the other will be executed because a boolean condition will evaluate to either true or false. Note that proper indentation is used again to communicate that the statements are part of the governing `if` statement.

> **key concept**
> An `if-else` statement allows a program to do one thing if a condition is true and another thing if the condition is false.

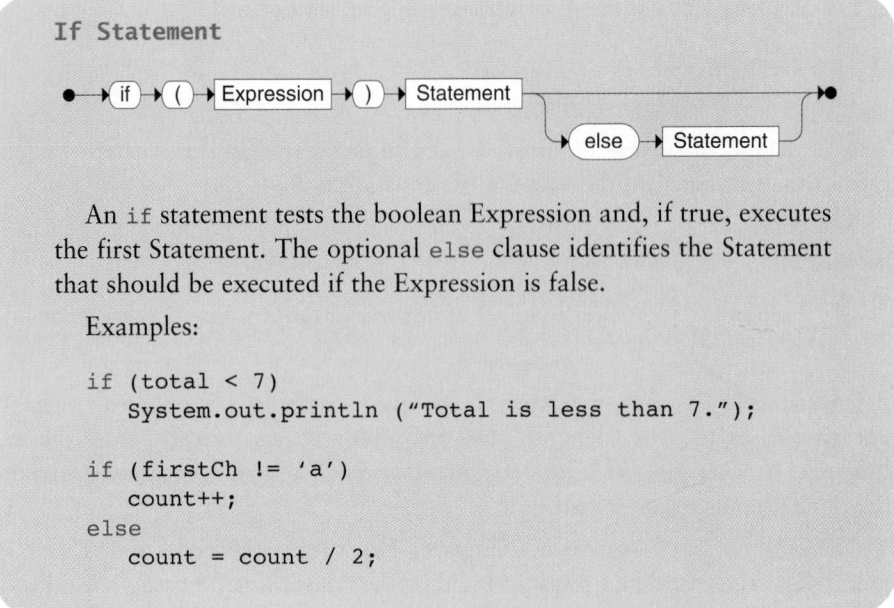

An `if` statement tests the boolean Expression and, if true, executes the first Statement. The optional `else` clause identifies the Statement that should be executed if the Expression is false.

Examples:

```
if (total < 7)
    System.out.println ("Total is less than 7.");

if (firstCh != 'a')
    count++;
else
    count = count / 2;
```

The `Wages` program shown in Listing 3.2 uses an `if-else` statement to compute the proper payment amount for an employee.

In the `Wages` program, if an employee works over 40 hours in a week, the payment amount takes into account the overtime hours. An `if-else` statement is used to determine whether the number of hours entered by the user is greater than 40. If it is, the extra hours are paid at a rate one and a half times the normal rate. If there are no overtime hours, the total payment is based simply on the number of hours worked and the standard rate.

Let's look at another example of an `if-else` statement:

```
if (roster.getSize() == FULL)
    roster.expand();
else
    roster.addName (name);
```

This example makes use of an object called `roster`. Even without knowing what `roster` represents, or from what class it was created, we can see that it has at least three methods: `getSize`, `expand`, and `addName`. The condition of the `if`

listing
    3.2

```java
//********************************************************************
//  Wages.java        Author: Lewis/Loftus
//
//  Demonstrates the use of an if-else statement.
//********************************************************************

import java.text.NumberFormat;
import cs1.Keyboard;

public class Wages
{
   //-----------------------------------------------------------------
   //  Reads the number of hours worked and calculates wages.
   //-----------------------------------------------------------------
   public static void main (String[] args)
   {
      final double RATE = 8.25;  // regular pay rate
      final int STANDARD = 40;   // standard hours in a work week

      double pay = 0.0;

      System.out.print ("Enter the number of hours worked: ");
      int hours = Keyboard.readInt();

      System.out.println ();

      // Pay overtime at "time and a half"
      if (hours > STANDARD)
         pay = STANDARD * RATE + (hours-STANDARD) * (RATE * 1.5);
      else
         pay = hours * RATE;

      NumberFormat fmt = NumberFormat.getCurrencyInstance();
      System.out.println ("Gross earnings: " + fmt.format(pay));
   }
}
```

output

```
Enter the number of hours worked: 46

Gross earnings: $404.25
```

statement calls `getSize` and compares the result to the constant `FULL`. If the condition is true, the `expand` method is invoked (apparently to expand the size of the roster). If the roster is not yet full, the variable `name` is passed as a parameter to the `addName` method.

using block statements

We may want to do more than one thing as the result of evaluating a boolean condition. In Java, we can replace any single statement with a *block statement*. A block statement is a collection of statements enclosed in braces. We've already seen these braces used to delimit the `main` method and a class definition. The program called `Guessing`, shown in Listing 3.3, uses an `if-else` statement in which the statement of the `else` clause is a block statement.

If the guess entered by the user equals the randomly chosen answer, an appropriate acknowledgement is printed. However, if the answer is incorrect, two statements are printed, one that states that the guess is wrong and one that prints the actual answer. A programming project at the end of this chapter expands the concept of this example into the Hi-Lo game, which can only be done after we explore loops in more detail.

Note that if the block braces were not used, the sentence stating that the answer is incorrect would be printed if the answer was wrong, but the sentence revealing the correct answer would be printed in all cases. That is, only the first statement would be considered part of the `else` clause.

Remember that indentation means nothing except to the human reader. Statements that are not blocked properly can lead to the programmer making improper assumptions about how the code will execute. For example, the following code is misleading:

```
if (depth > 36.238)
   delta = 100;
else
   System.out.println ("WARNING: Delta is being reset to ZERO");
   delta = 0;  // not part of the else clause!
```

The indentation (not to mention the logic of the code) implies that the variable `delta` is reset only when `depth` is less than `36.238`. However, without using a block, the assignment statement that resets `delta` to zero is not governed by the `if-else` statement at all. It is executed in either case, which is clearly not what is intended.

**listing
   3.3**

```java
//********************************************************************
//   Guessing.java        Author: Lewis/Loftus
//
//   Demonstrates the use of a block statement in an if-else.
//********************************************************************

import cs1.Keyboard;
import java.util.Random;

public class Guessing
{
   //-----------------------------------------------------------------
   //   Plays a simple guessing game with the user.
   //-----------------------------------------------------------------
   public static void main (String[] args)
   {
      final int MAX = 10;
      int answer, guess;

      Random generator = new Random();
      answer = generator.nextInt(MAX) + 1;

      System.out.print ("I'm thinking of a number between 1 and "
                        + MAX + ". Guess what it is: ");
      guess = Keyboard.readInt();

      if (guess == answer)
         System.out.println ("You got it! Good guessing!");
      else
      {
         System.out.println ("That is not correct, sorry.");
         System.out.println ("The number was " + answer);
      }
   }
}
```

output

```
I'm thinking of a number between 1 and 10. Guess what it is: 7
That is not correct, sorry.
The number was 4
```

A block statement can be used anywhere a single statement is called for in Java syntax. For example, the `if` portion of an `if-else` statement could be a block, or the `else` portion could be a block (as we saw in the `Guessing` program), or both parts could be block statements. For example:

```java
if (boxes != warehouse.getCount())
{
   System.out.println ("Inventory and warehouse do NOT match.");
   System.out.println ("Beginning inventory process again!");
   boxes = 0;
}
else
{
   System.out.println ("Inventory and warehouse MATCH.");
   warehouse.ship();
}
```

In this `if-else` statement, the value of `boxes` is compared to a value obtained by calling the `getCount` method of the `warehouse` object (whatever that is). If they do not match exactly, two `println` statements and an assignment statement are executed. If they do match, a different message is printed and the `ship` method of `warehouse` is invoked.

nested if statements

The statement executed as the result of an `if` statement could be another `if` statement. This situation is called a *nested if*. It allows us to make another decision after determining the results of a previous decision. The program in Listing 3.4, called `MinOfThree`, uses nested `if` statements to determine the smallest of three integer values entered by the user.

Carefully trace the logic of the `MinOfThree` program, using various input sets with the minimum value in all three positions, to see how it determines the lowest value.

An important situation arises with nested `if` statements. It may seem that an `else` clause after a nested `if` could apply to either `if` statement. For example:

```java
if (code == 'R')
   if (height <= 20)
      System.out.println ("Situation Normal");
   else
      System.out.println ("Bravo!");
```

listing
3.4

```java
//************************************************************************
//   MinOfThree.java       Author: Lewis/Loftus
//
//   Demonstrates the use of nested if statements.
//************************************************************************

import cs1.Keyboard;

public class MinOfThree
{
   //-----------------------------------------------------------------
   //   Reads three integers from the user and determines the smallest
   //   value.
   //-----------------------------------------------------------------
   public static void main (String[] args)
   {
      int num1, num2, num3, min = 0;

      System.out.println ("Enter three integers: ");
      num1 = Keyboard.readInt();
      num2 = Keyboard.readInt();
      num3 = Keyboard.readInt();

      if (num1 < num2)
         if (num1 < num3)
            min = num1;
         else
            min = num3;
      else
         if (num2 < num3)
            min = num2;
         else
            min = num3;

      System.out.println ("Minimum value: " + min);
   }
}
```

output

```
Enter three integers:
45    22    69
Minimum value: 22
```

Is the `else` clause matched to the inner `if` statement or the outer `if` statement? The indentation in this example implies that it is part of the inner `if` statement, and that is correct. An `else` clause is always matched to the closest unmatched `if` that preceded it. However, if we're not careful, we can easily mismatch it in our mind and imply our intentions, but not reality, by misaligned indentation. This is another reason why accurate, consistent indentation is crucial.

> **key concept**
>
> In a nested `if` statement, an `else` clause is matched to the closest unmatched `if`.

Braces can be used to specify the `if` statement to which an `else` clause belongs. For example, if the previous example should have been structured so that the string `"Bravo!"` is printed if `code` is not equal to `'R'`, we could force that relationship (and properly indent) as follows:

```java
if (code == 'R')
{
   if (height <= 20)
      System.out.println ("Situation Normal");
}
else
   System.out.println ("Bravo!");
```

By using the block statement in the first `if` statement, we establish that the `else` clause belongs to it.

3.3 the switch statement

Another conditional statement in Java is called the *switch statement*, which causes the executing program to follow one of several paths based on a single value. We also discuss the *break statement* in this section because it is usually used with a `switch` statement.

The `switch` statement evaluates an expression to determine a value and then matches that value with one of several possible *cases*. Each case has statements associated with it. After evaluating the expression, control jumps to the statement associated with the first case that matches the value. Consider the following example:

```java
switch (idChar)
{
   case 'A':
      aCount = aCount + 1;
      break;
   case 'B':
```

```
      bCount = bCount + 1;
      break;
   case 'C':
      cCount = cCount + 1;
      break;
   default:
      System.out.println ("Error in Identification Character.");
}
```

First, the expression is evaluated. In this example, the expression is a simple char variable. Execution then transfers to the first statement identified by the case value that matches the result of the expression. Therefore, if idChar contains an 'A', the variable aCount is incremented. If it contains a 'B', the case for 'A' is skipped and processing continues where bCount is incremented.

If no case value matches that of the expression, execution continues with the optional *default case,* indicated by the reserved word default. If no default case exists, no statements in the switch statement are executed and processing continues with the statement after the switch. It is often a good idea to include a default case, even if you don't expect it to be executed.

When a break statement is encountered, processing jumps to the statement following the switch statement. A break statement is usually used to break out of each case of a switch statement. Without a break statement, processing continues into the next case of the switch. Therefore if the break statement at the end of the 'A' case in the previous example was not there, both the aCount and bCount variables would be incremented when the idChar contains an 'A'. Usually we want to perform only one case, so a break statement is almost always used. Occasionally, though, the "pass through" feature comes in handy.

> **key concept**
>
> A break statement is usually used at the end of each case alternative of a switch statement to jump to the end of the switch.

The expression evaluated at the beginning of a switch statement must be an *integral type,* meaning that it is either an int or a char. It cannot evaluate to a boolean or floating point value, and even other integer types (byte, short, and long) cannot be used. Furthermore, each case value must be a constant; it cannot be a variable or other expression.

Note that the implicit boolean condition of a switch statement is based on equality. The expression at the beginning of the statement is compared to each case value to determine which one it equals. A switch statement cannot be used to determine other relational operations (such as less than), unless some preliminary processing is done. For example, the GradeReport program in Listing 3.5 prints a comment based on a numeric grade that is entered by the user.

Switch Statement

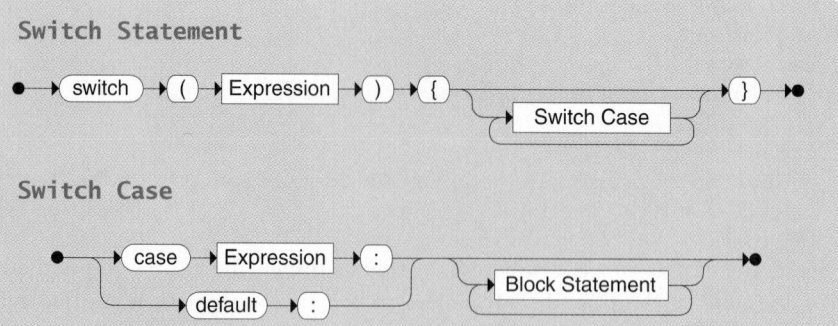

The `switch` statement evaluates the initial Expression and matches its value with one of the cases. Processing continues with the Statement corresponding to that case. The optional `default` case will be executed if no other case matches.

Example:

```
switch (numValues)
{
   case 0:
      System.out.println ("No values were entered.");
      break;
   case 1:
      System.out.println ("One value was entered.");
      break;
   case 2:
      System.out.println ("Two values were entered.");
      break;
   default:
      System.out.println ("Too many values were entered.");
}
```

listing
   3.5

```java
//********************************************************************
//   GradeReport.java       Author: Lewis/Loftus
//
//   Demonstrates the use of a switch statement.
//********************************************************************

import cs1.Keyboard;

public class GradeReport
{
   //-----------------------------------------------------------------
   //   Reads a grade from the user and prints comments accordingly.
   //-----------------------------------------------------------------
   public static void main (String[] args)
   {
      int grade, category;

      System.out.print ("Enter a numeric grade (0 to 100): ");
      grade = Keyboard.readInt();

      category = grade / 10;

      System.out.print ("That grade is ");

      switch (category)
      {
         case 10:
            System.out.println ("a perfect score. Well done.");
            break;
         case 9:
            System.out.println ("well above average. Excellent.");
            break;
         case 8:
            System.out.println ("above average. Nice job.");
            break;
         case 7:
            System.out.println ("average.");
            break;
         case 6:
            System.out.println ("below average. You should see the");
            System.out.println ("instructor to clarify the material "
                                + "presented in class.");
            break;
```

listing
3.5   continued

```
        default:
            System.out.println ("not passing.");
    }
  }
}
```

output

```
Enter a numeric grade (0 to 100): 86
That grade is above average. Nice job.
```

In `GradeReport`, the category of the grade is determined by dividing the grade by 10 using integer division, resulting in an integer value between 0 and 10 (assuming a valid grade is entered). This result is used as the expression of the `switch`, which prints various messages for grades 60 or higher and a default sentence for all other values.

> **key concept**
>
> A `switch` statement could be implemented as a series of `if-else` statements, but the `switch` is sometimes a more convenient and readable construct.

Note that any `switch` statement could be implemented as a set of nested `if` statements. However, nested `if` statements quickly become difficult for a human reader to understand and are error prone to implement and debug. But because a `switch` can evaluate only equality, sometimes nested `if` statements are necessary. It depends on the situation.

3.4 boolean expressions revisited

Let's examine a few more options regarding the use of boolean expressions.

logical operators

In addition to the equality and relational operators, Java has three *logical operators* that produce boolean results. They also take boolean operands. Figure 3.3 lists and describes the logical operators.

The ! operator is used to perform the *logical NOT* operation, which is also called the *logical complement*. The logical complement of a boolean value yields

Operator	Description	Example	Result
!	logical NOT	! a	true if a is false and false if a is true
&&	logical AND	a && b	true if a and b are both true and false otherwise
||	logical OR	a || b	true if a or b or both are true and false otherwise

figure 3.3   Java logical operators

its opposite value. That is, if a boolean variable called found has the value false, then !found is true. Likewise, if found is true, then !found is false. The logical NOT operation does not change the value stored in found.

A logical operation can be described by a *truth table* that lists all possible combinations of values for the variables involved in an expression. Because the logical NOT operator is unary, there are only two possible values for its one operand, true or false. Figure 3.4 shows a truth table that describes the ! operator.

The && operator performs a *logical AND* operation. The result is true if both operands are true, but false otherwise. Since it is a binary operator and each operand has two possible values, there are four combinations to consider.

The result of the *logical OR* operator (||) is true if one or the other or both operands are true, but false otherwise. It is also a binary operator. Figure 3.5 depicts a truth table that shows both the && and || operators.

The logical NOT has the highest precedence of the three logical operators, followed by logical AND, then logical OR.

Logical operators are often used as part of a condition for a selection or repetition statement. For example, consider the following if statement:

```
if (!done && (count > MAX))
    System.out.println ("Completed.");
```

Under what conditions would the println statement be executed? The value of the boolean variable done is either true or false, and the NOT operator

a	!a
false	true
true	false

figure 3.4   Truth table describing the logical NOT operator

a	b	a && b	a || b
false	false	false	false
false	true	false	true
true	false	false	true
true	true	true	true

figure 3.5   Truth table describing the logical AND and OR operators

> **key concept**
>
> Logical operators return a boolean value and are often used to construct sophisticated conditions.

reverses that value. The value of count is either greater than MAX or it isn't. The truth table in Fig. 3.6 breaks down all of the possibilities.

An important characteristic of the && and || operators is that they are "short-circuited." That is, if their left operand is sufficient to decide the boolean result of the operation, the right operand is not evaluated. This situation can occur with both operators but for different reasons. If the left operand of the && operator is false, then the result of the operation will be false no matter what the value of the right operand is. Likewise, if the left operand of the || is true, then the result of the operation is true no matter what the value of the right operand is.

Sometimes you can capitalize on the fact that the operation is short-circuited. For example, the condition in the following if statement will not attempt to divide by zero if the left operand is false. If count has the value zero, the left side of the && operation is false; therefore the whole expression is false and the right side is not evaluated.

```
if (count != 0 && total/count > MAX)
    System.out.println ("Testing.");
```

done	count > MAX	!done	!done && (count > MAX)
false	false	true	false
false	true	true	true
true	false	false	false
true	true	false	false

figure 3.6   A truth table for a specific condition

Be careful when you rely on these kinds of subtle programming language characteristics. Not all programming languages work the same way. As we have mentioned several times, you should always strive to make it extremely clear to the reader exactly how the logic of your program works.

comparing characters and strings

We know what it means when we say that one number is less than another, but what does it mean to say one character is less than another? As we discussed in Chapter 2, characters in Java are based on the Unicode character set, which defines an ordering of all possible characters that can be used. Because the character 'a' comes before the character 'b' in the character set, we can say that 'a' is less than 'b'.

We can use the equality and relational operators on character data. For example, if two character variables ch1 and ch2 hold the values of two characters, we might determine their relative ordering in the Unicode character set with an if statement as follows:

```
if (ch1 > ch2)
    System.out.println (ch1 + " is greater than " + ch2);
else
    System.out.println (ch1 + " is NOT greater than " + ch2);
```

The Unicode character set is structured so that all lowercase alphabetic characters ('a' through 'z') are contiguous and in alphabetical order. The same is true of uppercase alphabetic characters ('A' through 'Z') and characters that represent digits ('0' through '9'). The digits precede the uppercase alphabetic characters, which precede the lowercase alphabetic characters. Before, after, and in between these groups are other characters. (See the chart in Appendix C.)

> **key concept**
> The relative order of characters in Java is defined by the Unicode character set.

These relationships make it easy to sort characters and strings of characters. If you have a list of names, for instance, you can put them in alphabetical order based on the inherent relationships among characters in the character set.

However, you should not use the equality or relational operators to compare String objects. The String class contains a method called equals that returns a boolean value that is true if the two strings being compared contain exactly the same characters, and false otherwise. For example:

```
if (name1.equals(name2))
    System.out.println ("The names are the same.");
else
    System.out.println ("The names are not the same.");
```

Assuming that `name1` and `name2` are `String` objects, this condition determines whether the characters they contain are an exact match. Because both objects were created from the `String` class, they both respond to the `equals` message. Therefore the condition could have been written as `name2.equals(name1)` and the same result would occur.

It is valid to test the condition (`name1 == name2`), but that actually tests to see whether both reference variables refer to the same `String` object. That is, the `==` operator tests whether both reference variables contain the same address. That's different than testing to see whether two different `String` objects contain the same characters. We discuss this issue in more detail later in the book.

To determine the relative ordering of two strings, use the `compareTo` method of the `String` class. The `compareTo` method is more versatile than the equals method. Instead of returning a `boolean` value, the `compareTo` method returns an integer. The return value is negative if the `String` object through which the method is invoked precedes (is less than) the string that is passed in as a parameter. The return value is zero if the two strings contain the same characters. The return value is positive if the `String` object through which the method is invoked follows (is greater than) the string that is passed in as a parameter. For example:

```
int result = name1.compareTo(name2);
if (result < 0)
   System.out.println (name1 + " comes before " + name2);
else
   if (result == 0)
      System.out.println ("The names are equal.");
   else
      System.out.println (name1 + " follows " + name2);
```

Keep in mind that comparing characters and strings is based on the Unicode character set (see Appendix C). This is called a *lexicographic ordering*. If all alphabetic characters are in the same case (upper or lower), the lexicographic ordering will be alphabetic ordering as well. However, when comparing two strings, such as *"able"* and *"Baker"*, the `compareTo` method will conclude that *"Baker"* comes first because all of the uppercase letters come before all of the lowercase letters in the Unicode character set. A string that is the prefix of another, longer string is considered to precede the longer string. For example, when comparing two strings such as *"horse"* and *"horsefly"*, the `compareTo` method will conclude that *"horse"* comes first.

comparing floats

Another interesting situation occurs when comparing floating point data. Specifically, you should rarely use the equality operator (==) when comparing floating point values. Two floating point values are equal, according to the == operator, only if all the binary digits of their underlying representations match. If the compared values are the results of computation, it may be unlikely that they are exactly equal even if they are close enough for the specific situation.

A better way to check for floating point equality is to compute the absolute value of the difference between the two values and compare the result to some tolerance level. For example, we may choose a tolerance level of 0.00001. If the two floating point values are so close that their difference is less than the tolerance, then we are willing to consider them equal. Comparing two floating point values, f1 and f2, could be accomplished as follows:

```
if (Math.abs(f1 - f2) < TOLERANCE)
    System.out.println ("Essentially equal.");
```

The value of the constant TOLERANCE should be appropriate for the situation.

3.5   more operators

Before moving on to repetition statements, let's examine a few more Java operators to give us even more flexibility in the way we express our program commands. Some of these operators are commonly used in loop processing.

increment and decrement operators

The *increment operator* (++) adds 1 to any integer or floating point value. The two plus signs that make up the operator cannot be separated by white space. The *decrement operator* (--) is similar except that it subtracts 1 from the value. They are both unary operators because they operate on only one operand. The following statement causes the value of count to be incremented.

```
count++;
```

The result is stored back into the variable count. Therefore it is functionally equivalent to the following statement:

```
count = count + 1;
```

The increment and decrement operators can be applied after the variable (such as count++ or count--), creating what is called the *postfix form* of the operator. They can also be applied before the variable (such as ++count or --count), in what is called the *prefix form*. When used alone in a statement, the prefix and postfix forms are functionally equivalent. That is, it doesn't matter if you write

```
count++;
```

or

```
++count;
```

However, when such a form is written as a statement by itself, it is usually written in its postfix form.

When the increment or decrement operator is used in a larger expression, it can yield different results depending on the form used. For example, if the variable count currently contains the value 15, the following statement assigns the value 15 to total and the value 16 to count:

```
total = count++;
```

However, the following statement assigns the value 16 to both total and count:

```
total = ++count;
```

The value of count is incremented in both situations, but the value used in the larger expression depends on whether a prefix or postfix form of the increment operator is used, as described in Fig. 3.7.

Expression	Operation	Value of Expression
count++	add 1 to count	the original value of count
++count	add 1 to count	the new value of count
count--	subtract 1 from count	the original value of count
--count	subtract 1 from count	the new value of count

figure 3.7 Prefix and postfix forms of the increment and decrement operators

Because of the subtle differences between the prefix and postfix forms of the increment and decrement operators, they should be used with care. As always, favor the side of readability.

> The prefix and postfix increment and decrement operators have subtle effects on programs because of differences in when they are evaluated.

> key concept

assignment operators

As a convenience, several *assignment operators* have been defined in Java that combine a basic operation with assignment. For example, the += operator can be used as follows:

```
total += 5;
```

It performs the same operation as the following statement:

```
total = total + 5;
```

The right-hand side of the assignment operator can be a full expression. The expression on the right-hand side of the operator is evaluated, then that result is added to the current value of the variable on the left-hand side, and that value is stored in the variable. Therefore, the following statement:

```
total += (sum - 12) / count;
```

is equivalent to:

```
total = total + ((sum - 12) / count);
```

Many similar assignment operators are defined in Java, as listed in Fig. 3.8. (Appendix E discusses additional operators.)

All of the assignment operators evaluate the entire expression on the right-hand side first, then use the result as the right operand of the other operation. Therefore, the following statement:

```
result *= count1 + count2;
```

is equivalent to:

```
result = result * (count1 + count2);
```

Likewise, the following statement:

```
result %= (highest - 40) / 2;
```

is equivalent to:

```
result = result % ((highest - 40) / 2);
```

Operator	Description	Example	Equivalent Expression
=	assignment	x = y	x = y
+=	addition, then assignment	x += y	x = x + y
+=	string concatenation, then assignment	x += y	x = x + y
-=	subtraction, then assignment	x -= y	x = x - y
*=	multiplication, then assignment	x *= y	x = x * y
/=	division, then assignment	x /= y	x = x / y
%=	remainder, then assignment	x %= y	x = x % y
<<=	left shift, then assignment	x <<= y	x = x << y
>>=	right shift with sign, then assignment	x >>= y	x = x >> y
>>>=	right shift with zero, then assignment	x >>>= y	x = x >>> y
&=	bitwise AND, then assignment	x &= y	x = x & y
&=	boolean AND, then assignment	x &= y	x = x & y
^=	bitwise XOR, then assignment	x ^= y	x = x ^ y
^=	boolean XOR, then assignment	x ^= y	x = x ^ y
|=	bitwise OR, then assignment	x |= y	x = x | y
|=	boolean OR, then assignment	x |= y	x = x | y

figure 3.8   Java assignment operators

Some assignment operators perform particular functions depending on the types of the operands, just as their corresponding regular operators do. For example, if the operands to the += operator are strings, then the assignment operator performs string concatenation.

the conditional operator

The Java *conditional operator* is a *ternary operator* because it requires three operands. The symbol for the conditional operator is usually written ?:, but it is not like other operators in that the two symbols that make it up are always separated. The following is an example of an expression that contains the conditional operator:

```
(total > MAX) ? total + 1 : total * 2;
```

Preceding the ? is a boolean condition. Following the ? are two expressions separated by the : symbol. The entire conditional expression returns the value of the first expression if the condition is true, and the value of the second expression if the condition is false. Keep in mind that this is an expression that returns a value, and usually we want to do something with that value, such as assign it to a variable:

```
total = (total > MAX) ? total + 1 : total * 2;
```

In many ways, the ?: operator serves like an abbreviated if-else statement. Therefore the previous statement is functionally equivalent to, but sometimes more convenient than, the following:

```
if (total > MAX)
    total = total + 1;
else
    total = total * 2;
```

The two expressions that define the larger conditional expression must evaluate to the same type. Consider the following declaration:

```
int larger = (num1 > num2) ? num1 : num2;
```

If num1 is greater than num2, the value of num1 is returned and used to initialize the variable larger. If not, the value of num2 is returned and used. Similarly, the following statement prints the smaller of the two values:

```
System.out.println ("Smaller: " + ((num1 < num2) ? num1 : num2));
```

The conditional operator is occasionally helpful to evaluate a short condition and return a result. It is not a replacement for an if-else statement, however, because the operands to the ?: operator are expressions, not necessarily full statements. Even when the conditional operator is a viable alternative, you should use it sparingly because it is often less readable than an if-else statement.

3.6 the while statement

As we discussed earlier in this chapter, a repetition statement (or loop) allows us to execute another statement multiple times. A while *statement* is a loop that evaluates a boolean condition—just like an if statement does—and executes a statement (called the *body* of the loop) if the condition is true. However, unlike the if statement, after the body is executed, the condition is evaluated again. If it is still

A while statement allows a program to execute the same statement multiple times.

true, the body is executed again. This repetition continues until the condition becomes false; then processing continues with the statement after the body of the while loop. Figure 3.9 shows this processing.

The Counter program shown in Listing 3.6 simply prints the values from 1 to 5. Each iteration through the loop prints one value, then increments the counter. A constant called LIMIT is used to hold the maximum value that count is allowed to reach.

Note that the body of the while loop is a block containing two statements. Because the value of count is incremented each time, we are guaranteed that count will eventually reach the value of LIMIT.

Let's look at another program that uses a while loop. The Average program shown in Listing 3.7 reads a series of integer values from the user, sums them up, and computes their average.

We don't know how many values the user may enter, so we need to have a way to indicate that the user is done entering numbers. In this program, we designate zero to be a *sentinel value* that indicates the end of the input. The while loop continues to process input values until the user enters zero. This assumes that zero is not one of the valid numbers that should contribute to the average. A sentinel value must always be outside the normal range of values entered.

Note that in the Average program, a variable called sum is used to maintain a *running sum*, which means it is the sum of the values entered thus far. The variable sum is initialized to zero, and each value read is added to and stored back into sum.

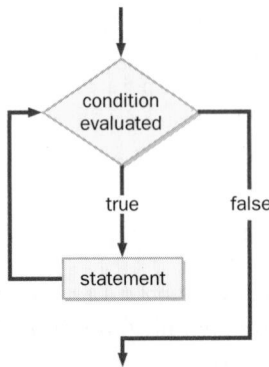

figure 3.9   The logic of a while loop

listing
   3.6

```java
//********************************************************************
//  Counter.java          Author: Lewis/Loftus
//
//  Demonstrates the use of a while loop.
//********************************************************************

public class Counter
{
   //-----------------------------------------------------------------
   //  Prints integer values from 1 to a specific limit.
   //-----------------------------------------------------------------
   public static void main (String[] args)
   {
      final int LIMIT = 5;
      int count = 1;

      while (count <= LIMIT)
      {
         System.out.println (count);
         count = count + 1;
      }

      System.out.println ("Done");
   }
}
```

output

```
1
2
3
4
5
Done
```

We also have to count the number of values that are entered so that after the loop concludes we can divide by the appropriate value to compute the average. Note that the sentinel value is not counted. Consider the unusual situation in which the user immediately enters the sentinel value before entering any valid values. The value of count in this case will still be zero and the computation of the average will result in a runtime error. Fixing this problem is left as a programming project.

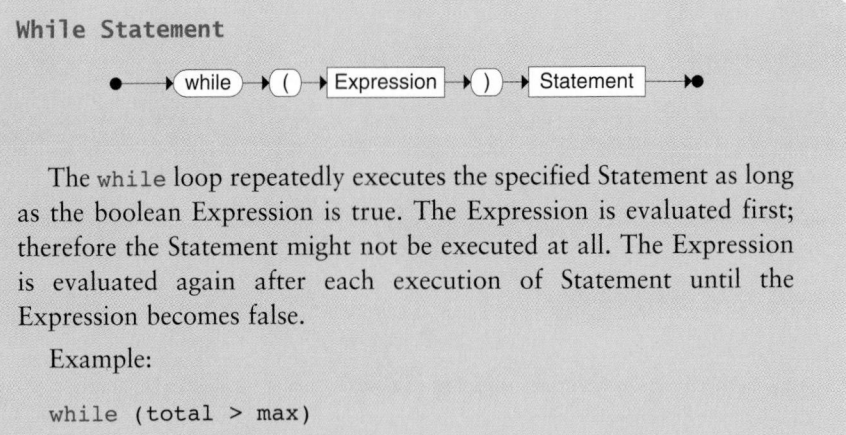

The `while` loop repeatedly executes the specified Statement as long as the boolean Expression is true. The Expression is evaluated first; therefore the Statement might not be executed at all. The Expression is evaluated again after each execution of Statement until the Expression becomes false.

Example:

```
while (total > max)
{
    total = total / 2;
    System.out.println ("Current total: " + total);
}
```

Let's examine yet another program that uses a `while` loop. The `WinPercentage` program shown in Listing 3.8 computes the winning percentage of a sports team based on the number of games won.

We use a `while` loop in the `WinPercentage` program to *validate the input*, meaning we guarantee that the user enters a value that we consider to be valid. In this example, that means that the number of games won must be greater than or equal to zero and less than or equal to the total number of games played. The `while` loop continues to execute, repeatedly prompting the user for valid input, until the entered number is indeed valid.

Validating input data, avoiding errors such as dividing by zero, and performing other actions that guarantee proper processing are important design steps. We generally want our programs to be *robust*, which means that they handle potential problems as elegantly as possible.

listing
    3.7

```java
//********************************************************************
//   Average.java          Author: Lewis/Loftus
//
//   Demonstrates the use of a while loop, a sentinel value, and a
//   running sum.
//********************************************************************

import java.text.DecimalFormat;
import cs1.Keyboard;

public class Average
{
   //-----------------------------------------------------------------
   //   Computes the average of a set of values entered by the user.
   //   The running sum is printed as the numbers are entered.
   //-----------------------------------------------------------------
   public static void main (String[] args)
   {
      int sum = 0, value, count = 0;
      double average;

      System.out.print ("Enter an integer (0 to quit): ");
      value = Keyboard.readInt();

      while (value != 0)  // sentinel value of 0 to terminate loop
      {
         count++;

         sum += value;
         System.out.println ("The sum so far is " + sum);

         System.out.print ("Enter an integer (0 to quit): ");
         value = Keyboard.readInt();
      }

      System.out.println ();
      System.out.println ("Number of values entered: " + count);

      average = (double)sum / count;

      DecimalFormat fmt = new DecimalFormat ("0.###");
```

listing
   3.7   continued

```
        System.out.println ("The average is " + fmt.format(average));
    }
}
```

output

```
Enter an integer (0 to quit): 25
The sum so far is 25
Enter an integer (0 to quit): 164
The sum so far is 189
Enter an integer (0 to quit): -14
The sum so far is 175
Enter an integer (0 to quit): 84
The sum so far is 259
Enter an integer (0 to quit): 12
The sum so far is 271
Enter an integer (0 to quit): -35
The sum so far is 236
Enter an integer (0 to quit): 0
Number of values entered: 6
The average is 39.333
```

infinite loops

It is the programmer's responsibility to ensure that the condition of a loop will eventually become false. If it doesn't, the loop body will execute forever, or at least until the program is interrupted. This situation, called an *infinite loop,* is a common mistake.

> **key concept**
>
> We must design our programs carefully to avoid infinite loops. The body of the loop must eventually make the loop condition false.

The program shown in Listing 3.9 demonstrates an infinite loop. If you execute this program, be prepared to interrupt it. On most systems, pressing the Control-C keyboard combination (hold down the Control key and press C) terminates a running program.

listing
 3.8

```java
//********************************************************************
//  WinPercentage.java        Author: Lewis/Loftus
//
//  Demonstrates the use of a while loop for input validation.
//********************************************************************

import java.text.NumberFormat;
import cs1.Keyboard;

public class WinPercentage
{
   //-----------------------------------------------------------------
   //  Computes the percentage of games won by a team.
   //-----------------------------------------------------------------
   public static void main (String[] args)
   {
      final int NUM_GAMES = 12;
      int won;
      double ratio;

      System.out.print ("Enter the number of games won (0 to "
                        + NUM_GAMES + "): ");
      won = Keyboard.readInt();

      while (won < 0 || won > NUM_GAMES)
      {
         System.out.print ("Invalid input. Please reenter: ");
         won = Keyboard.readInt();
      }

      ratio = (double)won / NUM_GAMES;

      NumberFormat fmt = NumberFormat.getPercentInstance();

      System.out.println ();
      System.out.println ("Winning percentage: " + fmt.format(ratio));
   }
}
```

listing
   3.8   continued

output

```
Enter the number of games won (0 to 12): -5
Invalid input. Please reenter: 13
Invalid input. Please reenter: 7

Winning percentage: 58%
```

In the Forever program, the initial value of count is 1 and it is decremented in the loop body. The while loop will continue as long as count is less than or equal to 25. Because count gets smaller with each iteration, the condition will always be true.

Let's look at some other examples of infinite loops:

```
int count = 1;
while (count != 50)
    count += 2;
```

In this code fragment, the variable count is initialized to 1 and is moving in a positive direction. However, note that it is being incremented by 2 each time. This loop will never terminate because count will never equal 50. It begins at 1 and then changes to 3, then 5, and so on. Eventually it reaches 49, then changes to 51, then 53, and continues forever.

Now consider the following situation:

```
double num = 1.0;
while (num != 0.0)
    num = num − 0.1;
```

Once again, the value of the loop control variable seems to be moving in the correct direction. And, in fact, it seems like num will eventually take on the value 0.0. However, this loop is infinite (at least on most systems) because num will never have a value *exactly* equal to 0.0. This situation is similar to one we discussed earlier in this chapter when we explored the idea of comparing floating point values in the condition of an if statement. Because of the way the values are represented in binary, minute computational deficiencies occur internally that make a direct comparison of floating point values (for equality) problematic.

listing
   3.9

```
//********************************************************************
//  Forever.java        Author: Lewis/Loftus
//
//  Demonstrates an INFINITE LOOP.  WARNING!!
//********************************************************************

public class Forever
{
   //----------------------------------------------------------------
   //  Prints ever-decreasing integers in an INFINITE LOOP!
   //----------------------------------------------------------------
   public static void main (String[] args)
   {
      int count = 1;

      while (count <= 25)
      {
         System.out.println (count);
         count = count - 1;
      }

      System.out.println ("Done");  // this statement is never reached
   }
}
```

output

```
1
0
-1
-2
-3
-4
-5
-6
-7
-8
-9
and so on until interrupted
```

nested loops

The body of a loop can contain another loop. This situation is called a *nested loop*. Keep in mind that for each iteration of the outer loop, the inner loop executes completely. Consider the following code fragment. How many times does the string "Here again" get printed?

```java
int count1, count2;
count1 = 1;
while (count1 <= 10)
{
   count2 = 1;
   while (count2 <= 50)
   {
      System.out.println ("Here again");
      count2++;
   }
   count1++;
}
```

The `println` statement is inside the inner loop. The outer loop executes 10 times, as `count1` iterates between 1 and 10. The inner loop executes 50 times, as `count2` iterates between 1 and 50. For each iteration of the outer loop, the inner loop executes completely. Therefore the `println` statement is executed 500 times.

As with any loop situation, we must be careful to scrutinize the conditions of the loops and the initializations of variables. Let's consider some small changes to this code. What if the condition of the outer loop were (`count1 < 10`) instead of (`count1 <= 10`)? How would that change the total number of lines printed? Well, the outer loop would execute 9 times instead of 10, so the `println` statement would be executed 450 times. What if the outer loop were left as it was originally defined, but `count2` were initialized to 10 instead of 1 before the inner loop? The inner loop would then execute 40 times instead of 50, so the total number of lines printed would be 400.

Let's look at another example of a nested loop. A *palindrome* is a string of characters that reads the same forward or backward. For example, the following strings are palindromes:

▶ radar

▶ drab bard

‣ ab cde xxxx edc ba

‣ kayak

‣ deified

‣ able was I ere I saw elba

Note that some palindromes have an even number of characters, whereas others have an odd number of characters. The `PalindromeTester` program shown in Listing 3.10 tests to see whether a string is a palindrome. The user may test as many strings as desired.

listing
3.10

```java
//********************************************************************
//   PalindromeTester.java        Author: Lewis/Loftus
//
//   Demonstrates the use of nested while loops.
//********************************************************************

import cs1.Keyboard;

public class PalindromeTester
{
   //-----------------------------------------------------------------
   //   Tests strings to see if they are palindromes.
   //-----------------------------------------------------------------
   public static void main (String[] args)
   {
      String str, another = "y";
      int left, right;

      while (another.equalsIgnoreCase("y")) // allows y or Y
      {
         System.out.println ("Enter a potential palindrome:");
         str = Keyboard.readString();

         left = 0;
         right = str.length() - 1;

         while (str.charAt(left) == str.charAt(right) && left < right)
         {
            left++;
```

listing
3.10   continued

```
            right--;
        }

        System.out.println();

        if (left < right)
            System.out.println ("That string is NOT a palindrome.");
        else
            System.out.println ("That string IS a palindrome.");

        System.out.println();
        System.out.print ("Test another palindrome (y/n)? ");
        another = Keyboard.readString();
        }
    }
}
```

output

```
Enter a potential palindrome:
radar

That string IS a palindrome.

Test another palindrome (y/n)? y
Enter a potential palindrome:
able was I ere I saw elba

That string IS a palindrome.

Test another palindrome (y/n)? y
Enter a potential palindrome:
abcddcba

That string IS a palindrome.

Test another palindrome (y/n)? y
Enter a potential palindrome:
abracadabra

That string is NOT a palindrome.

Test another palindrome (y/n)? n
```

The code for `PalindromeTester` contains two loops, one inside the other. The outer loop controls how many strings are tested, and the inner loop scans through each string, character by character, until it determines whether the string is a palindrome.

The variables `left` and `right` store the indexes of two characters. They initially indicate the characters on either end of the string. Each iteration of the inner loop compares the two characters indicated by `left` and `right`. We fall out of the inner loop when either the characters don't match, meaning the string is not a palindrome, or when the value of `left` becomes equal to or greater than the value of `right`, which means the entire string has been tested and it is a palindrome.

Note that the following phrases would not be considered palindromes by the current version of the program:

- A man, a plan, a canal, Panama.
- Dennis and Edna sinned.
- Rise to vote, sir.
- Doom an evil deed, liven a mood.
- Go hang a salami; I'm a lasagna hog.

These strings fail our current criteria for a palindrome because of the spaces, punctuation marks, and changes in uppercase and lowercase. However, if these characteristics were removed or ignored, these strings read the same forward and backward. Consider how the program could be changed to handle these situations. These modifications are included as a programming project at the end of the chapter.

the `StringTokenizer` class

Let's examine another useful class from the Java standard class library. The types of problems this class helps us solve are inherently repetitious. Therefore the solutions almost always involve loops.

To the Java compiler, a string is just a series of characters, but often we can identify separate, important elements within a string. Extracting and processing the data contained in a string is a common programming activity. The individual elements that comprise the string are referred to as *tokens*, and therefore the process of extracting these elements is called *tokenizing* the string. The characters that are used to separate one token from another are called *delimiters*.

For example, we may want to separate a sentence such as the following into individual words:

```
"The quick brown fox jumped over the lazy dog"
```

In this case, each word is a token and the space character is the delimiter. As another example, we may want to separate the elements of a URL such as:

```
"www.csc.villanova.edu/academics/courses"
```

The delimiters of interest in this case are the period (.) and the slash (/). In yet another situation we may want to extract individual data values from a string, such as:

```
"75.43 190.49 69.58 140.77"
```

The delimiter in this case is once again the space character. A second step in processing this data is to convert the individual token strings into numeric values. This kind of processing is performed by the code inside the Keyboard class. When we invoke a Keyboard method such as readDouble or readInt, the data is initially read as a string, then tokenized, and finally converted into the appropriate numeric form. If there are multiple values on one line, the Keyboard class keeps track of them and extracts them as needed. We discuss Keyboard class processing in more detail in Chapter 5.

The StringTokenizer class, which is part of the java.util package in the Java standard class library, is used to separate a string into tokens. The default delimiters used by the StringTokenizer class are the space, tab, carriage return, and newline characters. Figure 3.10 lists some methods of the StringTokenizer class. Note that the second constructor provides a way to specify another set of delimiters for separating tokens. Once the StringTokenizer object is created, a call to the nextToken method returns the next token from the string. The hasMoreTokens method, which returns a boolean value, is often used in the condition of a loop to determine whether more tokens are left to process in the string.

The CountWords program shown in Listing 3.11 uses the StringTokenizer class and a nested while loop to analyze several lines of text. The user types in as many lines of text as desired, terminating them with a line that contains only the word "DONE". Each iteration of the outer loop processes one line of text. The inner loop extracts and processes the tokens in the current line. The program counts the total number of words and the total number of characters in the words. After the sentinel value (which is not counted) is entered, the results are displayed.

```
StringTokenizer (String str)
    Constructor: creates a new StringTokenizer object to parse the specified
    string str based on white space.

StringTokenizer (String str, String delimiters)
    Constructor: creates a new StringTokenizer object to parse the specified
    string str based on the specified set of delimiters.

int countTokens ()
    Returns the number of tokens still left to be processed in the string.

boolean hasMoreTokens ()
    Returns true if there are tokens still left to be processed in the string.

String nextToken ()
    Returns the next token in the string.
```

figure 3.10   Some methods of the StringTokenizer class

Note that the punctuation characters in the strings are included with the tokenized words because the program uses only the default delimiters of the StringTokenizer class. Modifying this program to ignore punctuation is left as a programming project.

other loop controls

We've seen how the break statement can be used to break out of the cases of a switch statement. The break statement can also be placed in the body of any loop, even though this is usually inappropriate. Its effect on a loop is similar to its effect on a switch statement. The execution of the loop is stopped, and the statement following the loop is executed.

It is never necessary to use a break statement in a loop. An equivalent loop can always be written without it. Because the break statement causes program flow to jump from one place to another, using a break in a loop is not good practice. Its use is tolerated in a switch statement because an equivalent switch statement cannot be written without it. However, you can and should avoid it in a loop.

A *continue statement* has a similar effect on loop processing. The continue statement is similar to a break, but the loop condition is evaluated again, and the loop body is executed again if it is still true. Like the break statement, the continue statement can always be avoided in a loop, and for the same reasons, it should be.

listing
3.11

```java
//********************************************************************
//   CountWords.java          Author: Lewis/Loftus
//
//   Demonstrates the use of the StringTokenizer class and nested
//   loops.
//********************************************************************

import cs1.Keyboard;
import java.util.StringTokenizer;

public class CountWords
{
   //-----------------------------------------------------------------
   //  Reads several lines of text, counting the number of words
   //  and the number of non-space characters.
   //-----------------------------------------------------------------
   public static void main (String[] args)
   {
      int wordCount = 0, characterCount = 0;
      String line, word;
      StringTokenizer tokenizer;

      System.out.println ("Please enter text (type DONE to quit):");

      line = Keyboard.readString();
      while (!line.equals("DONE"))
      {
         tokenizer = new StringTokenizer (line);
         while (tokenizer.hasMoreTokens())
         {
            word = tokenizer.nextToken();
            wordCount++;
            characterCount += word.length();
         }
         line = Keyboard.readString();
      }

      System.out.println ("Number of words: " + wordCount);
      System.out.println ("Number of characters: " + characterCount);
   }
}
```

listing
    3.11   **continued**

output

```
Please enter text (type DONE to quit):
Mary had a little lamb; its fleece was white as snow.
And everywhere that Mary went, the fleece shed all
over and made quite a mess. Little lambs do not make
good house pets.
DONE
Number of words: 34
Number of characters: 141
```

web bonus

The book's Web site contains a discussion of the break and continue statements, but in general their use should be avoided.

3.7   the do statement

> A do statement executes its loop body at least once.
>
> **key concept**

The *do statement* is similar to the while statement except that its termination condition is at the end of the loop body. Like the while loop, the do loop executes the statement in the loop body until the condition becomes false. The condition is written at the end of the loop to indicate that it is not evaluated until the loop body is executed. Note that the body of a do loop is always executed at least once. Figure 3.11 shows this processing.

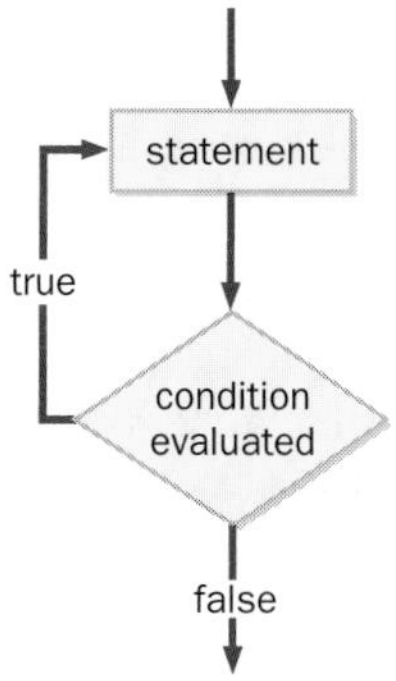

figure 3.11   The logic of a do loop

Do Statement

```
●──▶(do)──▶[Statement]──▶(while)──▶(()──▶[Expression]──▶())──▶(;)──▶●
```

The do loop repeatedly executes the specified Statement as long as the boolean Expression is true. The Statement is executed at least once, then the Expression is evaluated to determine whether the Statement should be executed again.

Example:

```
do
{
    System.out.print ("Enter a word:");
    word = Keyboard.readString();
    System.out.println (word);
}
while (!word.equals("quit"));
```

The program Counter2 shown in Listing 3.12 uses a do loop to print the numbers 1 to 5, just as we did in an earlier version of this program with a while loop.

Note that the do loop begins simply with the reserved word do. The body of the do loop continues until the *while clause* that contains the boolean condition that determines whether the loop body will be executed again. Sometimes it is difficult to determine whether a line of code that begins with the reserved word while is the beginning of a while loop or the end of a do loop.

Let's look at another example of the do loop. The program called ReverseNumber, shown in Listing 3.13, reads an integer from the user and reverses its digits mathematically.

The do loop in the ReverseNumber program uses the remainder operation to determine the digit in the 1's position, then adds it into the reversed number, then truncates that digit from the original number using integer division. The do loop terminates when we run out of digits to process, which corresponds to the point when the variable number reaches the value zero. Carefully trace the logic of this program with a few examples to see how it works.

If you know you want to perform the body of a loop at least once, then you probably want to use a do statement. A do loop has many of the same properties as a while statement, so it must also be checked for termination conditions to avoid infinite loops.

listing
    3.12

```java
//********************************************************************
//   Counter2.java        Author: Lewis/Loftus
//
//   Demonstrates the use of a do loop.
//********************************************************************

public class Counter2
{
   //-----------------------------------------------------------------
   //  Prints integer values from 1 to a specific limit.
   //-----------------------------------------------------------------
   public static void main (String[] args)
   {
      final int LIMIT = 5;
      int count = 0;

      do
      {
         count = count + 1;
         System.out.println (count);
      }
      while (count < LIMIT);

      System.out.println ("Done");
   }
}
```

output

```
1
2
3
4
5
Done
```

listing
    3.13

```
//********************************************************************
//  ReverseNumber.java        Author: Lewis/Loftus
//
//  Demonstrates the use of a do loop.
//********************************************************************

import cs1.Keyboard;

public class ReverseNumber
{
   //-----------------------------------------------------------------
   //  Reverses the digits of an integer mathematically.
   //-----------------------------------------------------------------
   public static void main (String[] args)
   {
      int number, lastDigit, reverse = 0;

      System.out.print ("Enter a positive integer: ");
      number = Keyboard.readInt();

      do
      {
         lastDigit = number % 10;
         reverse = (reverse * 10) + lastDigit;
         number = number / 10;
      }
      while (number > 0);

      System.out.println ("That number reversed is " + reverse);
   }
}
```

output

```
Enter a positive integer: 2846
That number reversed is 6482
```

3.8 the for statement

The while and the do statements are good to use when you don't initially know how many times you want to execute the loop body. The *for statement* is another repetition statement that is particularly well suited for executing the body of a loop a specific number of times that can be determined before the loop is executed.

The Counter3 program shown in Listing 3.14 once again prints the numbers 1 through 5, except this time we use a for loop to do it.

The header of a for loop contains three parts separated by semicolons. Before the loop begins, the first part of the header, called the *initialization,* is executed. The second part of the header is the boolean condition, which is evaluated before the loop body (like the while loop). If true, the body of the loop is executed, followed by the execution of the third part of the header, which is called the *increment*. Note that the initialization part is executed only once, but the

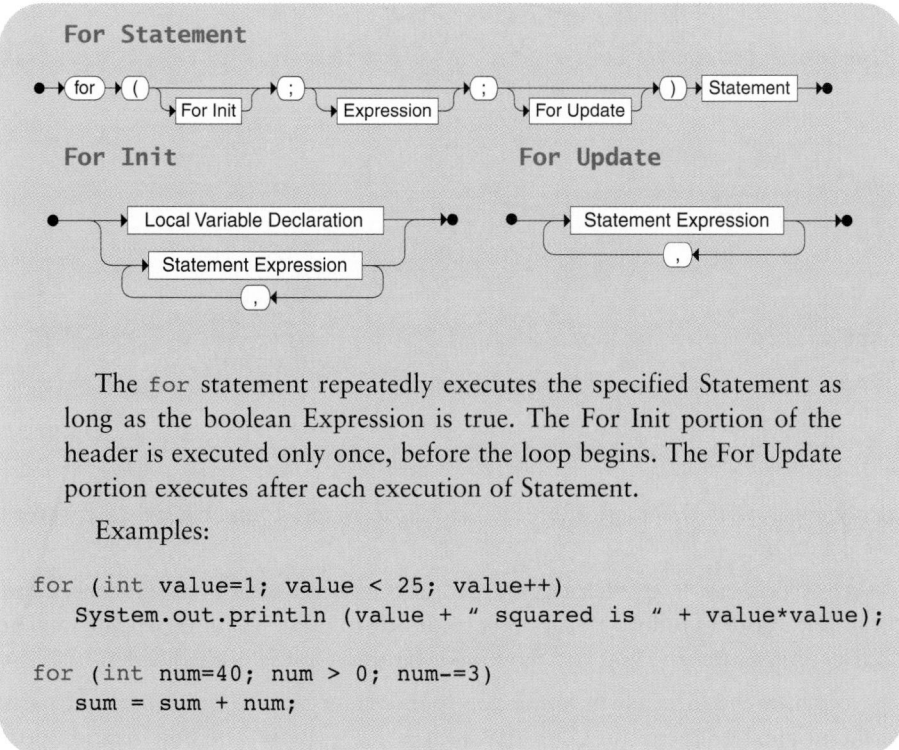

The for statement repeatedly executes the specified Statement as long as the boolean Expression is true. The For Init portion of the header is executed only once, before the loop begins. The For Update portion executes after each execution of Statement.

Examples:

```
for (int value=1; value < 25; value++)
    System.out.println (value + " squared is " + value*value);

for (int num=40; num > 0; num-=3)
    sum = sum + num;
```

listing
    3.14

```
//*****************************************************************
//   Counter3.java        Author: Lewis/Loftus
//
//   Demonstrates the use of a for loop.
//*****************************************************************

public class Counter3
{
   //--------------------------------------------------------------
   //   Prints integer values from 1 to a specific limit.
   //--------------------------------------------------------------
   public static void main (String[] args)
   {
      final int LIMIT = 5;

      for (int count=1; count <= LIMIT; count++)
         System.out.println (count);

      System.out.println ("Done");
   }
}
```

output

```
1
2
3
4
5
Done
```

increment part is executed after each iteration of the loop. Figure 3.12 shows this processing.

A for loop can be a bit tricky to read until you get used to it. The execution of the code doesn't follow a "top to bottom, left to right" reading. The increment code executes after the body of the loop even though it is in the header.

Note how the three parts of the for loop header map to the equivalent parts of the original Counter program that uses a while loop. The initialization por-

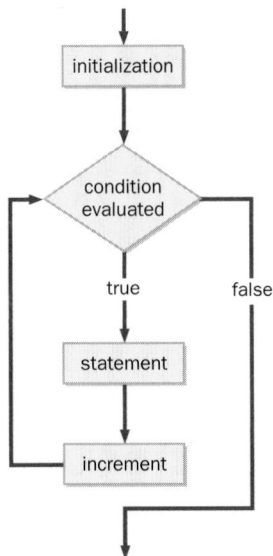

figure 3.12   The logic of a for loop

tion of the for loop header is used to declare the variable count as well as to give it an initial value. We are not required to declare a variable there, but it is common practice in situations where the variable is not needed outside of the loop. Because count is declared in the for loop header, it exists only inside the loop body and cannot be referenced elsewhere. The loop control variable is set up, checked, and modified by the actions in the loop header. It can be referenced inside the loop body, but it should not be modified except by the actions defined in the loop header.

The increment portion of the for loop header, despite its name, could decrement a value rather than increment it. For example, the following loop prints the integer values from 100 down to 1:

```
for (int num = 100; num > 0; num--)
    System.out.println (num);
```

In fact, the increment portion of the for loop can perform any calculation, not just a simple increment or decrement. Consider the program shown in Listing 3.15, which prints multiples of a particular value up to a particular limit.

listing
    3.15

```java
//********************************************************************
//  Multiples.java        Author: Lewis/Loftus
//
//  Demonstrates the use of a for loop.
//********************************************************************

import cs1.Keyboard;

public class Multiples
{
   //-----------------------------------------------------------------
   //  Prints multiples of a user-specified number up to a user-
   //  specified limit.
   //-----------------------------------------------------------------
   public static void main (String[] args)
   {
      final int PER_LINE = 5;
      int value, limit, mult, count = 0;

      System.out.print ("Enter a positive value: ");
      value = Keyboard.readInt();

      System.out.print ("Enter an upper limit: ");
      limit = Keyboard.readInt();

      System.out.println ();
      System.out.println ("The multiples of " + value + " between " +
                          value + " and " + limit + " (inclusive) are:");

      for (mult = value; mult <= limit; mult += value)
      {
         System.out.print (mult + "\t");

         // Print a specific number of values per line of output
         count++;
         if (count % PER_LINE == 0)
            System.out.println();
      }
   }
}
```

listing
3.15   continued

output

```
Enter a positive value: 7
Enter an upper limit: 400

The multiples of 7 between 7 and 400 (inclusive) are:
7        14       21       28       35
42       49       56       63       70
77       84       91       98       105
112      119      126      133      140
147      154      161      168      175
182      189      196      203      210
217      224      231      238      245
252      259      266      273      280
287      294      301      308      315
322      329      336      343      350
357      364      371      378      385
392      399
```

The increment portion of the for loop in the Multiples program adds the value entered by the user after each iteration. The number of values printed per line is controlled by counting the values printed and then moving to the next line whenever count is evenly divisible by the PER_LINE constant.

The Stars program in Listing 3.16 shows the use of nested for loops. The output is a triangle shape made of asterisk characters. The outer loop executes exactly 10 times. Each iteration of the outer loop prints one line of the output. The inner loop performs a different number of iterations depending on the line value controlled by the outer loop. Each iteration of the inner loop prints one star on the current line. Writing programs that print variations on this triangle configuration are included in the programming projects at the end of the chapter.

comparing loops

The three loop statements (while, do, and for) are functionally equivalent. Any particular loop written using one type of loop can be written using either of the other two loop types. Which type of loop we use depends on the situation.

listing
3.16

```java
//********************************************************************
//  Stars.java         Author: Lewis/Loftus
//
//  Demonstrates the use of nested for loops.
//********************************************************************

public class Stars
{
   //-----------------------------------------------------------------
   //  Prints a triangle shape using asterisk (star) characters.
   //-----------------------------------------------------------------
   public static void main (String[] args)
   {
      final int MAX_ROWS = 10;

      for (int row = 1; row <= MAX_ROWS; row++)
      {
         for (int star = 1; star <= row; star++)
            System.out.print ("*");

         System.out.println();
      }
   }
}
```

output

```
*
**
***
****
*****
******
*******
********
*********
**********
```

As we mentioned earlier, the primary difference between a while loop and a do loop is when the condition is evaluated. If we know we want to execute the loop body at least once, a do loop is usually the better choice. The body of a while loop, on the other hand, might not be executed at all if the condition is initially false. Therefore we say that the body of a while loop is executed zero or more times, but the body of a do loop is executed one or more times.

A for loop is like a while loop in that the condition is evaluated before the loop body is executed. Figure 3.13 shows the general structure of equivalent for and while loops.

We generally use a for loop when the number of times we want to iterate through a loop is fixed or can be easily calculated. In many situations, it is simply more convenient to separate the code that sets up and controls the loop iterations inside the for loop header from the body of the loop.

3.9 program development revisited

Now that we've added several more programming language statements and operators to our repertoire, let's apply them to the program development activities that we discussed at the beginning of this chapter. Suppose an instructor wants a program that will analyze exam scores. The initial requirements are given as follows. The program will:

▶ accept a series of test scores as input

▶ compute the average test score

▶ determine the highest and lowest test scores

▶ display the average, highest, and lowest test scores

Our first task is requirements analysis. The initial requirements raise questions that need to be answered before we can design a suitable solution. Clarifying

```
for (initialization; condition; increment)        initialization;
    statement;                                     while (condition)
                                                   {
                                                       statement;
                                                       increment;
                                                   }
```

figure 3.13   The general structure of equivalent for and while loops

requirements often involves an extended dialog with the client. The client may very well have a clear vision about what the program should do, but this list of requirements does not provide enough detail.

For example, how many test scores should be processed? Is this program intended to handle a particular class size or should it handle varying size classes? Is the input stored in a data file or should it be entered interactively? Should the average be computed to a specific degree of accuracy? Should the output be presented in any particular format?

Let's assume that after conferring with the client, we establish that the program needs to handle an arbitrary number of test scores each time it is run and that the input should be entered interactively. Furthermore, the client wants the average presented to two decimal places, but otherwise allows us (the developer) to specify the details of the output format.

Now let's consider some design questions. Because there is no limit to the number of grades that can be entered, how should the user indicate that there are no more grades? We can address this situation in several possible ways. The program could prompt the user after each grade is entered, asking if there are more grades to process. Or the program could prompt the user initially for the total number of grades that will be entered, then read exactly that many grades. A third option: When prompted for a grade, the instructor could enter a sentinel value that indicates that there are no more grades to be entered.

The first option requires a lot more input from the user and therefore is too cumbersome a solution. The second option seems reasonable, but it forces the user to have an exact count of the number of grades to enter and therefore may not be convenient. The third option is reasonable, but before we can pick an appropriate sentinel value to end the input, we must ask additional questions. What is the range of valid grades? What would be an appropriate value to use as a sentinel value? After conferring with the client again, we establish that a student cannot receive a negative grade, therefore the use of -1 as a sentinel value in this situation will work.

Let's sketch out an initial algorithm for this program. The pseudocode for a program that reads in a list of grades and computes their average might be expressed as follows:

```
prompt for and read the first grade.
while (grade does not equal -1)
{
    increment count.
    sum = sum + grade;
    prompt for and read another grade.
```

```
}
average = sum / count;
print average
```

This algorithm addresses only the calculation of the average grade. Now we must refine the algorithm to compute the highest and lowest grade. Further, the algorithm does not deal elegantly with the unusual case of entering −1 for the first grade. We can use two variables, max and min, to keep track of the highest and lowest scores. The augmented pseudocode is now as follows:

```
prompt for and read the first grade.
max = min = grade;
while (grade does not equal -1)
{
    increment count.
    sum = sum + grade;
    if (grade > max)
        max = grade;
    if (grade < min)
        min = grade;
    prompt for and read another grade.
}
if (count is not zero)
{
    average = sum / count;
    print average, highest, and lowest grades
}
```

Having planned out an initial algorithm for the program, the implementation can proceed. Consider the solution to this problem shown in Listing 3.17.

Let's examine how this program accomplishes the stated requirements and critique the implementation. After the variable declarations in the main method, we prompt the user to enter the value of the first grade. Prompts should provide information about any special input requirements. In this case, we inform the user that entering a value of −1 will indicate the end of the input.

The variables max and min are initially set to the first value entered. Note that this is accomplished using *chained assignments*. An assignment statement returns a value and can be used as an expression. The value returned by an assignment statement is the value that gets assigned. Therefore, the value of grade is first assigned to min, then that value is assigned to max. In the unusual case that no larger or smaller grade is ever entered, the initial values of max and min will not change.

listing
3.17

```java
//********************************************************************
//  ExamGrades.java        Author: Lewis/Loftus
//
//  Demonstrates the use of various control structures.
//********************************************************************

import java.text.DecimalFormat;
import cs1.Keyboard;

public class ExamGrades
{
   //-----------------------------------------------------------------
   //  Computes the average, minimum, and maximum of a set of exam
   //  scores entered by the user.
   //-----------------------------------------------------------------
   public static void main (String[] args)
   {
      int grade, count = 0, sum = 0, max, min;
      double average;

      //  Get the first grade and give max and min that initial value
      System.out.print ("Enter the first grade (-1 to quit): ");
      grade = Keyboard.readInt();

      max = min = grade;

      //  Read and process the rest of the grades
      while (grade >= 0)
      {
         count++;
         sum += grade;

         if (grade > max)
            max = grade;
         else
            if (grade < min)
               min = grade;

         System.out.print ("Enter the next grade (-1 to quit): ");
         grade = Keyboard.readInt ();
      }
```

listing
  3.17   continued

```java
      //  Produce the final results
      if (count == 0)
         System.out.println ("No valid grades were entered.");
      else
      {
         DecimalFormat fmt = new DecimalFormat ("0.##");
         average = (double)sum / count;
         System.out.println();
         System.out.println ("Total number of students: " + count);
         System.out.println ("Average grade: " + fmt.format(average));
         System.out.println ("Highest grade: " + max);
         System.out.println ("Lowest grade: " + min);
      }
   }
}
```

output

```
Enter the first grade (-1 to quit): 89
Enter the next grade (-1 to quit): 95
Enter the next grade (-1 to quit): 82
Enter the next grade (-1 to quit): 70
Enter the next grade (-1 to quit): 98
Enter the next grade (-1 to quit): 85
Enter the next grade (-1 to quit): 81
Enter the next grade (-1 to quit): 73
Enter the next grade (-1 to quit): 69
Enter the next grade (-1 to quit): 77
Enter the next grade (-1 to quit): 84
Enter the next grade (-1 to quit): 82
Enter the next grade (-1 to quit): -1

Total number of students: 12
Average grade: 82.08
Highest grade: 98
Lowest grade: 69
```

The while loop condition specifies that the loop body will be executed as long as the current grade being processed is greater than zero. Therefore, in this implementation, any negative value will indicate the end of the input, even though the prompt suggests a specific value. This change is a slight variation on the original design and ensures that no negative values will be counted as grades.

The implementation uses a nested `if` structure to determine if the new grade is a candidate for the highest or lowest grade. It cannot be both, so using an `else` clause is slightly more efficient. There is no need to ask whether the grade is a minimum if we already know it was a maximum.

If at least one positive grade was entered, then `count` is not equal to zero after the loop, and the `else` portion of the `if` statement is executed. The average is computed by dividing the sum of the grades by the number of grades. Note that the `if` statement prevents us from attempting to divide by zero in situations where no valid grades are entered. As we've mentioned before, we want to design robust programs that handle unexpected or erroneous input without causing a runtime error. The solution for this problem is robust up to a point because it processes any numeric input without a problem, but it will fail if a nonnumeric value (like a string) is entered at the grade prompt.

3.10 drawing using conditionals and loops

Although they are not specifically related to graphics, conditionals and loops greatly enhance our ability to generate interesting graphics.

The program called `Bullseye` shown in Listing 3.18 uses a loop to draw a specific number of rings of a target. The `Bullseye` program uses an `if` statement to alternate the colors between black and white. Note that each ring is actually drawn as a filled circle (an oval of equal width and length). Because we draw the circles on top of each other, the inner circles cover the inner part of the larger circles, creating the ring effect. At the end, a final red circle is drawn for the bull's-eye.

Listing 3.19 shows the `Boxes` applet, in which several randomly sized rectangles are drawn in random locations. If the width of a rectangle is below a certain thickness (5 pixels), the box is filled with the color yellow. If the height is less than the same minimal thickness, the box is filled with the color green. Otherwise, the box is drawn, unfilled, in white.

listing 3.18

```java
//********************************************************************
//  Bullseye.java         Author: Lewis/Loftus
//
//  Demonstrates the use of conditionals and loops to guide drawing.
//********************************************************************

import java.applet.Applet;
import java.awt.*;

public class Bullseye extends Applet
{
   //-----------------------------------------------------------------
   //  Paints a bullseye target.
   //-----------------------------------------------------------------
   public void paint (Graphics page)
   {
      final int MAX_WIDTH = 300, NUM_RINGS = 5, RING_WIDTH = 25;
      int x = 0, y = 0, diameter;

      setBackground (Color.cyan);

      diameter = MAX_WIDTH;
      page.setColor (Color.white);

      for (int count = 0; count < NUM_RINGS; count++)
      {
         if (page.getColor() == Color.black)  // alternate colors
            page.setColor (Color.white);
         else
            page.setColor (Color.black);

         page.fillOval (x, y, diameter, diameter);

         diameter -= (2 * RING_WIDTH);
         x += RING_WIDTH;
         y += RING_WIDTH;
      }
```

listing
    3.18   continued

```
    // Draw the red bullseye in the center
    page.setColor (Color.red);
    page.fillOval (x, y, diameter, diameter);
  }
}
```

display

```
//********************************************************************
//  Boxes.java          Author: Lewis/Loftus
//
//  Demonstrates the use of conditionals and loops to guide drawing.
//********************************************************************

import java.applet.Applet;
import java.awt.*;
import java.util.Random;

public class Boxes extends Applet
{
   //-----------------------------------------------------------------
   //  Paints boxes of random width and height in a random location.
   //  Narrow or short boxes are highlighted with a fill color.
   //-----------------------------------------------------------------
   public void paint(Graphics page)
   {
      final int NUM_BOXES = 50, THICKNESS = 5, MAX_SIDE = 50;
      final int MAX_X = 350, MAX_Y = 250;
      int x, y, width, height;

      setBackground (Color.black);
      Random generator = new Random();

      for (int count = 0; count < NUM_BOXES; count++)
      {
         x = generator.nextInt (MAX_X) + 1;
         y = generator.nextInt (MAX_Y) + 1;

         width = generator.nextInt (MAX_SIDE) + 1;
         height = generator.nextInt (MAX_SIDE) + 1;

         if (width <= THICKNESS)  // check for narrow box
         {
            page.setColor (Color.yellow);
            page.fillRect (x, y, width, height);
         }
         else
```

**listing
    3.19   continued**

```
if (height <= THICKNESS)   // check for short box
{
    page.setColor (Color.green);
    page.fillRect (x, y, width, height);
}
else
{
    page.setColor (Color.white);
    page.drawRect (x, y, width, height);
}
    }
  }
}
```

display

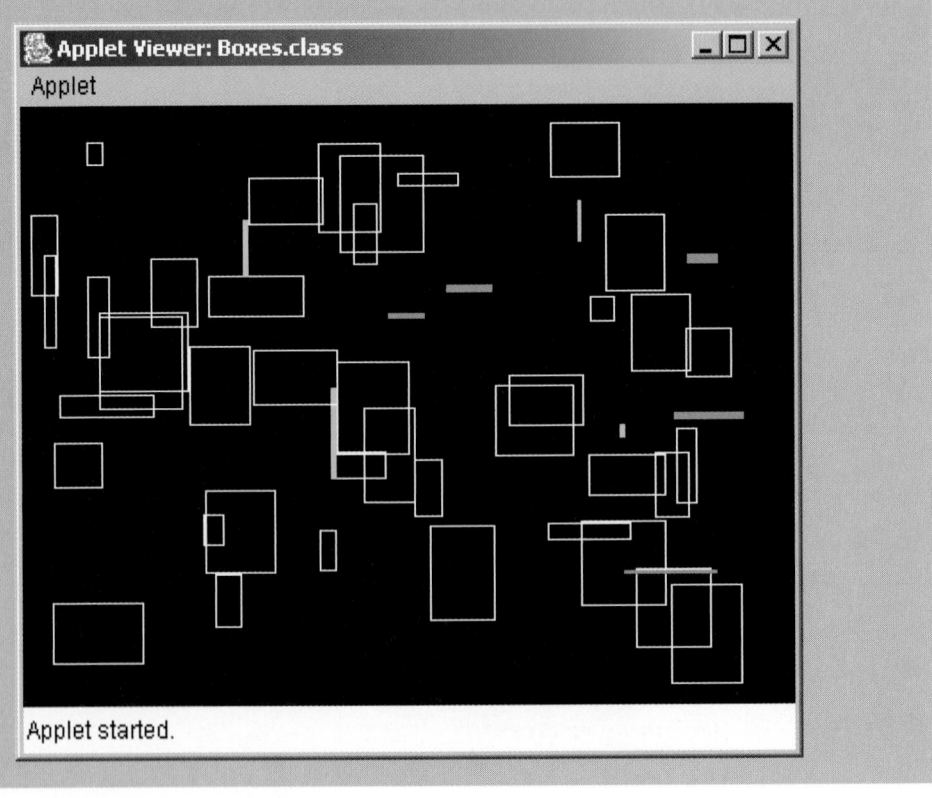

Note that in the Boxes program, the color is decided before each rectangle is drawn. In the BarHeights applet, shown in Listing 3.20, we handle the situation differently. The goal of BarHeights is to draw 10 vertical bars of random heights, coloring the tallest bar in red and the shortest bar in yellow.

listing
3.20

```java
//********************************************************************
//  BarHeights.java       Author: Lewis/Loftus
//
//  Demonstrates the use of conditionals and loops to guide drawing.
//********************************************************************

import java.applet.Applet;
import java.awt.*;
import java.util.Random;

public class BarHeights extends Applet
{
   //-----------------------------------------------------------------
   //  Paints bars of varying heights, tracking the tallest and
   //  shortest bars, which are redrawn in color at the end.
   //-----------------------------------------------------------------
   public void paint (Graphics page)
   {
      final int NUM_BARS = 10, WIDTH = 30, MAX_HEIGHT = 300, GAP =9;
      int tallX = 0, tallest = 0, shortX = 0, shortest = MAX_HEIGHT;
      int x, height;

      Random generator = new Random();
      setBackground (Color.black);

      page.setColor (Color.blue);
      x = GAP;

      for (int count = 0; count < NUM_BARS; count++)
      {
         height = generator.nextInt(MAX_HEIGHT) + 1;
         page.fillRect (x, MAX_HEIGHT-height, WIDTH, height);

         // Keep track of the tallest and shortest bars
         if (height > tallest)
```

listing
    3.20   **continued**

```
      {
         tallX = x;
         tallest = height;
      }

      if (height < shortest)
      {
         shortX = x;
         shortest = height;
      }

      x = x + WIDTH + GAP;
   }

   // Redraw the tallest bar in red
   page.setColor (Color.red);
   page.fillRect (tallX, MAX_HEIGHT-tallest, WIDTH, tallest);

   // Redraw the shortest bar in yellow
   page.setColor (Color.yellow);
   page.fillRect (shortX, MAX_HEIGHT-shortest, WIDTH, shortest);
   }
}
```

listing
3.20   continued

display

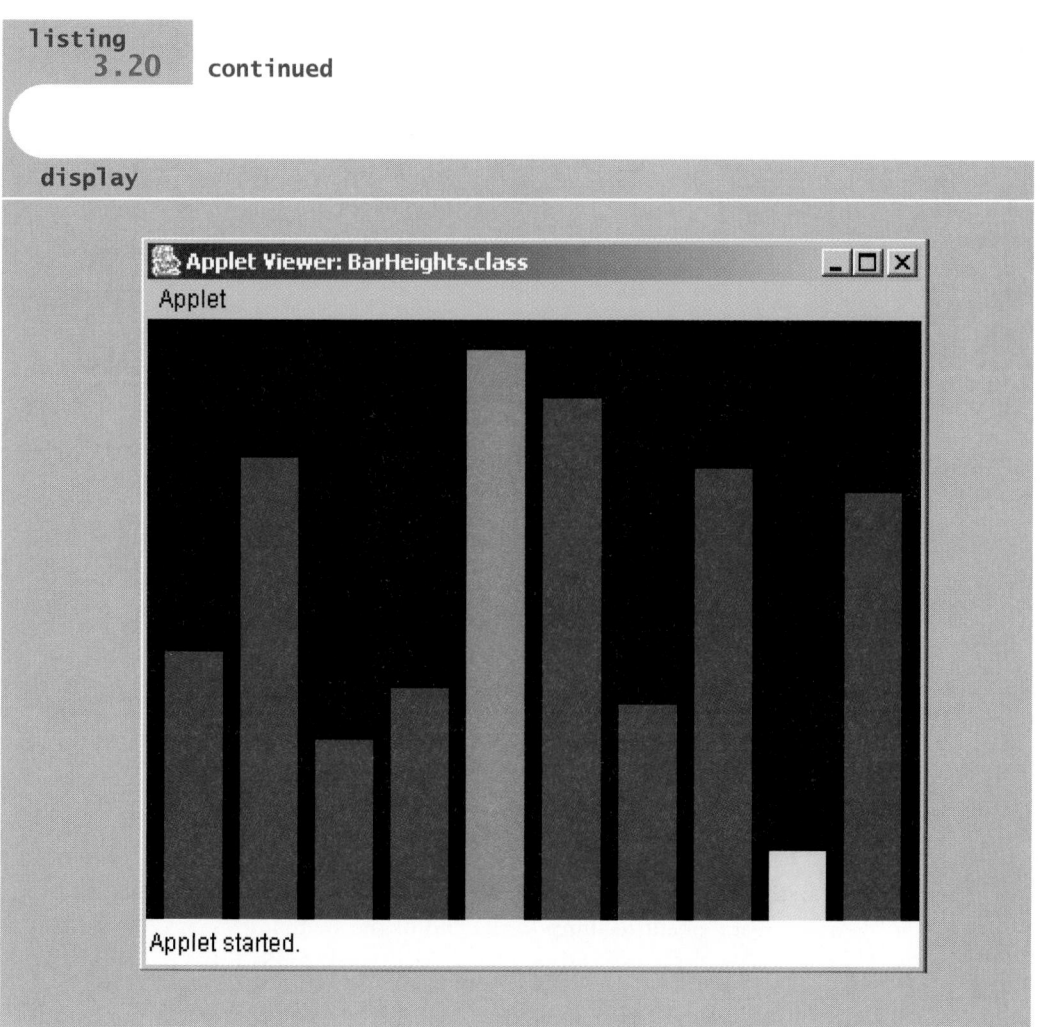

In the BarHeights program, we don't know if the bar we are about to draw is either the tallest or the shortest because we haven't created them all yet. Therefore we keep track of the position of both the tallest and shortest bars as they are drawn. After all the bars are drawn, the program goes back and redraws these two bars in the appropriate color.

- Software requirements specify *what* a program must accomplish.

- A software design specifies *how* a program will accomplish its requirements.

- An algorithm is a step-by-step process for solving a problem, often expressed in pseudocode.

- Implementation should be the least creative of all development activities.

- The goal of testing is to find errors. We can never really be sure that all errors have been found.

- Conditionals and loops allow us to control the flow of execution through a method.

- An `if` statement allows a program to choose whether to execute a particular statement.

- Even though the compiler does not care about indentation, proper indentation is important for human readability; it shows the relationship between one statement and another.

- An `if-else` statement allows a program to do one thing if a condition is true and another thing if the condition is false.

- In a nested `if` statement, an `else` clause is matched to the closest unmatched `if`.

- A `break` statement is usually used at the end of each case alternative of a `switch` statement to jump to the end of the switch.

- A `switch` statement could be implemented as a series of `if-else` statements, but the `switch` is sometimes a more convenient and readable construct.

- Logical operators return a boolean value and are often used to construct sophisticated conditions.

- The relative order of characters in Java is defined by the Unicode character set.

- The `compareTo` method can be used to determine the relative order of strings. It determines lexicographic order, which does not correspond exactly to alphabetical order.

▸ The prefix and postfix increment and decrement operators have subtle effects on programs because of differences in when they are evaluated.

▸ A `while` statement allows a program to execute the same statement multiple times.

▸ We must design our programs carefully to avoid infinite loops. The body of the loop must eventually make the loop condition false.

▸ A `do` statement executes its loop body at least once.

▸ A `for` statement is usually used when a loop will be executed a set number of times.

self-review questions

3.1 Name the four basic activities that are involved in a software development process.

3.2 What is an algorithm? What is pseudocode?

3.3 What is meant by the flow of control through a program?

3.4 What type of conditions are conditionals and loops based on?

3.5 What are the equality operators? The relational operators?

3.6 What is a nested `if` statement? A nested loop?

3.7 How do block statements help us in the construction of conditionals and loops?

3.8 What happens if a case in a `switch` does not end with a `break` statement?

3.9 What is a truth table?

3.10 How do we compare strings for equality?

3.11 Why must we be careful when comparing floating point values for equality?

3.12 What is an assignment operator?

3.13 What is an infinite loop? Specifically, what causes it?

3.14 Compare and contrast a `while` loop and a `do` loop.

3.15 When would we use a `for` loop instead of a `while` loop?

exercises

3.1   What happens in the MinOfThree program if two or more of the values are equal? If exactly two of the values are equal, does it matter whether the equal values are lower or higher than the third?

3.2   Write four different program statements that increment the value of an integer variable total.

3.3   What is wrong with the following code fragment? Rewrite it so that it produces correct output.

```
if (total == MAX)
   if (total < sum)
      System.out.println ("total == MAX and is < sum.");
else
   System.out.println ("total is not equal to MAX");
```

3.4   What is wrong with the following code fragment? Will this code compile if it is part of an otherwise valid program? Explain.

```
if (length = MIN_LENGTH)
   System.out.println ("The length is minimal.");
```

3.5   What output is produced by the following code fragment?

```
int num = 87, max = 25;
if (num >= max*2)
   System.out.println ("apple");
   System.out.println ("orange");
System.out.println ("pear");
```

3.6   What output is produced by the following code fragment?

```
int limit = 100, num1 = 15, num2 = 40;
if (limit <= limit)
{
   if (num1 == num2)
      System.out.println ("lemon");
   System.out.println ("lime");
}
System.out.println ("grape");
```

3.7   Put the following list of strings in lexicographic order as if determined by the compareTo method of the String class. Consult the Unicode chart in Appendix C.

```
"fred"
"Ethel"
"?-?-?-?"
"{([])}"
"Lucy"
"ricky"
"book"
"******"
"12345"
"         "
"HEPHALUMP"
"bookkeeper"
"6789"
";+<?"
"^^^^^^^^^^"
"hephalump"
```

3.8   What output is produced by the following code fragment?

```
int num = 0, max = 20;
while (num < max)
{
    System.out.println (num);
    num += 4;
}
```

3.9   What output is produced by the following code fragment?

```
int num = 1, max = 20;
while (num < max)
{
    if (num%2 == 0)
        System.out.println (num);
    num++;
}
```

3.10   What output is produced by the following code fragment?

```
for (int num = 0; num <= 200; num += 2)
    System.out.println (num);
```

3.11 What output is produced by the following code fragment?

```
for(int val = 200; val >= 0; val -= 1)
    if (val % 4 != 0)
        System.out.println (val);
```

3.12 Transform the following `while` loop into an equivalent `do` loop (make sure it produces the same output).

```
int num = 1;
while (num < 20)
{
    num++;
    System.out.println (num);
}
```

3.13 Transform the `while` loop from the previous exercise into an equivalent `for` loop (make sure it produces the same output).

3.14 What is wrong with the following code fragment? What are three distinct ways it could be changed to remove the flaw?

```
count = 50;
while (count >= 0)
{
    System.out.println (count);
    count = count + 1;
}
```

3.15 Write a `while` loop that verifies that the user enters a positive integer value.

3.16 Write a `do` loop that verifies that the user enters an even integer value.

3.17 Write a code fragment that reads and prints integer values entered by a user until a particular sentinel value (stored in `SENTINEL`) is entered. Do not print the sentinel value.

3.18 Write a `for` loop to print the odd numbers from 1 to 99 (inclusive).

3.19 Write a `for` loop to print the multiples of 3 from 300 down to 3.

3.20 Write a code fragment that reads 10 integer values from the user and prints the highest value entered.

3.21 Write a code fragment that determines and prints the number of times the character `'a'` appears in a `String` object called `name`.

3.22 Write a code fragment that prints the characters stored in a `String` object called `str` backward.

3.23 Write a code fragment that prints every other character in a `String` object called `word` starting with the first character.

programming projects

3.1 Create a modified version of the `Average` program that prevents a runtime error when the user immediately enters the sentinel value (without entering any valid values).

3.2 Design and implement an application that reads an integer value representing a year from the user. The purpose of the program is to determine if the year is a leap year (and therefore has 29 days in February) in the Gregorian calendar. A year is a leap year if it is divisible by 4, unless it is also divisible by 100 but not 400. For example, the year 2003 is not a leap year, but 2004 is. The year 1900 is not a leap year because it is divisible by 100, but the year 2000 is a leap year because even though it is divisible by 100, it is also divisible by 400. Produce an error message for any input value less than 1582 (the year the Gregorian calendar was adopted).

3.3 Modify the solution to the previous project so that the user can evaluate multiple years. Allow the user to terminate the program using an appropriate sentinel value. Validate each input value to ensure it is greater than or equal to 1582.

3.4 Design and implement an application that reads an integer value and prints the sum of all even integers between 2 and the input value, inclusive. Print an error message if the input value is less than 2. Prompt accordingly.

3.5 Design and implement an application that reads a string from the user and prints it one character per line.

3.6 Design and implement an application that determines and prints the number of odd, even, and zero digits in an integer value read from the keyboard.

3.7 Design and implement an application that produces a multiplication table, showing the results of multiplying the integers 1 through 12 by themselves.

3.8   Modify the `CountWords` program so that it does not include punctuation characters in its character count. *Hint*: This requires changing the set of delimiters used by the `StringTokenizer` class.

3.9   Create a revised version of the `Counter2` program such that the `println` statement comes before the counter increment in the body of the loop. Make sure the program still produces the same output.

3.10   Design and implement an application that prints the first few verses of the traveling song "One Hundred Bottles of Beer." Use a loop such that each iteration prints one verse. Read the number of verses to print from the user. Validate the input. The following are the first two verses of the song:

> 100 bottles of beer on the wall
>
> 100 bottles of beer
>
> If one of those bottles should happen to fall
>
> 99 bottles of beer on the wall
>
> 99 bottles of beer on the wall
>
> 99 bottles of beer
>
> If one of those bottles should happen to fall
>
> 98 bottles of beer on the wall

3.11   Design and implement an application that plays the Hi-Lo guessing game with numbers. The program should pick a random number between 1 and 100 (inclusive), then repeatedly prompt the user to guess the number. On each guess, report to the user that he or she is correct or that the guess is high or low. Continue accepting guesses until the user guesses correctly or chooses to quit. Use a sentinel value to determine whether the user wants to quit. Count the number of guesses and report that value when the user guesses correctly. At the end of each game (by quitting or a correct guess), prompt to determine whether the user wants to play again. Continue playing games until the user chooses to stop.

3.12   Create a modified version of the `PalindromeTester` program so that the spaces, punctuation, and changes in uppercase and lowercase are not considered when determining whether a string is a palindrome. *Hint*: These issues can be handled in several ways. Think carefully about your design.

3.13 Create modified versions of the stars program to print the following patterns. Create a separate program to produce each pattern. *Hint:* Parts b, c, and d require several loops, some of which print a specific number of spaces.

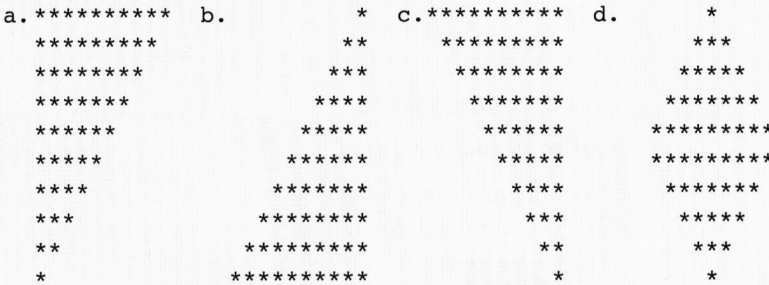

3.14 Design and implement an application that prints a table showing a subset of the Unicode characters and their numeric values. Print five number/character pairs per line, separated by tab characters. Print the table for numeric values from 32 (the space character) to 126 (the ~ character), which corresponds to the printable ASCII subset of the Unicode character set. Compare your output to the table in Appendix C. Unlike the table in Appendix C, the values in your table can increase as they go across a row.

3.15 Design and implement an application that reads a string from the user, then determines and prints how many of each lowercase vowel (a, e, i, o, and u) appear in the entire string. Have a separate counter for each vowel. Also count and print the number of nonvowel characters.

3.16 Design and implement an application that plays the Rock-Paper-Scissors game against the computer. When played between two people, each person picks one of three options (usually shown by a hand gesture) at the same time, and a winner is determined. In the game, Rock beats Scissors, Scissors beats Paper, and Paper beats Rock. The program should randomly choose one of the three options (without revealing it), then prompt for the user's selection. At that point, the program reveals both choices and prints a statement indicating if the user won, the computer won, or if it was a tie. Continue playing until the user chooses to stop, then print the number of user wins, losses, and ties.

3.17 Design and implement an application that prints the verses of the song "The Twelve Days of Christmas," in which each verse adds one line. The first two verses of the song are:

On the 1st day of Christmas my true love gave to me

A partridge in a pear tree.

On the 2nd day of Christmas my true love gave to me

Two turtle doves, and

A partridge in a pear tree.

Use a switch statement in a loop to control which lines get printed. *Hint:* Order the cases carefully and avoid the break statement. Use a separate switch statement to put the appropriate suffix on the day number (1st, 2nd, 3rd, etc.). The final verse of the song involves all 12 days, as follows:

On the 12th day of Christmas, my true love gave to me

Twelve drummers drumming,

Eleven pipers piping,

Ten lords a leaping,

Nine ladies dancing,

Eight maids a milking,

Seven swans a swimming,

Six geese a laying,

Five golden rings,

Four calling birds,

Three French hens,

Two turtle doves, and

A partridge in a pear tree.

3.18 Design and implement an application that simulates a simple slot machine in which three numbers between 0 and 9 are randomly selected and printed side by side. Print an appropriate statement if all three of the numbers are the same, or if any two of the numbers are the same. Continue playing until the user chooses to stop.

3.19 Create a modified version of the `ExamGrades` program to validate the grades entered to make sure they are in the range 0 to 100, inclusive. Print an error message if a grade is not valid, then continue to collect grades. Continue to use the sentinel value to indicate the end of the input, but do not print an error message when the sentinel value is entered. Do not count an invalid grade or include it as part of the running sum.

3.20 Design and implement an applet that draws 20 horizontal, evenly spaced parallel lines of random length.

3.21 Design and implement an applet that draws the side view of stair steps from the lower left to the upper right.

3.22 Design and implement an applet that draws 100 circles of random color and random diameter in random locations. Ensure that in each case the entire circle appears in the visible area of the applet.

3.23 Design and implement an applet that draws 10 concentric circles of random radius.

3.24 Design and implement an applet that draws a brick wall pattern in which each row of bricks is offset from the row above and below it.

3.25 Design and implement an applet that draws a quilt in which a simple pattern is repeated in a grid of squares.

3.26 Design and implement an applet that draws a simple fence with vertical, equally spaced slats backed by two horizontal support boards. Behind the fence show a simple house in the background. Make sure the house is visible between the slats in the fence.

3.27 Design and implement an applet that draws a rainbow. Use tightly spaced concentric arcs to draw each part of the rainbow in a particular color.

3.28 Design and implement an applet that draws 20,000 points in random locations within the visible area of the applet. Make the points on the left half of the applet appear in red and the points on the right half of the applet appear in green. Draw a point by drawing a line with a length of only one pixel.

3.29 Design and implement an applet that draws 10 circles of random radius in random locations. Fill in the largest circle in red.

answers to self-review questions

3.1   The four basic activities in software development are requirements
       analysis (deciding what the program should do), design (deciding
       how to do it), implementation (writing the solution in source code),
       and testing (validating the implementation).

3.2   An algorithm is a step-by-step process that describes the solution to
       a problem. Every program can be described in algorithmic terms. An
       algorithm is often expressed in pseudocode, a loose combination of
       English and code-like terms used to capture the basic processing
       steps informally.

3.3   The flow of control through a program determines the program
       statements that will be executed on a given run of the program.

3.4   Each conditional and loop is based on a boolean condition that eval-
       uates to either true or false.

3.5   The equality operators are equal (==) and not equal (!=). The rela-
       tional operators are less than (<), less than or equal to (<=), greater
       than (>), and greater than or equal to (>=).

3.6   A nested `if` occurs when the statement inside an `if` or `else` clause
       is an `if` statement. A nested `if` lets the programmer make a series of
       decisions. Similarly, a nested loop is a loop within a loop.

3.7   A block statement groups several statements together. We use them
       to define the body of an `if` statement or loop when we want to do
       multiple things based on the boolean condition.

3.8   If a case does not end with a `break` statement, processing continues
       into the statements of the next case. We usually want to use `break`
       statements in order to jump to the end of the `switch`.

3.9   A truth table is a table that shows all possible results of a boolean
       expression, given all possible combinations of variables and condi-
       tions.

3.10   We compare strings for equality using the `equals` method of the
       `String` class, which returns a boolean result. The `compareTo`
       method of the `String` class can also be used to compare strings. It
       returns a positive, 0, or negative integer result depending on the rela-
       tionship between the two strings.

3.11   Because they are stored internally as binary numbers, comparing
       floating point values for exact equality will be true only if they are

the same bit-by-bit. It's better to use a reasonable tolerance value and consider the difference between the two values.

3.12 An assignment operator combines an operation with assignment. For example, the += operator performs an addition, then stores the value back into the variable on the right-hand side.

3.13 An infinite loop is a repetition statement that never terminates. Specifically, the body of the loop never causes the condition to become false.

3.14 A while loop evaluates the condition first. If it is true, it executes the loop body. The do loop executes the body first and then evaluates the condition. Therefore the body of a while loop is executed zero or more times, and the body of a do loop is executed one or more times.

3.15 A for loop is usually used when we know, or can calculate, how many times we want to iterate through the loop body. A while loop handles a more generic situation.

In Chapters 2 and 3 we used objects and classes for the various services they provide. We also explored several fundamental programming statements. With that experience as a foundation, we are now ready to design more complex software by creating our own classes to define objects that perform whatever services we define. This chapter explores the details of class definitions, including the structure and semantics of methods and the scope and encapsulation of data.

chapter objectives

▶ Define classes that serve as blueprints for new objects, composed of variables and methods.

▶ Explain the advantages of encapsulation and the use of Java modifiers to accomplish it.

▶ Explore the details of method declarations.

▶ Revisit the concepts of method invocation and parameter passing.

▶ Explain and use method overloading to create versatile classes.

▶ Demonstrate the usefulness of method decomposition.

▶ Describe various relationships between objects.

▶ Create graphics-based objects.

4.0 objects revisited

Throughout Chapters 2 and 3 we created objects from classes in the Java standard class library in order to use the particular services they provide. We didn't need to know the details of how the classes did their jobs; we simply trusted them to do so. That, as we have discussed previously, is one of the advantages of abstraction. Now, however, we are ready to turn our attention to writing our own classes.

First, let's revisit the concept of an object and explore it in more detail. Think about objects in the world around you. How would you describe them? Let's use a ball as an example. A ball has particular characteristics such as its diameter, color, and elasticity. Formally, we say the properties that describe an object, called *attributes*, define the object's *state of being*. We also describe a ball by what it does, such as the fact that it can be thrown, bounced, or rolled. These activities define the object's *behavior*.

All objects have a state and a set of behaviors. We can represent these characteristics in software objects as well. The values of an object's variables describe the object's state, and the methods that can be invoked using the object define the object's behaviors.

Consider a computer game that uses a ball. The ball could be represented as an object. It could have variables to store its size and location, and methods that draw it on the screen and calculate how it moves when thrown, bounced, or rolled. The variables and methods defined in the ball object establish the state and behavior that are relevant to the ball's use in the computerized ball game.

Each object has its own state. Each ball object has a particular location, for instance, which typically is different from the location of all other balls.. Behaviors, though, tend to apply to all objects of a particular type. For instance, in general, any ball can be thrown, bounced, or rolled. The act of rolling a ball is generally the same for all balls.

The state of an object and that object's behaviors work together. How high a ball bounces depends on its elasticity. The action is the same, but the specific result depends on that particular object's state. An object's behavior often modifies its state. For example, when a ball is rolled, its location changes.

Any object can be described in terms of its state and behavior. Let's consider another example. In software that is used to manage a university, a student could be represented as an object. The collection of all such objects represents the entire student body at the university. Each student has a state. That is, each student object would contain the variables that store information about a particular student, such as name, address, major, courses taken, grades, and grade point average. A student object also has behaviors. For example, the class of the student object may contain a method to add a new course.

Although software objects often represent tangible items, they don't have to. For example, an error message can be an object, with its state being the text of the message and behaviors, including the process of issuing (printing) the error. A common mistake made by new programmers to the world of object-orientation is to limit the possibilities to tangible entities.

classes

An object is defined by a class. A class is the model, pattern, or blueprint from which an object is created. Consider the blueprint created by an architect when designing a house. The blueprint defines the important characteristics of the house—its walls, windows, doors, electrical outlets, and so on. Once the blueprint is created, several houses can be built using it, as depicted in Fig. 4.1.

In one sense, the houses built from the blueprint are different. They are in different locations, they have different addresses, contain different furniture, and different people live in them. Yet in many ways they are the "same" house. The layout of the rooms and other crucial characteristics are the same in each. To create a different house, we would need a different blueprint.

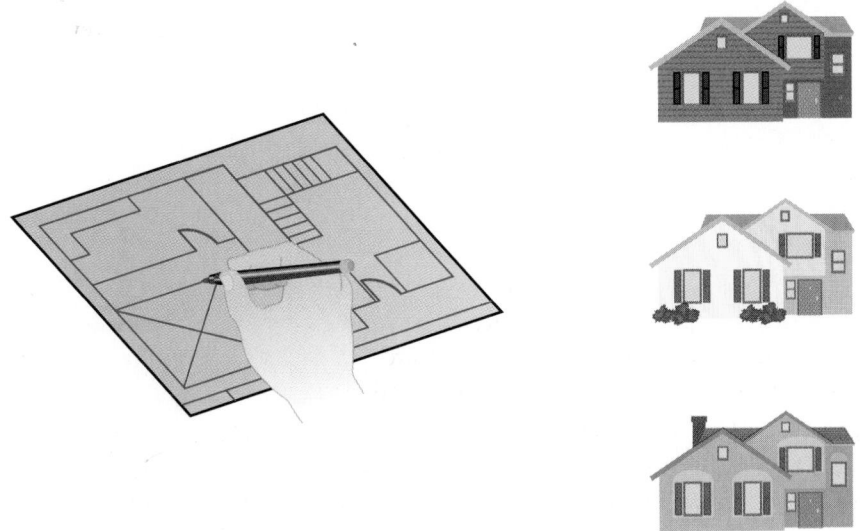

figure 4.1   A house blueprint and three houses created from it

A class is a blueprint of an object. However, a class is not an object any more than a blueprint is a house. In general, no space to store data values is reserved in a class. To allocate space to store data values, we must instantiate one or more objects from the class. (We discuss the exception to this rule in the next chapter.) Each object is an instance of a class. Each object has space for its own data, which is why each object can have its own state.

4.1   anatomy of a class

A class contains the declarations of the data that will be stored in each instantiated object and the declarations of the methods that can be invoked using an object. Collectively these are called the *members* of the class, as shown in Fig. 4.2.

Consider the CountFlips program shown in Listing 4.1. It uses an object that represents a coin that can be flipped to get a random result of "heads" or "tails." The CountFlips program simulates the flipping of a coin 1000 times to see how often it comes up heads or tails. The myCoin object is instantiated from a class called Coin.

Listing 4.2 shows the Coin class used by the CountFlips program. A class, and therefore any object created from it, is composed of data values (variables

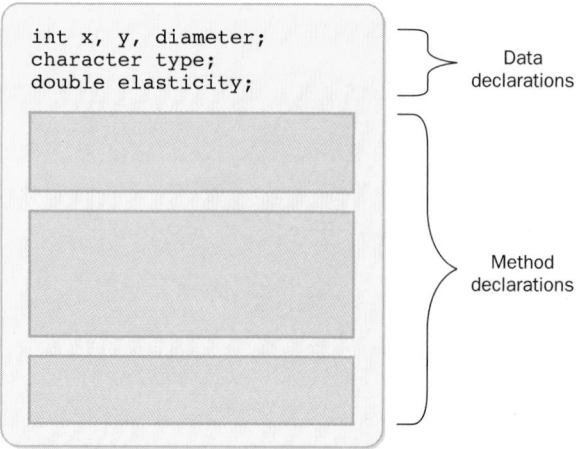

figure 4.2   The members of a class: data and method declarations

listing
  4.1

```java
//********************************************************************
//  CountFlips.java       Author: Lewis/Loftus
//
//  Demonstrates the use of a programmer-defined class.
//********************************************************************

public class CountFlips
{
   //-----------------------------------------------------------------
   //  Flips a coin multiple times and counts the number of heads
   //  and tails that result.
   //-----------------------------------------------------------------
   public static void main (String[] args)
   {
      final int NUM_FLIPS = 1000;
      int heads = 0, tails = 0;

      Coin myCoin = new Coin();   // instantiate the Coin object

      for (int count=1; count <= NUM_FLIPS; count++)
      {
         myCoin.flip();

         if (myCoin.isHeads())
            heads++;
         else
            tails++;
      }

      System.out.println ("The number flips: " + NUM_FLIPS);
      System.out.println ("The number of heads: " + heads);
      System.out.println ("The number of tails: " + tails);
   }
}
```

output

```
The number flips: 1000
The number of heads: 486
The number of tails: 514
```

and constants) and methods. In the Coin class, we have two integer constants, HEADS and TAILS, and one integer variable, face. The rest of the Coin class is composed of the Coin constructor and three regular methods: flip, isHeads, and toString.

You will recall from Chapter 2 that constructors are special methods that have the same name as the class. The Coin constructor gets called when the new opera-

listing
   4.2

```java
//************************************************************************
//  Coin.java          Author: Lewis/Loftus
//
//  Represents a coin with two sides that can be flipped.
//************************************************************************

public class Coin
{
   private final int HEADS = 0;
   private final int TAILS = 1;

   private int face;

   //-----------------------------------------------------------------
   //  Sets up the coin by flipping it initially.
   //-----------------------------------------------------------------
   public Coin ()
   {
      flip();
   }

   //-----------------------------------------------------------------
   //  Flips the coin by randomly choosing a face value.
   //-----------------------------------------------------------------
   public void flip ()
   {
      face = (int) (Math.random() * 2);
   }

   //-----------------------------------------------------------------
   //  Returns true if the current face of the coin is heads.
   //-----------------------------------------------------------------
```

listing
    4.2   continued

```java
    public boolean isHeads ()
    {
        return (face == HEADS);
    }

    //------------------------------------------------------------
    //  Returns the current face of the coin as a string.
    //------------------------------------------------------------
    public String toString()
    {
        String faceName;

        if (face == HEADS)
            faceName = "Heads";
        else
            faceName = "Tails";

        return faceName;
    }
}
```

tor is used to create a new instance of the Coin class. The rest of the methods in the Coin class define the various services provided by Coin objects.

Note that a header block of documentation is used to explain the purpose of each method in the class. This practice is not only crucial for anyone trying to understand the software, it also separates the code visually so that it's easy to jump visually from one method to the next while reading the code. The definitions of these methods have various parts, and we'll dissect them in later sections of this chapter.

Figure 4.3 lists the services defined in the Coin class. From this point of view, it looks no different from any other class that we've used in previous examples. The only important difference is that the Coin class was not provided for us by the Java standard class library. We wrote it ourselves.

For the examples in this book, we generally store each class in its own file. Java allows multiple classes to be stored in one file. If a file contains multiple classes, only one of those classes can be declared using the reserved word public. Furthermore, the name of the public class must correspond to the name of the file. For instance, class Coin is stored in a file called Coin.java.

```
Coin ()
   Constructor: sets up a new Coin object with a random initial face.

void flip ()
   Flips the coin.

boolean isHeads ()
   Returns true if the current face of the coin shows heads.

String toString ()
   Returns a string describing the current face of the coin.
```

figure 4.3   Some methods of the `Coin` class

instance data

Note that in the `Coin` class, the constants HEADS and TAILS and the variable `face` are declared inside the class, but not inside any method. The location at which a variable is declared defines its *scope*, which is the area within a program in which that variable can be referenced. By being declared at the class level (not within a method), these variables and constants can be referenced in any method of the class.

Attributes such as the variable `face` are also called *instance data* because memory space is created for each instance of the class that is created. Each `Coin` object, for example, has its own `face` variable with its own data space. Therefore at any point in time, two `Coin` objects can have their own states: one can be showing heads and the other can be showing tails, for instance.

The program `FlipRace` shown in Listing 4.3 declares two `Coin` objects. They are used in a race to see which coin will flip first to three heads in a row.

The output of the `FlipRace` program shows the results of each coin flip on each turn. The object reference variables, `coin1` and `coin2`, are used in the `println` statement. When an object is used as an operand of the string concatenation operator (+), that object's `toString` method is automatically called to get a string representation of the object. The `toString` method is also called if an object is sent to a `print` or `println` method by itself. If no `toString` method is defined for a particular class, a default version is called that returns a string that contains the name of the class, together with other information. It is usually a good idea to define a specific `toString` method for a class.

We have now used the same class, `Coin`, to create objects in two separate programs (`CountFlips` and `FlipRace`). This is no different from using the `String` class in whatever program we need it. When designing a class, it is always good

listing
    4.3

```java
//********************************************************************
//   FlipRace.java        Author: Lewis/Loftus
//
//   Demonstrates the existence of separate data space in multiple
//   instantiations of a programmer-defined class.
//********************************************************************

public class FlipRace
{
   //-----------------------------------------------------------------
   //   Flips two coins until one of them comes up heads three times
   //   in a row.
   //-----------------------------------------------------------------
   public static void main (String[] args)
   {
      final int GOAL = 3;
      int count1 = 0, count2 = 0;

      // Create two separate coin objects
      Coin coin1 = new Coin();
      Coin coin2 = new Coin();

      while (count1 < GOAL && count2 < GOAL)
      {
         coin1.flip();
         coin2.flip();

         // Print the flip results (uses Coin's toString method)
         System.out.print ("Coin 1: " + coin1);
         System.out.println ("   Coin 2: " + coin2);

         // Increment or reset the counters
         count1 = (coin1.isHeads()) ? count1+1 : 0;
         count2 = (coin2.isHeads()) ? count2+1 : 0;
      }

      // Determine the winner
      if (count1 < GOAL)
         System.out.println ("Coin 2 Wins!");
      else
         if (count2 < GOAL)
            System.out.println ("Coin 1 Wins!");
```

listing
    4.3   continued

```
        else
            System.out.println ("It's a TIE!");
    }
}
```

output

```
Coin 1: Heads    Coin 2: Tails
Coin 1: Heads    Coin 2: Tails
Coin 1: Tails    Coin 2: Heads
Coin 1: Tails    Coin 2: Heads
Coin 1: Heads    Coin 2: Tails
Coin 1: Tails    Coin 2: Heads
Coin 1: Heads    Coin 2: Tails
Coin 1: Heads    Coin 2: Heads
Coin 1: Heads    Coin 2: Tails
Coin 1 Wins!
```

to look to the future to try to give the class behaviors that may be beneficial in other programs, not just fit the specific purpose for which you are creating it at the moment.

Java automatically initializes any variables declared at the class level. For example, all variables of numeric types such as `int` and `double` are initialized to zero. However, despite the fact that the language performs this automatic initialization, it is good practice to initialize variables explicitly (usually in a constructor) so that anyone reading the code will clearly understand the intent.

UML diagrams

Throughout this book, we use *UML diagrams* to visualize relationships among classes and objects. UML stands for the *Unified Modeling Language*. Several types of UML diagrams exist, each designed to show specific aspects of object-oriented program design.

A UML *class diagram* consists of one or more classes, each with sections for the class name, attributes, and methods. Figure 4.4 depicts an example showing classes of the `FlipRace` program. Depending on the goal of the diagram, the attribute and/or method sections can be left out of any class.

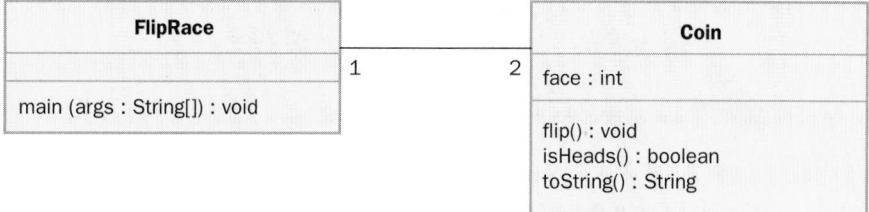

figure 4.4   A UML class diagram showing the classes
involved in the FlipRace program

The line connecting the FlipRace and Coin classes in Fig. 4.4 indicates that a relationship exists between the classes. This simple line represents a basic *association*, meaning that the classes are generally aware of each other within the program; that one may refer to and make use of the other. An association can show *multiplicity*, as this one does by annotating the connection with numeric values. In this case, it indicates that FlipRace is associated with exactly two Coin objects.

UML diagrams always show the type of an attribute, parameter, and the return value of a method after the attribute name, parameter name, or method header (separated by a colon). This may seem somewhat backward given that types in Java are generally shown before the entity of that type. We must keep in mind that UML is not designed specifically for Java programmers. It is intended to be language independent. UML has become the most popular notation in the world for the design of object-oriented software.

A UML *object diagram* consists of one or more instantiated objects. An object diagram is a snapshot of the objects at a given point in the executing program. For example, Fig. 4.5 shows the two Coin objects of the FlipRace program.

The notation for an object is similar to that for a class. However, the contents of the first section are underlined and often include the name of a specific object in addition to the class name. Another important difference between the notation of a class and an object is that the attributes shown in the second section of an object are shown with their current value. Because objects of the same class respond to the same methods, the third section is often left out.

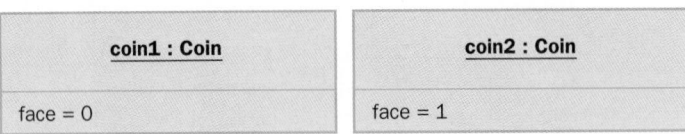

coin1 : Coin	**coin2 : Coin**
face = 0	face = 1

figure 4.5   A UML object diagram showing the
Coin objects of the FlipRace program

We should keep in mind that UML notation is not intended to describe a program after it is written. It's primarily a language-independent mechanism for visualizing and capturing the design of a program before it is written.

As we develop larger programs consisting of multiple classes and objects, UML diagrams will help us visualize them. UML diagrams have additional notations that represent various other program entities and relationships. We will explore new aspects of UML diagrams as the situation dictates.

encapsulation and visibility modifiers

We can think about an object in one of two ways. The view we take depends on what we are trying to accomplish at the moment. First, when we are designing and implementing an object, we need to think about the details of how an object works. That is, we have to design the class—we have to define the variables that will be held in the object and write the methods that make the object useful.

However, when we are designing a solution to a larger problem, we have to think in terms of how the objects in the program interact. At that level, we have to think only about the services that an object provides, not the details of how those services are provided. As we discussed in Chapter 2, an object provides a level of abstraction that allows us to focus on the larger picture when we need to.

This abstraction works only if we are careful to respect its boundaries. An object should be *self-governing*, which means that the variables contained in an object should be modified only within the object. Only the methods within an object should have access to the variables in that object. For example, the methods of the `Coin` class should be solely responsible for changing the value of the `face` variable. We should make it difficult, if not impossible, for code outside of a class to "reach in" and change the value of a variable that is declared inside the class.

In Chapter 2 we mentioned that the object-oriented term for this characteristic is encapsulation. An object should be encapsulated from the rest of the system. It should interact with other parts of a program only through the specific set of methods that define the services that that object provides. These methods define the *interface* between that object and the program that uses it.

> Objects should be encapsulated. The rest of a program should interact with an object only through a well-defined interface.
>
> **key concept**

Encapsulation is depicted graphically in Fig. 4.6. The code that uses an object, sometimes called the *client* of an object, should not be allowed to access variables directly. The client should interact with the object's methods, and those methods then interact with the data encapsulated within the object. For example, the `main` method in the `CountFlips` program calls the `flip` and `isHeads` methods of the `myCoin` object. The main method should not (and in fact cannot) access the `face` variable directly.

In Java, we accomplish object encapsulation using *modifiers*. A modifier is a Java reserved word that is used to specify particular characteristics of a programming language construct. We've already seen one modifier, `final`, which we use to declare a constant. Java has several modifiers that can be used in various ways. Some modifiers can be used together, but some combinations are invalid. We discuss various Java modifiers at appropriate points throughout this book, and all of them are summarized in Appendix F.

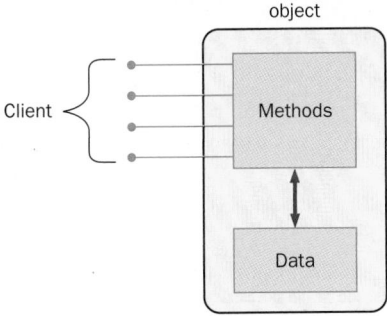

figure 4.6   A client interacting with the methods of an object

Some Java modifiers are called *visibility modifiers* because they control access to the members of a class. The reserved words `public` and `private` are visibility modifiers that can be applied to the variables and methods of a class. If a member of a class has *public visibility*, it can be directly referenced from outside of the object. If a member of a class has *private visibility*, it can be used anywhere inside the class definition but cannot be referenced externally. A third visibility modifier, `protected`, is relevant only in the context of inheritance. We discuss it in Chapter 7.

Public variables violate encapsulation. They allow code external to the class in which the data is defined to reach in and access or modify the value of the data. Therefore instance data should be defined with private visibility. Data that is declared as `private` can be accessed only by the methods of the class, which makes the objects created from that class self-governing. The visibility we apply to a method depends on the purpose of that method. Methods that provide services to the client of the class must be declared with public visibility so that they can be invoked by the client. These methods are sometimes referred to as *service methods*. A `private` method cannot be invoked from outside the class. The only purpose of a `private` method is to help the other methods of the class do their job. Therefore they are sometimes referred to as *support methods*. We discuss an example that makes use of several support methods later in this chapter.

key concept

Instance variables should be declared with private visibility to promote encapsulation.

The table in Fig. 4.7 summarizes the effects of public and private visibility on both variables and methods.

	`public`	`private`
Variables	Violate encapsulation	Enforce encapsulation
Methods	Provide services to clients	Support other methods in the class

figure 4.7 The effects of public and private visibility

Note that a client can still access or modify `private` data by invoking service methods that change the data. For example, although the `main` method of the `FlipRace` class cannot directly access the `face` variable, it can invoke the `flip` service method, which sets the value of `face`. A class must provide service methods for valid client operations. The code of those methods must be carefully designed to permit only appropriate access and valid changes.

Giving constants public visibility is generally considered acceptable because, although their values can be accessed directly, they cannot be changed because they were declared using the `final` modifier. Keep in mind that encapsulation means that data values should not be able to be *changed* directly by another part of the code. Because constants, by definition, cannot be changed, the encapsulation issue is largely moot. If we had thought it important to provide external access to the values of the constants `HEADS` and `TAILS` in the `Coin` class, we could have declared them with public visibility without violating the principle of encapsulation.

UML diagrams reflect the visibility of a class member with special notations. A member with public visibility is preceded by a plus sign (+), and a member with private visibility is preceded by a minus sign (-). We'll see these notations used in the next example.

4.2 anatomy of a method

We've seen that a class is composed of data declarations and method declarations. Let's examine method declarations in more detail.

As we stated in Chapter 1, a method is a group of programming language statements that is given a name. Every method in a Java program is part of a particular class. A *method declaration* specifies the code that is executed when the method is invoked.

When a method is called, the flow of control transfers to that method. One by one, the statements of that method are executed. When that method is done, control returns to the location where the call was made and execution continues. A method that is called might be part of the same object (defined in the same class) as the method that invoked it, or it might be part of a different object. If the called method is part of the same object, only the method name is needed to invoke it. If it is part of a different object, it is invoked through that object's name, as we've seen many times. Figure 4.8 presents this process.

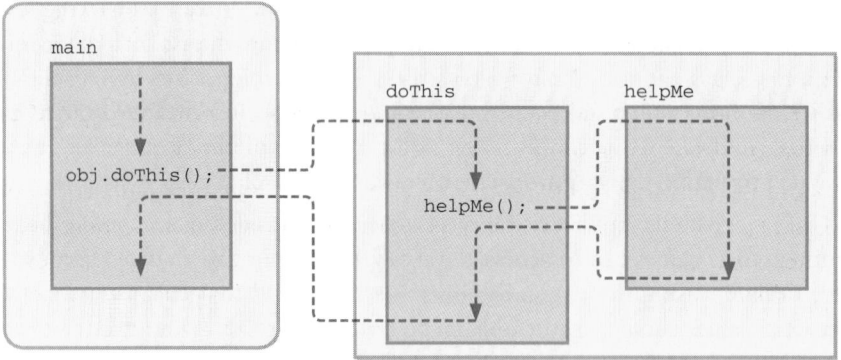

figure 4.8   The flow of control following method invocations

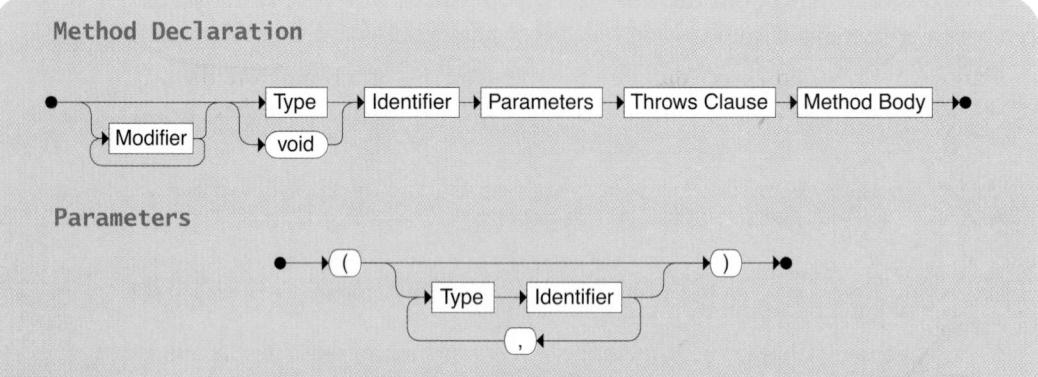

A method is defined by optional modifiers, followed by a return Type, followed by an Identifier that determines the method name, followed by a list of Parameters, followed by the Method Body. The return Type indicates the type of value that will be returned by the method, which may be void. The Method Body is a block of statements that executes when the method is invoked. The Throws Clause is optional and indicates the exceptions that may be thrown by this method.

Example:

```
public void instructions (int count)
{
    System.out.println ("Follow all instructions.");
    System.out.println ("Use no more than " + count +
                    " turns.");
}
```

We've defined the `main` method of a program many times in previous examples. Its definition follows the same syntax as all methods. The header of a method includes the type of the return value, the method name, and a list of parameters that the method accepts. The statements that make up the body of the method are defined in a block delimited by braces.

Let's look at another example as we explore the details of method declarations. The `Banking` class shown in Listing 4.4 contains a `main` method that creates a few `Account` objects and invokes their services. The `Banking` program doesn't really do anything useful except demonstrate how to interact with `Account` objects. Such programs are often called *driver programs* because all they do is drive the use of other, more interesting parts of our program. They are often used for testing purposes.

The `Account` class represents a basic bank account and is shown in Listing 4.5. It contains data values important to the management of a bank account: the account number, the balance, and the name of the account's owner. The interest rate is stored as a constant.

Figure 4.9 shows an object diagram for the `Banking` program. Note the use of the minus signs in front of the attributes to indicate that they have private visibility.

The methods of the `Account` class perform various services on a bank account, such as making deposits and withdrawals. Checks are made to ensure that the data used for the services are valid, such as preventing the withdrawal of a negative amount (which would essentially be a deposit). We explore the methods of the `Account` class in detail in the following sections.

the return statement

The return type specified in the method header can be a primitive type, class name, or the reserved word `void`. When a method does not return any value, `void` is used as the return type, as is always done with the `main` method.

A method that returns a value must have a *return statement*. When a `return` statement is executed, control is immediately returned to the statement in the calling method, and processing continues there. A `return` statement consists of the reserved word `return` followed by an expression that dictates the value to be returned. The expression must be consistent with the return type in the method header.

> **key concept**
> A method must return a value consistent with the return type specified in the method header.

listing
4.4

```java
//********************************************************************
//  Banking.java        Author: Lewis/Loftus
//
//  Driver to exercise the use of multiple Account objects.
//********************************************************************

public class Banking
{
   //-----------------------------------------------------------------
   //  Creates some bank accounts and requests various services.
   //-----------------------------------------------------------------
   public static void main (String[] args)
   {
      Account acct1 = new Account ("Ted Murphy", 72354, 102.56);
      Account acct2 = new Account ("Jane Smith", 69713, 40.00);
      Account acct3 = new Account ("Edward Demsey", 93757, 759.32);

      acct1.deposit (25.85);

      double smithBalance = acct2.deposit (500.00);
      System.out.println ("Smith balance after deposit: " +
                          smithBalance);

      System.out.println ("Smith balance after withdrawal: " +
                          acct2.withdraw (430.75, 1.50));

      acct3.withdraw (800.00, 0.0);   // exceeds balance

      acct1.addInterest();
      acct2.addInterest();
      acct3.addInterest();

      System.out.println ();
      System.out.println (acct1);
      System.out.println (acct2);
      System.out.println (acct3);
   }
}
```

listing
   4.4   continued

output

```
Smith balance after deposit: 540.0
Smith balance after withdrawal: 107.75

Error: Insufficient funds.
Account: 93757
Requested: $800.00
Available: $759.32

72354    Ted Murphy      $132.90
69713    Jane Smith      $111.52
93757    Edward Demsey   $785.90
```

listing
   4.5

```java
//********************************************************************
//   Account.java        Author: Lewis/Loftus
//
//   Represents a bank account with basic services such as deposit
//   and withdraw.
//********************************************************************

import java.text.NumberFormat;

public class Account
{
   private NumberFormat fmt = NumberFormat.getCurrencyInstance();

   private final double RATE = 0.035;  // interest rate of 3.5%

   private long acctNumber;
   private double balance;
   private String name;

   //-----------------------------------------------------------------
   //  Sets up the account by defining its owner, account number,
   //  and initial balance.
   //-----------------------------------------------------------------
   public Account (String owner, long account, double initial)
```

listing
   4.5   continued

```java
{
   name = owner;
   acctNumber = account;
   balance = initial;
}

//------------------------------------------------------------------
//  Validates the transaction, then deposits the specified amount
//  into the account. Returns the new balance.
//------------------------------------------------------------------
public double deposit (double amount)
{
   if (amount < 0)   // deposit value is negative
   {
      System.out.println ();
      System.out.println ("Error: Deposit amount is invalid.");
      System.out.println (acctNumber + "  " + fmt.format(amount));
   }
   else
      balance = balance + amount;

   return balance;
}

//------------------------------------------------------------------
//  Validates the transaction, then withdraws the specified amount
//  from the account. Returns the new balance.
//------------------------------------------------------------------
public double withdraw (double amount, double fee)
{
   amount += fee;

   if (amount < 0)   // withdraw value is negative
   {
      System.out.println ();
      System.out.println ("Error: Withdraw amount is invalid.");
      System.out.println ("Account: " + acctNumber);
      System.out.println ("Requested: " + fmt.format(amount));
   }
   else
      if (amount > balance)   // withdraw value exceeds balance
      {
         System.out.println ();
         System.out.println ("Error: Insufficient funds.");
```

listing
4.5   continued

```
            System.out.println ("Account: " + acctNumber);
            System.out.println ("Requested: " + fmt.format(amount));
            System.out.println ("Available: " + fmt.format(balance));
        }
        else
            balance = balance - amount;

     return balance;
  }

  //------------------------------------------------------------------
  //  Adds interest to the account and returns the new balance.
  //------------------------------------------------------------------
  public double addInterest ()
  {
     balance += (balance * RATE);
     return balance;
  }

  //------------------------------------------------------------------
  //  Returns the current balance of the account.
  //------------------------------------------------------------------
  public double getBalance ()
  {
     return balance;
  }

  //------------------------------------------------------------------
  //  Returns the account number.
  //------------------------------------------------------------------
  public long getAccountNumber ()
  {
     return acctNumber;
  }

  //------------------------------------------------------------------
  //  Returns a one-line description of the account as a string.
  //------------------------------------------------------------------
  public String toString ()
  {
     return (acctNumber + "\t" + name + "\t" + fmt.format(balance));
  }
}
```

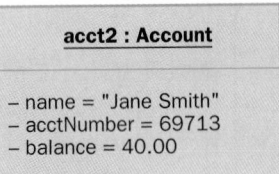

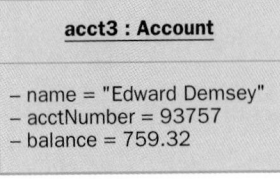

figure 4.9 A UML object diagram showing the objects of the `Banking` program

A method that does not return a value does not usually contain a `return` statement. The method automatically returns to the calling method when the end of the method is reached. A method with a `void` return type may, however, contain a `return` statement without an expression.

It is usually not good practice to use more than one `return` statement in a method, even though it is possible to do so. In general, a method should have one `return` statement as the last line of the method body, unless that makes the method overly complex.

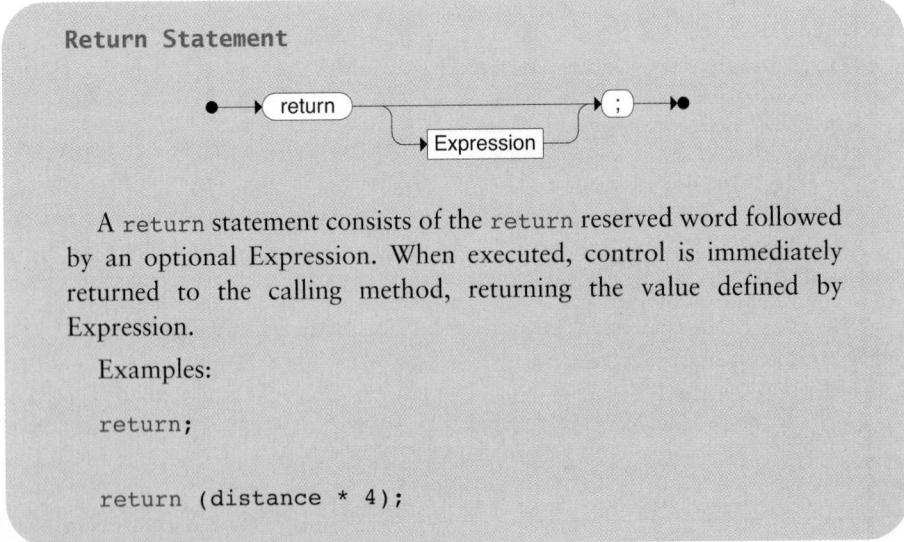

Return Statement

A `return` statement consists of the `return` reserved word followed by an optional Expression. When executed, control is immediately returned to the calling method, returning the value defined by Expression.

Examples:

```
return;
```

```
return (distance * 4);
```

Many of the methods of the `Account` class return a `double` that represents the balance of the account. Constructors do not have a return type at all (not even `void`), and therefore cannot have a `return` statement. We discuss constructors in more detail in a later section.

Note that a return value can be ignored when the invocation is made. In the `main` method of the `Banking` class, sometimes the value that is returned by a method is used in some way, and in other cases the value returned is simply ignored.

parameters

As we defined in Chapter 2, a parameter is a value that is passed into a method when it is invoked. The *parameter list* in the header of a method specifies the types of the values that are passed and the names by which the called method will refer to those values.

The names of the parameters in the header of the method declaration are called *formal parameters*. In an invocation, the values passed into a method are called *actual parameters*. A method invocation and definition always give the parameter list in parentheses after the method name. If there are no parameters, an empty set of parentheses is used.

The formal parameters are identifiers that serve as variables inside the method and whose initial values come from the actual parameters in the invocation. Sometimes they are called **automatic** variables. When a method is called, the value in each actual parameter is copied and stored in the corresponding formal parameter. Actual parameters can be literals, variables, or full expressions. If an expression is used as an actual parameter, it is fully evaluated before the method call and the result passed as the parameter.

> **key concept**
>
> When a method is called, the actual parameters are copied into the formal parameters. The types of the corresponding parameters must match.

The parameter lists in the invocation and the method declaration must match up. That is, the value of the first actual parameter is copied into the first formal parameter, the second actual parameter into the second formal parameter, and so on as shown in Fig. 4.10. The types of the actual parameters must be consistent with the specified types of the formal parameters.

The `deposit` method of the `Account` class, for instance, takes one formal parameter called `amount` of type `double` representing the amount to be deposited into the account. Each time the method is invoked in the `main` method of the `Banking` class, one literal value of type `double` is passed as an actual parameter. In the case of the `withdraw` method, two parameters of type `double` are expected. The types and number of parameters must be consistent or the compiler will issue an error message.

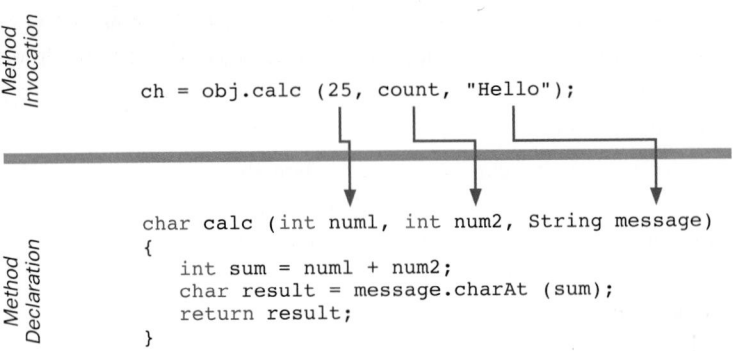

Method Invocation

Method Declaration

figure 4.10   Passing parameters from the method
invocation to the declaration

Constructors can also take parameters, as we discuss in the next section. We discuss parameter passing in more detail in Chapter 5.

constructors

As we stated in Chapter 2, a constructor is similar to a method that is invoked when an object is instantiated. When we define a class, we usually define a constructor to help us set up the class. In particular, we often use a constructor to initialize the variables associated with each object.

A constructor differs from a regular method in two ways. First, the name of a constructor is the same name as the class. Therefore the name of the constructor in the Coin class is Coin, and the name of the constructor of the Account class is Account. Second, a constructor cannot return a value and does not have a return type specified in the method header.

A common mistake made by programmers is to put a void return type on a constructor. As far as the compiler is concerned, putting any return type on a constructor, even void, turns it into a regular method that happens to have the same name as the class. As such, it cannot be invoked as a constructor. This leads to error messages that are sometimes difficult to decipher.

A constructor is generally used to initialize the newly instantiated object. For instance, the constructor of the Coin class calls the flip method initially to determine the face value of the coin. The constructor of the Account class explicitly sets the values of the instance variables to the values passed in as parameters to the constructor.

We don't have to define a constructor for every class. Each class has a *default constructor* that takes no parameters and is used if we don't provide our own. This default constructor generally has no effect on the newly created object.

local data

As we described earlier in this chapter, the scope of a variable (or constant) is the part of a program in which a valid reference to that variable can be made. A variable can be declared inside a method, making it *local data* as opposed to instance data. Recall that instance data is declared in a class but not inside any particular method. Local data has scope limited to only the method in which it is declared. The faceName variable declared in the toString method of the Coin class is local data. Any reference to faceName in any other method of the Coin class would cause the compiler to issue an error message. A local variable simply does not exist outside of the method in which it is declared. Instance data, declared at the class level, has a scope of the entire class; any method of the class can refer to it.

Because local data and instance data operate at different levels of scope, it's possible to declare a local variable inside a method using the same name as an instance variable declared at the class level. Referring to that name in the method will reference the local version of the variable. This naming practice obviously has the potential to confuse anyone reading the code, so it should be avoided.

The formal parameter names in a method header serve as local data for that method. They don't exist until the method is called, and they cease to exist when the method is exited. For example, although amount is the name of the formal parameter in both the deposit and withdraw method of the Account class, each is a separate piece of local data that doesn't exist until the method is invoked.

4.3 method overloading

As we've discussed, when a method is invoked, the flow of control transfers to the code that defines the method. After the method has been executed, control returns to the location of the call, and processing continues.

Often the method name is sufficient to indicate which method is being called by a specific invocation. But in Java, as in other object-oriented languages, you can use the same method name with different parameter lists for multiple methods. This technique is called *method overloading*. It is useful when you need to perform similar methods on different types of data.

key concept

The versions of an overloaded method are distinguished by their signature, which is the number, type, and order of the parameters.

The compiler must still be able to associate each invocation to a specific method declaration. If the method name for two or more methods is the same, then additional information is used to uniquely identify the version that is being invoked. In Java, a method name can be used for multiple methods as long as the number of parameters, the types of those parameters, and/or the order of the types of parameters is distinct. A method's name along with the number, type, and order of its parameters is called the method's *signature*. The compiler uses the complete method signature to *bind* a method invocation to the appropriate definition.

The compiler must be able to examine a method invocation, including the parameter list, to determine which specific method is being invoked. If you attempt to specify two method names with the same signature, the compiler will issue an appropriate error message and will not create an executable program. There can be no ambiguity.

Note that the return type of a method is not part of the method signature. That is, two overloaded methods cannot differ only by their return type. This is because the value returned by a method can be ignored by the invocation. The compiler would not be able to distinguish which version of an overloaded method is being referenced in such situations.

The `println` method is an example of a method that is overloaded several times, each accepting a single type. The following is a partial list of its various signatures:

▶ `println (String s)`

▶ `println (int i)`

▶ `println (double d)`

▶ `println (char c)`

▶ `println (boolean b)`

The following two lines of code actually invoke different methods that have the same name:

```
System.out.println ("The total number of students is: ");
System.out.println (count);
```

The first line invokes the `println` that accepts a string. The second line, assuming `count` is an integer variable, invokes the version of `println` that accepts an integer.

We often use a `println` statement that prints several distinct types, such as:

```
System.out.println ("The total number of students is: " +
                    count);
```

In this case, the plus sign is the string concatenation operator. First, the value in the variable `count` is converted to a string representation, then the two strings are concatenated into one longer string, and finally the definition of `println` that accepts a single string is invoked.

Constructors are a primary candidate for overloading. By providing multiple versions of a constructor, we provide several ways to set up an object. For example, the `SnakeEyes` program shown in Listing 4.6 instantiates two `Die` objects and initializes them using different constructors.

The purpose of the program is to roll the dice and count the number of times both dice show a 1 on the same throw (snake eyes). In this case, however, one die has 6 sides and the other has 20 sides. Each `Die` object is initialized using different constructors of the `Die` class. Listing 4.7 shows the `Die` class.

Both `Die` constructors have the same name, but one takes no parameters and the other takes an integer as a parameter. The compiler can examine the invocation and determine which version of the method is intended.

4.4 method decomposition

Occasionally, a service that an object provides is so complicated it cannot reasonably be implemented using one method. Therefore we sometimes need to decompose a method into multiple methods to create a more understandable design. As an example, let's examine a program that translates English sentences into Pig Latin.

Pig Latin is a made-up language in which each word of a sentence is modified, in general, by moving the initial sound of the word to the end and adding an "ay" sound. For example, the word *happy* would be written and pronounced *appyhay* and the word *birthday* would become *ithrdaybay*. Words that begin with vowels simply have a "yay" sound added on the end, turning the word *enough* into *enoughyay*. Consonant blends such as "ch" and "st" at the beginning of a word are moved to the end together before adding the "ay" sound. Therefore the word *grapefruit* becomes *apefruitgray*.

The `PigLatin` program shown in Listing 4.8 reads one or more sentences, translating each into Pig Latin.

```
listing
    4.6
```

```
//********************************************************************
//  SnakeEyes.java        Author: Lewis/Loftus
//
//  Demonstrates the use of a class with overloaded constructors.
//********************************************************************

public class SnakeEyes
{
   //-----------------------------------------------------------------
   //  Creates two die objects, then rolls both dice a set number of
   //  times, counting the number of snake eyes that occur.
   //-----------------------------------------------------------------
   public static void main (String[] args)
   {
      final int ROLLS = 500;
      int snakeEyes = 0, num1, num2;

      Die die1 = new Die();      // creates a six-sided die
      Die die2 = new Die(20);    // creates a twenty-sided die

      for (int roll = 1; roll <= ROLLS; roll++)
      {
         num1 = die1.roll();
         num2 = die2.roll();

         if (num1 == 1 && num2 == 1)   // check for snake eyes
            snakeEyes++;
      }

      System.out.println ("Number of rolls: " + ROLLS);
      System.out.println ("Number of snake eyes: " + snakeEyes);
      System.out.println ("Ratio: " + (float)snakeEyes/ROLLS);
   }
}
```

```
output

Number of rolls: 500
Number of snake eyes: 6
Ratio: 0.012
```

listing
    4.7

```java
//********************************************************************
//  Die.java        Author: Lewis/Loftus
//
//  Represents one die (singular of dice) with faces showing values
//  between 1 and the number of faces on the die.
//********************************************************************

public class Die
{
   private final int MIN_FACES = 4;

   private int numFaces;    // number of sides on the die
   private int faceValue;   // current value showing on the die

   //-------------------------------------------------------------
   //  Defaults to a six-sided die. Initial face value is 1.
   //-------------------------------------------------------------
   public Die ()
   {
      numFaces = 6;
      faceValue = 1;
   }

   //-------------------------------------------------------------
   //  Explicitly sets the size of the die. Defaults to a size of
   //  six if the parameter is invalid.  Initial face value is 1.
   //-------------------------------------------------------------
   public Die (int faces)
   {
      if (faces < MIN_FACES)
         numFaces = 6;
      else
         numFaces = faces;

      faceValue = 1;
   }

   //-------------------------------------------------------------
   //  Rolls the die and returns the result.
   //-------------------------------------------------------------
   public int roll ()
   {
      faceValue = (int) (Math.random() * numFaces) + 1;
      return faceValue;
   }
```

listing
4.7   **continued**

```
//-----------------------------------------------------------------
//   Returns the current die value.
//-----------------------------------------------------------------
public int getFaceValue ()
{
   return faceValue;
}
}
```

listing
4.8

```
//*********************************************************************
//   PigLatin.java        Author: Lewis/Loftus
//
//   Driver to exercise the PigLatinTranslator class.
//*********************************************************************

import cs1.Keyboard;

public class PigLatin
{
   //-----------------------------------------------------------------
   //   Reads sentences and translates them into Pig Latin.
   //-----------------------------------------------------------------
   public static void main (String[] args)
   {
      String sentence, result, another;
      PigLatinTranslator translator = new PigLatinTranslator();

      do
      {
         System.out.println ();
         System.out.println ("Enter a sentence (no punctuation):");
         sentence = Keyboard.readString();

         System.out.println ();
         result = translator.translate (sentence);
         System.out.println ("That sentence in Pig Latin is:");
         System.out.println (result);
```

listing 4.8   **continued**

```
        System.out.println ();
        System.out.print ("Translate another sentence (y/n)? ");
        another = Keyboard.readString();
    }
    while (another.equalsIgnoreCase("y"));
   }
}
```

output

```
Enter a sentence (no punctuation):
Do you speak Pig Latin

That sentence in Pig Latin is:
oday ouyay eakspay igpay atinlay

Translate another sentence (y/n)? y

Enter a sentence (no punctuation):
Play it again Sam

That sentence in Pig Latin is:
ayplay ityay againyay amsay

Translate another sentence (y/n)? n
```

The workhorse behind the `PigLatin` program is the `PigLatinTranslator` class, shown in Listing 4.9. An object of type `PigLatinTranslator` provides one fundamental service, a method called `translate`, which accepts a string and translates it into Pig Latin. Note that the `PigLatinTranslator` class does not contain a constructor because none is needed.

The act of translating an entire sentence into Pig Latin is not trivial. If written in one big method, it would be very long and difficult to follow. A better solution, as implemented in the `PigLatinTranslator` class, is to decompose the `translate` method and use several other support methods to help with the task.

The `translate` method uses a `StringTokenizer` object to separate the string into words. Recall that the primary role of the `StringTokenizer` class (discussed in Chapter 3) is to separate a string into smaller elements called tokens. In this case, the tokens are separated by space characters so we can use the default white

**listing
   4.9**

```java
//********************************************************************
//   PigLatinTranslator.java        Author: Lewis/Loftus
//
//   Represents a translation system from English to Pig Latin.
//   Demonstrates method decomposition and the use of StringTokenizer.
//********************************************************************

import java.util.StringTokenizer;

public class PigLatinTranslator
{
   //-----------------------------------------------------------------
   //   Translates a sentence of words into Pig Latin.
   //-----------------------------------------------------------------
   public String translate (String sentence)
   {
      String result = "";

      sentence = sentence.toLowerCase();
      StringTokenizer tokenizer = new StringTokenizer (sentence);

      while (tokenizer.hasMoreTokens())
      {
         result += translateWord (tokenizer.nextToken());
         result += " ";
      }

      return result;
   }

   //-----------------------------------------------------------------
   //   Translates one word into Pig Latin. If the word begins with a
   //   vowel, the suffix "yay" is appended to the word.  Otherwise,
   //   the first letter or two are moved to the end of the word,
   //   and "ay" is appended.
   //-----------------------------------------------------------------
   private String translateWord (String word)
   {
      String result = "";

      if (beginsWithVowel(word))
         result = word + "yay";
      else
```

listing
    4.9   continued

```java
        if (beginsWithBlend(word))
            result = word.substring(2) + word.substring(0,2) + "ay";
        else
            result = word.substring(1) + word.charAt(0) + "ay";

    return result;
}

//---------------------------------------------------------------------
//  Determines if the specified word begins with a vowel.
//---------------------------------------------------------------------
private boolean beginsWithVowel (String word)
{
    String vowels = "aeiou";

    char letter = word.charAt(0);

    return (vowels.indexOf(letter) != -1);
}

//---------------------------------------------------------------------
//  Determines if the specified word begins with a particular
//  two-character consonant blend.
//---------------------------------------------------------------------
private boolean beginsWithBlend (String word)
{
    return ( word.startsWith ("bl") || word.startsWith ("sc") ||
             word.startsWith ("br") || word.startsWith ("sh") ||
             word.startsWith ("ch") || word.startsWith ("sk") ||
             word.startsWith ("cl") || word.startsWith ("sl") ||
             word.startsWith ("cr") || word.startsWith ("sn") ||
             word.startsWith ("dr") || word.startsWith ("sm") ||
             word.startsWith ("dw") || word.startsWith ("sp") ||
             word.startsWith ("fl") || word.startsWith ("sq") ||
             word.startsWith ("fr") || word.startsWith ("st") ||
             word.startsWith ("gl") || word.startsWith ("sw") ||
             word.startsWith ("gr") || word.startsWith ("th") ||
             word.startsWith ("kl") || word.startsWith ("tr") ||
             word.startsWith ("ph") || word.startsWith ("tw") ||
             word.startsWith ("pl") || word.startsWith ("wh") ||
             word.startsWith ("pr") || word.startsWith ("wr") );
}
}
```

space delimiters. The `PigLatin` program assumes that no punctuation is included in the input.

The `translate` method passes each word to the private support method `translateWord`. Even the job of translating one word is somewhat involved, so the `translateWord` method makes use of two other private methods, `beginsWithVowel` and `beginsWithBlend`.

The `beginsWithVowel` method returns a `boolean` value that indicates whether the word passed as a parameter begins with a vowel. Note that instead of checking each vowel separately, the code for this method declares a string that contains all of the vowels, and then invokes the `String` method `indexOf` to determine whether the first character of the word is in the vowel string. If the specified character cannot be found, the `indexOf` method returns a value of −1.

The `beginsWithBlend` method also returns a `boolean` value. The body of the method contains only a `return` statement with one large expression that makes several calls to the `startsWith` method of the `String` class. If any of these calls returns true, then the `beginsWithBlend` method returns true as well.

Note that the `translateWord`, `beginsWithVowel`, and `beginsWithBlend` methods are all declared with private visibility. They are not intended to provide services directly to clients outside the class. Instead, they exist to help the `translate` method, which is the only true service method in this class, to do its job. By declaring them with private visibility, they cannot be invoked from outside this class. If the `main` method of the `PigLatin` class attempted to invoke the `translateWord` method, for instance, the compiler would issue an error message.

Figure 4.11 shows a UML class diagram for the `PigLatin` program. Note the notation showing the visibility of various methods.

Whenever a method becomes large or complex, we should consider decomposing it into multiple methods to create a more understandable class design.

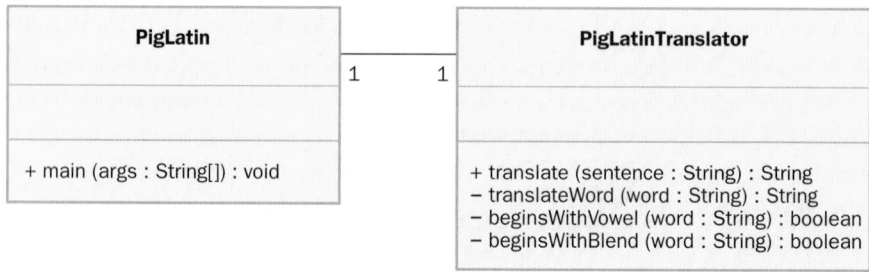

figure 4.11   A UML class diagram for the `PigLatin` program

First, however, we must consider how other classes and objects can be defined to create better overall system design. In an object-oriented design, method decomposition must be subordinate to object decomposition.

4.5 object relationships

Classes, and their associated objects, can have particular types of relationships to each other. This section revisits the idea of the general association and then extends that concept to include associations between objects of the same class. We then explore aggregation, in which one object is composed of other objects, creating a "has-a" relationship.

Inheritance, which we introduced in Chapter 2, is another important relationship between classes. It creates a generalization, or an "is-a" relationship, between classes. We examine inheritance in Chapter 7.

association

In previous examples of UML diagrams, we've seen the idea of two classes having a general association. This means that those classes are "aware" of each other. Objects of those classes may use each other for the specific services that each provides. This sometimes is referred to as a *use relationship*.

An association could be described in general terms, such as the fact that an Author object *writes* a Book object. The association connections between two classes in a UML diagram can be annotated with such comments, if desired. These kinds of annotations are called *adornments*.

As we've seen, associations can have a multiplicity associated with them. They don't always have to show specific values, however. The asterisk could be used to indicate a general zero-or-more value. Ranges of values could be given if appropriate, such as 1...5.

An association relationship is intended to be very general and therefore very versatile. We introduce additional uses of general associations throughout the book as appropriate.

web bonus

You can find additional discussion and examples of UML notation on the book's Web site.

association between objects of the same class

Some associations occur between two objects of the same class. That is, a method of one object takes as a parameter another object of the same class. The operation performed often involves the internal data of both objects.

The concat method of the String class is an example of this situation. The method is executed through one String object and is passed another String object as a parameter. For example:

```
str3 = str1.concat(str2);
```

The String object executing the method (str1) appends its characters to those of the String passed as a parameter (str2). A new String object is returned as a result (and stored as str3).

The RationalNumbers program shown in Listing 4.10 demonstrates a similar situation. Recall that a rational number is a value that can be represented as a ratio of two integers (a fraction). The RationalNumbers program creates two objects representing rational numbers and then performs various operations on them to produce new rational numbers.

listing
  4.10

```
//********************************************************************
//   RationalNumbers.java        Author: Lewis/Loftus
//
//   Driver to exercise the use of multiple Rational objects.
//********************************************************************

public class RationalNumbers
{
   //-----------------------------------------------------------------
   //   Creates some rational number objects and performs various
   //   operations on them.
   //-----------------------------------------------------------------
   public static void main (String[] args)
   {
      Rational r1 = new Rational (6, 8);
      Rational r2 = new Rational (1, 3);
      Rational r3, r4, r5, r6, r7;

      System.out.println ("First rational number: " + r1);
      System.out.println ("Second rational number: " + r2);
```

listing
    4.10   continued

```
        if (r1.equals(r2))
            System.out.println ("r1 and r2 are equal.");
        else
            System.out.println ("r1 and r2 are NOT equal.");

        r3 = r1.reciprocal();
        System.out.println ("The reciprocal of r1 is: " + r3);

        r4 = r1.add(r2);
        r5 = r1.subtract(r2);
        r6 = r1.multiply(r2);
        r7 = r1.divide(r2);

        System.out.println ("r1 + r2: " + r4);
        System.out.println ("r1 - r2: " + r5);
        System.out.println ("r1 * r2: " + r6);
        System.out.println ("r1 / r2: " + r7);
    }
}
```

output

```
First rational number: 3/4
Second rational number: 1/3
r1 and r2 are NOT equal.
r1 + r2: 13/12
r1 - r2: 5/12
r1 * r2: 1/4
r1 / r2: 9/4
```

The Rational class is shown in Listing 4.11. Each object of type Rational represents one rational number. The Rational class contains various operations on rational numbers, such as addition and subtraction.

The methods of the Rational class, such as add, subtract, multiply, and divide, use the Rational object that is executing the method as the first (left) operand and the Rational object passed as a parameter as the second (right) operand.

Note that some of the methods in the Rational class, including reduce and gcd, are declared with private visibility. These methods are private because we don't want them executed directly from outside a Rational object. They exist only to support the other services of the object.

listing
    4.11

```
//***********************************************************************
//   Rational.java        Author: Lewis/Loftus
//
//   Represents one rational number with a numerator and denominator.
//***********************************************************************

public class Rational
{
   private int numerator, denominator;

   //-----------------------------------------------------------------
   //   Sets up the rational number by ensuring a nonzero denominator
   //   and making only the numerator signed.
   //-----------------------------------------------------------------
   public Rational (int numer, int denom)
   {
      if (denom == 0)
         denom = 1;

      // Make the numerator "store" the sign
      if (denom < 0)
      {
         numer = numer * -1;
         denom = denom * -1;
      }

      numerator = numer;
      denominator = denom;

      reduce();
   }

   //-----------------------------------------------------------------
   //   Returns the numerator of this rational number.
   //-----------------------------------------------------------------
   public int getNumerator ()
   {
      return numerator;
   }

   //-----------------------------------------------------------------
   //   Returns the denominator of this rational number.
   //-----------------------------------------------------------------
```

listing
4.11   continued

```java
public int getDenominator ()
{
   return denominator;
}

//-----------------------------------------------------------------
//  Returns the reciprocal of this rational number.
//-----------------------------------------------------------------
public Rational reciprocal ()
{
   return new Rational (denominator, numerator);
}

//-----------------------------------------------------------------
//  Adds this rational number to the one passed as a parameter.
//  A common denominator is found by multiplying the individual
//  denominators.
//-----------------------------------------------------------------
public Rational add (Rational op2)
{
   int commonDenominator = denominator * op2.getDenominator();
   int numerator1 = numerator * op2.getDenominator();
   int numerator2 = op2.getNumerator() * denominator;
   int sum = numerator1 + numerator2;

   return new Rational (sum, commonDenominator);
}

//-----------------------------------------------------------------
//  Subtracts the rational number passed as a parameter from this
//  rational number.
//-----------------------------------------------------------------
public Rational subtract (Rational op2)
{
   int commonDenominator = denominator * op2.getDenominator();
   int numerator1 = numerator * op2.getDenominator();
   int numerator2 = op2.getNumerator() * denominator;
   int difference = numerator1 - numerator2;

   return new Rational (difference, commonDenominator);
}
```

listing
    4.11   continued

```
//-------------------------------------------------------------------
//  Multiplies this rational number by the one passed as a
//  parameter.
//-------------------------------------------------------------------
public Rational multiply (Rational op2)
{
   int numer = numerator * op2.getNumerator();
   int denom = denominator * op2.getDenominator();

   return new Rational (numer, denom);
}


//-------------------------------------------------------------------
//  Divides this rational number by the one passed as a parameter
//  by multiplying by the reciprocal of the second rational.
//-------------------------------------------------------------------
public Rational divide (Rational op2)
{
   return multiply (op2.reciprocal());
}


//-------------------------------------------------------------------
//  Determines if this rational number is equal to the one passed
//  as a parameter.  Assumes they are both reduced.
//-------------------------------------------------------------------
public boolean equals (Rational op2)
{
   return ( numerator == op2.getNumerator() &&
            denominator == op2.getDenominator() );
}


//-------------------------------------------------------------------
//  Returns this rational number as a string.
//-------------------------------------------------------------------
public String toString ()
{
   String result;

   if (numerator == 0)
      result = "0";
   else
      if (denominator == 1)
```

listing
    4.11   continued

```
            result = numerator + "";
        else
            result = numerator + "/" + denominator;

    return result;
}

//----------------------------------------------------------------------
//  Reduces this rational number by dividing both the numerator
//  and the denominator by their greatest common divisor.
//----------------------------------------------------------------------
private void reduce ()
{
    if (numerator != 0)
    {
        int common = gcd (Math.abs(numerator), denominator);

        numerator = numerator / common;
        denominator = denominator / common;
    }
}

//----------------------------------------------------------------------
//  Computes and returns the greatest common divisor of the two
//  positive parameters. Uses Euclid's algorithm.
//----------------------------------------------------------------------
private int gcd (int num1, int num2)
{
    while (num1 != num2)
        if (num1 > num2)
            num1 = num1 - num2;
        else
            num2 = num2 - num1;

    return num1;
}
}
```

aggregation

Some objects are made up of other objects. A car, for instance, is made up of its engine, its chassis, its wheels, and several other parts. Each of these other parts could be considered separate objects. Therefore we can say that a car is an *aggregation*—it is composed, at least in part, of other objects. Aggregation is sometimes described as a *has-a relationship*. For instance, a car has a chassis.

In the software world, we define an *aggregate object* as any object that contains references to other objects as instance data. For example, an Account object contains, among other things, a String object that represents the name of the account owner. We sometimes forget that strings are objects, but technically that makes each Account object an aggregate object.

Let's consider another example. The program StudentBody shown in Listing 4.12 creates two Student objects. Each Student object is composed, in part, of two Address objects, one for the student's address at school and another for the student's home address. The main method does nothing more than create these objects and print them out. Note that we once again pass objects to the println method, relying on the automatic call to the toString method to create a valid representation of the object suitable for printing.

listing
4.12

```
//********************************************************************
//   StudentBody.java       Author: Lewis/Loftus
//
//   Demonstrates the use of an aggregate class.
//********************************************************************

public class StudentBody
{
    //-----------------------------------------------------------------
    //   Creates some Address and Student objects and prints them.
    //-----------------------------------------------------------------
    public static void main (String[] args)
    {
        Address school = new Address ("800 Lancaster Ave.", "Villanova",
                            "PA", 19085);

        Address jHome = new Address ("21 Jump Street", "Lynchburg",
                            "VA", 24551);
        Student john = new Student ("John", "Smith", jHome, school);
```

listing
4.12   **continued**

```
        Address mHome = new Address ("123 Main Street", "Euclid", "OH",
                                     44132);
        Student marsha = new Student ("Marsha", "Jones", mHome, school);

        System.out.println (john);
        System.out.println ();
        System.out.println (marsha);
    }
}
```

output

```
John Smith
Home Address:
21 Jump Street
Lynchburg, VA  24551
School Address:
800 Lancaster Ave.
Villanova, PA  19085

Marsha Jones
Home Address:
123 Main Street
Euclid, OH  44132
School Address:
800 Lancaster Ave.
Villanova, PA  19085
```

The Student class shown in Listing 4.13 represents a single student. This class would have to be greatly expanded if it were to represent all aspects of a student. We deliberately keep it simple for now so that the object aggregation is clearly shown. The instance data of the Student class includes two references to Address objects. We refer to those objects in the toString method as we create a string representation of the student. By concatenating an Address object to another string, the toString method in Address is automatically invoked.

The Address class is shown in Listing 4.14. It contains only the parts of a street address. Note that nothing about the Address class indicates that it is part of a Student object. The Address class is kept generic by design and therefore could be used in any situation in which a street address is needed.

listing
    4.13

```java
//************************************************************************
//   Student.java         Author: Lewis/Loftus
//
//   Represents a college student.
//************************************************************************

public class Student
{
   private String firstName, lastName;
   private Address homeAddress, schoolAddress;

   //-----------------------------------------------------------------
   //   Sets up this Student object with the specified initial values.
   //-----------------------------------------------------------------
   public Student (String first, String last, Address home,
                   Address school)
   {
      firstName = first;
      lastName = last;
      homeAddress = home;
      schoolAddress = school;
   }

   //-----------------------------------------------------------------
   //   Returns this Student object as a string.
   //-----------------------------------------------------------------
   public String toString()
   {
      String result;

      result = firstName + " " + lastName + "\n";
      result += "Home Address:\n" + homeAddress + "\n";
      result += "School Address:\n" + schoolAddress;

      return result;
   }
}
```

listing
    4.14

```java
//********************************************************************
//  Address.java        Author: Lewis/Loftus
//
//  Represents a street address.
//********************************************************************

public class Address
{
   private String streetAddress, city, state;
   private long zipCode;

   //-----------------------------------------------------------------
   //  Sets up this Address object with the specified data.
   //-----------------------------------------------------------------
   public Address (String street, String town, String st, long zip)
   {
      streetAddress = street;
      city = town;
      state = st;
      zipCode = zip;
   }

   //-----------------------------------------------------------------
   //  Returns this Address object as a string.
   //-----------------------------------------------------------------
   public String toString()
   {
      String result;

      result = streetAddress + "\n";
      result += city + ", " + state + "   " + zipCode;

      return result;
   }
}
```

The more complex an object, the more likely it will need to be represented as an aggregate object. In UML, aggregation is represented by a connection between two classes, with an open diamond at the end near the class that is the aggregate. Figure 4.12 shows a UML class diagram for the StudentBody program.

Note that in previous UML diagram examples, strings were not represented as separate classes with aggregation relationships, though technically they could be. Strings are so fundamental to programming that they are usually represented the same way a primitive attribute is represented.

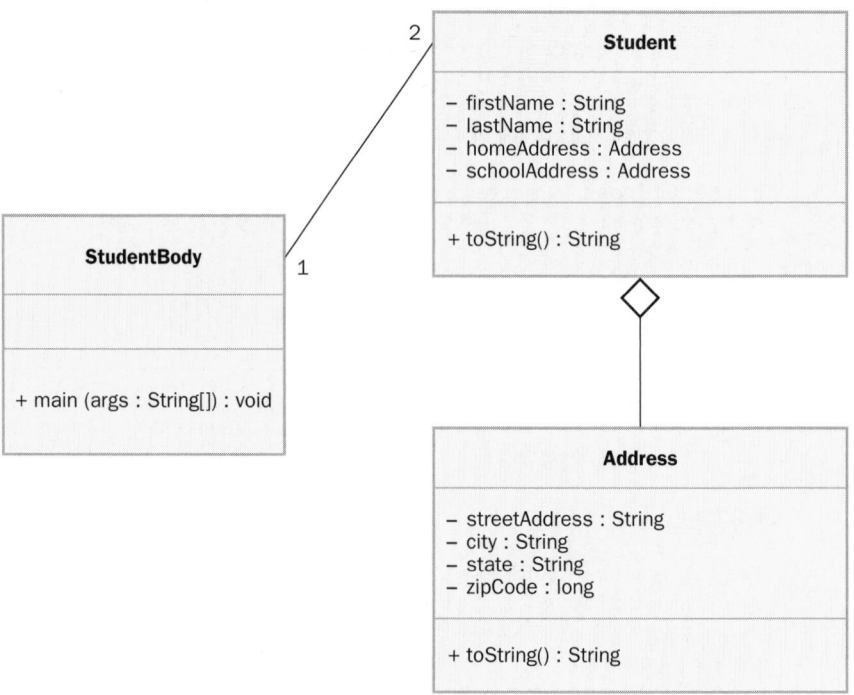

figure 4.12   A UML class diagram showing aggregation

4.6 applet methods

In applets presented in previous chapters, we've seen the use of the `paint` method to draw the contents of the applet on the screen. An applet has several other methods that perform specific duties. Because an applet is designed to work with Web pages, some applet methods are specifically designed with that concept in mind. Figure 4.13 lists several applet methods.

> **key concept**
>
> Several methods of the `Applet` class are designed to facilitate their execution in a Web browser.

The `init` method is executed once when the applet is first loaded, such as when the browser or appletviewer initially view the applet. Therefore the `init` method is the place to initialize the applet's environment and permanent data.

The `start` and `stop` methods of an applet are called when the applet becomes active or inactive, respectively. For example, after we use a browser to initially

```
public void init ()
    Initializes the applet. Called just after the applet is loaded.

public void start ()
    Starts the applet. Called just after the applet is made active.

public void stop ()
    Stops the applet. Called just after the applet is made inactive.

public void destroy ()
    Destroys the applet. Called when the browser is exited.

public URL getCodeBase ()
    Returns the URL at which this applet's bytecode is located.

public URL getDocumentBase ()
    Returns the URL at which the HTML document containing this applet is
    located.

public AudioClip getAudioClip (URL url, String name)
    Retrieves an audio clip from the specified URL.

public Image getImage (URL url, String name)
    Retrieves an image from the specified URL.
```

figure 4.13   Some methods of the `Applet` class

load an applet, the applet's `start` method is called. We may then leave that page to visit another one, at which point the applet becomes inactive and the `stop` method is called. If we return to the applet's page, the applet becomes active again and the `start` method is called again. Note that the `init` method is called once when the applet is loaded, but `start` may be called several times as the page is revisited. It is good practice to implement `start` and `stop` for an applet if it actively uses CPU time, such as when it is showing an animation, so that CPU time is not wasted on an applet that is not visible.

Note that reloading the Web page in the browser does not necessarily reload the applet. To force the applet to reload, most browsers provide some key combination for that purpose. For example, in Netscape Navigator, holding down the shift key while pressing the reload button with the mouse will not only reload the Web page, it will also reload (and reinitialize) all applets linked to that page.

The `getCodeBase` and `getDocumentBase` methods are useful to determine where the applet's bytecode or HTML document resides. An applet could use the appropriate URL to retrieve additional resources, such as an image or audio clip using the applet methods `getImage` or `getAudioClip`.

We use the various applet methods as appropriate throughout this book.

4.7 graphical objects

Often an object has a graphical representation. Consider the `LineUp` applet shown in Listing 4.15. It creates several `StickFigure` objects, of varying color and random height. The `StickFigure` objects are instantiated in the `init` method of the applet, so they are created only once when the applet is initially loaded.

The `paint` method of `LineUp` simply requests that the stick figures redraw themselves whenever the method is called. The `paint` method is called whenever an event occurs that might influence the graphic representation of the applet itself. For instance, when the window that the applet is displayed in is moved, `paint` is called to redraw the applet contents.

The `StickFigure` class is shown in Listing 4.16. Like any other object, a `StickFigure` object contains data that defines its state, such as the position, color, and height of the figure. The `draw` method contains the individual commands that draw the figure itself, relative to the position and height.

listing
4.15

```
//************************************************************************
//   LineUp.java         Author: Lewis/Loftus
//
//   Demonstrates the use of a graphical object.
//************************************************************************

import java.util.Random;
import java.applet.Applet;
import java.awt.*;

public class LineUp extends Applet
{
   private final int APPLET_WIDTH = 400;
   private final int APPLET_HEIGHT = 150;
   private final int HEIGHT_MIN = 100;
   private final int VARIANCE = 40;

   private StickFigure figure1, figure2, figure3, figure4;

   //----------------------------------------------------------------
   //   Creates several stick figures with varying characteristics.
   //----------------------------------------------------------------
   public void init ()
   {
      int h1, h2, h3, h4;  // heights of stick figures
      Random generator = new Random();

      h1 = HEIGHT_MIN + generator.nextInt(VARIANCE);
      h2 = HEIGHT_MIN + generator.nextInt(VARIANCE);
      h3 = HEIGHT_MIN + generator.nextInt(VARIANCE);
      h4 = HEIGHT_MIN + generator.nextInt(VARIANCE);

      figure1 = new StickFigure (100, 150, Color.red, h1);
      figure2 = new StickFigure (150, 150, Color.cyan, h2);
      figure3 = new StickFigure (200, 150, Color.green, h3);
      figure4 = new StickFigure (250, 150, Color.yellow, h4);

      setBackground (Color.black);
      setSize (APPLET_WIDTH, APPLET_HEIGHT);
   }
```

listing
4.15   **continued**

```
//-------------------------------------------------------------------
//  Paints the stick figures on the applet.
//-------------------------------------------------------------------
public void paint (Graphics page)
{
    figure1.draw (page);
    figure2.draw (page);
    figure3.draw (page);
    figure4.draw (page);
}
}
```

display

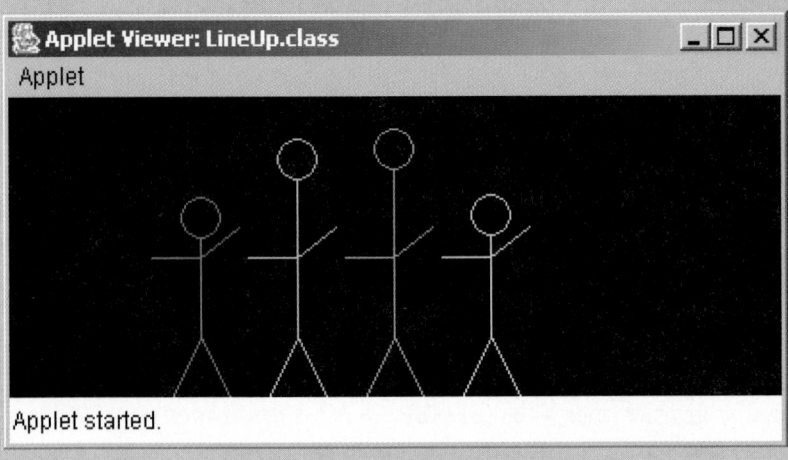

listing
   4.16

```java
//********************************************************************
//  StickFigure.java          Author: Lewis/Loftus
//
//  Represents a graphical stick figure.
//********************************************************************

import java.awt.*;

public class StickFigure
{
   private int baseX;        // center of figure
   private int baseY;        // floor (bottom of feet)
   private Color color;      // color of stick figure
   private int height;       // height of stick figure

   //-----------------------------------------------------------------
   //  Sets up the stick figure's primary attributes.
   //-----------------------------------------------------------------
   public StickFigure (int center, int bottom, Color shade, int size)
   {
      baseX = center;
      baseY = bottom;
      color = shade;
      height = size;
   }

   //-----------------------------------------------------------------
   //  Draws this figure relative to baseX, baseY, and height.
   //-----------------------------------------------------------------
   public void draw (Graphics page)
   {
      int top = baseY - height;  // top of head

      page.setColor (color);

      page.drawOval (baseX-10, top, 20, 20);  // head

      page.drawLine (baseX, top+20, baseX, baseY-30);  // trunk
```

listing
    4.16   continued

```
    page.drawLine (baseX, baseY-30, baseX-15, baseY);   // legs
    page.drawLine (baseX, baseY-30, baseX+15, baseY);

    page.drawLine (baseX, baseY-70, baseX-25, baseY-70);   // arms
    page.drawLine (baseX, baseY-70, baseX+20, baseY-85);
  }
}
```

summary of
key concepts

▸ Each object has a state and a set of behaviors. The values of an object's variables define its state. The methods to which an object responds define its behaviors.

▸ A class is a blueprint for an object; it reserves no memory space for data. Each object has its own data space, thus its own state.

▸ The scope of a variable, which determines where it can be referenced, depends on where it is declared.

▸ A UML diagram is a software design tool that helps us visualize the classes and objects of a program and the relationships among them.

▸ Objects should be encapsulated. The rest of a program should interact with an object only through a well-defined interface.

▸ Instance variables should be declared with private visibility to promote encapsulation.

▸ A method must return a value consistent with the return type specified in the method header.

▸ When a method is called, the actual parameters are copied into the formal parameters. The types of the corresponding parameters must match.

▸ A constructor cannot have any return type, even `void`.

▸ A variable declared in a method is local to that method and cannot be used outside of it.

▸ The versions of an overloaded method are distinguished by their signatures. The number, type, and order of their parameters must be distinct.

▸ A complex service provided by an object can be decomposed to can make use of private support methods.

▸ A method invoked through one object may take as a parameter another object of the same class.

▸ An aggregate object is composed, in part, of other objects, forming a has-a relationship.

▸ Several methods of the `Applet` class are designed to facilitate their execution in a Web browser.

self-review questions

4.1   What is the difference between an object and a class?

4.2   What is the scope of a variable?

4.3   What are UML diagrams designed to do?

4.4   Objects should be self-governing. Explain.

4.5   What is a modifier?

4.6   Describe each of the following:

a. public method

b. private method

c. public variable

d. private variable

4.7   What does the `return` statement do?

4.8   Explain the difference between an actual parameter and a formal parameter.

4.9   What are constructors used for? How are they defined?

4.10 How are overloaded methods distinguished from each other?

4.11 What is method decomposition?

4.12 Explain how a class can have an association with itself.

4.13 What is an aggregate object?

4.14 What do the `start` and `stop` methods of an applet do?

exercises

4.1   Write a method called `powersOfTwo` that prints the first 10 powers of 2 (starting with 2). The method takes no parameters and doesn't return anything.

4.2   Write a method called `alarm` that prints the string "`Alarm!`" multiple times on separate lines. The method should accept an integer parameter that specifies how many times the string is printed. Print an error message if the parameter is less than 1.

4.3   Write a method called `sum100` that returns the sum of the integers from 1 to 100, inclusive.

4.4   Write a method called `maxOfTwo` that accepts two integer parameters and returns the larger of the two.

4.5   Write a method called `sumRange` that accepts two integer parameters that represent a range. Issue an error message and return zero if the second parameter is less than the first. Otherwise, the method should return the sum of the integers in that range (inclusive).

4.6   Write a method called `larger` that accepts two floating point parameters (of type `double`) and returns true if the first parameter is greater than the second, and false otherwise.

4.7   Write a method called `countA` that accepts a `String` parameter and returns the number of times the character `'A'` is found in the string.

4.8   Write a method called `evenlyDivisible` that accepts two integer parameters and returns true if the first parameter is evenly divisible by the second, or vice versa, and false otherwise. Return false if either parameter is zero.

4.9   Write a method called `average` that accepts two integer parameters and returns their average as a floating point value.

4.10 Overload the `average` method of Exercise 4.9 such that if three integers are provided as parameters, the method returns the average of all three.

4.11 Overload the `average` method of Exercise 4.9 to accept four integer parameters and return their average.

4.12 Write a method called `multiConcat` that takes a `String` and an integer as parameters. Return a `String` that consists of the string parameter concatenated with itself `count` times, where `count` is the integer parameter. For example, if the parameter values are `"hi"` and `4`, the return value is `"hihihihi"`. Return the original string if the integer parameter is less than 2.

4.13 Overload the `multiConcat` method from Exercise 4.12 such that if the integer parameter is not provided, the method returns the string concatenated with itself. For example, if the parameter is `"test"`, the return value is `"testtest"`.

4.14 Write a method called `isAlpha` that accepts a character parameter and returns true if that character is either an uppercase or lowercase alphabetic letter.

4.15 Write a method called `floatEquals` that accepts three floating point values as parameters. The method should return true if the first two parameters are equal within the tolerance of the third parameter. *Hint*: See the discussion in Chapter 3 on comparing floating point values for equality.

4.16 Write a method called `reverse` that accepts a `String` parameter and returns a string that contains the characters of the parameter in reverse order. Note that there is a method in the `String` class that performs this operation, but for the sake of this exercise, you are expected to write your own.

4.17 Write a method called `isIsoceles` that accepts three integer parameters that represent the lengths of the sides of a triangle. The method returns true if the triangle is isosceles but not equilateral (meaning that exactly two of the sides have an equal length), and false otherwise.

4.18 Write a method called `randomInRange` that accepts two integer parameters representing a range. The method should return a random integer in the specified range (inclusive). Return zero if the first parameter is greater than the second.

4.19 Write a method called `randomColor` that creates and returns a `Color` object that represents a random color. Recall that a `Color` object can be defined by three integer values between 0 and 255, representing the contributions of red, green, and blue (its RGB value).

4.20 Write a method called `drawCircle` that draws a circle based on the method's parameters: a `Graphics` object through which to draw the circle, two integer values representing the (x, y) coordinates of the center of the circle, another integer that represents the circle's radius, and a `Color` object that defines the circle's color. The method does not return anything.

4.21 Overload the `drawCircle` method of Exercise 4.20 such that if the `Color` parameter is not provided, the circle's color will default to black.

4.22 Overload the `drawCircle` method of Exercise 4.20 such that if the radius is not provided, a random radius in the range 10 to 100 (inclusive) will be used.

4.23 Overload the `drawCircle` method of Exercise 4.20 such that if both the color and the radius of the circle are not provided, the color will default to red and the radius will default to 40.

4.24 Draw a UML class diagram for the `SnakeEyes` program.

4.25 Draw a UML object diagram showing the `Die` objects of the `SnakeEyes` program at a specific point in the program.

4.26 Draw a UML object diagram for the objects of the `StudentBody` program.

4.27 Draw UML class and object diagrams for the `BoxCars` program described in Programming Project 4.3.

4.28 Draw UML class and object diagrams for the `Pig` program described in Programming Project 4.4.

programming projects

4.1 Modify the `Account` class to provide a service that allows funds to be transferred from one account to another. Note that a transfer can be thought of as withdrawing money from one account and depositing it into another. Modify the `main` method of the `Banking` class to demonstrate this new service.

4.2 Modify the `Account` class so that it also permits an account to be opened with just a name and an account number, assuming an initial balance of zero. Modify the `main` method of the `Banking` class to demonstrate this new capability.

4.3 Design and implement a class called `PairOfDice`, composed of two six-sided `Die` objects. Create a driver class called `BoxCars` with a `main` method that rolls a `PairOfDice` object 1000 times, counting the number of box cars (two sixes) that occur.

4.4 Using the `PairOfDice` class from Programming Project 4.3, design and implement a class to play a game called Pig. In this game, the user competes against the computer. On each turn, the current player rolls a pair of dice and accumulates points. The goal is to reach 100 points before your opponent does. If, on any turn, the player rolls a 1, all points accumulated for that round are forfeited and control of the dice moves to the other player. If the player rolls two 1s in one turn, the player loses all points accumulated thus far in the game and loses control of the dice. The player may voluntarily turn over the dice after each roll. Therefore the player must decide to either roll again (be a pig) and risk losing points, or relinquish control of the dice, possibly allowing the other player to win. Implement the computer player such that it always relinquishes the dice after accumulating 20 or more points in any given round.

4.5 Design and implement a class called `Card` that represents a standard playing card. Each card has a suit and a face value. Create a program that deals 20 random cards.

4.6 Modify the `Student` class presented in this chapter as follows. Each student object should also contain the scores for three tests. Provide a constructor that sets all instance values based on parameter values. Overload the constructor such that each test score is assumed to be initially zero. Provide a method called `setTestScore` that accepts two parameters: the test number (1 through 3) and the score. Also provide a method called `getTestScore` that accepts the test number and returns the appropriate score. Provide a method called `average` that computes and returns the average test score for this student. Modify the `toString` method such that the test scores and average are included in the description of the student. Modify the driver class `main` method to exercise the new `Student` methods.

4.7   Design and implement a class called `Course` that represents a course taken at a school. A course object should keep track of up to five students, as represented by the modified `Student` class from the previous programming project. The constructor of the `Course` class should accept only the name of the course. Provide a method called `addStudent` that accepts one `Student` parameter (the `Course` object should keep track of how many valid students have been added to the course). Provide a method called `average` that computes and returns the average of all students' test score averages. Provide a method called `roll` that prints all students in the course. Create a driver class with a `main` method that creates a course, adds several students, prints a roll, and prints the overall course test average.

4.8   Design and implement a class called `Building` that represents a graphical depiction of a building. Allow the parameters to the constructor to specify the building's width and height. Each building should be colored black, and contain a few random windows of yellow. Create an applet that draws a random skyline of buildings.

4.9   A programming project in Chapter 3 describes an applet that draws a quilt with a repeating pattern. Design and implement an applet that draws a quilt using a separate class called `Pattern` that represents a particular pattern. Allow the constructor of the Pattern class to vary some characteristics of the pattern, such as its color scheme. Instantiate two separate Pattern objects and incorporate them in a checkerboard layout in the quilt.

4.10   Write an applet that displays a graphical seating chart for a dinner party. Create a class called `Diner` (as in one who dines) that stores the person's name, gender, and location at the dinner table. A diner is graphically represented as a circle, color-coded by gender, with the person's name printed in the circle.

4.11   Create a class called `Crayon` that represents one crayon of a particular color and length (height). Design and implement an applet that draws a box of crayons.

4.12   Create a class called `Star` that represents a graphical depiction of a star. Let the constructor of the star accept the number of points in the star (4, 5, or 6), the radius of the star, and the center point location. Write an applet that draws a sky full of various types of stars.

4.13 Enhance the concept of the LineUp program to create a PoliceLineUp class. Instead of a stick figure, create a class called Thug that has a more realistic graphical representation. In addition to varying the person's height, vary the clothes and shoes by color, and add a hat or necktie for some thugs.

answers to self-review questions

4.1   A class is the blueprint of an object. It defines the variables and methods that will be a part of every object that is instantiated from it. But a class reserves no memory space for variables. Each object has its own data space and therefore its own state.

4.2   The scope of a variable is the area within a program in which the variable can be referenced. An instance variable, declared at the class level, can be referenced in any method of the class. Local variables, including the formal parameters, declared within a particular method, can be referenced only in that method.

4.3   A UML diagram helps us visualize the entities (classes and objects) in a program as well as the relationships among them. UML diagrams are tools that help us capture the design of a program prior to writing it.

4.4   A self-governing object is one that controls the values of its own data. Encapsulated objects, which don't allow an external client to reach in and change its data, are self-governing.

4.5   A modifier is a Java reserved word that can be used in the definition of a variable or method and that specifically defines certain characteristics of its use. For example, by declaring a variable with private visibility, the variable cannot be directly accessed outside of the object in which it is defined.

4.6   The modifiers affect the methods and variables in the following ways:

a. A public method is called a service method for an object because it defines a service that the object provides.

b. A private method is called a support method because it cannot be invoked from outside the object and is used to support the activities of other methods in the class.

c. A public variable is a variable that can be directly accessed and modified by a client. This explicitly violates the principle of encapsulation and therefore should be avoided.

d. A private variable is a variable that can be accessed and modified only from within the class. Variables almost always are declared with private visibility.

4.7 An explicit `return` statement is used to specify the value that is returned from a method. The type of the return value must match the return type specified in the method definition.

4.8 An actual parameter is a value sent to a method when it is invoked. A formal parameter is the corresponding variable in the header of the method declaration; it takes on the value of the actual parameter so that it can be used inside the method.

4.9 Constructors are special methods in an object that are used to initialize the object when it is instantiated. A constructor has the same name as its class, and it does not return a value.

4.10 Overloaded methods are distinguished by having a unique signature, which includes the number, order, and type of the parameters. The return type is not part of the signature.

4.11 Method decomposition is the process of dividing a complex method into several support methods to get the job done. This simplifies and facilitates the design of the program.

4.12 A method executed through an object might take as a parameter another object created from the same class. For example, the `concat` method of the String class is executed through one String object and takes another String object as a parameter.

4.13 An aggregate object is an object that has other objects as instance data. That is, an aggregate object is one that is made up of other objects.

4.14 The `Applet start` method is invoked automatically every time the applet becomes active, such as when a browser returns to the page it is on. The `stop` method is invoked automatically when the applet becomes inactive.

This chapter explores a variety of issues related to the design and implementation of classes. First we revisit the concept of an object reference to explore what it is and how it affects our processing. Then we examine the `static` modifier to see how it can be applied to variables and to methods. We define the concept and usefulness of a wrapper class and see how the `Keyboard` class uses them to help process input. We also explore the ability to nest one class definition within another. We then examine the use of an interface construct to formalize the interaction between classes. Finally, in the graphics track of this chapter we examine the use of dialog boxes and then explore the basic elements that are used in every Java graphical user interface (GUI).

chapter
objectives

▶ Define reference aliases and explore Java garbage collection.

▶ Explore the effects of passing object references as parameters.

▶ Define the use and effects of the `static` modifier.

▶ Examine the wrapper classes defined in the Java standard class library.

▶ Discover the fundamental aspects of keyboard input.

▶ Define nested classes and inner classes and explore their appropriate use.

▶ Define formal interfaces and their class implementations.

▶ Determine how to present basic graphical user interfaces.

5.0 references revisited

In previous examples we've declared many *object reference variables* through which we access particular objects. In this chapter we need to examine this relationship in more detail. Object references play an important role in a program. We need to have a careful understanding of how they work in order to write sophisticated object-oriented software.

An object reference variable and an object are two separate things. Remember that the declaration of the reference variable and the creation of the object that it refers to are separate steps. Although we often declare the reference variable and create an object for it to refer to on the same line, keep in mind that we don't have to do so. In fact, in many cases, we won't want to.

> **Key concept**
>
> An object reference variable stores the address of an object.

An object reference variable stores the address of an object even though the address never is disclosed to us. When we use the dot operator to invoke an object's method, we are actually using the address in the reference variable to locate the representation of the object in memory, to look up the appropriate method, and to invoke it.

the null reference

A reference variable that does not currently point to an object is called a *null reference*. When a reference variable is initially declared as an instance variable, it is a null reference. If we try to follow a null reference, a `NullPointerException` is thrown, indicating that there is no object to reference. For example, consider the following situation:

```
class NameIsNull
{
    String name; // not initialized, therefore null

    void printName()
    {
        System.out.println (name.length()); // causes an exception
    }
}
```

The declaration of the instance variable name asserts it to be a reference to a `String` object but doesn't create any `String` object for it to refer to. The variable name, therefore, contains a null reference. When the method attempts to invoke the length method of the object to which name refers, an exception is thrown because no object exists to execute the method.

Note that this situation can arise only in the case of instance variables. Suppose, for instance, the following two lines of code were in a method:

```
String name;
System.out.println (name.length());
```

In this case, the variable name is local to whatever method we are in. The compiler would complain that we were using the name variable before it had been initialized. In the case of instance variables, however, the compiler can't determine whether a variable had been initialized; therefore, the danger of attempting to follow a null reference is a problem.

The identifier null is a reserved word in Java and represents a null reference. We can explicitly set a reference to null to ensure that it doesn't point to any object. We can also use it to check to see whether a particular reference currently points to an object. For example, we could have used the following code in the printName method to keep us from following a null reference:

```
if (name == null)
    System.out.println ("Invalid Name");
else
    System.out.println (name.length());
```

> **key concept**
>
> The reserved word null represents a reference that does not point to a valid object.

the this reference

Another special reference for Java objects is called the this reference. The word this is a reserved word in Java. It allows an object to refer to itself. As we have discussed, a method is always invoked through (or by) a particular object or class. Inside that method, the this reference can be used to refer to the currently executing object.

> **key concept**
>
> The this reference always refers to the currently executing object.

For example, in a class called ChessPiece there could be a method called move, which could contain the following line:

```
if (this.position == piece2.position)
    result = false;
```

In this situation, the this reference is being used to clarify which position is being referenced. The this reference refers to the object through which the method was invoked. So when the following line is used to invoke the method, the `this` reference refers to `bishop1`:

```
bishop1.move();
```

However, when another object is used to invoke the method, the `this` reference refers to it. Therefore, when the following invocation is used, the `this` reference in the move method refers to `bishop2`:

```
bishop2.move();
```

The `this` reference can also be used to distinguish the parameters of a constructor from their corresponding instance variable with the same names. For example, the constructor of the `Account` class was presented in Chapter 4 as follows:

```
public Account (String owner, long account, double initial)
{
    name = owner;
    acctNumber = account;
    balance = initial;
}
```

When writing this constructor, we deliberately came up with different names for the parameters to distinguish them from the instance variables `name`, `acctNumber`, and `balance`. This distinction is arbitrary. The constructor could have been written as follows using the `this` reference:

```
public Account (String name, long acctNumber, double balance)
{
    this.name = name;
    this.acctNumber = acctNumber;
    this.balance = balance;
}
```

In this version of the constructor, the `this` reference specifically refers to the instance variables of the object. The variables on the right-hand side of the assignment statements refer to the formal parameters. This approach eliminates the need to come up with different yet equivalent names. This situation sometimes occurs in other methods but comes up often in constructors.

aliases

Because an object reference variable stores an address, a programmer must be careful when managing objects. In particular, you must understand the semantics of an assignment statement for objects. First, let's revisit the concept of assignment for primitive types. Consider the following declarations of primitive data:

```
int num1 = 5;
int num2 = 12;
```

In the following assignment statement, a copy of the value that is stored in num1 is stored in num2:

```
num2 = num1;
```

The original value of 12 in num2 is overwritten by the value 5. The variables num1 and num2 still refer to different locations in memory, and both of those locations now contain the value 5. Figure 5.1 depicts this situation.

Now consider the following object declarations:

```
ChessPiece bishop1 = new ChessPiece();
ChessPiece bishop2 = new ChessPiece();
```

Initially, the references bishop1 and bishop2 refer to two different ChessPiece objects. The following assignment statement copies the value in bishop1 into bishop2.

```
bishop2 = bishop1;
```

The key issue is that when an assignment like this is made, the address stored in bishop1 is copied into bishop2. Originally, the two references referred to different objects. After the assignment, both bishop1 and bishop2 contain the same address and therefore refer to the same object. Figure 5.2 depicts this process.

The bishop1 and bishop2 references are now *aliases* of each other because they are two names that refer to the same object. All references to the object that

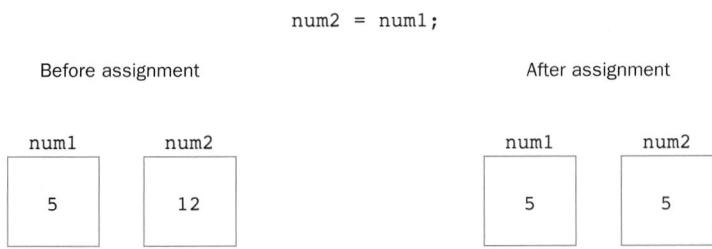

figure 5.1   Primitive data assignment

```
bishop2 = bishop1;
```

Before assignment   After assignment

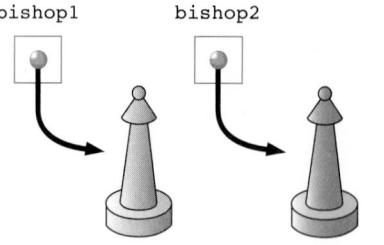
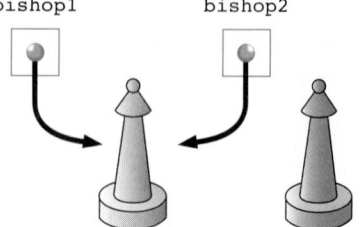

figure 5.2   Reference assignment

was originally referenced by `bishop2` are now gone; that object cannot be used again in the program.

One important implication of aliases is that when we use one reference to change the state of the object, it is also changed for the other because there is really only one object. If you change the state of `bishop1`, for instance, you change the state of `bishop2` because they both refer to the same object. Aliases can produce undesirable effects unless they are managed carefully.

Another important aspect of references is the way they affect how we determine whether two objects are equal. The `==` operator that we use for primitive data can be used with object references, but it returns true only if the two references being compared are aliases of each other. It does not "look inside" the objects to see whether they contain the same data.

Thus the following expression is true only if `bishop1` and `bishop2` currently refer to the same object:

```
bishop1 == bishop2
```

A method called `equals` is defined for all objects, but unless we replace it with a specific definition when we write a class, it has the same semantics as the `==` operator. That is, the `equals` method returns a `boolean` value that, by default, will be true if the two objects being compared are aliases of each other. The `equals` method is invoked through one object, and takes the other one as a parameter. Therefore, the following expression returns true if both references refer to the same object:

```
bishop1.equals(bishop2)
```

However, we could define the `equals` method in the `ChessPiece` class to define equality for `ChessPiece` objects any way we would like. That is, we could define the `equals` method to return true under whatever conditions we think are appropriate to mean that one `ChessPiece` is equal to another.

> **key concept**
> The `equals` method can be defined to determine equality between objects in any way we consider appropriate.

As we discussed in Chapter 3, the `equals` method has been given an appropriate definition in the `String` class. When comparing two `String` objects, the `equals` method returns true only if both strings contain the same characters. A common mistake is to use the `==` operator to compare strings, which compares the references for equality, when most of the time we want to compare the characters inside the string objects for equality. We discuss the `equals` method in more detail in Chapter 7.

garbage collection

All interaction with an object occurs through a reference variable, so we can use an object only if we have a reference to it. When all references to an object are lost (perhaps by reassignment), that object can no longer participate in the program. The program can no longer invoke its methods or use its variables. At this point the object is called *garbage* because it serves no useful purpose.

Java performs *automatic garbage collection*. When the last reference to an object is lost, the object becomes a candidate for garbage collection. Occasionally, the Java runtime executes a method that "collects" all of the objects marked for garbage collection and returns their allocated memory to the system for future use. The programmer does not have to worry about explicitly returning memory that has become garbage.

> **key concept**
> If an object has no references to it, a program cannot use it. Java performs automatic garbage collection by periodically reclaiming the memory space occupied by these objects.

If there is an activity that a programmer wants to accomplish in conjunction with the object being destroyed, the programmer can define a method called `finalize` in the object's class. The `finalize` method takes no parameters and has a `void` return type. It will be executed by the Java runtime after the object is marked for garbage collection and before it is actually destroyed. The `finalize` method is not often used because the garbage collector performs most normal cleanup operations. However, it is useful for performing activities that the garbage collector does not address, such as closing files (discussed in Chapter 8).

web
bonus

The Web site of the text contains a detailed discussion of the `finalize` method.

passing objects as parameters

Another important issue related to object references comes up when we want to pass an object to a method. Java passes all parameters to a method *by value*. That is, the current value of the actual parameter (in the invocation) is copied into the formal parameter in the method header. Essentially, parameter passing is like an assignment statement, assigning to the formal parameter a copy of the value stored in the actual parameter.

This issue must be considered when making changes to a formal parameter inside a method. The formal parameter is a separate copy of the value that is passed in, so any changes made to it have no effect on the actual parameter. After control returns to the calling method, the actual parameter will have the same value as it did before the method was called.

However, when an object is passed to a method, we are actually passing a reference to that object. The value that gets copied is the address of the object. Therefore, the formal parameter and the actual parameter become aliases of each other. If we change the state of the object through the formal parameter reference inside the method, we are changing the object referenced by the actual parameter because they refer to the same object. On the other hand, if we change the formal parameter reference itself (to make it point to a new object, for instance), we have not changed the fact that the actual parameter still refers to the original object.

> **key concept**
>
> When an object is passed to a method, the actual and formal parameters become aliases of each other.

The program in Listing 5.1 illustrates the nuances of parameter passing. Carefully trace the processing of this program and note the values that are output. The `ParameterPassing` class contains a `main` method that calls the `changeValues` method in a `ParameterTester` object. Two of the parameters to `changeValues` are `Num` objects, each of which simply stores an integer value. The other parameter is a primitive integer value.

listing
   5.1

```
//********************************************************************
//  ParameterPassing.java        Author: Lewis/Loftus
//
//  Demonstrates the effects of passing various types of parameters.
//********************************************************************

public class ParameterPassing
{
   //-----------------------------------------------------------------
   //  Sets up three variables (one primitive and two objects) to
   //  serve as actual parameters to the changeValues method. Prints
   //  their values before and after calling the method.
   //-----------------------------------------------------------------
   public static void main (String[] args)
   {
      ParameterTester tester = new ParameterTester();

      int a1 = 111;
      Num a2 = new Num (222);
      Num a3 = new Num (333);

      System.out.println ("Before calling changeValues:");
      System.out.println ("a1\ta2\ta3");
      System.out.println (a1 + "\t" + a2 + "\t" + a3 + "\n");

      tester.changeValues (a1, a2, a3);

      System.out.println ("After calling changeValues:");
      System.out.println ("a1\ta2\ta3");
      System.out.println (a1 + "\t" + a2 + "\t" + a3 + "\n");
   }
}
```

listing
   5.1   continued

output

```
Before calling changeValues:
a1        a2        a3
111       222       333

Before changing the values:
f1        f2        f3
111       222       333

After changing the values:
f1        f2        f3
999       888       777

After calling changeValues:
a1        a2        a3
111       888       333
```

Listing 5.2 shows the `ParameterTester` class, and Listing 5.3 shows the `Num` class. Inside the `changeValues` method, a modification is made to each of the three formal parameters: the integer parameter is set to a different value, the value stored in the first `Num` parameter is changed using its `setValue` method, and a new `Num` object is created and assigned to the second `Num` parameter. These changes are reflected in the output printed at the end of the `changeValues` method.

However, note the final values that are printed after returning from the method. The primitive integer was not changed from its original value because the change was made to a copy inside the method. Likewise, the last parameter still refers to its original object with its original value. This is because the new `Num` object created in the method was referred to only by the formal parameter. When the method returned, that formal parameter was destroyed and the `Num` object it referred to was marked for garbage collection. The only change that is "permanent" is the change made to the state of the second parameter. Figure 5.3 shows the step-by-step processing of this program.

```
listing
    5.2
```

```java
//********************************************************************
//   ParameterTester.java        Author: Lewis/Loftus
//
//   Demonstrates the effects of passing various types of parameters.
//********************************************************************

public class ParameterTester
{
   //------------------------------------------------------------------
   //   Modifies the parameters, printing their values before and
   //   after making the changes.
   //------------------------------------------------------------------
   public void changeValues (int f1, Num f2, Num f3)
   {
      System.out.println ("Before changing the values:");
      System.out.println ("f1\tf2\tf3");
      System.out.println (f1 + "\t" + f2 + "\t" + f3 + "\n");

      f1 = 999;
      f2.setValue (888);
      f3 = new Num (777);

      System.out.println ("After changing the values:");
      System.out.println ("f1\tf2\tf3");
      System.out.println (f1 + "\t" + f2 + "\t" + f3 + "\n");
   }
}
```

listing
    5.3

```java
//********************************************************************
//   Num.java        Author: Lewis/Loftus
//
//   Represents a single integer as an object.
//********************************************************************

public class Num
{
   private int value;

   //-----------------------------------------------------------------
   //   Sets up the new Num object, storing an initial value.
   //-----------------------------------------------------------------
   public Num (int update)
   {
      value = update;
   }

   //-----------------------------------------------------------------
   //   Sets the stored value to the newly specified value.
   //-----------------------------------------------------------------
   public void setValue (int update)
   {
      value = update;
   }

   //-----------------------------------------------------------------
   //   Returns the stored integer value as a string.
   //-----------------------------------------------------------------
   public String toString ()
   {
      return value + "";
   }
}
```

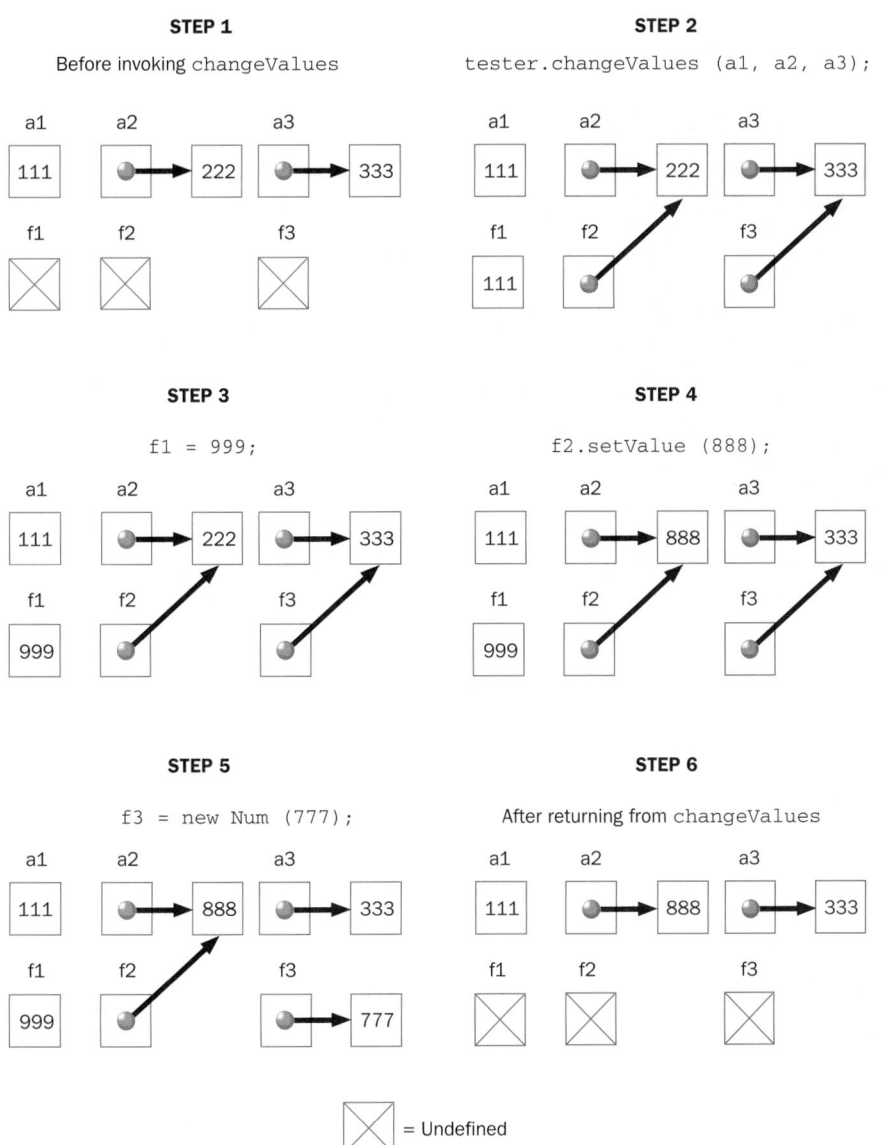

figure 5.3   Tracing the parameters in the ParameterPassing program

5.1   the static modifier

We've seen how visibility modifiers allow us to specify the encapsulation characteristics of variables and methods in a class. Java has several other modifiers that determine other characteristics. For example, the `static` modifier associates a variable or method with its class rather than with an object of the class.

static variables

So far, we've seen two categories of variables: local variables that are declared inside a method and instance variables that are declared in a class but not inside a method. The term *instance variable* is used because an instance variable is accessed through a particular instance (an object) of a class. In general, each object has distinct memory space for each variable so that each object can have a distinct value for that variable.

Another kind of variable, called a *static variable* or *class variable*, is shared among all instances of a class. There is only one copy of a static variable for all objects of a class. Therefore, changing the value of a static variable in one object changes it for all of the others. The reserved word `static` is used as a modifier to declare a static variable as follows:

> **key concept**
>
> A `static` variable is shared among all instances of a class.

```
private static int count = 0;
```

Memory space for a static variable is established when the class that contains it is referenced for the first time in a program. A local variable declared within a method cannot be static.

Constants, which are declared using the `final` modifier, are also often declared using the `static` modifier as well. Because the value of constants cannot be changed, there might as well be only one copy of the value across all objects of the class.

static methods

In Chapter 2 we introduced the concept of a *static method* (also called a *class method*). We noted, for instance, that all of the methods of the `Math` class are static methods, meaning that they can be invoked through the class name. We don't have to instantiate an object of the class to invoke a static method. For example, in the following line of code the `sqrt` method is invoked through the `Math` class name:

```
System.out.println ("Square root of 27: " + Math.sqrt(27));
```

A method is made static by using the `static` modifier in the method declaration. As we've seen many times, the `main` method of a Java program must be declared with the `static` modifier; this is so `main` can be executed by the interpreter without instantiating an object from the class that contains `main`.

Because static methods do not operate in the context of a particular object, they cannot reference instance variables, which exist only in an instance of a class. The compiler will issue an error if a static method attempts to use a nonstatic variable. A static method can, however, reference static variables because static variables exist independent of specific objects. Therefore, the `main` method can access only static or local variables.

The methods in the `Math` class perform basic computations based on values passed as parameters. There is no object state to maintain in these situations; therefore there is no good reason to force us to create an object in order to request these services.

The program in Listing 5.4 uses a loop to instantiate several objects of the `Slogan` class, printing each one out in turn. At the end of the program it invokes a method called `getCount` through the class name, which returns the number of `Slogan` objects that were instantiated in the program.

Listing 5.5 shows the `Slogan` class. The constructor of `Slogan` increments a static variable called `count`, which is initialized to zero when it is declared. Therefore, `count` serves to keep track of the number of instances of `Slogan` that are created.

The `getCount` method of `Slogan` is also declared as `static`, which allows it to be invoked through the class name in the `main` method. Note that the only data referenced in the `getCount` method is the integer variable `count`, which is static. The `getCount` method could have been declared without the `static` modifier, but then its invocation in the `main` method would have to have been done through an instance of the `Slogan` class instead of the class itself.

5.2 wrapper classes

In some object-oriented programming languages, everything is represented using classes and the objects that are instantiated from them. In Java, as we've discussed previously, there are primitive types (such as `int`, `double`, `char`, and `boolean`) in addition to classes and objects.

listing
   5.4

```java
//********************************************************************
//  CountInstances.java        Author: Lewis/Loftus
//
//  Demonstrates the use of the static modifier.
//********************************************************************

public class CountInstances
{
   //----------------------------------------------------------------
   //  Creates several Slogan objects and prints the number of
   //  objects that were created.
   //----------------------------------------------------------------
   public static void main (String[] args)
   {
      Slogan obj;

      obj = new Slogan ("Remember the Alamo.");
      System.out.println (obj);

      obj = new Slogan ("Don't Worry. Be Happy.");
      System.out.println (obj);

      obj = new Slogan ("Live Free or Die.");
      System.out.println (obj);

      obj = new Slogan ("Talk is Cheap.");
      System.out.println (obj);

      obj = new Slogan ("Write Once, Run Anywhere.");
      System.out.println (obj);

      System.out.println();
      System.out.println ("Slogans created: " + Slogan.getCount());
   }
}
```

output

```
Remember the Alamo.
Don't Worry. Be Happy.
Live Free or Die.
Talk is Cheap.
Write Once, Run Anywhere.

Slogans created: 5
```

listing
   5.5

```java
//********************************************************************
//   Slogan.java        Author: Lewis/Loftus
//
//   Represents a single slogan string.
//********************************************************************

public class Slogan
{
   private String phrase;
   private static int count = 0;

   //----------------------------------------------------------------
   //   Sets up the slogan and counts the number of instances created.
   //----------------------------------------------------------------
   public Slogan (String str)
   {
      phrase = str;
      count++;
   }

   //----------------------------------------------------------------
   //   Returns this slogan as a string.
   //----------------------------------------------------------------
   public String toString()
   {
      return phrase;
   }

   //----------------------------------------------------------------
   //   Returns the number of instances of this class that have been
   //   created.
   //----------------------------------------------------------------
   public static int getCount ()
   {
      return count;
   }
}
```

Having two categories of data to manage (primitive values and object references) can present a challenge in some circumstances. For example, we might create an object that serves as a container to hold various types of other objects. However, in a specific situation, you may want it to hold a simple integer value. In these cases we need to "wrap" a primitive type into a class so that it can be treated as an object.

A *wrapper class* represents a particular primitive type. For instance, the `Integer` class represents a simple integer value. An object created from the `Integer` class stores a single `int` value. The constructors of the wrapper classes accept the primitive value to store. For example:

```
Integer ageObj = new Integer(45);
```

> **key concept**
>
> A wrapper class represents a primitive value so that it can be treated as an object.

Once this declaration and instantiation are performed, the `ageObj` object effectively represents the integer 45 as an object. It can be used wherever an object is called for in a program instead of a primitive type.

For each primitive type in Java there exists a corresponding wrapper class in the Java class library. All wrapper classes are defined in the `java.lang` package. Figure 5.4 shows the wrapper class that corresponds to each primitive type.

Note that there is even a wrapper class that represents the type `void`. However, unlike the other wrapper classes, the `Void` class cannot be instantiated. It simply represents the concept of a void reference.

The wrapper classes also provide various methods related to the management of the associated primitive type. For example, the `Integer` class contains methods that return the `int` value stored in the object and that convert the stored value to other primitive types. Figure 5.5 lists some of the methods found in the

Primitive Type	Wrapper Class
byte	Byte
short	Short
int	Integer
long	Long
float	Float
double	Double
char	Character
boolean	Boolean
void	Void

figure 5.4   Wrapper classes in the Java class library

```
Integer (int value)
   Constructor: creates a new Integer object storing the specified value.

byte byteValue ()
double doubleValue ()
float floatValue ()
int intValue ()
long longValue ()
   Return the value of this Integer as the corresponding primitive type.

static int ParseInt (String str)
   Returns the int corresponding to the value stored in the
   specified string.

static String toBinaryString (int num)
static String tohexString (int num)
static String toOctalString (int num)
   Returns a string representation of the specified integer value in the
   corresponding base.
```

figure 5.5   Some methods of the Integer class

Integer class. The other wrapper classes have similar methods. Appendix M includes details of all wrapper classes.

Note that the wrapper classes also contain static methods that can be invoked independent of any instantiated object. For example, the Integer class contains a static method called parseInt to convert an integer that is stored in a String to its corresponding int value. If the String object str holds the string "987", the following line of code converts the string into the integer value 987 and stores that value the int variable num:

```
num = Integer.parseInt(str);
```

The Java wrapper classes often contain static constants that are helpful as well. For example, the Integer class contains two constants, MIN_VALUE and MAX_VALUE, which hold the smallest and largest int values, respectively. The other wrapper classes contain similar constants for their types.

5.3 keyboard input revisited

The Keyboard class was presented in Chapter 2 to facilitate reading input entered at the keyboard. Recall that the authors of this text wrote the Keyboard class. It is not part of the Java standard class library. Our goal was to make the initial exploration of Java programming a bit easier. Now that we have explored several aspects of object-oriented programming, let's revisit the concept of keyboard input. Let's see, at least in part, what the Keyboard class has been doing for us and how we can write code that accepts keyboard input without using the Keyboard class.

The program in Listing 5.6 is generally equivalent to the Wages program presented in Chapter 3. It accomplishes the same task—determining the wages for an employee based on the number of hours worked—but it does so without relying on the Keyboard class.

Java input and output (I/O) is accomplished using objects that represent streams of data. A *stream* is an ordered sequence of bytes. The System.out object represents a standard *output stream*, which defaults to the monitor screen. We've been able to use that object (with its print and println methods) all along because it requires no special setup or processing. Reading input from the keyboard, however, is a bit more involved.

First we must establish the *input stream* from which we will read the incoming data. The first line of the main method in the Wages2 program is a declaration of the standard input stream object in a useful form. The System.in object is used to create an InputStreamReader object, which is used in turn to create a BufferedReader object. This declaration creates an input stream that treats the input as characters (rather than arbitrary bits) and buffers the input so that it can be read one line at a time.

The readLine method of the BufferedReader class reads an entire line of input as a String. A line of input is terminated by the enter key. If we want to treat the input as a numeric value, we must convert it. For example, in two places in this program, we use the parseInt method of the Integer wrapper class and the parseDouble method of the Double class to convert the input string to the appropriate numeric type.

Also, several things could go wrong in the process of reading or converting a value. These problems will manifest themselves as exceptions. Some exceptions in Java have to be handled explicitly—or at least acknowledged that they could occur—by the program. The Wages2 program acknowledges that the main method may throw an IOException using a *throws clause* in the method header.

The Keyboard class hides these aspects of keyboard input. It declares and manages the standard input stream. It provides methods that read and convert specific data types. It catches exceptions if they occur and handles them gracefully. In addition, the Keyboard class allows multiple values to be put on one line of input and uses the StringTokenizer class to separate the data items.

listing
    5.6

```
//************************************************************************
//  Wages2.java        Author: Lewis/Loftus
//
//  Demonstrates the use of Java I/O classes for keyboard input.
//************************************************************************

import java.io.*;
import java.text.NumberFormat;

public class Wages2
{
   //-----------------------------------------------------------------
   //  Reads pertinent information and calculates wages.
   //-----------------------------------------------------------------
   public static void main (String[] args) throws IOException
   {
      BufferedReader in =
         new BufferedReader (new InputStreamReader (System.in));

      String name;
      int hours;
      double rate, pay;

      System.out.print ("Enter your name: ");
      name = in.readLine ();

      System.out.print ("Enter the number of hours worked: ");
      hours = Integer.parseInt (in.readLine());

      System.out.print ("Enter pay rate per hour: ");
      rate = Double.parseDouble (in.readLine());

      System.out.println ();

      pay = hours * rate;

      NumberFormat fmt = NumberFormat.getCurrencyInstance();
      System.out.println (name + ", your pay is: " + fmt.format(pay));
   }
}
```

output

```
Enter the number of hours worked: 46

Gross earnings: $404.25
```

Exceptions and I/O are further explored in Chapter 8. It is important to learn how keyboard input is accomplished in Java without any special third-party classes. Keep in mind that any general Java programming environment will not have the `Keyboard` class to use. However, the `Keyboard` class does represent a nice abstraction of these issues. We will continue to use it as appropriate in examples throughout this book.

5.4 nested classes

A class can be declared inside another class. Just as a loop written inside another loop is called a nested loop, a class written inside another class is called a *nested class*. The nested class is considered a member of the enclosing class, just like a variable or method.

Just like any other class, a nested class produces a separate bytecode file. The name of the bytecode file is the name of the enclosing class followed by the $ character followed by the name of the nested class. Like any other bytecode file, it has an extension of `.class`. A class called `Nested` that is declared inside a class called `Enclosing` will result in a compiled bytecode file called `Enclosing$Nested.class`.

Because it is a member of the enclosing class, a nested class has access to the enclosing class's instance variables and methods, even if they are declared with private visibility. Now let's look at it from the other direction. The enclosing class can directly access data in the nested class only if the data is declared public. In general, we've always said that public data is a bad idea because it violates encapsulation. However, nested classes provide an exception to that rule. It is reasonable to declare the data of a private nested class with public visibility because only the enclosing class can get to that data (despite its public declaration).

Such a privileged relationship should be reserved for appropriate situations. A class should be nested inside another only if it makes sense in the context of the enclosing class. In such cases, the nesting reinforces the relationship yet simplifies the implementation by allowing direct access to the data.

The `static` modifier can be applied to a class, but only if the class is nested inside another. Like static methods, a static nested class cannot reference instance variables or methods defined in its enclosing class.

inner classes

A nonstatic nested class is called an *inner class*. Because it is not static, an inner class is associated with each instance of the enclosing class. Therefore no member inside an inner class can be declared `static`. An instance of an inner class can exist only within an instance of the enclosing class.

Let's look at an example that shows the access capabilities of nested classes. The program shown in Listing 5.7 contains a `main` method that creates one `Outer` object, prints it, calls its `changeMessages` method, and then prints it again.

listing
  5.7

```java
//********************************************************************
//   TestInner.java        Author: Lewis/Loftus
//
//   Demonstrates the access capabilities of inner classes.
//********************************************************************

public class TestInner
{
   //-----------------------------------------------------------------
   //   Creates and manipulates an Outer object.
   //-----------------------------------------------------------------
   public static void main (String[] args)
   {
      Outer out = new Outer();

      System.out.println (out);
      System.out.println();

      out.changeMessages();

      System.out.println (out);
   }
}
```

output

```
Half of the problem is 90% mental.
Outer num = 9877
Another deadline. Another miracle.
Outer num = 9878

Life is uncertain. Eat dessert first.
Outer num = 9879
One seventh of your life is spent on Mondays.
Outer num = 9880
```

The Outer class, shown in Listing 5.8, contains some private instance data, some public methods, and a private inner class called Inner. The instance data of the Outer class includes two references to Inner objects.

listing
   5.8

```
//***************************************************************
//  Outer.java        Author: Lewis/Loftus
//
//  Represents a class that encapsulates an inner class.
//***************************************************************

public class Outer
{
   private int num;
   private Inner in1, in2;

   //-----------------------------------------------------------
   //  Sets up this object, initializing one int and two objects
   //  created from the inner class.
   //-----------------------------------------------------------
   public Outer()
   {
     num = 9876;
     in1 = new Inner ("Half of the problem is 90% mental.");
     in2 = new Inner ("Another deadline. Another miracle.");
   }

   //-----------------------------------------------------------
   //  Changes the messages in the Inner objects (directly).
   //-----------------------------------------------------------
   public void changeMessages()
   {
      in1.message = "Life is uncertain. Eat dessert first.";
      in2.message = "One seventh of your life is spent on Mondays.";
   }

   //-----------------------------------------------------------
   //  Returns this object as a string.
   //-----------------------------------------------------------
   public String toString()
   {
      return in1 + "\n" + in2;
   }
```

listing
5.8   continued

```
//*****************************************************************
//  Represents an inner class.
//*****************************************************************
private class Inner
{
   public String message;

   //---------------------------------------------------------------
   //  Sets up this Inner object with the specified string.
   //---------------------------------------------------------------
   public Inner (String str)
   {
      message = str;
   }

   //---------------------------------------------------------------
   //  Returns this object as a string, including a value from
   //  the outer class.
   //---------------------------------------------------------------
   public String toString()
   {
      num++;
      return message + "\nOuter num = " + num;
   }
}
}
```

Each Inner object contains a public String called message. Because it is public, the changeMessages of the Outer class can reach in and modify the contents. As we've stressed many times, giving data public access should be avoided in general. However, in this case, since Inner is a private class, no class other than Outer can refer to it. Therefore no class other than Outer can directly access the public data inside it either.

> **key concept**
> If designed properly, inner classes preserve encapsulation while simplifying the implementation of related classes.

Using inner classes with public data should be done only in situations in which the outer class is completely dependent on the inner class for its existence. The nuances of nested and inner classes go beyond the scope of this text, but their basic concepts will prove useful in certain examples, particularly in the graphics track at the end of this chapter.

5.5   interfaces

We've used the term interface to refer to the public methods through which we can interact with an object. That definition is consistent with our use of it in this section, but now we are going to formalize this concept using a particular language construct in Java.

A Java *interface* is a collection of constants and abstract methods. An *abstract method* is a method that does not have an implementation. That is, there is no body of code defined for an abstract method. The header of the method, including its parameter list, is simply followed by a semicolon. An interface cannot be instantiated.

> **key concept**
> An interface is a collection of abstract methods. It cannot be instantiated.

Listing 5.9 shows an interface called `Complexity`. It contains two abstract methods: `setComplexity` and `getComplexity`.

An abstract method can be preceded by the reserved word `abstract`, though in interfaces it usually is not. Methods in interfaces have public visibility by default.

> **key concept**
> A class implements an interface, which formally defines a set of methods used to interact with objects of that class.

A class *implements* an interface by providing method implementations for each of the abstract methods defined in the interface. A class that implements an interface uses the reserved word `implements`

> **listing
> 5.9**

```
//********************************************************************
//  Complexity.java       Author: Lewis/Loftus
//
//  Represents the interface for an object that can be assigned an
//  explicit complexity.
//********************************************************************

public interface Complexity
{
    public void setComplexity (int complexity);
    public int getComplexity();
}
```

followed by the interface name in the class header. If a class asserts that it implements a particular interface, it must provide a definition for all methods in the interface. The compiler will produce errors if any of the methods in the interface are not given a definition in the class.

The Question class, shown in Listing 5.10, implements the Complexity interface. Both the setComplexity and getComplexity methods are implemented. They must be declared with the same signatures as their abstract counterparts in the interface. In the Question class, the methods are defined simply to set or return a numeric value representing the complexity level of the question that the object represents.

listing
5.10

```java
//********************************************************************
//   Question.java        Author: Lewis/Loftus
//
//   Represents a question (and its answer).
//********************************************************************

public class Question implements Complexity
{
   private String question, answer;
   private int complexityLevel;

   //-----------------------------------------------------------------
   //   Sets up the question with a default complexity.
   //-----------------------------------------------------------------
   public Question (String query, String result)
   {
      question = query;
      answer = result;
      complexityLevel = 1;
   }

   //-----------------------------------------------------------------
   //   Sets the complexity level for this question.
   //-----------------------------------------------------------------
   public void setComplexity (int level)
   {
      complexityLevel = level;
   }
```

listing
    5.10   continued

```java
    //-----------------------------------------------------------------
    //  Returns the complexity level for this question.
    //-----------------------------------------------------------------
    public int getComplexity()
    {
        return complexityLevel;
    }

    //-----------------------------------------------------------------
    //  Returns the question.
    //-----------------------------------------------------------------
    public String getQuestion()
    {
        return question;
    }

    //-----------------------------------------------------------------
    //  Returns the answer to this question.
    //-----------------------------------------------------------------
    public String getAnswer()
    {
        return answer;
    }

    //-----------------------------------------------------------------
    //  Returns true if the candidate answer matches the answer.
    //-----------------------------------------------------------------
    public boolean answerCorrect (String candidateAnswer)
    {
        return answer.equals(candidateAnswer);
    }

    //-----------------------------------------------------------------
    //  Returns this question (and its answer) as a string.
    //-----------------------------------------------------------------
    public String toString()
    {
        return question + "\n" + answer;
    }
}
```

Note that the Question class also implements additional methods that are not part of the Complexity interface. Specifically, it defines methods called getQuestion, getAnswer, answerCorrect, and toString, which have nothing to do with the interface. The interface guarantees that the class implements certain methods, but it does not restrict it from having others. It is common for a class that implements an interface to have other methods.

Listing 5.11 shows a program called MiniQuiz, which uses some Question objects.

listing
5.11

```java
//********************************************************************
//  MiniQuiz.java        Author: Lewis/Loftus
//
//  Demonstrates the use of a class that implements an interface.
//********************************************************************

import cs1.Keyboard;

public class MiniQuiz
{
   //-----------------------------------------------------------------
   //  Presents a short quiz.
   //-----------------------------------------------------------------
   public static void main (String[] args)
   {
      Question q1, q2;
      String possible;

      q1 = new Question ("What is the capital of Jamaica?",
                         "Kingston");
      q1.setComplexity (4);

      q2 = new Question ("Which is worse, ignorance or apathy?",
                         "I don't know and I don't care");
      q2.setComplexity (10);

      System.out.print (q1.getQuestion());
      System.out.println (" (Level: " + q1.getComplexity() + ")");
      possible = Keyboard.readString();
      if (q1.answerCorrect(possible))
         System.out.println ("Correct");
      else
         System.out.println ("No, the answer is " + q1.getAnswer());
```

listing
    5.11   continued

```
        System.out.println();
        System.out.print (q2.getQuestion());
        System.out.println (" (Level: " + q2.getComplexity() + ")");
        possible = Keyboard.readString();
        if (q2.answerCorrect(possible))
            System.out.println ("Correct");
        else
            System.out.println ("No, the answer is " + q2.getAnswer());
    }
}
```

output

```
What is the capital of Jamaica? (Level: 4)
Kingston
Correct

Which is worse, ignorance or apathy? (Level: 10)
apathy
No, the answer is I don't know and I don't care
```

An interface—as well as its relationship to a class that implements it—can be shown in a UML diagram. An interface is represented similarly to a class node except that the designation <<interface>> is inserted above the class name. A dotted arrow with an open arrowhead is drawn from the class to the interface that it implements. Figure 5.6 shows a UML class diagram for the MiniQuiz program.

Multiple classes can implement the same interface, providing alternative definitions for the methods. For example, we could implement a class called Task that also implements the Complexity interface. In it we could choose to manage the complexity of a task in a different way (though it would still have to implement all the methods of the interface).

A class can implement more than one interface. In these cases, the class must provide an implementation for all methods in all interfaces listed. To show that a class implements multiple interfaces, they are listed in the implements clause, separated by commas. For example:

```
class ManyThings implements interface1, interface2, interface3
{
    // all methods of all interfaces
}
```

In addition to, or instead of, abstract methods, an interface can also contain constants, defined using the `final` modifier. When a class implements an interface, it gains access to all of the constants defined in it. This mechanism allows multiple classes to share a set of constants that are defined in a single location.

The interface construct formally defines the ways in which we can interact with a class. It also serves as a basis for a powerful programming technique called polymorphism, which we discuss in Chapter 7.

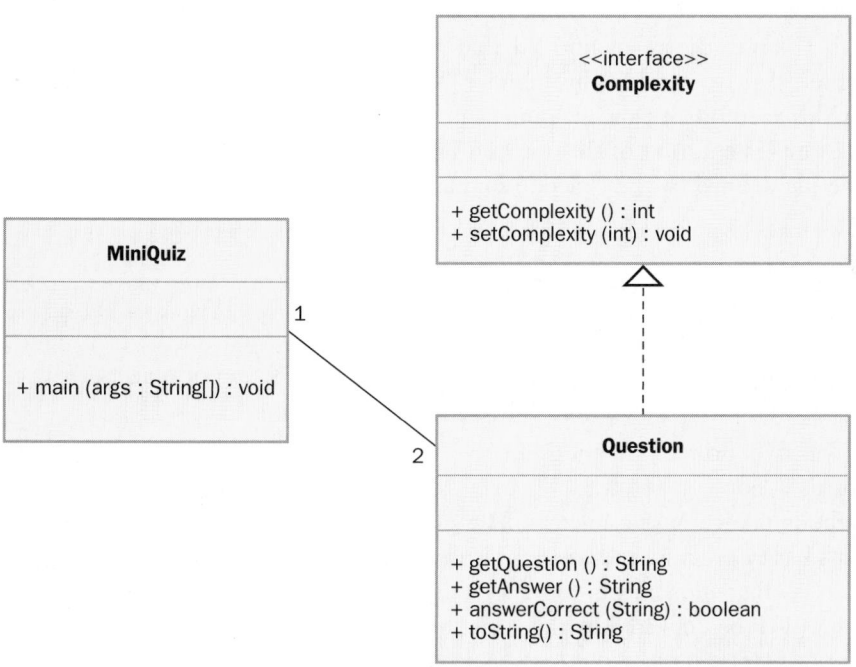

figure 5.6   A UML class diagram for the MiniQuiz program

the `Comparable` interface

The Java standard class library contains interfaces as well as classes. The `Comparable` interface, for example, is defined in the `java.lang` package. It contains only one method, `compareTo`, which takes an object as a parameter and returns an integer.

The intention of this interface is to provide a common mechanism for comparing one object to another. One object calls the method and passes another as a parameter as follows:

```
if (obj1.compareTo(obj2) < 0)
    System.out.println ("obj1 is less than obj2");
```

As specified by the documentation for the interface, the integer that is returned from the `compareTo` method should be negative if `obj1` is less than `obj2`, 0 if they are equal, and positive if `obj1` is greater than `obj2`. It is up to the designer of each class to decide what it means for one object of that class to be less than, equal to, or greater than another.

In Chapter 3, we mentioned that the `String` class contains a `compareTo` method that operates in this manner. Now we can clarify that the `String` class has this method because it implements the `Comparable` interface. The `String` class implementation of this method bases the comparison on the lexicographic ordering defined by the Unicode character set.

the `Iterator` interface

The `Iterator` interface is another interface defined as part of the Java standard class library. It is used by classes that represent a collection of objects, providing a means to move through the collection one object at a time.

The two primary methods in the `Iterator` interface are `hasNext`, which returns a boolean result, and `next`, which returns an object. Neither of these methods takes any parameters. The `hasNext` method returns true if there are items left to process, and `next` returns the next object. It is up to the designer of the class that implements the `Iterator` interface to decide the order in which objects will be delivered by the `next` method.

We should note that, according to the spirit of the interface, the `next` method does not remove the object from the underlying collection; it simply returns a reference to it. The `Iterator` interface also has a method called `remove`, which takes no parameters and has a `void` return type. A call to the `remove` method removes the object that was most recently returned by the `next` method from the underlying collection.

The Iterator interface is an improved version of an older interface called Enumeration, which is still part of the Java standard class library. The Enumeration interface does not have a remove method. Generally, the Iterator interface is the preferred choice between the two.

We explore an example that uses the Iterator interface later in this text.

5.6 dialog boxes

A *dialog box* is a graphical window that pops up on top of any currently active window so that the user can interact with it. A dialog box can serve a variety of purposes, such as conveying some information, confirming an action, or allowing the user to enter some information. Usually a dialog box has a solitary purpose, and the user's interaction with it is brief.

The Swing package (javax.swing) of the Java class library contains a class called JOptionPane that simplifies the creation and use of basic dialog boxes. Figure 5.7 lists some of the methods of JOptionPane.

The basic formats for a JOptionPane dialog box fall into three categories. A *message dialog* simply displays an output string. An *input dialog* presents a prompt and a single input text field into which the user can enter one string of data. A *confirm dialog* presents the user with a simple yes-or-no question.

> **key concept**
>
> JOptionPane is a Swing class that facilitates the creation of dialog boxes.

Let's look at a program that uses each of these types of dialog boxes. Listing 5.12 shows a program that first presents the user with an input dialog box requesting that an integer be entered. After the user presses the OK button on the

---

```
static String showInputDialog (Object msg)
    Displays a dialog box containg the specified message and an input text
field. The contents of the text field are returned.

static int showConfirmDialog (Component parent, Object msg)
    Displays a dialog box containing the specified message and Yes/No
button options. If the parent component is null, the box is centered on the screen.

static int showMessageDialog (Component parent, Object msg)
    Displays a dialog box containing the specified message. If the parent
component is null, the box is centered on the screen.
```

figure 5.7   Some methods of the JOptionPane class

listing
5.12

```java
//********************************************************************
//  EvenOdd.java        Author: Lewis/Loftus
//
//  Demonstrates the use of the JOptionPane class.
//********************************************************************

import javax.swing.JOptionPane;

public class EvenOdd
{
   //-----------------------------------------------------------------
   //  Determines if the value input by the user is even or odd.
   //  Uses multiple dialog boxes for user interaction.
   //-----------------------------------------------------------------
   public static void main (String[] args)
   {
      String numStr, result;
      int num, again;

      do
      {
         numStr = JOptionPane.showInputDialog ("Enter an integer: ");

         num = Integer.parseInt(numStr);

         result = "That number is " + ((num%2 == 0) ? "even" : "odd");

         JOptionPane.showMessageDialog (null, result);

         again = JOptionPane.showConfirmDialog (null, "Do Another?");
      }
      while (again == JOptionPane.YES_OPTION);
   }
}
```

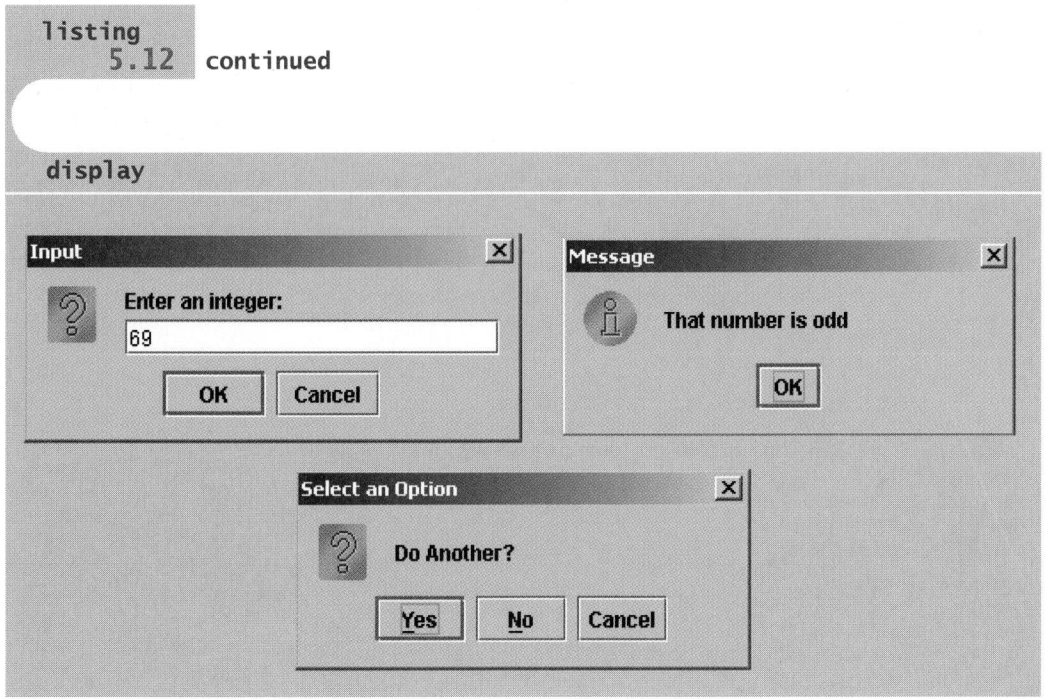

input dialog, a second dialog box (this time a message dialog) appears informing the user whether the number entered was even or odd. After the user dismisses that box, a third dialog box appears to determine if the user would like to test another number. If the user presses the button labeled Yes, the series of dialog boxes repeats. Otherwise the program terminates.

The first parameter to the showMessageDialog and the showConfirmDialog methods specifies the governing parent component for the dialog. Using a null reference as this parameter causes the dialog box to appear centered on the screen.

Many of the JOptionPane methods are overloaded in various ways to allow the programmer to tailor the contents of the dialog box. Furthermore, the showOptionDialog method can be used to create dialog boxes that combine characteristics of the three basic formats for more elaborate interactions. Details of these methods can be found in the class summary in Appendix M.

5.7 graphical user interfaces

Dialog boxes provide a brief glimpse into the world of graphical user interfaces (GUIs) by permitting a user to interact with graphical elements such as buttons and text boxes. However, in general, their interaction is limited by the predefined nature of the dialog boxes. Furthermore, a GUI is far more than a series of dialog boxes that pop up as needed. A GUI is a well-designed layout of interactive graphical components. There is usually significant programming logic designed to respond to the various ways a user can interact with a GUI.

essential GUI elements

A GUI in Java is created with at least three kinds of objects:

- components
- events
- listeners

A GUI *component* is an object that defines a screen element to display information or allow the user to interact with a program in a certain way. Examples of GUI components include push buttons, text fields, labels, scroll bars, and menus. A *container* is a special type of component that is used to hold and organize other components. A dialog box and an applet are examples of container components.

An *event* is an object that represents some occurrence in which we may be interested. Often, events correspond to user actions, such as pressing a mouse button or typing a key on the keyboard. Most GUI components generate events to indicate a user action related to that component. For example, a component representing a button will generate an event to indicate that it has been pushed. A program that is oriented around a GUI, responding to events from the user, is called *event-driven*.

> **key concept**
>
> A GUI is made up of graphical components, events that represent user actions, and listeners that respond to those events.

A *listener* is an object that is "waiting" for an event to occur and that can respond in some way when it does. The programmer must carefully establish the relationships among the listener, the event it listens for, and the component that will generate the event.

The remainder of this chapter introduces these essential elements of a GUI. The graphic tracks in subsequent chapters expand on each of these topics, and discuss additional events and components as well as additional features of components already introduced. Chapter 9 is devoted to a complete discussion of GUI issues, building on your evolving understanding of these topics.

creating GUIs

To create a Java program that uses a GUI, we must:

▶ define and set up the necessary components,

▶ create listener objects and establish the relationship between the listeners and the components which generate the events of interest, and

▶ define what happens as a result of the various user interactions that could occur.

Let's look at an example that performs these activities. The PushCounter program shown in Listing 5.13 is an applet that presents the user with a single push button (labeled "Push Me!"). Each time the button is pushed, a counter is updated and displayed.

listing
  5.13

```
//********************************************************************
//  PushCounter.java        Authors: Lewis/Loftus
//
//  Demonstrates a graphical user interface and an event listener.
//********************************************************************

import java.awt.*;
import java.awt.event.*;
import javax.swing.*;

public class PushCounter extends JApplet
{
   private int APPLET_WIDTH = 300, APPLET_HEIGHT = 35;
   private int pushes;
   private JLabel label;
   private JButton push;

   //-----------------------------------------------------------
   //  Sets up the GUI.
   //-----------------------------------------------------------
   public void init ()
   {
      pushes = 0;

      push = new JButton ("Push Me!");
      push.addActionListener (new ButtonListener());
```

listing
5.13   continued

```java
    label = new JLabel ("Pushes: " + Integer.toString (pushes));

    Container cp = getContentPane();
    cp.setBackground (Color.cyan);
    cp.setLayout (new FlowLayout());
    cp.add (push);
    cp.add (label);

    setSize (APPLET_WIDTH, APPLET_HEIGHT);
  }


  //**********************************************************************
  //  Represents a listener for button push (action) events.
  //**********************************************************************
  private class ButtonListener implements ActionListener
  {
    //-------------------------------------------------------------------
    //  Updates the counter when the button is pushed.
    //-------------------------------------------------------------------
    public void actionPerformed (ActionEvent event)
    {
      pushes++;
      label.setText("Pushes: " + Integer.toString (pushes));
      repaint ();
    }
  }
}
```

display

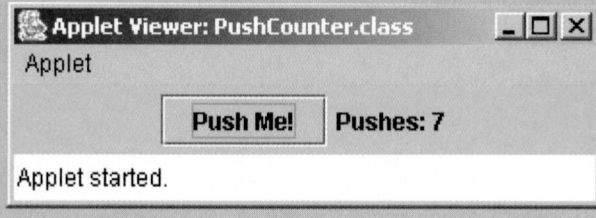

The components used in this program include a button, a label, and the applet window that contains them. These components are defined by the classes JButton, JLabel, and JApplet, respectively. These components are all part of the Swing package (javax.swing). In Chapter 1 we mentioned that the Swing package contains components that surpass those defined in the original AWT package. These include JApplet, which is the Swing version of the Applet class that we've used previously.

A *push button* is a component that allows the user to initiate an action with a press of the mouse. A *label* is a component that displays a line of text in a GUI. Labels are generally used to display information or to identify other components in the GUI. Both push buttons and labels are fundamental components that can be found in almost any GUI.

The init method of the applet sets up the GUI. The JButton constructor takes a String parameter that specifies the label on the button. The JLabel constructor also takes a String parameter, which defines the initial content of the label.

The only event of interest in this program occurs when the button is pushed. To respond to an event, we must do two things: create a listener object for the event and add that listener to the graphical component that generates the event. The listener object can contain a method that is called by the component whenever that event occurs.

> A listener object contains a method that is called whenever an event occurs.
>
> *key concept*

A JButton generates an *action event* when it is pushed. Therefore we need an action event listener. In this program, we define the ButtonListener class as the listener for this event. In the init method, the listener object is instantiated and then added to the button using the addActionListener method.

GUI components must be added to the container in which they are displayed. In this example, the init method adds each component to the applet container. More precisely, the button and label components are added to the *content pane* that represents the primary container for the applet. The content pane is retrieved using the getContentPane method of the JApplet class. The components are then added to the content pane using the add method. The background color of the content pane is set using the setBackground method. The layout manager for the pane is set to a flow layout so that components are placed top to bottom and left to right in each row as permitted by the width of the pane. (We discuss layout managers in detail in Chapter 9.)

Now let's take a closer look at the ButtonListener class. A common technique for creating a listener object is to define a class that implements a *listener interface.* The Java standard class library contains a set of interfaces for various event categories. For example, the interface for an action event is called `ActionListener`. Recall from the discussion of interfaces earlier in this chapter that an interface defines a set of methods that a class must implement. The `ActionListener` interface specifies only one method, called `actionPerformed`.

key concept

Inner classes are often used to define listener objects.

Therefore the `ButtonListener` class implements the `ActionListener` interface. The `actionPerformed` method takes one parameter of type `ActionEvent`. Note that `ButtonListener` is implemented as an inner class, nested inside the primary applet class. Inner classes are often used to define listener objects.

When the button is pushed, the `JButton` object invokes the `actionPerformed` method of any listener that has been added to it. The `JButton` object generates an `ActionEvent` object and passes it into the `actionPerformed` method. If necessary, a listener can get information about the event from this parameter. In this program, however, it is sufficient to know that the button was pushed. The `actionPerformed` method responds by updating the counter used to keep track of the number of times the button has been pushed, updating the content of the label using the `setText` method of the `JLabel` class, and causing the applet to repaint itself (so that the label is displayed correctly).

GUI applications

Let's look at another example that uses some additional components. The `Fahrenheit` program shown in Listing 5.14 is implemented as an application, not an applet. The `main` method of the program instantiates the `FahrenheitGUI` class and invokes its `display` method.

The program converts a temperature on the Fahrenheit scale into its equivalent Celsius value. The user types an input value into a text field. A *text field* is a component that displays an area into which the user can type a single line of information. Text fields are commonly used in GUI programs as a means to accept input. In this program, when the user enters a value and presses the enter key, the result is computed and displayed using a label.

key concept

A frame is a container that is often used to display the interface for a standalone GUI application.

In the `PushCounter` applet, the applet window served as the primary container of the GUI. However, because the `Fahrenheit` program is an application, we need a different container. A *frame* is a container component that is generally used for standalone GUI-based applications. A

listing
    5.14

```
//*************************************************************************
//   Fahrenheit.java        Author: Lewis/Loftus
//
//   Demonstrates the use of JFrame and JTextArea GUI components.
//*************************************************************************

public class Fahrenheit
{
   //----------------------------------------------------------------
   //  Creates and displays the temperature converter GUI.
   //----------------------------------------------------------------
   public static void main (String[] args)
   {
      FahrenheitGUI converter = new FahrenheitGUI();
      converter.display();
   }
}
```

display

frame is displayed as a separate window with its own title bar. The Fahrenheit
program is executed just like any other application, but instead of interacting
with it through prompts in the command window, the application displays its
own frame containing the program's graphical interface.

Listing 5.15 shows the FahrenheitGUI class. Its constructor sets up the GUI.
First it creates a frame using the JFrame class. The JFrame constructor accepts a
String parameter that will be shown in the title bar of the frame when it is displayed. The setDefaultCloseOperation method is used to specify what will
happen when the close button on the frame is pushed. In this case, we specify that

listing
    5.15

```java
//********************************************************************
//   FahrenheitGUI.java        Author: Lewis/Loftus
//
//   Demonstrates the use of JFrame and JTextArea GUI components.
//********************************************************************

import java.awt.*;
import java.awt.event.*;
import javax.swing.*;

public class FahrenheitGUI
{
    private int WIDTH = 300;
    private int HEIGHT = 75;

    private JFrame frame;
    private JPanel panel;
    private JLabel inputLabel, outputLabel, resultLabel;
    private JTextField fahrenheit;

    //-----------------------------------------------------------------
    //   Sets up the GUI.
    //-----------------------------------------------------------------
    public FahrenheitGUI()
    {
        frame = new JFrame ("Temperature Conversion");
        frame.setDefaultCloseOperation (JFrame.EXIT_ON_CLOSE);

        inputLabel = new JLabel ("Enter Fahrenheit temperature:");
        outputLabel = new JLabel ("Temperature in Celcius: ");
        resultLabel = new JLabel ("---");

        fahrenheit = new JTextField (5);
        fahrenheit.addActionListener (new TempListener());

        panel = new JPanel();
        panel.setPreferredSize (new Dimension(WIDTH, HEIGHT));
        panel.setBackground (Color.yellow);
        panel.add (inputLabel);
        panel.add (fahrenheit);
        panel.add (outputLabel);
        panel.add (resultLabel);

        frame.getContentPane().add (panel);
    }
```

listing
   5.15 continued

```java
//-----------------------------------------------------------------
//  Displays the primary application frame.
//-----------------------------------------------------------------
public void display()
{
    frame.pack();
    frame.show();
}

//*****************************************************************
//  Represents an action listener for the temperature input field.
//*****************************************************************
private class TempListener implements ActionListener
{
    //-----------------------------------------------------------------
    //  Performs the conversion when the enter key is pressed in
    //  the text field.
    //-----------------------------------------------------------------
    public void actionPerformed (ActionEvent event)
    {
        int fahrenheitTemp, celciusTemp;

        String text = fahrenheit.getText();

        fahrenheitTemp = Integer.parseInt (text);
        celciusTemp = (fahrenheitTemp-32) * 5/9;

        resultLabel.setText (Integer.toString (celciusTemp));
    }
}
}
```

the program should terminate (exit) when the frame is closed. This is a typical way to define the end of an event-driven application.

Another container used in this program is created using the JPanel class. A *panel* is a container; however, unlike a frame, it cannot be displayed on its own. A panel must be added to another container. Its role is to help organize the components in a GUI.

The size of a panel can be specified using its `setPreferredSize` method, which takes as a parameter a `Dimension` object. (A `Dimension` object encapsulates the height and width of a component into one object.) The background color of a panel can be set using the `setBackground` method. Components are added to the panel using the `add` method. In the `Fahrenheit` example, once the entire panel is set up, it is added to the content pane of the frame.

The components added to the panel in this program are three labels and a text field. A text field is defined by the `JTextField` class. The constructor of the `JTextField` class accepts an integer that indicates how many characters the text field should be able to display.

Note that the order in which the labels and text field are added to the panel dictates the order in which they appear. The size of the panel determines how the components line up relative to each other. This is actually a function of the layout manager. Panels, by default, are governed by a flow layout, which we explore in detail in Chapter 9.

The `display` method of the `FahrenheitGUI` class invokes the `pack` and `show` methods of the frame. The `pack` method sizes the frame to fit the components that have been added to it, which in this case is the panel. The `show` method causes the frame to be displayed on the monitor screen.

Note that the program responds only when the user presses the enter key inside the text field. A `JTextField` object generates an action event when the enter key is pressed. This is the same event that occurs when a button is pressed, as we saw in the `PushCounter` example. The `TempListener` class is set up as the action listener for this program. Note that it is implemented as an inner class, which gives it easy access to the components stored in the enclosing class.

In the `actionPerformed` method, the input string is obtained using the `getText` method of the `JTextField` class. Then the input text is converted to a numeric value, the equivalent Celsius temperature is computed, and the text of the output label is set.

summary of
key concepts

▸ An object reference variable stores the address of an object.

▸ The reserved word `null` represents a reference that does not point to a valid object.

▸ The `this` reference always refers to the currently executing object.

▸ Several references can refer to the same object. These references are aliases of each other.

▸ The `==` operator compares object references for equality, returning true if the references are aliases of each other.

▸ The `equals` method can be defined to determine equality between objects in any way we consider appropriate.

▸ If an object has no references to it, a program cannot use it. Java performs automatic garbage collection by periodically reclaiming the memory space occupied by these objects.

▸ When an object is passed to a method, the actual and formal parameters become aliases of each other.

▸ A static variable is shared among all instances of a class.

▸ A method is made static by using the `static` modifier in the method declaration.

▸ A wrapper class represents a primitive value so that it can be treated as an object.

▸ If designed properly, inner classes preserve encapsulation while simplifying the implementation of related classes.

▸ An interface is a collection of abstract methods. It cannot be instantiated.

▸ A class implements an interface, which formally defines a set of methods used to interact with objects of that class.

▸ `JOptionPane` is a Swing class that facilitates the creation of dialog boxes.

▸ A GUI is made up of graphical components, events that represent user actions, and listeners that respond to those events.

▸ A listener object contains a method that is called whenever an event occurs.

▸ Inner classes are often used to define listener objects.

▶ A frame is a container that is often used to display the interface for a standalone GUI application.

▶ A panel is a container used to organize other components. It cannot be displayed on its own.

self-review questions

5.1   What is a null reference?

5.2   What does the `this` reference refer to?

5.3   What is an alias? How does it relate to garbage collection?

5.4   How are objects passed as parameters?

5.5   What is the difference between a static variable and an instance variable?

5.6   How can we represent a primitive value as an object?

5.7   What are some of the issues of Java keyboard input that the `Keyboard` class hides?

5.8   Why might you declare an inner class?

5.9   What is the difference between a class and an interface?

5.10   What is a dialog box?

5.11   What is the relationship between an event and a listener?

5.12   Can a GUI-based program be implemented as a standalone application? Explain.

exercises

5.1   Discuss the manner in which Java passes parameters to a method. Is this technique consistent between primitive types and objects? Explain.

5.2   Explain why a static method cannot refer to an instance variable.

5.3   Can a class implement two interfaces that each contains the same method signature? Explain.

5.4   Create an interface called `Visible` that includes two methods: `makeVisible` and `makeInvisible`. Both methods should take no parameters and should return a `boolean` result. Describe how a class might implement this interface.

5.5   Draw a UML class diagram that shows the relationships among the elements of Exercise 5.4.

5.6   Create an interface called `VCR` that has methods that represent the standard operations on a video cassette recorder (play, stop, etc.). Define the method signatures any way you desire. Describe how a class might implement this interface.

5.7   Draw a UML class diagram that shows the relationships among the elements of Exercise 5.6.

5.8   Draw a UML class diagram that shows the relationships among the classes used in the `PushCounter` program.

5.9   Draw a UML class diagram that shows the relationships among the classes used in the `Fahrenheit` program.

programming projects

5.1   Modify the `PigLatinTranslator` class from Chapter 4 so that its `translate` method is static. Modify the `PigLatin` class so that it invokes the method correctly.

5.2   Modify the `Rational` class from Chapter 4 so that it implements the `Comparable` interface. To perform the comparison, compute an equivalent floating point value from the numerator and denominator for both `Rational` objects, then compare them using a tolerance value of 0.0001. Write a main driver to test your modifications.

5.3   Design a Java interface called `Priority` that includes two methods: `setPriority` and `getPriority`. The interface should define a way to establish numeric priority among a set of objects. Design and implement a class called `Task` that represents a task (such as on a to-do list) that implements the `Priority` interface. Create a driver class to exercise some `Task` objects.

5.4   Modify the `Task` class from Programming Project 5.3 so that it also implements the `Complexity` interface defined in this chapter. Modify the driver class to show these new features of `Task` objects.

5.5   Modify the `Task` class from Programming Projects 5.3 and 5.4 so that it also implements the `Comparable` interface from the Java standard class library. Implement the interface such that the tasks are ranked by priority. Create a driver class whose `main` method shows these new features of `Task` objects.

5.6   Design a Java interface called `Lockable` that includes the following methods: `setKey`, `lock`, `unlock`, and `locked`. The `setKey`, `lock`, and `unlock` methods take an integer parameter that represents the key. The `setKey` method establishes the key. The `lock` and `unlock` methods lock and unlock the object, but only if the key passed in is correct. The `locked` method returns a boolean that indicates whether or not the object is locked. A `Lockable` object represents an object whose regular methods are protected: if the object is locked, the methods cannot be invoked; if it is unlocked, they can be invoked. Redesign and implement a version of the `Coin` class from Chapter 4 so that it is `Lockable`.

5.7   Redesign and implement a version of the `Account` class from Chapter 4 so that it is `Lockable` as defined by Programming Project 5.6.

5.8   Design and implement an application that uses dialog boxes to obtain two integer values (one dialog box for each value) and display the sum and product of the values. Use another dialog box to see whether the user wants to process another pair of values.

5.9   Redesign and implement a version of the `PalindromeTester` program from Chapter 3 so that it uses dialog boxes to obtain the input string, display the results, and prompt to continue.

5.10 Modify the `Fahrenheit` program from this chapter so that it displays a button that, when pressed, also causes the conversion calculation to take place. (That is, the user will now have the option of pressing enter in the text field or pressing the button.) Have the listener that is already defined for the text field also listen for the button push.

5.11 Design and implement an application that displays a button and a label. Every time the button is pushed, the label should display a random number between 1 and 100, inclusive.

5.12 Redesign and implement a version of the `PigLatin` program from Chapter 4 so that it uses a GUI. Accept the sentence using a text field and display the results using a label.

5.13 Design and implement an application that presents two buttons and a label to the user. Label the buttons Increment and Decrement, respectively. Display a numeric value (initially 50) using the label. Each time the increment button is pushed, increment the value displayed. Likewise, each time the decrement button is pressed, decrement the value displayed.

5.14 Design and implement an application that serves as a mortgage calculator. Accept the mortgage amount, the interest rate, and the loan duration (number of years) using three text fields. When the user presses a button, determine and display the total of the monthly payments and the amount of interest that will be paid.

answers to self-review questions

5.1 A null reference is a reference that does not refer to any object. The reserved word null can be used to check for null references before following them.

5.2 The this reference always refers to the currently executing object. A non-static method of a class is written generically for all objects of the class, but it is invoked through a particular object. The this reference, therefore, refers to the object through which that method is currently being executed.

5.3 Two references are aliases of each other if they refer to the same object. Changing the state of the object through one reference changes it for the other because there is actually only one object. An object is marked for garbage collection only when there are no valid references to it.

5.4 Objects are passed to methods by copying the reference to the object (its address). Therefore the actual and formal parameters of a method become aliases of each other.

5.5 Memory space for an instance variable is created for each object that is instantiated from a class. A static variable is shared among all objects of a class.

5.6 A wrapper class is defined in the Java standard class library for each primitive type. In situations where objects are called for, an object created from a wrapper class may suffice.

5.7   The Keyboard class hides the declaration of a useful standard input stream, handles exceptions that may occur, and performs data type conversions.

5.8   An inner class is useful when two classes are tightly related and one regularly changes the state of the other. If designed properly, an inner class can preserve encapsulation while simplifying the implementations of both classes.

5.9   A class can be instantiated; an interface cannot. An interface contains a set of abstract methods for which a class provides the implementation.

5.10 A dialog box is a small window that appears for the purpose of conveying information, confirming an action, or accepting input. Generally, dialog boxes are used in specific situations for brief user interactions.

5.11 Events usually represent user actions. A listener object is set up to listen for a certain event to be generated from a particular component.

5.12 A GUI-based program can be implemented as a standalone application. The application needs a window such as a frame to serve as a container for the GUI elements of the program.

In our programming efforts, we often want to organize objects or primitive data in a form that is easy to access and modify. This chapter introduces arrays, which are programming constructs that group data into lists. Arrays are a fundamental component of most high-level languages. We also explore the `ArrayList` class in the Java standard class library, which provides capabilities similar to arrays, with additional features.

chapter
objectives

▶ Define and use arrays for basic data organization.

▶ Describe how arrays and array elements are passed as parameters.

▶ Explore how arrays and other objects can be combined to manage complex information.

▶ Describe the use of multidimensional arrays.

▶ Examine the `ArrayList` class and the costs of its versatility.

6.0 arrays

An *array* is a simple but powerful programming language construct used to group and organize data. When writing a program that manages a large amount of information, such as a list of 100 names, it is not practical to declare separate variables for each piece of data. Arrays solve this problem by letting us declare one variable that can hold multiple, individually accessible values.

array indexing

An array is a list of values. Each value is stored at a specific, numbered position in the array. The number corresponding to each position is called an *index* or a *subscript*. Figure 6.1 shows an array of integers and the indexes that correspond to each position. The array is called `height`; it contains integers that represent several peoples' heights in inches.

In Java, array indexes always begin at zero. Therefore the value stored at index 5 is actually the sixth value in the array. The array shown in Fig. 6.1 has 11 values, indexed from 0 to 10.

To access a value in an array, we use the name of the array followed by the index in square brackets. For example, the following expression refers to the ninth value in the array `height`:

```
height[8]
```

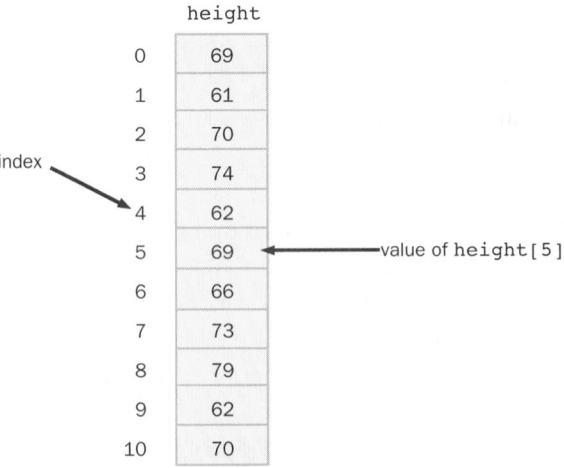

figure 6.1   An array called `height` containing integer values

According to Fig. 6.1, `height[8]` (pronounced height-sub-eight) contains the value 79. Don't confuse the value of the index, in this case 8, with the value stored in the array at that index, in this case 79.

The expression `height[8]` refers to a single integer stored at a particular memory location. It can be used wherever an integer variable can be used. Therefore you can assign a value to it, use it in calculations, print its value, and so on. Furthermore, because array indexes are integers, you can use integer expressions to specify the index used to access an array. These concepts are demonstrated in the following lines of code:

```
height[2] = 72;
height[count] = feet * 12;
average = (height[0] + height[1] + height[2]) / 3;
System.out.println ("The middle value is " + height[MAX/2]);
pick = height[rand.nextInt(11)];
```

declaring and using arrays

In Java, arrays are objects. To create an array, the reference to the array must be declared. The array can then be instantiated using the `new` operator, which allocates memory space to store values. The following code represents the declaration for the array shown in Fig. 6.1:

> **key concept**
>
> In Java, an array is an object. Memory space for the array elements is reserved by instantiating the array using the `new` operator.

```
int[] height = new int[11];
```

The variable `height` is declared to be an array of integers whose type is written as `int[]`. All values stored in an array have the same type (or are at least compatible). For example, we can create an array that can hold integers or an array that can hold strings, but not an array that can hold both integers and strings. An array can be set up to hold any primitive type or any object (class) type. A value stored in an array is sometimes called an *array element*, and the type of values that an array holds is called the *element type* of the array.

Note that the type of the array variable (`int[]`) does not include the size of the array. The instantiation of `height`, using the `new` operator, reserves the memory space to store 11 integers indexed from 0 to 10. Once an array is declared to be a certain size, the number of values it can hold cannot be changed.

The example shown in Listing 6.1 creates an array called `list` that can hold 15 integers, which it loads with successive increments of 10. It then changes the value of the sixth element in the array (at index 5). Finally, it prints all values stored in the array.

```
//********************************************************************
//   BasicArray.java         Author: Lewis/Loftus
//
//   Demonstrates basic array declaration and use.
//********************************************************************

public class BasicArray
{
   final static int LIMIT = 15;
   final static int MULTIPLE = 10;

   //-----------------------------------------------------------------
   //   Creates an array, fills it with various integer values,
   //   modifies one value, then prints them out.
   //-----------------------------------------------------------------
   public static void main (String[] args)
   {
      int[] list = new int[LIMIT];

      //   Initialize the array values
      for (int index = 0; index < LIMIT; index++)
         list[index] = index * MULTIPLE;

      list[5] = 999;   // change one array value

      for (int index = 0; index < LIMIT; index++)
         System.out.print (list[index] + "   ");

      System.out.println ();
   }
}
```

output

0   10   20   30   40   999   60   70   80   90   100   110   120   130   140

Figure 6.2 shows the array as it changes during the execution of the BasicArray program. It is often convenient to use for loops when handling arrays because the number of positions in the array is constant. Note that a constant called LIMIT is used in several places in the BasicArray program. This con-

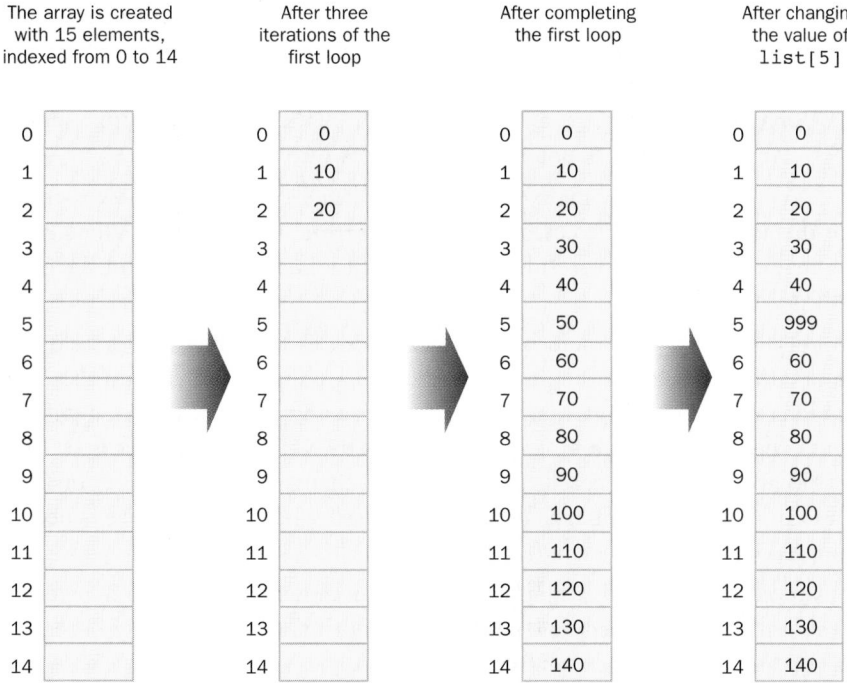

figure 6.2   The array `list` as it changes in the `BasicArray` program

stant is used to declare the size of the array, to control the `for` loop that initializes the array values, and to control the `for` loop that prints the values. The use of constants in this way is a good practice. It makes a program more readable and easier to modify. For instance, if the size of the array needed to change, only one line of code (the constant declaration) would need to be modified. We'll see another way to handle this situation in upcoming examples in this chapter.

The square brackets used to indicate the index of an array are treated as an operator in Java. Therefore, just like the + operator or the <= operator, the index operator (`[ ]`) has a precedence relative to the other Java operators that determines when it is executed. It has the highest precedence of all Java operators.

The index operator performs *automatic bounds checking*. Bounds checking ensures that the index is in range for the array being referenced. Whenever a reference to an array element is made, the index must be greater than or equal to zero and less than the size of the array. For example, suppose an array called `prices` is created with 25 elements. The valid indexes for the array are from 0 to

key concept

> Bounds checking ensures that an index used to refer to an array element is in range. The Java index operator performs automatic bounds checking.

24. Whenever a reference is made to a particular element in the array (such as prices[count]), the value of the index is checked. If it is in the valid range of indexes for the array (0 to 24), the reference is carried out. If the index is not valid, an exception called ArrayIndexOutOfBoundsException is thrown.

Because array indexes begin at zero and go up to one less than the size of the array, it is easy to create *off-by-one errors* in a program. When referencing array elements, be careful to ensure that the index stays within the array bounds.

Another important characteristic of Java arrays is that their size is held in a constant called length in the array object. It is a public constant and therefore can be referenced directly. For example, after the array prices is created with 25 elements, the constant prices.length contains the value 25. Its value is set once when the array is first created and cannot be changed. The length constant, which is an integral part of each array, can be used when the array size is needed without having to create a separate constant.

Let's look at another example. The program shown in Listing 6.2 reads 10 integers into an array called numbers, and then prints them in reverse order.

listing
  6.2

```
//********************************************************************
//  ReverseOrder.java        Author: Lewis/Loftus
//
//  Demonstrates array index processing.
//********************************************************************

import cs1.Keyboard;

public class ReverseOrder
{
    //-----------------------------------------------------------------
    //  Reads a list of numbers from the user, storing them in an
    //  array, then prints them in the opposite order.
    //-----------------------------------------------------------------
    public static void main (String[] args)
    {
        double[] numbers = new double[10];

        System.out.println ("The size of the array: " + numbers.length);
```

listing
    6.2   continued

```
for (int index = 0; index < numbers.length; index++)
{
    System.out.print ("Enter number " + (index+1) + ": ");
    numbers[index] = Keyboard.readDouble();
}

System.out.println ("The numbers in reverse order:");

for (int index = numbers.length-1; index >= 0; index--)
    System.out.print (numbers[index] + "  ");

System.out.println ();
    }
}
```

output

```
The size of the array: 10
Enter number 1: 18.36
Enter number 2: 48.9
Enter number 3: 53.5
Enter number 4: 29.06
Enter number 5: 72.404
Enter number 6: 34.8
Enter number 7: 63.41
Enter number 8: 45.55
Enter number 9: 69.0
Enter number 10: 99.18
The numbers in reverse order:
99.18   69.0   45.55   63.41   34.8   72.404   29.06   53.5   48.9   18.36
```

Note that in the ReverseOrder program, the array numbers is declared to have 10 elements and therefore is indexed from 0 to 9. The index range is controlled in the for loops by using the length field of the array object. You should carefully set the initial value of loop control variables and the conditions that terminate loops to guarantee that all intended elements are processed and only valid indexes are used to reference an array element.

The LetterCount example, shown in Listing 6.3, uses two arrays and a String object. The array called upper is used to store the number of times each uppercase alphabetic letter is found in the string. The array called lower serves the same purpose for lowercase letters.

listing
    6.3

```
//*****************************************************************
//  LetterCount.java         Author: Lewis/Loftus
//
//  Demonstrates the relationship between arrays and strings.
//*****************************************************************

import cs1.Keyboard;

public class LetterCount
{
   //---------------------------------------------------------------
   //  Reads a sentence from the user and counts the number of
   //  uppercase and lowercase letters contained in it.
   //---------------------------------------------------------------
   public static void main (String[] args)
   {
      final int NUMCHARS = 26;

      int[] upper = new int[NUMCHARS];
      int[] lower = new int[NUMCHARS];

      char current;    // the current character being processed
      int other = 0;   // counter for non-alphabetics

      System.out.println ("Enter a sentence:");
      String line = Keyboard.readString();

      //  Count the number of each letter occurence
      for (int ch = 0; ch < line.length(); ch++)
      {
         current = line.charAt(ch);
         if (current >= 'A' && current <= 'Z')
            upper[current-'A']++;
         else
            if (current >= 'a' && current <= 'z')
               lower[current-'a']++;
            else
               other++;
      }

      //  Print the results
      System.out.println ();
      for (int letter=0; letter < upper.length; letter++)
```

listing
6.3   continued

```
    {
        System.out.print ( (char) (letter + 'A') );
        System.out.print (": " + upper[letter]);
        System.out.print ("\t\t" + (char) (letter + 'a') );
        System.out.println (": " + lower[letter]);
    }

    System.out.println ();
    System.out.println ("Non-alphabetic characters: " + other);
    }
}
```

output

```
Enter a sentence:
In Casablanca, Humphrey Bogart never says "Play it again, Sam."
A: 0              a: 10
B: 1              b: 1
C: 1              c: 1
D: 0              d: 0
E: 0              e: 3
F: 0              f: 0
G: 0              g: 2
H: 1              h: 1
I: 1              i: 2
J: 0              j: 0
K: 0              k: 0
L: 0              l: 2
M: 0              m: 2
N: 0              n: 4
O: 0              o: 1
P: 1              p: 1
Q: 0              q: 0
R: 0              r: 3
S: 1              s: 3
T: 0              t: 2
U: 0              u: 1
V: 0              v: 1
W: 0              w: 0
X: 0              x: 0
Y: 0              y: 3
Z: 0              z: 0

Non-alphabetic characters: 14
```

Because there are 26 letters in the English alphabet, both the `upper` and `lower` arrays are declared with 26 elements. Each element contains an integer that is initially zero by default. The `for` loop scans through the string one character at a time. The appropriate counter in the appropriate array is incremented for each character found in the string.

Both of the counter arrays are indexed from 0 to 25. We have to map each character to a counter. A logical way to do this is to use `upper[0]` to count the number of `'A'` characters found, `upper[1]` to count the number of `'B'` characters found, and so on. Likewise, `lower[0]` is used to count `'a'` characters, `lower[1]` is used to count `'b'` characters, and so on. A separate variable called `other` is used to count any nonalphabetic characters that are encountered.

We use the current character to calculate which index in the array to reference. Remember that each character has a numeric value based on the Unicode character set, and that the uppercase and lowercase alphabetic letters are continuous and in order (see Appendix C). Therefore, taking the numeric value of an uppercase letter such as `'E'` (which is 69) and subtracting the numeric value of the character `'A'` (which is 65) yields 4, which is the correct index for the counter of the character `'E'`. Note that nowhere in the program do we actually need to know the specific numeric values for each letter.

alternate array syntax

Syntactically, there are two ways to declare an array reference in Java. The first technique, which is used in the previous examples and throughout this text, is to associate the brackets with the type of values stored in the array. The second technique is to associate the brackets with the name of the array. Therefore the following two declarations are equivalent:

```
int[] grades;
int grades[];
```

Although there is no difference between these declaration techniques as far as the compiler is concerned, the first is consistent with other types of declarations. Consider the following declarations:

```
int total, sum, result;
int[] grade1, grade2, grade3;
```

In the first declaration, the type of the three variables, `int`, is given at the beginning of the line. Similarly, in the second declaration, the type of the three variables, `int[]`, is also given at the beginning of the line. In both cases, the type applies to all variables in that particular declaration.

When the alternative form of array declaration is used, it can lead to potentially confusing situations, such as the following:

```
int grade1[], grade2, grade3[];
```

The variables `grade1` and `grade3` are declared to be arrays of integers, whereas `grade2` is a single integer. Although most declarations declare variables of the same type, this example declares variables of two different types. Why did the programmer write a declaration in this way? Is it a mistake? Should `grade2` be an array? This confusion is eliminated if the array brackets are associated with the element type. Therefore we associate the brackets with the element type throughout this text.

initializer lists

An important alternative technique for instantiating arrays is using an *initializer list* that provides the initial values for the elements of the array. It is essentially the same idea as initializing a variable of a primitive data type in its declaration except that an array requires several values.

The items in an initializer list are separated by commas and delimited by braces (`{}`). When an initializer list is used, the `new` operator is not used. The size of the array is determined by the number of items in the initializer list. For example, the following declaration instantiates the array `scores` as an array of eight integers, indexed from 0 to 7 with the specified initial values:

```
int[] scores = {87, 98, 69, 54, 65, 76, 87, 99};
```

An initializer list can be used only when an array is first declared.

> **key concept**
>
> An initializer list can be used to instantiate an array object instead of using the `new` operator. The size of the array and its initial values are determined by the initializer list.

The type of each value in an initializer list must match the type of the array elements. Let's look at another example:

```
char[] letterGrades = {'A', 'B', 'C', 'D', 'F'};
```

In this case, the variable `letterGrades` is declared to be an array of five characters, and the initializer list contains character literals. The program shown in Listing 6.4 demonstrates the use of an initializer list to instantiate an array.

listing
6.4

```java
//********************************************************************
//  Primes.java          Author: Lewis/Loftus
//
//  Demonstrates the use of an initializer list for an array.
//********************************************************************

public class Primes
{
   //-----------------------------------------------------------------
   //  Stores some prime numbers in an array and prints them.
   //-----------------------------------------------------------------
   public static void main (String[] args)
   {
      int[] primeNums = {2, 3, 5, 7, 11, 13, 17, 19};

      System.out.println ("Array length: " + primeNums.length);

      System.out.println ("The first few prime numbers are:");

      for (int scan = 0; scan < primeNums.length; scan++)
         System.out.print (primeNums[scan] + "  ");

      System.out.println ();
   }
}
```

output

```
Array length: 8
The first few prime numbers are:
2   3   5   7   11   13   17   19
```

arrays as parameters

An entire array can be passed as a parameter to a method. Because an array is an object, when an entire array is passed as a parameter, a copy of the reference to the original array is passed. We discussed this issue as it applies to all objects in Chapter 5.

> **Key concept**
>
> An entire array can be passed as a parameter, making the formal parameter an alias of the original.

A method that receives an array as a parameter can permanently change an element of the array because it is referring to the original element value. The method cannot permanently change the reference to the array itself because a copy of the original reference is sent to the method. These rules are consistent with the rules that govern any object type.

An element of an array can be passed to a method as well. If the element type is a primitive type, a copy of the value is passed. If that element is a reference to an object, a copy of the object reference is passed. As always, the impact of changes made to a parameter inside the method depends on the type of the parameter. We discuss arrays of objects further in the next section.

6.1 arrays of objects

In previous examples, the arrays stored primitive types such as integers and characters. Arrays can also store references to objects as elements. Fairly complex information management structures can be created using only arrays and other objects. For example, an array could contain objects, and each of those objects could consist of several variables and the methods that use them. Those variables could themselves be arrays, and so on. The design of a program should capitalize on the ability to combine these constructs to create the most appropriate representation for the information.

arrays of string objects

Consider the following declaration:

```
String[] words = new String[25];
```

The variable words is an array of references to String objects. The new operator in the declaration instantiates the array and reserves space for 25 String references. Note that this declaration does not create any String objects; it merely creates an array that holds references to String objects.

The program called GradeRange shown in Listing 6.5 creates an array of String objects called grades, which stores letter grades for a course. The String objects are created using string literals in the initializer list. Note that this array could not have been declared as an array of characters because the plus and minus grades create two-character strings. The output for the GradeRange program shown in Listing 6.5 lists various letter grades and their corresponding lower numeric cutoff values, which have been stored in a corresponding array of integers.

**listing
   6.5**

```java
//********************************************************************
//  GradeRange.java        Author: Lewis/Loftus
//
//  Demonstrates the use of an array of String objects.
//********************************************************************

public class GradeRange
{
   //-----------------------------------------------------------------
   //  Stores the possible grades and their numeric lowest value,
   //  then prints them out.
   //-----------------------------------------------------------------
   public static void main (String[] args)
   {
      String[] grades = {"A", "A-", "B+", "B", "B-", "C+", "C", "C-",
                         "D+", "D", "D-", "F"};

      int[] cutoff = {95, 90, 87, 83, 80, 77, 73, 70, 67, 63, 60, 0};

      for (int level = 0; level < cutoff.length; level++)
         System.out.println (grades[level] + "\t" + cutoff[level]);
   }
}
```

output

```
A       95
A-      90
B+      87
B       83
B-      80
C+      77
C       73
C-      70
D+      67
D       63
D-      60
F        0
```

Sometimes two arrays with corresponding elements are called *parallel arrays*. The danger of parallel arrays is that one may become out of synch with the other. In an object-oriented approach, we would generally be better off creating one array that held a single object containing all necessary information. For example, the GradeRange program could be changed to use a single array of objects that contain both the grade string and the numeric cutoff value. This modification is left as a programming project.

command-line arguments

The formal parameter to the main method of a Java application is always an array of String objects. We've ignored that parameter in previous examples, but now we can discuss how it might occasionally be useful.

The Java runtime environment invokes the main method when an application is submitted to the interpreter. The String[] parameter, which we typically call args, represents *command-line arguments* that are provided when the interpreter is invoked. Any extra information on the command line when the interpreter is invoked is stored in the args array for use by the program. This technique is another way to provide input to a program.

> **key concept**
>
> Command-line arguments are stored in an array of String objects and are passed to the main method.

The program shown in Listing 6.6 uses command-line arguments to print a nametag. It assumes the first argument represents some type of greeting and the second argument represents a person's name.

If two strings are not provided on the command line for the NameTag program, the args array will not contain enough (if any) elements, and the references in the program will cause an ArrayIndexOutOfBoundsException to be thrown. If extra information is included on the command line, it would be stored in the args array but ignored by the program.

Remember that the parameter to the main method is always an array of String objects. If you want numeric information to be input as a command-line argument, the program has to convert it from its string representation.

You also should be aware that in some program development environments a command line is not used to submit a program to the interpreter. In such situations, the command-line information can be specified in some other way. Consult the documentation for these specifics if necessary.

filling arrays of objects

We must always take into account an important characteristic of object arrays: The creation of the array and the creation of the objects that we store in the array are two separate steps. When we declare an array of String objects, for example,

listing
  6.6

```
//********************************************************************
//   NameTag.java        Author: Lewis/Loftus
//
//   Demonstrates the use of command line arguments.
//********************************************************************

public class NameTag
{
   //-----------------------------------------------------------------
   //   Prints a simple name tag using a greeting and a name that is
   //   specified by the user.
   //-----------------------------------------------------------------
   public static void main (String[] args)
   {
      System.out.println ();
      System.out.println ("      " + args[0]);
      System.out.println ("My name is " + args[1]);
      System.out.println ();
   }
}
```

output

```
>java NameTag Howdy John

      Howdy
My name is John

>java NameTag Hello William

      Hello
My name is William
```

key concept

Instantiating an array of objects reserves room to store references only. The objects that are stored in each element must be instantiated separately.

we create an array that holds String references. The String objects themselves must be created separately. In previous examples, the String objects were created using string literals in an initializer list, or, in the case of command-line arguments, they were created by the Java runtime environment.

This issue is demonstrated in the Tunes program and its accompanying classes. Listing 6.7 shows the Tunes class, which contains a main method that creates, modifies, and examines a compact disc (CD) collection. Each CD added to the collection is specified by its title, artist, purchase price, and number of tracks.

listing
6.7

```java
//********************************************************************
//  Tunes.java        Author: Lewis/Loftus
//
//  Driver for demonstrating the use of an array of objects.
//********************************************************************

public class Tunes
{
   //-----------------------------------------------------------------
   //  Creates a CDCollection object and adds some CDs to it. Prints
   //  reports on the status of the collection.
   //-----------------------------------------------------------------
   public static void main (String[] args)
   {
      CDCollection music = new CDCollection ();

      music.addCD ("Storm Front", "Billy Joel", 14.95, 10);
      music.addCD ("Come On Over", "Shania Twain", 14.95, 16);
      music.addCD ("Soundtrack", "Les Miserables", 17.95, 33);
      music.addCD ("Graceland", "Paul Simon", 13.90, 11);

      System.out.println (music);

      music.addCD ("Double Live", "Garth Brooks", 19.99, 26);
      music.addCD ("Greatest Hits", "Jimmy Buffet", 15.95, 13);

      System.out.println (music);
   }
}
```

output

```
&&&&&&&&&&&&&&&&&&&&&&&&&&&&&&&&&&&&&&&&&&&
My CD Collection

Number of CDs: 4
Total value: $61.75
Average cost: $15.44

CD List:

$14.95   10      Storm Front     Billy Joel
$14.95   16      Come On Over    Shania Twain
$17.95   33      Soundtrack      Les Miserables
$13.90   11      Graceland       Paul Simon
```

listing
6.7   continued

```
&&&&&&&&&&&&&&&&&&&&&&&&&&&&&&&&&&&&&&&&&&&&&
My CD Collection

Number of CDs: 6
Total value: $97.69
Average cost: $16.28

CD List:

$14.95   10      Storm Front      Billy Joel
$14.95   16      Come On Over     Shania Twain
$17.95   33      Soundtrack       Les Miserables
$13.90   11      Graceland        Paul Simon
$19.99   26      Double Live      Garth Brooks
$15.95   13      Greatest Hits    Jimmy Buffet
```

Listing 6.8 shows the CDCollection class. It contains an array of CD objects representing the collection. It maintains a count of the CDs in the collection and their combined value. It also keeps track of the current size of the collection array so that a larger array can be created if too many CDs are added to the collection.

The collection array is instantiated in the CDCollection constructor. Every time a CD is added to the collection (using the addCD method), a new CD object is created and a reference to it is stored in the collection array.

Each time a CD is added to the collection, we check to see whether we have reached the current capacity of the collection array. If we didn't perform this check, an exception would eventually be thrown when we try to store a new CD object at an invalid index. If the current capacity has been reached, the private increaseSize method is invoked, which first creates an array that is twice as big as the current collection array. Each CD in the existing collection is then copied into the new array. Finally, the collection reference is set to the larger array. Using this technique, we theoretically never run out of room in our CD collection. The user of the CDCollection object (the main method) never has to worry about running out of space because it's all handled internally.

Figure 6.3 shows a UML class diagram of the Tunes program. Recall that the open diamond indicates aggregation (a has-a relationship). The cardinality of the relationship is also noted: a CDCollection object contains zero or more CD objects.

listing
  6.8

```java
//********************************************************************
//   CDCollection.java        Author: Lewis/Loftus
//
//   Represents a collection of compact discs.
//********************************************************************

import java.text.NumberFormat;

public class CDCollection
{
   private CD[] collection;
   private int count;
   private double totalCost;

   //-----------------------------------------------------------------
   //  Creates an initially empty collection.
   //-----------------------------------------------------------------
   public CDCollection ()
   {
      collection = new CD[100];
      count = 0;
      totalCost = 0.0;
   }

   //-----------------------------------------------------------------
   //  Adds a CD to the collection, increasing the size of the
   //  collection if necessary.
   //-----------------------------------------------------------------
   public void addCD (String title, String artist, double cost,
                      int tracks)
   {
      if (count == collection.length)
         increaseSize();

      collection[count] = new CD (title, artist, cost, tracks);
      totalCost += cost;
      count++;
   }
```

listing
    6.8   continued

```java
//-----------------------------------------------------------------
//  Returns a report describing the CD collection.
//-----------------------------------------------------------------
public String toString()
{
    NumberFormat fmt = NumberFormat.getCurrencyInstance();

    String report = "&&&&&&&&&&&&&&&&&&&&&&&&&&&&&&&&&&&&&&&&&&&&&&\n";
    report += "My CD Collection\n\n";

    report += "Number of CDs: " + count + "\n";
    report += "Total cost: " + fmt.format(totalCost) + "\n";
    report += "Average cost: " + fmt.format(totalCost/count);

    report += "\n\nCD List:\n\n";


    for (int cd = 0; cd < count; cd++)
        report += collection[cd].toString() + "\n";

    return report;
}

//-----------------------------------------------------------------
//  Doubles the size of the collection by creating a larger array
//  and copying the existing collection into it.
//-----------------------------------------------------------------
private void increaseSize ()
{
    CD[] temp = new CD[collection.length * 2];

    for (int cd = 0; cd < collection.length; cd++)
        temp[cd] = collection[cd];

    collection = temp;
}
}
```

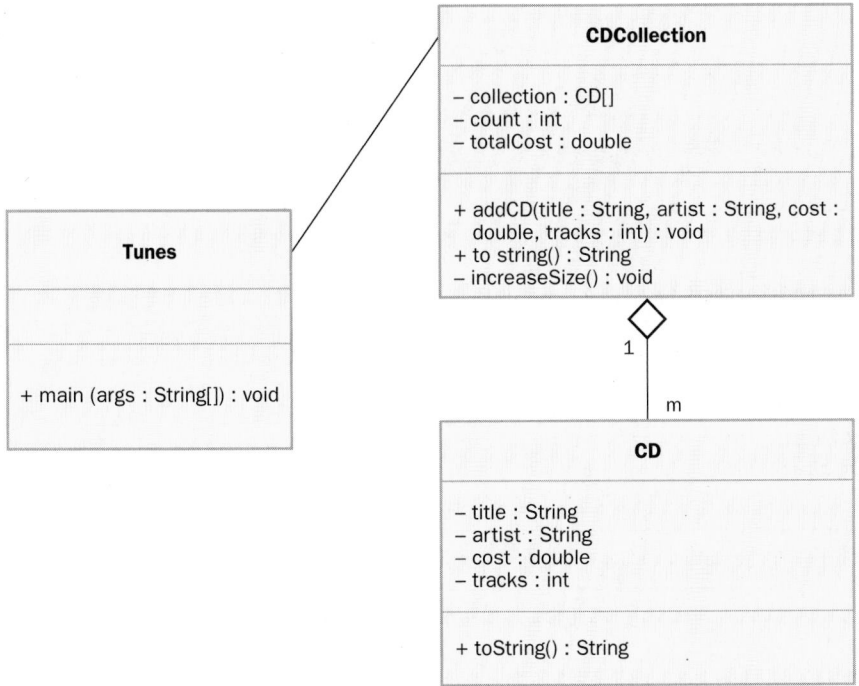

figure 6.3   A UML class diagram of the Tunes program

The toString method of the CDCollection class returns an entire report summarizing the collection. The report is created, in part, using calls to the toString method of each CD object stored in the collection. Listing 6.9 shows the CD class.

6.2 sorting

Sorting is the process of arranging a list of items in a well-defined order. For example, you may want to alphabetize a list of names or put a list of survey results into descending numeric order. Many sorting algorithms have been developed and critiqued over the years. In fact, sorting is considered to be a classic area of study in computer science.

listing
    6.9

```java
//********************************************************************
//  CD.java          Author: Lewis/Loftus
//
//  Represents a compact disc.
//********************************************************************

import java.text.NumberFormat;

public class CD
{
   private String title, artist;
   private double cost;
   private int tracks;

   //------------------------------------------------------------------
   //  Creates a new CD with the specified information.
   //------------------------------------------------------------------
   public CD (String name, String singer, double price, int numTracks)
   {
      title = name;
      artist = singer;
      cost = price;
      tracks = numTracks;
   }


   //------------------------------------------------------------------
   //  Returns a description of this CD.
   //------------------------------------------------------------------
   public String toString()
   {
      NumberFormat fmt = NumberFormat.getCurrencyInstance();

      String description;

      description = fmt.format(cost) + "\t" + tracks + "\t";
      description += title + "\t" + artist;

      return description;
   }
}
```

This section examines two sorting algorithms: selection sort and insertion sort. Complete coverage of various sorting techniques is beyond the scope of this text. Instead we introduce the topic and establish some of the fundamental ideas involved. We do not delve into a detailed analysis of the algorithms but instead focus on the strategies involved and general characteristics.

> **key concept**
>
> Selection sort and insertion sort are two sorting algorithms that define the processing steps for putting a list of values into a well-defined order.

selection sort

The *selection sort* algorithm sorts a list of values by successively putting particular values in their final, sorted positions. In other words, for each position in the list, the algorithm selects the value that should go in that position and puts it there. Let's consider the problem of putting a list of numeric values into ascending order.

> **key concept**
>
> Selection sort works by putting each value in its final position, one at a time.

The general strategy of selection sort is: Scan the entire list to find the smallest value. Exchange that value with the value in the first position of the list. Scan the rest of the list (all but the first value) to find the smallest value, then exchange it with the value in the second position of the list. Scan the rest of the list (all but the first two values) to find the smallest value, then exchange it with the value in the third position of the list. Continue this process for all but the last position in the list (which will end up containing the largest value). When the process is complete, the list is sorted. Figure 6.4 demonstrates the use of the selection sort algorithm.

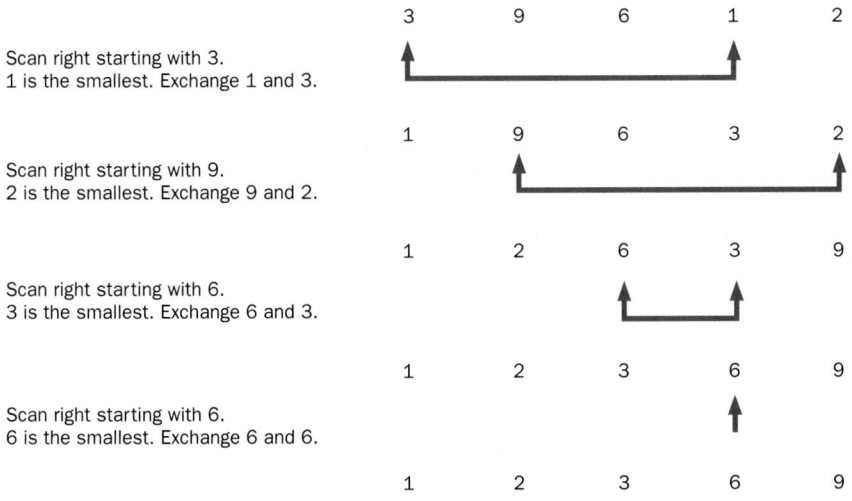

figure 6.4   Selection sort processing

The program shown in Listing 6.10 uses a selection sort to arrange a list of values into ascending order. The SortGrades class contains a main method that creates an array of integers. It calls the static method selectionSort in the Sorts class to put them in ascending order.

Listing 6.11 shows the Sorts class. It contains three static sorting algorithms. The SortGrades program uses only the selectionSort method. The other methods are discussed later in this section.

The implementation of the selectionSort method uses two for loops to sort an array of integers. The outer loop controls the position in the array where the next smallest value will be stored. The inner loop finds the smallest value in the rest of the list by scanning all positions greater than or equal to the index specified by the outer loop. When the smallest value is determined, it is exchanged with the value stored at the index. This exchange is done in three assignment statements by using an extra variable called temp. This type of exchange is often called *swapping*.

listing
6.10

```
//********************************************************************
//  SortGrades.java       Author: Lewis/Loftus
//
//  Driver for testing a numeric selection sort.
//********************************************************************

public class SortGrades
{
    //----------------------------------------------------------------
    //  Creates an array of grades, sorts them, then prints them.
    //----------------------------------------------------------------
    public static void main (String[] args)
    {
        int[] grades = {89, 94, 69, 80, 97, 85, 73, 91, 77, 85, 93};

        Sorts.selectionSort (grades);

        for (int index = 0; index < grades.length; index++)
            System.out.print (grades[index] + "   ");
    }
}
```

output

```
69   73   77   80   85   85   89   91   93   94   97
```

listing
   6.11

```java
//********************************************************************
//  Sorts.java         Author: Lewis/Loftus
//
//  Demonstrates the selection sort and insertion sort algorithms,
//  as well as a generic object sort.
//********************************************************************

public class Sorts
{
   //-----------------------------------------------------------------
   //  Sorts the specified array of integers using the selection
   //  sort algorithm.
   //-----------------------------------------------------------------
   public static void selectionSort (int[] numbers)
   {
      int min, temp;

      for (int index = 0; index < numbers.length-1; index++)
      {
         min = index;
         for (int scan = index+1; scan < numbers.length; scan++)
            if (numbers[scan] < numbers[min])
               min = scan;

         // Swap the values
         temp = numbers[min];
         numbers[min] = numbers[index];
         numbers[index] = temp;
      }
   }

   //-----------------------------------------------------------------
   //  Sorts the specified array of integers using the insertion
   //  sort algorithm.
   //-----------------------------------------------------------------
   public static void insertionSort (int[] numbers)
   {
      for (int index = 1; index < numbers.length; index++)
      {
         int key = numbers[index];
         int position = index;
```

listing
6.11   **continued**

```
        // shift larger values to the right
        while (position > 0 && numbers[position-1] > key)
        {
            numbers[position] = numbers[position-1];
            position--;
        }

        numbers[position] = key;
    }
}

//-----------------------------------------------------------------
//  Sorts the specified array of objects using the insertion
//  sort algorithm.
//-----------------------------------------------------------------
public static void insertionSort (Comparable[] objects)
{
    for (int index = 1; index < objects.length; index++)
    {
        Comparable key = objects[index];
        int position = index;

        // shift larger values to the right
        while (position > 0 && objects[position-1].compareTo(key) > 0)
        {
            objects[position] = objects[position-1];
            position--;
        }

        objects[position] = key;
    }
}
}
```

Note that because this algorithm finds the smallest value during each iteration, the result is an array sorted in ascending order (that is, smallest to largest). The algorithm can easily be changed to put values in descending order by finding the largest value each time.

insertion sort

The `Sorts` class also contains a method that performs an insertion sort on an array of integers. If used to sort the array of grades in the `SortGrades` program, it would produce the same results as the selection sort did. However, the processing to put the numbers in order is different.

The *insertion sort* algorithm sorts a list of values by repetitively inserting a particular value into a subset of the list that has already been sorted. One at a time, each unsorted element is inserted at the appropriate position in that sorted subset until the entire list is in order.

> Insertion sort works by inserting each value into a previously sorted subset of the list.
>
> key concept

The general strategy of insertion sort is: Begin with a "sorted" list containing only one value. Sort the first two values in the list relative to each other by exchanging them if necessary. Insert the list's third value into the appropriate position relative to the first two (sorted) values. Then insert the fourth value into its proper position relative to the first three values in the list. Each time an insertion is made, the number of values in the sorted subset increases by one. Continue this process until all values are inserted in their proper places, at which point the list is completely sorted.

The insertion process requires that the other values in the array shift to make room for the inserted element. Figure 6.5 demonstrates the behavior of the insertion sort algorithm.

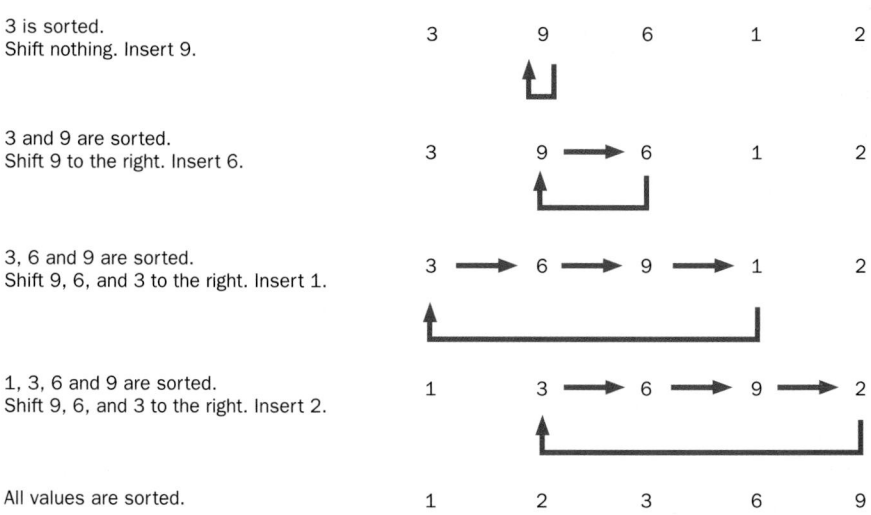

figure 6.5   Insertion sort processing

Similar to the selection sort implementation, the insertionSort method uses two for loops to sort an array of integers. In the insertion sort, however, the outer loop controls the index in the array of the next value to be inserted. The inner loop compares the current insert value with values stored at lower indexes (which make up a sorted subset of the entire list). If the current insert value is less than the value at position, that value is shifted to the right. Shifting continues until the proper position is opened to accept the insert value. Each iteration of the outer loop adds one more value to the sorted subset of the list, until the entire list is sorted.

sorting an array of objects

The Sorts class in Listing 6.11 contains an overloaded version of the insertionSort method. This version of the method accepts an array of Comparable objects and uses the insertion sort algorithm to put the objects in sorted order. Note the similarities in the general logic of both versions of the insertionSort method.

The main difference between the two versions of the insertionSort method is that one sorts an array of integers, whereas the other sorts an array of objects. We know what it means for one integer to be less than another integer, but what does it mean for one object to be less than another object? Basically, that decision depends on the objects being sorted and the characteristics on which the objects are to be ordered.

The key is that the parameter to the method is an array of Comparable objects. That is, the array is filled with objects that have implemented the Comparable interface, which we discussed in Chapter 5. Recall that the Comparable interface contains one method, compareTo, which is designed to return an integer that is less than zero, equal to zero, or greater than zero if the executing object is less than, equal to, or greater than the object to which it is being compared, respectively.

Let's look at an example. The SortPhoneList program shown in Listing 6.12 creates an array of Contact objects, sorts these objects using a call to the insertionSort method, and prints the sorted list.

Each Contact object represents a person with a last name, a first name, and a phone number. Listing 6.13 shows the Contact class.

listing
6.12

```
//********************************************************************
//   SortPhoneList.java          Author: Lewis/Loftus
//
//   Driver for testing an object sort.
//********************************************************************

public class SortPhoneList
{
    //-----------------------------------------------------------------
    //  Creates an array of Contact objects, sorts them, then prints
    //  them.
    //-----------------------------------------------------------------
    public static void main (String[] args)
    {
        Contact[] friends = new Contact[7];

        friends[0] = new Contact ("John", "Smith", "610-555-7384");
        friends[1] = new Contact ("Sarah", "Barnes", "215-555-3827");
        friends[2] = new Contact ("Mark", "Riley", "733-555-2969");
        friends[3] = new Contact ("Laura", "Getz", "663-555-3984");
        friends[4] = new Contact ("Larry", "Smith", "464-555-3489");
        friends[5] = new Contact ("Frank", "Phelps", "322-555-2284");
        friends[6] = new Contact ("Marsha", "Grant", "243-555-2837");

        Sorts.insertionSort(friends);

        for (int index = 0; index < friends.length; index++)
            System.out.println (friends[index]);
    }
}
```

output

```
Barnes, Sarah    215-555-3827
Getz, Laura      663-555-3984
Grant, Marsha    243-555-2837
Phelps, Frank    322-555-2284
Riley, Mark      733-555-2969
Smith, John      610-555-7384
Smith, Larry     464-555-3489
```

listing
6.13

```java
//********************************************************************
//  Contact.java        Author: Lewis/Loftus
//
//  Represents a phone contact.
//********************************************************************

public class Contact implements Comparable
{
   private String firstName, lastName, phone;

   //-----------------------------------------------------------------
   //  Sets up this contact with the specified information.
   //-----------------------------------------------------------------
   public Contact (String first, String last, String telephone)
   {
      firstName = first;
      lastName = last;
      phone = telephone;
   }

   //-----------------------------------------------------------------
   //  Returns a description of this contact as a string.
   //-----------------------------------------------------------------
   public String toString ()
   {
      return lastName + ", " + firstName + "\t" + phone;
   }

   //-----------------------------------------------------------------
   //  Uses both last and first names to determine lexical ordering.
   //-----------------------------------------------------------------
   public int compareTo (Object other)
   {
      int result;

      if (lastName.equals(((Contact)other).lastName))
         result = firstName.compareTo(((Contact)other).firstName);
      else
         result = lastName.compareTo(((Contact)other).lastName);

      return result;
   }
}
```

The Contact class implements the Comparable interface and therefore provides a definition of the compareTo method. In this case, the contacts are sorted by last name; if two contacts have the same last name, their first names are used.

When the insertionSort method executes, it relies on the compareTo method of each object to determine the order. We are guaranteed that the objects in the array have implemented the compareTo method because they are all Comparable objects (according to the parameter type). The compiler will issue an error message if we attempt to pass an array to this method that does not contain Comparable objects. Therefore this version of the insertionSort method can be used to sort any array of objects as long as the objects have implemented the Comparable interface. This example demonstrates a classic and powerful use of interfaces to create generic algorithms that work on a variety of data.

comparing sorts

There are various reasons for choosing one sorting algorithm over another, including the algorithm's simplicity, its level of efficiency, the amount of memory it uses, and the type of data being sorted. An algorithm that is easier to understand is also easier to implement and debug. However, often the simplest sorts are the most inefficient ones. Efficiency is usually considered to be the primary criterion when comparing sorting algorithms. In general, one sorting algorithm is less efficient than another if it performs more comparisons than the other. There are several algorithms that are more efficient than the two we examined, but they are also more complex.

> **key concept**
> Sorting algorithms are ranked according to their efficiency, which is usually defined as the number of comparisons required to perform the sort.

Both selection sort and insertion sort have essentially the same level of efficiency. Both have an outer loop and an inner loop with similar properties, if not purposes. The outer loop is executed once for each value in the list, and the inner loop compares the value in the outer loop with most, if not all, of the values in the rest of the list. Therefore, both algorithms perform approximately n^2 number of comparisons, where n is the number of values in the list. We say that both selection sort and insertion sort are algorithms of *order* n^2. More efficient sorts perform fewer comparisons and are of a smaller order, such as $n \log_2 n$.

> **key concept**
> Both selection sort and insertion sort algorithms are of order n^2. Other sorts are more efficient.

Because both selection sort and insertion sort have the same general efficiency, the choice between them is almost arbitrary. However, there are some additional issues to consider. Selection sort is usually easy to understand and will often suffice in many situations. Further, each value moves exactly once to its final place in the list. That is, although the selection and insertion sorts are equivalent (generally) in the number of comparisons made, selection sort makes fewer swaps.

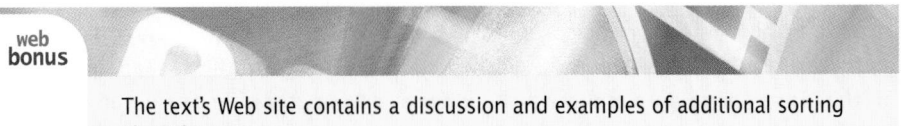

web bonus

The text's Web site contains a discussion and examples of additional sorting algorithms.

6.3 two-dimensional arrays

The arrays we've examined so far have all been *one-dimensional arrays* in the sense that they represent a simple list of values. As the name implies, a *two-dimensional array* has values in two dimensions, which are often thought of as the rows and columns of a table. Figure 6.6 graphically compares a one-dimensional array with a two-dimensional array. We must use two indexes to refer to a value in a two-dimensional array, one specifying the row and another the column.

Brackets are used to represent each dimension in the array. Therefore the type of a two-dimensional array that stores integers is `int[][]`. Technically, Java represents two-dimensional arrays as an array of arrays. A two-dimensional integer array is really a one-dimensional array of references to one-dimensional integer arrays.

The `TwoDArray` program shown in Listing 6.14 instantiates a two-dimensional array of integers. As with one-dimensional arrays, the size of the dimensions is specified when the array is created. The size of the dimensions can be different.

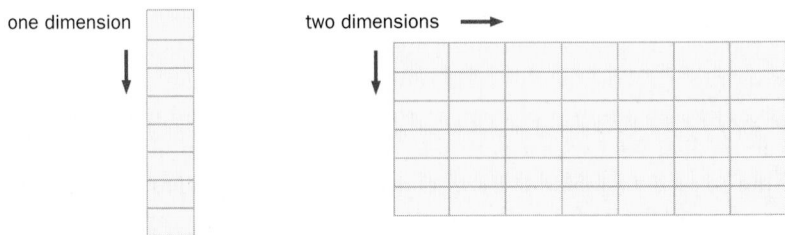

figure 6.6   A one-dimensional array and a two-dimensional array

listing
    6.14

```java
//********************************************************************
//  TwoDArray.java   Author: Lewis/Loftus
//
//  Demonstrates the use of a two-dimensional array.
//********************************************************************

public class TwoDArray
{
   //-----------------------------------------------------------------
   //  Creates a 2D array of integers, fills it with increasing
   //  integer values, then prints them out.
   //-----------------------------------------------------------------
   public static void main (String[] args)
   {
      int[][] table = new int[5][10];

      // Load the table with values
      for (int row=0; row < table.length; row++)
         for (int col=0; col < table[row].length; col++)
            table[row][col] = row * 10 + col;

      // Print the table
      for (int row=0; row < table.length; row++)
      {
         for (int col=0; col < table[row].length; col++)
            System.out.print (table[row][col] + "\t");
         System.out.println();
      }
   }
}
```

output

0	1	2	3	4	5	6	7	8	9
10	11	12	13	14	15	16	17	18	19
20	21	22	23	24	25	26	27	28	29
30	31	32	33	34	35	36	37	38	39
40	41	42	43	44	45	46	47	48	49

Nested `for` loops are used in the `TwoDArray` program to load the array with values and also to print those values in a table format. Carefully trace the processing to see how the nested loops eventually visit each element in the two-dimensional array. Note that the outer loops are governed by `table.length`, which represents the number of rows, and the inner loops are governed by `table[row].length`, which represents the number of columns in that row.

As with one-dimensional arrays, an initializer list can be used to instantiate a two-dimensional array, where each element is itself an array initializer list. This technique is used in the `SodaSurvey` program, which is shown in Listing 6.15.

listing
6.15

```java
//********************************************************************
//   SodaSurvey.java        Author: Lewis/Loftus
//
//   Demonstrates the use of a two-dimensional array.
//********************************************************************

import java.text.DecimalFormat;

public class SodaSurvey
{
    //-----------------------------------------------------------------
    //   Determines and prints the average of each row (soda) and each
    //   column (respondent) of the survey scores.
    //-----------------------------------------------------------------
    public static void main (String[] args)
    {
        int[][] scores = { {3, 4, 5, 2, 1, 4, 3, 2, 4, 4},
                           {2, 4, 3, 4, 3, 3, 2, 1, 2, 2},
                           {3, 5, 4, 5, 5, 3, 2, 5, 5, 5},
                           {1, 1, 1, 3, 1, 2, 1, 3, 2, 4} };

        final int SODAS = scores.length;
        final int PEOPLE = scores[0].length;

        int[] sodaSum = new int[SODAS];
        int[] personSum = new int[PEOPLE];
```

listing
  6.15 continued

```java
        for (int soda=0; soda < SODAS; soda++)
           for (int person=0; person < PEOPLE; person++)
           {
              sodaSum[soda] += scores[soda][person];
              personSum[person] += scores[soda][person];
           }

        DecimalFormat fmt = new DecimalFormat ("0.#");
        System.out.println ("Averages:\n");

        for (int soda=0; soda < SODAS; soda++)
           System.out.println ("Soda #" + (soda+1) + ": " +
                      fmt.format ((float)sodaSum[soda]/PEOPLE));

        System.out.println ();
        for (int person =0; person < PEOPLE; person++)
           System.out.println ("Person #" + (person+1) + ": " +
                      fmt.format ((float)personSum[person]/SODAS));
   }
}
```

output

```
Averages:

Soda #1: 3.2
Soda #2: 2.6
Soda #3: 4.2
Soda #4: 1.9

Person #1: 2.2
Person #2: 3.5
Person #3: 3.2
Person #4: 3.5
Person #5: 2.5
Person #6: 3
Person #7: 2
Person #8: 2.8
Person #9: 3.2
Person #10: 3.8
```

Suppose a soda manufacturer held a taste test for four new flavors to see how people liked them. The manufacturer got 10 people to try each new flavor and give it a score from 1 to 5, where 1 equals poor and 5 equals excellent. The two-dimensional array called `scores` in the `SodaSurvey` program stores the results of that survey. Each row corresponds to a soda and each column in that row corresponds to the person who tasted it. More generally, each row holds the responses that all testers gave for one particular soda flavor, and each column holds the responses of one person for all sodas.

The `SodaSurvey` program computes and prints the average responses for each soda and for each respondent. The sums of each soda and person are first stored in one-dimensional arrays of integers. Then the averages are computed and printed.

multidimensional arrays

An array can have one, two, three, or even more dimensions. Any array with more than one dimension is called a *multidimensional array.*

It's fairly easy to picture a two-dimensional array as a table. A three-dimensional array could be drawn as a cube. However, once you are past three dimensions, multidimensional arrays might seem hard to visualize. Yet, consider that each subsequent dimension is simply a subdivision of the previous one. It is often best to think of larger multidimensional arrays in this way.

For example, suppose we wanted to store the number of students attending universities across the United States, broken down in a meaningful way. We might represent it as a four-dimensional array of integers. The first dimension represents the state. The second dimension represents the universities in each state. The third dimension represents the colleges in each university. Finally, the fourth dimension represents departments in each college. The value stored at each location is the number of students in one particular department. Figure 6.7 shows these subdivisions.

Two-dimensional arrays are fairly common. However, care should be taken when deciding to create multidimensional arrays in a program. When dealing with large amounts of data that are managed at multiple levels, additional information and the methods needed to manage that information will probably be required. It is far more likely, for instance, that in the previous example, each state would be represented by an object, which may contain, among other things, an array to store information about each university, and so on.

Key concept

Using an array with more than two dimensions is rare in an object-oriented system because intermediate levels are usually represented as separate objects.

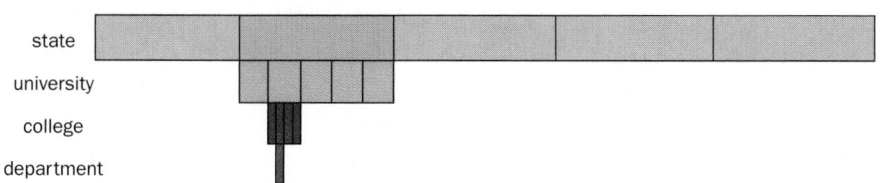

figure 6.7   Visualization of a four-dimensional array

There is one other important characteristic of Java arrays to consider. As we established previously, Java does not directly support multidimensional arrays. Instead, they are represented as arrays of references to array objects. Those arrays could themselves contain references to other arrays. This layering continues for as many dimensions as required. Because of this technique for representing each dimension, the arrays in any one dimension could be of different lengths. These are sometimes called *ragged arrays*. For example, the number of elements in each row of a two-dimensional array may not be the same. In such situations, care must be taken to make sure the arrays are managed appropriately.

> **key concept**
>
> Each array in a given dimension of a multidimensional array could have a different length.

6.4 the ArrayList class

The ArrayList class is part of the java.util package of the Java standard class library. It provides a service similar to an array in that it can store a list of values and reference them by an index. However, whereas an array remains a fixed size throughout its existence, an ArrayList object dynamically grows and shrinks as needed. A data element can be inserted into or removed from any location (index) of an ArrayList object with a single method invocation.

> **key concept**
>
> An ArrayList object is similar to an array, but it dynamically changes size as needed, and elements can be inserted and removed.

The ArrayList class is part of the Collections API, a group of classes that serve to organize and manage other objects. We discuss collection classes further in Chapter 12.

Unlike an array, an ArrayList is not declared to store a particular type. An ArrayList object stores a list of references to the Object class. A reference to any type of object can be added to an ArrayList object. Because an ArrayList stores references, a primitive value must be stored in an appropriate wrapper class in order to be stored in an ArrayList. Figure 6.8 lists several methods of the ArrayList class.

```
ArrayList()
   Constructor: creates an initially empty list.

boolean add (Object obj)
   Inserts the specified object to the end of this list.

void add (int index, Object obj)
   Inserts the specified object into this list at the specified index.

void clear()
   Removes all elements from this list.

Object remove (int index)
   Removes the element at the specified index in this list and returns it.

Object get (int index)
   Returns the object at the specified index in this list without removing it.

int indexOf (Object obj)
   Returns the index of the first occurrence of the specified object.

boolean contains (Object obj)
   Returns true if this list contains the specified object.

boolean isEmpty()
   Returns true if this list contains no elements.

int size()
   Returns the number of elements in this list.
```

figure 6.8   Some methods of the `ArrayList` class

The program shown in Listing 6.16 instantiates an `ArrayList` called `band`. The method `add` is used to add several `String` objects to the `ArrayList` in a specific order. Then one particular string is deleted and another is inserted at a particular index. As with any other object, the `toString` method of the `ArrayList` class is automatically called whenever it is sent to the `println` method.

Note that when an element from an `ArrayList` is deleted, the list of elements "collapses" so that the indexes are kept continuous for the remaining elements. Likewise, when an element is inserted at a particular point, the indexes of the other elements are adjusted accordingly.

The objects stored in an `ArrayList` object can be of different reference types. The methods of the `ArrayList` class are designed to accept references to the `Object` class as parameters, thus allowing a reference to any kind of object to be passed to it. Note that an implication of this implementation is that the

listing
    6.16

```java
//***********************************************************************
//  Beatles.java        Author: Lewis/Loftus
//
//  Demonstrates the use of a ArrayList object.
//***********************************************************************

import java.util.ArrayList;

public class Beatles
{
   //-------------------------------------------------------------------
   //  Stores and modifies a list of band members.
   //-------------------------------------------------------------------
   public static void main (String[] args)
   {
      ArrayList band = new ArrayList();

      band.add ("Paul");
      band.add ("Pete");
      band.add ("John");
      band.add ("George");

      System.out.println (band);

      int location = band.indexOf ("Pete");
      band.remove (location);

      System.out.println (band);
      System.out.println ("At index 1: " + band.get(1));

      band.add (2, "Ringo");

      System.out.println (band);
      System.out.println ("Size of the band: " + band.size());
   }
}
```

output

```
[Paul, Pete, John, George]
[Paul, John, George]
At index 1: John
Size of the band: 4
```

elementAt method's return type is an Object reference. In order to retrieve a specific object from the ArrayList, the returned object must be cast to its original class. We discuss the Object class and its relationship to other classes in Chapter 7.

ArrayList efficiency

The ArrayList class is implemented, as you might imagine, using an array. That is, the ArrayList class stores as instance data an array of Object references. The methods provided by the class manipulate that array so that the indexes remain continuous as elements are added and removed.

When an ArrayList object is instantiated, the internal array is created with an initial capacity that defines the number of references it can currently handle. Elements can be added to the list without needing to allocate more memory until it reaches this capacity. When required, the capacity is expanded to accommodate the new need. We performed a similar operation in the Tunes program earlier in this chapter.

When an element is inserted into an ArrayList, all of the elements at higher indexes are copied into their new locations to make room for the new element. Figure 6.9 illustrates this process. Similar processing occurs when an element is removed from an ArrayList, except that the items are shifted in the other direction, closing the gap created by the deleted element to keep the indexes continuous. If several elements are inserted or deleted, this copying is repeated many times over.

If, in general, elements are added to or removed from the end of an ArrayList, it's efficiency is not affected. But if elements are added to and/or removed from the front part of a long ArrayList, a huge amount of element copying will occur. An ArrayList, with its dynamic characteristics, is a useful abstraction of an array, but the abstraction masks some underlying activity that can be fairly inefficient depending on how it is used.

> **Key concept**
>
> ArrayList processing can be inefficient depending on how it is used.

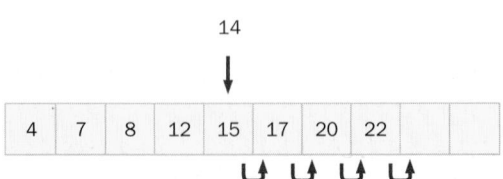

figure 6.9   Inserting an element into an ArrayList object

6.5 polygons and polylines

Arrays are helpful when drawing complex shapes. A polygon, for example, is a multisided shape that is defined in Java using a series of (x, y) points that indicate the vertices of the polygon. Arrays are often used to store the list of coordinates.

Polygons are drawn using methods of the `Graphics` class, similar to how we draw rectangles and ovals. Like these other shapes, a polygon can be drawn filled or unfilled. The methods used to draw a polygon are called `drawPolygon` and `fillPolygon`. Both of these methods are overloaded. One version uses arrays of integers to define the polygon, and the other uses an object of the `Polygon` class to define the polygon. We discuss the `Polygon` class later in this section.

In the version that uses arrays, the `drawPolygon` and `fillPolygon` methods take three parameters. The first is an array of integers representing the x coordinates of the points in the polygon, the second is an array of integers representing the corresponding y coordinates of those points, and the third is an integer that indicates how many points are used from each of the two arrays. Taken together, the first two parameters represent the (x, y) coordinates of the vertices of the polygons.

A polygon is always closed. A line segment is always drawn from the last point in the list to the first point in the list.

> **key concept**
> A polygon is always a closed shape. The last point is automatically connected back to the first one.

Similar to a polygon, a *polyline* contains a series of points connected by line segments. Polylines differ from polygons in that the first and last coordinates are not automatically connected when it is drawn. Since a polyline is not closed, it cannot be filled. Therefore there is only one method, called `drawPolyline`, used to draw a polyline.

> **key concept**
> A polyline is similar to a polygon except that a polyline is not a closed shape.

As with the `drawPolygon` method, the first two parameters of the `drawPolyline` method are both arrays of integers. Taken together, the first two parameters represent the (x, y) coordinates of the end points of the line segments of the polyline. The third parameter is the number of points in the coordinate list.

The program shown in Listing 6.17 uses polygons to draw a rocket. The arrays called `xRocket` and `yRocket` define the points of the polygon that make up the main body of the rocket. The first point in the arrays is the upper tip of the rocket, and they progress clockwise from there. The `xWindow` and `yWindow` arrays specify the points for the polygon that form the window in the rocket. Both the rocket and the window are drawn as filled polygons.

listing
   6.17

```
//********************************************************************
//   Rocket.java        Author: Lewis/Loftus
//
//   Demonstrates the use of polygons and polylines.
//********************************************************************

import javax.swing.JApplet;
import java.awt.*;

public class Rocket extends JApplet
{
   private final int APPLET_WIDTH = 200;
   private final int APPLET_HEIGHT = 200;

   private int[] xRocket = {100, 120, 120, 130, 130, 70, 70, 80, 80};
   private int[] yRocket = {15, 40, 115, 125, 150, 150, 125, 115, 40};

   private int[] xWindow = {95, 105, 110, 90};
   private int[] yWindow = {45, 45, 70, 70};

   private int[] xFlame = {70, 70, 75, 80, 90, 100, 110, 115, 120,
                           130, 130};
   private int[] yFlame = {155, 170, 165, 190, 170, 175, 160, 185,
                           160, 175, 155};

   //-----------------------------------------------------------------
   //   Sets up the basic applet environment.
   //-----------------------------------------------------------------
   public void init()
   {
      setBackground (Color.black);
      setSize (APPLET_WIDTH, APPLET_HEIGHT);
   }

   //-----------------------------------------------------------------
   //   Draws a rocket using polygons and polylines.
   //-----------------------------------------------------------------
   public void paint (Graphics page)
   {
      page.setColor (Color.cyan);
      page.fillPolygon (xRocket, yRocket, xRocket.length);

      page.setColor (Color.gray);
```

listing
6.17 continued

```
        page.fillPolygon (xWindow, yWindow, xWindow.length);

        page.setColor (Color.red);
        page.drawPolyline (xFlame, yFlame, xFlame.length);
    }
}
```

display

Applet started.

The xFlame and yFlame arrays define the points of a polyline that are used to create the image of flame shooting out of the tail of the rocket. Because it is drawn as a polyline, and not a polygon, the flame is not closed or filled.

the Polygon class

A polygon can also be defined explicitly using an object of the Polygon class, which is defined in the java.awt package of the Java standard class library. Two versions of the overloaded drawPolygon and fillPolygon methods take a single Polygon object as a parameter.

A `Polygon` object encapsulates the coordinates of the polygon sides. The constructors of the `Polygon` class allow the creation of an initially empty polygon, or one defined by arrays of integers representing the point coordinates. The `Polygon` class contains methods to add points to the polygon and to determine whether a given point is contained within the polygon shape. It also contains methods to get a representation of a bounding rectangle for the polygon, as well as a method to translate all of the points in the polygon to another position. Figure 6.10 lists these methods.

```
Polygon ()
    Constructor: Creates an empty polygon.

Polygon (int[] xpoints, int[] ypoints, int npoints)
    Constructor: Creates a polygon using the (x, y) coordinate pairs
    in corresponding entries of xpoints and ypoints.

void addPoint (int x, int y)
    Appends the specified point to this polygon.

boolean contains (int x, int y)
    Returns true if the specified point is contained in this polygon.

boolean contains (Point p)
    Returns true if the specified point is contained in this polygon.

Rectangle getBounds ()
    Gets the bounding rectangle for this polygon.

void translate (int deltaX, int deltaY)
    Translates the vertices of this polygon by deltaX along the x axis
    and deltaY along the y axis.
```

figure 6.10   Some methods of the `Polygon` class

6.6 other button components

In the graphics track of Chapter 5, we introduced the basics of graphical user interface (GUI) construction: components, events, and listeners. Recall that the JButton class represents a push button. When pushed, an action event is generated and we can set up a listener to respond accordingly. Let's now examine some additional components—buttons of a different kind.

check boxes

A *check box* is a button that can be toggled on or off using the mouse, indicating that a particular boolean condition is set or unset. For example, a check box labeled Collate might be used to indicate whether the output of a print job should be collated. Although you might have a group of check boxes indicating a set of options, each check box operates independently. That is, each can be set to on or off and the status of one does not influence the others.

The program in Listing 6.18 displays two check boxes and a label. The check boxes determine whether the text of the label is displayed in bold, italic, both, or neither. Any combination of bold and italic is valid. For example, both check boxes could be checked (on), in which case the text is displayed in both bold and italic. If neither is checked, the text of the label is displayed in a plain style.

The GUI for the StyleOptions program is embodied in the StyleGUI class shown in Listing 6.19. This organization is somewhat different than that used in the Fahrenheit program in the previous chapter. In this example, the frame is created in the main method. The StyleGUI object creates a panel on which the label and check boxes are arranged. The panel is returned to the main method using a call to getPanel and is added to the application frame.

A check box is represented by the JCheckBox class. When a check box changes state from selected (checked) to deselected (unchecked), or vice versa, it generates an *item event*. The ItemListener interface contains a single method called itemStateChanged. In this example, we use the same listener object to handle both check boxes.

listing
    6.18

```
//********************************************************************
//   StyleOptions.java        Author: Lewis/Loftus
//
//   Demonstrates the use of check boxes.
//********************************************************************

import javax.swing.*;

public class StyleOptions
{
   //-----------------------------------------------------------------
   //   Creates and presents the program frame.
   //-----------------------------------------------------------------
   public static void main (String[] args)
   {
      JFrame styleFrame = new JFrame ("Style Options");
      styleFrame.setDefaultCloseOperation (JFrame.EXIT_ON_CLOSE);

      StyleGUI gui = new StyleGUI();
      styleFrame.getContentPane().add (gui.getPanel());

      styleFrame.pack();
      styleFrame.show();
   }
}
```

display

listing
    6.19

```
//************************************************************************
//   StyleGUI.java          Author: Lewis/Loftus
//
//   Represents the user interface for the StyleOptions program.
//************************************************************************

import javax.swing.*;
import java.awt.*;
import java.awt.event.*;

public class StyleGUI
{
   private final int WIDTH = 300, HEIGHT = 100, FONT_SIZE = 36;
   private JLabel saying;
   private JCheckBox bold, italic;
   private JPanel primary;

   //-----------------------------------------------------------------
   //   Sets up a panel with a label and some check boxes that
   //   control the style of the label's font.
   //-----------------------------------------------------------------
   public StyleGUI()
   {
      saying = new JLabel ("Say it with style!");
      saying.setFont (new Font ("Helvetica", Font.PLAIN, FONT_SIZE));

      bold = new JCheckBox ("Bold");
      bold.setBackground (Color.cyan);
      italic = new JCheckBox ("Italic");
      italic.setBackground (Color.cyan);

      StyleListener listener = new StyleListener();
      bold.addItemListener (listener);
      italic.addItemListener (listener);

      primary = new JPanel();
      primary.add (saying);
      primary.add (bold);
      primary.add (italic);
      primary.setBackground (Color.cyan);
      primary.setPreferredSize (new Dimension(WIDTH, HEIGHT));
   }
```

listing
      6.19   **continued**

```java
//--------------------------------------------------------------
//  Returns the primary panel containing the GUI.
//--------------------------------------------------------------
public JPanel getPanel()
{
   return primary;
}

//*************************************************************
//  Represents the listener for both check boxes.
//*************************************************************
private class StyleListener implements ItemListener
{
   //-----------------------------------------------------------
   //  Updates the style of the label font style.
   //-----------------------------------------------------------
   public void itemStateChanged (ItemEvent event)
   {
      int style = Font.PLAIN;

      if (bold.isSelected())
         style = Font.BOLD;

      if (italic.isSelected())
         style += Font.ITALIC;

      saying.setFont (new Font ("Helvetica", style, FONT_SIZE));
   }
}
}
```

This program also uses the Font class, which represents a particular *character font*. A Font object is defined by the font name, the font style, and the font size. The font name establishes the general visual characteristics of the characters. We are using the Helvetica font in this program. The style of a Java font can be plain, bold, italic, or bold and italic combined. The check boxes in our graphical user interface are set up to change the characteristics of our font style.

The style of a font is represented as an integer, and integer constants defined in the Font class are used to represent the various aspects of the style. The constant PLAIN is used to represent a plain style. The constants BOLD and ITALIC are used to represent bold and italic, respectively. The sum of the BOLD and ITALIC constants indicates a style that is both bold and italic.

The itemStateChanged method of the listener determines what the revised style should be now that one of the check boxes has changed state. It initially sets the style to be plain. Then each check box is consulted in turn using the isSelected method, which returns a boolean value. First, if the bold check box is selected (checked), then the style is set to bold. Then, if the italic check box is selected, the ITALIC constant is added to the style variable. Finally, the font of the label is set to a new font with its revised style.

Note that, given the way the listener is written in this program, it doesn't matter which check box was clicked to generate the event. Both check boxes are processed by the same listener. It also doesn't matter whether the changed check box was toggled from selected to unselected or vice versa. The state of both check boxes is examined if either is changed.

radio buttons

A *radio button* is used with other radio buttons to provide a set of mutually exclusive options. Unlike a check box, a radio button is not useful by itself. It has meaning only when it is used with one or more other radio buttons. Only one option out of the group is valid. At any point in time, one and only one button of the group of radio buttons is selected (on). When a radio button from the group is pushed, the other button in the group that is currently on is automatically toggled off.

> **key concept**
>
> Radio buttons operate as a group, providing a set of mutually exclusive options. When one button is selected, the currently selected button is toggled off.

The term radio buttons comes from the way the buttons worked on an old-fashioned car radio. At any point, one button was pushed to specify the current choice of station; when another was pushed, the current one automatically popped out.

The QuoteOptions program, shown in Listing 6.20, displays a label and a group of radio buttons. The radio buttons determine which quote is displayed in the label. Because only one of the quotes can be displayed at a time, the use of radio buttons is appropriate. For example, if the Comedy radio button is selected, the comedy quote is displayed in the label. If the Philosophy button is then pressed, the Comedy radio button is automatically toggled off and the comedy quote is replaced by a philosophical one.

listing
    6.20

```java
//********************************************************************
//   QuoteOptions.java        Author: Lewis/Loftus
//
//   Demonstrates the use of radio buttons.
//********************************************************************

import javax.swing.*;

public class QuoteOptions
{
   //-----------------------------------------------------------------
   //   Creates and presents the program frame.
   //-----------------------------------------------------------------
   public static void main (String[] args)
   {
      JFrame quoteFrame = new JFrame ("Quote Options");
      quoteFrame.setDefaultCloseOperation (JFrame.EXIT_ON_CLOSE);

      QuoteGUI gui = new QuoteGUI();
      quoteFrame.getContentPane().add (gui.getPanel());

      quoteFrame.pack();
      quoteFrame.show();
   }
}
```

display

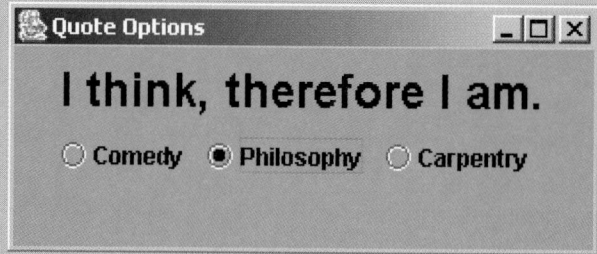

The structure of this program is similar to that of the `StyleOptions` program from the previous section. The label and radio buttons are displayed on a panel defined in the `QuoteGUI` class, shown in Listing 6.21. A radio button is represented by the `JRadioButton` class. Because the radio buttons in a set work together, the `ButtonGroup` class is used to define a set of related radio buttons.

listing
6.21

```java
//***********************************************************************
//  QuoteGUI.java        Author: Lewis/Loftus
//
//  Represents the user interface for the QuoteOptions program.
//***********************************************************************

import javax.swing.*;
import java.awt.*;
import java.awt.event.*;

public class QuoteGUI
{
    private final int WIDTH = 300, HEIGHT = 100;
    private JPanel primary;
    private JLabel quote;
    private JRadioButton comedy, philosophy, carpentry;
    private String comedyQuote = "Take my wife, please.";
    private String philosophyQuote = "I think, therefore I am.";
    private String carpentryQuote = "Measure twice. Cut once.";

    //-------------------------------------------------------------------
    //  Sets up a panel with a label and a set of radio buttons
    //  that control its text.
    //-------------------------------------------------------------------
    public QuoteGUI()
    {
        quote = new JLabel (comedyQuote);
        quote.setFont (new Font ("Helvetica", Font.BOLD, 24));

        comedy = new JRadioButton ("Comedy", true);
        comedy.setBackground (Color.green);
        philosophy = new JRadioButton ("Philosophy");
        philosophy.setBackground (Color.green);
        carpentry = new JRadioButton ("Carpentry");
        carpentry.setBackground (Color.green);
```

listing
    6.21   continued

```java
        ButtonGroup group = new ButtonGroup();
        group.add (comedy);
        group.add (philosophy);
        group.add (carpentry);

        QuoteListener listener = new QuoteListener();
        comedy.addActionListener (listener);
        philosophy.addActionListener (listener);
        carpentry.addActionListener (listener);

        primary = new JPanel();
        primary.add (quote);
        primary.add (comedy);
        primary.add (philosophy);
        primary.add (carpentry);
        primary.setBackground (Color.green);
        primary.setPreferredSize (new Dimension(WIDTH, HEIGHT));
    }

    //-----------------------------------------------------------------
    //   Returns the primary panel containing the GUI.
    //-----------------------------------------------------------------
    public JPanel getPanel()
    {
        return primary;
    }

    //*****************************************************************
    //   Represents the listener for all radio buttons
    //*****************************************************************
    private class QuoteListener implements ActionListener
    {
        //-----------------------------------------------------------
        //   Sets the text of the label depending on which radio
        //   button was pressed.
        //-----------------------------------------------------------
        public void actionPerformed (ActionEvent event)
        {
            Object source = event.getSource();
```

```
listing
   6.21   continued

        if (source == comedy)
           quote.setText (comedyQuote);
        else
           if (source == philosophy)
              quote.setText (philosophyQuote);
           else
              quote.setText (carpentryQuote);
      }
    }
}
```

Note that each button is added to the button group, and also that each button is added individually to the panel. A `ButtonGroup` object is not a container to organize and display components; it is simply a way to define the group of radio buttons that work together to form a set of dependent options. The `ButtonGroup` object ensures that the currently selected radio button is turned off when another in the group is selected.

A radio button produces an action event when it is selected. The `actionPerformed` method of the listener first determines the source of the event using the `getSource` method, and then compares it to each of the three radio buttons in turn. Depending on which button was selected, the text of the label is set to the appropriate quote.

Note that unlike push buttons, both check boxes and radio buttons are *toggle buttons*, meaning that at any time they are either on or off. The difference is in how they are used. Independent options (choose any combination) are controlled with check boxes. Dependent options (choose one of a set) are controlled with radio buttons. If there is only one option to be managed, a check box can be used by itself. As we mentioned earlier, a radio button, on the other hand, makes sense only in conjunction with one or more other radio buttons.

Also note that check boxes and radio buttons produce different types of events. A check box produces an item event and a radio button produces an action event. The use of different event types is related to the differences in button functionality. A check box produces an event when it is selected or deselected, and the listener could make the distinction if desired. A radio button, on the other hand, only produces an event when it is selected (the currently selected button from the group is deselected automatically).

summary of
key concepts

- An array of size N is indexed from 0 to $N-1$.

- In Java, an array is an object. Memory space for the array elements is reserved by instantiating the array using the `new` operator.

- Bounds checking ensures that an index used to refer to an array element is in range. The Java index operator performs automatic bounds checking.

- An initializer list can be used to instantiate an array object instead of using the `new` operator. The size of the array and its initial values are determined by the initializer list.

- An entire array can be passed as a parameter, making the formal parameter an alias of the original.

- Command-line arguments are stored in an array of `String` objects and are passed to the `main` method.

- Instantiating an array of objects reserves room to store references only. The objects that are stored in each element must be instantiated separately.

- Selection sort and insertion sort are two sorting algorithms that define the processing steps for putting a list of values into a well-defined order.

- Selection sort works by putting each value in its final position, one at a time.

- Swapping is the process of exchanging two values. Swapping requires three assignment statements.

- Insertion sort works by inserting each value into a previously sorted subset of the list.

- Sorting algorithms are ranked according to their efficiency, which is usually defined as the number of comparisons required to perform the sort.

- Both selection sort and insertion sort algorithms are of order n^2. Other sorts are more efficient.

- Using an array with more than two dimensions is rare in an object-oriented system because intermediate levels are usually represented as separate objects.

- Each array in a given dimension of a multidimensional array could have a different length.

- An `ArrayList` object is similar to an array, but it dynamically changes size as needed, and elements can be inserted and removed.
- `ArrayList` processing can be inefficient depending on how it is used.
- A polygon is always a closed shape. The last point is automatically connected back to the first one.
- A polyline is similar to a polygon except that a polyline is not a closed shape.
- A check box allows the user to set the status of a boolean condition.
- Radio buttons operate as a group, providing a set of mutually exclusive options. When one button is selected, the currently selected button is toggled off.

self-review questions

6.1 Explain the concept of array bounds checking. What happens when a Java array is indexed with an invalid value?

6.2 Describe the process of creating an array. When is memory allocated for the array?

6.3 What is an off-by-one error? How does it relate to arrays?

6.4 What does an array initializer list accomplish?

6.5 Can an entire array be passed as a parameter? How is this accomplished?

6.6 How is an array of objects created?

6.7 What is a command-line argument?

6.8 What are parallel arrays?

6.9 Which is better: selection sort or insertion sort? Explain.

6.10 How are multidimensional arrays implemented in Java?

6.11 What are the advantages of using an `ArrayList` object as opposed to an array? What are the disadvantages?

6.12 What is a polyline? How do we specify its shape?

6.13 Compare and contrast check boxes and radio buttons.

6.14 How does the `Timer` class help us perform animations in Java?

exercises

6.1   Which of the following are valid declarations? Which instantiate an array object? Explain your answers.

```
int primes = {2, 3, 4, 5, 7, 11};
float elapsedTimes[] = {11.47, 12.04, 11.72, 13.88};
int[] scores = int[30];
int[] primes = new {2,3,5,7,11};
int[] scores = new int[30];
char grades[] = {'a', 'b', 'c', 'd', 'f'};
char[] grades = new char[];
```

6.2   Describe five programs that are difficult to implement without using arrays.

6.3   Describe what problem occurs in the following code. What modifications should be made to it to eliminate the problem?

```
int[] numbers = {3, 2, 3, 6, 9, 10, 12, 32, 3, 12, 6};
for (int count = 1; count <= numbers.length; count++)
   System.out.println (numbers[count]);
```

6.4   Write an array declaration and any necessary supporting classes to represent the following statements:

a. students' names for a class of 25 students

b. students' test grades for a class of 40 students

c. credit-card transactions that contain a transaction number, a merchant name, and a charge

d. students' names for a class and homework grades for each student

e. for each employee of the L&L International Corporation: the employee number, hire date, and the amount of the last five raises

6.5   Write a method called sumArray that accepts an array of floating point values and returns the sum of the values stored in the array.

6.6   Write a method called switchThem that accepts two integer arrays as parameters and switches the contents of the arrays. Take into account that the arrays may be of different sizes.

6.7   Describe a program for which you would use the ArrayList class instead of arrays to implement choices. Describe a program for which you would use arrays instead of the ArrayList class. Explain your choices.

6.8   Explain what would happen if the radio buttons used in the
      QuoteOptions program were not organized into a ButtonGroup
      object. Modify the program to test your answer.

programming projects

6.1   Design and implement an application that reads an arbitrary number
      of integers that are in the range 0 to 50 inclusive and counts how
      many occurrences of each are entered. After all input has been
      processed, print all of the values (with the number of occurrences)
      that were entered one or more times.

6.2   Modify the program from Programming Project 6.1 so that it works
      for numbers in the range between –25 and 25.

6.3   Rewrite the Sorts class so that both sorting algorithms put the val-
      ues in descending order. Create a driver class with a main method to
      exercise the modifications.

6.4   Design and implement an application that creates a histogram that
      allows you to visually inspect the frequency distribution of a set of
      values. The program should read in an arbitrary number of integers
      that are in the range 1 to 100 inclusive; then produce a chart similar
      to the one below that indicates how many input values fell in the
      range 1 to 10, 11 to 20, and so on. Print one asterisk for each value
      entered.

```
1   - 10  | *****
11  - 20  | **
21  - 30  | ********************
31  - 40  |
41  - 50  | ***
51  - 60  | ********
61  - 70  | **
71  - 80  | *****
81  - 90  | *******
91  - 100 | ********
```

6.5   The lines in the histogram in Programming Project 6.4 will be too
      long if a large number of values is entered. Modify the program so
      that it prints an asterisk for every five values in each category. Ignore

leftovers. For example, if a category had 17 values, print three asterisks in that row. If a category had 4 values, do not print any asterisks in that row.

6.6 Design and implement an application that computes and prints the mean and standard deviation of a list of integers x_1 through x_n. Assume that there will be no more than 50 input values. Compute both the mean and standard deviation as floating point values, using the following formulas.

$$\text{mean} = \frac{\sum_{i=1}^{n} x_i}{n}$$

$$\text{sd} = \sqrt{\frac{\sum_{i=1}^{n} (x_i - \text{mean})^2}{n-1}}$$

6.7 The L&L Bank can handle up to 30 customers who have savings accounts. Design and implement a program that manages the accounts. Keep track of key information and allow each customer to make deposits and withdrawals. Produce appropriate error messages for invalid transactions. *Hint*: you may want to base your accounts on the Account class from Chapter 4. Also provide a method to add 3 percent interest to all accounts whenever the method is invoked.

6.8 Modify the GradeRange program from this chapter so that it eliminates the use of parallel arrays. Instead, design a new class called Grade that stores both the grade string and its cutoff value. Set both values using the Grade constructor and provide methods that return the values. In the main method of the revised GradeRange program, populate a single array with Grade objects, and then produce the same output as the original GradeRange program did.

6.9 The programming projects of Chapter 4 discussed a Card class that represents a standard playing card. Create a class called DeckOfCards that stores 52 objects of the Card class. Include methods to shuffle the deck, deal a card, and report the number of cards left in the deck. The shuffle method should assume a full deck.

Create a driver class with a `main` method that deals each card from a shuffled deck, printing each card as it is dealt.

6.10 Use the `Question` class from Chapter 5 to define a `Quiz` class. A quiz can be composed of up to 25 questions. Define the `add` method of the `Quiz` class to add a question to a quiz. Define the `giveQuiz` method of the `Quiz` class to present each question in turn to the user, accept an answer for each one, and keep track of the results. Define a class called `QuizTime` with a `main` method that populates a quiz, presents it, and prints the final results.

6.11 Modify your answer to Programming Project 6.10 so that the complexity level of the questions given in the quiz is taken into account. Overload the `giveQuiz` method so that it accepts two integer parameters that specify the minimum and maximum complexity levels for the quiz questions and only presents questions in that complexity range. Modify the `main` method to demonstrate this feature.

6.12 Modify the `Tunes` program so that it keeps the CDs sorted by title. Use the general object sort defined in the `Sorts` class from this chapter.

6.13 Modify the `Sorts` class to include an overloaded version of the `SelectionSort` method that performs a general object sort. Modify the `SortPhoneList` program to test the new sort.

6.14 Design and implement an applet that graphically displays the processing of a selection sort. Use bars of various heights to represent the values being sorted. Display the set of bars after each swap. Put a delay in the processing of the sort to give the human observer a chance to see how the order of the values changes.

6.15 Repeat Programming Project 6.14 using an insertion sort.

6.16 Design a class that represents a star with a specified radius and color. Use a filled polygon to draw the star. Design and implement an applet that draws 10 stars of random radius in random locations.

6.17 Design a class that represents the visual representation of a car. Use polylines and polygons to draw the car in any graphics context and at any location. Create a main driver to display the car.

6.18 Modify the solution to Programming Project 6.17 so that it uses the `Polygon` class to represent all polygons used in the drawing.

6.19 Modify the `Fahrenheit` program from Chapter 5 so that it uses a structure similar to the `StyleOptions` and `QuoteOptions` programs from this chapter. Specifically, create the application frame in the `main` method and add the GUI panel to it.

6.20 Modify the `StyleOptions` program in this chapter to allow the user to specify the size of the font. Use a text field to obtain the size.

6.21 Modify the `QuoteOptions` program in this chapter so that it provides three additional quote options. Use an array to store all of the quote strings.

6.22 Design and implement an applet that draws 20 circles, with the radius and location of each circle determined at random. If a circle does not overlap any other circle, draw that circle in black. If a circle overlaps one or more other circles, draw it in cyan. Use an array to store a representation of each circle, then determine the color of each circle. Two circles overlap if the distance between their center points is less than the sum of their radii.

6.23 Design and implement an applet that draws a checkerboard with five red and eight black checkers on it in various locations. Store the checkerboard as a two-dimensional array.

6.24 Modify the applet from Programming Project 6.23 so that the program determines whether any black checkers can jump any red checkers. Under the checkerboard, print (using `drawString`) the row and column position of all black checkers that have possible jumps.

answers to self-review questions

6.1 Whenever a reference is made to a particular array element, the index operator (the brackets that enclose the subscript) ensures that the value of the index is greater than or equal to zero and less than the size of the array. If it is not within the valid range, an `ArrayIndexOutOfBoundsException` is thrown.

6.2 Arrays are objects. Therefore, as with all objects, to create an array we first create a reference to the array (its name). We then instantiate the array itself, which reserves memory space to store the array elements. The only difference between a regular object instantiation and an array instantiation is the bracket syntax.

6.3 An off-by-one error occurs when a program's logic exceeds the boundary of an array (or similar structure) by one. These errors include forgetting to process a boundary element as well as attempting to process a nonexistent element. Array processing is susceptible to off-by-one errors because their indexes begin at zero and run to one less than the size of the array.

6.4   An array initializer list is used in the declaration of an array to set up the initial values of its elements. An initializer list instantiates the array object, so the new operator is needed.

6.5   An entire array can be passed as a parameter. Specifically, because an array is an object, a reference to the array is passed to the method. Any changes made to the array elements will be reflected outside of the method.

6.6   An array of objects is really an array of object references. The array itself must be instantiated, and the objects that are stored in the array must be created separately.

6.7   A command-line argument is data that is included on the command line when the interpreter is invoked to execute the program. Command-line arguments are another way to provide input to a program. They are accessed using the array of strings that is passed into the main method as a parameter.

6.8   Parallel arrays are two or more arrays whose corresponding elements are related in some way. Because parallel arrays can easily get out of synch if not managed carefully, it is often better to create a single array of objects that encapsulate the related elements.

6.9   Selection sort and insertion sort are generally equivalent in efficiency, because they both take about n^2 number of comparisons to sort a list of n numbers. Selection sort, though, generally makes fewer swaps. Several sorting algorithms are more efficient than either of these.

6.10 A multidimensional array is implemented in Java as an array of array objects. The arrays that are elements of the outer array could also contain arrays as elements. This nesting process could continue for as many levels as needed.

6.11 An ArrayList keeps the indexes of its objects continuous as they are added and removed, and an ArrayList dynamically increases its capacity as needed. In addition, an ArrayList is implemented so that it stores references to the Object class, which allows any object to be stored in it. A disadvantage of the ArrayList class is that it copies a significant amount of data in order to insert and delete elements, and this process is inefficient.

6.12 A polyline is defined by a series of points that represent its vertices. The drawPolyline method takes three parameters to specify its shape. The first is an array of integers that represent the x coordinates of the points. The second is an array of integers that represent the y coordinates of the points. The third parameter is a single integer that indicates the number of points to be used from the arrays.

6.13 Both check boxes and radio buttons show a toggled state: either on or off. However, radio buttons work as a group in which only one can be toggled on at any point in time. Check boxes, on the other hand, represent independent options. They can be used alone or in a set in which any combination of toggled states is valid.

6.14 The Timer class represents an object that generates an action event at regular intervals. The programmer sets the interval delay. An animation can be set up to change its display every time the timer goes off.

This chapter explains inheritance, a fundamental technique for organizing and creating classes. It is a simple but powerful idea that influences the way we design object-oriented software. Furthermore, inheritance enhances our ability to reuse classes in other situations and programs. We explore how classes can be related to form inheritance hierarchies and how these relationships allow us to create polymorphic references. This chapter also revisits the concept of a formal Java interface. Finally, we discuss how inheritance affects various issues related to graphical user interfaces (GUIs) in Java.

chapter
objectives

▶ Derive new classes from existing ones.

▶ Explain how inheritance supports software reuse.

▶ Add and modify methods in child classes.

▶ Discuss how to design class hierarchies.

▶ Define polymorphism and determine how it can be accomplished.

▶ Examine inheritance hierarchies for interfaces.

▶ Discuss the use of inheritance in Java GUI frameworks.

▶ Examine and use the GUI component class hierarchy.

7.0 creating subclasses

In Chapter 4 we presented the analogy that a class is to an object as a blueprint is to a house. A class establishes the characteristics and behaviors of an object but reserves no memory space for variables (unless those variables are declared as `static`). Classes are the plan, and objects are the embodiment of that plan.

Many houses can be created from the same blueprint. They are essentially the same house in different locations with different people living in them. But suppose you want a house that is similar to another but with some different or additional features. You want to start with the same basic blueprint but modify it to suit your needs and desires. Many housing developments are created this way. The houses in the development have the same core layout, but they have unique features. For instance, they might all be split-level homes with the same bedroom, kitchen, and living-room configuration, but some have a fireplace or full basement while others do not, or an attached garage instead of a carport.

It's likely that the housing developer commissioned a master architect to create a single blueprint to establish the basic design of all houses in the development, then a series of new blueprints that include variations designed to appeal to different buyers. The act of creating the series of blueprints was simplified since they all begin with the same underlying structure, while the variations give them unique characteristics that may be important to the prospective owners.

Creating a new blueprint that is based on an existing blueprint is analogous to the object-oriented concept of inheritance, which is a powerful software development technique and a defining characteristic of object-oriented programming.

derived classes

Inheritance is the process in which a new class is derived from an existing one. The new class automatically contains some or all of the variables and methods in the original class. Then, to tailor the class as needed, the programmer can add new variables and methods to the derived class or modify the inherited ones.

> **key concept**
>
> Inheritance is the process of deriving a new class from an existing one.

In general, new classes can be created via inheritance faster, easier, and cheaper than by writing them from scratch. At the heart of inheritance is the idea of *software reuse*. By using existing software components to create new ones, we capitalize on the effort that went into the design, implementation, and testing of the existing software.

Keep in mind that the word *class* comes from the idea of classifying groups of objects with similar characteristics. Classification schemes often use levels of classes that relate to each other. For example, all mammals share certain characteristics: They are warmblooded, have hair, and bear live offspring. Now consider a subset of mammals, such as horses. All horses are mammals and have all of the characteristics of mammals, but they also have unique features that make them different from other mammals.

> One purpose of inheritance is to reuse existing software.
>
> **key concept**

If we translate this idea into software terms, an existing class called `Mammal` would have certain variables and methods that describe the state and behavior of mammals. A `Horse` class could be derived from the existing `Mammal` class, automatically inheriting the variables and methods contained in `Mammal`. The `Horse` class can refer to the inherited variables and methods as if they had been declared locally in that class. New variables and methods can then be added to the derived class to distinguish a horse from other mammals. Inheritance thus nicely models many situations found in the natural world.

> Inherited variables and methods can be used in the derived class as if they had been declared locally.
>
> **key concept**

The original class that is used to derive a new one is called the *parent class, superclass,* or *base class.* The derived class is called a *child class,* or *subclass.* Java uses the reserved word `extends` to indicate that a new class is being derived from an existing class.

The derivation process should establish a specific kind of relationship between two classes: an *is-a relationship.* This type of relationship means that the derived class should be a more specific version of the original. For example, a horse is a mammal. Not all mammals are horses, but all horses are mammals.

> Inheritance creates an is-a relationship between all parent and child classes.
>
> **key concept**

Let's look at an example. The program shown in Listing 7.1 instantiates an object of class `Dictionary`, which is derived from a class called `Book`. In the `main` method, two methods are invoked through the `Dictionary` object: one that was declared locally in the `Dictionary` class and one that was inherited from the `Book` class.

The `Book` class (see Listing 7.2) is used to derive the `Dictionary` class (see Listing 7.3) using the reserved word `extends` in the header of `Dictionary`. The `Dictionary` class automatically inherits the definition of the `pageMessage` method and the `pages` variable. It is as if the `pageMessage` method and the `pages` variable were declared inside the `Dictionary` class. Note that the `definitionMessage` method refers explicitly to the `pages` variable.

```
listing
   7.1
```

```
//********************************************************************
//   Words.java        Author: Lewis/Loftus
//
//   Demonstrates the use of an inherited method.
//********************************************************************

public class Words
{
   //-----------------------------------------------------------------
   //   Instantiates a derived class and invokes its inherited and
   //   local methods.
   //-----------------------------------------------------------------
   public static void main (String[] args)
   {
      Dictionary webster = new Dictionary ();

      webster.pageMessage();
      webster.definitionMessage();
   }
}
```

output

```
Number of pages: 1500
Number of definitions: 52500
Definitions per page: 35
```

Also, note that although the Book class is needed to create the definition of Dictionary, no Book object is ever instantiated in the program. An instance of a child class does not rely on an instance of the parent class.

Inheritance is a one-way street. The Book class cannot use variables or methods that are declared explicitly in the Dictionary class. For instance, if we created an object from the Book class, it could not be used to invoke the definitionMessage method. This restriction makes sense because a child class is a more specific version of the parent class. A dictionary has pages because all books have pages; but although a dictionary has definitions, not all books do.

Inheritance relationships are often represented in UML class diagrams. Figure 7.1 shows the inheritance relationship between the Book and Dictionary classes. An arrow with an open arrowhead is used to show inheritance in a UML diagram, with the arrow pointing from the child class to the parent class.

```
//**********************************************************************
//   Book.java        Author: Lewis/Loftus
//
//   Represents a book. Used as the parent of a derived class to
//   demonstrate inheritance.
//**********************************************************************

public class Book
{
   protected int pages = 1500;

   //-----------------------------------------------------------------
   //  Prints a message about the pages of this book.
   //-----------------------------------------------------------------
   public void pageMessage ()
   {
      System.out.println ("Number of pages: " + pages);
   }
}
```

the protected modifier

Not all variables and methods are inherited in a derivation. The visibility modifiers used to declare the members of a class determine which ones are inherited and which ones are not. Specifically, the child class inherits variables and methods that are declared public and does not inherit those that are declared private. The pageMessage method is inherited by Dictionary because it is declared with public visibility.

However, if we declare a variable with public visibility so that a derived class can inherit it, we violate the principle of encapsulation. Therefore, Java provides a third visibility modifier: protected. Note that the variable pages is declared with protected visibility in the Book class. When a variable or method is declared with protected visibility, a derived class will inherit it, retaining some of its encapsulation properties. The encapsulation with protected visibility is not as tight as it would be if the variable or method were declared private, but it is better than if it were declared public. Specifically, a variable or method declared with protected

> key concept
>
> Visibility modifiers determine which variables and methods are inherited. Protected visibility provides the best possible encapsulation that permits inheritance.

listing
    7.3

```
//*******************************************************************
//  Dictionary.java        Author: Lewis/Loftus
//
//  Represents a dictionary, which is a book. Used to demonstrate
//  inheritance.
//*******************************************************************

public class Dictionary extends Book
{
    private int definitions = 52500;

    //----------------------------------------------------------------
    //  Prints a message using both local and inherited values.
    //----------------------------------------------------------------
    public void definitionMessage ()
    {
        System.out.println ("Number of definitions: " + definitions);

        System.out.println ("Definitions per page: " + definitions/pages);
    }
}
```

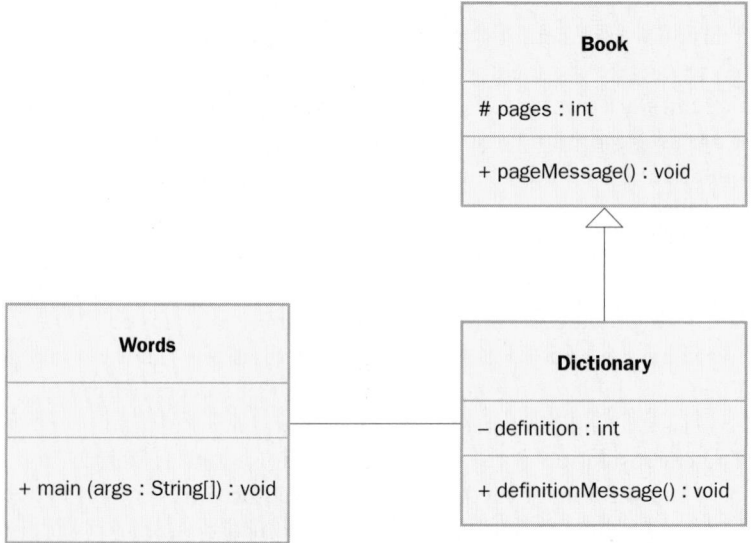

figure 7.1   A UML class diagram showing an inheritance relationship

visibility may be accessed by any class in the same package. The relationships among all Java modifiers are explained completely in Appendix F.

In a UML diagram, protected visibility can be indicated by proceeding the protected member with a hash mark (#). The `pages` variable of the `Book` class has this annotation in Fig. 7.1.

Each inherited variable or method retains the effect of its original visibility modifier. For example, the `pageMessage` method is still considered to be public in its inherited form.

Constructors are not inherited in a derived class, even though they have public visibility. This is an exception to the rule about public members being inherited. Constructors are special methods that are used to set up a particular type of object, so it wouldn't make sense for a class called `Dictionary` to have a constructor called `Book`.

the `super` reference

The reserved word `super` can be used in a class to refer to its parent class. Using the `super` reference, we can access a parent's members, even if they aren't inherited. Like the `this` reference, what the word `super` refers to depends on the class in which it is used. However, unlike the `this` reference, which refers to a particular instance of a class, `super` is a general reference to the members of the parent class.

One use of the `super` reference is to invoke a parent's constructor. Let's look at an example. Listing 7.4 shows a modification of the original `Words` program shown in Listing 7.1. Similar to the original version, we use a class called `Book2` (see Listing 7.5) as the parent of the derived class `Dictionary2` (see Listing 7.6). However, unlike earlier versions of these classes, `Book2` and `Dictionary2` have explicit constructors used to initialize their instance variables. The output of the `Words2` program is the same as it is for the original `Words` program.

> **key concept**
> A parent's constructor can be invoked using the `super` reference.

The `Dictionary2` constructor takes two integer values as parameters, representing the number of pages and definitions in the book. Because the `Book2` class already has a constructor that performs the work to set up the parts of the dictionary that were inherited, we rely on that constructor to do that work. However, since the constructor is not inherited, we cannot invoke it directly, and so we use the `super` reference to get to it in the parent class. The `Dictionary2` constructor then proceeds to initialize its `definitions` variable.

**listing
7.4**

```
//********************************************************************
//  Words2.java        Author: Lewis/Loftus
//
//  Demonstrates the use of the super reference.
//********************************************************************

public class Words2
{
   //-----------------------------------------------------------------
   //  Instantiates a derived class and invokes its inherited and
   //  local methods.
   //-----------------------------------------------------------------
   public static void main (String[] args)
   {
      Dictionary2 webster = new Dictionary2 (1500, 52500);

      webster.pageMessage();
      webster.definitionMessage();
   }
}
```

output

```
Number of pages: 1500
Number of definitions: 52500
Definitions per page: 35
```

In this case, it would have been just as easy to set the pages variable explicitly in the Dictionary2 constructor instead of using super to call the Book2 constructor. However, it is good practice to let each class "take care" of itself. If we choose to change the way that the Book2 constructor sets up its pages variable, we would also have to remember to make that change in Dictionary2. By using the super reference, a change made in Book2 is automatically reflected in Dictionary2.

A child's constructor is responsible for calling its parent's constructor. Generally, the first line of a constructor should use the super reference call to a constructor of the parent class. If no such call exists, Java will automatically make a call to super() at the beginning of the constructor. This rule ensures that a parent class initializes its variables before the child class constructor begins to execute. Using the super reference to invoke a parent's constructor can be done in

```
listing
   7.5
```

```
//*******************************************************************
//  Book2.java        Author: Lewis/Loftus
//
//  Represents a book. Used as the parent of a dervied class to
//  demonstrate inheritance and the use of the super reference.
//*******************************************************************

public class Book2
{
   protected int pages;

   //-------------------------------------------------------------
   //  Sets up the book with the specified number of pages.
   //-------------------------------------------------------------
   public Book2 (int numPages)
   {
      pages = numPages;
   }

   //-------------------------------------------------------------
   //  Prints a message about the pages of this book.
   //-------------------------------------------------------------
   public void pageMessage ()
   {
      System.out.println ("Number of pages: " + pages);
   }
}
```

only the child's constructor, and if included it must be the first line of the constructor.

The super reference can also be used to reference other variables and methods defined in the parent's class. We discuss this technique later in this chapter.

multiple inheritance

Java's approach to inheritance is called *single inheritance*. This term means that a derived class can have only one parent. Some object-oriented languages allow a child class to have multiple parents. This approach is called *multiple inheritance* and is occasionally useful for describing objects that are in between two

listing
   7.6

```
//***********************************************************************
//  Dictionary2.java       Author: Lewis/Loftus
//
//  Represents a dictionary, which is a book. Used to demonstrate
//  the use of the super reference.
//***********************************************************************

public class Dictionary2 extends Book2
{
    private int definitions;

    //----------------------------------------------------------------
    //  Sets up the dictionary with the specified number of pages
    //  (maintained by the Book parent class) and defintions.
    //----------------------------------------------------------------
    public Dictionary2 (int numPages, int numDefinitions)
    {
        super (numPages);

        definitions = numDefinitions;
    }

    //----------------------------------------------------------------
    //  Prints a message using both local and inherited values.
    //----------------------------------------------------------------
    public void definitionMessage ()
    {
        System.out.println ("Number of definitions: " + definitions);

        System.out.println ("Definitions per page: " + definitions/pages);
    }
}
```

categories or classes. For example, suppose we had a class Car and a class Truck and we wanted to create a new class called PickupTruck. A pickup truck is somewhat like a car and somewhat like a truck. With single inheritance, we must decide whether it is better to derive the new class from Car or Truck. With multiple inheritance, it can be derived from both, as shown in Fig. 7.2.

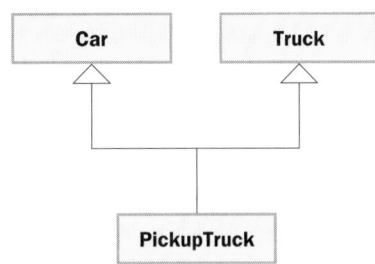

figure 7.2   A UML class diagram showing multiple inheritance

Multiple inheritance works well in some situations, but it comes with a price. What if both `Truck` and `Car` have methods with the same name? Which method would `PickupTruck` inherit? The answer to this question is complex, and it depends on the rules of the language that supports multiple inheritance.

Java does not support multiple inheritance, but interfaces provide some of the abilities of multiple inheritance. Although a Java class can be derived from only one parent class, it can implement many different interfaces. Therefore, we can interact with a particular class in particular ways while inheriting the core information from one particular parent.

7.1 overriding methods

When a child class defines a method with the same name and signature as a method in the parent class, we say that the child's version *overrides* the parent's version in favor of its own. The need for overriding occurs often in inheritance situations.

> **key concept**
>
> A child class can override (redefine) the parent's definition of an inherited method.

The program in Listing 7.7 provides a simple demonstration of method overriding in Java. The `Messages` class contains a `main` method that instantiates two objects: one from class `Thought` and one from class `Advice`. The `Thought` class is the parent of the `Advice` class.

Both the `Thought` class (see Listing 7.8) and the `Advice` class (see Listing 7.9) contain a definition for a method called `message`. The version of `message` defined in the `Thought` class is inherited by `Advice`, but `Advice` overrides it with an alternative version. The new version of the method prints out an entirely different message and then invokes the parent's version of the `message` method using the `super` reference.

```
listing
   7.7
```

```
//************************************************************
//   Messages.java          Author: Lewis/Loftus
//
//   Demonstrates the use of an overridden method.
//************************************************************

public class Messages
{
    //--------------------------------------------------------
    //   Instatiates two objects a invokes the message method in each.
    //--------------------------------------------------------
    public static void main (String[] args)
    {
        Thought parked = new Thought();
        Advice dates = new Advice();

        parked.message();

        dates.message();   // overridden
    }
}
```

output

```
I feel like I'm diagonally parked in a parallel universe.

Warning: Dates in calendar are closer than they appear.

I feel like I'm diagonally parked in a parallel universe.
```

The object that is used to invoke a method determines which version of the method is actually executed. When message is invoked using the parked object in the main method, the Thought version of message is executed. When message is invoked using the dates object, the Advice version of message is executed. This flexibility allows two objects that are related by inheritance to use the same naming conventions for methods that accomplish the same general task in different ways.

A method can be defined with the final modifier. A child class cannot override a final method. This technique is used to ensure that a derived class uses a particular definition for a method.

```
listing
   7.8

//**********************************************************************
//  Thought.java          Author: Lewis/Loftus
//
//  Represents a stray thought. Used as the parent of a derived
//  class to demonstrate the use of an overridden method.
//**********************************************************************

public class Thought
{
   //-----------------------------------------------------------------
   //  Prints a message.
   //-----------------------------------------------------------------
   public void message()
   {
      System.out.println ("I feel like I'm diagonally parked in a " +
                             "parallel universe.");

      System.out.println();
   }
}
```

The concept of method overriding is important to several issues related to inheritance. We explore these issues throughout this chapter.

shadowing variables

It is possible, although not recommended, for a child class to declare a variable with the same name as one that is inherited from the parent. This technique is called *shadowing variables*. It is similar to the process of overriding methods but creates confusing subtleties. Note the distinction between redeclaring a variable and simply giving an inherited variable a particular value.

Because an inherited variable is already available to the child class, there is usually no good reason to redeclare it. Someone reading code with a shadowed variable will find two different declarations that seem to apply to a variable used in the child class. This confusion causes problems and serves no purpose. A redeclaration of a particular variable name could change its type, but that is usually unnecessary. In general, shadowing variables should be avoided.

listing
   7.9

```
//********************************************************************
//  Advice.java        Author: Lewis/Loftus
//
//  Represents a piece of advice. Used to demonstrate the use of an
//  overridden method.
//********************************************************************

public class Advice extends Thought
{
    //-----------------------------------------------------------------
    //  Prints a message. This method overrides the parent's version.
    //  It also invokes the parent's version explicitly using super.
    //-----------------------------------------------------------------
    public void message()
    {
        System.out.println ("Warning: Dates in calendar are closer " +
                            "than they appear.");

        System.out.println();

        super.message();
    }
}
```

7.2   class hierarchies

A child class derived from one parent can be the parent of its own child class. Furthermore, multiple classes can be derived from a single parent. Therefore, inheritance relationships often develop into *class hierarchies*. The UML class diagram in Fig. 7.3 shows a class hierarchy that incorporates the inheritance relationship between the `Mammal` and `Horse` classes.

There is no limit to the number of children a class can have or to the number of levels to which a class hierarchy can extend. Two children of the same parent are called *siblings*. Although siblings share the characteristics passed on by their common parent, they are not related by inheritance because one is not used to derive the other.

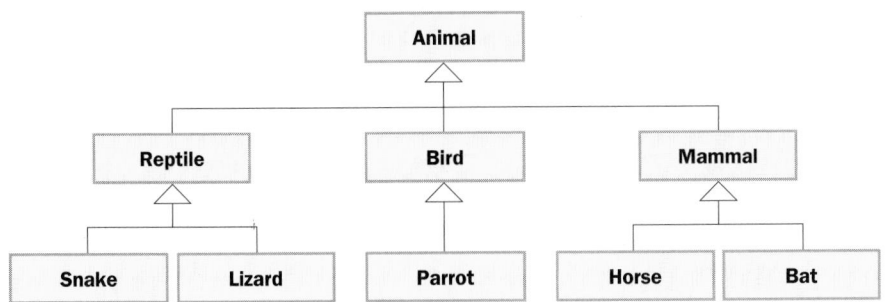

figure 7.3   A UML class diagram showing a class hierarchy

In class hierarchies, common features should be kept as high in the hierarchy as reasonably possible. That way, the only characteristics explicitly established in a child class are those that make the class distinct from its parent and from its siblings. This approach maximizes the potential to reuse classes. It also facilitates maintenance activities because when changes are made to the parent, they are automatically reflected in the descendents. Always remember to maintain the is-a relationship when building class hierarchies.

> Common features should be located as high in a class hierarchy as is reasonably possible, minimizing maintenance efforts.
>
> *key concept*

The inheritance mechanism is transitive. That is, a parent passes along a trait to a child class, and that child class passes it along to its children, and so on. An inherited feature might have originated in the immediate parent or possibly several levels higher in a more distant ancestor class.

There is no single best hierarchy organization for all situations. The decisions you make when you are designing a class hierarchy restrict and guide more detailed design decisions and implementation options, so you must make them carefully.

Earlier in this chapter we discussed a class hierarchy that organized animals by their major biological classifications, such as `Mammal`, `Bird`, and `Reptile`. However, in a different situation, the same animals might logically be organized in a different way. For example, as shown in Fig. 7.4, the class hierarchy might be organized around a function of the animals, such as their ability to fly. In this case, a `Parrot` class and a `Bat` class would be siblings derived from a general `FlyingAnimal` class. This class hierarchy is as valid and reasonable as the original one. The needs of the programs that use the classes will determine which is best for the particular situation.

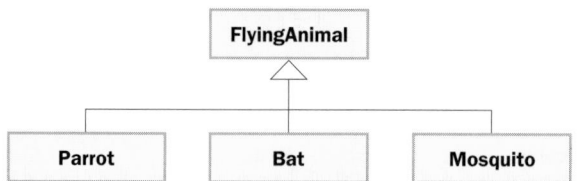

figure 7.4   An alternative hierarchy for organizing animals

the Object class

In Java, all classes are derived ultimately from the Object class. If a class defi-nition doesn't use the extends clause to derive itself explicitly from another class, then that class is automatically derived from the Object class by default. Therefore, the following two class definitions are equivalent:

```
class Thing
{
   // whatever
}
```

and

```
class Thing extends Object
{
   // whatever
}
```

key concept

All Java classes are derived, directly or indirectly, from the Object class.

Because all classes are derived from Object, any public method of Object can be invoked through any object created in any Java pro-gram. The Object class is defined in the java.lang package of the Java standard class library. Figure 7.5 lists some of the methods of the Object class.

As it turns out, we've been using Object methods quite often in our examples. The toString method, for instance, is defined in the Object class, so the toString method can be called on any object. As we've seen several times, when a println method is called with an object parameter, toString is called to deter-mine what to print.

The definition for toString that is provided by the Object class returns a string containing the object's class name followed by a numeric value that is unique for that object. Usually, we override the Object version of toString to

```
boolean equals (Object obj)
    Returns true if this object is an alias of the specified object.

String toString ()
    Returns a string representation of this object.

Object clone ()
    Creates and returns a copy of this object.
```

figure 7.5   Some methods of the `Object` class

fit our own needs. The `String` class has overridden the `toString` method so that it returns its stored string value.

The `equals` method of the `Object` class is also useful. As we've discussed previously, its purpose is to determine whether two objects are equal. The definition of the `equals` method provided by the `Object` class returns true if the two object references actually refer to the same object (that is, if they are aliases). Classes often override the inherited definition of the `equals` method in favor of a more appropriate definition. For instance, the `String` class overrides `equals` so that it returns true only if both strings contain the same characters in the same order.

> **key concept**
>
> The `toString` and `equals` methods are defined in the `Object` class and therefore are inherited by every class in every Java program.

Listing 7.10 shows the program called `Academia`. In this program, a `Student` object and a `GradStudent` object are instantiated. The `Student` class (see Listing 7.11) is the parent of `GradStudent` (see Listing 7.12). A graduate student is a student that has a potential source of income, such as being a graduate teaching assistant (GTA).

The `GradStudent` class inherits the variables `name` and `numCourses`, as well as the method `toString` that was defined in `Student` (overriding the version from `Object`). The `GradStudent` constructor uses the `super` reference to invoke the constructor of `Student`, and then initializes its own variables.

The `GradStudent` class augments its inherited definition with variables concerning financial support, and it overrides `toString` (yet again) to print additional information. Note that the `GradStudent` version of `toString` explicitly invokes the `Student` version of `toString` using the `super` reference.

listing
    7.10

```
//***********************************************************************
//   Academia.java        Author: Lewis/Loftus
//
//   Demonstrates the use of methods inherited from the Object class.
//***********************************************************************

public class Academia
{
   //----------------------------------------------------------------
   //   Creates objects of two student types, prints some information
   //   about them, then checks them for equality.
   //----------------------------------------------------------------
   public static void main (String[] args)
   {
      Student susan = new Student ("Susan", 5);
      GradStudent frank = new GradStudent ("Frank", 3, "GTA", 12.75);

      System.out.println (susan);
      System.out.println ();

      System.out.println (frank);
      System.out.println ();

      if (! susan.equals(frank))
         System.out.println ("These are two different students.");
   }
}
```

output

```
Student name: Susan
Number of courses: 5

Student name: Frank
Number of courses: 3
Support source: GTA
Hourly pay rate: 12.75

These are two different students.
```

listing
   7.11

```java
//********************************************************************
//  Student.java        Author: Lewis/Loftus
//
//  Represents a student. Used to demonstrate inheritance.
//********************************************************************

public class Student
{
   protected String name;
   protected int numCourses;

   //-----------------------------------------------------------------
   //  Sets up a student with the specified name and number of
   //  courses.
   //-----------------------------------------------------------------
   public Student (String studentName, int courses)
   {
      name = studentName;
      numCourses = courses;
   }

   //-----------------------------------------------------------------
   //  Returns information about this student as a string.
   //-----------------------------------------------------------------
   public String toString()
   {
      String result = "Student name: " + name + "\n";

      result += "Number of courses: " + numCourses;

      return result;
   }
}
```

listing
    7.12

```
//********************************************************************
//  GradStudent.java        Author: Lewis/Loftus
//
//  Represents a graduate student with financial support. Used to
//  demonstrate inheritance.
//********************************************************************

public class GradStudent extends Student
{
   private String source;
   private double rate;

   //-----------------------------------------------------------------
   //  Sets up the graduate student using the specified information.
   //-----------------------------------------------------------------
   public GradStudent (String studentName, int courses,
                       String support, double payRate)
   {
      super (studentName, courses);

      source = support;
      rate = payRate;
   }

   //-----------------------------------------------------------------
   //  Returns a description of this graduate student as a string.
   //-----------------------------------------------------------------
   public String toString()
   {
      String result = super.toString();

      result += "\nSupport source: " + source + "\n";
      result += "Hourly pay rate: " + rate;

      return result;
   }
}
```

abstract classes

An *abstract class* represents a generic concept in a class hierarchy. An abstract class cannot be instantiated and usually contains one or more abstract methods, which have no definition. In this sense, an abstract class is similar to an interface. Unlike interfaces, however, an abstract class can contain methods that are not abstract. It can also contain data declarations other than constants.

A class is declared as abstract by including the `abstract` modifier in the class header. Any class that contains one or more abstract methods must be declared as abstract. In abstract classes (unlike interfaces) the `abstract` modifier must be applied to each abstract method. A class declared as abstract does not have to contain abstract methods.

Abstract classes serve as placeholders in a class hierarchy. As the name implies, an abstract class represents an abstract entity that is usually insufficiently defined to be useful by itself. Instead, an abstract class may contain a partial description that is inherited by all of its descendants in the class hierarchy. Its children, which are more specific, fill in the gaps.

> **key concept**
>
> An abstract class cannot be instantiated. It represents a concept on which other classes can build their definitions.

Consider the class hierarchy shown in Fig. 7.6. The `Vehicle` class at the top of the hierarchy may be too generic for a particular application. Therefore we may choose to implement it as an abstract class. In UML diagram, abstract class names are shown in italic. Concepts that apply to all vehicles can be represented in the `Vehicle` class and are inherited by its descendants. That way, each of its descendants doesn't have to define the same concept redundantly (and perhaps inconsistently.) For example, we may say that all vehicles have a particular speed. Therefore we declare a `speed` variable in the `Vehicle` class, and all specific vehicles below it in the hierarchy automatically have that variable because of inheritance. Any change we make to the representation of the speed of a vehicle is automatically reflected in all descendant classes. Similarly, we may declare an abstract

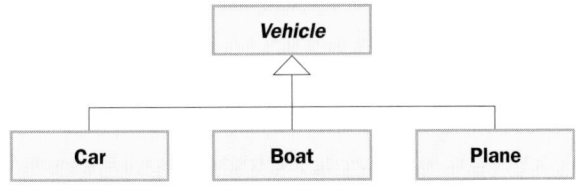

figure 7.6   A `vehicle` class hierarchy

method called `fuelConsumption`, whose purpose is to calculate how quickly fuel is being consumed by a particular vehicle. The details of the `fuelConsumption` method must be defined by each type of vehicle, but the `Vehicle` class establishes that all vehicles consume fuel and provides a consistent way to compute that value.

Some concepts don't apply to all vehicles, so we wouldn't represent those concepts at the `Vehicle` level. For instance, we wouldn't include a variable called `numberOfWheels` in the `Vehicle` class, because not all vehicles have wheels. The child classes for which wheels are appropriate can add that concept at the appropriate level in the hierarchy.

There are no restrictions as to where in a class hierarchy an abstract class can be defined. Usually they are located at the upper levels of a class hierarchy. However, it is possible to derive an abstract class from a nonabstract parent.

> **Key concept**
>
> A class derived from an abstract parent must override all of its parent's abstract methods, or the derived class will also be considered abstract.

Usually, a child of an abstract class will provide a specific definition for an abstract method inherited from its parent. Note that this is just a specific case of overriding a method, giving a different definition than the one the parent provides. If a child of an abstract class does not give a definition for every abstract method that it inherits from its parent, the child class is also considered abstract.

Note that it would be a contradiction for an abstract method to be modified as `final` or `static`. Because a final method cannot be overridden in subclasses, an abstract final method would have no way of being given a definition in subclasses. A static method can be invoked using the class name without declaring an object of the class. Because abstract methods have no implementation, an abstract static method would make no sense.

Choosing which classes and methods to make abstract is an important part of the design process. You should make such choices only after careful consideration. By using abstract classes wisely, you can create flexible, extensible software designs. We present an example later in this chapter that relies on an abstract class to organize a class hierarchy.

7.3   indirect use of class members

There is a subtle feature of inheritance that is worth noting at this point. The visibility modifiers determine whether a variable or method is inherited into a subclass. If a variable or method is inherited, it can be referenced directly in the subclass by name, as if it were declared locally in the subclass. However, all variables and methods that are defined in a parent class exist for an object of a derived class, even though they can't be referenced directly. They can, however, be referenced indirectly.

Let's look at an example that demonstrates this situation. The program shown in Listing 7.13 contains a `main` method that instantiates a `Pizza` object and invokes a method to determine how many calories the pizza has per serving due to its fat content.

The `FoodItem` class shown in Listing 7.14 represents a generic type of food. The constructor of `FoodItem` accepts the number of grams of fat and the number of servings of that food. The `calories` method returns the number of calories due to fat, which the `caloriesPerServing` method invokes to help compute the number of fat calories per serving.

listing
7.13

```
//************************************************************************
//   FoodAnalysis.java        Author: Lewis/Loftus
//
//   Demonstrates indirect referencing through inheritance.
//************************************************************************

public class FoodAnalysis
{
    //---------------------------------------------------------------
    //   Instantiates a Pizza object and prints its calories per
    //   serving.
    //---------------------------------------------------------------
    public static void main (String[] args)
    {
        Pizza special = new Pizza (275);

        System.out.println ("Calories per serving: " +
                            special.caloriesPerServing());
    }
}
```

output

```
Calories per serving: 309
```

listing
    7.14

```
//********************************************************************
//   FoodItem.java        Author: Lewis/Loftus
//
//   Represents an item of food. Used as the parent of a derived class
//   to demonstrate indirect referencing through inheritance.
//********************************************************************

public class FoodItem
{
   final private int CALORIES_PER_GRAM = 9;
   private int fatGrams;
   protected int servings;

   //----------------------------------------------------------------
   //   Sets up this food item with the specified number of fat grams
   //   and number of servings.
   //----------------------------------------------------------------
   public FoodItem (int numFatGrams, int numServings)
   {
      fatGrams = numFatGrams;
      servings = numServings;
   }

   //----------------------------------------------------------------
   //   Computes and returns the number of calories in this food item
   //   due to fat.
   //----------------------------------------------------------------
   private int calories()
   {
      return fatGrams * CALORIES_PER_GRAM;
   }

   //----------------------------------------------------------------
   //   Computes and returns the number of fat calories per serving.
   //----------------------------------------------------------------
   public int caloriesPerServing()
   {
      return (calories() / servings);
   }
}
```

The `Pizza` class, shown in Listing 7.15, is derived from `FoodItem` class, but it adds no special functionality or data. Its constructor calls the constructor of `FoodItem`, using the `super` reference assuming that there are eight servings per pizza.

Note that the `Pizza` object called `special` in the `main` method is used to invoke the method `caloriesPerServing`, which is defined as a public method of `FoodItem` and is therefore inherited by `Pizza`. However, `caloriesPerServing` calls `calories`, which is declared private, and is therefore not inherited by `Pizza`. Furthermore, `calories` references the variable `fatGrams` and the constant `CALORIES_PER_GRAM`, which are also declared with private visibility.

> **key concept**
>
> All members of a superclass exist for a subclass, but they are not necessarily inherited. Only inherited members can be referenced by name in the subclass.

Even though `Pizza` did not inherit `calories`, `fatGrams`, or `CALORIES_PER_GRAM`, they are available for use indirectly when the `Pizza` object needs them. The `Pizza` class cannot refer to them directly by name because they are not inherited, but they do exist. Note that a `FoodItem` object was never created or needed.

listing 7.15

```
//********************************************************************
//  Pizza.java          Author: Lewis/Loftus
//
//  Represents a pizza, which is a food item. Used to demonstrate
//  indirect referencing through inheritance.
//********************************************************************

public class Pizza extends FoodItem
{
   //-----------------------------------------------------------------
   //  Sets up a pizza with the specified amount of fat (assumes
   //  eight servings).
   //-----------------------------------------------------------------
   public Pizza (int fatGrams)
   {
      super (fatGrams, 8);
   }
}
```

Figure 7.7 lists each variable and method declared in the `FoodItem` class and indicates whether it exists in or is inherited by the `Pizza` class. Note that every `FoodItem` member exists in the `Pizza` class, no matter how it is declared. The items that are not inherited can be referenced only indirectly.

7.4   polymorphism

Usually, the type of a reference variable matches exactly the class of the object to which it refers. That is, if we declare a reference as follows, the `bishop` reference is used to refer to an object created by instantiating the `ChessPiece` class.

```
ChessPiece bishop;
```

However, the relationship between a reference variable and the object it refers to is more flexible than that.

> **key concept**
>
> A polymorphic reference can refer to different types of objects over time.

The term *polymorphism* can be defined as "having many forms." A *polymorphic reference* is a reference variable that can refer to different types of objects at different points in time. The specific method invoked through a polymorphic reference can change from one invocation to the next.

Consider the following line of code:

```
obj.doIt();
```

Declared in `FoodItem` **class**	Defined in `Pizza` **class**	Inherited in `Pizza` **class**
`CALORIES_PER_GRAM`	yes	no, because the constant is private
`fatGrams`	yes	no, because the variable is private
`servings`	yes	yes, because the variable is protected
`FoodItem`	yes	no, because the constructors are not inherited
`calories`	yes	no, because the method is private
`caloriesPerServing`	yes	yes, because the method is public

figure 7.7   The relationship between `FoodItem` members and the `Pizza` class

If the reference `obj` is polymorphic, it can refer to different types of objects at different times. If that line of code is in a loop or in a method that is called more than once, that line of code might call a different version of the `doIt` method each time it is invoked.

At some point, the commitment is made to execute certain code to carry out a method invocation. This commitment is referred to as *binding* a method invocation to a method definition. In most situations, the binding of a method invocation to a method definition can occur at compile time. For polymorphic references, however, the decision cannot be made until run time. The method definition that is used is based on the object that is being referred to by the reference variable at that moment. This deferred commitment is called *late binding* or *dynamic binding*. It is less efficient than binding at compile time because the decision must be made during the execution of the program. This overhead is generally acceptable in light of the flexibility that a polymorphic reference provides.

We can create a polymorphic reference in Java in two ways: using inheritance and using interfaces. This section describes how we can accomplish polymorphism using inheritance. Later in the chapter we revisit the issue of interfaces and describe how polymorphism can be accomplished using interfaces as well.

references and class hierarchies

In Java, a reference that is declared to refer to an object of a particular class can also be used to refer to an object of any class related to it by inheritance. For example, if the class `Mammal` is used to derive the class `Horse`, then a `Mammal` reference can be used to refer to an object of class `Horse`. This ability is shown in the following code segment:

> A reference variable can refer to any object created from any class related to it by inheritance.

```
Mammal pet;
Horse secretariat = new Horse();
pet = secretariat;  // a valid assignment
```

The reverse operation, assigning the `Mammal` object to a `Horse` reference, is also valid but requires an explicit cast. Assigning a reference in this direction is generally less useful and more likely to cause problems because although a horse has all the functionality of a mammal (because a horse *is-a* mammal), the reverse is not necessarily true.

This relationship works throughout a class hierarchy. If the `Mammal` class were derived from a class called `Animal`, the following assignment would also be valid:

```
Animal creature = new Horse();
```

Carrying this to the limit, an `Object` reference can be used to refer to any object because ultimately all classes are descendants of the `Object` class. An `ArrayList`, for example, uses polymorphism in that it is designed to hold `Object` references. That's why an `ArrayList` can be used to store any kind of object. In fact, a particular `ArrayList` can be used to hold several different types of objects at one time because, in essence, they are all `Object` objects.

polymorphism via inheritance

The reference variable `creature`, as defined in the previous section, can be polymorphic because at any point in time it can refer to an `Animal` object, a `Mammal` object, or a `Horse` object. Suppose that all three of these classes have a method called move that is implemented in different ways (because the child class overrode the definition it inherited). The following invocation calls the move method, but the particular version of the method it calls is determined at runtime:

```
creature.move();
```

key concept

A polymorphic reference uses the type of the object, not the type of the reference, to determine which version of a method to invoke.

At the point when this line is executed, if `creature` currently refers to an `Animal` object, the move method of the `Animal` class is invoked. Likewise, if `creature` currently refers to a `Mammal` or `Horse` object, the `Mammal` or `Horse` version of move is invoked, respectively.

Of course, since `Animal` and `Mammal` represent general concepts, they may be defined as abstract classes. This situation does not eliminate the ability to have polymorphic references. Suppose the move method in the `Mammal` class is abstract, and is given unique definitions in the `Horse`, `Dog`, and `Whale` classes (all derived from `Mammal`). A `Mammal` reference variable can be used to refer to any objects created from any of the `Horse`, `Dog`, and `Whale` classes, and can be used to execute the move method on any of them.

Let's look at another situation. Consider the class hierarchy shown in Fig. 7.8. The classes in it represent various types of employees that might be employed at a particular company. Let's explore an example that uses this hierarchy to demonstrate several inheritance issues, including polymorphism.

The `Firm` class shown in Listing 7.16 contains a main driver that creates a `Staff` of employees and invokes the `payday` method to pay them all. The program output includes information about each employee and how much each is paid (if anything).

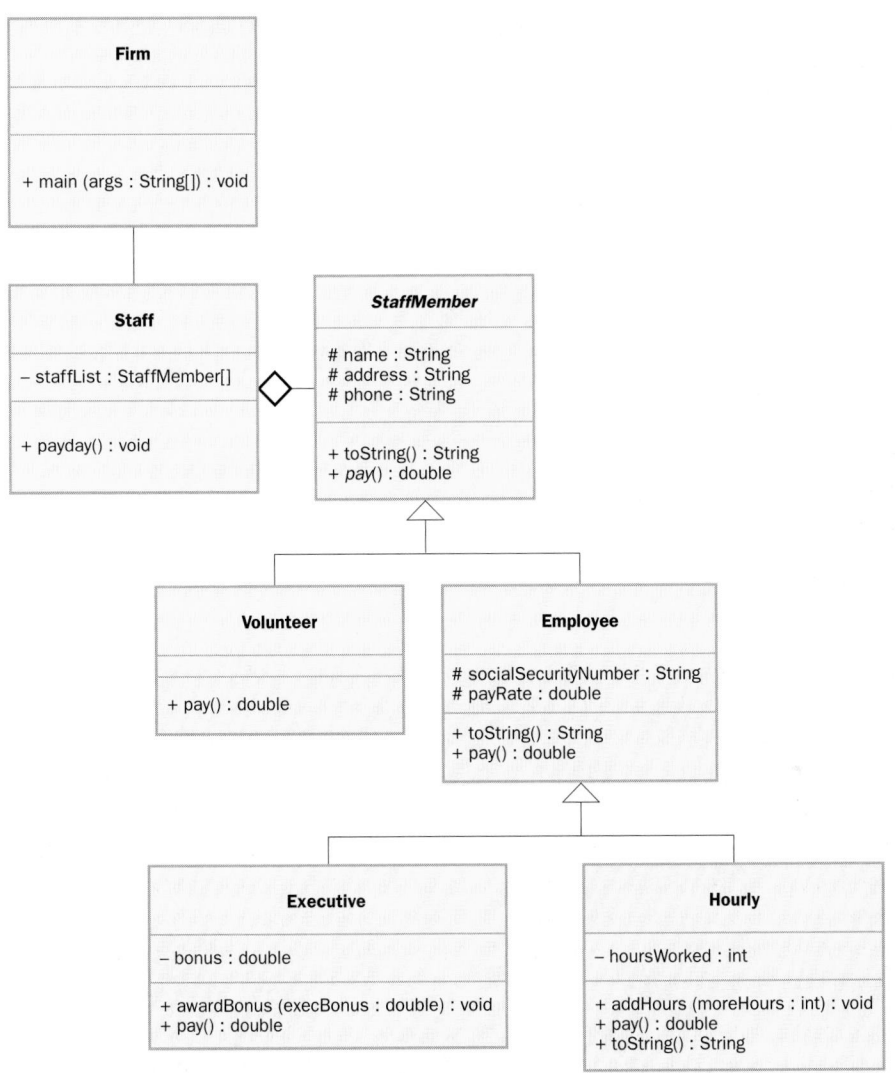

figure 7.8   A class hierarchy of employees

listing
   7.16

```
//********************************************************************
//  Firm.java        Author: Lewis/Loftus
//
//  Demonstrates polymorphism via inheritance.
//********************************************************************

public class Firm
{
   //-----------------------------------------------------------------
   //  Creates a staff of employees for a firm and pays them.
   //-----------------------------------------------------------------
   public static void main (String[] args)
   {
      Staff personnel = new Staff();

      personnel.payday();
   }
}
```

output

```
Name: Sam
Address: 123 Main Line
Phone: 555-0469
Social Security Number: 123-45-6789
Paid: 2923.07
------------------------------------
Name: Carla
Address: 456 Off Line
Phone: 555-0101
Social Security Number: 987-65-4321
Paid: 1246.15
------------------------------------
Name: Woody
Address: 789 Off Rocker
Phone: 555-0000
Social Security Number: 010-20-3040
Paid: 1169.23
------------------------------------
Name: Diane
Address: 678 Fifth Ave.
Phone: 555-0690
Social Security Number: 958-47-3625
Current hours: 40
Paid: 422.0
```

listing
7.16 continued

```
-------------------------------------
Name: Norm
Address: 987 Suds Blvd.
Phone: 555-8374
Thanks!
-------------------------------------
Name: Cliff
Address: 321 Duds Lane
Phone: 555-7282
Thanks!
-------------------------------------
```

The `Staff` class shown in Listing 7.17 maintains an array of objects that represent individual employees of various kinds. Note that the array is declared to hold `StaffMember` references, but it is actually filled with objects created from several other classes, such as `Executive` and `Employee`. These classes are all descendants of the `StaffMember` class, so the assignments are valid.

The `payday` method of the `Staff` class scans through the list of employees, printing their information and invoking their `pay` methods to determine how much each employee should be paid. The invocation of the `pay` method is polymorphic because each class has its own version of the `pay` method.

The `StaffMember` class shown in Listing 7.18 is abstract. It does not represent a particular type of employee and is not intended to be instantiated. Rather, it serves as the ancestor of all employee classes and contains information that applies to all employees. Each employee has a name, address, and phone number, so variables to store these values are declared in the `StaffMember` class and are inherited by all descendants.

The `StaffMember` class contains a `toString` method to return the information managed by the `StaffMember` class. It also contains an abstract method called `pay`, which takes no parameters and returns a value of type `double`. At the generic `StaffMember` level, it would be inappropriate to give a definition for this method. The descendants of `StaffMember`, however, each provide their own

listing
    7.17

```
//************************************************************************
//  Staff.java          Author: Lewis/Loftus
//
//  Represents the personnel staff of a particular business.
//************************************************************************

public class Staff
{
    private StaffMember[] staffList;

    //----------------------------------------------------------------
    //  Sets up the list of staff members.
    //----------------------------------------------------------------
    public Staff ()
    {
        staffList = new StaffMember[6];

        staffList[0] = new Executive ("Sam", "123 Main Line",
            "555-0469", "123-45-6789", 2423.07);

        staffList[1] = new Employee ("Carla", "456 Off Line",
            "555-0101", "987-65-4321", 1246.15);
        staffList[2] = new Employee ("Woody", "789 Off Rocker",
            "555-0000", "010-20-3040", 1169.23);

        staffList[3] = new Hourly ("Diane", "678 Fifth Ave.",
            "555-0690", "958-47-3625", 10.55);

        staffList[4] = new Volunteer ("Norm", "987 Suds Blvd.",
            "555-8374");
        staffList[5] = new Volunteer ("Cliff", "321 Duds Lane",
            "555-7282");

        ((Executive)staffList[0]).awardBonus (500.00);

        ((Hourly)staffList[3]).addHours (40);
    }

    //----------------------------------------------------------------
    //  Pays all staff members.
    //----------------------------------------------------------------
```

listing
    7.17 continued

```
    public void payday ()
    {
        double amount;

        for (int count=0; count < staffList.length; count++)
        {
            System.out.println (staffList[count]);

            amount = staffList[count].pay();   // polymorphic

            if (amount == 0.0)
                System.out.println ("Thanks!");
            else
                System.out.println ("Paid: " + amount);

            System.out.println ("--------------------------------");
        }
    }
}
```

specific definition for pay. By defining pay abstractly in StaffMember, the payday method of Staff can polymorphically pay each employee.

The Volunteer class shown in Listing 7.19 represents a person that is not compensated monetarily for his or her work. We keep track only of a volunteer's basic information, which is passed into the constructor of Volunteer, which in turn passes it to the StaffMember constructor using the super reference. The pay method of Volunteer simply returns a zero pay value. If pay had not been overridden, the Volunteer class would have been considered abstract and could not have been instantiated.

Note that when a volunteer gets "paid" in the payday method of Staff, a simple expression of thanks is printed. In all other situations, where the pay value is greater than zero, the payment itself is printed.

The Employee class shown in Listing 7.20 represents an employee that gets paid at a particular rate each pay period. The pay rate, as well as the employee's social security number, is passed along with the other basic information to the Employee constructor. The basic information is passed to the constructor of StaffMember using the super reference.

listing
    7.18

```java
//***********************************************************************
//   StaffMember.java          Author: Lewis/Loftus
//
//   Represents a generic staff member.
//***********************************************************************

abstract public class StaffMember
{
   protected String name;
   protected String address;
   protected String phone;

   //-----------------------------------------------------------------
   //   Sets up a staff member using the specified information.
   //-----------------------------------------------------------------
   public StaffMember (String eName, String eAddress, String ePhone)
   {
      name = eName;
      address = eAddress;
      phone = ePhone;
   }

   //-----------------------------------------------------------------
   //   Returns a string including the basic employee information.
   //-----------------------------------------------------------------
   public String toString()
   {
      String result = "Name: " + name + "\n";

      result += "Address: " + address + "\n";
      result += "Phone: " + phone;

      return result;
   }

   //-----------------------------------------------------------------
   //   Derived classes must define the pay method for each type of
   //   employee.
   //-----------------------------------------------------------------
   public abstract double pay();
}
```

```
//********************************************************************
//  Volunteer.java        Author: Lewis/Loftus
//
//  Represents a staff member that works as a volunteer.
//********************************************************************

public class Volunteer extends StaffMember
{
    //-----------------------------------------------------------------
    //  Sets up a volunteer using the specified information.
    //-----------------------------------------------------------------
    public Volunteer (String eName, String eAddress, String ePhone)
    {
        super (eName, eAddress, ePhone);
    }

    //-----------------------------------------------------------------
    //  Returns a zero pay value for this volunteer.
    //-----------------------------------------------------------------
    public double pay()
    {
        return 0.0;
    }
}
```

The toString method of Employee is overridden to concatenate the additional information that Employee manages to the information returned by the parent's version of toString, which is called using the super reference. The pay method of an Employee simply returns the pay rate for that employee.

The Executive class shown in Listing 7.21 represents an employee that may earn a bonus in addition to his or her normal pay rate. The Executive class is derived from Employee and therefore inherits from both StaffMember and Employee. The constructor of Executive passes along its information to the Employee constructor and sets the executive bonus to zero.

listing
    7.20

```java
//********************************************************************
//   Employee.java         Author: Lewis/Loftus
//
//   Represents a general paid employee.
//********************************************************************

public class Employee extends StaffMember
{
   protected String socialSecurityNumber;
   protected double payRate;

   //-----------------------------------------------------------------
   //  Sets up an employee with the specified information.
   //-----------------------------------------------------------------
   public Employee (String eName, String eAddress, String ePhone,
                    String socSecNumber, double rate)
   {
      super (eName, eAddress, ePhone);

      socialSecurityNumber = socSecNumber;
      payRate = rate;
   }

   //-----------------------------------------------------------------
   //  Returns information about an employee as a string.
   //-----------------------------------------------------------------
   public String toString()
   {
      String result = super.toString();

      result += "\nSocial Security Number: " + socialSecurityNumber;

      return result;
   }

   //-----------------------------------------------------------------
   //  Returns the pay rate for this employee.
   //-----------------------------------------------------------------
   public double pay()
   {
      return payRate;
   }
}
```

listing
7.21

```java
//********************************************************************
//  Executive.java       Author: Lewis/Loftus
//
//  Represents an executive staff member, who can earn a bonus.
//********************************************************************

public class Executive extends Employee
{
   private double bonus;

   //-----------------------------------------------------------------
   //  Sets up an executive with the specified information.
   //-----------------------------------------------------------------
   public Executive (String eName, String eAddress, String ePhone,
                   String socSecNumber, double rate)
   {
      super (eName, eAddress, ePhone, socSecNumber, rate);

      bonus = 0;  // bonus has yet to be awarded
   }

   //-----------------------------------------------------------------
   //  Awards the specified bonus to this executive.
   //-----------------------------------------------------------------
   public void awardBonus (double execBonus)
   {
      bonus = execBonus;
   }

   //-----------------------------------------------------------------
   //  Computes and returns the pay for an executive, which is the
   //  regular employee payment plus a one-time bonus.
   //-----------------------------------------------------------------
   public double pay()
   {
      double payment = super.pay() + bonus;

      bonus = 0;

      return payment;
   }
}
```

A bonus is awarded to an executive using the `awardBonus` method. This method is called in the `payday` method in `Staff` for the only executive that is part of the `personnel` array. Note that the generic `StaffMember` reference must be cast into an `Executive` reference to invoke the `awardBonus` method (which doesn't exist for a `StaffMember`).

The `Executive` class overrides the `pay` method so that it first determines the payment as it would for any employee, then adds the bonus. The `pay` method of the `Employee` class is invoked using `super` to obtain the normal payment amount. This technique is better than using just the `payRate` variable because if we choose to change how `Employee` objects get paid, the change will automatically be reflected in `Executive`. After the bonus is awarded, it is reset to zero.

The `Hourly` class shown in Listing 7.22 represents an employee whose pay rate is applied on an hourly basis. It keeps track of the number of hours worked in the current pay period, which can be modified by calls to the `addHours` method. This method is called from the `payday` method of `Staff`. The `pay` method of `Hourly` determines the payment based on the number of hours worked, and then resets the hours to zero.

listing
7.22

```java
//********************************************************************
//  Hourly.java          Author: Lewis/Loftus
//
//  Represents an employee that gets paid by the hour.
//********************************************************************

public class Hourly extends Employee
{
   private int hoursWorked;

   //-----------------------------------------------------------------
   //  Sets up this hourly employee using the specified information.
   //-----------------------------------------------------------------
   public Hourly (String eName, String eAddress, String ePhone,
                  String socSecNumber, double rate)
   {
      super (eName, eAddress, ePhone, socSecNumber, rate);

      hoursWorked = 0;
   }
```

listing
7.22 **continued**

```java
    //-------------------------------------------------------------
    //  Adds the specified number of hours to this employee's
    //  accumulated hours.
    //-------------------------------------------------------------
    public void addHours (int moreHours)
    {
        hoursWorked += moreHours;
    }

    //-------------------------------------------------------------
    //  Computes and returns the pay for this hourly employee.
    //-------------------------------------------------------------
    public double pay()
    {
        double payment = payRate * hoursWorked;

        hoursWorked = 0;

        return payment;
    }

    //-------------------------------------------------------------
    //  Returns information about this hourly employee as a string.
    //-------------------------------------------------------------
    public String toString()
    {
        String result = super.toString();

        result += "\nCurrent hours: " + hoursWorked;

        return result;
    }
}
```

7.5   `interfaces revisited`

We introduced interfaces in Chapter 5. We revisit them here because they have a lot in common with the topic of inheritance. Like classes, interfaces can be organized into inheritance hierarchies. And just as we can accomplish polymorphism using the inheritance relationship, we can also accomplish it using interfaces. This section discusses both of these topics.

interface hierarchies

The concept of inheritance can be applied to interfaces as well as classes. That is, one interface can be derived from another interface. These relationships can form an *interface hierarchy,* which is similar to a class hierarchy. Inheritance relationships between interfaces are shown in UML using the same connection (an arrow with an open arrowhead) as they are with classes.

> **key concept**
>
> Inheritance can be applied to interfaces so that one interface can be derived from another.

When a parent interface is used to derive a child interface, the child inherits all abstract methods and constants of the parent. Any class that implements the child interface must implement all of the methods. There are no restrictions on the inheritance between interfaces, as there are with protected and private members of a class, because all members of an interface are public.

Class hierarchies and interface hierarchies do not overlap. That is, an interface cannot be used to derive a class, and a class cannot be used to derive an interface. A class and an interface interact only when a class is designed to implement a particular interface.

polymorphism via interfaces

> **key concept**
>
> An interface name can be used to declare an object reference variable. An interface reference can refer to any object of any class that implements that interface.

As we've seen many times, a class name is used to declare the type of an object reference variable. Similarly, an interface name can be used as the type of a reference variable as well. An interface reference variable can be used to refer to any object of any class that implements that interface.

Suppose we declare an interface called `Speaker` as follows:

```
public interface Speaker
{
   public void speak();
   public void announce (String str);
}
```

The interface name, `Speaker`, can now be used to declare an object reference variable:

```
Speaker current;
```

The reference variable `current` can be used to refer to any object of any class that implements the `Speaker` interface. For example, if we define a class called `Philosopher` such that it implements the `Speaker` interface, we can then assign a `Philosopher` object to a `Speaker` reference as follows:

```
current = new Philosopher();
```

This assignment is valid because a `Philosopher` is, in fact, a `Speaker`.

The flexibility of an interface reference allows us to create polymorphic references. As we saw earlier in this chapter, using inheritance, we can create a polymorphic reference that can refer to any one of a set of objects related by inheritance. Using interfaces, we can create similar polymorphic references, except that the objects being referenced, instead of being related by inheritance, are related by implementing the same interface.

> **key concept**
>
> Interfaces allow us to make polymorphic references in which the method that is invoked is based on the particular object being referenced at the time.

For example, if we create a class called `Dog` that also implements the `Speaker` interface, it can be assigned to a `Speaker` reference variable. The same reference, in fact, can at one point refer to a `Philosopher` object and then later refer to a `Dog` object. The following lines of code illustrate this:

```
Speaker guest;
guest = new Philosopher();
guest.speak();
guest = new Dog();
guest.speak();
```

In this code, the first time the speak method is called, it invokes the speak method defined in the Philosopher class. The second time it is called, it invokes the speak method of the Dog class. As with polymorphic references via inheritance, it is not the type of the reference that determines which method gets invoked; it depends on the type of the object that the reference points to at the moment of invocation.

Note that when we are using an interface reference variable, we can invoke only the methods defined in the interface, even if the object it refers to has other methods to which it can respond. For example, suppose the Philosopher class also defined a public method called pontificate. The second line of the following code would generate a compiler error, even though the object can in fact respond to the pontificate method:

```
Speaker special = new Philosopher();
special.pontificate();   // generates a compiler error
```

The problem is that the compiler can determine only that the object is a Speaker, and therefore can guarantee only that the object can respond to the speak and announce methods. Because the reference variable special could refer to a Dog object (which cannot pontificate), it does not allow the reference. If we know in a particular situation that such an invocation is valid, we can cast the object into the appropriate reference so that the compiler will accept it as follows:

```
((Philosopher)special).pontificate();
```

Similar to polymorphic references based in inheritance, an interface name can be used as the type of a method parameter. In such situations, any object of any class that implements the interface can be passed into the method. For example, the following method takes a Speaker object as a parameter. Therefore both a Dog object and a Philosopher object can be passed into it in separate invocations:

```
public void sayIt (Speaker current)
{
   current.speak();
}
```

7.6 inheritance and GUIs

The concept of inheritance affects our use of graphics and GUIs. This section explores some of these issues.

It's important in these discussions to recall that there are two primary GUI APIs used in Java: the Abstract Windowing Toolkit (AWT) and the Swing classes. The AWT is the original set of graphics classes in Java. Swing classes were introduced later, adding components that provided much more functionality than their AWT counterparts. In general, we use Swing components in our examples in this book.

applets revisited

In previous chapters, we've created applets using inheritance. Initially, we extended the `Applet` class, which is an original AWT component that is part of the `java.applet` package. In Chapter 5 and beyond, we've derived our applets from the `JApplet` class, which is the Swing version. The primary difference between these two classes is that a `JApplet` has a content pane to which GUI components are added. Also, in general, a `JApplet` component should not be drawn on directly. It's better to draw on a panel and add that panel to the applet to be displayed, especially if there is to be user interaction.

The extension of an applet class demonstrates a classic use of inheritance, allowing the parent class to shoulder the responsibilities that apply to all of its descendants. The `JApplet` class is already designed to handle all of the details concerning applet creation and execution. For

> **key concept**
>
> An applet is a good example of inheritance. The `JApplet` parent class handles characteristics common to all applets.

example, an applet program interacts with a browser, can accept parameters through HTML code, and is constrained by certain security limitations. The `JApplet` class already takes care of these details in a generic way that applies to all applets.

Because of inheritance, the applet class that we write (the one derived from `JApplet`) is ready to focus on the purpose of that particular program. In other words, the only issues that we address in our applet code are those that make it different from other applets.

Note that we've been using applets even before we examined what inheritance accomplishes for us and what the parent applet class does in particular. We used the parent applet classes simply for the services it provides. Therefore applets are another wonderful example of abstraction in which certain details can be ignored.

the component class hierarchy

All of the Java classes that define GUI components are part of a class hierarchy, shown in part in Fig. 7.9. Almost all Swing GUI components are derived from the JComponent class, which defines how all components work in general. JComponent is derived from the Container class, which in turn is derived from the Component class.

Both Container and Component are original AWT classes. The Component class contains much of the general functionality that applies to all GUI components, such as basic painting and event handling. So although we may prefer to use some of the specific Swing components, they are based on core AWT concepts and respond to the same events as AWT components. Because they are derived from Container, many Swing components can serve as containers, though in most circumstances those abilities are curtailed. For example, a JLabel object can contain an image (as described in the next chapter) but it cannot be used as a generic container to which any component can be added.

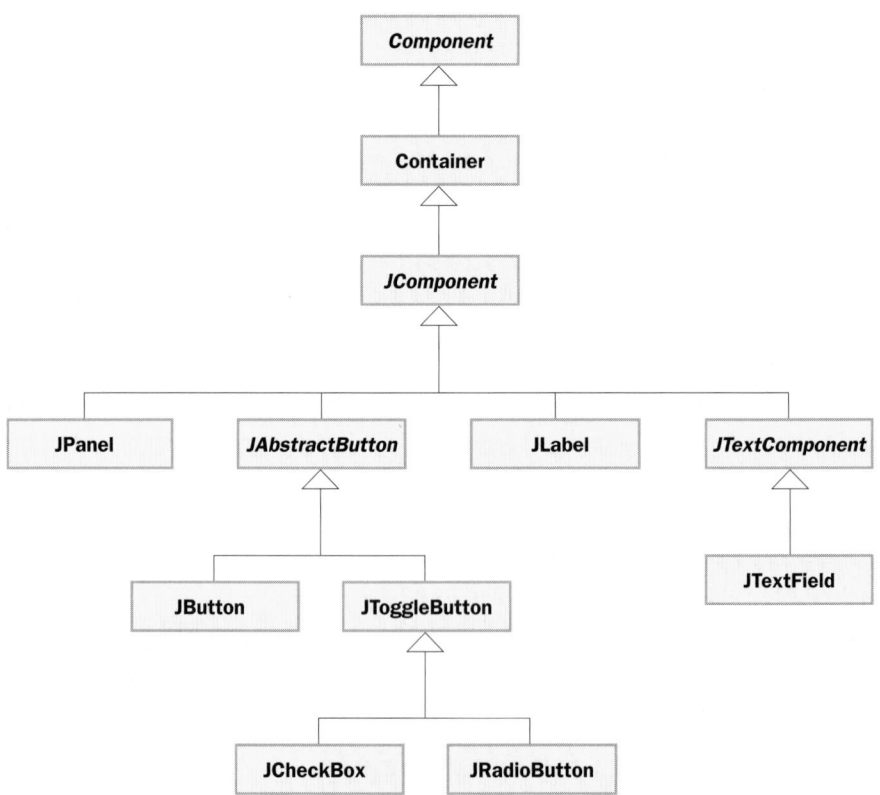

figure 7.9   Part of the GUI component class hierarchy

Many features that apply to all Swing components are defined in the `JComponent` class and are inherited into its descendants. For example, we have the ability to put a border on any Swing component (we discuss this more in Chapter 9). This ability is defined, only once, in the `JComponent` class and is inherited by any class that is derived, directly or indirectly, from it.

Some component classes, such as `JPanel` and `JLabel`, are derived directly from `JComponent`. Other component classes are nested further down in the inheritance hierarchy structure. For example, the `JAbstractButton` class is an abstract class that defines the functionality that applies to all types of GUI buttons. `JButton` is derived directly from it. However, note that `JCheckBox` and `JRadioButton` are both derived from a class called `JToggleButton`, which embodies the common characteristics for buttons that can be in one of two states. The set of classes that define GUI buttons shows once again how common characteristics are put at appropriately high levels of the class hierarchy rather than duplicated in multiple classes.

The world of text components demonstrates this as well. The `JTextField` class that we've used in previous examples is one of many Java GUI components that support the management of text data. They are organized under a class called `JTextComponent`. Keep in mind that there are many GUI component classes that are not shown in the diagram in Fig. 7.9.

Painting is another GUI feature affected by the inheritance hierarchy. The `paint` method we've used in applets is defined in the `Component` class. The `Applet` class inherits the default version of this method, which we have regularly overridden in our applet programs to paint particular shapes. Most Swing classes, however, use a method called `paintComponent` to perform custom painting. Usually, we will draw on a `JPanel` using its `paintComponent` method and use the `super` reference to invoke the version of the `paintComponent` method defined in `JComponent`, which draws the background and outline of the component. This technique is demonstrated in the next section.

7.7 mouse events

Let's examine the events that are generated when using a mouse. Java divides these events into two categories: *mouse events* and *mouse motion events*. The table in Fig. 7.10 defines these events.

Mouse Event	Description
mouse pressed	The mouse button is pressed down.
mouse released	The mouse button is released.
mouse clicked	The mouse button is pressed down and released without moving the mouse in between.
mouse entered	The mouse pointer is moved onto (over) a component.
mouse exited	The mouse pointer is moved off of a component.

Mouse Motion Event	Description
mouse moved	The mouse is moved.
mouse dragged	The mouse is moved while the mouse button is pressed down.

figure 7.10   Mouse events and mouse motion events

When you click the mouse button over a Java GUI component, three events are generated: one when the mouse button is pushed down (*mouse pressed*) and two when it is let up (*mouse released* and *mouse clicked*). A mouse click is defined as pressing and releasing the mouse button in the same location. If you press the mouse button down, move the mouse, and then release the mouse button, a mouse clicked event is not generated.

A component will generate a *mouse entered* event when the mouse pointer passes into its graphical space. Likewise, it generates a *mouse exited* event when the mouse pointer leaves.

> **key concept**
> Moving the mouse and clicking the mouse button generate mouse events to which a program can respond.

Mouse motion events, as the name implies, occur while the mouse is in motion. The *mouse moved* event indicates simply that the mouse is in motion. The *mouse dragged* event is generated when the user has pressed the mouse button down and moved the mouse without releasing the button. Mouse motion events are generated many times, very quickly, while the mouse is in motion.

In a specific situation, we may care about only one or two mouse events. What we listen for depends on what we are trying to accomplish.

The Dots program shown in Listing 7.23 responds to one mouse event. Specifically, it draws a green dot at the location of the mouse pointer whenever the mouse button is pressed.

listing
   7.23

```
//********************************************************************
//  Dots.java          Author: Lewis/Loftus
//
//  Demonstrates mouse events and drawing on a panel.
//********************************************************************

import javax.swing.*;

public class Dots
{
   //-----------------------------------------------------------------
   //  Creates and displays the application frame.
   //-----------------------------------------------------------------
   public static void main (String[] args)
   {
      JFrame dotsFrame = new JFrame ("Dots");
      dotsFrame.setDefaultCloseOperation (JFrame.EXIT_ON_CLOSE);

      dotsFrame.getContentPane().add (new DotsPanel());

      dotsFrame.pack();
      dotsFrame.show();
   }
}
```

display

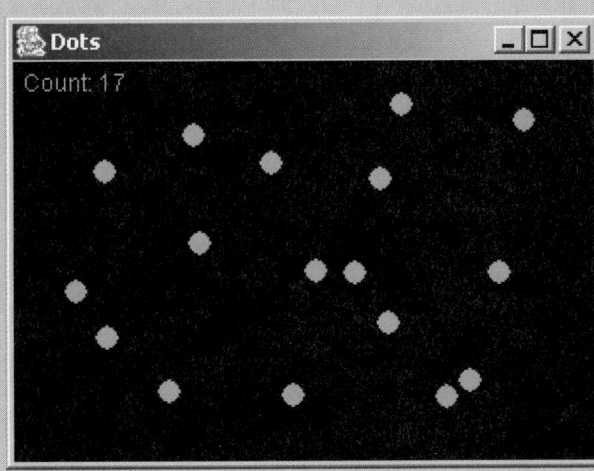

The `main` method of the `Dots` class creates a frame and adds one panel to it. That panel is defined by the `DotsPanel` class shown in Listing 7.24. The `DotsPanel` class is derived from `JPanel`. This panel serves as the surface on which the dots are drawn.

listing
    7.24

```
//********************************************************************
//  DotsPanel.java          Author: Lewis/Loftus
//
//  Represents the primary panel for the Dots program on which the
//  dots are drawn.
//********************************************************************

import javax.swing.*;
import java.awt.*;
import java.awt.event.*;
import java.util.*;

public class DotsPanel extends JPanel
{
   private final int WIDTH = 300, HEIGHT = 200;
   private final int RADIUS = 6;

   private ArrayList pointList;
   private int count;

   //-----------------------------------------------------------------
   //  Sets up this panel to listen for mouse events.
   //-----------------------------------------------------------------
   public DotsPanel()
   {
      pointList = new ArrayList();
      count = 0;

      addMouseListener (new DotsListener());

      setBackground (Color.black);
      setPreferredSize (new Dimension(WIDTH, HEIGHT));
   }

   //-----------------------------------------------------------------
   //  Draws all of the dots stored in the list.
   //-----------------------------------------------------------------
```

listing
7.24 continued

```java
    public void paintComponent (Graphics page)
    {
        super.paintComponent(page);

        page.setColor (Color.green);

        // Retrieve an iterator for the ArrayList of points
        Iterator pointIterator = pointList.iterator();

        while (pointIterator.hasNext())
        {
            Point drawPoint = (Point) pointIterator.next();
            page.fillOval (drawPoint.x - RADIUS, drawPoint.y - RADIUS,
                        RADIUS * 2, RADIUS * 2);
        }

        page.drawString ("Count: " + count, 5, 15);
    }

    //*****************************************************************
    //  Represents the listener for mouse events.
    //*****************************************************************
    private class DotsListener implements MouseListener
    {
        //------------------------------------------------------------
        //  Adds the current point to the list of points and redraws
        //  whenever the mouse button is pressed.
        //------------------------------------------------------------
        public void mousePressed (MouseEvent event)
        {
            pointList.add (event.getPoint());
            count++;
            repaint();
        }

        //------------------------------------------------------------
        //  Provide empty definitions for unused event methods.
        //------------------------------------------------------------
        public void mouseClicked (MouseEvent event) {}
        public void mouseReleased (MouseEvent event) {}
        public void mouseEntered (MouseEvent event) {}
        public void mouseExited (MouseEvent event) {}
    }
}
```

The `DotsPanel` class keeps track of a list of `Point` objects that represent all of the locations at which the user has clicked the mouse. A `Point` class represents the (*x*, *y*) coordinates of a given point in two-dimensional space. It provides public access to the instance variables x and y for the point. Each time the panel is painted, all of the points stored in the list are drawn. The list is maintained as an `ArrayList` object. To draw the points, an `Iterator` object is obtained from the `ArrayList` so that each point can be processed in turn. We discussed the `ArrayList` class in Chapter 6 and the `Iterator` interface in Chapter 5.

The listener for the mouse pressed event is defined as a private inner class that implements the `MouseListener` interface. The `mousePressed` method is invoked by the panel each time the user presses down on the mouse button while it is over the panel.

A mouse event always occurs at some point in space, and the object that represents that event keeps track of that location. In a mouse listener, we can get and use that point whenever we need it. In the `Dots` program, each time the `mousePressed` method is called, the location of the event is obtained using the `getPoint` method of the `MouseEvent` object. That point is stored in the `ArrayList`, and the panel is then repainted.

Note that, unlike the `ActionListener` and `ItemListener` interfaces that we've used in previous examples, which contain one method each, the `MouseListener` interface contains five methods. For this program, the only event in which we are interested is the mouse pressed event. Therefore, the only method in which we have any interest is the `mousePressed` method. However, implementing an interface means we must provide definitions for all methods in the interface. Therefore we provide empty methods corresponding to the other events. When those events are generated, the empty methods are called, but no code is executed.

Let's look at an example that responds to two mouse-oriented events. The `RubberLines` program shown in Listing 7.25 draws a line between two points. The first point is determined by the location at which the mouse is first pressed down. The second point changes as the mouse is dragged while the mouse button is held down. When the button is released, the line remains fixed between the first and second points. When the mouse button is pressed again, a new line is started. This program is implemented as an applet.

The panel on which the lines are drawn is represented by the `RubberLinesPanel` class shown in Listing 7.26. Because we need to listen for both a mouse pressed event and a mouse dragged event, we need a listener that responds to both mouse events and mouse motion events. Note that the listener class implements both the `MouseListener` and `MouseMotionListener` inter-

listing
    7.25

```
//********************************************************************
//  RubberLines.java        Author: Lewis/Loftus
//
//  Demonstrates mouse events and rubberbanding.
//********************************************************************

import javax.swing.*;

public class RubberLines extends JApplet
{
   private final int WIDTH = 300, HEIGHT = 200;

   //-----------------------------------------------------------------
   //  Sets up the applet to contain the drawing panel.
   //-----------------------------------------------------------------
   public void init()
   {
      getContentPane().add (new RubberLinesPanel());

      setSize (WIDTH, HEIGHT);
   }
}
```

display

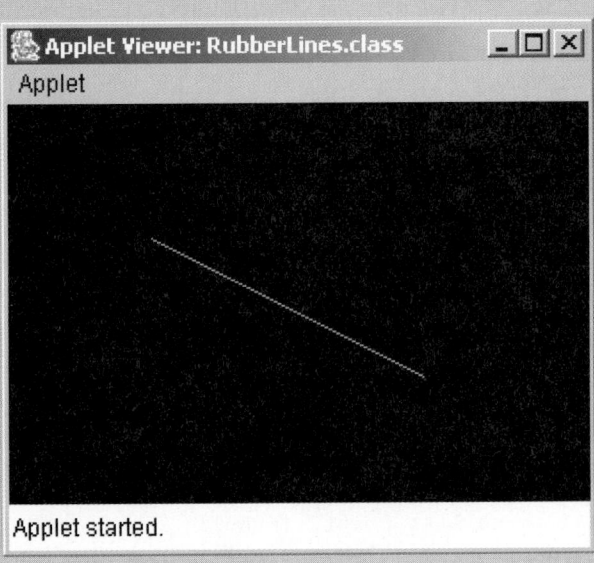

faces. It must therefore implement all methods of both classes. The two methods of interest, mousePressed and mouseDragged, are implemented, and the rest are given empty definitions.

listing
   7.26

```java
//********************************************************************
//   RubberLinesPanel.java       Author: Lewis/Loftus
//
//   Represents the primary drawing panel for the RubberLines applet.
//********************************************************************

import java.awt.*;
import java.awt.event.*;
import javax.swing.*;

public class RubberLinesPanel extends JPanel
{
   private Point point1 = null, point2 = null;

   //-----------------------------------------------------------------
   //   Sets up the applet to listen for mouse events.
   //-----------------------------------------------------------------
   public RubberLinesPanel()
   {
      LineListener listener = new LineListener();
      addMouseListener (listener);
      addMouseMotionListener (listener);

      setBackground (Color.black);
   }

   //-----------------------------------------------------------------
   //   Draws the current line from the intial mouse down point to
   //   the current position of the mouse.
   //-----------------------------------------------------------------
   public void paintComponent (Graphics page)
   {
      super.paintComponent (page);

      page.setColor (Color.green);
      if (point1 != null && point2 != null)
         page.drawLine (point1.x, point1.y, point2.x, point2.y);
   }
```

listing
7.26 continued

```java
//*****************************************************************
//  Represents the listener for all mouse events.
//*****************************************************************
private class LineListener implements MouseListener,
                                      MouseMotionListener
{
   //-------------------------------------------------------------
   //  Captures the initial position at which the mouse button is
   //  pressed.
   //-------------------------------------------------------------
   public void mousePressed (MouseEvent event)
   {
      point1 = event.getPoint();
   }

   //-------------------------------------------------------------
   //  Gets the current position of the mouse as it is dragged and
   //  draws the line to create the rubberband effect.
   //-------------------------------------------------------------
   public void mouseDragged (MouseEvent event)
   {
      point2 = event.getPoint();
      repaint();
   }

   //-------------------------------------------------------------
   //  Provide empty definitions for unused event methods.
   //-------------------------------------------------------------
   public void mouseClicked (MouseEvent event) {}
   public void mouseReleased (MouseEvent event) {}
   public void mouseEntered (MouseEvent event) {}
   public void mouseExited (MouseEvent event) {}
   public void mouseMoved (MouseEvent event) {}
}
}
```

When the `mousePressed` method is called, the variable `point1` is set. Then, as the mouse is dragged, the variable `point2` is continually reset and the panel repainted. Therefore the line is constantly being redrawn as the mouse is dragged, giving the appearance that one line is being stretched between a fixed point and a moving point. This effect is called *rubberbanding* and is common in graphical programs.

Note that, in the `RubberLinesPanel` constructor, the listener object is added to the panel twice: once as a mouse listener and once as a mouse motion listener. The method called to add the listener must correspond to the object passed as the parameter. In this case, we had one object that served as a listener for both categories of events. We could have had two listener classes if desired: one listening for mouse events and one listening for mouse motion events. A component can have multiple listeners for various event categories.

Also note that this program draws one line at a time. That is, when the user begins to draw another line with a new mouse click, the previous one disappears. This is because the `paintComponent` method redraws its background, eliminating the line every time. To see the previous lines, we'd have to keep track of them, perhaps using an `ArrayList` as was done in the `Dots` program. This modification to the `RubberLines` program is left as a programming project.

extending event adapter classes

In previous event-based examples, we've created the listener classes by implementing a particular listener interface. For instance, to create a class that listens for mouse events, we created a listener class that implements the `MouseListener` interface. As we saw in the `Dots` and `RubberLines` programs, a listener interface often contains event methods that are not important to a particular program, in which case we provided empty definitions to satisfy the interface requirement.

An alternative technique for creating a listener class is to extend an *event adapter class*. Each listener interface that contains more than one method has a corresponding adapter class that already contains empty definitions for all of the methods in the interface. To create a listener, we can derive a new listener class from the appropriate adapter class and override any event methods in which we are interested. Using this technique, we no longer must provide empty definitions for unused methods.

The program shown in Listing 7.27 is an applet that responds to mouse click events. Whenever the mouse button is clicked over the applet, a line is drawn from the location of the mouse pointer to the center of the applet. The distance that line represents in pixels is displayed.

The structure of the OffCenter program is similar to that of the RubberLines program. It loads a display panel, represented by the OffCenterPanel class shown in Listing 7.28 into the applet window.

The listener class, instead of implementing the MouseListener interface directly as we have done in previous examples, extends the MouseAdapter class, which is defined in the java.awt.event package of the Java standard class library. The MouseAdapter class implements the MouseListener interface and contains empty definitions for all of the mouse event methods. In our listener class, we override the definition of the mouseClicked method to suit our needs.

listing
   7.27

```
//********************************************************************
//  OffCenter.java        Author: Lewis/Loftus
//
//  Demonstrates the use of an event adatpter class.
//********************************************************************

import javax.swing.*;

public class OffCenter extends JApplet
{
   private final int WIDTH = 300, HEIGHT = 300;

   //-----------------------------------------------------------------
   //  Sets up the applet.
   //-----------------------------------------------------------------
   public void init()
   {
      getContentPane().add(new OffCenterPanel (WIDTH, HEIGHT));

      setSize (WIDTH, HEIGHT);
   }
}
```

listing
7.27   continued

display

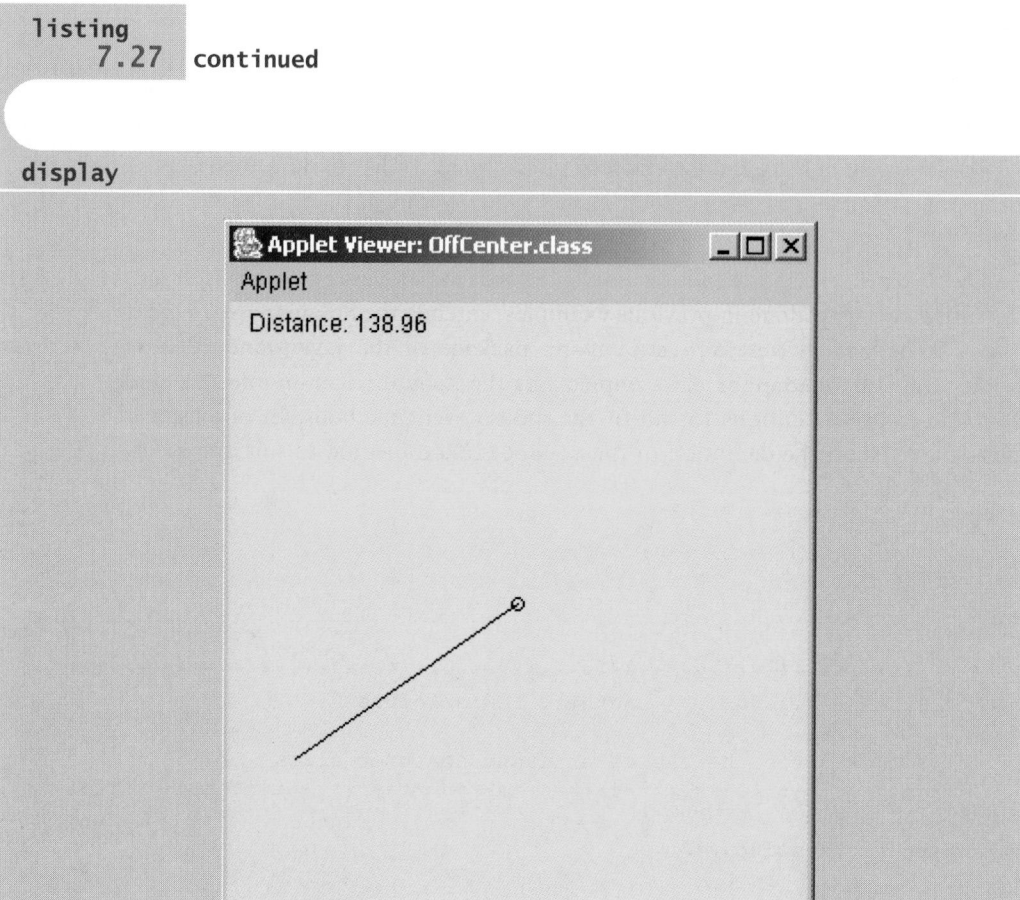

Because we inherit the other empty methods corresponding to the rest of the mouse events, we don't have to provide our own empty definitions.

Because of inheritance, we now have a choice when it comes to creating event listeners. We can implement an event listener interface, or we can extend an event adapter class. This is a design decision that should be considered carefully. The best technique depends on the situation.

listing
    7.28

```
//************************************************************************
//  OffCenterPanel.java          Author: Lewis/Loftus
//
//  Represents the primary drawing panel for the OffCenter applet.
//************************************************************************

import java.awt.*;
import java.awt.event.*;
import java.text.DecimalFormat;
import javax.swing.*;

public class OffCenterPanel extends JPanel
{
   private DecimalFormat fmt;
   private Point current;
   private int centerX, centerY;
   private double length;

   //-----------------------------------------------------------------
   //  Sets up the panel and necessary data.
   //-----------------------------------------------------------------
   public OffCenterPanel (int width, int height)
   {
      addMouseListener (new OffCenterListener());

      centerX = width / 2;
      centerY = height / 2;

      fmt = new DecimalFormat ("0.##");

      setBackground (Color.yellow);
   }

   //-----------------------------------------------------------------
   //  Draws a line from the mouse pointer to the center point of
   //  the applet and displays the distance.
   //-----------------------------------------------------------------
   public void paintComponent (Graphics page)
   {
      super.paintComponent (page);

      page.setColor (Color.black);
      page.drawOval (centerX-3, centerY-3, 6, 6);
```

listing
    7.28   **continued**

```java
        if (current != null)
        {
            page.drawLine (current.x, current.y, centerX, centerY);
            page.drawString ("Distance: " + fmt.format(length), 10, 15);
        }
    }

    //****************************************************************
    //   Represents the listener for mouse events.
    //****************************************************************
    private class OffCenterListener extends MouseAdapter
    {
        //-------------------------------------------------------------
        //   Computes the distance from the mouse pointer to the center
        //   point of the applet.
        //-------------------------------------------------------------
        public void mouseClicked (MouseEvent event)
        {
            current = event.getPoint();
            length = Math.sqrt(Math.pow((current.x-centerX), 2) +
                              Math.pow((current.y-centerY), 2));
            repaint();
        }
    }
}
```

summary of
key concepts

- Inheritance is the process of deriving a new class from an existing one.

- One purpose of inheritance is to reuse existing software.

- Inherited variables and methods can be used in the derived class as if they had been declared locally.

- Inheritance creates an is-a relationship between all parent and child classes.

- Visibility modifiers determine which variables and methods are inherited. Protected visibility provides the best possible encapsulation that permits inheritance.

- A parent's constructor can be invoked using the `super` reference.

- A child class can override (redefine) the parent's definition of an inherited method.

- The child of one class can be the parent of one or more other classes, creating a class hierarchy.

- Common features should be located as high in a class hierarchy as is reasonably possible, minimizing maintenance efforts.

- All Java classes are derived, directly or indirectly, from the `Object` class.

- The `toString` and `equals` methods are defined in the `Object` class and therefore are inherited by every class in every Java program.

- An abstract class cannot be instantiated. It represents a concept on which other classes can build their definitions.

- A class derived from an abstract parent must override all of its parent's abstract methods, or the derived class will also be considered abstract.

- All members of a superclass exist for a subclass, but they are not necessarily inherited. Only inherited members can be referenced by name in the subclass.

- A polymorphic reference can refer to different types of objects over time.

- A reference variable can refer to any object created from any class related to it by inheritance.

- A polymorphic reference uses the type of the object, not the type of the reference, to determine which version of a method to invoke.

- Inheritance can be applied to interfaces so that one interface can be derived from another.

▸ An interface name can be used to declare an object reference variable. An interface reference can refer to any object of any class that implements that interface.

▸ Interfaces allow us to make polymorphic references in which the method that is invoked is based on the particular object being referenced at the time.

▸ An applet is a good example of inheritance. The `JApplet` parent class handles characteristics common to all applets.

▸ The classes that represent Java GUI components are organized into a class hierarchy.

▸ Moving the mouse and clicking the mouse button generate mouse events to which a program can respond.

▸ Rubberbanding is the visual effect created when a graphical shape seems to expand and contract as the mouse is dragged.

▸ A listener class can be created by deriving it from an event adapter class.

self-review questions

7.1   Describe the relationship between a parent class and a child class.

7.2   How does inheritance support software reuse?

7.3   What relationship should every class derivation represent?

7.4   Why would a child class override one or more of the methods of its parent class?

7.5   Why is the `super` reference important to a child class?

7.6   What is the significance of the `Object` class?

7.7   What is the role of an abstract class?

7.8   Are all members of a parent class inherited by the child? Explain.

7.9   What is polymorphism?

7.10 How does inheritance support polymorphism?

7.11 How is overriding related to polymorphism?

7.12 What is an interface hierarchy?

7.13 How can polymorphism be accomplished using interfaces?

7.14 What is an adapter class?

exercises

7.1 Draw a UML class diagram showing an inheritance hierarchy containing classes that represent different types of clocks. Show the variables and method names for two of these classes.

7.2 Show an alternative diagram for the hierarchy in Exercise 7.1. Explain why it may be a better or worse approach than the original.

7.3 Draw and annotate a class hierarchy that represents various types of faculty at a university. Show what characteristics would be represented in the various classes of the hierarchy. Explain how polymorphism could play a role in the process of assigning courses to each faculty member.

7.4 Experiment with a simple derivation relationship between two classes. Put `println` statements in constructors of both the parent and child classes. Do not explicitly call the constructor of the parent in the child. What happens? Why? Change the child's constructor to explicitly call the constructor of the parent. Now what happens?

7.5 What would happen if the `pay` method were not defined as an abstract method in the `StaffMember` class of the `Firm` program?

7.6 What would happen if, in the `Dots` program, we did not provide empty definitions for one or more of the unused mouse events?

7.7 The `Dots` program listens for a mouse pressed event to draw a dot. How would the program behave differently if it listened for a mouse released event instead? A mouse clicked event?

7.8 What would happen if the call to `super.paintComponent` were removed from the `paintComponent` method of the `DotsPanel` class? Remove it and run the program to test your answer.

7.9 What would happen if the call to `super.paintComponent` were removed from the `paintComponent` method of the `RubberLinesPanel` class? Remove it and run the program to test your answer. In what ways is the answer different from the answer to Exercise 7.8?

7.10 Explain how a call to the `addMouseListener` method represents a polymorphic situation.

programming projects

7.1   Design and implement a class called MonetaryCoin that is derived from the Coin class presented in Chapter 4. Store a value in the monetary coin that represents its value and add a method that returns its value. Create a main driver class to instantiate and compute the sum of several MonetaryCoin objects. Demonstrate that a monetary coin inherits its parent's ability to be flipped.

7.2   Design and implement a set of classes that define the employees of a hospital: doctor, nurse, administrator, surgeon, receptionist, janitor, and so on. Include methods in each class that are named according to the services provided by that person and that print an appropriate message. Create a main driver class to instantiate and exercise several of the classes.

7.3   Design and implement a set of classes that define various types of reading material: books, novels, magazines, technical journals, textbooks, and so on. Include data values that describe various attributes of the material, such as the number of pages and the names of the primary characters. Include methods that are named appropriately for each class and that print an appropriate message. Create a main driver class to instantiate and exercise several of the classes.

7.4   Design and implement a set of classes that keeps track of various sports statistics. Have each low-level class represent a specific sport. Tailor the services of the classes to the sport in question, and move common attributes to the higher-level classes as appropriate. Create a main driver class to instantiate and exercise several of the classes.

7.5   Design and implement a set of classes that keeps track of demographic information about a set of people, such as age, nationality, occupation, income, and so on. Design each class to focus on a particular aspect of data collection. Create a main driver class to instantiate and exercise several of the classes.

7.6   Modify the StyleOptions program from Chapter 6 so that it accomplishes the same task but derives its primary panel using inheritance. Specifically, replace the StyleGUI class with one called StylePanel that extends the JPanel class. Eliminate the getPanel method.

7.7   Perform the same modifications described in Programming Project 7.6 to the QuoteOptions program from Chapter 6.

7.8 Design and implement an application that draws a traffic light and uses a push button to change the state of the light. Derive the drawing surface from the `JPanel` class and use another panel to organize the drawing surface and the button.

7.9 Modify the `RubberLines` program from this chapter so that it shows all of the lines drawn. Show only the final lines (from initial mouse press to mouse release), not the intermediate lines drawn to show the rubberbanding effect. *Hint*: Keep track of a list of objects that represent the lines similar to how the `Dots` program kept track of multiple dots.

7.10 Design and implement an applet that counts the number of times the mouse has been clicked. Display that number in the center of the applet window.

7.11 Design and implement an application that creates a polyline shape dynamically using mouse clicks. Each mouse click adds a new line segment from the previous point. Include a button below the drawing area to clear the current polyline and begin another.

7.12 Design and implement an application that draws a circle using a rubberbanding technique. The circle size is determined by a mouse drag. Use the original mouse click location as a fixed center point. Compute the distance between the current location of the mouse pointer and the center point to determine the current radius of the circle.

7.13 Design and implement an application that serves as a mouse odometer, continually displaying how far, in pixels, the mouse has moved (while it is over the program window). Display the current odometer value using a label. *Hint*: Use the mouse movement event to determine the current position, and compare it to the last position of the mouse. Use the distance formula to see how far the mouse has traveled, and add that to a running total distance.

7.14 Design and implement an applet whose background changes color depending on where the mouse pointer is located. If the mouse pointer is on the left half of the applet window, display red; if it is on the right half, display green.

7.15 Design and implement a class that represents a spaceship, which can be drawn (side view) in any particular location. Create an applet that displays the spaceship so that it follows the movement of the mouse. When the mouse button is pressed down, have a laser beam shoot out of the front of the spaceship (one continuous beam, not a moving projectile) until the mouse button is released.

answers to self-review questions

7.1   A child class is derived from a parent class using inheritance. The methods and variables of the parent class automatically become a part of the child class, subject to the rules of the visibility modifiers used to declare them.

7.2   Because a new class can be derived from an existing class, the characteristics of the parent class can be reused without the error-prone process of copying and modifying code.

7.3   Each inheritance derivation should represent an is-a relationship: the child *is-a* more specific version of the parent. If this relationship does not hold, then inheritance is being used improperly.

7.4   A child class may prefer its own definition of a method in favor of the definition provided for it by its parent. In this case, the child overrides (redefines) the parent's definition with its own.

7.5   The super reference can be used to call the parent's constructor, which cannot be invoked directly by name. It can also be used to invoke the parent's version of an overridden method.

7.6   All classes in Java are derived, directly or indirectly, from the Object class. Therefore all public methods of the Object class, such as equals and toString, are available to every object.

7.7   An abstract class is a representation of a general concept. Common characteristics and method signatures can be defined in an abstract class so that they are inherited by child classes derived from it.

7.8   A class member is not inherited if it has private visibility, meaning that it cannot be referenced by name in the child class. However, such members do exist for the child and can be referenced indirectly.

7.9   Polymorphism is the ability of a reference variable to refer to objects of various types at different times. A method invoked through such a reference is bound to different method definitions at different times, depending on the type of the object referenced.

7.10   In Java, a reference variable declared using a parent class can be used to refer to an object of the child class. If both classes contain a method with the same signature, the parent reference can be polymorphic.

7.11 When a child class overrides the definition of a parent's method, two versions of that method exist. If a polymorphic reference is used to invoke the method, the version of the method that is invoked is determined by the type of the object being referred to, not by the type of the reference variable.

7.12 A new interface can be derived from an existing interface using inheritance, just as a new class can be derived from an existing class.

7.13 An interface name can be used as the type of a reference. Such a reference variable can refer to any object of any class that implements that interface. Because all classes implement the same interface, they have methods with common signatures, which can be dynamically bound.

7.14 An adapter class is a class that implements a listener interface, providing empty definitions for all of its methods. A listener class can be created by extending the appropriate adapter class and overriding the methods of interest.

This chapter addresses two related topics: exceptions and input/output (I/O) streams. Exceptions represent problems that can occur in software and allow us to handle them appropriately. The ability to handle exceptions is essential to being able to perform various I/O operations. Java supports many ways for a program to read information from an external source and to write information to an external destination. The source or destination could be main memory, a file, another program, a network connection, or other options. Several classes in the Java standard class library support the management of exceptions and I/O.

chapter
objectives

▶ Examine the try-catch statement for handling exceptions.

▶ Create a new exception.

▶ Define an I/O stream.

▶ Explore the classes used to create streams.

▶ Discuss the standard input and output streams.

▶ Further explore the processing of the Keyboard class.

▶ Determine how to read and write text files.

▶ Determine how to serialize and deserialize objects.

8.0 exceptions

As we've discussed briefly in other parts of the text, problems that arise in a Java program may generate exceptions or errors. Recall from Chapter 2 that an *exception* is an object that defines an unusual or erroneous situation. An exception is thrown by a program or the runtime environment and can be caught and handled appropriately if desired. An *error* is similar to an exception except that an error generally represents an unrecoverable situation and should not be caught.

Java has a predefined set of exceptions and errors that may occur during the execution of a program. Appendix K contains a list of many of the errors and exceptions defined in the Java standard class library.

We have several options when it comes to dealing with exceptions. A program can be designed to process an exception in one of three ways. It can:

▸ not handle the exception at all,

▸ handle the exception where it occurs, or

▸ handle the exception at another point in the program.

We explore each of these approaches in the following sections.

exception messages

If a program does not handle the exception at all, it will terminate (abnormally) and produce a message that describes what exception occurred and where it was produced. The information associated with an exception is often helpful in tracking down the cause of a problem.

Let's look at the output of an exception. The program shown in Listing 8.1 throws an `ArithmeticException` when an invalid arithmetic operation is attempted. In this case, the program attempts to divide by zero.

Because there is no code in the program in Listing 8.1 to handle the exception explicitly, the program terminates when the exception occurs, printing specific information about the exception. Note that the last `println` statement in the program never executes because the exception occurs first.

The first line of the exception output indicates which exception was thrown and provides some information about why it was thrown. The remaining lines are the *call stack trace*; they indicate where the exception occurred. In this case, there

```
//********************************************************************
//   Zero.java          Author: Lewis/Loftus
//
//   Demonstrates an uncaught exception.
//********************************************************************

public class Zero
{
   //-----------------------------------------------------------------
   //   Deliberately divides by zero to produce an exception.
   //-----------------------------------------------------------------
   public static void main (String[] args)
   {
      int numerator = 10;
      int denominator = 0;

      System.out.println (numerator / denominator);

      System.out.println ("This text will not be printed.");
   }
}
```

output

```
Exception in thread "main" java.lang.ArithmeticException: / by zero
        at Zero.main(Zero.java:17)
```

is only one line in the call stack trace, but there may be several depending on where the exception originated. The first trace line indicates the method, file, and line number where the exception occurred. The other trace lines, if present, indicate the methods that were called to get to the method that produced the exception. In this program, there is only one method, and it produced the exception; therefore there is only one line in the trace.

> **key concept**
>
> The messages printed by a thrown exception indicate the nature of the problem and provide a method call stack trace.

The call stack trace information is also available by calling methods of the exception class that is being thrown. The method `getMessage` returns a string explaining the reason the exception was thrown. The method `printStackTrace` prints the call stack trace.

the `try` statement

Let's now examine how we catch and handle an exception when it is thrown. The *try statement* identifies a block of statements that may throw an exception. A *catch clause*, which follows a `try` block, defines how a particular kind of exception is handled. A `try` block can have several `catch` clauses associated with it. Each `catch` clause is called an *exception handler*.

> Each `catch` clause on a `try` statement handles a particular kind of exception that may be thrown within the `try` block.

When a `try` statement is executed, the statements in the `try` block are executed. If no exception is thrown during the execution of the `try` block, processing continues with the statement following the `try` statement (after all of the `catch` clauses). This situation is the normal execution flow and should occur most of the time.

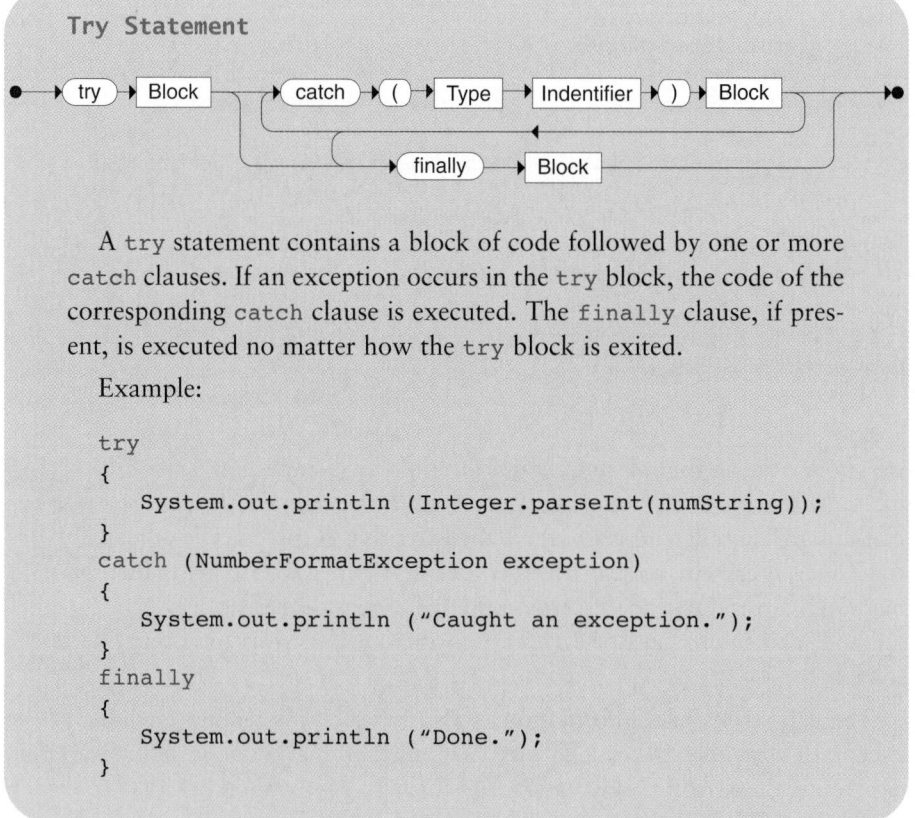

A `try` statement contains a block of code followed by one or more `catch` clauses. If an exception occurs in the `try` block, the code of the corresponding `catch` clause is executed. The `finally` clause, if present, is executed no matter how the `try` block is exited.

Example:

```
try
{
    System.out.println (Integer.parseInt(numString));
}
catch (NumberFormatException exception)
{
    System.out.println ("Caught an exception.");
}
finally
{
    System.out.println ("Done.");
}
```

If an exception is thrown at any point during the execution of the `try` block, control is immediately transferred to the appropriate catch handler if it is present. That is, control transfers to the first `catch` clause whose exception class corresponds to the class of the exception that was thrown. After executing the statements in the `catch` clause, control transfers to the statement after the entire `try` statement.

Let's look at an example. Suppose a hypothetical company uses codes to represent its various products. A product code includes, among other information, a character in the tenth position that represents the zone from which that product was made, and a four-digit integer in positions 4 through 7 that represents the district in which it will be sold. Due to some reorganization, products from zone R are banned from being sold in districts with a designation of 2000 or higher. The program shown in Listing 8.2 reads product codes from the user and counts the number of banned codes entered.

listing
8.2

```java
//********************************************************************
//  ProductCodes.java        Author: Lewis/Loftus
//
//  Demonstrates the use of a try-catch block.
//********************************************************************

import cs1.Keyboard;

public class ProductCodes
{
   //-----------------------------------------------------------------
   //  Counts the number of product codes that are entered with a
   //  zone of R and and district greater than 2000.
   //-----------------------------------------------------------------
   public static void main (String[] args)
   {
      String code;
      char zone;
      int district, valid = 0, banned = 0;

      System.out.print ("Enter product code (XXX to quit): ");
      code = Keyboard.readString();

      while (!code.equals ("XXX"))
      {
```

```
        try
        {
            zone = code.charAt(9);
            district = Integer.parseInt(code.substring(3, 7));
            valid++;
            if (zone == 'R' && district > 2000)
                banned++;
        }
        catch (StringIndexOutOfBoundsException exception)
        {
            System.out.println ("Improper code length: " + code);
        }
        catch (NumberFormatException exception)
        {
            System.out.println ("District is not numeric: " + code);
        }

        System.out.print ("Enter product code (XXX to quit): ");
        code = Keyboard.readString();
    }

    System.out.println ("# of valid codes entered: " + valid);
    System.out.println ("# of banned codes entered: " + banned);
  }
}
```

output

```
Enter product code (XXX to quit): TRV2475A5R-14
Enter product code (XXX to quit): TRD1704A7R-12
Enter product code (XXX to quit): TRL2k74A5R-11
District is not numeric: TRL2k74A5R-11
Enter product code (XXX to quit): TRQ2949A6M-04
Enter product code (XXX to quit): TRV2105A2
Improper code length: TRV2105A2
Enter product code (XXX to quit): TRQ2778A7R-19
Enter product code (XXX to quit): XXX
# of valid codes entered: 4
# of banned codes entered: 2
```

The programming statements in the `try` block attempt to pull out the zone and district information, and then determine whether it represents a banned product code. If there is any problem extracting the zone and district information, the product code is considered to be invalid and is not processed further. For example, a `StringIndexOutOfBoundsException` could be thrown by either the `charAt` or `substring` methods. Furthermore, a `NumberFormatException` could be thrown by the `parseInt` method if the `substring` does not contain a valid integer. A particular message is printed depending on which exception is thrown. In either case, since the exception is caught and handled, processing continues normally.

Note that, for each code examined, the integer `valid` is incremented only if no exception is thrown. If an exception is thrown, control transfers immediately to the appropriate `catch` clause. Likewise, the zone and district are tested by the `if` statement only if no exception is thrown.

the `finally` clause

A `try` statement can have an optional *finally clause*. The `finally` clause defines a section of code that is executed no matter how the `try` block is exited. Most often, a `finally` clause is used to manage resources or to guarantee that particular parts of an algorithm are executed.

If no exception is generated, the statements in the `finally` clause are executed after the `try` block is complete. If an exception is generated in the `try` block, control first transfers to the appropriate catch clause. After executing the exception-handling code, control transfers to the `finally` clause and its statements are executed. A `finally` clause, if present, must be listed following the `catch` clauses.

> **key concept**
> The `finally` clause of a try block is executed whether or not the `try` block is exited normally or because of a thrown exception.

Note that a `try` block does not need to have a `catch` clause at all. If there are no `catch` clauses, a `finally` clause may used by itself if that is appropriate for the situation.

exception propagation

If an exception is not caught and handled where it occurs, control is immediately returned to the method that invoked the method that produced the exception. We can design our software so that the exception is caught and handled at this outer level. If it isn't caught there, control returns to the method that called it. This process is called *propagating*

> **key concept**
> If an exception is not caught and handled where it occurs, it is propagated to the calling method.

the exception. This propagation continues until the exception is caught and handled or until it is passed out of the `main` method, which terminates the program and produces an exception message. To catch an exception at an outer level, the method that produces the exception must be invoked inside a `try` block that has `catch` clauses to handle it.

The `Propagation` program shown in Listing 8.3 succinctly demonstrates the process of exception propagation. The `main` method invokes method `level1` in the `ExceptionScope` class (see Listing 8.4), which invokes `level2`, which invokes `level3`, which produces an exception. Method `level3` does not catch and handle the exception, so control is transferred back to `level2`. The `level2` method does not catch and handle the exception either, so control is transferred back to `level1`. Because the invocation of `level2` is made inside a `try` block (in method `level1`), the exception is caught and handled at that point.

Note that the output does not include the messages indicating that the methods `level3` and `level2` are ending. These `println` statements are never executed because an exception occurred and had not yet been caught. However, after method `level1` handles the exception, processing continues normally from that point, printing the messages indicating that method `level1` and the program are ending.

Note also that the `catch` clause that handles the exception uses the `getMessage` and `printStackTrace` methods to output that information. The stack trace shows the methods that were called when the exception occurred.

A programmer must pick the most appropriate level at which to catch and handle an exception. There is no single best answer. It depends on the situation and the design of the system. Sometimes the right approach will be not to catch an exception at all and let the program terminate.

the exception class hierarchy

The classes that define various exceptions are related by inheritance, creating a class hierarchy that is shown in part in Fig. 8.1.

The `Throwable` class is the parent of both the `Error` class and the `Exception` class. Many types of exceptions are derived from the `Exception` class, and these classes also have many children. Though these high-level classes are defined in the `java.lang` package, many child classes that define specific exceptions are part of several other packages. Inheritance relationships can span package boundaries.

listing
   8.3

```
//********************************************************************
//   Propagation.java          Author: Lewis/Loftus
//
//   Demonstrates exception propagation.
//********************************************************************

public class Propagation
{
   //-------------------------------------------------------------
   //   Invokes the level1 method to begin the exception demonstation.
   //-------------------------------------------------------------
   static public void main (String[] args)
   {
      ExceptionScope demo = new ExceptionScope();

      System.out.println("Program beginning.");
      demo.level1();
      System.out.println("Program ending.");
   }
}
```

output

```
Program beginning.
Level 1 beginning.
Level 2 beginning.
Level 3 beginning.

The exception message is: / by zero

The call stack trace:
java.lang.ArithmeticException: / by zero
        at ExceptionScope.level3(ExceptionScope.java:54)
        at ExceptionScope.level2(ExceptionScope.java:41)
        at ExceptionScope.level1(ExceptionScope.java:18)
        at Propagation.main(Propagation.java:17)

Level 1 ending.
Program ending.
```

listing
    8.4

```
//********************************************************************
//   ExceptionScope.java          Author: Lewis/Loftus
//
//   Demonstrates exception propagation.
//********************************************************************

public class ExceptionScope
{
   //-----------------------------------------------------------------
   //  Catches and handles the exception that is thrown in level3.
   //-----------------------------------------------------------------
   public void level1()
   {
      System.out.println("Level 1 beginning.");

      try
      {
         level2();
      }
      catch (ArithmeticException problem)
      {
         System.out.println ();
         System.out.println ("The exception message is: " +
                              problem.getMessage());
         System.out.println ();
         System.out.println ("The call stack trace:");
         problem.printStackTrace();
         System.out.println ();
      }

      System.out.println("Level 1 ending.");
   }

   //-----------------------------------------------------------------
   //  Serves as an intermediate level.  The exception propagates
   //  through this method back to level1.
   //-----------------------------------------------------------------
   public void level2()
   {
      System.out.println("Level 2 beginning.");
      level3 ();
      System.out.println("Level 2 ending.");
   }
```

listing
8.4   continued

```
//----------------------------------------------------------------
//  Performs a calculation to produce an exception.  It is not
//  caught and handled at this level.
//----------------------------------------------------------------
public void level3 ()
{
   int numerator = 10, denominator = 0;

   System.out.println("Level 3 beginning.");
   int result = numerator / denominator;
   System.out.println("Level 3 ending.");
}
}
```

We can define our own exceptions by deriving a new class from Exception or one of its descendants. The class we choose as the parent depends on what situation or condition the new exception represents.

> **Key concept**
> A new exception is defined by deriving a new class from the Exception class or one of its descendants.

The program in Listing 8.5 instantiates an exception object and throws it. The exception is created from the OutOfRangeException class, which is shown in Listing 8.6. Note that this exception is not part of the Java standard class library. It was created to represent the situation in which a value is outside a particular valid range.

After reading in an input value, the main method evaluates it to see whether it is in the valid range. If not, the *throw statement* is executed. A throw statement is used to begin exception propagation. Because the main method does not catch and handle the exception, the program will terminate if the exception is thrown, printing the message associated with the exception.

We create the OutOfRangeException class by extending the Exception class. Often, a new exception is nothing more than what you see in this example: an extension of some existing exception class that stores a particular message describing the situation it represents. The important point is that the class is ultimately a descendant of the Exception class and the Throwable class, which gives it the ability to be thrown using a throw statement.

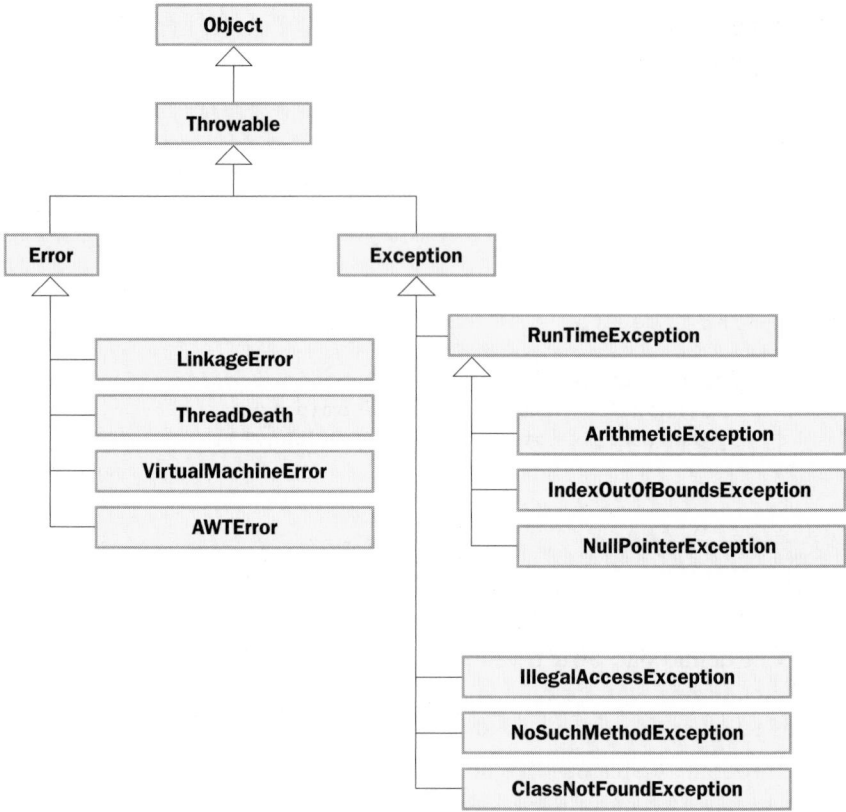

figure 8.1   Part of the Error and Exception class hierarchy

The type of situation handled by this program, in which a value is out of range, does not need to be represented as an exception. We've previously handled such situations using conditionals or loops. Whether you handle a situation using an exception or whether you take care of it in the normal flow of your program is an important design decision.

**listing
   8.5**

```
//************************************************************************
//  CreatingExceptions.java        Author: Lewis/Loftus
//
//  Demonstrates the ability to define an exception via inheritance.
//************************************************************************

import cs1.Keyboard;

public class CreatingExceptions
{
   //----------------------------------------------------------------
   //  Creates an exception object and possibly throws it.
   //----------------------------------------------------------------
   public static void main (String[] args) throws OutOfRangeException
   {
      final int MIN = 25, MAX = 40;

      OutOfRangeException problem =
         new OutOfRangeException ("Input value is out of range.");

      System.out.print ("Enter an integer value between " + MIN +
                        " and " + MAX + ", inclusive: ");
      int value = Keyboard.readInt();

      //  Determines if the exception should be thrown
      if (value < MIN || value > MAX)
         throw problem;

      System.out.println ("End of main method.");  // may never reach
   }
}
```

output

```
Enter an integer value between 25 and 40, inclusive: 69
Exception in thread "main" OutOfRangeException:
      Input value is out of range.
      at CreatingExceptions.main(CreatingExceptions.java:20)
```

```
//***********************************************************************
//  OutOfRangeException.java          Author: Lewis/Loftus
//
//  Represents an exceptional condition in which a value is out of
//  some particular range.
//***********************************************************************

public class OutOfRangeException extends Exception
{
   //-----------------------------------------------------------------
   //  Sets up the exception object with a particular message.
   //-----------------------------------------------------------------
   OutOfRangeException (String message)
   {
      super (message);
   }
}
```

checked and unchecked exceptions

There is one other issue concerning exceptions that we should explore. Some exceptions are checked, whereas others are unchecked. A *checked exception* must either be caught by a method or it must be listed in the *throws clause* of any method that may throw or propagate it. A throws clause is appended to the header of a method definition to formally acknowledge that the method will throw or propagate a particular exception if it occurs. An *unchecked exception* generally should not be caught and requires no throws clause.

> The throws clause on a method header must be included for checked exceptions that are not caught and handled in the method.

The only unchecked exceptions in Java are objects of type RuntimeException or any of its descendants. All other exceptions are considered checked exceptions. The main method of the CreatingExceptions program has a throws clause, indicating that it may throw an OutOfRangeException. This throws clause is required because the OutOfRangeException was derived from the Exception class, making it a checked exception.

Errors are similar to RuntimeException and its descendants in that they should not be caught and do not require a throws clause.

8.1 input/output streams

A *stream* is an ordered sequence of bytes. The term stream comes from the analogy that as we read and write information, the data flows from a source to a destination (or *sink*) as water flows down a stream. The source of the information is like a spring filling the stream, and the destination is like a cave into which the stream flows.

> **key concept**
>
> A stream is a sequential sequence of bytes, it can be used as a source of input or a destination for output.

In a program, we treat a stream as either an *input stream,* from which we read information, or as an *output stream,* to which we write information. That is, a program serves either as the spring filling the stream or as the cave receiving the stream. A program can deal with multiple input and output streams at one time. A particular store of data, such as a file, can serve either as an input stream or as an output stream to a program, but it cannot be both at the same time.

The `java.io` package of the Java standard class library provides many classes that let us define streams with particular characteristics. Some of the classes deal with files, others with memory, and others with strings. Some classes assume that the data they handle consists of characters, whereas others assume the data consists of raw bytes of binary information. Some classes provide the means to manipulate the data in the stream in some way, such as buffering the information or numbering it. By combining classes in appropriate ways, we can create objects that represent a stream of information that has the exact characteristics we want for a particular situation.

The sheer number of classes in the `java.io` package prohibits us from discussing them all in detail. Instead, our goal is to provide an overview of the classes involved, and then explore a few specific situations that are particularly useful.

In addition to dividing the classes in the `java.io` package into input and output streams, they can be subdivided in two other primary ways. First, we can divide the classes by the type of information on which they operate. There are basically two categories of classes in this regard: those that operate on character data and those that operate on byte data. We can also divide the classes in the `java.io` package by the role they play. Again we have two categories: those that represent a particular type of source or sink for information, such as a file or network connection, and those that provide the means to alter or manage the basic data in the stream. Most of the classes in the `java.io` package fall into one of the subdivisions created by these categories, as shown in Fig. 8.2.

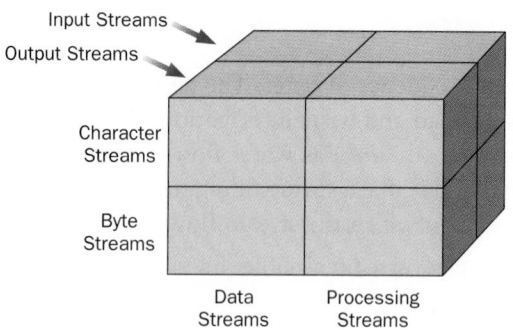

figure 8.2   Dividing the Java I/O classes into categories

character streams versus byte streams

A *character stream* is designed to manage 16-bit Unicode characters. The stream is nothing more than a lengthy series of characters, though they can be read and written in chunks (such as one line at a time) if we set up the stream with the proper characteristics. A *byte stream,* on the other hand, manages 8-bit bytes of raw binary data. How the bytes are interpreted and used once read depends on the program that reads them. Although they can be used to read and write any data, byte streams are typically used to read and write binary data such as sounds and images.

The classes that manage character streams and byte streams are cleanly divided in the I/O class inheritance hierarchy. The `InputStream` and `OutputStream` classes and all their descendants represent byte streams. The `Reader` and `Writer` classes and all their descendants represent character streams. Figure 8.3 shows this relationship.

The two class hierarchies share some basic similarities. For example, the `Reader` and `InputStream` classes provide similar methods but for different types of data. For example, they both provide a basic `read` method. The `read` method of `Reader` reads one character or an array of characters; the `read` method of `InputStream` reads one byte or an array of bytes. Such paired classes are common between the hierarchies but are not always consistent.

data streams versus processing streams

A *data stream* is a stream that represents a particular source or destination stream, such as a string in memory or a file on disk. A *processing stream* (sometimes called

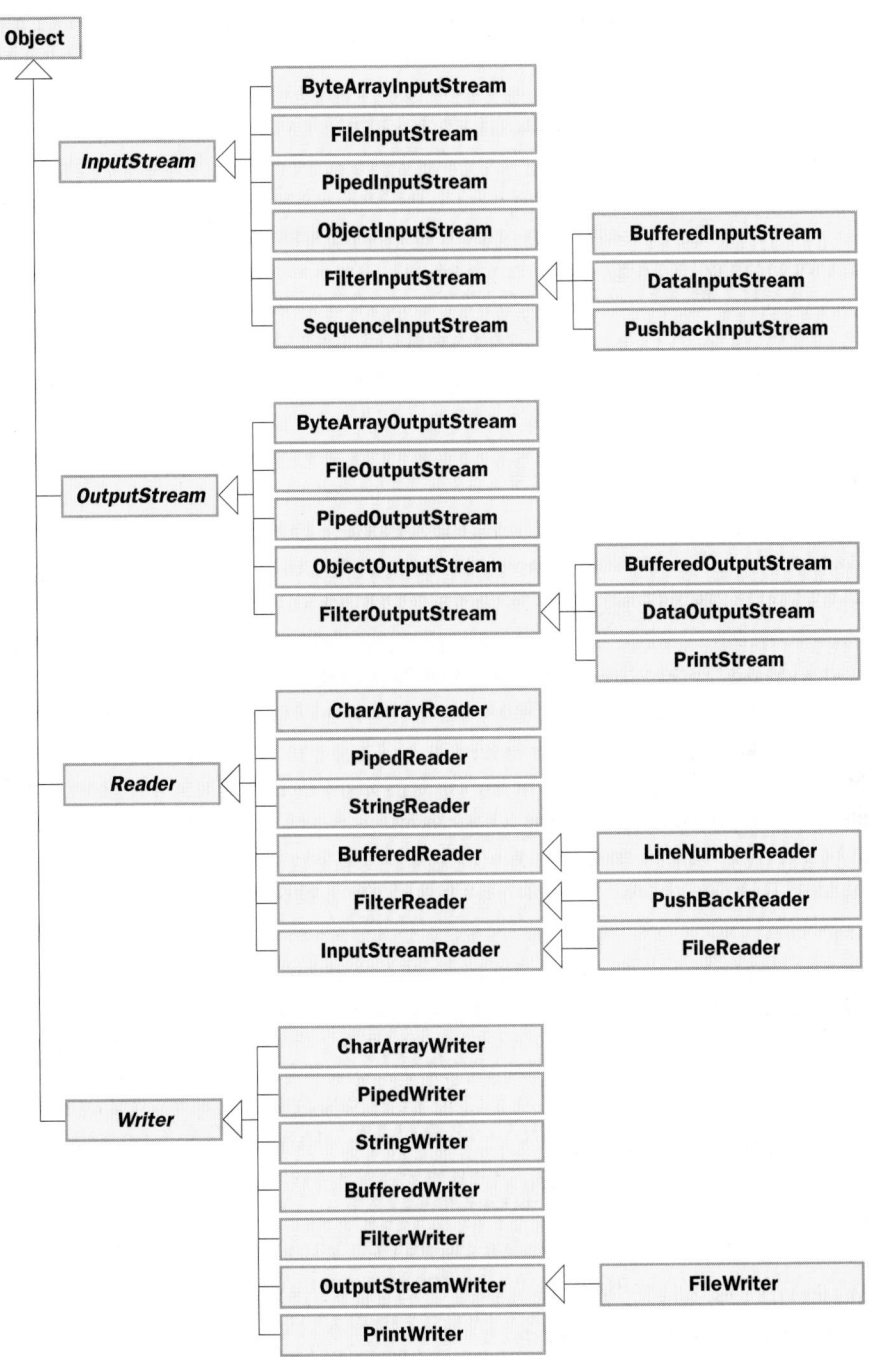

figure 8.3   The Java I/O class hierarchy

a *filtering stream*) performs some sort of manipulation on the data in a stream, such as converting it from one format to another or buffering the input to deliver it in chunks. By combining data streams with processing streams we can create an input or output stream that behaves exactly as we wish.

The classes that represent data streams and processing streams are the same classes that represent character streams and byte streams. It is just another way to categorize them. The data streams and processing streams cut across the class hierarchies, however. That is, all four of the primary class hierarchies in the Java I/O classes can be further subdivided into those that represent data streams and those that represent processing streams.

the IOException class

Many operations performed by I/O classes can potentially throw an IOException. The IOException class is the parent of several exception classes that represent problems when trying to perform I/O.

An IOException is a checked exception. As described earlier in this chapter that means that either the exception must be caught, or all methods that propagate it must list it in a throws clause of the method header.

Because I/O often deals with external resources, many problems can arise in programs that attempt to perform I/O operations. For example, a file from which we want to read might not exist; when we attempt to open the file, an exception will be thrown because that file can't be found. In general, we should try to design programs to be as robust as possible when dealing with potential problems.

8.2   standard I/O

Three streams are often called the *standard I/O streams*. They are listed in Fig. 8.4. The System class contains three object reference variables (in, out, and err)

that represent the three standard I/O streams. These references are declared as both public and static, which allows them to be accessed directly through the System class.

We've been using the standard output stream, with calls to System.out.prinln for instance, in examples throughout this book. Finally we can explain the details underlying that method invocation. In Chapter

Standard I/O Stream	Description
System.in	Standard input stream.
System.out	Standard output stream.
System.err	Standard error stream (output for error messages)

figure 8.4   Standard I/O streams

5 we explored some of the details of the Keyboard class, which masks the use of the standard input stream. We can now explore those issues in more detail as well.

The standard I/O streams, by default, represent particular I/O devices. System.in typically represents keyboard input, whereas System.out and System.err typically represent a particular window on the monitor screen. The System.out and System.err streams write output to the same window by default (usually the one in which the program was executed), though they could be set up to write to different places. The System.err stream is usually where error messages are sent.

All three of these streams are created and open by default, and in one sense are ready for use by any Java program. Both the System.out and System.err reference variables are declared to be of type PrintStream. The System.in reference is declared to be a generic InputStream.

PrintStream objects automatically have print and println methods defined for them. This makes the System.out object useful without any further manipulations. Note that PrintStream is technically a byte stream that converts objects and numbers into text for easy output. It is typically used for debugging and simple examples. PrintStream does not handle advanced internationalization and error checking; the PrintWriter class is a better choice for this.

The System.in reference is deliberately declared to be a generic InputStream reference so that it is not restricted in its use. This means, however, that it must usually be mapped into a stream with more useful characteristics. This is one of the reasons we created the Keyboard class.

the Keyboard class revisited

Recall that the Keyboard class was written by the authors of this text to make reading values from the standard input stream easier, especially when we were

The Keyboard class, though not part of the Java standard class library, provides an abstraction for several I/O operations on the standard input stream.

just getting started and had other issues to worry about. The Keyboard class provides methods such as readInt, readFloat, and readString to obtain a particular type of input value. In Chapter 5, we explored some of the details that the Keyboard class took care of for us. Now we can peel back the cover even more, revealing the underlying standard Java features used to write the Keyboard class.

The Keyboard class hides the following I/O operations:

▶ the declaration of the standard input stream in a useful form

▶ the handling of any IOException that may be thrown

▶ the parsing of an input line into separate tokens

▶ the conversion of an input value to its expected type

▶ the handling of conversion problems

Because System.in is defined as a reference to a generic InputStream object, it has by default only the basic ability to read and write byte data. To modify it into a more useful form, the Keyboard class performs the following declaration:

```
InputStreamReader isr = new InputStreamReader (System.in);
BufferedReader stdin = new BufferedReader (isr);
```

The first line creates an InputStreamReader object, which converts the original byte input stream into a character input stream. The second line transforms it into a BufferedReader, which allows us to use the readLine method to get an entire line of character input in one operation.

In the Keyboard class, each invocation of readLine is performed inside a try block so that an IOException, if it is thrown, can be caught and handled. The readLine method returns a string that includes all characters included in the input line. If that input line contains multiple values, they must be separated into individual tokens. Recall that the StringTokenizer class performs just that kind of service. The Keyboard class constantly keeps track of the current input line and uses a StringTokenizer object to extract the next token when requested.

On top of all of this, each token, as it is extracted from the input line, may be needed as a particular primitive type, such as an int. Therefore each method of the Keyboard class performs the proper conversion. For example, the readInt method of the Keyboard class takes the next token from the input line and calls the parseInt method of the Integer wrapper class to convert the string to an int. Similar processing can be seen in the file I/O examples in the next section.

8.3 text files

Another common programming requirement is to read from and write to files on disk. Information is stored in a file as either byte or character (text) data and should be read in the same way. This section focuses on text files.

reading text files

The `FileReader` class represents an input file that contains character data. Its constructors set up the relationship between the program and the file, opening a stream from which data can be read. Its ability to read data is limited to the `read` method, which is inherited from its parent class `InputStreamReader`. If we want to read something other than character arrays, we have to use another input class.

As we discussed in the previous section, the `BufferedReader` class does not represent any particular data source but filters data on a given stream by buffering it into more accessible units. In particular, the `BufferedReader` class provides the `readLine` method, which allows us to read an entire line of characters in one operation. Recall that the `readLine` method returns a string, which must be processed if individual data values are to be extracted from it.

> **key concept**
>
> The `FileReader` and `BufferedReader` classes can be used together to create a convenient text file output stream.

Let's examine a program that reads data from a particular input file and processes it. Suppose a text data file called `inventory.dat` contained the following information:

```
Widget 14 3.35
Spoke 132 0.32
Wrap 58 1.92
Thing 28 4.17
Brace 25 1.75
Clip 409 0.12
Cog 142 2.08
```

Suppose this data represents the inventory of a warehouse. Each line contains an item name, the number of available units, and the price of that item. Each value on a line is separated from the other values by at least one space. The program in

Listing 8.7 reads this data file, creates an array of objects based on that data, and prints the information.

listing
    8.7

```java
//********************************************************************
//  CheckInventory.java        Author: Lewis/Loftus
//
//  Demonstrates the use of a character file input stream.
//********************************************************************

import java.io.*;
import java.util.StringTokenizer;

public class CheckInventory
{
   //-----------------------------------------------------------------
   //  Reads data about a store inventory from an input file,
   //  creating an array of InventoryItem objects, then prints them.
   //-----------------------------------------------------------------
   public static void main (String[] args)
   {
      final int MAX = 100;
      InventoryItem[] items = new InventoryItem[MAX];
      StringTokenizer tokenizer;
      String line, name, file = "inventory.dat";
      int units, count = 0;
      float price;

      try
      {
         FileReader fr = new FileReader (file);
         BufferedReader inFile = new BufferedReader (fr);

         line = inFile.readLine();
         while (line != null)
         {
            tokenizer = new StringTokenizer (line);
            name = tokenizer.nextToken();
            try
            {
               units = Integer.parseInt (tokenizer.nextToken());
               price = Float.parseFloat (tokenizer.nextToken());
               items[count++] = new InventoryItem (name, units, price);
            }
```

```
listing
   8.7    continued

            catch (NumberFormatException exception)
            {
                System.out.println ("Error in input. Line ignored:");
                System.out.println (line);
            }
            line = inFile.readLine();
        }

        inFile.close();

        for (int scan = 0; scan < count; scan++)
            System.out.println (items[scan]);
    }
    catch (FileNotFoundException exception)
    {
        System.out.println ("The file " + file + " was not found.");
    }
    catch (IOException exception)
    {
        System.out.println (exception);
    }
  }
}
```

output

```
Widget: 14 at 3.35 = 46.9
Spoke:  132 at 0.32 = 42.24
Wrap:   58 at 1.92 = 111.36
Thing:  28 at 4.17 = 116.76
Brace:  25 at 1.75 = 43.75
Clip:   409 at 0.12 = 49.08
Cog:    142 at 2.08 = 295.36
```

The program uses the data it reads from the file to create several InventoryItem objects (see Listing 8.8). The data read from the file is passed to the InventoryItem constructor.

Certain parts of the processing in the CheckInventory program are performed within try blocks to handle exceptions that may arise. The declaration of the input file stream is accomplished at the top of the outer try block. If the file cannot be located when the FileReader constructor is executed, a

listing
   8.8

```
//********************************************************************
//   InventoryItem.java        Author: Lewis/Loftus
//
//   Represents an item in the inventory.
//********************************************************************

import java.text.DecimalFormat;

public class InventoryItem
{
   private String name;
   private int units;       // number of available units of this item
   private float price;     // price per unit of this item
   private DecimalFormat fmt;

   //-----------------------------------------------------------------
   //   Sets up this item with the specified information.
   //-----------------------------------------------------------------
   public InventoryItem (String itemName, int numUnits, float cost)
   {
      name = itemName;
      units = numUnits;
      price = cost;
      fmt = new DecimalFormat ("0.##");
   }

   //-----------------------------------------------------------------
   //   Returns information about this item as a string.
   //-----------------------------------------------------------------
   public String toString()
   {
      return name + ":\t" + units + " at " + price + " = " +
            fmt.format ((units * price));
   }
}
```

FileNotFoundException is thrown. If at any point during the processing an IOException is thrown, it is caught and processing is neatly terminated.

Once the input stream is set up, the program begins to read and process one line of input at a time. The readLine method reads an entire line of text until a line terminator character is found. When the end of the file is encountered, readLine returns a null reference, which is used as a termination condition for the loop.

Each line is separated into distinct values using a StringTokenizer object. First the name of the item is stored, then the number of units and the unit price are separated and converted into numeric values. A NumberFormatException will be thrown if the string does not represent a valid numeric value, so the inner try block catches and handles it. If a conversion error is encountered, the input line is ignored but processing continues.

Note that BufferedReader is serving the same purpose in this program as it does in the Keyboard class—to buffer input and provide the readLine method—even though the actual source of the information is quite different in each case. This situation illustrates why the designers of the java.io package separated the responsibilities as they did. The Java I/O classes can be combined in many different ways to provide exactly the kind of interaction and character manipulation needed for a particular situation.

writing text files

Writing output to a text file requires simply that we use the appropriate classes to create the output stream, then call the appropriate methods to write the data. As with standard I/O, file output seems to be a little more straightforward than file input.

The FileWriter class represents a text output file, but, like FileReader, it has minimal method support for manipulating data. The PrintWriter class provides print and println methods similar to the standard I/O PrintStream class.

Suppose we want to test a program we are writing, but don't have the real data available. We could write a program that generates a test data file that contains random values. The program shown in Listing 8.9 generates a file that contains random integer values within a particular range. The one line of standard text output for the TestData program, confirming that the data file has been written, is also shown.

listing
8.9

```java
//********************************************************************
//   TestData.java         Author: Lewis/Loftus
//
//   Demonstrates the use of a character file output stream.
//********************************************************************

import java.util.Random;
import java.io.*;

public class TestData
{
   //------------------------------------------------------------------
   //   Creates a file of test data that consists of ten lines each
   //   containing ten integer values in the range 10 to 99.
   //------------------------------------------------------------------
   public static void main (String[] args) throws IOException
   {
      final int MAX = 10;

      int value;
      String file = "test.dat";

      Random rand = new Random();

      FileWriter fw = new FileWriter (file);
      BufferedWriter bw = new BufferedWriter (fw);
      PrintWriter outFile = new PrintWriter (bw);

      for (int line=1; line <= MAX; line++)
      {
         for (int num=1; num <= MAX; num++)
         {
            value = rand.nextInt (90) + 10;
            outFile.print (value + "    ");
         }
         outFile.println ();
      }
```

```
listing
   8.9    continued

      outFile.close();
      System.out.println ("Output file has been created: " + file);
   }
}
```

output

```
Output file has been created: test.dat
```

Although we do not need to do so for the program to work, we have added a layer in the file stream configuration to include a `BufferedWriter`. This addition simply gives the output stream buffering capabilities, which makes the processing more efficient. While buffering is not crucial in this situation, it is usually a good idea when writing text files.

Note that in the `TestData` program, we have eliminated explicit exception handling. That is, if something goes wrong, we simply allow the program to terminate instead of specifically catching and handling the problem. Because all `IOExceptions` are checked exceptions, we must include the `throws` clause on the method header to indicate that they may be thrown. For each program, we must carefully consider how best to handle the exceptions that may be thrown. This requirement is especially important when dealing with I/O, which is fraught with potential problems that cannot always be foreseen.

The `TestData` program uses nested `for` loops to compute a random value and print it to the file. After all values are printed, the file is closed. Output files must be closed explicitly to ensure that the data is retained. In general, it is good practice to close all file streams explicitly when they are no longer needed.

> **key concept**
> Output file streams should be explicitly closed or they may not correctly retain the data written to them.

The data that is contained in the file `test.dat` after the `TestData` program is run might look like this:

```
85  90  93  15  82  79  52  71  70  98
74  57  41  66  22  16  67  65  24  84
86  61  91  79  18  81  64  41  68  81
98  47  28  40  69  10  85  82  64  41
23  61  27  10  59  89  88  26  24  76
```

```
33  89  73  36  54  91  42  73  95  58
19  41  18  14  63  80  96  30  17  28
24  37  40  64  94  23  98  10  78  50
89  28  64  54  59  23  61  15  80  88
51  28  44  48  73  21  41  52  35  38
```

8.4 object serialization

When a program terminates, the data it used is destroyed unless an effort is made to store the data externally. We've seen how we can read and write primitive data to and from a file. But what happens when we want to store an object, an array of objects, or some other complex structure? We could write code that stores all the pieces of an object separately and reconstruct the object when that data is read back in. However, the more complex the information, the more difficult and tedious this process becomes.

Persistence is the concept that an object can exist separate from the executing program that creates it. Java contains a mechanism called *object serialization* for creating persistent objects. When an object is serialized, it is transformed into a sequence of bytes; this sequence is raw binary representation of the object. Later, this representation can be restored to the original object. Once serialized, the object can be stored in a file for later use.

In Java, object serialization is accomplished with the help of an interface and two classes. Any object we want to serialize must implement the Serializable interface. This interface contains no methods; it serves instead as a flag to the compiler that objects of this type might be serialized. To serialize an object, we invoke the writeObject method of an ObjectOutputStream. To deserialize the object, we invoke the readObject method of an ObjectInputStream.

ObjectOutputStream and ObjectInputStream are processing streams; they must be wrapped around an OutputStream or InputStream of some kind, respectively. Therefore the actual data streams to which the serialized object is written can represent a file, network communication, or some other type of stream.

Let's look at an example. The program shown in Listing 8.10 creates several CountryInfo objects and prints them to standard output. It also serializes the objects as it writes them to a file called countries.dat.

listing
8.10

```
//********************************************************************
//   WriteCountryInfo.java          Author: Lewis/Loftus
//
//   Demonstrates object serialization.
//********************************************************************

import java.io.*;

public class WriteCountryInfo
{
   //-----------------------------------------------------------------
   //  Creates several objects, prints them to standard output, and
   /// serializes them to a file.
   //-----------------------------------------------------------------
   public static void main (String[] args) throws IOException
   {
      FileOutputStream file = new FileOutputStream ("countries.dat");
      ObjectOutputStream outStream = new ObjectOutputStream (file);

      CountryInfo[] countries = new CountryInfo[5];

      countries[0] = new CountryInfo ("United States of America",
                        "USA", "Washington, D.C.", 9629091L, 278058900L);
      countries[1] = new CountryInfo ("Russia", "RUS", "Moscow",
                        17075200L, 145470200L);
      countries[2] = new CountryInfo ("Italy", "ITA", "Rome",
                        301230L, 57679800L);
      countries[3] = new CountryInfo ("Sweden", "SWE", "Stockholm",
                        449964L, 8875100L);
      countries[4] = new CountryInfo ("Poland", "POL", "Warsaw",
                        312685L, 38633900L);

      int scan;

      //  Print the objects
      for (scan = 0; scan < countries.length; scan++)
         System.out.println (countries[scan]);

      //  Serialize the objects to a file
      for (scan = 0; scan < countries.length; scan++)
         outStream.writeObject (countries[scan]);
   }
}
```

listing
   8.10   continued

output

```
Name: United States of America
Abbreviation: USA
Capitol: Washington, D.C.
Area: 9629091 square kilometers
Population: 278058900
^^^^^^^^^^^^^^^^^^^^^^^^^^^^^^^^^^^^^^^^^^^^^^^^^^^^
Name: Russia
Abbreviation: RUS
Capitol: Moscow
Area: 17075200 square kilometers
Population: 145470200
^^^^^^^^^^^^^^^^^^^^^^^^^^^^^^^^^^^^^^^^^^^^^^^^^^^^
Name: Italy
Abbreviation: ITA
Capitol: Rome
Area: 301230 square kilometers
Population: 57679800
^^^^^^^^^^^^^^^^^^^^^^^^^^^^^^^^^^^^^^^^^^^^^^^^^^^^
Name: Sweden
Abbreviation: SWE
Capitol: Stockholm
Area: 449964 square kilometers
Population: 8875100
^^^^^^^^^^^^^^^^^^^^^^^^^^^^^^^^^^^^^^^^^^^^^^^^^^^^
Name: Poland
Abbreviation: POL
Capitol: Warsaw
Area: 312685 square kilometers
Population: 38633900
^^^^^^^^^^^^^^^^^^^^^^^^^^^^^^^^^^^^^^^^^^^^^^^^^^^^
```

The CountryInfo class is shown in Listing 8.11. Note that it implements the Serializable interface but otherwise has no special features that relate to its persistence.

listing
   8.11

```
//********************************************************************
//  CountryInfo.java        Author: Lewis/Loftus
//
//  Represents a country's demographic information.
//********************************************************************

import java.io.Serializable;

public class CountryInfo implements Serializable
{
   private String name, abbreviation, capitol;
   private long area, population;

   //-------------------------------------------------------------------
   //  Sets up this object by storing the specified information.
   //-------------------------------------------------------------------
   public CountryInfo (String cName, String cAbbreviation,
                       String cCapitol, long cArea, long cPopulation)
   {
      name = cName;
      abbreviation = cAbbreviation;
      capitol = cCapitol;
      area = cArea;   // measured in square kilometers
      population = cPopulation;
   }

   //-------------------------------------------------------------------
   //  Returns the information in this object as a string.
   //-------------------------------------------------------------------
   public String toString()
   {
      String result = "Name: " + name + "\n";
      result += "Abbreviation: " + abbreviation + "\n";
      result += "Capitol: " + capitol + "\n";
      result += "Area: " + area + " square kilometers\n";
      result += "Population: " + population + "\n";
      result += "^^^^^^^^^^^^^^^^^^^^^^^^^^^^^^^^^^^^^^^^^^^^^^^^^^";

      return result;
   }
}
```

The act of serialization automatically takes into account any additional referenced objects. That is, it automatically follows all references contained in the object being serialized and serializes them. Thus, if a `Car` object contains a reference to an `Engine` object, for instance, the `Engine` object is automatically serialized as part of the act of serializing the car. For this to work, the `Engine` class must also implement the `Serializable` interface. This processing continues as needed for any level of aggregate objects. If an `Engine` object, for instance, contains references to other objects, they are serialized as well (and so on).

Many classes of the Java standard class library implement the `Serializable` interface so that they can be serialized as needed. The `String` class, for example, implements `Serializable` so that any class containing references to `String` objects can be serialized without complications. This situation occurs in the `CountryInfo` class.

Now let's examine a program that reverses this process. That is, now that the `CountryInfo` objects have been serialized and written out to a file, let's deserialize them. The program shown in Listing 8.12 creates the appropriate input stream and reads the objects. It then prints them. Note that the output is the same as that of the `WriteCountryInfo` program.

The `ArrayList` class also implements the `Serializable` interface, so we can store an entire list of objects in one operation. So if we had stored the `CountryInfo` objects in an `ArrayList` (instead of a regular array) in the `WriteCountryInfo` program, we could have written the entire set of objects out in one operation. Likewise, the `ReadCountryInfo` program could have then read the entire `ArrayList` of `CountryInfo` objects from the file in one operation. Keep in mind that the objects stored in the `ArrayList` must also implement the `Serializable` interface for this to work.

the transient modifier

Sometimes we may prefer to exclude particular information when we serialize an object. For example, we may want to exclude a password so that it is not part of the information that is stored or transferred over the network. The danger is that, even though we declare the password with private visibility, once it is serialized, it could be read and accessed by some unfriendly source. Another reason we may want to exclude particular information from the serialization process is if it is simply not needed or can easily be reproduced when the object is deserialized. That way, the byte stream representing the serialized object does not contain unnecessary information that will increase its size.

listing
   8.12

```java
//********************************************************************
//  ReadCountryInfo.java        Author: Lewis/Loftus
//
//  Demonstrates object deserialization.
//********************************************************************

import java.io.*;

public class ReadCountryInfo
{
   //-----------------------------------------------------------------
   //  Reads objects from a serialized file and prints them.
   //-----------------------------------------------------------------
   public static void main (String[] args) throws Exception
   {
      FileInputStream file = new FileInputStream ("countries.dat");
      ObjectInputStream inStream = new ObjectInputStream (file);

      CountryInfo[] countries = new CountryInfo[5];

      int scan;

      // Deserialize the objects
      for (scan = 0; scan < countries.length; scan++)
         countries[scan] = (CountryInfo) inStream.readObject();

      // Print the objects
      for (scan = 0; scan < countries.length; scan++)
         System.out.println (countries[scan]);
   }
}
```

output

```
Name: United States of America
Abbreviation: USA
Capitol: Washington, D.C.
Area: 9629091 square kilometers
Population: 278058900
^^^^^^^^^^^^^^^^^^^^^^^^^^^^^^^^^^^^^^^^^^^^^^^^^^^^^^^

Name: Russia
Abbreviation: RUS
Capitol: Moscow
Area: 17075200 square kilometers
Population: 145470200
^^^^^^^^^^^^^^^^^^^^^^^^^^^^^^^^^^^^^^^^^^^^^^^^^^^^^^^
```

listing
8.12 **continued**

```
Name: Italy
Abbreviation: ITA
Capitol: Rome
Area: 301230 square kilometers
Population: 57679800
^^^^^^^^^^^^^^^^^^^^^^^^^^^^^^^^^^^^^^^^^^^^^^^^^^^

Name: Sweden
Abbreviation: SWE
Capitol: Stockholm
Area: 449964 square kilometers
Population: 8875100
^^^^^^^^^^^^^^^^^^^^^^^^^^^^^^^^^^^^^^^^^^^^^^

Name: Poland
Abbreviation: POL
Capitol: Warsaw
Area: 312685 square kilometers
Population: 38633900
^^^^^^^^^^^^^^^^^^^^^^^^^^^^^^^^^^^^^^^^^^^^^^
```

The reserved word `transient` can be used to modify the declaration of a variable so that it will not be represented as part of the byte stream when the object containing it is serialized. For example, suppose an object contains the following declaration:

```
private transient int password;
```

That variable, when the object in which it is contained is serialized, will not be included in the representation.

8.5 files and GUIs

Programs that use graphical user interfaces (GUIs) often must deal with external files in one way or another. This section explores several of these issues, and presents some additional GUI components and events as well.

file choosers

Dialog boxes were introduced in Chapter 5. We used the JOptionPane class to create several specialized dialog boxes to present information, accept input, and confirm actions.

The JFileChooser class represents another specialized dialog box, a *file chooser*, which allows the user to select a file from a hard disk or other storage medium. You have probably run many programs that allow you to open a file using a similar dialog box.

The program shown in Listing 8.13 uses a JFileChooser dialog box to select a file. This program also demonstrates the use of another GUI component, a *text area*, which is similar to a text field but can display multiple lines of text at one time. Once the user has selected a file using the file chooser dialog box, the text contained in that file is displayed in a text area.

The file chooser dialog box is displayed when the showOpenDialog method is invoked. It automatically presents the list of files contained in a particular directory. The user can use the controls on the dialog box to navigate to other directories, change the way the files are viewed, and specify which types of files are displayed.

> **key concept**
>
> A file chooser allows the user to browse a disk or other storage device in order to select a file.

The showOpenDialog method returns an integer representing the status of the operation, which can be checked against constants defined in the JFileChooser class. In this program, if a file was not selected (perhaps by pressing the Cancel button), a default message is displayed in the text area. If the user chose a file, it is opened and its contents are read. Note that this program assumes the selected file contains text, and that no exceptions are caught. If the user selects an inappropriate file, the program will terminate when the exception is thrown.

A text area component is defined by the JTextArea class. In this program, we pass two parameters to its constructor, specifying the size of the text area in terms of the number of characters (rows and columns) it should display. The text it is to display is set using the setText method. A text area component, like a text field, can be set so that it is either editable or noneditable. The user can change the contents of an editable text area by clicking on the text area and typing with the mouse. If the text area is noneditable, it is used to display text only. By default, a JTextArea component is editable.

> **key concept**
>
> A text area component displays multiple rows of text.

A JFileChooser component makes it easy to allow users to specify a specific file to use. Another specialized dialog box—one that allows the user to choose a color—is discussed in the next section.

listing
   8.13

```
//********************************************************************
//   DisplayFile.java        Author: Lewis/Loftus
//
//   Demonstrates the use of a file chooser and a text area.
//********************************************************************

import java.io.*;
import javax.swing.*;

public class DisplayFile
{
   //-----------------------------------------------------------------
   //  Opens a file chooser dialog, reads the selected file and
   //  loads it into a text area.
   //-----------------------------------------------------------------
   public static void main (String[] args) throws IOException
   {
      JFrame frame = new JFrame ("Display File");
      frame.setDefaultCloseOperation (JFrame.EXIT_ON_CLOSE);

      JTextArea ta = new JTextArea (20, 30);
      JFileChooser chooser = new JFileChooser();

      int status = chooser.showOpenDialog (null);

      if (status != JFileChooser.APPROVE_OPTION)
         ta.setText ("No File Chosen");
      else
      {
         File file = chooser.getSelectedFile();
         FileReader fr = new FileReader (file);
         BufferedReader inFile = new BufferedReader (fr);

         String info = "";
         String line = inFile.readLine();
         while (line != null)
         {
            info += line + "\n";
            line = inFile.readLine();
         }
```

listing
    8.13 **continued**

```
        ta.setText (info);
    }

    frame.getContentPane().add (ta);
    frame.pack();
    frame.show();
  }
}
```

display

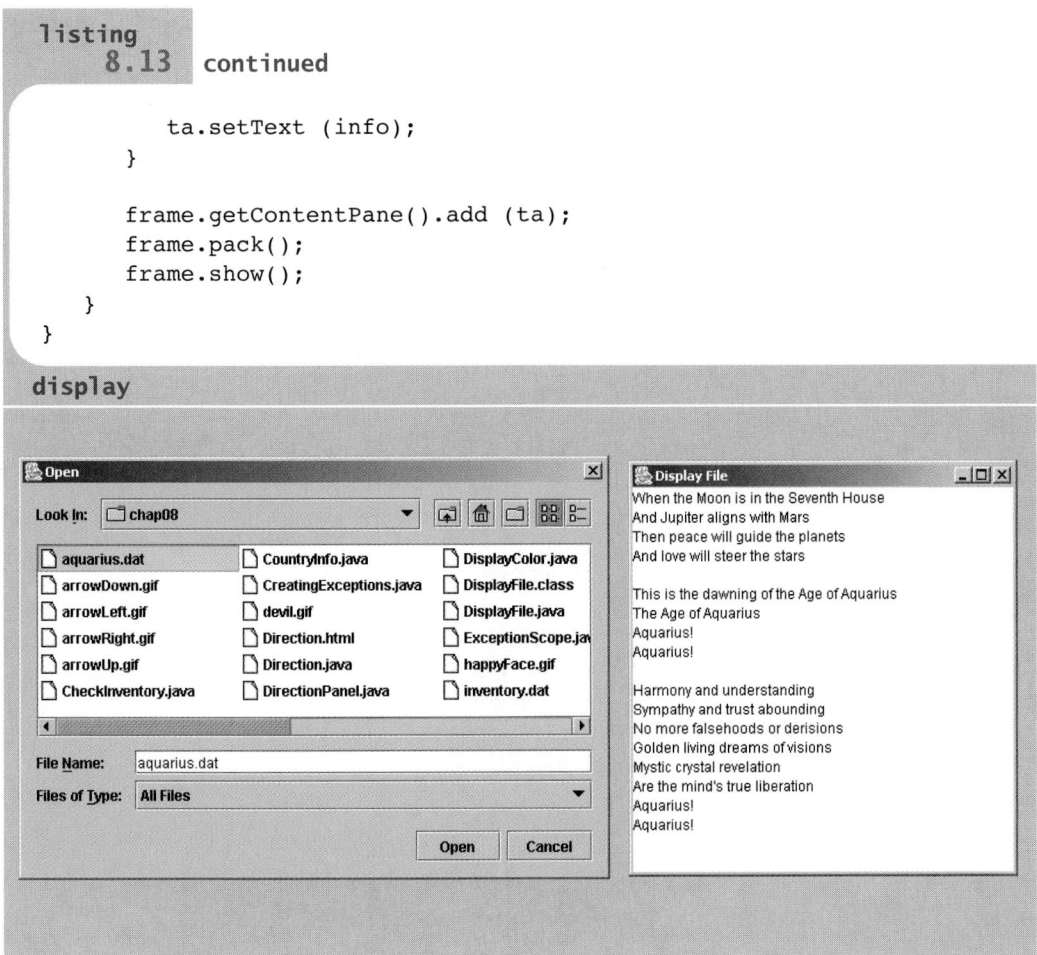

color choosers

In many situations we may want to give the user of a program the ability to choose a color. We could accomplish this in various ways. We could, for instance, provide a list of colors using a set of radio buttons. However, with the wide variety of colors available, it's nice to have an easier and more flexible technique to accomplish this common task.

The `JColorChooser` class represents a component that allows the user to specify a color. It can be used to display a dialog box that lets the user click on a color of choice from a palette presented for that purpose. The user could also specify a color using RGB values or other color representation techniques.

> **key concept**
>
> A color chooser allows the user to select a color from a palette or using RGB values.

The program shown in Listing 8.14 uses a color chooser dialog box to specify the color of a panel that is displayed in a separate frame.

listing
   8.14

```
//********************************************************************
//  DisplayColor.java        Author: Lewis/Loftus
//
//  Demonstrates the use of a color chooser.
//********************************************************************

import javax.swing.*;
import java.awt.*;

public class DisplayColor
{
   //-----------------------------------------------------------------
   //  Presents a frame with a colored panel, then allows the user
   //  to change the color multiple times using a color chooser.
   //-----------------------------------------------------------------
   public static void main (String[] args)
   {
      JFrame frame = new JFrame ("Display Color");
      frame.setDefaultCloseOperation (JFrame.EXIT_ON_CLOSE);

      JPanel colorPanel = new JPanel();
      colorPanel.setBackground (Color.white);
      colorPanel.setPreferredSize (new Dimension (300, 100));

      frame.getContentPane().add (colorPanel);
      frame.pack();
      frame.show();

      Color shade = Color.white;
      int again;

      do
      {
         shade = JColorChooser.showDialog (frame, "Pick a Color!",
                                           shade);

         colorPanel.setBackground (shade);
```

listing
    8.14 continued

```
        again = JOptionPane.showConfirmDialog (null,
            "Change color again?");
    }
    while (again == JOptionPane.YES_OPTION);
  }
}
```

display

After choosing a color, the new color is displayed in the primary frame and another dialog box (this one created using JOptionPane as discussed in Chapter 5) is used to determine if the user wants to change the color again. If so, another color chooser dialog box is displayed. This cycle can continue as long as the user desires.

Invoking the static showDialog method of the JColorChooser class causes the color chooser dialog box to appear. The parameters to that method specify the parent component for the dialog box, the title that appears in the dialog box frame, and the initial color showing in the color chooser. By using the variable shade as the third parameter, the color showing in the color chooser will always be the current color of the panel.

image icons

As we've seen in previous examples, a label, defined by the JLabel class, is used to provide information to the user or describe other components in an interface. A JLabel can also contain an image. That is, a label can be composed of text, an image, or both.

An ImageIcon object is used to represent an image that is used in a label. The ImageIcon constructor takes the name of the image file and loads it into the object. ImageIcon objects can be made using either JPEG or GIF images.

The alignment of the text and image within the label can be set explicitly, using either the JLabel constructor or specific methods. Similarly, we can set the position of the text relative to the image.

The program shown in Listing 8.15 displays several labels. Each label shows the text and image in different orientations.

The labels are set up and displayed using the LabelPanel class shown in Listing 8.16. Its constructor loads the image used in the labels, creates three label objects, and then sets their characteristics.

The third parameter passed to the JLabel constructor defines the horizontal positioning of the label within the space allowed for the label. The SwingConstants interface contains several constants used by various Swing components, making it easier to refer to them.

The orientation of the label's text and image is explicitly set using the setHorizontalTextPosition and setVerticalTextPosition methods. As shown in the case of the first label, the default horizontal position for text is on the right (image on the left), and the default vertical position for text is centered relative to the image.

listing
    8.15

```
//********************************************************************
//   LabelDemo.java          Author: Lewis/Loftus
//
//   Demonstrates the use of image icons in labels.
//********************************************************************

import javax.swing.*;

public class LabelDemo
{
   //-----------------------------------------------------------------
   //   Creates and displays the primary application frame.
   //-----------------------------------------------------------------
   public static void main (String[] args)
   {
      JFrame frame = new JFrame ("Label Demo");
      frame.setDefaultCloseOperation (JFrame.EXIT_ON_CLOSE);

      frame.getContentPane().add(new LabelPanel());

      frame.pack();
      frame.show();
   }
}
```

display

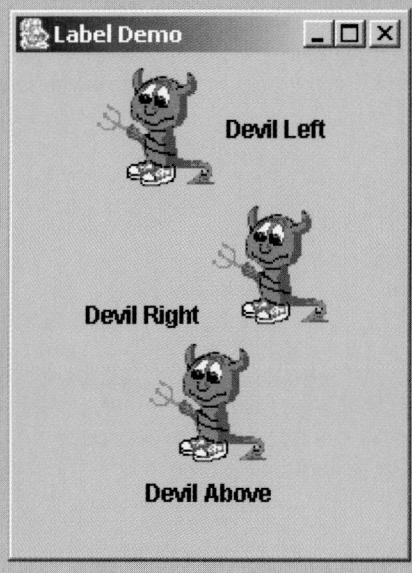

listing
   8.16

```java
//********************************************************************
//  LabelPanel.java        Author: Lewis/Loftus
//
//  Represents the primary display for the LabelDemo program.
//********************************************************************

import java.awt.*;
import javax.swing.*;

public class LabelPanel extends JPanel
{
   private ImageIcon icon;
   private JLabel label1, label2, label3;

   //-----------------------------------------------------------------
   //  Displays three labels with different text/icon orientations.
   //-----------------------------------------------------------------
   public LabelPanel ()
   {
      icon = new ImageIcon ("devil.gif");

      label1 = new JLabel ("Devil Left", icon, SwingConstants.LEFT);

      label2 = new JLabel ("Devil Right", icon, SwingConstants.LEFT);
      label2.setHorizontalTextPosition (SwingConstants.LEFT);
      label2.setVerticalTextPosition (SwingConstants.BOTTOM);

      label3 = new JLabel ("Devil Above", icon, SwingConstants.LEFT);
      label3.setHorizontalTextPosition (SwingConstants.CENTER);
      label3.setVerticalTextPosition (SwingConstants.BOTTOM);

      add (label1);
      add (label2);
      add (label3);

      setBackground (Color.cyan);
      setPreferredSize (new Dimension (200, 250));
   }
}
```

Don't confuse the horizontal positioning of the label in its allotted space with the setting of the orientation between the text and the image. The third parameter of the constructor determines the first, and the explicit method calls determine the second. In this program, the layout manager of the program overrides the horizontal positioning of the labels anyway, centering them in each row of the panel. Layout managers are discussed in detail in Chapter 9.

Images can also be used in `JButton` objects. That is, a button can contain text, an image, or both, just as a label can. The orientations between the text and image in a button can also be set explicitly if desired.

> **key concept**
> An image icon can be added to other components such as a label or a button.

key events

A *key event* is generated when a keyboard key is pressed. Key events allow a program to respond immediately to the user while he or she is typing or pressing other keyboard keys such as the arrow keys. There is no need to wait for the Enter key to be pressed or some other component to be activated.

> **key concept**
> Key events allow a program to immediately respond to the user typing keyboard keys.

The `Direction` program shown in Listing 8.17 responds to key events. An image of an arrow is displayed and the image moves across the screen as the arrow keys are pressed. This program is implemented as an applet.

The `DirectionPanel` class, shown in Listing 8.18, represents the panel on which the arrow image is displayed. The program actually loads four separate images of arrows pointing in the four primary directions (up, down, right, and left). The image that is displayed corresponds to the arrow key that was most recently pressed. For example, if the up arrow is pressed, the image with the arrow pointing up is displayed. If an arrow key is continually pressed, the appropriate image "moves" in the appropriate direction until the boundary of the applet window is encountered.

The arrow images are managed as `ImageIcon` objects. In this example, the image is drawn using the `paintIcon` method each time the panel is repainted. The `paintIcon` method takes four parameters: a component to serve as an *image observer*, the graphics context on which the image will be drawn, and the (x, y) coordinates where the image is drawn. An image observer is a component that serves to manage image loading; in this case we use the panel as the image observer.

listing
8.17

```java
//********************************************************************
//  Direction.java        Author: Lewis/Loftus
//
//  Demonstrates the use of key events.
//********************************************************************

import javax.swing.*;

public class Direction extends JApplet
{
   //-----------------------------------------------------------------
   //  Adds the display panel to the applet.
   //-----------------------------------------------------------------
   public void init()
   {
      getContentPane().add (new DirectionPanel(this));
   }
}
```

display

listing
8.18

```
//*********************************************************************
//  DirectionPanel.java        Author: Lewis/Loftus
//
//  Represents the primary display panel for the Direction program.
//*********************************************************************

import javax.swing.*;
import java.awt.*;
import java.awt.event.*;

public class DirectionPanel extends JPanel
{
   private final int WIDTH = 300, HEIGHT = 200;
   private final int JUMP = 10;  // increment for image movement

   private final int IMAGE_SIZE = 31;

   private ImageIcon up, down, right, left, currentImage;
   private int x, y;

   //-----------------------------------------------------------------
   //  Sets up this panel and loads the images.
   //-----------------------------------------------------------------
   public DirectionPanel (JApplet applet)
   {
      applet.addKeyListener (new DirectionListener());

      x = WIDTH / 2;
      y = HEIGHT / 2;

      up = new ImageIcon ("arrowUp.gif");
      down = new ImageIcon ("arrowDown.gif");
      left = new ImageIcon ("arrowLeft.gif");
      right = new ImageIcon ("arrowRight.gif");

      currentImage = right;

      setBackground (Color.black);
      setPreferredSize (new Dimension(WIDTH, HEIGHT));
   }
```

listing
8.18 continued

```java
//-----------------------------------------------------------------
//  Draws the image in the current location.
//-----------------------------------------------------------------
public void paintComponent (Graphics page)
{
   super.paintComponent (page);
   currentImage.paintIcon (this, page, x, y);
}

//*****************************************************************
//  Represents the listener for keyboard activity.
//*****************************************************************
private class DirectionListener implements KeyListener
{
   //-----------------------------------------------------------------
   //  Responds to the user pressing arrow keys by adjusting the
   //  image location accordingly.
   //-----------------------------------------------------------------
   public void keyPressed (KeyEvent event)
   {
      switch (event.getKeyCode())
      {
         case KeyEvent.VK_UP:
            currentImage = up;
            if (y > 0)
               y -= JUMP;
            break;
         case KeyEvent.VK_DOWN:
            currentImage = down;
            if (y < HEIGHT-IMAGE_SIZE)
               y += JUMP;
            break;
         case KeyEvent.VK_LEFT:
            currentImage = left;
            if (x > 0)
               x -= JUMP;
            break;
         case KeyEvent.VK_RIGHT:
            currentImage = right;
            if (x < WIDTH-IMAGE_SIZE)
               x += JUMP;
            break;
      }
```

listing
8.18 continued

```
        repaint();
    }

    //----------------------------------------------------------------
    //  Provide empty definitions for unused event methods.
    //----------------------------------------------------------------
    public void keyTyped (KeyEvent event) {}
    public void keyReleased (KeyEvent event) {}
  }
}
```

The private inner class called DirectionListener is set up to respond to key events. It implements the KeyListener interface, which defines three methods that we can use to respond to keyboard activity. Figure 8.5 lists these methods.

Specifically, the Direction program responds to key pressed events. Because the listener class must implement all methods defined in the interface, we provide empty methods for the other events.

The KeyEvent object passed to the keyPressed method of the listener can be used to determine which key was pressed. In the example, we call the getKey-Code method of the event object to get a numeric code that represents the key that was pressed. We use a switch statement to determine which key was pressed and

```
void keyPressed (KeyEvent event)
   Called when a key is pressed.

void keyReleased (KeyEvent event)
   Called when a key is released.

void keyTyped (KeyEvent event)
   Called when a pressed key or key combination produces
   a key character.
```

figure 8.5   The methods of the KeyListener interface

to respond accordingly. The `KeyEvent` class contains constants that correspond to the numeric code that is returned from the `getKeyCode` method. If any key other than an arrow key is pressed it is ignored.

Key events fire whenever a key is pressed, but most systems enable the concept of *key repetition*. That is, when a key is pressed and held down, its as if that key is being pressed repeatedly and quickly. Key events are generated in the same way. In the `Direction` program, the user can hold down an arrow key and watch the image move across the screen quickly.

The component that generates key events is the one that currently has the *keyboard focus*. Usually the keyboard focus is held by the primary "active" component. A component usually gets the keyboard focus when the user clicks on it with the mouse. When the `Direction` program is first executed, the user may have to click on the applet window with the mouse before it will respond to the arrow keys.

Getting the keyboard focus can be a tricky thing because the manner in which it is handled is system dependent. Note that in the `Direction` program, the listener is added to the applet itself, not the panel.

8.6　animations

An *animation* is a series of images or drawings that gives the appearance of movement on the screen. A cartoon is animated by drawing several images such that, when shown in progression at an appropriate speed, they fool the human eye into thinking there is one image in continuous motion.

We can create animations in a Java program in a similar way. For example, we can make it seem that a single image is moving across the screen. We created this effect somewhat with the `Direction` program described in the previous section of this chpater, but in that case the speed of the "movement" was determined by the user pressing the arrow keys.

In a true animation, the program controls the speed at which the scene changes. To create the illusion of movement, the program draws an image in one location, waits long enough for the human eye to see it, then redraws it in a slightly different location. To create the necessary pause during our animation, we can use the `Timer` class.

the `Timer` class

A *timer* object, created from the `Timer` class of the `javax.swing` package, can be thought of as a GUI component. However, unlike other components, it does not have a visual representation that appears on the screen. Instead, as the name implies, it helps us manage an activity over time.

A timer object generates an action event at regular intervals. To perform an animation, we set up a timer to generate an action event periodically, then update the animation graphics in the action listener. The methods of the `Timer` class are shown in Fig. 8.6.

The `Rebound` applet, shown in Listing 8.19, displays the image of a smiling face that seems to glide across the applet window at an angle, bouncing off of the window edges.

> A `Timer` object generates an action event at regular intervals and can be used to control an animation.
>
> **key concept**

The timer is created in the `init` method of the applet. The first parameter to the `Timer` constructor is the delay in milliseconds. Usually, the second parameter to the constructor is the listener that handles the action events of the timer. In this example, we defer the creation of that listener and pass the `Timer` constructor a `null` reference instead. The timer object is passed to the constructor of the `ReboundPanel` class, shown in Listing 8.20.

The methods `start` and `stop` are implemented in the applet to start and stop the timer, respectively. This causes the animation to pause or resume as needed. It is appropriate to implement the `stop` method of an applet if the applet performs continuous processing, such as an animation. Recall from Chapter 4 that

```
Timer (int delay, ActionListener listener)
    Constructor: Creates a timer that generates an action event at
    regular intervals, specified by the delay. The event will be handled
    by the specified listener.

void addActionListener (ActionListener listener)
    Adds an action listener to the timer.

boolean isRunning ()
    Returns true if the timer is running.

void setDelay (int delay)
    Sets the delay of the timer.

void start ()
    Starts the timer, causing it to generate action events.

void stop ()
    Stops the timer, causing it to stop generating action events.
```

figure 8.6   Some methods of the `Timer` class

listing
   8.19

```java
//********************************************************************
//   Rebound.java         Author: Lewis/Loftus
//
//   Demonstrates an animation and the use of the Timer class.
//********************************************************************

import java.awt.*;
import java.awt.event.*;
import javax.swing.*;

public class Rebound extends JApplet
{
   private final int DELAY = 20;
   private Timer timer;

   //-----------------------------------------------------------------
   //   Sets up the applet, including the timer for the animation.
   //-----------------------------------------------------------------
   public void init()
   {
      timer = new Timer (DELAY, null);

      getContentPane().add (new ReboundPanel(timer));
   }

   //-----------------------------------------------------------------
   //   Starts the animation when the applet is started.
   //-----------------------------------------------------------------
   public void start ()
   {
      timer.start();
   }

   //-----------------------------------------------------------------
   //   Stops the animation when the applet is stopped.
   //-----------------------------------------------------------------
   public void stop ()
   {
      timer.stop();
   }
}
```

listing
  8.19   continued

display

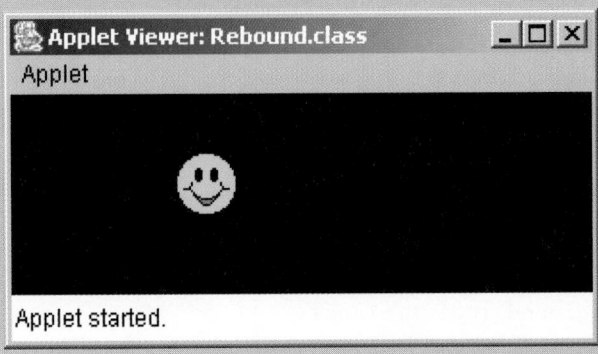

listing
  8.20

```
//********************************************************************
//  ReboundPanel.java        Author: Lewis/Loftus
//
//  Represents the primary panel for the Rebound applet.
//********************************************************************

import java.awt.*;
import java.awt.event.*;
import javax.swing.*;

public class ReboundPanel extends JPanel
{
   private final int WIDTH = 300, HEIGHT = 100;
   private final int IMAGE_SIZE = 35;

   private ImageIcon image;
   private Timer timer;
   private int x, y, moveX, moveY;
```

listing
   8.20   continued

```java
//----------------------------------------------------------------
//  Sets up the applet, including the timer for the animation.
//----------------------------------------------------------------
public ReboundPanel (Timer countdown)
{
    timer = countdown;
    timer.addActionListener (new ReboundListener());

    image = new ImageIcon ("happyFace.gif");

    x = 0;
    y = 40;
    moveX = moveY = 3;

    setBackground (Color.black);
    setPreferredSize (new Dimension(WIDTH, HEIGHT));
}

//----------------------------------------------------------------
//  Draws the image in the current location.
//----------------------------------------------------------------
public void paintComponent (Graphics page)
{
    super.paintComponent (page);
    image.paintIcon (this, page, x, y);
}

//****************************************************************
//  Represents the action listener for the timer.
//****************************************************************
private class ReboundListener implements ActionListener
{
    //----------------------------------------------------------------
    //  Updates the position of the image and possibly the direction
    //  of movement whenever the timer fires an action event.
    //----------------------------------------------------------------
    public void actionPerformed (ActionEvent event)
    {
        x += moveX;
        y += moveY;
```

listing
    8.20 continued

```
            if (x <= 0 || x >= WIDTH-IMAGE_SIZE)
                moveX = moveX * -1;

            if (y <= 0 || y >= HEIGHT-IMAGE_SIZE)
                moveY = moveY * -1;

            repaint();
        }
    }
}
```

the `stop` method of an applet is called automatically when the user leaves the browser page of the applet. Therefore the animation is automatically paused when the user can't see it. This is considered to be the polite way to implement an applet, so that the user's machine isn't wasting CPU time on unproductive activity. The `start` method will resume the animation where it left off when the applet again becomes active.

In the constructor of the `ReboundPanel` class, the action listener is created and added to the timer. The constructor also sets up the initial position for the image and the number of pixels it will move, in both the vertical and horizontal directions, each time the image is redrawn.

The `actionPerformed` method of the listener updates the current x and y coordinate values, then checks to see if those values cause the image to "run into" the edge of the panel. If so, the movement is adjusted so that the image will make future moves in the opposite direction horizontally, vertically, or both. Note that this calculation takes the image size into account.

The speed of the animation in the `Rebound` applet is a function of two factors: the pause between the action events and the distance the image is shifted each time. In this example, the timer is set to generate an action event every 20 milliseconds, and the image is shifted 3 pixels each time it is updated. You can experiment with these values to change the speed of the animation. The goal should be to create the illusion of movement that is pleasing to the eye.

summary of
key concepts

▸ Errors and exceptions represent unusual or invalid processing.

▸ The messages printed by a thrown exception indicate the nature of the problem and provide a method call stack trace.

▸ Each `catch` clause on a `try` statement handles a particular kind of exception that may be thrown within the `try` block.

▸ The `finally` clause of a `try` block is executed whether the `try` block is exited normally or because of a thrown exception.

▸ If an exception is not caught and handled where it occurs, it is propagated to the calling method.

▸ A programmer must carefully consider how exceptions should be handled, if at all, and at what level of the method-calling hierarchy.

▸ A new exception is defined by deriving a new class from the `Exception` class or one of its descendants.

▸ The `throws` clause on a method header must be included for checked exceptions that are not caught and handled in the method.

▸ A stream is a sequential sequence of bytes; it can be used as a source of input or a destination for output.

▸ A character stream manages Unicode characters, whereas a byte stream manages 8-bit bytes.

▸ Java I/O classes can be divided into data streams, which represent a particular source or destination, or processing streams, which perform operations on data in an existing stream.

▸ Three variables in the `System` class represent the standard I/O streams.

▸ The `Keyboard` class, though not part of the Java standard class library, provides an abstraction for several I/O operations on the standard input stream.

▸ The `FileReader` and `BufferedReader` classes can be used together to create a convenient text file output stream.

▸ The `readLine` method returns `null` when the end of a file is encountered.

▸ Output file streams should be explicitly closed or they may not correctly retain the data written to them.

- Object serialization represents an object as a sequence of bytes that can be stored in a file or transferred to another computer.

- A file chooser allows the user to browse a disk or other storage device in order to select a file.

- A text area component displays multiple rows of text.

- A color chooser allows the user to select a color from a palette or using RGB values.

- An image icon can be added to other components such as a label or a button.

- Key events allow a program to immediately respond to the user typing keyboard keys.

- A `Timer` object generates an action event at regular intervals and can be used to control an animation.

self-review questions

8.1 In what ways might a thrown exception be handled?

8.2 What is a `catch` phrase?

8.3 What happens if an exception is not caught?

8.4 What is a stream?

8.5 What is the difference between a character stream and a byte stream?

8.6 What are the standard I/O streams?

8.7 Who wrote the `Keyboard` class? Why?

8.8 What types of processing does the `Keyboard` class hide?

8.9 How is reading and writing files different from reading and writing text using standard I/O?

8.10 How can we detect the end of an input file?

8.11 How is object persistence accomplished in Java?

8.12 What is a file chooser?

8.13 What are two ways an image can be displayed on a Java panel?

8.14 What does a `Timer` object do?

exercises

8.1   Describe the general purpose of each of the following Java I/O classes. Classify each as character stream or byte stream and as data stream or processing stream.

a. `BufferedReader`

b. `FileInputStream`

c. `ObjectOutputStream`

d. `FileReader`

8.2   Carefully explain the processing of the `readFloat` method of the `Keyboard` class.

8.3   Create a UML class diagram for the `ProductCodes` program.

8.4   Create a UML class diagram for the `CheckInventory` program.

8.5   Create a UML class diagram for the `WriteCountryInfo` program.

8.6   Create a UML class diagram for the `Direction` program.

8.7   What would happen if the `try` statement were removed from the `level1` method of the `ExceptionScope` class in the `Propagation` program?

8.8   What would happen if the `try` statement described in the previous exercise were moved to the `level2` method?

8.9   What would happen if the `implements` clause were removed from the header of the `CountryInfo` class?

programming projects

8.1   Design and implement a program that creates an exception class called `StringTooLongException`, designed to be thrown when a string is discovered that has too many characters in it. In the `main` driver of the program, read strings from the user until the user enters "DONE". If a string is entered that has too many characters (say 20), throw the exception. Allow the thrown exception to terminate the program.

8.2   Modify the solution to Programming Project 8.1 such that it catches and handles the exception if it is thrown. Handle the exception by printing an appropriate message, and then continue processing more strings.

8.3 Modify the ProductCodes program such that it reads the data from a file. Eliminate the interactive prompt. Write the output to an output file, except for the messages about the error conditions that are detected (regarding banned codes), which should be printed to the screen.

8.4 Design and implement a program to process golf scores. The scores of four golfers are stored in a text file. Each line represents one hole, and the file contains 18 lines. Each line contains five values: par for the hole followed by the number of strokes each golfer used on that hole. Determine the winner and produce a table showing how well each golfer did (compared to par).

8.5 Design and implement a program to produce a random, but reasonable, test file for the golf program described in Programming Project 8.4.

8.6 Design and implement a program that compares two text input files, line by line, for equality. Print any lines that are not equivalent.

8.7 Design and implement a program that counts the number of punctuation marks in a text input file. Produce a table that shows how many times each symbol occurred.

8.8 Design and implement a program that helps a hospital analyze the flow of patients through the emergency room. A text input file contains integers that represent the number of patients that entered the emergency room during each hour of each day for four weeks. Read the information and store it in a three dimensional array. Then analyze it to compare the total number of patients per week, per day, and per hour. Display the results of the analysis.

8.9 Modify the WriteCountryInfo program such that it uses an ArrayList object to store the CountryInfo objects. Serialize the entire list in one operation. Modify the ReadCountryInfo program accordingly.

8.10 Design and implement a program that creates an array of objects created from the Rational class from Chapter 4, then serializes the objects and stores them in a file. Create another program that reads the objects and exercises some of their methods.

8.11 Modify the DisplayFile program to add a button labeled Save above the text area. When the button is pushed, write the contents back out to the file.

8.12 Modify the LabelDemo program so that it displays a fourth label, with the text of the label centered above the image.

8.13 Modify the Direction program from this chapter so that, in addition to responding to the arrow keys, it also responds to four other keys that move the image in diagonal directions. When the 't' key is pressed, move the image up and to the left. Likewise, use 'u' to move up and right, 'g' to move down and left, and 'j' to move down and right. Do not move the image if it has reached a window boundary.

8.14 Modify the Rebound applet from this chapter such that when the mouse button is clicked the animation stops, and when it is clicked again the animation resumes.

8.15 Modify the StickFigure class from Chapter 4 to include methods setX and setY to set the x and y coordinate of the figure. Use the Timer class to create an applet animation that lets a stick figure glide across the floor from left to right. When the figure reaches the right edge of the window, have it reappear on the left side again. Implement the start and stop methods for polite browsing.

8.16 Design and implement an application that displays an animation of a car (side view) moving across the screen from left to right. Create a Car class that represents the car (or use one that was created for a programming project in Chapter 6).

8.17 Design and implement an application that displays an animation of a horizontal line segment moving across the screen, eventually passing across a vertical line. As the vertical line is passed, the horizontal line should change color. The change of color should occur while the horizontal line crosses the vertical one; therefore, while crossing, the horizontal line will be two different colors.

8.18 Design and implement an application that plays a game called Catch-the-Creature. Use an image to represent the creature. Have the creature appear at a random location for a random duration, then disappear and reappear somewhere else. The goal is to "catch" the creature by pressing the mouse button while the mouse pointer is on the creature image. Create a separate class to represent the creature, and include in it a method that determines if the location of the mouse click corresponds to the current location of the creature. Display a count of the number of times the creature is caught.

answers to self-review questions

8.1 A thrown exception can be handled in one of three ways: it can be ignored, which will cause a program to terminate, it can be handled where it occurs using a `try` statement, or it can be caught and handled higher in the method calling hierarchy.

8.2 A `catch` phrase of a `try` statement defines the code that will handle a particular type of exception.

8.3 If an exception is not caught immediately when thrown, it begins to propagate up through the methods that were called to get to the point where it was generated. The exception can be caught and handled at any point during that propagation. If it propagates out of the `main` method, the program terminates.

8.4 A stream is a sequential series of bytes that serves as a source of input or a destination for output.

8.5 A character stream manages Unicode character data, whereas a byte stream manages 8-bit bytes.

8.6 The standard I/O streams in Java are `System.in`, the standard input stream; `System.out`, the standard output stream; and `System.err`, the standard error stream. Usually, standard input comes from the keyboard and standard output and error go to a default window on the monitor screen.

8.7 The authors of this text wrote the `Keyboard` class to facilitate reading input from the keyboard.

8.8 The `Keyboard` class hides many details of standard input such as stream declaration, error handling, parsing input, and value conversions.

8.9 All Java I/O operations are similar in that the stream is set up, the data is read or written, and the stream is closed. The primary difference between standard I/O and file I/O are the classes used to create the streams.

8.10 The `readLine` method returns a `null` reference if an attempt is made to read past the end of the input file.

8.11 Object persistence is the process of keeping an object viable outside of the program that created it. Persistence is accomplished in Java by serializing the object into a sequence of bytes using special processing stream classes. Once serialized, the object can be stored in a file, sent across the network, and so on.

8.12 A file chooser is a GUI component that allows the user to navigate a disk or other storage structure and select a file. The program using the file chooser can then use the file as needed.

8.13 An image, represented as an `ImageIcon` object, can be drawn on a panel in a specific location using the `paintIcon` method. Or it can be displayed as part of another GUI component such as a label or button.

8.14 An object created from the `Timer` class produces an action event at regular intervals. It can be used to control the speed of an animation.

This chapter extends the material that is covered in the graphics track sections of preceding chapters and provides a comprehensive exploration of the development of graphical user interfaces (GUIs) in Java. In particular, it examines several of the layout managers provided by the Java standard class library. It discusses techniques for organizing GUI containers into component hierarchies. It also explores some of the special features available with some components to tailor their use appropriately. Finally, this chapter explores several new GUI components and events.

graphical user interfaces

chapter objectives

- Review the GUI concepts established in previous chapters.

- Discuss GUI design guidelines.

- Explore the functionality of a layout manager and explore some layout managers in detail.

- Examine the use of nested containers to organize components.

- Explore the use of borders, tool tips, mnemonics, and other special component features.

- Explore new GUI components and events.

9.0 preliminaries

This chapter assumes a familiarity with the material on GUIs covered in the graphics track sections of Chapters 5 through 8. That gradual introduction now allows us to explore Java GUIs in a more comprehensive fashion. The previous chapters established a fundamental vocabulary regarding GUIs and explored many of the basic concepts involved in their construction. Let's review briefly the GUI issues covered in those chapters. You may want to revisit some of this material before continuing.

GUI review

Chapter 5 described the three basic elements that compose any Java GUI: components, events, and listeners. A programmer sets up these objects to interact in precise ways. Components generate events, usually because of a user action, and listeners handle the events when they occur. The components examined in Chapter 5 were push buttons (`JButton`), labels (`JLabel`), and text fields (`JTextField`). Push buttons and text fields generate action events (`ActionEvent`). Listeners are often constructed using listener interfaces such as `ActionListener`. Containers are special components that hold and organize other components, and include applets (`JApplet`), frames (`JFrame`), and panels (`JPanel`).

Chapter 6 introduced two new categories of button components: check boxes and radio buttons. Both are toggle buttons, meaning that at any time they are either set (on) or not set (off). A radio button (`JRadioButton`) is used in conjunction with other radio buttons to provide a set of mutually exclusive options. A set of radio buttons is defined by a `ButtonGroup` object. Only one radio button in the set can be on at any time. When one is selected, the currently set option is automatically turned off. A check box (`JCheckBox`) provides an independent option that can be selected or not without any effect on other options. If used among other check boxes, any combination of selections is valid. Both check boxes and radio buttons generate action events. In addition, a check box generates an item event (`ItemEvent`), which lets the listener determine whether the button was selected or deselected by the most recent mouse click.

Chapter 7 examined inheritance, which allowed for the exploration of the component class hierarchy. Inheritance further provides a second way to create listener objects: by deriving the listener from the appropriate adapter class instead of implementing the corresponding listener interface. Chapter 7 also introduced mouse events and mouse motion events, which are generated by all components. Objects of the MouseEvent class are used to represent both categories of events, but they have separate listener interfaces and adapter classes. A mouse event is generated when the mouse button is clicked or when the mouse moves into or out of a component's drawing area. Mouse motion events are generated as the mouse position is changed (moved or dragged) over a component.

Chapter 8 introduced some additional components, including a text area (JTextArea) that provides a viewing and editing area larger than a text field. It also explored the use of special dialog boxes that let the user select a particular file (JFileChooser) and color (JColorChooser). The use of images and the ImageIcon class were also explored, including their use in conjunction with other components such as labels and buttons. Chapter 8 also examined key events (KeyEvent), which are generated when the user presses a keyboard key.

GUI design

As we focus on the details that allow us to create GUIs, we may sometimes lose sight of the big picture. As we continue to explore GUI construction, we should keep in mind that our goal is to solve a problem. Specifically, we want to create software that is useful. Knowing the details of components, events, and other language elements gives us the tools to put GUIs together, but we must guide that knowledge with fundamental ideas of good GUI design:

‣ Know the user.

‣ Prevent user errors.

‣ Optimize user abilities.

‣ Be consistent.

The software designer must understand the user's needs and potential activities in order to develop an interface that will serve that user well. Keep in mind that, to the user, the interface *is* the software. It is the only way the user interacts with the system. As such, the interface must satisfy the user's needs.

> The design of any GUI should adhere to basic guidelines regarding consistency and usability.

> **key concept**

Whenever possible, we should design interfaces so that the user can make as few mistakes as possible. In many situations, we have the flexibility to choose one of several components to accomplish a specific task. We should always try to choose components that will prevent inappropriate actions and avoid invalid input. For example, if an input value must be one of a set of particular values, we should use components that allow the user to make only a valid choice. That is, constraining the user to a few valid choices with, for instance, a set of radio buttons is better than allowing the user to type arbitrary and possibly invalid data into a text field. We cover additional components appropriate for specific situations in this chapter.

Not all users are alike. Some are more adept at using a particular GUI or GUI components in general than others. We shouldn't design with only the lowest common denominator in mind. For example, we should provide shortcuts whenever reasonable. That is, in addition to a normal series of actions that will allow a user to accomplish a task, we should also provide redundant ways to accomplish the same task. Sometimes these additional mechanisms are less intuitive, but they may be faster for the experienced user.

Finally, consistency is important when dealing with large systems or multiple systems in a common environment. Users become familiar with a particular organization or color scheme; these should not be changed arbitrarily.

9.1 layout managers

In addition to the components, events, and listeners that comprise the backbone of a GUI, the most important activity in GUI design is the use of layout managers.

A *layout manager* is an object that governs how components are arranged in a container. It determines the size and position of each component and may take many factors into account to do so. Every container has a default layout manager, although we can replace it if we prefer another one.

> **key concept**
> The layout manager of a container determines how components are visually presented.

A container's layout manager is consulted whenever a change to the visual appearance of its contents might be needed. When the size of a container is adjusted, for example, the layout manager is consulted to determine how all of the components in the container should appear in the resized container. Every time a component is added to a container, the layout manager determines how the addition affects all of the existing components.

> **key concept**
> When changes occur, the components in a container reorganize themselves according to the layout manager's policy.

The table in Fig. 9.1 describes several of the predefined layout managers provided by the Java standard class library.

Layout Manager	Description
Border Layout	Organizes components into five areas (North, South, East, West and Center).
Box Layout	Organizes components into a single row or column.
Card Layout	Organizes components into one area such that only one is visible at any time.
Flow Layout	Organizes components from left to right, starting new rows as necessary.
Grid Layout	Organizes components into a grid of rows and columns.
GridBag Layout	Organizes components into a grid of cells, allowing components to span more than one cell.

figure 9.1   Some predefined Java layout managers

Every layout manager has its own particular properties and rules governing the layout of components. For some layout managers, the order in which you add the components affects their positioning, whereas others provide more specific control. Some layout managers take a component's preferred size or alignment into account, whereas others don't. To develop good GUIs in Java, it is important to become familiar with features and characteristics of various layout managers.

We can use the `setLayout` method of a container to change its layout manager. We've done this a few times in examples. For example, the following code sets the layout manager of a `JPanel`, which has a flow layout by default, so that it uses a border layout instead:

```
JPanel panel = new JPanel();
panel.setLayout (new BorderLayout());
```

Let's explore some of these layout managers in more detail. We'll focus on the most popular layout managers at this point: flow, border, box, and grid. The class presented in Listing 9.1 contains the `main` method of an application that demonstrates the use and effects of these layout managers.

> The layout manager for each container can be explicitly set.
>
> key concept

listing
    9.1

```
//********************************************************************
//  LayoutDemo.java          Authors: Lewis/Loftus
//
//  Demonstrates the use of flow, border, grid, and box layouts.
//********************************************************************

import javax.swing.*;

public class LayoutDemo
{
    //-----------------------------------------------------------------
    //  Sets up a frame containing a tabbed pane. The panel on each
    //  tab demonstrates a different layout manager.
    //-----------------------------------------------------------------
    public static void main (String[] args)
    {
        JFrame frame = new JFrame ("Layout Manager Demo");
        frame.setDefaultCloseOperation (JFrame.EXIT_ON_CLOSE);

        JTabbedPane tp = new JTabbedPane();
        tp.addTab ("Intro", new IntroPanel());
        tp.addTab ("Flow", new FlowPanel());
        tp.addTab ("Border", new BorderPanel());
        tp.addTab ("Grid", new GridPanel());
        tp.addTab ("Box", new BoxPanel());

        frame.getContentPane().add(tp);
        frame.pack();
        frame.show();
    }
}
```

The LayoutDemo program introduces the use of a *tabbed pane*, a container that allows the user to select (by clicking on a tab) which of several panes are currently visible. A tabbed pane is defined by the JTabbedPane class. The addTab method creates a tab, specifying the name that appears on the tab and the component to be displayed on that pane when it achieves focus by being "brought to the front" and made visible to the user.

key concept

A tabbed pane presents a set of cards from which the user can choose.

Interestingly, there is an overlap in the functionality provided by tabbed panes and the card layout manager. Similar to the tabbed pane, a card layout allows several layers to be defined, and only one of those layers is displayed at any given point. However, a container managed by a card layout can be adjusted only under program control, whereas tabbed panes allow the user to indicate directly which tab should be displayed.

In this example, each tab of the tabbed pane contains a panel that is controlled by a different layout manager. The first tab simply contains a panel with an introductory message, as shown in Listing 9.2. As we explore each layout manager in more detail, we examine the class that defines the corresponding panel of this program and discuss its visual effect.

flow layout

Flow layout is one of the easiest layout managers to use. The `JPanel` class uses flow layout by default. Flow layout puts as many components as possible on a row, at their preferred size. When a component cannot fit on a row, it is put on the next row. As many rows as needed are added to fit all components that have been added to the container. Figure 9.2 depicts a container governed by a flow layout manager.

The class in Listing 9.3 represents the panel that demonstrates the flow layout in the `LayoutDemo` program. It explicitly sets the layout to be a flow layout (though in this case that is unnecessary because `JPanel` defaults to flow layout). The buttons are then created and added to the panel.

The size of each button is made large enough to accommodate the size of the label that is put on it. As we mentioned earlier, flow layout puts as many of these buttons as possible on one row within the panel, and then starts putting components on another row. When the size of the frame is widened (by dragging the lower-right corner with the mouse, for example), the panel grows as well, and more buttons can fit on a row. When the frame is resized, the layout manager is consulted and the components are reorganized automatically. Note that on each row the components are centered within the window by default.

> In a flow layout, the width of the container determines how many components fit on a row.
>
> key concept

listing
  9.2

```java
//********************************************************************
//  IntroPanel.java          Authors: Lewis/Loftus
//
//  Represents the introduction panel for the LayoutDemo program.
//********************************************************************

import java.awt.*;
import javax.swing.*;

public class IntroPanel extends JPanel
{
   //-----------------------------------------------------------------
   //  Sets up this panel with two labels.
   //-----------------------------------------------------------------
   public IntroPanel()
   {
      setBackground (Color.green);

      JLabel l1 = new JLabel ("Layout Manger Demonstration");
      JLabel l2 = new JLabel ("Choose a tab to see an example of " +
                              "a layout manager.");

      add (l1);
      add (l2);
   }
}
```

display

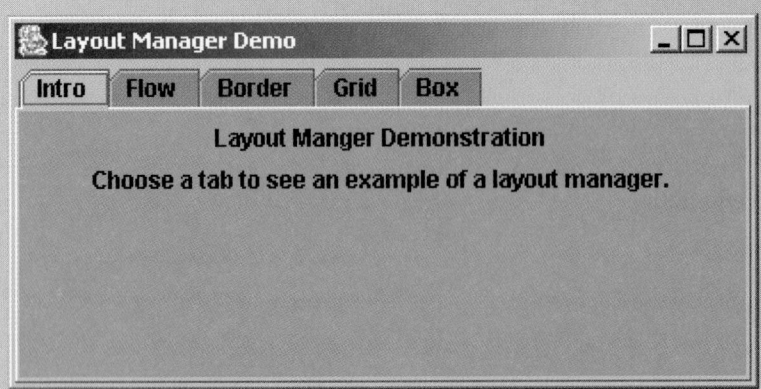

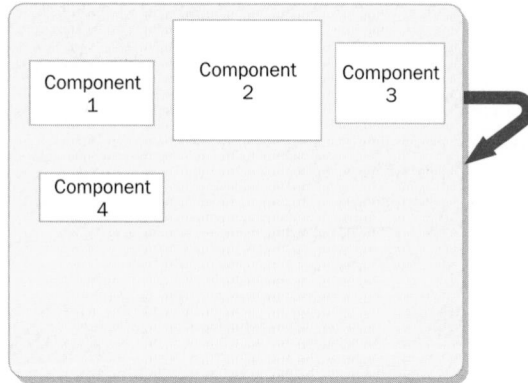

figure 9.2   Flow layout puts as many components as possible on a row

listing 9.3

```java
//********************************************************************
//  FlowPanel.java        Authors: Lewis/Loftus
//
//  Represents the panel in the LayoutDemo program that demonstrates
//  the flow layout manager.
//********************************************************************

import java.awt.*;
import javax.swing.*;

public class FlowPanel extends JPanel
{
    //-----------------------------------------------------------------
    //  Sets up this panel with some buttons to show how flow layout
    //  affects their position.
    //-----------------------------------------------------------------
    public FlowPanel ()
    {
        setLayout (new FlowLayout());

        setBackground (Color.green);
```

listing
    9.3   continued

```java
        JButton b1 = new JButton ("BUTTON 1");
        JButton b2 = new JButton ("BUTTON 2");
        JButton b3 = new JButton ("BUTTON 3");
        JButton b4 = new JButton ("BUTTON 4");
        JButton b5 = new JButton ("BUTTON 5");

        add (b1);
        add (b2);
        add (b3);
        add (b4);
        add (b5);
    }
}
```

display

The constructor of the `FlowLayout` class is overloaded to allow the programmer to tailor the characteristics of the layout manager. Within each row, components are either centered, left aligned, or right aligned. The alignment defaults to center. The horizontal and vertical gap size between components also can be specified when the layout manager is created. The `FlowLayout` class also has methods to set the alignment and gap sizes after the layout manager is created.

border layout

A *border layout* has five areas to which components can be added: North, South, East, West, and Center. The areas have a particular positional relationship to each other, as shown in Fig. 9.3.

The four outer areas become as big as needed in order to accommodate the component they contain. If no components are added to the North, South, East, or West areas, these areas do not take up any room in the overall layout. The Center area expands to fill any available space.

A particular container might use only a few areas, depending on the functionality of the system. For example, a program might use only the Center, South, and West areas. This versatility makes border layout a very useful layout manager.

> **key concept**
> Not all areas of a border layout must be used; the areas that contain components fill in the unused space.

The `add` method for a container governed by a border layout takes as its first parameter the component to be added. The second parameter indicates the area to which it is added. The area is specified using constants defined in the `BorderLayout` class. Listing 9.4 shows the panel used by the `LayoutDemo` program to demonstrate the border layout.

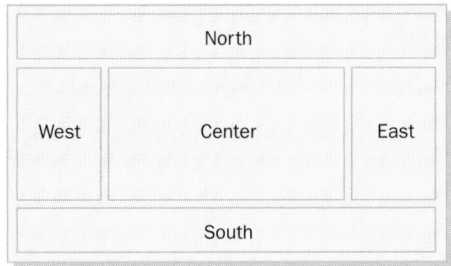

figure 9.3   Border layout organizes components in five areas

listing
    9.4

```java
//********************************************************************
//  BorderPanel.java        Authors: Lewis/Loftus
//
//  Represents the panel in the LayoutDemo program that demonstrates
//  the border layout manager.
//********************************************************************

import java.awt.*;
import javax.swing.*;

public class BorderPanel extends JPanel
{
   //-----------------------------------------------------------------
   //  Sets up this panel with a button in each area of a border
   //  layout to show how it affects their position, shape, and size.
   //-----------------------------------------------------------------
   public BorderPanel()
   {
      setLayout (new BorderLayout());

      setBackground (Color.green);

      JButton b1 = new JButton ("BUTTON 1");
      JButton b2 = new JButton ("BUTTON 2");
      JButton b3 = new JButton ("BUTTON 3");
      JButton b4 = new JButton ("BUTTON 4");
      JButton b5 = new JButton ("BUTTON 5");

      add (b1, BorderLayout.CENTER);
      add (b2, BorderLayout.NORTH);
      add (b3, BorderLayout.SOUTH);
      add (b4, BorderLayout.EAST);
      add (b5, BorderLayout.WEST);
   }
}
```

listing
9.4 continued

display

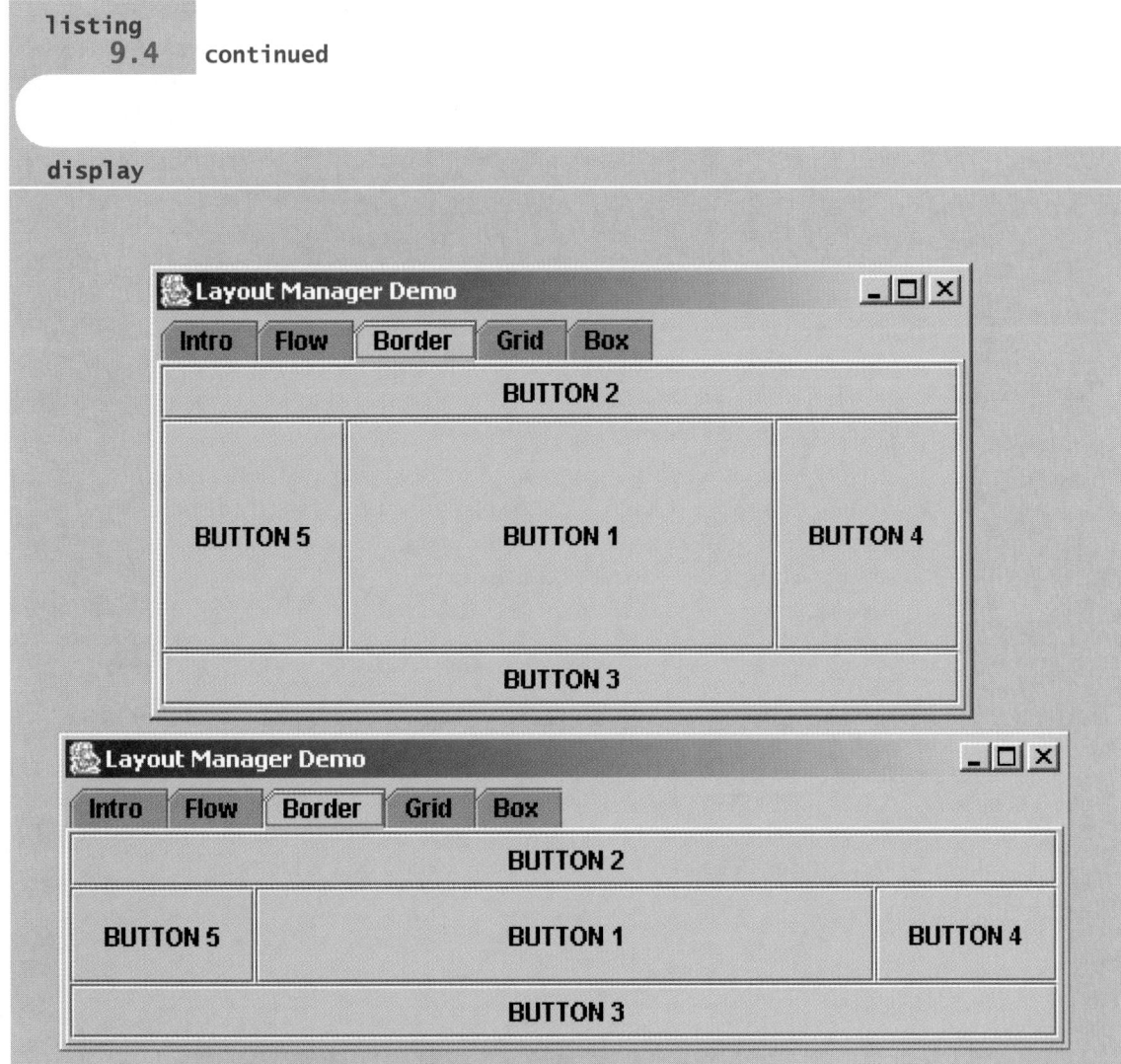

In the `BorderPanel` class constructor, the layout manager of the panel is explicitly set to be border layout. The buttons are then created and added to specific panel areas. By default, each button is made is wide enough to accommodate its label and tall enough to fill the area to which it has been assigned. As the frame (and the panel) is resized, the size of each button adjusts as needed, with the button in the Center area filling any unused space.

Each area in a border layout displays only one component. That is, only one component is added to each area of a given border layout. A common error is to add two components to a particular area of a border layout, in which case the first component added is replaced by the second, and only the second is seen when the container is displayed. To add multiple components to an area within a border layout, we first add the components to another container, such as a `JPanel`, then add the panel to the area.

Note that although the panel used to display the buttons has a green background, no green is visible in the display for Listing 9.4. By default there are no horizontal or vertical gaps between the areas of a border layout. These gaps can be set with an overloaded constructor or with explicit methods of the `BorderLayout` class. If the gaps are increased, the underlying panel will show through.

grid layout

A *grid layout* presents a container's components in a rectangular grid of rows and columns. One component is placed in each grid cell, and all cells are the same size. Figure 9.4 shows the general organization of a grid layout.

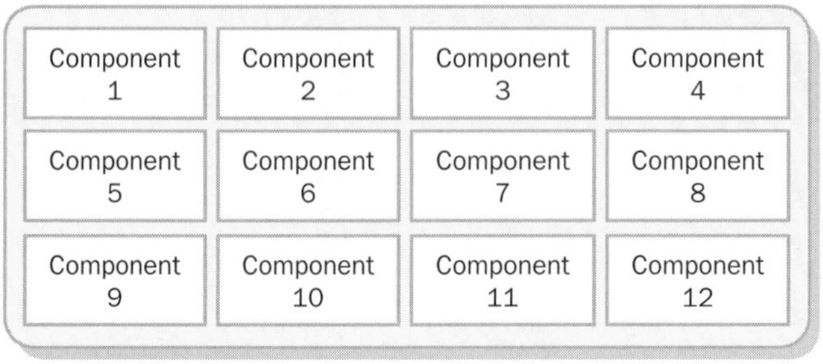

figure 9.4 Grid layout creates a rectangular grid of equal-sized cells

The number of rows and columns in a grid layout is established using parameters to the constructor when the layout manager is created. The class in Listing 9.5 shows the panel used by the LayoutDemo program to demonstrate a grid layout. It specifies that the panel should be managed using a grid of two rows and three columns.

listing
  9.5

```
//*********************************************************************
//  GridPanel.java         Authors: Lewis/Loftus
//
//  Represents the panel in the LayoutDemo program that demonstrates
//  the grid layout manager.
//*********************************************************************

import java.awt.*;
import javax.swing.*;

public class GridPanel extends JPanel
{
   //-----------------------------------------------------------------
   //  Sets up this panel with some buttons to show how grid
   //  layout affects their position, shape, and size.
   //-----------------------------------------------------------------
   public GridPanel()
   {
      setLayout (new GridLayout (2, 3));

      setBackground (Color.green);

      JButton b1 = new JButton ("BUTTON 1");
      JButton b2 = new JButton ("BUTTON 2");
      JButton b3 = new JButton ("BUTTON 3");
      JButton b4 = new JButton ("BUTTON 4");
      JButton b5 = new JButton ("BUTTON 5");

      add (b1);
      add (b2);
      add (b3);
      add (b4);
      add (b5);
   }
}
```

listing
   9.5   continued

display

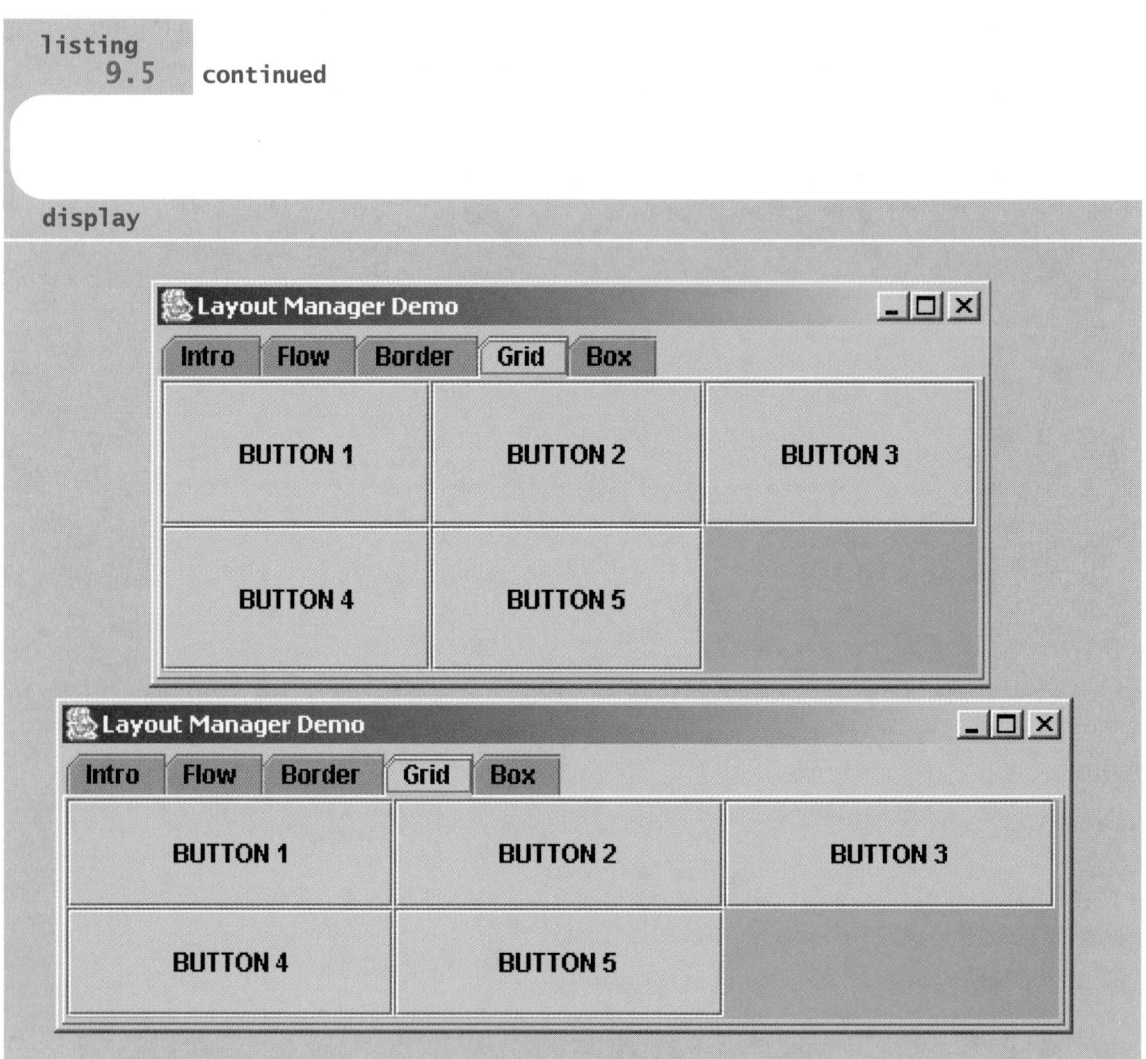

key concept

The cells of a grid layout are filled in order as components are added to the container.

As buttons are added to the container, they fill the grid (by default) from left-to-right and top-to-bottom. There is no way to explicitly assign a component to a particular location in the grid other than the order in which they are added to the container.

The size of each cell is determined by the container's overall size. When the container is resized, all of the cells change size proportionally to fill the container.

If the value used to specify either the number of rows or the number of columns is zero, the grid expands as needed in that dimension to accommodate the number of components added to the container. The values for the number of rows and columns cannot both be zero.

By default, there are no horizontal and vertical gaps between the grid cells. The gap sizes can be specified using an overloaded constructor or with the appropriate `GridLayout` methods.

box layout

A *box layout* organizes components either vertically or horizontally, in one row or one column, as shown in Fig. 9.5. It is easy to use, yet when combined with other box layouts, it can produce complex GUI designs similar to those that can be accomplished with a `GridBagLayout`, which in general is far more difficult to master.

When a `BoxLayout` object is created, we specify that it will follow either the *X* axis (horizontal) or the *Y* axis (vertical), using constants defined in the `BoxLayout` class. Unlike other layout managers, the constructor of a `BoxLayout` takes as its first parameter the component that it will govern. Therefore a new `BoxLayout` object must be created for each component. Listing 9.6 shows the panel used by the `LayoutDemo` program to demonstrate the box layout.

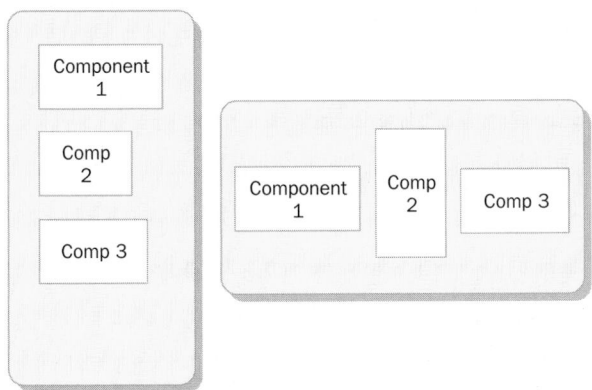

figure 9.5   Box layout organizes components either
vertically or horizontally

listing
9.6

```java
//********************************************************************
//   BoxPanel.java          Authors: Lewis/Loftus
//
//   Represents the panel in the LayoutDemo program that demonstrates
//   the box layout manager.
//********************************************************************

import java.awt.*;
import javax.swing.*;

public class BoxPanel extends JPanel
{
   //-----------------------------------------------------------------
   //  Sets up this panel with some buttons to show how a vertical
   //  box layout (and invisible components) affects their position.
   //-----------------------------------------------------------------
   public BoxPanel()
   {
      setLayout (new BoxLayout (this, BoxLayout.Y_AXIS));

      setBackground (Color.green);

      JButton b1 = new JButton ("BUTTON 1");
      JButton b2 = new JButton ("BUTTON 2");
      JButton b3 = new JButton ("BUTTON 3");
      JButton b4 = new JButton ("BUTTON 4");
      JButton b5 = new JButton ("BUTTON 5");

      add (b1);
      add (Box.createRigidArea (new Dimension (0, 10)));
      add (b2);
      add (Box.createVerticalGlue());
      add (b3);
      add (b4);
      add (Box.createRigidArea (new Dimension (0, 20)));
      add (b5);
   }
}
```

**listing
9.6** continued

display

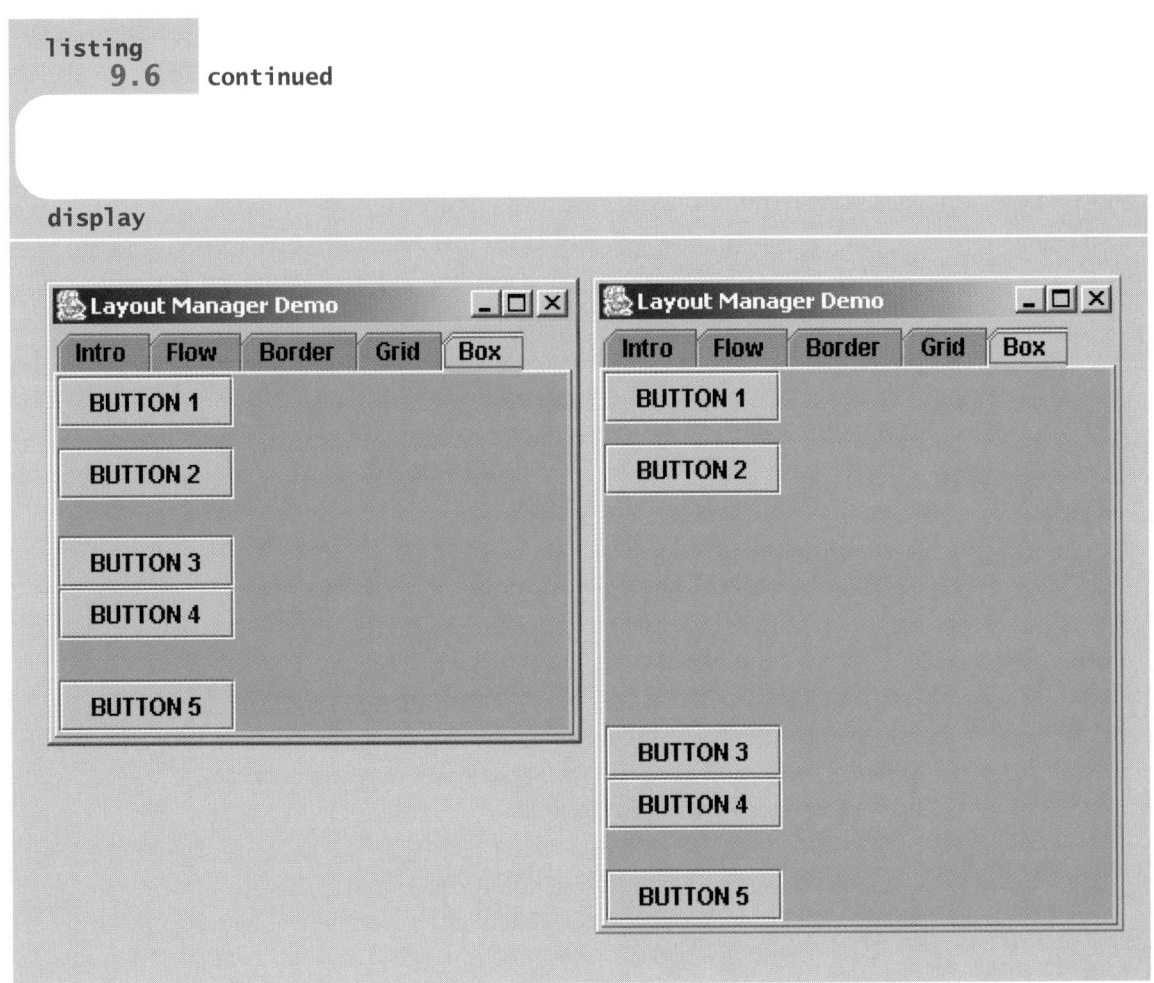

Components in containers governed by a box layout are organized (top-to-bottom or left-to-right) in the order in which they are added to the container.

There are no gaps between the components in a box layout. Unlike previous layout managers we've explored, a box layout does not have a specific vertical or horizontal gap that can be specified for the entire container. Instead, we can add *invisible components* to the container that take up space between other components. The Box class, which is also part of the Java standard class library, contains static methods that can be used to create these invisible components.

> A box layout can use invisible components to provide space between components.
>
> **key concept**

The two types of invisible components used in the `BoxPanel` class are *rigid areas*, which have a fixed size, and *glue*, which specifies where excess space in a container should go. A rigid area is created using the `createRigidArea` method of the `Box` class, and takes a `Dimension` object as a parameter to define the size of the invisible area. Glue is created using the `createHorizontalGlue` or `createVerticalGlue` methods, as appropriate.

Note that in our example, the space between buttons separated by a rigid area remains constant even when the container is resized. Glue, on the other hand, expands or contracts as needed to fill the space.

A box layout—more than most of the other layout managers—respects the alignments and the minimum, maximum, and preferred sizes of the components it governs. Therefore setting the characteristics of the components that go into the container is another way to tailor the visual effect.

9.2 containment hierarchies

The way components are grouped into containers, and the way those containers are nested within each other, establishes the *containment hierarchy* for a GUI. There is generally one primary container, called a *top-level container*, such as a frame or applet. The top-level container of a program often contains one or more other containers, such as panels. These panels may contain other panels to organize the other components as desired.

> **Key concept**
>
> A GUIs appearance is a function of the containment hierarchy and the layout managers of each of the containers.

Each container can have its own layout manager. The final appearance of a GUI is a function of the layout managers chosen for each of the containers and the design of the containment hierarchy. Many combinations are possible, and there is rarely a single best option. As always, we should be guided by the desired system goals and general GUI design guidelines.

Figure 9.6 shows a GUI application that has been annotated to describe its containment hierarchy. Several components used in this program have been discussed previously in this text; others are discussed later in this chapter.

Note that in many cases, the use of some containers is not obvious just by looking at the GUI. We also use invisible components to provide specific spacing between components. These elements are all part of the containment hierarchy, even though they are not visible to the user.

A particular program's containment hierarchy can be represented as a tree structure, such as the one shown in Fig. 9.7. The root of the tree is the top-level

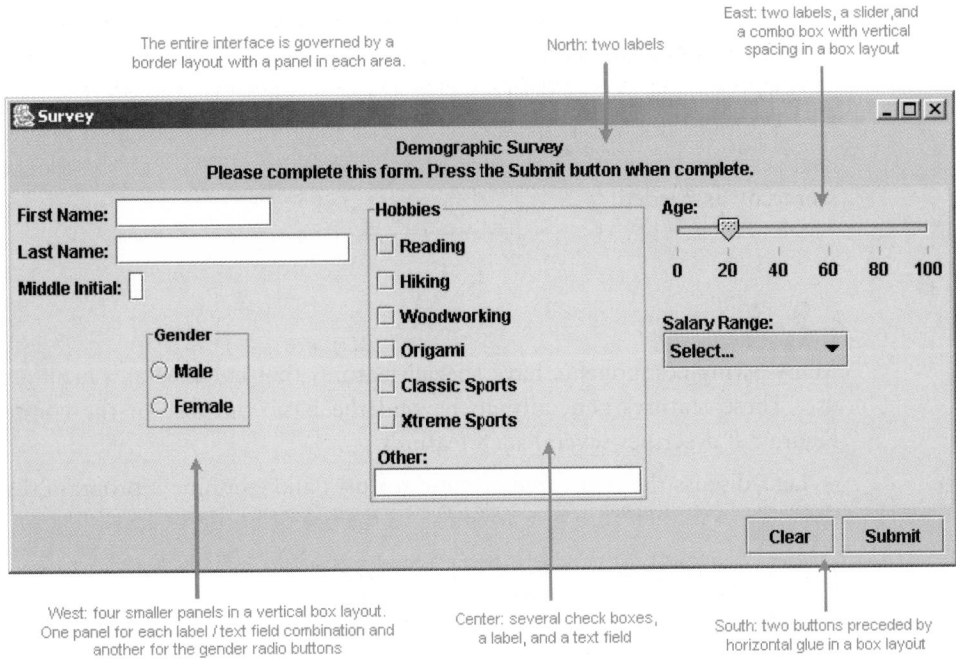

figure 9.6   The containment hierarchy of a GUI

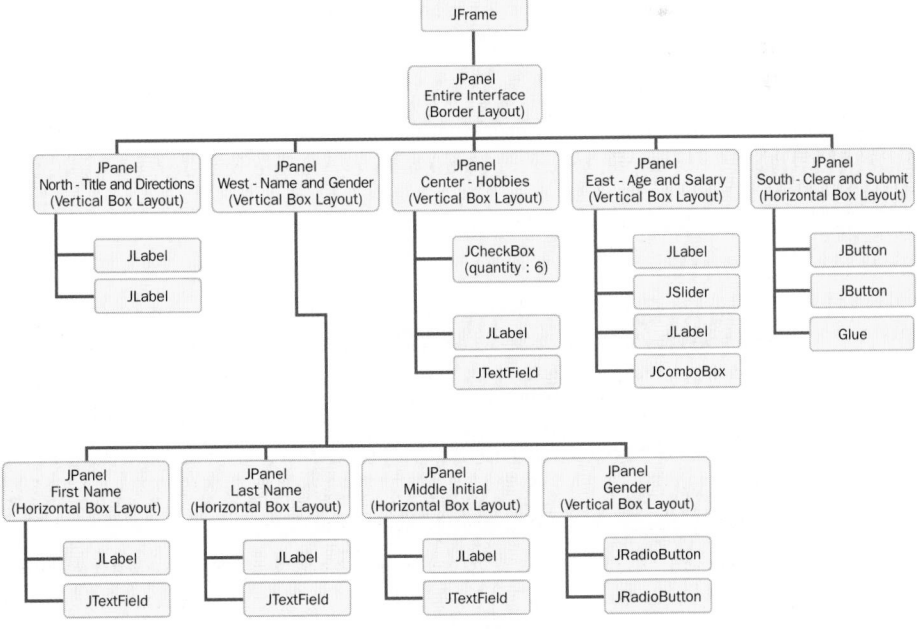

figure 9.7   The containment hierarchy tree

container. Each level of the tree shows the containers and components held in the containers of the level above.

When changes are made that might affect the visual layout of the components in a program, the layout managers of each container are consulted in turn. The changes in one may affect another. These changes ripple through the containment hierarchy as needed.

9.3 special features

Many Swing components have special features that enhance and facilitate their use. These features generally go beyond the basic purpose of the component. Figure 9.8 describes several such features.

Let's discuss the first three of these features and examine a program that uses them. We will then turn our attention to the use of borders.

Any Swing component can be assigned a *tool tip*, which is a short line of text that will appear when the cursor is rested momentarily on top of the component. Tool tips are usually used to inform the user about the component, such as the purpose of a particular button. A tool tip can be assigned using the setToolTipText method of a Swing component. For example:

```
JButton button = new JButton ("Compute");
button.setToolTipText ("Calculates the area under the curve.");
```

> **key concept**
>
> Using the special features of various components often improves a GUI's functionality.

A *mnemonic* is a character that allows the user to push a button or make a menu choice using the keyboard in addition to the mouse. For example, when a mnemonic has been defined for a button, the user can

Special Feature	Description
Tool tip	Causes a line of text to appear when the mouse cursor stops over a component.
Mnemonic	Allows an action such as a button push to occur in response to a keyboard key combination.
Enabled/Disabled	Allows a component to be enabled and disabled as appropriate. When disabled, the component does not respond to user interaction.
Border	Surrounds a component with a border. Several border styles are available.

figure 9.8   Special features available with many Java GUI components

hold down the ALT key and press the mnemonic character to activate the button. Using the mnemonic is no different from using the mouse to press the button.

A mnemonic character should be chosen from the label on a button or menu item. Once the mnemonic has been established using the `setMnemonic` method, the character in the label will appear underlined to indicate that it can be used as a shortcut. If a letter is chosen that is not in the label, nothing will be underlined and the user won't know how to use the shortcut. The following is an example of setting a mnemonic:

```
JButton button = new JButton ("Calculate");
button.setMnemonic ('C');
```

Some components can be *disabled* if they should not be used. A disabled component will appear "grayed out," and nothing will happen if the user attempts to interact with it. To disable and enable components, we invoke the `setEnabled` method of the component, passing it a boolean value to indicate whether the component should be disabled (false) or enabled (true). For example:

```
JButton button = new JButton ("Do It");
button.setEnabled (false);
```

Disabling components is a good idea when users should not be allowed to use the functionality of a component. The grayed appearance of the disabled component is an indication that using the component is inappropriate (and, in fact, impossible) at the current time.

Let's look at an example that uses tool tips, mnemonics, and disabled components. The program in Listing 9.7 presents the image of a light bulb and provides a button to turn the light bulb on and a button to turn the light bulb off.

There are actually two images of the light bulb: one showing it turned on and one showing it turned off. These images are brought in as `ImageIcon` objects. The `setIcon` method of the label that displays the image is used to set the appropriate image, depending on the current status. This processing is controlled in the `LightBulbPanel` class shown in Listing 9.8.

The `LightBulbControls` class shown in Listing 9.9 is a panel that contains the on and off buttons. Both of these buttons have tool tips assigned to them, and both use mnemonics. Also, when one of the buttons is enabled, the other is disabled, and vice versa. When the light bulb is on, there is no reason for the On button to be enabled. Likewise, when the light bulb is off, there is no reason for the Off button to be enabled.

listing
9.7

```java
//********************************************************************
//  LightBulb.java         Author: Lewis/Loftus
//
//  Demonstrates some special component features such as disabled
//  buttons, mnemonics, tool tips, and borders.
//********************************************************************

import javax.swing.*;
import java.awt.*;

public class LightBulb
{
   //-----------------------------------------------------------------
   //  Sets up a frame that displays a light bulb image that can be
   //  turned on and off.
   //-----------------------------------------------------------------
   public static void main (String[] args)
   {
      JFrame lightBulbFrame = new JFrame ("Light Bulb");
      lightBulbFrame.setDefaultCloseOperation (JFrame.EXIT_ON_CLOSE);

      LightBulbPanel bulb = new LightBulbPanel();
      LightBulbControls controls = new LightBulbControls (bulb);

      JPanel panel = new JPanel();
      panel.setBackground (Color.black);
      panel.setLayout (new BoxLayout(panel, BoxLayout.Y_AXIS));
      panel.add (Box.createRigidArea (new Dimension (0, 20)));
      panel.add (bulb);
      panel.add (Box.createRigidArea (new Dimension (0, 10)));
      panel.add (controls);
      panel.add (Box.createRigidArea (new Dimension (0, 10)));

      lightBulbFrame.getContentPane().add(panel);
      lightBulbFrame.pack();
      lightBulbFrame.show();
   }
}
```

listing
   9.7   continued

display

listing
   9.8

```
//********************************************************************
//  LightBulbPanel.java        Author: Lewis/Loftus
//
//  Represents the image for the LightBulb program.
//********************************************************************

import javax.swing.*;
import java.awt.*;
```

listing
   9.8   continued

```java
public class LightBulbPanel extends JPanel
{
   private boolean on;
   private ImageIcon lightOn, lightOff;
   private JLabel imageLabel;

   //-----------------------------------------------------------------
   //  Sets up the images and the initial state of the panel.
   //-----------------------------------------------------------------
   public LightBulbPanel()
   {
      lightOn = new ImageIcon ("lightBulbOn.gif");
      lightOff = new ImageIcon ("lightBulbOff.gif");

      setBackground (Color.black);

      on = true;
      imageLabel = new JLabel (lightOff);
      add (imageLabel);
   }

   //-----------------------------------------------------------------
   //  Paints the panel using the appropriate image.
   //-----------------------------------------------------------------
   public void paintComponent (Graphics page)
   {
      super.paintComponent(page);

      if (on)
         imageLabel.setIcon (lightOn);
      else
         imageLabel.setIcon (lightOff);
   }

   //-----------------------------------------------------------------
   //  Sets the status of the light bulb.
   //-----------------------------------------------------------------
   public void setOn (boolean lightBulbOn)
   {
      on = lightBulbOn;
   }
}
```

listing
  9.9

```java
//***********************************************************************
//   LightBulbControls.java        Author: Lewis/Loftus
//
//   Represents the control panel for the LightBulb program.
//***********************************************************************

import javax.swing.*;
import java.awt.*;
import java.awt.event.*;

public class LightBulbControls extends JPanel
{
   private LightBulbPanel bulb;
   private JButton onButton, offButton;

   //-----------------------------------------------------------------
   //  Sets up the lightbulb control panel.
   //-----------------------------------------------------------------
   public LightBulbControls (LightBulbPanel bulbPanel)
   {
      bulb = bulbPanel;

      onButton = new JButton ("On");
      onButton.setEnabled (false);
      onButton.setMnemonic ('n');
      onButton.setToolTipText ("Turn it on!");
      onButton.addActionListener (new OnListener());

      offButton = new JButton ("Off");
      offButton.setEnabled (true);
      offButton.setMnemonic ('f');
      offButton.setToolTipText ("Turn it off!");
      offButton.addActionListener (new OffListener());

      setBackground (Color.black);
      add (onButton);
      add (offButton);
   }
```

```java
//****************************************************************
//   Represents the listener for the On button.
//****************************************************************
private class OnListener implements ActionListener
{
    //--------------------------------------------------------------
    //   Turns the bulb on and repaints the bulb panel.
    //--------------------------------------------------------------
    public void actionPerformed (ActionEvent event)
    {
        bulb.setOn (true);
        onButton.setEnabled (false);
        offButton.setEnabled (true);
        bulb.repaint();
    }
}


//****************************************************************
//   Represents the listener for the Off button.
//****************************************************************
private class OffListener implements ActionListener
{
    //--------------------------------------------------------------
    //   Turns the bulb off and repaints the bulb panel.
    //--------------------------------------------------------------
    public void actionPerformed (ActionEvent event)
    {
        bulb.setOn (false);
        onButton.setEnabled (true);
        offButton.setEnabled (false);
        bulb.repaint();
    }
}
}
```

Each button has its own listener class. The `actionPerformed` method of each sets the bulb's status, toggles the enabled state of both buttons, and causes the panel with the image to repaint itself.

Note that the mnemonic characters used for each button are underlined in the display. When you run the program, note that the tool tip displayed when the mouse cursor rests over a button automatically includes an indication of the mnemonic that can be used for that button.

borders

Java also provides the ability to put a *border* around any Swing component. A border is not a component itself but defines how the edge of any component should be drawn. A border provides visual cues as to how GUI components are organized, and can be used to give titles to components. Figure 9.9 lists the predefined borders in the Java standard class library.

> **key concept**
>
> Various borders can be applied to Swing components to group objects and to enhance the visual effect.

The `BorderFactory` class is useful for creating borders for components. It has many methods for creating specific types of borders. A border is applied to a component using the component's `setBorder` method.

The program in Listing 9.10 demonstrates several types of borders. It simply creates several panels, sets a different border for each, and then displays them in a larger panel using a grid layout.

Border	Description
Empty Border	Puts buffering space around the edge of a component, but otherwise has no visual effect.
Line Border	A simple line surrounding the component.
Etched Border	Creates the effect of an etched groove around a component.
Bevel Border	Creates the effect of a component raised above the surface or sunken below it.
Titled Border	Includes a text title on or around the border.
Matte Border	Allows the size of each edge to be specified. Uses either a soild color or an image.
Compound Border	A combination of two borders.

figure 9.9   Component borders

listing
   9.10

```java
//********************************************************************
//  BorderDemo.java        Authors: Lewis/Loftus
//
//  Demonstrates the various types of borders.
//********************************************************************

import java.awt.*;
import javax.swing.*;
import javax.swing.border.*;

public class BorderDemo
{
   //-----------------------------------------------------------------
   //  Creates several bordered panels and displays them in a frame.
   //-----------------------------------------------------------------
   public static void main (String[] args)
   {
      JFrame frame = new JFrame ("Border Demo");
      frame.setDefaultCloseOperation (JFrame.EXIT_ON_CLOSE);

      JPanel panel = new JPanel();
      panel.setLayout (new GridLayout (0, 2, 5, 10));
      panel.setBorder (BorderFactory.createEmptyBorder (5, 5, 5, 5));

      JPanel p1 = new JPanel();
      p1.setBorder (BorderFactory.createLineBorder (Color.red, 3));
      p1.add (new JLabel ("Line Border"));
      panel.add (p1);

      JPanel p2 = new JPanel();
      p2.setBorder (BorderFactory.createEtchedBorder ());
      p2.add (new JLabel ("Etched Border"));
      panel.add (p2);

      JPanel p3 = new JPanel();
      p3.setBorder (BorderFactory.createRaisedBevelBorder ());
      p3.add (new JLabel ("Raised Bevel Border"));
      panel.add (p3);
```

listing
    9.10   continued

```java
    JPanel p4 = new JPanel();
    p4.setBorder (BorderFactory.createLoweredBevelBorder ());
    p4.add (new JLabel ("Lowered Bevel Border"));
    panel.add (p4);

    JPanel p5 = new JPanel();
    p5.setBorder (BorderFactory.createTitledBorder ("Title"));
    p5.add (new JLabel ("Titled Border"));
    panel.add (p5);

    JPanel p6 = new JPanel();
    TitledBorder tb = BorderFactory.createTitledBorder ("Title");
    tb.setTitleJustification (TitledBorder.RIGHT);
    p6.setBorder (tb);
    p6.add (new JLabel ("Titled Border (right)"));
    panel.add (p6);

    JPanel p7 = new JPanel();
    Border b1 = BorderFactory.createLineBorder (Color.blue, 2);
    Border b2 = BorderFactory.createEtchedBorder ();
    p7.setBorder (BorderFactory.createCompoundBorder (b1, b2));
    p7.add (new JLabel ("Compound Border"));
    panel.add (p7);

    JPanel p8 = new JPanel();
    Border mb = BorderFactory.createMatteBorder (1, 5, 1, 1,
                                                 Color.yellow);
    p8.setBorder (mb);
    p8.add (new JLabel ("Matte Border"));
    panel.add (p8);

    frame.getContentPane().add (panel);
    frame.pack();
    frame.show();
  }
}
```

listing
9.10   continued

display

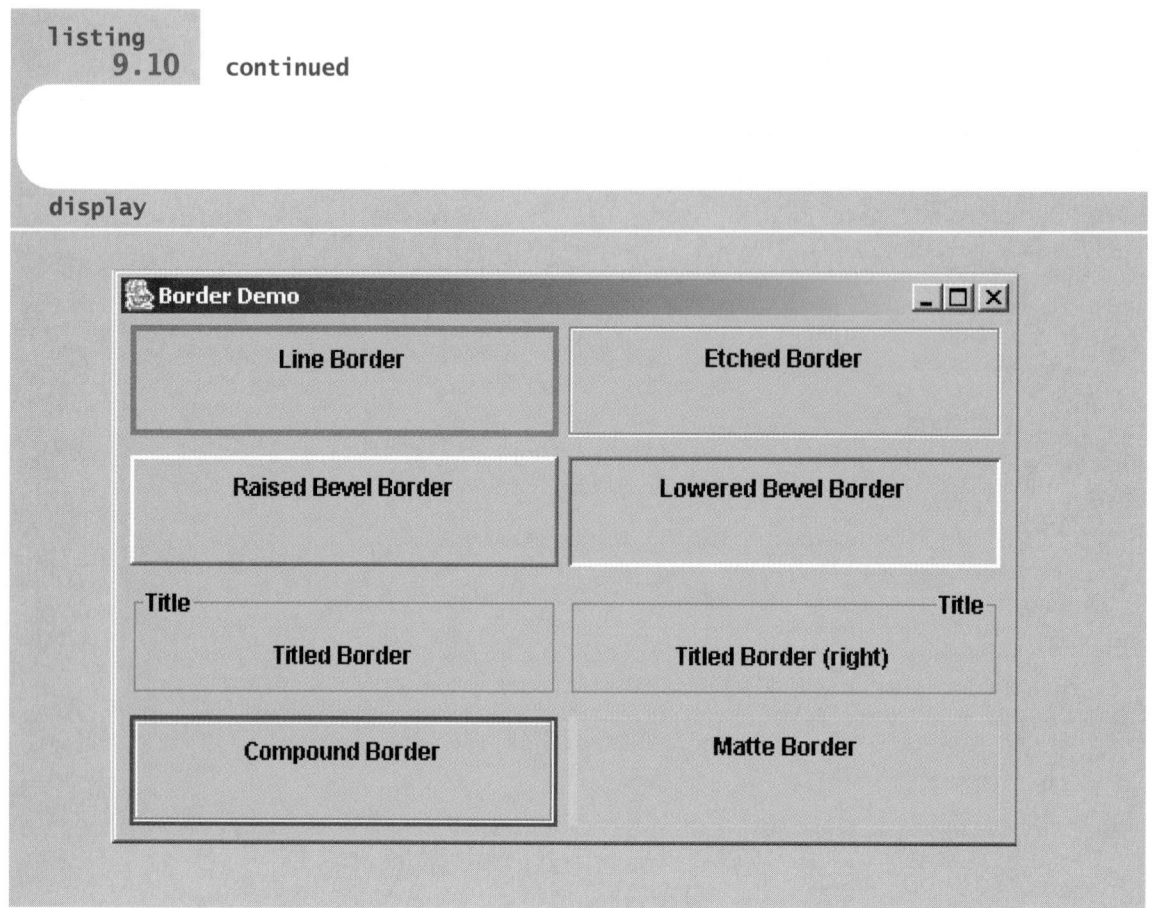

Let's look at each type of border created in this program. An *empty border* is applied to the larger panel that holds all of the others to create a buffer of space around the outer edge of the frame. The sizes of the top, left, bottom, and right edges of the empty border is specified in pixels. The *line border* is created using a particular color and specifies the line thickness in pixels (3 in this case). The line thickness defaults to 1 pixel if left unspecified. The *etched border* created in this program uses default colors for the highlight and shadow of the etching, but both could be explicitly set if desired.

A *bevel border* can be either raised or lowered. The default coloring is used in this program, although the coloring of each aspect of the bevel can be tailored as desired, including the outer highlight, inner highlight, outer shadow, and inner shadow. Each of these aspects could be a different color if desired.

A *titled border* places a title on or around the border. The default position for the title is on the border at the top left edge. Using the `setTitleJustification` method of the `TitledBorder` class, this position can be set to many other places above, below, on, or to the left, right, or center of the border. (Two titled borders were used in Fig. 9.6 also.)

A *compound border* is a combination of two or more borders. The example in this program creates a compound border using a line border and an etched border. The `createCompoundBorder` method accepts two borders as parameters and makes the first parameter the outer border and the second parameter the inner border. Combinations of three or more borders are created by first creating a compound border using two borders, then making another compound border using it and yet another one.

A *matte border* specifies the sizes, in pixels, of the top, left, bottom, and right edges of the border. Those edges can be composed of a single color, as they are in this example, or an image icon can be used.

Borders should be used carefully. They can be helpful in drawing attention to appropriate parts of your GUI and can conceptually group related items together. However, if used inappropriately, they can also detract from the elegance of the presentation. Borders should enhance the interface, not complicate or compete with it.

9.4 additional components

At various points in this text, we've examined specific containers and components, discussing the events they generate and how they can help us present useful GUIs. Let's explore a few more.

scroll pane

Sometimes we need to deal with images or information too large to fit in a reasonable area. A *scroll pane* is often helpful in these situations. A scroll pane is a container that offers a limited view of a component, and provides vertical or horizontal scroll bars to change that view. At any point, only part of the underlying component can be seen, but the scrollbars allow the user to navigate to any part of the component. Scrollbars are useful when space within a GUI is limited or when the component being viewed is large or can change in size dynamically.

> **key concept**
> A scroll pane is useful if you want to view large objects or large amounts of data.

The program in Listing 9.11 presents a frame that contains a single scroll pane. The scroll pane is used to view an image of a fairly large transit map for Philadelphia and the surrounding areas. The image is put into a label. The label is added to the scroll pane using the JScrollPane constructor.

listing
   9.11

```
//********************************************************************
//  TransitMap.java         Authors: Lewis/Loftus
//
//  Demonstrates the use a scroll pane.
//********************************************************************

import java.awt.*;
import javax.swing.*;

public class TransitMap
{
   //-----------------------------------------------------------------
   //  Presents a frame containing a scroll pane used to view a large
   //  image of a Philadelphia subway system map. (SEPTA stands for
   //  the SouthEast Pennsylvania Transit Authority)
   //-----------------------------------------------------------------
   public static void main (String[] args)
   {
      JFrame frame = new JFrame ("SEPTA Transit Map");
      frame.setDefaultCloseOperation (JFrame.EXIT_ON_CLOSE);

      ImageIcon image = new ImageIcon ("septa.jpg");
      JLabel imageLabel = new JLabel (image);

      JScrollPane sp = new JScrollPane (imageLabel);
      sp.setPreferredSize (new Dimension (450, 400));

      frame.getContentPane().add (sp);
      frame.pack();
      frame.show();
   }
}
```

listing
9.11   continued

display

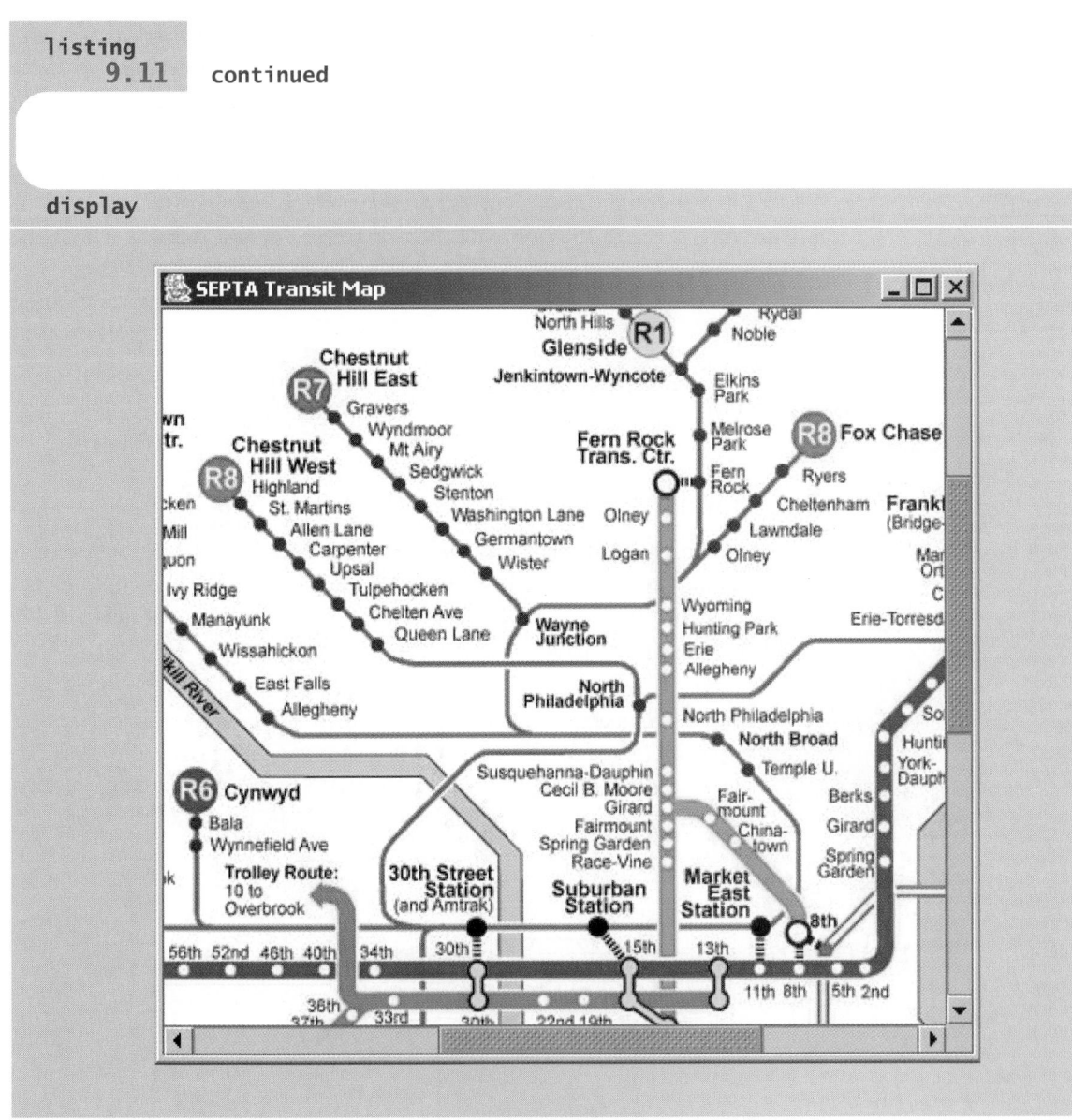

A scroll pane can have a vertical scrollbar on the right of the container as well as a horizontal scrollbar at the bottom of the container. For each of these, the programmer can specify that the scrollbars are always used, never used, or used as needed to view the underlying component. By default, both the vertical and horizontal scrollbars are used as needed. The `TransitMap` program relies on these defaults, and both scrollbars are used because the image is too large in both height and width.

To move a scrollbar, the user can click on and drag the box (called the *knob*) in the scrollbar that indicates its current location (in that dimension: up/down or right/left). Alternatively, the user can click in the bar to the right or left of the knob, or on the arrows at either end of the scrollbar, to adjust the location. The programmer can determine how much each of these actions changes the viewing area.

Note that no event listeners need to be set up to use a scroll pane in this manner. A scroll pane responds automatically to the adjustments of its scrollbars.

split panes

A *split pane* is a container that displays two components separated by a moveable divider bar. Depending on how the split pane is set up, the two components are displayed either side by side or one on top of the other, as shown in Fig. 9.10. In Java, we create a split pane using the `JSplitPane` class.

key concept

> A split pane displays two components separated by a movable divider bar. The components can be displayed either horizontally or vertically.

The orientation of a split pane is set using constants in the `JSplitPane` class, and can be set when the container is created or explicitly later on. The constant `HORIZONTAL_SPLIT` specifies that the components be displayed side by side. In contrast, `VERTICAL_SPLIT` specifies that the components be displayed one on top of the other.

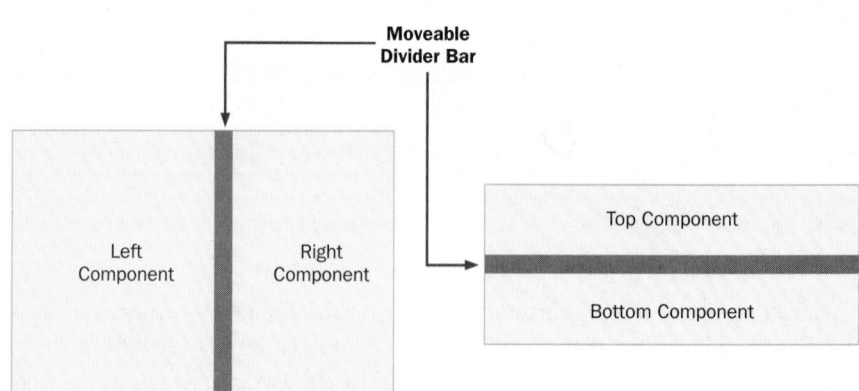

figure 9.10   The configurations of a split pane

The location of the divider bar determines how much visible area is devoted to each component in the split pane. The divider bar can be dragged across the container area using the mouse. As it moves, the visible space is increased for one component and decreased for the other. The total space allotted for both components changes only if the size of the entire split pane changes.

A `JSplitPane` respects the minimum size set for the components it displays. Therefore the divider bar may not allow a section to be reduced in size beyond a particular point. To adjust this aspect, the minimum sizes of the components displayed can be changed.

The divider bar of a `JSplitPane` object can be set so that it can be expanded, one direction or the other, with one click of the mouse. By default, the divider bar does not have this feature and can only be moved by dragging it. If this feature is turned on, the divider bar appears with two small arrows pointing in opposite directions. Clicking either of these arrows causes the divider bar to move fully in that direction, maximizing the space allotted to one of the components. This feature is set using the `setOneTouchExpandable` method, which takes a boolean parameter. The size of the divider bar and the initial location of the divider bar can be set explicitly as well.

Another feature that can be set on a `JSplitPane` is whether or not the components are continuously adjusted and repainted as the divider bar is being moved. If this feature is not set, the components' layout managers will only be consulted after the divider bar stops moving. This feature is off by default, and can be turned on when the `JSplitPane` object is created or using the `setContinuousLayout` method.

Split panes can be nested by putting a split pane into one or both sides of another split pane. For example, we could divide a container into three sections by putting a split pane into the top component of another split pane. There would then be two divider bars, one that separates the total area into two main sections, and another that separates one of those sections into two others. How much visible area is shown in each would depend on where the divider bars are placed.

The next section contains an example that uses a split pane.

lists

The Swing `JList` class represents a *list* of items from which the user can choose. In general, all of the options in a list are visible. When the user selects an item using the mouse, it is highlighted. When a new item is selected, the previously selected item is automatically unhighlighted.

The contents of a JList can be specified using an array of objects passed into the constructor. Methods of the JList class are used to manage the list in various ways, including retrieving the currently selected item.

The program shown in Listing 9.12 uses a list in the left side of a split pane to present a set of image file names to the user. When one of the file names is selected, the corresponding image is displayed in the right side of the split pane.

listing
   9.12

```
//********************************************************************
//  PickImage.java        Authors: Lewis/Loftus
//
//  Demonstrates the use a split pane and a list.
//********************************************************************

import java.awt.*;
import javax.swing.*;

public class PickImage
{
   //-----------------------------------------------------------------
   //  Creates and displays a frame containing a split pane. The
   //  user selects an image name from the list to be displayed.
   //-----------------------------------------------------------------
   public static void main (String[] args)
   {
      JFrame frame = new JFrame ("Pick Image");
      frame.setDefaultCloseOperation (JFrame.EXIT_ON_CLOSE);

      JLabel imageLabel = new JLabel();
      JPanel imagePanel = new JPanel();
      imagePanel.add (imageLabel);
      imagePanel.setBackground (Color.white);

      ListPanel imageList = new ListPanel (imageLabel);

      JSplitPane sp = new JSplitPane(JSplitPane.HORIZONTAL_SPLIT,
                                     imageList, imagePanel);
```

listing
   9.12   continued

```
      sp.setOneTouchExpandable (true);

      frame.getContentPane().add (sp);
      frame.pack();
      frame.show();
   }
}
```

display

The split pane is created in the main method and added to the frame to be displayed. The split pane is oriented, using the HORIZONTAL_SPLIT constant, such that the panel containing the list and the label containing the image to be displayed are side by side. The call to the setOneTouchExpandable method causes the divider bar of the split pane to display the arrows that permit the user to expand the panes one way or the other with one click of the mouse.

The ListPanel class shown in Listing 9.13 defines the panel that contains the list of file names. The list contents are set up as an array of String objects, which are passed into the JList constructor.

listing
   9.13

```java
//********************************************************************
//  ListPanel.java         Authors: Lewis/Loftus
//
//  Represents the list of images for the PickImage program.
//********************************************************************

import java.awt.*;
import javax.swing.*;
import javax.swing.event.*;

public class ListPanel extends JPanel
{
   private JLabel label;
   private JList list;

   //----------------------------------------------------------------
   //  Loads the list of image names into the list.
   //----------------------------------------------------------------
   public ListPanel (JLabel imageLabel)
   {
      label = imageLabel;

      String[] fileNames = { "circuit.gif",
                             "duke.gif",
                             "hammock.gif",
                             "justin.jpg",
                             "kayla.jpg",
                             "tiger.jpg",
                             "toucan.gif",
                             "worldmap.gif" };

      list = new JList (fileNames);
      list.addListSelectionListener (new ListListener());
      list.setSelectionMode (ListSelectionModel.SINGLE_SELECTION);

      add (list);
      setBackground (Color.white);
   }
```

<table>
<tr><td>listing
  9.13</td><td>continued</td></tr>
</table>

```
//***************************************************************
//   Represents the listener for the list of images.
//***************************************************************
private class ListListener implements ListSelectionListener
{
   public void valueChanged (ListSelectionEvent event)
   {
      if (list.isSelectionEmpty())
         label.setIcon (null);
      else
      {
         String fileName = (String)list.getSelectedValue();
         ImageIcon image = new ImageIcon (fileName);
         label.setIcon (image);
      }
   }
}
}
```

A JList object generates a *list selection event* whenever the current selection of the list changes. The ListSelectionListener interface contains one method called valueChanged. In this program, the private inner class called ListListener defines the listener for the list of file names.

The valueChanged method of the listener calls the isSelectionEmpty method of the JList object to determine if there is any value currently selected. If not, the icon of the label is set to null. If so, the file name is obtained using the getSelectedValue method. Then the corresponding image icon is created and displayed in the label.

A JList object can be set so that multiple items can be selected at the same time. The *list selection mode* can be one of three options, as shown in the table in Fig. 9.11.

The list selection mode is defined by a ListSelectionModel object. By default, a list allows multiple interval selection. A call to the setSelectionMode method, using a constant defined in the ListSelectionModel class, will explicitly set the list selection mode.

> **A list can be set up to allow multiple selections.**
>
> key concept

List Selection Mode	Description
Single Selection	Only one item can be selected at a time.
Single Interval Selection	Multiple, contiguous items can be selected at a time.
Multiple Interval Selection	Any combination of items can be selected.

figure 9.11   List selection modes

In the `PickImage` program, we set the list selection mode to single selection because only one image can be displayed at a time. However, even if multiple selections were allowed in this program, the `getSelectedValue` method returns the first item selected, so that would be the image displayed. A similar method called `getSelectedValues` returns an array of objects representing the items selected when multiple selections are permitted.

Instead of an array of `String` objects, the `JList` constructor could be passed an array of `ImageIcon` objects instead. In that case, the images would be displayed in the list.

combo boxes

key concept

A combo box provides a list of options from which to choose and displays the current selection.

A *combo box* allows the user to select one of several options. When the user presses a combo box using the mouse, a list of options is displayed from which the user can choose. The current choice is displayed in the combo box. A combo box is defined by the `JComboBox` class.

Note the similarities and differences between a combo box and a `JList` object (described in the previous section). Both allow the user to select an item from a set of choices. However, the choices on a list are always displayed, with the current choice highlighted, whereas a combo box presents its options only when the user presses it with the mouse. The only item displayed all the time in a combo box is the current selection.

A combo box can be either *editable* or *uneditable*. By default, a combo box is uneditable. Changing the value of an uneditable combo box can be accomplished only by selecting an item from the list. If the combo box is editable, however, the user can change the value by either selecting an item from the list or by typing a particular value into the combo box area.

The options in a combo box list can be established in one of two ways. We can create an array of strings and pass it into the constructor of the JComboBox class. Alternatively, we can use the addItem method to add an item to the combo box after it has been created. Like a JList, a JComboBox can also display ImageIcon objects as options as well.

The JukeBox program shown in Listing 9.14 demonstrates the use of a combo box. The user chooses a song to play using the combo box, and then presses the Play button to begin playing the song. The Stop button can be pressed at any time to stop the song. Selecting a new song while one is playing also stops the current song.

The JukeBoxControls class shown in Listing 9.15 is a panel that contains the components that make up the jukebox GUI. The constructor of the class also loads the audio clips that will be played. An audio clip is obtained first by creating a URL object that corresponds to the wav or au file that defines the clip. The first two parameters to the URL constructor should be "file" and "localhost" respectively, if the audio clip is stored on the same machine on which the program is executing. Creating URL objects can potentially throw an exception; therefore they are created in a try block. However, this program assumes the audio clips will be loaded successfully and therefore does nothing if an exception is thrown.

Once created, the URL objects are used to create AudioClip objects using the static newAudioClip method of the JApplet class. The audio clips are stored in an array. The first entry in the array, at index 0, is set to null. This entry corresponds to the initial combo box option, which simply encourages the user to make a selection.

The list of songs that are displayed in the combo box is defined in an array of strings. The first entry of the array will appear in the combo box by default and is often used to direct the user. We must take care that the rest of the program does not try to use that option as a valid song.

The play and stop buttons are displayed with both a text label and an image icon. They are also given mnemonics so that the jukebox can be controlled partially from the keyboard.

A combo box generates an action event whenever the user makes a selection from it. The JukeBox program uses one action listener class for the combo box and another for both of the push buttons. They could be combined if desired.

The actionPerformed method of the ComboListener class is executed when a selection is made from the combo box. The current audio selection that is playing, if any, is stopped. The current clip is then updated to reflect the new selection. Note that the audio clip is not immediately played at that point. The user must press the play button to hear the new selection.

```
//********************************************************************
//   JukeBox.java        Author: Lewis/Loftus
//
//   Demonstrates the use of a combo box.
//********************************************************************

import javax.swing.*;

public class JukeBox
{
   //-----------------------------------------------------------------
   //  Creates and displays the controls for the juke box.
   //-----------------------------------------------------------------
   public static void main (String[] args)
   {
      JFrame frame = new JFrame ("Java Juke Box");
      frame.setDefaultCloseOperation (JFrame.EXIT_ON_CLOSE);

      JukeBoxControls controlPanel = new JukeBoxControls();

      frame.getContentPane().add(controlPanel);
      frame.pack();
      frame.show();
   }
}
```

display

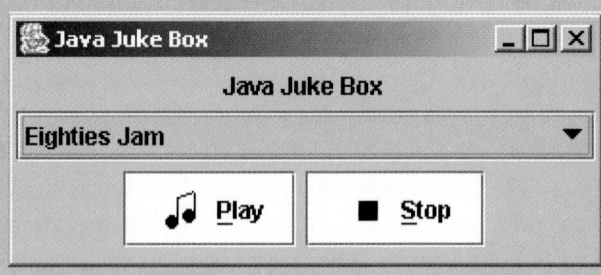

listing
  9.15

```java
//********************************************************************
//   JukeBoxControls.java         Author: Lewis/Loftus
//
//   Represents the control panel for the juke box.
//********************************************************************

import java.awt.*;
import java.awt.event.*;
import javax.swing.*;
import java.applet.AudioClip;
import java.net.URL;

public class JukeBoxControls extends JPanel
{
    private JComboBox musicCombo;
    private JButton stopButton, playButton;
    private AudioClip[] music;
    private AudioClip current;

    //----------------------------------------------------------------
    //   Sets up the GUI for the juke box.
    //----------------------------------------------------------------
    public JukeBoxControls()
    {
        URL url1, url2, url3, url4, url5, url6;
        url1 = url2 = url3 = url4 = url5 = url6 = null;

        // Obtain and store the audio clips to play
        try
        {
            url1 = new URL ("file", "localhost", "westernBeat.wav");
            url2 = new URL ("file", "localhost", "classical.wav");
            url3 = new URL ("file", "localhost", "jeopardy.au");
            url4 = new URL ("file", "localhost", "newAgeRythm.wav");
            url5 = new URL ("file", "localhost", "eightiesJam.wav");
            url6 = new URL ("file", "localhost", "hitchcock.wav");
        }
        catch (Exception exception) {}

        music = new AudioClip[7];
        music[0] = null;  // Corresponds to "Make a Selection..."
        music[1] = JApplet.newAudioClip (url1);
        music[2] = JApplet.newAudioClip (url2);
        music[3] = JApplet.newAudioClip (url3);
```

listing
9.15   continued

```
music[4] = JApplet.newAudioClip (url4);
music[5] = JApplet.newAudioClip (url5);
music[6] = JApplet.newAudioClip (url6);

JLabel titleLabel = new JLabel ("Java Juke Box");
titleLabel.setAlignmentX (Component.CENTER_ALIGNMENT);

// Create the list of strings for the combo box options
String[] musicNames = {"Make A Selection...", "Western Beat",
        "Classical Melody", "Jeopardy Theme", "New Age Rythm",
        "Eighties Jam", "Alfred Hitchcock's Theme"};

musicCombo = new JComboBox (musicNames);
musicCombo.setAlignmentX (Component.CENTER_ALIGNMENT);

//  Set up the buttons
playButton = new JButton ("Play", new ImageIcon ("play.gif"));
playButton.setBackground (Color.white);
playButton.setMnemonic ('p');
stopButton = new JButton ("Stop", new ImageIcon ("stop.gif"));
stopButton.setBackground (Color.white);
stopButton.setMnemonic ('s');

JPanel buttons = new JPanel();
buttons.setLayout (new BoxLayout (buttons, BoxLayout.X_AXIS));
buttons.add (playButton);
buttons.add (Box.createRigidArea (new Dimension(5,0)));
buttons.add (stopButton);
buttons.setBackground (Color.cyan);

//  Set up this panel
setPreferredSize (new Dimension (300, 100));
setBackground (Color.cyan);
setLayout (new BoxLayout (this, BoxLayout.Y_AXIS));
add (Box.createRigidArea (new Dimension(0,5)));
add (titleLabel);
add (Box.createRigidArea (new Dimension(0,5)));
add (musicCombo);
add (Box.createRigidArea (new Dimension(0,5)));
add (buttons);
add (Box.createRigidArea (new Dimension(0,5)));

musicCombo.addActionListener (new ComboListener());
stopButton.addActionListener (new ButtonListener());
```

listing
9.15   continued

```java
      playButton.addActionListener (new ButtonListener());

      current = null;
   }

   //****************************************************************
   //   Represents the action listener for the combo box.
   //****************************************************************
   private class ComboListener implements ActionListener
   {
      //----------------------------------------------------------
      //   Stops playing the current selection (if any) and resets
      //   the current selection to the one chosen.
      //----------------------------------------------------------
      public void actionPerformed (ActionEvent event)
      {
         if (current != null)
            current.stop();

         current = music[musicCombo.getSelectedIndex()];
      }
    }

   //****************************************************************
   //   Represents the action listener for both control buttons.
   //****************************************************************
   private class ButtonListener implements ActionListener
   {
      //----------------------------------------------------------
      //   Stops the current selection (if any) in either case. If
      //   the play button was pressed, start playing it again.
      //----------------------------------------------------------
      public void actionPerformed (ActionEvent event)
      {
         if (current != null)
            current.stop();

         if (event.getSource() == playButton)
            if (current != null)
               current.play();
      }
   }
}
```

The `actionPerformed` method of the `ButtonListener` class is executed when either of the buttons is pushed. The current audio selection that is playing, if any, is stopped. If it was the stop button that was pressed, the task is complete. If the play button was pressed, the current audio selection is played again from the beginning.

sliders

key concept

A slider lets the user specify a numeric value within a bounded range.

A *slider* is a component that allows the user to specify a numeric value within a bounded range. A slider can be presented either vertically or horizontally and can have optional tick marks and labels indicating the range of values.

A program called `ViewColors` is shown in Listing 9.16. It presents three sliders that control the RGB components of a color. The color specified by the values of the sliders is shown in a square that is displayed to the right of the sliders.

listing 9.16

```
//********************************************************************
//  ViewColors.java          Authors: Lewis/Loftus
//
//  Demonstrates the use slider components.
//********************************************************************

import java.awt.*;
import javax.swing.*;

public class ViewColors
{
   //-----------------------------------------------------------------
   //  Presents up a frame with a control panel and a panel that
   //  changes color as the sliders are adjusted.
   //-----------------------------------------------------------------
   public static void main (String[] args)
   {
      JFrame frame = new JFrame ("View Colors");
      frame.setDefaultCloseOperation (JFrame.EXIT_ON_CLOSE);
```

listing
9.16 continued

```
        JPanel colorPanel = new JPanel();
        colorPanel.setPreferredSize (new Dimension (100, 100));
        colorPanel.setBackground (new Color (0, 0, 0));

        Container cp = frame.getContentPane();
        cp.setLayout (new FlowLayout());
        cp.add (new ViewSliderPanel(colorPanel));
        cp.add (colorPanel);

        frame.pack();
        frame.show();
    }
}
```

display

The panel called colorPanel defined in the main method is used to display (by setting its background color) the color specified by the sliders. Initially, the settings of the sliders are all zero, which correspond to the initial color displayed (black).

The `ViewSliderPanel` class shown in Listing 9.17 is a panel used to display the three sliders. Each is created from the `JSlider` class, which accepts four parameters. The first determines the orientation of the slider using one of two `JSlider` constants (`HORIZONTAL` or `VERTICAL`). The second and third parameters specify the maximum and minimum values of the slider, which are set to 0 and 255 for each of the sliders in the example. The last parameter of the `JSlider` constructor specifies the slider's initial value. In our example, the initial value of each slider is zero, which puts the slider knob to the far left when the program initially executes.

listing
   9.17

```
//********************************************************************
//  ViewSliderPanel.java        Authors: Lewis/Loftus
//
//  Represents the slider control panel for the ViewColors program.
//********************************************************************

import java.awt.*;
import javax.swing.*;
import javax.swing.event.*;

public class ViewSliderPanel extends JPanel
{
   private JPanel colorPanel;
   private JSlider rSlider, gSlider, bSlider;
   private JLabel rLabel, gLabel, bLabel;

   //-----------------------------------------------------------------
   //  Sets up the sliders and their labels, aligning them along
   //  their left edge using a box layout.
   //-----------------------------------------------------------------
   public ViewSliderPanel (JPanel panel)
   {
      colorPanel = panel;
```

listing
9.17 continued

```
        rSlider = new JSlider (JSlider.HORIZONTAL, 0, 255, 0);
        rSlider.setMajorTickSpacing (50);
        rSlider.setMinorTickSpacing (10);
        rSlider.setPaintTicks (true);
        rSlider.setPaintLabels (true);
        rSlider.setAlignmentX (Component.LEFT_ALIGNMENT);

        gSlider = new JSlider (JSlider.HORIZONTAL, 0, 255, 0);
        gSlider.setMajorTickSpacing (50);
        gSlider.setMinorTickSpacing (10);
        gSlider.setPaintTicks (true);
        gSlider.setPaintLabels (true);
        gSlider.setAlignmentX (Component.LEFT_ALIGNMENT);

        bSlider = new JSlider (JSlider.HORIZONTAL, 0, 255, 0);
        bSlider.setMajorTickSpacing (50);
        bSlider.setMinorTickSpacing (10);
        bSlider.setPaintTicks (true);
        bSlider.setPaintLabels (true);
        bSlider.setAlignmentX (Component.LEFT_ALIGNMENT);

        SliderListener listener = new SliderListener();
        rSlider.addChangeListener (listener);
        gSlider.addChangeListener (listener);
        bSlider.addChangeListener (listener);

        rLabel = new JLabel ("Red: 0");
        rLabel.setAlignmentX (Component.LEFT_ALIGNMENT);
        gLabel = new JLabel ("Green: 0");
        gLabel.setAlignmentX (Component.LEFT_ALIGNMENT);
        bLabel = new JLabel ("Blue: 0");
        bLabel.setAlignmentX (Component.LEFT_ALIGNMENT);

        setLayout (new BoxLayout (this, BoxLayout.Y_AXIS));
        add (rLabel);
        add (rSlider);
        add (Box.createRigidArea (new Dimension (0, 20)));
        add (gLabel);
        add (gSlider);
        add (Box.createRigidArea (new Dimension (0, 20)));
        add (bLabel);
        add (bSlider);
    }
```

listing
9.17 continued

```
//***************************************************************
//  Represents the listener for all three sliders.
//***************************************************************
private class SliderListener implements ChangeListener
{
    //------------------------------------------------------------
    //  Gets the value of each slider, then updates the labels and
    //  the color panel.
    //------------------------------------------------------------
    public void stateChanged (ChangeEvent event)
    {
        int red, green, blue;

        red = rSlider.getValue();
        green = gSlider.getValue();
        blue = bSlider.getValue();

        rLabel.setText ("Red: " + red);
        gLabel.setText ("Green: " + green);
        bLabel.setText ("Blue: " + blue);

        colorPanel.setBackground (new Color (red, green, blue));
    }
}
}
```

The JSlider class has several methods that allow the programmer to tailor the look of a slider. Major tick marks can be set at specific intervals using the setMajorTickSpacing method. Intermediate minor tick marks can be set using the setMinorTickSpacing method. Neither is displayed, however, unless the setPaintTicks method, with a parameter of true, is invoked as well. Labels indicating the value of the major tick marks are displayed if indicated by a call to the setPaintLabels method.

Note that in this example, the major tick spacing is set to 50. Starting at zero, each increment of 50 is labeled. The last label is therefore 250, even though the slider value can reach 255.

A slider produces a *change event*, indicating that the position of the slider and the value it represents has changed. The `ChangeListener` interface contains a single method called `stateChanged`. In the `ViewColors` program, the same listener object is used for all three sliders. In the `stateChanged` method, which is called whenever any of the sliders is adjusted, the value of each slider is obtained, the labels of all three are updated, and the background color of the display panel is revised. It is actually necessary to update only one of the labels (the one whose corresponding slider changed). However, the effort to determine which slider was adjusted is not warranted. It's easier—and probably more efficient—to update all three labels each time. Another alternative is to have a unique listener for each slider, though that extra coding effort is not needed either.

A slider is often a good choice when a large range of values is possible but strictly bounded on both ends. Compared to alternatives such as a text field, sliders convey more information to the user and eliminate input errors.

9.5 events revisited

Throughout the graphics track sections of previous chapters, and continuing into this chapter, we've discussed various events that components might generate. At this point it is worth taking a moment to put the event/component relationship into context.

The events listed in Fig. 9.12 are generated by every Swing component. That is, we can set up a listener for any of these events on any component.

> **key concept**
> Some events are generated by every Swing component; others are generated only by a few.

Some events are generated only by certain components. The table in Fig. 9.13 maps the components to the events that they can generate. Keep in mind

Event	Represents
Component Event	Changing a component's size, position, or visibility.
Focus Event	Gaining or losing the keyboard focus.
Key Event	Pressing, releasing, and clicking keyboard keys.
Mouse Event	Clicking the mouse button and moving the mouse into and out of a component's drawing area.
Mouse Motion Event	Moving or dragging a mouse over a component.

figure 9.12 Events that are generated by every Swing component

that these events are in addition to the ones that all components generate. If a component does not generate a particular kind of event, a listener for that event cannot be added to that component.

We have discussed some of the events in Figs. 9.10 and 9.11 at appropriate points in this text; we have left others for your independent exploration. Applying the basic concept of component/event/listener interaction is often just a matter of knowing which components generate which events under which circumstances.

| | **Event** | | | | | | | |
Component	Action	Caret	Change	Document	Item	List Selection	Window	*Other*
JButton	√		√		√			
JCheckBox	√		√		√			
JColorChooser			√					
JComboBox	√				√			
JDialog							√	
JEditorPane		√		√				√
JFileChooser	√							
JFrame							√	
JInternalFrame								√
JList						√		√
JMenu								√
JMenuItem	√		√		√			√
JOptionPane								
JPasswordField	√	√		√				
JPopupMenu								√
JProgessBar			√		√			
JRadioButton	√		√					
JSlider			√					
JTabbedPane			√					
JTable						√		√
JTextArea		√		√				
JTextField	√	√		√				
JTextPane		√		√				√
JToggleButton	√		√		√			
JTree								√

figure 9.13   Specific events generated by specific components

Of course, many events occur in a GUI that have no bearing on the current program. For example, every time a mouse is moved across a component, many mouse motion events are generated. However, this doesn't mean we must listen for them. A GUI is defined in part by the events to which we choose to respond.

9.6 more about GUIs

Even though we've used several graphics track sections from earlier chapters to discuss GUIs, and have devoted this entire chapter to GUIs as well, we've still only scratched the surface of Java GUI possibilities. The constraints of space limit us, though additional GUI topics and examples can be found on the text's Web site.

web bonus

The text's Web site contains additional examples and explanations of Java GUI topics.

Let's briefly describe, but not explore, a few other Java GUI containers that are not covered in depth in this text:

- A *tool bar* is a container that groups several components into a row or column. A tool bar usually contains buttons that correspond to tasks that can also be accomplished in other ways. Tool bars can be dragged away from the container in which they initially exist into their own window.

- An *internal frame* is a container that operates like a regular frame but only within another window. An internal frame can be moved around within the window and overlapped with other internal frames. Internal frames can be used to create the feel of a GUI desktop in which components can be arranged as the user chooses.

- A *layered pane* is a container that takes into account a third dimension, depth, for organizing the components it contains. When a component is added to a layered pane, its depth is specified. If components overlap, the depth value of each component determines which is on top.

You may also be interested in a few other regular GUI components provided by the Swing API:

- A *progress bar* can be used to indicate the progress of a particular activity. The user does not generally interact with a progress bar other than to view it to determine how far along a task, such as the loading of images, has progressed.

- A *table* is a Java GUI component that displays data in a table format. A Java table can be completely tailored to provide a precise organization and presentation. It can allow the user to edit the data as well. A Java table does not actually contain or store the data; it simply presents it to the user in an organized manner.

- A *tree* is a component that presents a hierarchical view of data. Like a table, it doesn't actually store the data; it provides an organized view that allows the user to traverse the data from a high-level root node down through the various branches.

- Another area for which Java provides rich support is *text processing*. We've made use of basic text components such as text fields and text areas, but that's only the beginning. The Java standard class library, and particularly the Swing API, has a huge number of classes that support the display, editing, and manipulation of text.

As with all topics introduced in this book, we encourage you to explore these issues in more detail. The world of Java GUIs, in particular, has many opportunities still to discover.

summary of
key concepts

▶ The design of any GUI should adhere to basic guidelines regarding consistency and usability.

▶ The layout manager of a container determines how components are visually presented.

▶ When changes occur, the components in a container reorganize themselves according to the layout manager's policy.

▶ The layout manager for each container can be explicitly set.

▶ A tabbed pane presents a set of cards from which the user can choose.

▶ In a flow layout, the width of the container determines how many components fit on a row.

▶ Not all areas of a border layout must be used; the areas that contain components fill in the unused space.

▶ The cells of a grid layout are filled in order as components are added to the container.

▶ A box layout can use invisible components to provide space between components.

▶ A GUI's appearance is a function of the containment hierarchy and the layout managers of each of the containers.

▶ Using the special features of various components often improves a GUI's functionality.

▶ Various borders can be applied to Swing components to group objects and to enhance the visual effect.

▶ A scroll pane is useful if you want to view large objects or large amounts of data.

▶ A split pane displays two components separated by a movable divider bar. The components can be displayed either horizontally or vertically.

▶ A list can be set up to allow multiple selections.

▶ A combo box provides a list of options from which to choose and displays the current selection.

▶ A slider lets the user specify a numeric value within a bounded range.

▶ Some events are generated by every Swing component; others are generated only by a few.

self-review questions

9.1   What general guidelines for GUI design are presented in this chapter?

9.2   When is a layout manager consulted?

9.3   How does the flow layout manager behave?

9.4   Describe the areas of a border layout.

9.5   What effect does a glue component in a box layout have?

9.6   What is the containment hierarchy for a GUI?

9.7   What is a tool tip?

9.8   What is a mnemonic and how is it used?

9.9   Why might you want to disable a component?

9.10 What is the role of the `BorderFactory` class?

9.11 Describe the use of scrollbars on a scroll pane.

9.12 What is a combo box?

9.13 Why is a slider a better choice than a text field in some cases?

9.14 Can we add any kind of listener to any component? Explain.

exercises

9.1   Draw the containment hierarchy tree for the `LayoutDemo` program.

9.2   Draw the containment hierarchy tree for the `LightBulb` program.

9.3   Draw the containment hierarchy tree for the `PickImage` program.

9.4   Draw the containment hierarchy tree for the `JukeBox` program.

9.5   Draw the containment hierarchy tree for the `ViewColors` program.

9.6   What visual effect would result by changing the horizontal and vertical gaps on the border layout used in the `LayoutDemo` program? Make the change to test your answer.

9.7   Write the lines of code that will define a compound border using three borders. Use a line border on the inner edge, an etched border on the outer edge, and a raised bevel border in between.

9.8   What effect would removing the call to `setSelectionMode` in the `ListPanel` class have? Make the change to test your answer.

programming projects

9.1   Modify the `IntroPanel` class of the `LayoutDemo` program so that it uses a box layout manager. Use invisible components to put space before and between the two labels on the panel.

9.2   Modify the `QuoteOptions` program from Chapter 6 to change its visual appearance. Present the radio buttons in a vertical column with a surrounding border to the left of the quote label.

9.3   Modify the `JukeBox` program such that it plays a song immediately after it has been selected using the combo box.

9.4   Modify the `StyleOptions` program from Chapter 6 so that it uses a split pane. Orient the split pane such that the label is on the top and the style check boxes are in the bottom. Add tool tips to the check boxes to explain their purpose.

9.5   Modify the `PickImage` program so that it presents several additional image options. Display the list within a scroll pane with a vertical scroll bar that is always displayed. Display the image in a scroll pane that uses both horizontal and vertical scroll bars, but only when necessary.

9.6   Design and implement a program that displays a numeric keypad that might appear on a phone. Above the keypad buttons, show a label that displays the numbers as they are picked. To the right of the keypad buttons, include another button to clear the display. Use a border layout to manage the overall presentation, and a grid layout to manage the keypad buttons. Put a border around the keypad buttons to group them visually, and a border around the display. Include a tool tip for the clear button, and mnemonics for all buttons in the program.

9.7   Design and implement a program that combines the functionality of the `StyleOptions` and `QuoteOptions` programs from Chapter 6. That is, the new program should present the appropriate quote (using radio buttons) whose style can be changed (using checkboxes). Also include a slider that regulates the size of the quotation font. Design the containment hierarchy carefully and use layout managers as appropriate to create a nice interface.

9.8   Design and implement an application that works as a stopwatch. Include a display that shows the time (in seconds) as it increments. Include buttons that allow the user to start and stop the time, and reset the display to zero. Arrange the components to present a nice interface. Include mnemonics for the buttons. *Hint*: use the `Timer` class (described in Chapter 8) to control the timing of the stopwatch.

9.9   Design and implement an application that draws the graph of the equation $ax^2 + bx + c$, where the values of a, b, and c are set using three sliders.

9.10 Design and implement an application that performs flashcard testing of simple mathematical problems. Allow the user to pick the category. Repetitively display a problem and get the user's answer. Indicate whether the user's answer is right or wrong for each problem, and display an ongoing score.

9.11 Design and implement an application that helps a pizza restaurant take orders. Use a tabbed pane for different categories of food (pizza, beverages, special items). Collect information about quantity and size. Display the cost of the order as information is gathered. Use appropriate components for collecting the various kinds of information. Structure the interface carefully using the containment hierarchy and layout managers.

answers to self-review questions

9.1   The general guidelines for GUI design include: know the needs and characteristics of the user, prevent user errors when possible, optimize user abilities by providing shortcuts and other redundant means to accomplish a task, and be consistent in GUI layout and coloring schemes.

9.2   A layout manager is consulted whenever the visual appearance of its components might be affected, such as when the container is resized or when a new component is added to the container.

9.3   Flow layout attempts to put as many components on a row as possible. Multiple rows are created as needed.

9.4   Border layout is divided into five areas: North, South, East, West, and Center. The North and South areas are at the top and bottom of the container, respectively, and span the entire width of the container. Sandwiched between them, from left to right, are the West, Center, and East areas. Any unused area takes up no space, and the others fill in as needed.

9.5 A glue component in a box layout dictates where any extra space in the layout should go. It expands as necessary, but takes up no space if there is no extra space to distribute.

9.6 The containment hierarchy for a GUI is the set of nested containers and the other components they contain. The containment hierarchy can be described as a tree.

9.7 A tool tip is a small amount of text that can be set up to appear when the cursor comes to rest on a component. It usually gives information about that component.

9.8 A mnemonic is a character that can be used to activate a control such as a button as if the user had used to mouse to do so. The user activates a mnemonic by holding down the ALT key and pressing the appropriate character.

9.9 A component should be disabled if it is not a viable option for the user at a given time. Not only does this prevent user error, it helps clarify what the current valid actions are.

9.10 The `BorderFactory` class contains several methods used to create borders that can be applied to components.

9.11 A scroll pane can have a vertical scrollbar on the right side and/or a horizontal scrollbar along the bottom. The programmer can determine, in either case, whether the scrollbar should always appear, never appear, or appear as needed to be able to view the underlying component.

9.12 A combo box is a component that allows the user to choose from a set of options in a pull-down list. An editable combo box also allows the user to enter a specific value.

9.13 If in a specific situation user input should be a numeric value from a bounded range, a slider is probably a better choice than a text field. A slider prevents an improper value from being entered and conveys the valid range to the user.

9.14 No, we cannot add any listener to any component. Each component generates a certain set of events, and only listeners of those types can be added to the component.

software engineering

The quality of software is only as good as the process used to create it. In Chapter 3, we introduced four basic phases that should characterize any software development effort: requirements, design, implementation, and testing. In subsequent chapters, we've learned to design and implement classes and objects with various characteristics, including those that support systems with graphical user interfaces (GUIs). To successfully develop large systems, however, we must refine these development activities into a well-defined process that can be applied repeatedly and consistently. This chapter explores models for developing software and defines an evolutionary approach that specifically takes object-oriented issues into account. This approach is illustrated using an extended example that synthesizes many of the programming concepts explored thus far in the text.

chapter
objectives

- Explore several different software development models.

- Explain the life cycle of a software system and its implications for software development.

- Contrast linear and iterative development approaches.

- Discuss prototypes and their various uses.

- Consider the goals and techniques of testing.

- Define an evolutionary approach to object-oriented design and implementation.

- Demonstrate evolutionary development using a nontrivial example.

10.0 software development models

A program goes through many phases from its initial conception to its ultimate demise. This sequence is often called the *life cycle* of a program. Too often programmers focus so much on the particular issues involved in getting a program to run that they ignore other important characteristics. Developing high-quality software requires an appreciation for many issues, and those issues must be considered in the day-to-day activities of a programmer. We explore these issues as we discuss the software life cycle and software development models in this chapter.

software life cycle

All programs go through three fundamental stages: development (with its four basic phases), followed by use, and maintenance. Figure 10.1 shows the life cycle of a program. Initially, the idea for a program is conceived by a software developer or by a user who has a particular need. The new program is created in the *development* stage. At some point the new program is considered to be complete and is turned over to users. The version of the program that is made available to users is often called an initial *release* of the program.

Almost certainly, users discover problems with the program. Often they also have suggestions for new features that they would like to see added to the program in order to make it more useful. These defects and ideas for new features are conveyed back to the developer, and the program undergoes maintenance.

Software maintenance is the process of modifying a program in order to enhance it or eliminate deficiencies. Unlike hardware, software does not degrade over time. Thus, the goal of software maintenance is to produce an improved program rather than a program that is "almost like new." The changes are made to a copy of the program, so that the user can still use the current release while

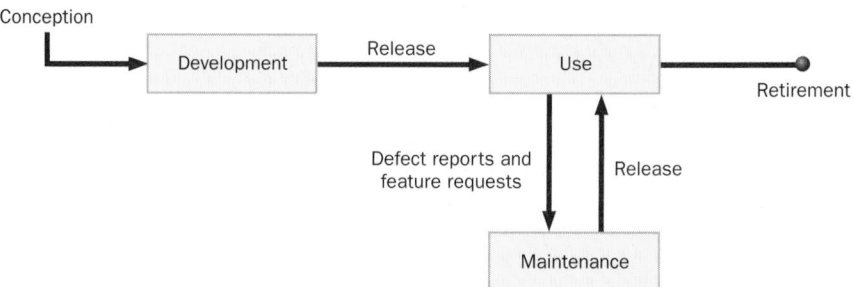

figure 10.1   The life cycle of a program

the program is being maintained. When the changes are serious or numerous enough, a new version of the program is released for use. A program might be maintained many times over, resulting in several releases.

For a variety of reasons, a developer may decide that it is no longer worth the effort to maintain an existing program and therefore releases no further versions of it. A program eventually reaches the end of its useful life. Users abandon it or seek another solution. This eventual demise is sometimes referred to as the program's *retirement* from active use.

The duration of a program's life cycle varies greatly depending on the purpose of the program, how useful the program is, and how well it is constructed. The time taken for the development portion of a program can vary from a few weeks to several years. Likewise, a program may be used and maintained for many years.

One important aspect of software development is the relationship between development effort and maintenance effort. Figure 10.2 shows a typical ratio of development effort to maintenance effort. This may seem contrary to intuition because it seems that the initial development of a program is where the real work is done, but this isn't actually the case. Much more effort is expended overall to enhance and fix an existing system than to develop it.

For various reasons, maintenance is often more difficult than the original development effort. For instance, the original developers are rarely the same people as the ones who maintain it. A significant amount of time often elapses between the initial development and the maintenance tasks, and often the responsibilities of personnel change. Therefore, maintainers often do not understand the software as well as

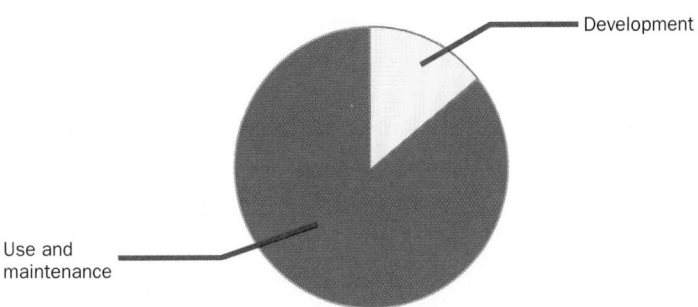

figure 10.2   A typical ratio of development effort to maintenance effort

the original developers did. The effort involved in a maintenance task, such as fixing a defect, depends on the maintainer's ability to understand the program, determine the cause of the problem, and correct it.

The ability to read and understand a program depends on how clearly the requirements are established, and how well it is designed, implemented, and documented. It depends on how classes are organized and how objects are used. It depends on how elegantly methods accomplish their goals and how closely coding guidelines are followed. In short, the ability to read and understand a program depends on the effort put into the initial development process.

When requirements are not clearly established and when designs are not carefully thought out, software can be unnecessarily complex and difficult to understand. The more complex a program is, the easier it is to introduce errors during development, and the more difficult it is to remove these errors when they are found. The earlier the problems are discovered, the easier and less costly they are to correct.

Designing a solution without establishing clear requirements is as unreasonable as creating a blueprint for a house without first determining what purposes the house must serve. While the blueprint may qualify as a design for a house, the design may be entirely unsuitable for a particular family. Writing a program without establishing a careful design first is as absurd as building the house without creating a blueprint. The builder may actually create some kind of structure, even one that looks good on a superficial examination. However, it is possible that the structure will fail to meet the safety requirements of the local building code, or it will not stand up to the local weather nearly as well as a house that has been carefully designed. It is almost certain that the resulting structure will not satisfy a particular family's requirements. Likewise, a program that is created in an ad hoc fashion, with little or no attention to requirements or design, is likely to contain many defects and will not perform well when used.

The relationship between development effort and maintenance effort is not linear. Small changes in the development effort can greatly reduce the effort necessary during maintenance. The bars in Fig. 10.3 show the relationship between the development effort and the maintenance effort. The bottom bar shows that if a small increase in effort is expended during development, significantly higher savings in maintenance effort can be realized. The effort put into the development stage is an investment that will reduce the overall effort required throughout the life cycle of the program. Thus, a good programmer keeps long-term effects in mind while performing near-term activities.

In some ways, this issue centers on maturity. An experienced software developer realizes the long-term advantages of certain development activities. This sit-

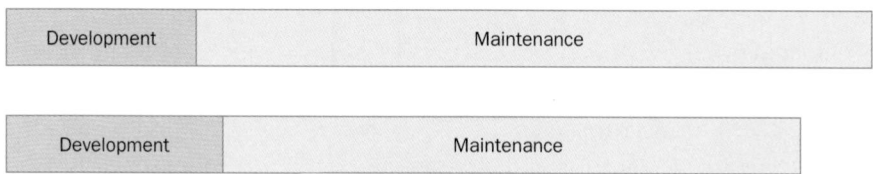

figure 10.3   The relationship between development effort
and maintenance effort

uation is analogous in many ways to the maturity differences between a child and an adult. For instance, consider the task of brushing your teeth. To many children, brushing teeth may be seen as a chore with no obvious advantages. To an adult, brushing teeth is simply part of a daily routine, necessary for a lifetime of healthy teeth. Similarly, the mature software developer realizes that even small, unobtrusive activities can have a dramatic effect over the life of the program, even if the results are not immediately apparent.

Always keep in mind that a working program is not necessarily a good program. The goal of writing software is not to minimize the amount of time it takes to develop a program, but to minimize the overall amount of effort required to create and maintain a useful program for the long term. With this goal in mind, the development process should be well defined and rigorously followed.

software development models

A *software development model* is an organized strategy for executing the steps necessary to create high-quality software. All development models incorporate, in various ways, the basic development activities of establishing requirements, creating a design, implementing the design, and testing the implementation. We discussed these basic activities in Chapter 3.

Too often, however, programmers follow the build-and-fix approach depicted in Fig. 10.4. In this approach, a programmer creates an initial version of a program, and then continually modifies it until it has reached some level of acceptance. Often, testing activities are not systematic or carefully planned, and therefore problems often go undiscovered. In a build-and-fix approach, the programmer is reacting to problems as opposed to participating in an effort to create a quality product in the first place.

In the build-and-fix approach, although some problems might be eliminated during development, the overall quality of the product is never really addressed.

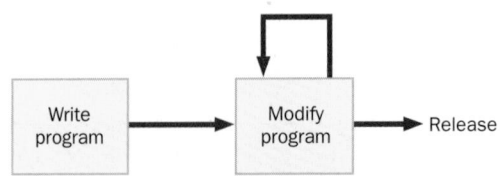

figure 10.4   The build-and-fix approach

Defects that still exist in the software will be difficult to isolate and correct. Enhancements to the program will be challenging because the system was not designed well.

A program produced using the build-and-fix approach is a product of ad hoc, reckless activities. It is reactive rather than proactive. Therefore, the build-and-fix approach is not really a development model at all.

One of the first true development process models, called the *waterfall model*, was introduced in the early 1970s. It is depicted in Fig. 10.5. The waterfall model is linear, with one stage followed directly by the next. In fact, the model gets its name from the implication that development flows in one direction from stage to stage until the final release is created. This model does not allow for an earlier stage to be revisited after a new stage is begun any more than water can be made to flow up a waterfall.

Although the waterfall model formalizes the stages of development, it ultimately is not realistic because it doesn't acknowledge the fact that developers sometimes need to revisit previous stages. It would be nice if all program require-

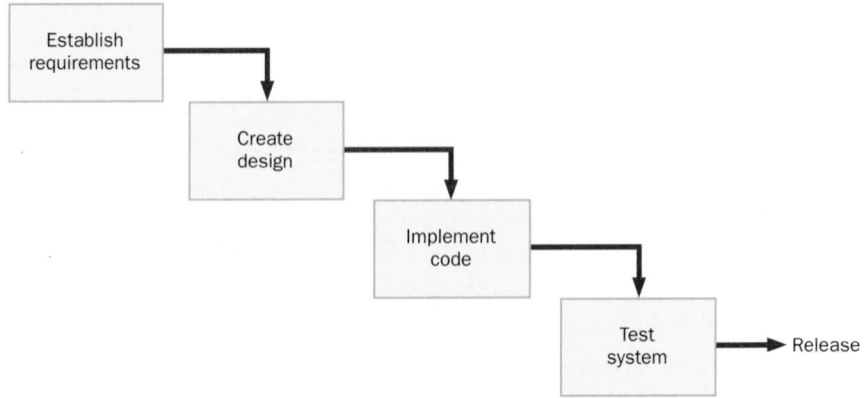

figure 10.5   The waterfall model

ments were completely specified and analyzed before design activities started. Likewise, it would be nice to have all design decisions made before implementation begins. Unfortunately, it almost never works out that way. No matter how carefully the requirements are established or how carefully the design is created, it is impossible to consider every eventuality, and there will always come a time when the developer realizes that an earlier decision was in error.

> The waterfall model does not recognize the inherently iterative nature of development activities.
>
> **key concept**

iterative development

A realistic model must take into account that development activities are somewhat overlapping. We need a flexible development model with interacting activities. However, we must be careful not to allow such flexibility to degenerate into a build-and-fix approach. We must still focus rigorous attention on each stage, ensuring the quality of the overall product.

> Added flexibility in the development process must not be allowed to degenerate into a build-and-fix approach.
>
> **key concept**

An *iterative development process* is one that allows a software developer to cycle through the different development activities. Earlier stages can be formally revisited, allowing proper changes to be made. Figure 10.6 shows an initial version of an iterative development process.

The process in Fig. 10.6 is essentially the waterfall model leveled out to permit backtracking. That is, when new information is uncovered that changes the requirements or design, we have a way to formally go back and modify the affected stages. The appropriate documents are updated to reflect these new decisions.

The danger of backtracking is that the developer might rely on it too much. This model is not intended to reduce the amount of effort that goes into developing the initial requirements before starting on the design. Likewise, the design

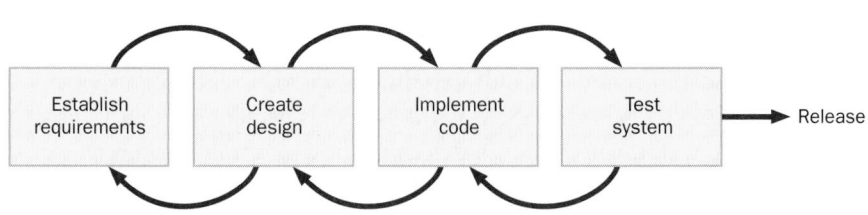

figure 10.6   An iterative development process

of a program should still be well established before beginning implementation. Backtracking activity should primarily be used to correct problems uncovered in later stages.

Any realistic development model will include the prospect of revisiting previous activities in some iterative manner. It will also include formal test strategies and prototyping, as we discuss in the next sections.

10.1 testing

The term *testing* can be applied in many ways to software development. Testing certainly includes its traditional definition: the act of running a completed program with various inputs to discover problems. But it also includes any evaluation that is performed by human or machine to assess the quality of the developing system. These evaluations should occur long before a single line of code is written.

Before moving on to the next stage of the development process, the results of the current stage should be evaluated. For instance, before moving on to creating a design, the requirements should be carefully evaluated to ensure that they are complete, consistent, and unambiguous. Prior to implementation, the design should be evaluated to make sure that each requirement is adequately addressed.

walkthroughs

One technique used to evaluate design or code is called a *walkthrough,* which is a meeting in which several people carefully review a design document or section of code. Presenting our design or code to others causes us to think more carefully about it and permits others to share their suggestions with us. The participants discuss its merits and problems, and create a list of issues that must be addressed. The goal of a walkthrough is to identify problems, not to solve them, which usually takes much more time.

> **key concept**
>
> A design or code walkthrough is a meeting in which several people review and critique a software design or implementation.

A design walkthrough should determine whether the requirements are addressed. It should also assess the way the system is decomposed into classes and objects. A code walkthrough should determine how faithfully the design satisfies the requirements and how faithfully the implementation represents the design. It should identify any specific problems that would cause the design or the implementation to fail in its responsibilities.

defect testing

As we mentioned in Chapter 3, the goal of testing is to find errors. This can generally be referred to as *defect testing*. With that goal in mind, a good test is one that uncovers any deficiencies in a program. This might seem strange because we ultimately don't want to have problems in our system. But keep in mind that errors almost certainly exist. Our testing efforts should make every attempt to find them. We want to increase the reliability of our program by finding and fixing the errors that exist, rather than letting users discover them.

> **key concept**
> The goal of testing is to find errors; therefore a good test is one that uncovers the deficiencies in a program.

It is possible to prove that a program is correct, but that technique is enormously complex for large systems, and errors can be made in the proof itself. Therefore, we generally rely on testing to determine the quality of a program. We run specific tests in an attempt to find problems. As more tests are run and fewer errors are found, our confidence in a program increases.

A *test case* is a set of inputs, user actions, or other initial conditions, and the expected output. A test case should be appropriately documented so that it can be repeated later as needed. Developers often create a complete *test suite,* which is a set of test cases that cover various aspects of the system.

Because programs operate on a large number of possible inputs, it is not feasible to create test cases for all possible input or user actions. Nor is it usually necessary to test every single situation. Two specific test cases may be so similar that they actually do not test unique aspects of the program. To do both would be a wasted effort. We'd rather execute a test case that stresses the program in some new way. Therefore, we want to choose our test cases carefully. To that end, let's examine two approaches to defect testing: black-box testing and white-box testing.

> **key concept**
> Because programs operate on a large number of possible inputs, it is not feasible to create test cases for all possible input or user actions.

As the name implies, *black-box testing* treats the thing being tested as a black box. That is, test cases are developed without regard to the internal workings. Black-box tests are based on inputs and outputs. An entire program can be tested using a black-box technique, in which case the inputs are the user-provided information and user actions such as button pushes. A test case is successful only if the input produces the expected output. A single class can also be tested using a black-box technique, which focuses on the system interface (its public methods) of the class. Certain parameters are passed in, producing certain results. Black-box test cases are often derived directly from the requirements of the system or from the stated purpose of a method.

The input data for a black-box test case are often selected by defining equivalence categories. An *equivalence category* is a collection of inputs that are expected to produce similar outputs. Generally, if a method will work for one value in the equivalence category, we have every reason to believe it will work for the others. For example, the input to a method that computes the square root of an integer can be divided into two equivalence categories: nonnegative integers and negative integers. If it works appropriately for one nonnegative value, it will likely work for all nonnegative values. Likewise, if it works appropriately for one negative value, it will likely work for all negative values.

Equivalence categories have defined boundaries. Because all values of an equivalence category essentially test the same features of a program, only one test case inside the equivalence boundary is needed. However, because programming often produces "off by one" errors, the values on and around the boundary should be tested exhaustively. For an integer boundary, a good test suite would include at least the exact value of the boundary, the boundary minus 1, and the boundary plus 1. Test cases that use these cases, plus at least one from within the general field of the category should be defined.

Let's look at an example. Consider a method whose purpose is to validate that a particular integer value is in the range 0 and 99, inclusive. There are three equivalence categories in this case: values below 0, values in the range of 0 to 99, and values above 99. Black-box testing dictates that we use test values that surround and fall on the boundaries, as well as some general values from the equivalence categories. Therefore, a set of black-box test cases for this situation might be: −500, −1, 0, 1, 50, 98, 99, 100, and 500.

White-box testing, also known as *glass-box testing,* exercises the internal structure and implementation of a method. A white-box test case is based on the logic of the code. The goal is to ensure that every path through a program is executed at least once. A white-box test maps the possible paths through the code and ensures that the test cases cause every path to be executed. This type of testing is often called *statement coverage.*

Paths through code are controlled by various control flow statements that use conditional expressions, such as `if` statements. In order to have every path through the program executed at least once, the input data values for the test cases need to control the values for the conditional expressions. The input data of one or more test cases should cause the condition of an `if` statement to evaluate to true in at least one case and to false in at least one case. Covering both true and false values in an `if` statement guarantees that both the paths through the `if` statement will be executed. Similar situations can be created for loops and other constructs.

In both black-box and white-box testing, the expected output for each test should be established prior to running the test. It's too easy to be persuaded that the results of a test are appropriate if you haven't first carefully determined what the results should be.

10.2 prototypes

A *prototype* is a program or a representation of a program that is created to explore particular characteristics of the proposed or evolving system. Sometimes a programmer simply doesn't know how to accomplish a particular task, whether a certain requirement is feasible, or whether the user interface is acceptable to the client. Prototypes can be used to explore all of these issues instead of proceeding on an assumption that may later prove unwise.

> **key concept**
>
> A prototype can be used to explore the feasibility of a decision instead of proceeding on an assumption that may later prove unwise.

For example, a programmer might have no experience using a particular set of classes provided by a library. Before committing to its use, the programmer may produce a small program that exercises the classes in order to establish that they are a viable choice for use, providing the functionality needed in an acceptable manner. If the classes prove unreasonable, the design could then take into account that new classes must be developed from scratch.

Another prototype might be created to show a simplified version of the user interface. The developer and the client can then discuss the interaction between the user and the program to determine whether it is acceptable. Keep in mind that this prototype need not be a program. A set of diagrams that show the layout of buttons and other components may be enough to explore the issues involved.

Another prototype might be created to test the feasibility of a specific requirement. For example, suppose the requirements state that the program should perform a certain task and print the results within one second. A prototype that explores this issue would focus exclusively on the ability to satisfy that requirement. If it can be accomplished, the design can proceed with confidence; if not, the feasibility of the requirements can be questioned. It is better to question requirements early because any changes might have a significant impact on the entire system.

A prototype often calls attention to problems that a list of requirements might obscure or miss altogether. A prototype can be used to reject certain design or implementation decisions before they become a problem, and it can clarify the user's intentions. It is not uncommon for a client to make a statement such as: "I know that's what I said I wanted, but that's not what I meant."

throw-away vs. evolutionary prototypes

Often, a prototype is a "quick-and-dirty" test of an idea or concept. As such, a prototype is created with little regard to software engineering principles, and not intended to be a part of the final system. This type of prototype is sometimes called a *throw-away prototype* because once it has been written and has served its purpose, it is discarded.

A throw-away prototype takes relatively little effort to develop because good design and coding techniques are not a priority. Nevertheless, it provides an invaluable service by helping the developer avoid improper and costly decisions.

The problem with a throw-away prototype is that programmers sometimes feel like they're wasting the effort it took to create it and want to incorporate the prototype into their final system. Sometimes they are pressured to do so by managers or clients who don't know any better. The solution to this problem is to realize that the prototype has served its purpose and that its inclusion at this point will likely cause more problems than it solves. We should take what we learn from a throw-away prototype and incorporate that knowledge into a sound design.

An *evolutionary prototype*, on the other hand, is carefully designed. It takes longer to develop than a throw-away version but can be incorporated into the final product with confidence. An evolutionary prototype serves two purposes: it allows specific aspects of a program to be explored, and if that exploration proves fruitful, it can be made part of an evolving software system. This concept is the underlying basis of evolutionary development, which has become one of the most popular and successful development models. We discuss evolutionary development in detail next.

10.3 evolutionary development

Let's examine a realistic development model that specifically takes object-oriented issues into account. Figure 10.7 depicts this object-oriented software development process. A key part of this model is the *refinement cycle*. Each refinement focuses on fleshing out one aspect of the overall system. Part or all of a refinement can also be devoted to addressing problems that were established during the testing of a previous refinement. The system evolves rather than being created in one large effort. Therefore, not only is this process iterative, it is *evolutionary*.

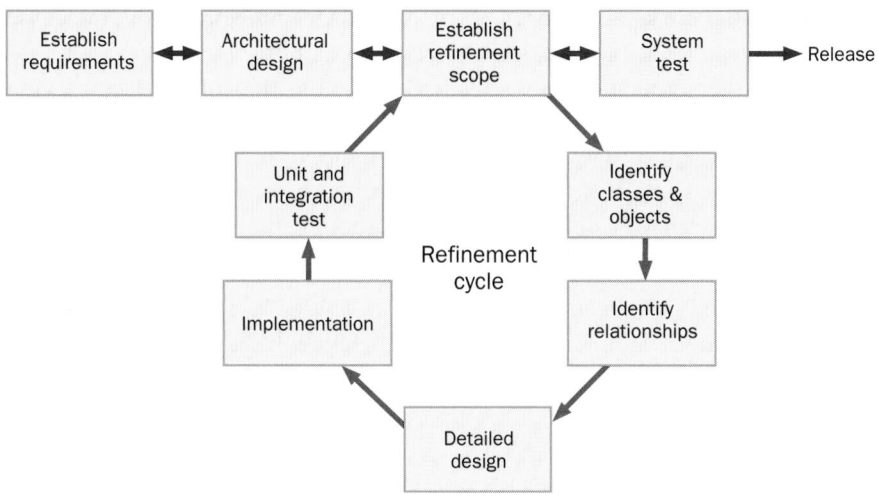

figure 10.7   An object-oriented software development process

The refinement cycle is performed many times until all parts of a program are completed, tested, and integrated. At this point the entire system is tested and the software is released to the user. Usually, the iterations continue until the program is considered to be "good enough" for release. What "good enough" means is different for every situation and depends in part on the client's expectations.

In this development model, design activity is divided into multiple steps. An *architectural design* (also called a high-level design) establishes the general structure and responsibilities of system elements; it is done at the beginning of the software development process. The refinement stages include various design issues, including identifying the classes and objects needed in the refinement as well as the relationships between them. The refinement cycle also includes a *detailed design* stage, which focuses on specific issues such as the methods and algorithms used in a particular class.

> **key concept**
>
> An architectural design establishes the general structure of a system, whereas a detailed design focuses on specific methods and algorithms.

Because the design activities are divided into subtasks, the interactions between design and implementation are more controlled and focused. Because each refinement concentrates on one aspect of a program, such as designing the user interface, the design steps in the refinement are focused on only that aspect. This reduces the overall level of complexity the design needs to address during each refinement.

By following these smaller design efforts with their implementation, the consequences of design decisions are detected at a more appropriate time, soon after the design of that refinement is completed but before the entire design is completed. In this way, the information uncovered during implementation can affect changes in the design of the current refinement and all future refinements. Also, by defining refinements that are independent of each other, several refinements can be done in parallel by different implementation teams.

Object-oriented programming is particularly well suited for this approach since it supports many types of abstraction. These abstraction techniques make it possible for the design and implementation to work hand-in-hand. By using techniques such as encapsulation to isolate what has not yet been specified by a refinement, an implementation for a refinement can be completed and tested.

Let's examine the details of each step in the refinement cycle.

establish refinement scope

The *refinement scope* is the set of objectives to be addressed in a particular refinement. The scope can be very broad, addressing a large portion of a program, or it might be focused on a particular detail of the program. Typical refinements might include the following:

- Create part of the user interface for the program.
- Develop a particular functional feature of the program.
- Test the feasibility of a particular program requirement.
- Establish a specific algorithm to be used in the program.
- Develop utility classes to provide general support for the program.
- Add non-essential but helpful features to the program.

The scope of a particular refinement is a tradeoff between the resources available to write the program and the complexity of the program. If there are many programmers that will be writing and designing the parts of a particular program, the scope of one refinement for this team of programmers can be larger than if there is only one programmer. The task of each member of the team is defined to assure that the goals of the refinement cycle will be achieved. In any case, the goals of each refinement must be well defined.

Refinements allow a programmer to focus on specific issues without having to embrace the complexities of the entire system at once. Careful separation of refinement responsibilities can significantly facilitate the overall development effort. After the scope of the refinement has been established and documented, the design process can begin.

identifying classes and objects

At this stage, we must first determine which requirements relate to the current refinement and then associate them with the part of the software that will fulfill that requirement. To do this, we must expand the architectural design of the system in ways that address the goals of the particular refinement. We must determine what classes and objects we need to fulfill the refinement goals and assign functional responsibilities to each.

It is usually easier to brainstorm about some of the objects we need and generalize to determine the classes from which they will be instantiated. Keep in mind that although an object tends to be a noun (a person, place, or thing), it does not have to represent something tangible. An error and a midterm score are perfectly good objects, even though we can't touch them.

Candidates for objects can come in a variety of categories. The following list shows some categories you should consider when attempting to identify objects in which you are interested. Examples of each category are shown in parentheses.

- physical things (ball, book, car)
- people (student, clerk, author)
- places (room, school, airport)
- containers of things (cash register, bookcase, transaction list)
- occurrences (sale, meeting, accident)
- information stores (catalog, ledger, event log)

Some of these categories overlap, which is fine. We're not trying to categorize the objects at this point; we're trying to use categories to uncover the need to represent the object. Any means that we can use to discover them is helpful.

Another technique for identifying objects is to review the requirements document and highlight the noun phrases. Each of these phrases could indicate an object or class that we may want to represent. Likewise, the verb phrases in the document might indicate a service that an object should provide. Don't hesitate to write down anything that may be a candidate object. It is better to identify more objects than we need than to forget a crucial one. We can always discard it later.

> **key concept**
> One way to identify objects is to consider various object categories; another is to examine the noun phrases of the requirements document.

Once we have the objects identified, we need to consider the classes used to define them. Often, the classes for some objects will be obvious. In other cases, thought needs to be put into the best way to represent them. For example, we may initially assume that a Student class is sufficient to represent the students in our system, only to discover after some thought that we'd be better off with two separate classes to distinguish graduate students from undergraduate students.

identifying relationships

Once a basic set of classes and objects is identified, we need to identify the way in which each class relates to the others. As we've discussed at various points in the book, there are three primary relationships to consider:

- general association (uses)
- aggregation (has-a)
- inheritance (is-a)

General relationships between classes and objects are called associations, as we discussed in Chapter 4. Associated objects often use each other for the services they provide. That is, one will likely invoke one or more methods of another. For example, a Driver object might invoke the accelerate method of the Car class.

We also discussed the aggregation relationship in Chapter 4. Aggregation is sometimes referred to as composition because some objects contain references to other objects, and therefore one object can be thought of as part of another. Sometimes the cardinality of the relationship should be noted, indicating the numeric relationship between the objects. For example, a Car could have between one and four Passenger objects associated with it.

We discussed the inheritance relationship in detail in Chapter 7. Sometimes a proper inheritance relationship is difficult to see. In particular, we should specifically think about the common characteristics of objects. This may lead to the creation of a new class whose sole purpose is to serve as the parent of the others, gathering common data and methods in one place. For example, a Vehicle class may serve well as the parent of the Car class and the Boat class, even though we have no intention of instantiating any objects of class Vehicle.

All of these relationships can be described using UML class diagrams. We've used class diagrams in other chapters. UML diagrams are even more important when developing large software systems in which it is crucial to carefully determine and capture the design of a program.

detailed design

Once we understand how the program will work with respect to classes and objects, we need to flesh out the details. We need to identify all of the methods of a class. These include all the methods necessary to satisfy the assumptions of any previous refinement phases. Though we are primarily concerned with public methods, we can also identify methods that will be used to support the others.

We must determine the data that each class and object will contain, and the manner in which that data will be modified. That includes the manner in which the data will be given an initial value and any methods that will change the value. It is not imperative that every piece of data be painstakingly identified at this stage, but the key elements should be.

Finally, the algorithms of any methods that perform unusual or crucial tasks should be carefully thought out and documented. Pseudocode is often a good choice for capturing these design decisions.

implementation

The implementation should be a concrete representation of the design. If we've done a good job with previous steps, the implementation of the classes should come together nicely. As we mentioned in Chapter 3, implementation should be the least creative part of the process. Any important decisions should have been made earlier. Of course, this isn't always the case, and some problems will arise. Care should be taken to follow all coding guidelines and to produce readable, clear source code.

If serious obstacles are discovered during implementation, the impact on the overall system should be considered. The appropriate decision at this point may be to resolve the issue in a future refinement.

Often during a refinement, a program will need to use a class, method, or object that is not part of the current refinement. Because we need to test the current refinement, we often use a *stub* object or method as a placeholder. A stub provides enough information for the rest of the refinement code to work. It is replaced in a future refinement with a fully implemented version.

For example, perhaps the system design includes a method that will display a dialog box and then accept and validate some user input. The current refinement calls the method, but it has not yet been created. For testing purposes, it can be temporarily replaced with a stub method that simply returns a particular integer value.

We should try to avoid defining our refinements so that such dependencies exist. However, other more important issues sometimes require that we deal with these situations.

unit and integration testing

Until now we've primarily concentrated on testing an entire program. For smaller programs, that may be sufficient. As our programs grow, however, it is important to focus on specific pieces and the nuances involved in making those pieces interact.

Once the classes for a particular refinement are written, they must be tested. Initially, the individual pieces that were created should be tested separately. A test that specifically targets one particular piece of a system, such as a class or method, is called a *unit test*.

Eventually, the classes of the refinement are integrated together and the entire refinement is integrated with previous refinements. Integrating one piece of code with another will often uncover errors, even if the code seemed to work correctly on its own. Separate testing efforts should be made to specifically explore the interaction among the integrated elements. Such a test is called an *integration test*. Full system testing is really just the ultimate integration test.

10.4   the PaintBox project

Let's examine a larger software development project than any other described in this text. As we explore this program, we will walk through most of the steps described in the evolutionary development model that are described in previous sections of this chapter.

Our example program allows the user to create drawings with various shapes and colors. This type of project encompasses a variety of issues that are commonly found in large-scale software development and provides a good basis for exploring our development model. We call this example the PaintBox project.

PaintBox requirements

Suppose the client provides the following set of initial requirements. The program will:

- Present a graphical user interface that is primarily mouse driven for all user actions.
- Allow the user to draw lines, ovals, circles, rectangles, and squares.
- Allow the user to change the drawing color.
- Display the current drawing color.
- Allow the user to fill a shape, except for a line, with a color.
- Allow the user to select a shape in order to move it, modify its color, or reshape it.
- Allow the user to cut, copy, and paste individual shapes in a drawing.
- Allow the user to save a drawing in a file and load a previously stored drawing from a file for further editing.
- Allow the user to begin a new drawing at any time.

After examining these general requirements, we might sit down with the client and discuss some of the details to ensure that there are no misunderstandings. We might create a new requirements document that gets much more specific about the issues involved.

During these interactions with the client, we might create a sketch, such as the one shown in Fig. 10.8, of a user interface for the system. This sketch serves as a basic prototype of the interface, and gives us something to refer to in our discussions with the client. For other systems there may be many such sketches for each screen of the program.

The interface sketch shows a main drawing area where the user will create a drawing. The top edge contains a set of buttons used to select various tools, such as the oval tool to draw an oval or circle, the color tool to change the current drawing color, and a select tool to select a previously drawn shape in order to modify or move it. Two menu headings are shown along the top edge. The File menu contains operations to begin a new drawing, save a drawing, and exit the program. The Edit menu contains editing operations such as cut, copy, and paste.

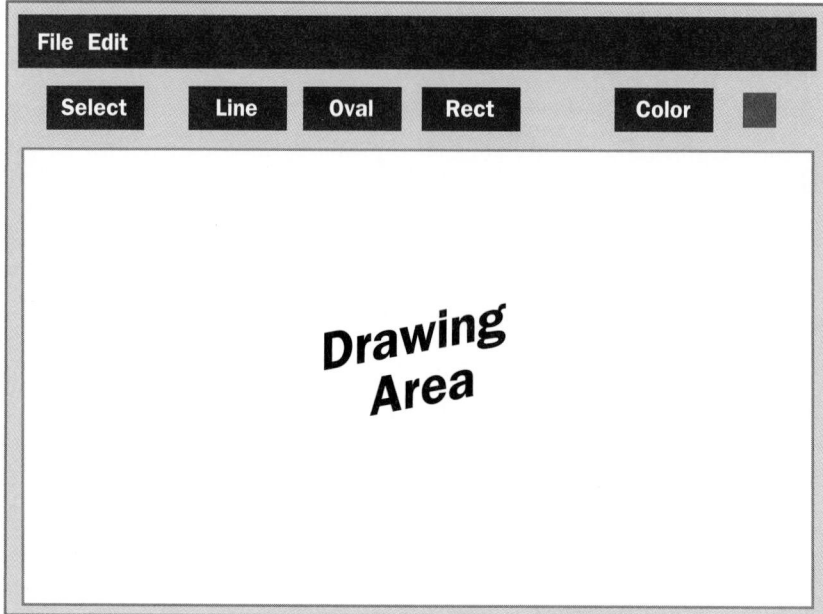

figure 10.8   A sketch of the user interface for the `PaintBox` program

As a result of the discussions with the client, several additional requirements issues are established:

- There is no need to have separate user interactions for a circle or square because they are subsets of ovals and rectangles, respectively.
- The user should also be able to create polyline shapes.
- The buttons used to select drawing tools should have icons instead of words.
- The system should make a distinction between the stroke color (the outline) and the fill color (the interior) of a shape. Therefore, each shape will have a separate stroke and fill color. Lines and polylines will have only a stroke color because they cannot be filled.
- An option to save a drawing under a particular name should be provided (the traditional "save as" operation).

- Traditional keyboard shortcuts for operations such as cut, copy, and paste should be included.
- The system should perform checks to ensure that the user does not lose unsaved changes to a drawing.
- The system should present an initial "splash screen" to introduce the program when it is executed.

These issues must be integrated into the formal description of the requirements document for the project. Several discussions with the client, with additional screen sketches, may be necessary before we have an accurate and solid set of program requirements. If we proceed to design and implementation too quickly, we run the risk of degenerating our process into the build-and-fix approach.

PaintBox architectural design

After we have clarified the requirements with the client, we can begin to think about some of the elements of the architectural design of the system. For example, many of the classes needed for the user interface can come from the Java standard class library in the Swing package.

It also seems reasonable that a separate class could be used to represent each shape type. Further, each individually drawn shape should be an instantiation of the appropriate shape class. For example, we could define an Oval class to represent an oval, a Line class to represent a line, and so on. Each class should be responsible for keeping track of the information it needs to define it, and it should provide methods to draw itself.

A drawing may be composed of many shapes, so we need a way to keep track of all of them. An ArrayList might be a good choice for this. As each new shape is drawn, we can add the object that represents it to the list. The list will also inherently define the order in which shapes are drawn. Since some shapes will be drawn on top of others, the list will also keep track of the order in which shapes are "stacked."

The process of defining an architectural design could take a while. The key is to make the most important and fundamental decisions that will affect the entire system without skipping ahead to decisions that are better left to individual refinements of the system.

PaintBox refinements

After some consideration, we might decide that the evolution of the PaintBox project could be broken down into the following refinement steps:

> Establish the basic user interface.
> Allow the user to draw basic shapes using different stroke colors.
> Allow the user to cut, copy, and paste shapes.
> Allow the user to select, move, and fill shapes.
> Allow the user to modify the dimensions of shapes.
> Allow the user to save and reload drawings.
> Include final touches such as the splash screen.

Note, first of all, that these refinements focus on breaking down the functionality of the system. Additional refinements may be necessary as we get into the iterative process. For instance, we may decide that we need a refinement to address problems that were discovered in previous refinements.

The listed refinements could have been broken down further. For example, one refinement could have been devoted to the ability to draw one particular type of shape. The level of refinement, just like many other decisions when developing a software system, is a judgment call. The developer must decide what is best in any particular situation.

The order in which we tackle the refinements is also important. The user interface refinement seems to be a logical first step because all other activity relies on it. We may decide that the ability to save and reload a drawing would be nice to have early for testing purposes. We might also note that being able to select an object is fundamental to operations such as move and cut/copy/paste. After further analysis, we end up with the set of refinements shown in Fig. 10.9.

PaintBox refinement #1

Most of the classes used for the interface come from predefined libraries. We use Swing technology whenever reasonable. For example, we can use a JPanel for the overall interface space, as well as separate JPanel objects to organize the button tools and the drawing area. The JButton class will serve well for the buttons. Classes such as JMenuBar and JMenuItem will serve to implement the menus.

Refinement	Description
1	Present the basic graphical user interface, including the main frame, buttons, menus, menu items, and the drawing area. The select and shape buttons work together as a radio button set (only one can be chosen at a time). No functionality for these interface elements is included at this time. Exiting the program is provided only by the frame's window close button.
2	Add support for drawing the four basic shapes: lines, ovals, rectangles, and polylines. The chosen shape button determines what shape is drawn. The stroke color button can be used to set the stroke color for the next shape drawn. The color button causes a separate dialog box to appear to allow color selection.
3	Add support for saving and loading drawings. This includes the functionality of the *open, save,* and *save as* File menu items. When the *open, new,* or *exit* File menu options are chosen, check to see if the current drawing has been modified since last saved, and if so prompt to see if the user wants to save the drawing.
4	Provide the ability to select and move shapes on the drawing surface. Simple graphic selection blocks should be presented on the shape's outline to indicate the currently selected shape. Once selected, the mouse can be used to drag the shape to another location on the drawing surface.
5	Add the functionality for the *cut, copy* and *paste* Edit menu items. Once selected, a shape can be cut or copied. Once a shape has been cut or copied, it can be pasted (perhaps multiple times) onto the drawing surface at a fixed offset to the original position. Edit menu items that are not valid at any given time are disabled. For example, unless a shape is selected, the cut and copy menu items cannot be chosen.
6	Add support for filling and reshaping a shape. Once a shape has been selected, the fill color button can be used to determine its fill color. A menu item on the Edit menu can be used to remove the fill of any filled object (make it transparent). The currently selected shape will now have a reshape handle that can be used to change the dimensions of the shape.
7	Add some extra functionality to the program. These additions include a splash screen that appears when the system is initially executed, an *about* dialog box, keyboard shortcuts for all menu items, and packaging the application into an executable JAR file.

figure 10.9   Functional refinements for the PaintBox project

Figure 10.10 shows a class diagram that represents the classes important to the first refinement of the PaintBox project. Note that it does not include all classes that might be needed, nor does it address anything other than the needs of this one refinement. We'll create additional diagrams that augment our understanding of the system design as further refinements are developed.

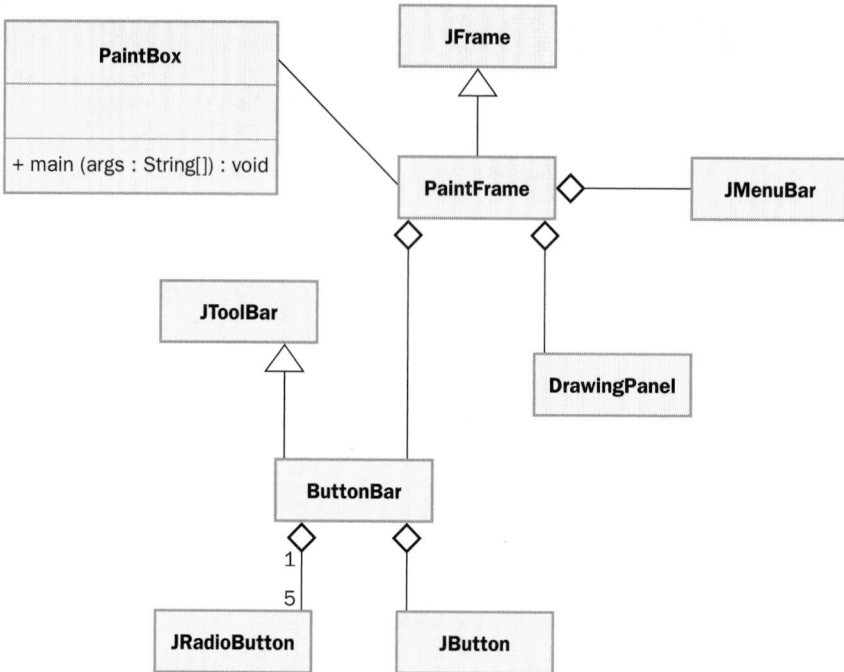

figure 10.10   A class diagram for the interface refinement of the `PaintBox` project

The detailed design and implementation for the interface refinement might develop similarly to other graphical projects we've developed in previous chapters. We can create listener objects and methods as appropriate but not concern ourselves with their inner workings at this time. That is, our focus in this refinement is to present the user interface, not create any of the functionality behind the interface. During the development of this refinement, we modify the details of the user interface until it appears just the way we'd like it.

At the end of the first refinement, we are left with a completely implemented program that presents only the user interface. The buttons do nothing when pushed and the menu items do nothing when selected. We have no way of creating a drawing yet.

What we do have, however, is a complete entity that has been debugged and tested to the level of this refinement. We may show it to the client at this point and get further input. Any changes that result from these discussions can be incorporated into future refinements. Figure 10.11 shows the `PaintBox` program after the first refinement has been completed.

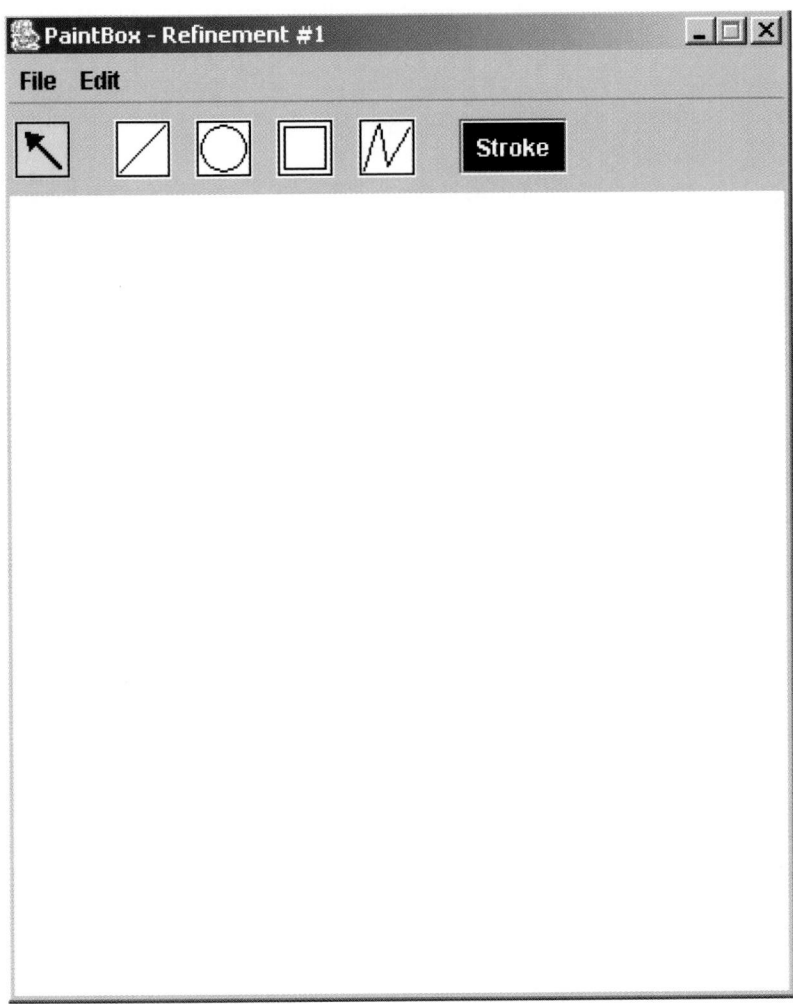

figure 10.11   The PaintBox program after refinement #1 is complete

PaintBox refinement #2

The next refinement to address is the ability to draw basic shapes, because all other operations use drawn shapes in one way or another. Therefore, in this refinement we focus on providing the processing power behind the buttons that draw shapes and specify color.

Most of the objects and classes that we will use in this refinement are not predefined as they were in the interface refinement. We might consider using the `Rectangle` class from the Java standard class library, but on further investigation we realize that its role is not really consistent with our goals. In addition, no other classes are defined for the other shapes we need.

So, as we envisioned in our architectural design, we consider having one class per shape type: `Line`, `Oval`, `Rect`, and `Poly`. Remember that circles and squares will just be specific instances of the `Oval` and `Rect` classes, respectively. Each shape class will have a `draw` method that draws that kind of shape on the screen.

Now let's consider the kind of information that each shape needs to store to be able to draw itself. A line needs two points: a starting point and an ending point. Each polyline, on the other hand, needs a list of points to define the start and end points of each line segment. Both ovals and rectangles are defined by a bounded rectangle, storing an upper left corner and the width and height of the shape.

This analysis leads to the conclusion that `Oval` and `Rect` objects have some common characteristics that we could exploit using inheritance. They could both, for instance, be derived from a class called `BoundedShape`. Furthermore, because all shapes have to be stored in the `ArrayList` object that we'll use to keep track of the entire drawing, it would simplify the refinement to have a generic `Shape` class from which all drawn shapes are derived.

The `Shape` and `BoundedShape` classes are used for organizational purposes. We do not intend to instantiate them; therefore they probably should be abstract classes. In fact, if we define an `abstract` method called `draw` in the `Shape` class, we could capitalize on polymorphism to simplify the drawing of the shapes in the drawing area. A loop can move through the `ArrayList`, having each shape (whatever it may be) draw itself.

After some consideration, we achieve the class diagram shown in Fig. 10.12. This diagram specifically represents the classes important to the second refinement of the `PaintBox` project.

Selecting a current color can be relegated to the `JColorChooser` component provided by the Swing package. The color button will bring up the `JColorChooser` dialog box and respond accordingly to the user's selection.

Multiple shapes will accumulate on the drawing surface. We could define a class to serve as a collection of the drawn shape objects. It could use an `ArrayList` to keep track of the list of shapes. Whenever the drawing area needs to be refreshed, we can iterate through the list of shapes and draw each one in turn.

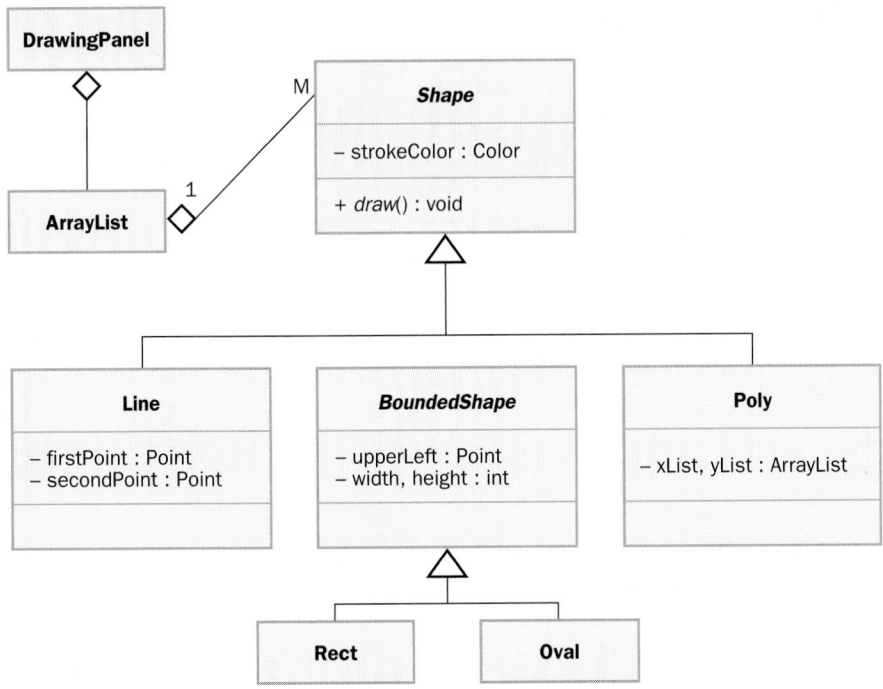

figure 10.12 A class diagram for the second refinement of the PaintBox project

Figure 10.13 shows the PaintBox program after the first two refinements have been completed. Once again, we could visit with the client at this point to determine whether the evolution of the system meets with his or her satisfaction.

remaining PaintBox refinements

For space reasons, the code for the various PaintBox refinements is not presented in the text. The full implementation of the first two refinements can be downloaded from the book's Web site. The remaining refinements are left as projects.

figure 10.13   The PaintBox program after the interface and shapes refinements

---

web
bonus

The program code for the PaintBox project can be obtained from the book's Web site.

The refinements of the `PaintBox` program continue until all requirement issues and problems have been addressed. This type of evolutionary development is crucial for medium- and large-scale development efforts.

Figure 10.14 shows the `PaintBox` program after all of the seven refinements described in this chapter have been completed.

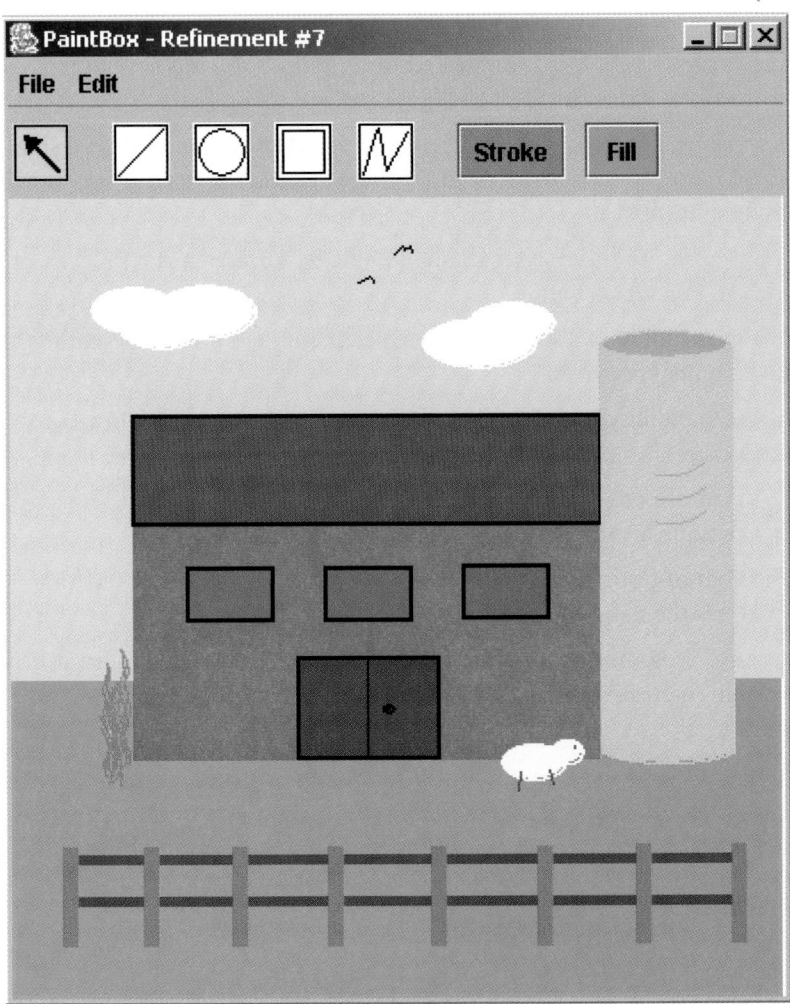

figure 10.14   The completed `PaintBox` program

summary of
key concepts

- Maintaining software is the process of modifying a program in order to enhance it or eliminate deficiencies.

- Often the maintainers of a program are not the program's original developers; thus maintainers must be able to understand a program that they didn't design.

- The earlier a problem is discovered during the software development process, the easier and less costly it is to correct.

- A working program is not necessarily a good program. Our goal should be to minimize the efforts required to create and maintain a program for the long term.

- A program produced using the build-and-fix approach is a product of ad hoc, reckless activities.

- The waterfall model does not recognize the inherent iterative nature of development activities.

- Added flexibility in the development process must not be allowed to degenerate into a build-and-fix approach.

- A design or code walkthrough is a meeting in which several people review and critique a software design or implementation.

- The goal of testing is to find errors; therefore a good test is one that uncovers the deficiencies in a program.

- Because programs operate on a large number of possible inputs, it is not feasible to create test cases for all possible input or user actions.

- Test cases can be organized into equivalence categories to get the most value out of the limited number of tests conducted.

- A prototype can be used to explore the feasibility of a decision instead of proceeding on an assumption that may later prove unwise.

- A refinement focuses on a single aspect of a program, such as the user interface or a particular algorithm.

- An architectural design establishes the general structure of a system, whereas a detailed design focuses on specific methods and algorithms.

- Object-oriented programming is particularly well suited for the refinement process because it supports many types of abstraction, such as modularity and encapsulation.

▶ The scope of a refinement is a tradeoff between the resources available to write the program and the complexity of the program.

▶ One way to identify objects is to consider various object categories; another is to examine the noun phrases of the requirements document.

self-review questions

10.1 What is the relationship between development effort and maintenance effort?

10.2 Describe the build-and-fix approach to software development.

10.3 What is the main problem with the waterfall model?

10.4 What is a code walkthrough?

10.5 How is white-box testing different from black-box testing?

10.6 What is a prototype?

10.7 What is evolutionary software development?

10.8 What is a program refinement?

10.9 What refinements might come up during the evolutionary process?

exercises

10.1 Develop a UML class diagram that captures the design of refinement #3 of the PaintBox project as described in Fig. 10.9.

10.2 Develop a UML class diagram that captures the design of refinement #4 of the PaintBox project as described in Fig. 10.9.

10.3 Develop a UML class diagram that captures the design of refinement #5 of the PaintBox project as described in Fig. 10.9.

10.4 Develop a UML class diagram that captures the design of refinement #6 of the PaintBox project as described in Fig. 10.9.

10.5 Develop a UML class diagram that captures the design of refinement #7 of the PaintBox project as described in Fig. 10.9.

10.6 Define the black-box testing equivalence categories for the Wages program in Chapter 3 and determine a set of appropriate test cases.

10.7 Determine a white-box set of test cases for the Wages program in Chapter 3.

10.8   Define the black-box testing equivalence categories for the `WinPercentage` program in Chapter 3 and determine a set of appropriate test cases.

10.9   Determine a white-box set of test cases for the `WinPercentage` program in Chapter 3.

10.10 Consider the development of a software program to perform library book management. The system should be able to catalog all books, record books being borrowed and returned, and deal with associated fines related to books returned late.

   a. Identify several possible refinements, such as book-borrowing, for the system.

   b. Identify several objects and classes for the book-borrowing refinement.

   c. Identify possible relationships between classes and objects in the book-borrowing refinement.

   d. Draw a UML class diagram for the book-borrowing refinement.

10.11 Consider the development of a software program to manage a household budget. The system should be able to apply debits and credits, add and remove budget items, and produce a report describing the current status.

   a. Identify several possible refinements, such as adding budget items, for the system.

   b. Identify several objects and classes for the budget item refinement.

   c. Identify possible relationships between classes and objects in the budget item refinement.

   d. Draw a UML class diagram for the budget item refinement.

10.12 Consider the development of a software program to simulate an airport. The system should be able to simulate takeoffs and landings of planes on different runways, simulate an air-traffic controller's screen, and allow an operator to control the takeoff, landing, and flying attributes of planes (such as course and speed).

   a. Identify several possible refinements, such as plane simulation, for the system.

   b. Identify several objects and classes for the plane-simulation refinement.

c. Identify possible relationships among classes and objects in the plane-simulation refinement.

d. Draw a UML class diagram for the plane-simulation refinement.

programming projects

10.1 Develop `PaintBox` refinement #3 as defined in Fig. 10.9 to save and load drawings.

10.2 Develop `PaintBox` refinement #4 as defined in Fig. 10.9 to select and move drawn shapes.

10.3 Develop `PaintBox` refinement #5 as defined in Fig. 10.9 to copy, cut, and paste shapes.

10.4 Develop `PaintBox` refinement #6 as defined in Fig. 10.9 to fill and reshape shapes.

10.5 Develop `PaintBox` refinement #7 as defined in Fig. 10.9 to add final touches.

10.6 Develop an additional `PaintBox` refinement of your own design.

answers to self-review questions

10.1 Much more effort is traditionally put into maintenance tasks than development tasks. Small, fundamental improvements in development efforts can greatly reduce the overall maintenance effort.

10.2 The build-and-fix approach is the ad hoc process of creating software without attention to important efforts such as requirements and design, then modifying the software until it reaches some minimal level of acceptance. It is not really a development model.

10.3 The traditional waterfall model assumes that development activities fundamentally progress in a linear fashion. The truth is that medium- and large-scale systems cannot be developed that way, and should be created using a model that allows backtracking as the system evolves.

10.4 A code walkthrough is a meeting in which developers carefully go over parts of a software system to search for problems.

10.5 White-box testing focuses on the internal details of a module (such as a method) to ensure that the logic of the module is thoroughly tested. Black-box testing focuses on different categories of input to determine if the predicted output is produced.

10.6 A prototype is a program, drawing, or mockup of some kind that allows the developer to explore an idea before committing to it in the developing system.

10.7 Evolutionary software development is a controlled iterative process that creates a program as a series of well-defined refinements. Evolutionary development acknowledges our limited ability to initially conceptualize all details of the program design and implementation.

10.8 Each refinement in an iterative development process focuses on one particular aspect of a software system. For example, one refinement may be to develop the user interface. A refinement allows a programmer to target a particular task while keeping the overall architectural design in mind.

10.9 A refinement might be defined dynamically during the evolution of a system to address some problems that were discovered in previous refinements.

Recursion is a powerful programming technique that provides elegant solutions to certain problems. This chapter provides an introduction to recursive processing. It contains an explanation of the basic concepts underlying recursion and then explores the use of recursion in programming. Several specific problems are solved using recursion, demonstrating its versatility, simplicity, and elegance.

chapter objectives

▶ Explain the underlying concepts of recursion.

▶ Examine recursive methods and unravel their processing steps.

▶ Define infinite recursion and discuss ways to avoid it.

▶ Explain when recursion should and should not be used.

▶ Demonstrate the use of recursion to solve problems.

11.0 recursive thinking

We've seen many times in previous examples that one method can call another method to accomplish a goal. What we haven't seen yet, however, is that a method can call itself. *Recursion* is a programming technique in which a method calls itself in order to fulfill its purpose. But before we get into the details of how we use recursion in a program, we need to explore the general concept of recursion. The ability to think recursively is essential to being able to use recursion as a programming technique.

In general, recursion is the process of defining something in terms of itself. For example, consider the following definition of the word *decoration*:

> **decoration:** n. any ornament or adornment used to decorate something

The word *decorate* is used to define the word *decoration*. You may recall your grade school teacher telling you to avoid such recursive definitions when explaining the meaning of a word. However, in many situations, recursion is an appropriate way to express an idea or definition. For example, suppose we wanted to formally define a list of one or more numbers, separated by commas. Such a list can be defined recursively as either a number or as a number followed by a comma followed by a list. This definition can be expressed as follows:

```
A List is a:  number
      or a:  number    comma    List
```

This recursive definition of *List* defines each of the following lists of numbers:

```
24, 88, 40, 37
96, 43
14, 64, 21, 69, 32, 93, 47, 81, 28, 45, 81, 52, 69
70
```

No matter how long a list is, the recursive definition describes it. A list of one element, such as in the last example, is defined completely by the first (non-recursive) part of the definition. For any list longer than one element, the recursive part of the definition (the part which refers to itself) is used as many times as necessary until the last element is reached. The last element in the list is always defined by the non-recursive part of the definition. Figure 11.1 shows how one particular list of numbers corresponds to the recursive definition of *List*.

LIST: number   comma   LIST

24   ,   88, 40, 37

                     number   comma   LIST

                         88   ,   40, 37

                                     number   comma   LIST

                                       40   ,   37

                                                number

                                                37

figure 11.1   Tracing the recursive definition of *List*

infinite recursion

Note that the definition of *List* contains one option that is recursive and one option that is not. The part of the definition that is not recursive is called the *base case*. If all options had a recursive component, the recursion would never end. For example, if the definition of *List* was simply "a number followed by a comma followed by a *List*," no list could ever end. This problem is called *infinite recursion*. It is similar to an infinite loop except that the "loop" occurs in the definition itself.

> Any recursive definition must have a non-recursive part, called the base case, which permits the recursion to eventually end.
>
> **key concept**

As in the infinite loop problem, a programmer must be careful to design algorithms so that they avoid infinite recursion. Any recursive definition must have a base case that does not result in a recursive option. The base case of the *List* definition is a single number that is not followed by anything. In other words, when the last number in the list is reached, the base case option terminates the recursive path.

recursion in math

Let's look at an example of recursion in mathematics. The value referred to as *N*! (pronounced *N factorial*) is defined for any positive integer *N* as the product of all integers between 1 and *N* inclusive. Therefore, 3! is defined as:

3! = 3*2*1 = 6

and 5! is defined as:

```
5!  =  5*4*3*2*1  =  120.
```

Mathematical formulas are often expressed recursively. The definition of $N!$ can be expressed recursively as:

```
1! = 1
N! = N * (N-1)! for N > 1
```

The base case of this definition is $1!$, which is defined as 1. All other values of $N!$ (for $N > 1$) are defined recursively as N times the value $(N-1)!$. The recursion is that the factorial function is defined in terms of the factorial function.

Using this definition, $50!$ is equal to $50 * 49!$. And $49!$ is equal to $49 * 48!$. And $48!$ is equal to $48 * 47!$. This process continues until we get to the base case of 1. Because $N!$ is defined only for positive integers, this definition is complete and will always conclude with the base case.

The next section describes how recursion is accomplished in programs.

11.1 recursive programming

Let's use a simple mathematical operation to demonstrate the concept of recursive programming. Consider the process of summing the values between 1 and N inclusive, where N is any positive integer. The sum of the values from 1 to N can be expressed as N plus the sum of the values from 1 to $N-1$. That sum can be expressed similarly, as shown in Fig. 11.2.

For example, the sum of the values between 1 and 20 is equal to 20 plus the sum of the values between 1 and 19. Continuing this approach, the sum of the values between 1 and 19 is equal to 19 plus the sum of the values between 1 and 18. This may sound like a strange way to think about this problem, but it is a straightforward example that can be used to demonstrate how recursion is programmed.

As we mentioned earlier, in Java, as in many other programming languages, a method can call itself. Each call to the method creates a new environment in which to work. That is, all local variables and parameters are newly defined with their own unique data space every time the method is called. Each parameter is

given an initial value based on the new call. Each time a method terminates, processing returns to the method that called it (which may be an earlier invocation of the same method). These rules are no different from those governing any "regular" method invocation.

$$\sum_{i=1}^{N} i \;=\; N \,+\, \sum_{i=1}^{N-1} i \;=\; N \,+\, N-1 \,+\, \sum_{i=1}^{N-2} i$$

$$=\; N \,+\, N-1 \,+\, N-2 \,+\, \sum_{i=1}^{N-3} i$$

$$\vdots$$

$$=\; N \,+\, N-1 \,+\, N-2 \,+\, \cdots \,+\, 2 \,+\, 1$$

figure 11.2   The sum of the numbers 1 through N, defined recursively

A recursive solution to the summation problem is defined by the following recursive method called sum:

```
// This method returns the sum of 1 to num
public int sum (int num)
{
   int result;
   if (num == 1)
      result = 1;
   else
      result = num + sum (num-1);
   return result;
}
```

Note that this method essentially embodies our recursive definition that the sum of the numbers between 1 and N is equal to N plus the sum of the numbers between 1 and N–1. The sum method is recursive because sum calls itself. The parameter passed to sum is decremented each time sum is called until it reaches the base case of 1. Recursive methods invariably contain an if-else statement, with one of the branches, usually the first one, representing the base case, as in this example.

Suppose the main method calls sum, passing it an initial value of 1, which is stored in the parameter num. Since num is equal to 1, the result of 1 is returned to main and no recursion occurs.

Now let's trace the execution of the sum method when it is passed an initial value of 2. Since num does not equal 1, sum is called again with an argument of num-1, or 1. This is a new call to the method sum, with a new parameter num and a new local variable result. Since this num is equal to 1 in this invocation, the result of 1 is returned without further recursive calls. Control returns to the first version of sum that was invoked. The return value of 1 is added to the initial value of num in that call to sum, which is 2. Therefore, result is assigned the value 3, which is returned to the main method. The method called from main correctly calculates the sum of the integers from 1 to 2 and returns the result of 3.

The base case in the summation example is when N equals 1, at which point no further recursive calls are made. The recursion begins to fold back into the earlier versions of the sum method, returning the appropriate value each time. Each return value contributes to the computation of the sum at the higher level. Without the base case, infinite recursion would result. Each call to a method requires additional memory space; therefore infinite recursion often results in a runtime error indicating that memory has been exhausted.

Trace the sum function with different initial values of num until this processing becomes familiar. Figure 11.3 illustrates the recursive calls when main invokes sum to determine the sum of the integers from 1 to 4. Each box represents a copy of the method as it is invoked, indicating the allocation of space to store the formal parameters and any local variables. Invocations are shown as solid lines, and returns as dotted lines. The return value result is shown at each step. The recur-

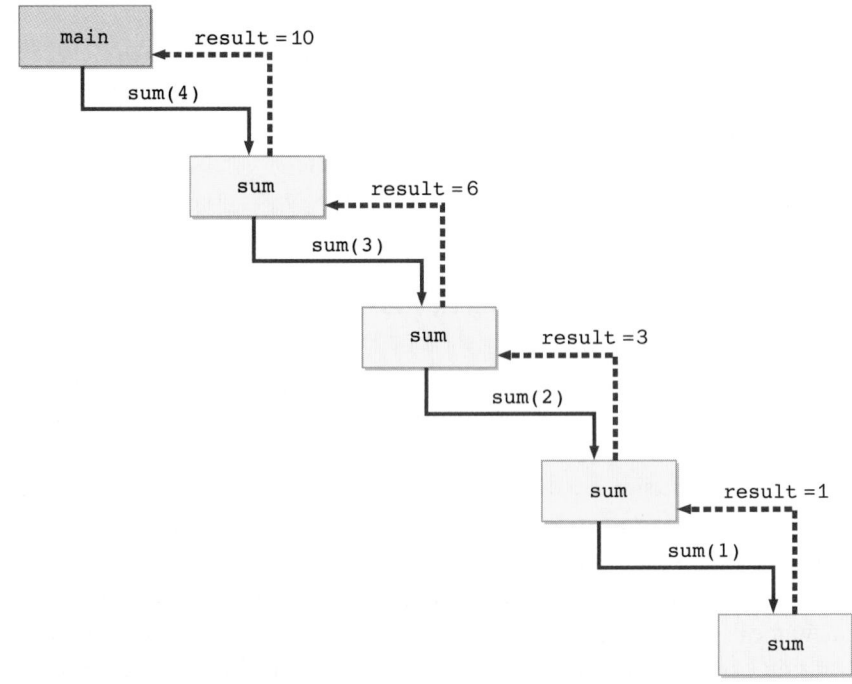

figure 11.3 Recursive calls to the sum method

sive path is followed completely until the base case is reached; the calls then begin to return their result up through the chain.

recursion vs. iteration

Of course, there is a non-recursive solution to the summation problem we just explored. One way to compute the sum of the numbers between 1 and num inclusive in an iterative manner is as follows:

```
sum = 0;
for (int number = 1; number <= num; number++)
    sum += number;
```

This solution is certainly more straightforward than the recursive version. We used the summation problem to demonstrate recursion because it is simple, not because you would use recursion to solve it under normal conditions. Recursion has the overhead of multiple method invocations and, in this case, presents a more complicated solution than its iterative counterpart.

A programmer must learn when to use recursion and when not to use it. Determining which approach is best depends on the problem being solved. All problems can be solved in an iterative manner, but in some cases the iterative version is much more complicated. Recursion, for some problems, allows us to create relatively short, elegant programs.

> **key concept**
> Recursion is the most elegant and appropriate way to solve some problems, but for others it is less intuitive than an iterative solution.

direct vs. indirect recursion

Direct recursion occurs when a method invokes itself, such as when sum calls sum. *Indirect recursion* occurs when a method invokes another method, eventually resulting in the original method being invoked again. For example, if method m1 invokes method m2, and m2 invokes method m1, we can say that m1 is indirectly recursive. The amount of indirection could be several levels deep, as when m1 invokes m2, which invokes m3, which invokes m4, which invokes m1. Figure 11.4 depicts a situation with indirect recursion. Method invocations are shown with solid lines, and returns are shown with dotted lines. The entire invocation path is followed, and then the recursion unravels following the return path.

Indirect recursion requires all of the same attention to base cases that direct recursion requires. Furthermore, indirect recursion can be more difficult to trace because of the intervening method calls. Therefore extra care is warranted when designing or evaluating indirectly recursive methods. Ensure that the indirection is truly necessary and clearly explained in documentation.

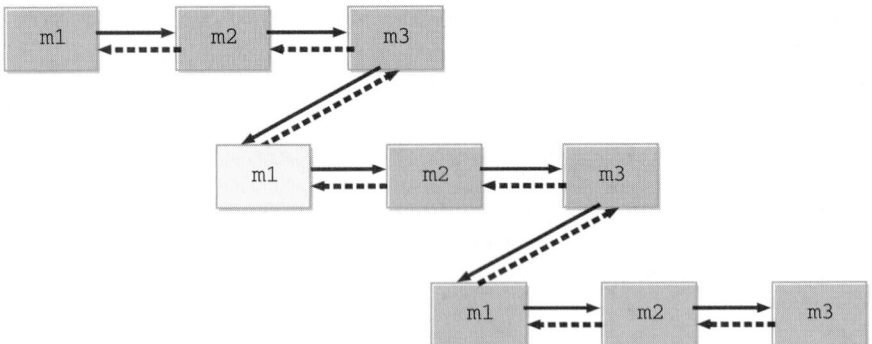

figure 11.4   Indirect recursion

11.2 using recursion

Each of the following sections describes a particular recursive problem. For each one, we examine exactly how recursion plays a role in the solution and how a base case is used to terminate the recursion. As you examine these examples, consider how complicated a non-recursive solution for each problem would be.

traversing a maze

Solving a maze involves a great deal of trial and error: following a path, backtracking when you cannot go farther, and trying other untried options. Such activities often are handled nicely using recursion. The program shown in Listing 11.1 creates a Maze object and attempts to traverse it.

The Maze class shown in Listing 11.2 uses a two-dimensional array of integers to represent the maze. The goal is to move from the top-left corner (the entry point) to the bottom-right corner (the exit point). Initially, a 1 indicates a clear path and a 0 indicates a blocked path. As the maze is solved, these array elements are changed to other values to indicate attempted paths and ultimately a successful path through the maze if one exists.

The only valid moves through the maze are in the four primary directions: down, right, up, and left. No diagonal moves are allowed. In this example, the maze is 8 rows by 13 columns, although the code is designed to handle a maze of any size.

listing
   11.1

```
//********************************************************************
//  MazeSearch.java        Author: Lewis/Loftus
//
//  Demonstrates recursion.
//********************************************************************

public class MazeSearch
{
   //----------------------------------------------------------------
   //  Creates a new maze, prints its original form, attempts to
   //  solve it, and prints out its final form.
   //----------------------------------------------------------------
   public static void main (String[] args)
   {
      Maze labyrinth = new Maze();

      System.out.println (labyrinth);

      if (labyrinth.traverse (0, 0))
         System.out.println ("The maze was successfully traversed!");
      else
         System.out.println ("There is no possible path.");

      System.out.println (labyrinth);
   }
}
```

output

```
1110110001111
1011101111001
0000101010100
1110111010111
1010000111001
1011111101111
1000000000000
111111111111
```

listing
11.1   continued

The maze was successfully traversed!

```
7770110001111
3077707771001
0000707070300
7770777070333
7070000773003
7077777703333
7000000000000
7777777777777
```

listing
11.2

```
//********************************************************************
//   Maze.java         Author: Lewis/Loftus
//
//   Represents a maze of characters. The goal is to get from the
//   top left corner to the bottom right, following a path of 1s.
//********************************************************************

public class Maze
{
    private final int TRIED = 3;
    private final int PATH = 7;

    private int[][] grid = { {1,1,1,0,1,1,0,0,0,1,1,1,1},
                             {1,0,1,1,1,0,1,1,1,1,0,0,1},
                             {0,0,0,0,1,0,1,0,1,0,1,0,0},
                             {1,1,1,0,1,1,1,0,1,0,1,1,1},
                             {1,0,1,0,0,0,0,1,1,1,0,0,1},
                             {1,0,1,1,1,1,1,1,1,0,1,1,1,1},
                             {1,0,0,0,0,0,0,0,0,0,0,0,0,0},
                             {1,1,1,1,1,1,1,1,1,1,1,1,1,1} };
```

listing
    11.2   continued

```java
//-------------------------------------------------------------------
//   Attempts to recursively traverse the maze. Inserts special
//   characters indicating locations that have been tried and that
//   eventually become part of the solution.
//-------------------------------------------------------------------
public boolean traverse (int row, int column)
{
   boolean done = false;

   if (valid (row, column))
   {
      grid[row][column] = TRIED;  // this cell has been tried

      if (row == grid.length-1 && column == grid[0].length-1)
         done = true;  // the maze is solved
      else
      {
         done = traverse (row+1, column);     // down
         if (!done)
            done = traverse (row, column+1);  // right
         if (!done)
            done = traverse (row-1, column);  // up
         if (!done)
            done = traverse (row, column-1);  // left
      }

      if (done)  // this location is part of the final path
         grid[row][column] = PATH;
   }

   return done;
}


//-------------------------------------------------------------------
//   Determines if a specific location is valid.
//-------------------------------------------------------------------
private boolean valid (int row, int column)
{
   boolean result = false;
```

listing
11.2   continued

```
    // check if cell is in the bounds of the matrix
    if (row >= 0 && row < grid.length &&
        column >= 0 && column < grid[row].length)

        //  check if cell is not blocked and not previously tried
        if (grid[row][column] == 1)
            result = true;

    return result;
}

//------------------------------------------------------------------
//  Returns the maze as a string.
//------------------------------------------------------------------
public String toString ()
{
    String result = "\n";

    for (int row=0; row < grid.length; row++)
    {
        for (int column=0; column < grid[row].length; column++)
            result += grid[row][column] + "";
        result += "\n";
    }

    return result;
}
}
```

Let's think this through recursively. The maze can be traversed successfully if it can be traversed successfully from position (0, 0). Therefore, the maze can be traversed successfully if it can be traversed successfully from any positions adjacent to (0, 0), namely position (1, 0), position (0, 1), position (–1, 0), or position (0, –1). Picking a potential next step, say (1, 0), we find ourselves in the same type of situation we did before. To successfully traverse the maze from the new current position, we must successfully traverse it from an adjacent position. At any point, some of the adjacent positions may be invalid, may be blocked, or may represent a possible successful path. We continue this process recursively. If the base case, position (7, 12) is reached, the maze has been traversed successfully.

The recursive method in the Maze class is called traverse. It returns a boolean value that indicates whether a solution was found. First the method determines whether a move to the specified row and column is valid. A move is considered valid if it stays within the grid boundaries and if the grid contains a 1 in that location, indicating that a move in that direction is not blocked. The initial call to traverse passes in the upper-left location (0, 0).

If the move is valid, the grid entry is changed from a 1 to a 3, marking this location as visited so that later we don't retrace our steps. The traverse method then determines whether the maze has been completed by having reached the bottom-right location. Therefore, there are actually three possibilities of the base case for this problem that will terminate any particular recursive path:

- an invalid move because the move is out of bounds
- an invalid move because the move has been tried before
- a move that arrives at the final location

If the current location is not the bottom-right corner, we search for a solution in each of the primary directions, if necessary. First, we look down by recursively calling the traverse method and passing in the new location. The logic of the traverse method starts all over again using this new position. A solution is either ultimately found by first attempting to move down from the current location, or it's not found. If it's not found, we try moving right. If that fails, we try up. Finally, if no other direction has yielded a correct path, we try left. If no direction from the current location yields a correct solution, then there is no path from this location, and traverse returns false.

If a solution is found from the current location, the grid entry is changed to a 7. The first 7 is placed in the bottom-right corner. The next 7 is placed in the location that led to the bottom-right corner, and so on until the final 7 is placed in the upper-left corner. Therefore, when the final maze is printed, the zeros still indicate a blocked path, a 1 indicates an open path that was never tried, a 3 indicates a path that was tried but failed to yield a correct solution, and a 7 indicates a part of the final solution of the maze.

Note that there are several opportunities for recursion in each call to the traverse method. Any or all of them might be followed, depending on the maze configuration. Although there may be many paths through the maze, the recursion terminates when a path is found. Carefully trace the execution of this code while following the maze array to see how the recursion solves the problem. Then consider the difficulty of producing a non-recursive solution.

the Towers of Hanoi

The *Towers of Hanoi* puzzle was invented in the 1880s by Edouard Lucas, a French mathematician. It has become a favorite among computer scientists because its solution is an excellent demonstration of recursive elegance.

The puzzle consists of three upright pegs and a set of disks with holes in the middle so that they slide onto the pegs. Each disk has a different diameter. Initially, all of the disks are stacked on one peg in order of size such that the largest disk is on the bottom, as shown in Fig. 11.5.

The goal of the puzzle is to move all of the disks from their original (first) peg to the destination (third) peg. We can use the "extra" peg as a temporary place to put disks, but we must obey the following three rules:

▸ We can move only one disk at a time.

▸ We cannot place a larger disk on top of a smaller disk.

▸ All disks must be on some peg except for the disk in transit between pegs.

These rules imply that we must move smaller disks "out of the way" in order to move a larger disk from one peg to another. Figure 11.6 shows the step-by-step solution for the Towers of Hanoi puzzle using three disks. In order to ultimately move all three disks from the first peg to the third peg, we first have to get to the point where the smaller two disks are out of the way on the second peg so that the largest disk can be moved from the first peg to the third peg.

The first three moves shown in Fig. 11.6 can be thought of as moving the smaller disks out of the way. The fourth move puts the largest disk in its final place. The last three moves then put the smaller disks to their final place on top of the largest one.

Let's use this idea to form a general strategy. To move a stack of N disks from the original peg to the destination peg:

▸ Move the topmost $N-1$ disks from the original peg to the extra peg.

▸ Move the largest disk from the original peg to the destination peg.

▸ Move the $N-1$ disks from the extra peg to the destination peg.

figure 11.5   The Towers of Hanoi puzzle

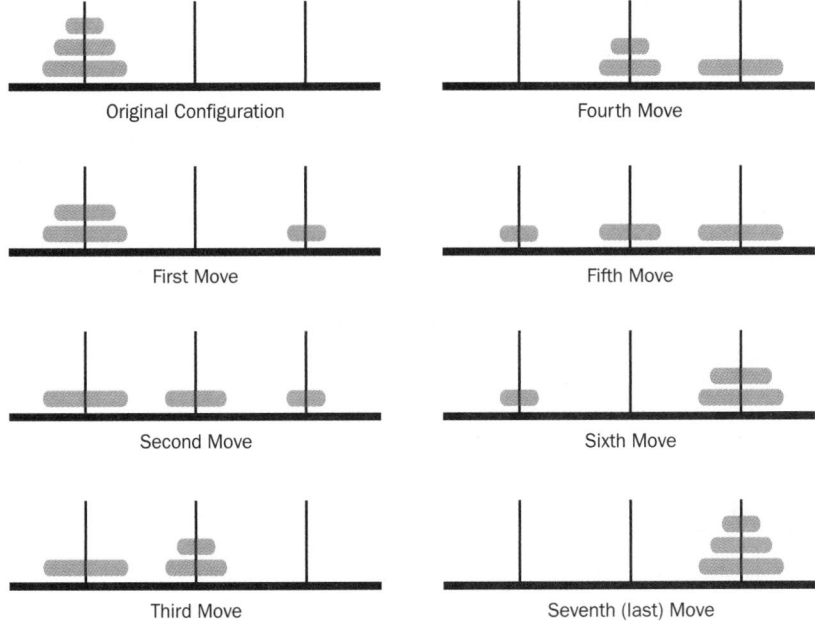

figure 11.6   A solution to the three-disk Towers of Hanoi puzzle

This strategy lends itself nicely to a recursive solution. The step to move the $N-1$ disks out of the way is the same problem all over again: moving a stack of disks. For this subtask, though, there is one less disk, and our destination peg is what we were originally calling the extra peg. An analogous situation occurs after we've moved the largest disk, and we have to move the original $N-1$ disks again.

The base case for this problem occurs when we want to move a "stack" that consists of only one disk. That step can be accomplished directly and without recursion.

The program in Listing 11.3 creates a `TowersOfHanoi` object and invokes its `solve` method. The output is a step-by-step list of instructions that describe how the disks should be moved to solve the puzzle. This example uses four disks, which is specified by a parameter to the `TowersOfHanoi` constructor.

The `TowersOfHanoi` class shown in Listing 11.4 uses the `solve` method to make an initial call to `moveTower`, the recursive method. The initial call indicates that all of the disks should be moved from peg 1 to peg 3, using peg 2 as the extra position.

listing
11.3

```
//********************************************************************
//   SolveTowers.java        Author: Lewis/Loftus
//
//   Demonstrates recursion.
//********************************************************************

public class SolveTowers
{
   //-----------------------------------------------------------------
   //  Creates a TowersOfHanoi puzzle and solves it.
   //-----------------------------------------------------------------
   public static void main (String[] args)
   {
      TowersOfHanoi towers = new TowersOfHanoi (4);

      towers.solve();
   }
}
```

output

```
Move one disk from 1 to 2
Move one disk from 1 to 3
Move one disk from 2 to 3
Move one disk from 1 to 2
Move one disk from 3 to 1
Move one disk from 3 to 2
Move one disk from 1 to 2
Move one disk from 1 to 3
Move one disk from 2 to 3
Move one disk from 2 to 1
Move one disk from 3 to 1
Move one disk from 2 to 3
Move one disk from 1 to 2
Move one disk from 1 to 3
Move one disk from 2 to 3
```

listing
11.4

```java
//********************************************************************
//  TowersOfHanoi.java        Author: Lewis/Loftus
//
//  Represents the classic Towers of Hanoi puzzle.
//********************************************************************

public class TowersOfHanoi
{
   private int totalDisks;

   //-----------------------------------------------------------------
   //  Sets up the puzzle with the specified number of disks.
   //-----------------------------------------------------------------
   public TowersOfHanoi (int disks)
   {
      totalDisks = disks;
   }

   //-----------------------------------------------------------------
   //  Performs the initial call to moveTower to solve the puzzle.
   //  Moves the disks from tower 1 to tower 3 using tower 2.
   //-----------------------------------------------------------------
   public void solve ()
   {
      moveTower (totalDisks, 1, 3, 2);
   }

   //-----------------------------------------------------------------
   //  Moves the specified number of disks from one tower to another
   //  by moving a subtower of n-1 disks out of the way, moving one
   //  disk, then moving the subtower back. Base case of 1 disk.
   //-----------------------------------------------------------------
   private void moveTower (int numDisks, int start, int end, int temp)
   {
      if (numDisks == 1)
         moveOneDisk (start, end);
      else
      {
         moveTower (numDisks-1, start, temp, end);
         moveOneDisk (start, end);
         moveTower (numDisks-1, temp, end, start);
      }
   }
```

listing
    11.4   **continued**

```
//----------------------------------------------------------------
//  Prints instructions to move one disk from the specified start
//  tower to the specified end tower.
//----------------------------------------------------------------
private void moveOneDisk (int start, int end)
{
   System.out.println ("Move one disk from " + start + " to " +
                       end);
}
}
```

The moveTower method first considers the base case (a "stack" of one disk). When that occurs, it calls the moveOneDisk method that prints a single line describing that particular move. If the stack contains more than one disk, we call moveTower again to get the $N-1$ disks out of the way, then move the largest disk, then move the $N-1$ disks to their final destination with yet another call to moveTower.

Note that the parameters to moveTower describing the pegs are switched around as needed to move the partial stacks. This code follows our general strategy and uses the moveTower method to move all partial stacks. Trace the code carefully for a stack of three disks to understand the processing. Compare the processing steps to Fig. 11.6.

Contrary to its short and elegant implementation, the solution to the Towers of Hanoi puzzle is terribly inefficient. To solve the puzzle with a stack of N disks, we have to make 2^N-1 individual disk moves. This situation is an example of *exponential complexity*. As the number of disks increases, the number of required moves increases exponentially.

> **key concept**
>
> The Towers of Hanoi solution has exponential complexity, which is very inefficient. Yet the implementation of the solution is incredibly short and elegant.

Legend has it that priests of Brahma are working on this puzzle in a temple at the center of the world. They are using 64 gold disks, moving them between pegs of pure diamond. The downside is that when the priests finish the puzzle, the world will end. The upside is that even if they move one disk every second of every day, it will take them over 584 billion years to complete it. That's with a puzzle of only 64 disks! It is certainly an indication of just how intractable exponential algorithmic complexity is.

11.3 recursion in graphics

The concept of recursion has several uses in images and graphics. The following section explores some image and graphics-based recursion examples.

tiled pictures

Carefully examine the display for the `TiledPictures` applet shown in Listing 11.5. There are actually three unique images among the menagerie. The entire area is divided into four equal quadrants. A picture of the world (with a circle indicating the Himalayan mountain region) is shown in the bottom-right quadrant. The bottom-left quadrant contains a picture of Mt. Everest. In the top-right quadrant is a picture of a mountain goat.

The interesting part of the picture is the top-left quadrant. It contains a copy of the entire collage, including itself. In this smaller version you can see the three simple pictures in their three quadrants. And again, in the top-left corner, the picture is repeated (including itself). This repetition continues for several levels. It is similar to the effect you can create when looking at a mirror in the reflection of another mirror.

This visual effect is created quite easily using recursion. The applet's `init` method initially loads the three images. The `paint` method then invokes the `drawPictures` method, which accepts a parameter that defines the size of the area in which pictures are displayed. It draws the three images using the `drawImage` method, with parameters that scale the picture to the correct size and location. The `drawPictures` method is then called recursively to draw the upper-left quadrant.

On each invocation, if the drawing area is large enough, the `drawPictures` method is invoked again, using a smaller drawing area. Eventually, the drawing area becomes so small that the recursive call is not performed. Note that `drawPictures` assumes the origin (0, 0) coordinate as the relative location of the new images, no matter what their size is.

The base case of the recursion in this problem specifies a minimum size for the drawing area. Because the size is decreased each time, the base case eventually is reached and the recursion stops. This is why the upper-left corner is empty in the smallest version of the collage.

listing
    11.5

```java
//********************************************************************
//   TiledPictures.java        Author: Lewis/Loftus
//
//   Demonstrates the use of recursion.
//********************************************************************

import java.awt.*;
import javax.swing.JApplet;

public class TiledPictures extends JApplet
{
   private final int APPLET_WIDTH = 320;
   private final int APPLET_HEIGHT = 320;
   private final int MIN = 20;  // smallest picture size

   private Image world, everest, goat;

   //-----------------------------------------------------------------
   //   Loads the images.
   //-----------------------------------------------------------------
   public void init()
   {
      world = getImage (getDocumentBase(), "world.gif");
      everest = getImage (getDocumentBase(), "everest.gif");
      goat = getImage (getDocumentBase(), "goat.gif");

      setSize (APPLET_WIDTH, APPLET_HEIGHT);
   }

   //-----------------------------------------------------------------
   //   Draws the three images, then calls itself recursively.
   //-----------------------------------------------------------------
   public void drawPictures (int size, Graphics page)
   {
      page.drawImage (everest, 0, size/2, size/2, size/2, this);
      page.drawImage (goat, size/2, 0, size/2, size/2, this);
      page.drawImage (world, size/2, size/2, size/2, size/2, this);

      if (size > MIN)
         drawPictures (size/2, page);
   }
```

listing
    11.5   continued

```
//-----------------------------------------------------------------
//  Performs the initial call to the drawPictures method.
//-----------------------------------------------------------------
public void paint (Graphics page)
{
    drawPictures (APPLET_WIDTH, page);
}
}
```

display

fractals

A *fractal* is a geometric shape that can be made up of the same pattern repeated at different scales and orientations. The nature of a fractal lends itself to a recursive definition. Interest in fractals has grown immensely in recent years, largely due to Benoit Mandelbrot, a Polish mathematician born in 1924. He demonstrated that fractals occur in many places in mathematics and nature. Computers have made fractals much easier to generate and investigate.

Over the past quarter century, the bright, interesting images that can be created with fractals have come to be considered as much an art form as a mathematical interest.

One particular example of a fractal is called the *Koch snowflake*, named after Helge von Koch, a Swedish mathematician. It begins with an equilateral triangle, which is considered to be the Koch fractal of order 1. Koch fractals of higher orders are constructed by repeatedly modifying all of the line segments in the shape.

To create the next higher order Koch fractal, each line segment in the shape is modified by replacing its middle third with a sharp protrusion made of two line segments, each having the same length as the replaced part. Relative to the entire shape, the protrusion on any line segment always points outward. Figure 11.7 shows several orders of Koch fractals. As the order increases, the shape begins to look like a snowflake.

The applet shown in Listing 11.6 draws a Koch snowflake of several different orders. The buttons at the top of the applet allow the user to increase and decrease the order of the fractal. Each time a button is pressed, the fractal image is redrawn. The applet serves as the listener for the buttons.

The fractal image is drawn on a canvas defined by the `KochPanel` class shown in Listing 11.7. The `paint` method makes the initial calls to the recursive method `drawFractal`. The three calls to `drawFractal` in the `paint` method represent the original three sides of the equilateral triangle that make up a Koch fractal of order 1.

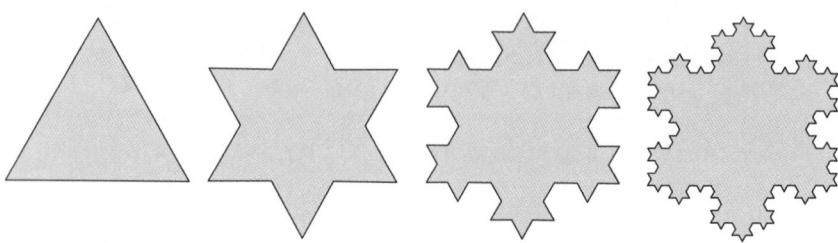

figure 11.7   Several orders of the Koch snowflake

listing
   11.6

```
//*****************************************************************
//   KochSnowflake.java        Author: Lewis/Loftus
//
//   Demonstrates the use of recursion.
//*****************************************************************

import java.awt.*;
import java.awt.event.*;
import javax.swing.*;

public class KochSnowflake extends JApplet implements ActionListener
{
    private final int APPLET_WIDTH = 400;
    private final int APPLET_HEIGHT = 440;

    private final int MIN = 1, MAX = 9;

    private JButton increase, decrease;
    private JLabel titleLabel, orderLabel;
    private KochPanel drawing;
    private JPanel appletPanel, tools;

    //----------------------------------------------------------------
    //   Sets up the components for the applet.
    //----------------------------------------------------------------
    public void init()
    {
        tools = new JPanel ();
        tools.setLayout (new BoxLayout(tools, BoxLayout.X_AXIS));
        tools.setBackground (Color.yellow);
        tools.setOpaque (true);

        titleLabel = new JLabel ("The Koch Snowflake");
        titleLabel.setForeground (Color.black);

        increase = new JButton (new ImageIcon ("increase.gif"));
        increase.setPressedIcon (new ImageIcon ("increasePressed.gif"));
        increase.setMargin (new Insets (0, 0, 0, 0));
        increase.addActionListener (this);
```

listing
11.6   **continued**

```
decrease = new JButton (new ImageIcon ("decrease.gif"));
decrease.setPressedIcon (new ImageIcon ("decreasePressed.gif"));
decrease.setMargin (new Insets (0, 0, 0, 0));
decrease.addActionListener (this);

orderLabel = new JLabel ("Order: 1");
orderLabel.setForeground (Color.black);

tools.add (titleLabel);
tools.add (Box.createHorizontalStrut (20));
tools.add (decrease);
tools.add (increase);
tools.add (Box.createHorizontalStrut (20));
tools.add (orderLabel);

drawing = new KochPanel (1);

appletPanel = new JPanel();
appletPanel.add (tools);
appletPanel.add (drawing);

getContentPane().add (appletPanel);

setSize (APPLET_WIDTH, APPLET_HEIGHT);
}

//----------------------------------------------------------------
//  Determines which button was pushed, and sets the new order
//  if it is in range.
//----------------------------------------------------------------
public void actionPerformed (ActionEvent event)
{
   int order = drawing.getOrder();

   if (event.getSource() == increase)
      order++;
   else
      order--;

   if (order >= MIN && order <= MAX)
   {
      orderLabel.setText ("Order: " + order);
      drawing.setOrder (order);
```

listing
11.6   continued

```
        repaint();
    }
  }
}
```

display

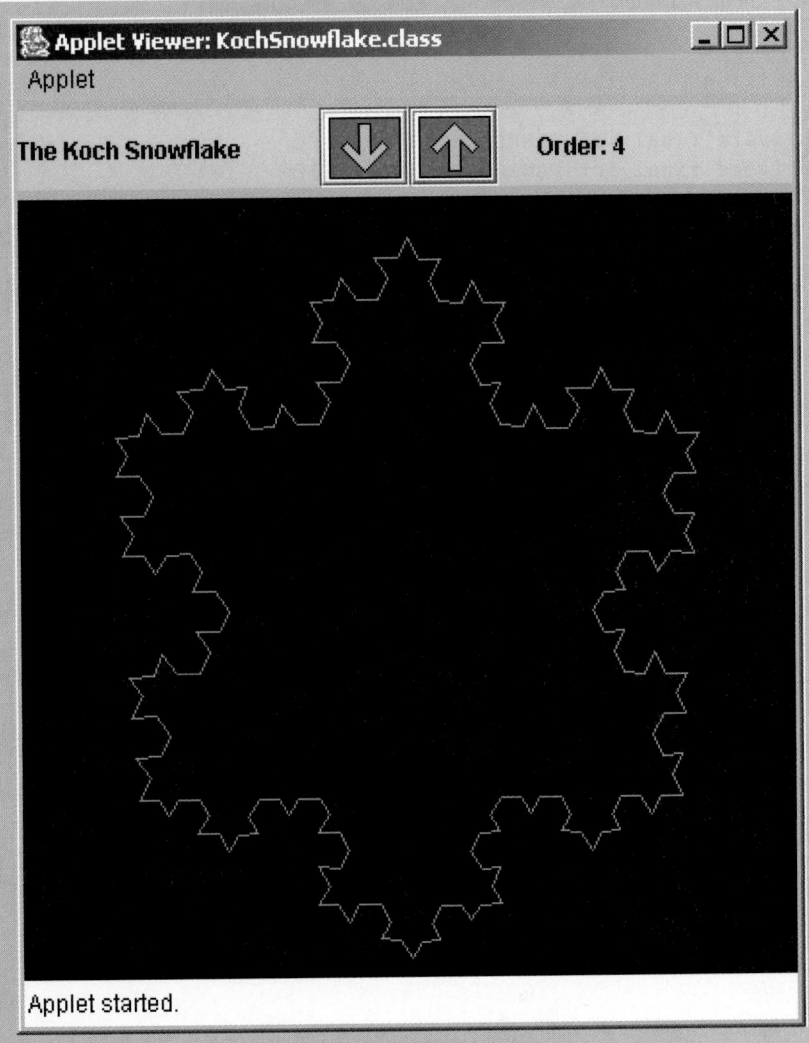

listing
    11.7

```
//*********************************************************************
//  KochPanel.java          Author: Lewis/Loftus
//
//  Represents a drawing surface on which to paint a Koch Snowflake.
//*********************************************************************

import java.awt.*;
import javax.swing.JPanel;

public class KochPanel extends JPanel
{
    private final int PANEL_WIDTH = 400;
    private final int PANEL_HEIGHT = 400;

    private final double SQ = Math.sqrt(3.0) / 6;

    private final int TOPX = 200, TOPY = 20;
    private final int LEFTX = 60, LEFTY = 300;
    private final int RIGHTX = 340, RIGHTY = 300;

    private int current; //current order

    //-----------------------------------------------------------------
    //  Sets the initial fractal order to the value specified.
    //-----------------------------------------------------------------
    public KochPanel (int currentOrder)
    {
        current = currentOrder;
        setBackground (Color.black);
        setPreferredSize (new Dimension(PANEL_WIDTH, PANEL_HEIGHT));
    }

    //-----------------------------------------------------------------
    //  Draws the fractal recursively. Base case is an order of 1 for
    //  which a simple straight line is drawn. Otherwise three
    //  intermediate points are computed, and each line segment is
    //  drawn as a fractal.
    //-----------------------------------------------------------------
```

listing
    11.7   continued

```java
public void drawFractal (int order, int x1, int y1, int x5, int y5,
                         Graphics page)
{
   int deltaX, deltaY, x2, y2, x3, y3, x4, y4;

   if (order == 1)
      page.drawLine (x1, y1, x5, y5);
   else
   {
      deltaX = x5 - x1;   // distance between end points
      deltaY = y5 - y1;

      x2 = x1 + deltaX / 3;   // one third
      y2 = y1 + deltaY / 3;

      x3 = (int) ((x1+x5)/2 + SQ * (y1-y5));   // tip of projection
      y3 = (int) ((y1+y5)/2 + SQ * (x5-x1));

      x4 = x1 + deltaX * 2/3;   // two thirds
      y4 = y1 + deltaY * 2/3;

      drawFractal (order-1, x1, y1, x2, y2, page);
      drawFractal (order-1, x2, y2, x3, y3, page);
      drawFractal (order-1, x3, y3, x4, y4, page);
      drawFractal (order-1, x4, y4, x5, y5, page);
   }
}

//--------------------------------------------------------------------
//  Performs the initial calls to the drawFractal method.
//--------------------------------------------------------------------
public void paintComponent (Graphics page)
{
   super.paintComponent (page);

   page.setColor (Color.green);

   drawFractal (current, TOPX, TOPY, LEFTX, LEFTY, page);
   drawFractal (current, LEFTX, LEFTY, RIGHTX, RIGHTY, page);
   drawFractal (current, RIGHTX, RIGHTY, TOPX, TOPY, page);
}
```

listing
   11.7   **continued**

```
//----------------------------------------------------------------
//  Sets the fractal order to the value specified.
//----------------------------------------------------------------
public void setOrder (int order)
{
    current = order;
}


//----------------------------------------------------------------
//  Returns the current order.
//----------------------------------------------------------------
public int getOrder ()
{
    return current;
}
}
```

The variable `current` represents the order of the fractal to be drawn. Each recursive call to `drawFractal` decrements the order by 1. The base case of the recursion occurs when the order of the fractal is 1, which results in a simple line segment between the coordinates specified by the parameters.

If the order of the fractal is higher than 1, three additional points are computed. In conjunction with the parameters, these points form the four line segments of the modified fractal. Figure 11.8 shows the transformation.

Based on the position of the two end points of the original line segment, a point one-third of the way and a point two-thirds of the way between them are computed. The calculation of $<x_3, y_3>$, the point at the tip of the protrusion, is more convoluted and uses a simplifying constant that incorporates multiple geometric relationships. The calculations to determine the three new points actually have nothing to do with the recursive technique used to draw the fractal, and so won't discuss the details of these computations here.

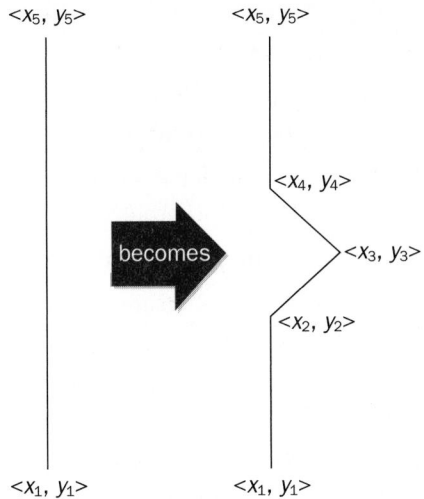

figure 11.8 The transformation of each line segment of a Koch snowflake

An interesting mathematical feature of a Koch snowflake is that it has an infinite perimeter but a finite area. As the order of the fractal increases, the perimeter grows exponentially larger, with a mathematical limit of infinity. However, a rectangle large enough to surround the second-order fractal for the Koch snowflake is large enough to contain all higher-order fractals. The shape is restricted forever in area, but its perimeter gets infinitely longer.

summary of
key concepts

▸ Recursion is a programming technique in which a method calls itself. A key to being able to program recursively is to be able to think recursively.

▸ Any recursive definition must have a non-recursive part, called the base case, which permits the recursion to eventually end.

▸ Mathematical problems and formulas are often expressed recursively.

▸ Each recursive call to a method creates new local variables and parameters.

▸ A careful trace of recursive processing can provide insight into the way it is used to solve a problem.

▸ Recursion is the most elegant and appropriate way to solve some problems, but for others it is less intuitive than an iterative solution.

▸ The Towers of Hanoi solution has exponential complexity, which is very inefficient. Yet the implementation of the solution is incredibly short and elegant.

▸ A fractal is a geometric shape that can be defined naturally in a recursive manner.

self-review questions

11.1 What is recursion?

11.2 What is infinite recursion?

11.3 When is a base case needed for recursive processing?

11.4 Is recursion necessary?

11.5 When should recursion be avoided?

11.6 What is indirect recursion?

11.7 Explain the general approach to solving the Towers of Hanoi puzzle. How does it relate to recursion?

11.8 What is a fractal? What does it have to do with recursion?

exercises

11.1 Write a recursive definition of a valid Java identifier (see Chapter 1).

11.2 Write a recursive definition of x^y (x raised to the power y), where x and y are integers and $y > 0$.

11.3 Write a recursive definition of $i * j$ (integer multiplication), where $i > 0$. Define the multiplication process in terms of integer addition. For example, 4 * 7 is equal to 7 added to itself 4 times.

11.4 Write a recursive definition of the Fibonacci numbers. The Fibonacci numbers are a sequence of integers, each of which is the sum of the previous two numbers. The first two numbers in the sequence are 0 and 1. Explain why you would not normally use recursion to solve this problem.

11.5 Modify the method that calculates the sum of the integers between 1 and N shown in this chapter. Have the new version match the following recursive definition: The sum of 1 to N is the sum of 1 to ($N/2$) plus the sum of ($N/2 + 1$) to N. Trace your solution using an N of 7.

11.6 Write a recursive method that returns the value of $N!$ (N factorial) using the definition given in this chapter. Explain why you would not normally use recursion to solve this problem.

11.7 Write a recursive method to reverse a string. Explain why you would not normally use recursion to solve this problem.

11.8 Design or generate a new maze for the MazeSearch program in this chapter and rerun the program. Explain the processing in terms of your new maze, giving examples of a path that was tried but failed, a path that was never tried, and the ultimate solution.

11.9 Annotate the lines of output of the SolveTowers program in this chapter to show the recursive steps.

11.10 Produce a chart showing the number of moves required to solve the Towers of Hanoi puzzle using the following number of disks: 2, 3, 4, 5, 6, 7, 8, 9, 10, 15, 20, and 25.

11.10 How many line segments are used to construct a Koch snowflake of order N? Produce a chart showing the number of line segments that make up a Koch snowflake for orders 1 through 9.

programming projects

11.1 Design and implement a recursive version of the `PalindromeTester` program from Chapter 3.

11.2 Design and implement a program that implements Euclid's algorithm for finding the greatest common divisor of two positive integers. The greatest common divisor is the largest integer that divides both values without producing a remainder. An iterative version of this method was part of the `Rational` class presented in Chapter 4. In a class called `DivisorCalc`, define a `static` method called `gcd` that accepts two integers, num1 and num2. Create a driver to test your implementation. The recursive algorithm is defined as follows:

a. gcd (num1, num2) is num2 if num2 <= num1 and num2 divides num1

b. gcd (num1, num2) is gcd (num2, num1) if num1 < num2

c. gcd (num1, num2) is gcd (num2, num1%num2) otherwise

11.3 Modify the `Maze` class so that it prints out the path of the final solution as it is discovered without storing it.

11.4 Design and implement a program that traverses a 3D maze.

11.5 Modify the `TiledPictures` program so that the repeated images appear in the lower-right quadrant.

11.6 Design and implement a recursive program that solves the Non-Attacking Queens problem. That is, write a program to determine how eight queens can be positioned on an eight-by-eight chessboard so that none of them are in the same row, column, or diagonal as any other queen. There are no other chess pieces on the board.

11.7 In the language of an alien race, all words take the form of Blurbs. A Blurb is a Whoozit followed by one or more Whatzits. A Whoozit is the character 'x' followed by zero or more 'y's. A Whatzit is a 'q' followed by either a 'z' or a 'd', followed by a Whoozit. Design and implement a recursive program that generates random Blurbs in this alien language.

11.8 Design and implement a recursive program to determine whether a string is a valid Blurb as defined in Programming Project 11.7.

11.9 Design and implement a recursive program to determine and print the Nth line of Pascal's Triangle, as shown below. Each interior value is the sum of the two values above it. *Hint*: use an array to store the values on each line.

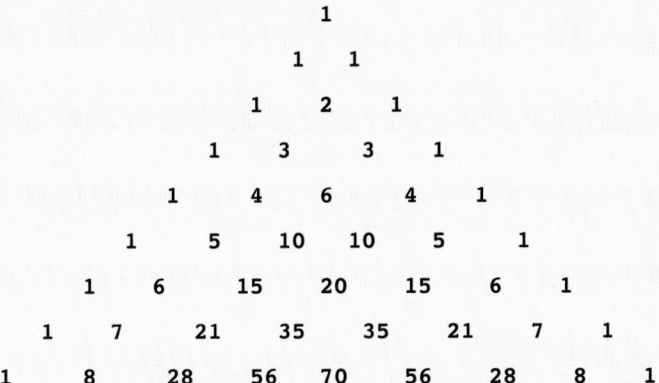

```
                    1
                1       1
            1       2       1
        1       3       3       1
    1       4       6       4       1
1       5      10      10      5       1
1   6      15      20      15      6       1
1   7      21      35      35      21      7       1
1   8      28      56      70      56      28      8       1
```

11.10 Design and implement an applet that generalizes the KochSnowflake program. Allow the user to choose a fractal design from a menu item and to pick the background and drawing colors. The buttons to increase and decrease the order of the fractal will apply to whichever fractal design is chosen. In addition to the Koch snowflake, include a *C-curve fractal* whose order 1 is a straight line. Each successive order is created by replacing all line segments by two line segments, both half of the size of the original, and which meet at a right angle. Specifically, a C-curve of order N from $<x_1, y_1>$ to $<x_3, y_3>$ is replaced by two C-curves from $<x_1, y_1>$ to $<x_2, y_2>$ and from $<x_2, y_2>$ to $<x_3, y_3>$ where:

‣ x2 = (x1 + x3 + y1 - y3) / 2;

‣ y2 = (x3 + y1 + y3 - x1) / 2;

11.11 Design and implement a graphic version of the Towers of Hanoi puzzle. Allow the user to set the number of disks used in the puzzle. The user should be able to interact with the puzzle in two main ways. The user can move the disks from one peg to another using the mouse, in which case the program should ensure that each move is legal. The user can also watch a solution take place as an animation, with pause/resume buttons. Permit the user to control the speed of the animation.

answers to self-review questions

11.1 Recursion is a programming technique in which a method calls itself, solving a smaller version of the problem each time, until the terminating condition is reached.

11.2 Infinite recursion occurs when there is no base case that serves as a terminating condition or when the base case is improperly specified. The recursive path is followed forever. In a recursive program, infinite recursion will often result in an error that indicates that available memory has been exhausted.

11.3 A base case is always required to terminate recursion and begin the process of returning through the calling hierarchy. Without the base case, infinite recursion results.

11.4 Recursion is not necessary. Every recursive algorithm can be written in an iterative manner. However, some problem solutions are much more elegant and straightforward when written recursively.

11.5 Avoid recursion when the iterative solution is simpler and more easily understood and programmed. Recursion has the overhead of multiple method calls and is not always intuitive.

11.6 Indirect recursion occurs when a method calls another method, which calls another method, and so on until one of the called methods invokes the original. Indirect recursion is usually more difficult to trace than direct recursion, in which a method calls itself.

11.7 The Towers of Hanoi puzzle of N disks is solved by moving $N-1$ disks out of the way onto an extra peg, moving the largest disk to its destination, then moving the $N-1$ disks from the extra peg to the destination. This solution is inherently recursive because, to move the substack of $N-1$ disks, we can use the same process.

11.8 A fractal is a geometric shape that can be composed of multiple versions of the same shape at different scales and different angles of orientation. Recursion can be used to draw the repetitive shapes over and over again.

12

data structures

Problem solving often requires techniques for organizing and managing information. The term *data structures* refers to the various ways information can be organized and used. Many data structures have been developed over the years, and some of them have become classics. Often, a data structure can be implemented in a variety of ways. This chapter explains how data structures can be implemented using references to link one object to another. It also serves as an introduction to some specific data structures.

chapter objectives

- Explore the concept of a collection.

- Examine the difference between fixed and dynamic implementations.

- Define and use dynamically linked lists.

- Define queue and stack data structures.

- Examine the organization of non-linear data structures.

- Introduce the predefined collection classes in the Java standard class library.

12.0 collections

A *collection* is an object that serves as a repository for other objects. It is a generic term that can be applied to many situations, but we usually use it when discussing an object whose specific role is to provide services to add, remove, and otherwise manage the elements that are contained within. For example, the `ArrayList` class (discussed in Chapter 6) represents a collection. It provides methods to add elements to the end of a list or to a particular location in the list based on an index value. It provides methods to remove specific elements as needed.

Some collections maintain their elements in a specific order, while others do not. Some collections are *homogeneous,* meaning that they can contain all of the same type of object; other collections are *heterogeneous,* which means they can contain objects of various types. An `ArrayList` is heterogeneous because it can hold an object of any type. Its heterogeneous nature comes from the fact that an `ArrayList` stores `Object` references, which means it can store any object because of inheritance and polymorphism (as discussed in Chapter 7).

separating interface from implementation

A crucial aspect of collections is that they can be implemented in a variety of ways. That is, the underlying data structure that stores the objects can be implemented using various techniques. The `ArrayList` class from the Java standard library, for instance, is implemented using an array. All operations on an `ArrayList` are accomplished by invoking methods that perform the appropriate operations on the underlying array.

An *abstract data type* (ADT) is a collection of data and the particular operations that are allowed on that data. An ADT has a name, a domain of values, and a set of operations that can be performed. An ADT is considered abstract because the operations you can perform on it are separated from the underlying implementation. That is, the details of how an ADT stores its data and accomplishes its methods are separate from the concept that it embodies.

Objects, therefore, are perfectly suited for defining ADTs. An object, by definition, has a well-defined interface whose implementation is hidden in the class. The data that is represented, and the operations that manage the data, are encapsulated together inside the object. This type of encapsulated ADT is reusable and reliable, because its interaction with the rest of the system is controlled.

12.1 representing data structures

An array is only one way in which a list can be represented. Arrays are limited in one sense because they have a fixed size throughout their existence. Sometimes we don't know how big to make an array because we don't know how much information we will store. The ArrayList class handles this by creating a larger array and copying everything over whenever necessary. This is not necessarily an efficient implementation.

A *dynamic data structure* is implemented using links. Using references as links between objects, we can create whatever type of structure is appropriate for the situation. If implemented carefully, the structure can be quite efficient to search and modify. Structures created this way are considered to be dynamic because their size is determined dynamically, as they are used, and not by their declaration.

> **key concept**
>
> A fixed data structure has a specific size for the duration of its existence, whereas a dynamic data structure grows and shrinks as needed.

dynamic structures

Recall from Chapter 4 that all objects are created dynamically using the new operator. A variable used to keep track of an object is actually a reference to the object, meaning that it stores the address of the object. Recall that a declaration such as:

```
House home = new House ("602 Greenbriar Court");
```

actually accomplishes two things: it declares home to be a reference to a House object, and it instantiates an object of class House. Now consider an object that contains a reference to another object of the same type. For example:

```
class Node
{
   int info;
   Node next;
}
```

Two objects of this class can be instantiated and chained together by having the next reference of one Node object refer to the other Node object. The second object's next reference can refer to a third Node object, and so on, creating a *linked list*. The first node in the list could be referenced using a separate variable. The last node in the list would have a next reference that is null, indicating the end of the list. Figure 12.1 depicts this situation. For this example, the information stored in each Node class is a simple integer, but keep in mind that we could define a class to contain any amount of information of any type.

> **key concept**
>
> A dynamically linked list is managed by storing and updating references to objects.

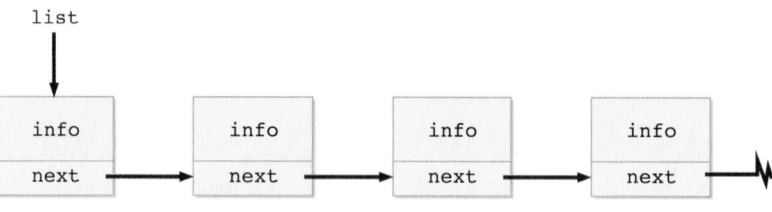

figure 12.1   A linked list

a dynamically linked list

The program in Listing 12.1 sets up a list of Magazine objects and then prints the list. The list of magazines is encapsulated inside the MagazineList class shown in Listing 12.2 and is maintained as a dynamically linked list.

The MagazineList class represents the list of magazines. From outside of the class (an external view), we do not focus on how the list is implemented. We don't know, for instance, whether the list of magazines is stored in an array or in a linked list. The MagazineList class provides a set of methods that allows the user to maintain the list of books. That set of methods, specifically add and toString, defines the operations to the MagazineList ADT.

The MagazineList class uses an inner class called MagazineNode to represent a node in the linked list. Each node contains a reference to one magazine and a reference to the next node in the list. Because MagazineNode is an inner class, it is reasonable to allow the data values in the class to be public. Therefore the code in the MagazineList class refers to those data values directly.

The Magazine class shown in Listing 12.3 is well encapsulated, with all data declared as private and methods provided to accomplish any updates necessary. Note that, because we use a separate class to represent a node in the list, the Magazine class itself does not need to contain a link to the next Magazine in the list. That allows the Magazine class to be free of any issues regarding its containment in a list.

Other methods could be included in the MagazineList ADT. For example, in addition to the add method provided, which always adds a new magazine to the end of the list, another method called insert could be defined to add a node anywhere in the list (to keep it sorted, for instance). A parameter to insert could indicate the value of the node after which the new node should be inserted. Figure 12.2 shows how the references would be updated to insert a new node.

listing
12.1

```
//********************************************************************
//   MagazineRack.java        Author: Lewis/Loftus
//
//   Driver to exercise the MagazineList collection.
//********************************************************************

public class MagazineRack
{
    //-----------------------------------------------------------------
    //   Creates a MagazineList object, adds several magazines to the
    //   list, then prints it.
    //-----------------------------------------------------------------
    public static void main (String[] args)
    {
        MagazineList rack = new MagazineList();

        rack.add (new Magazine("Time"));
        rack.add (new Magazine("Woodworking Today"));
        rack.add (new Magazine("Communications of the ACM"));
        rack.add (new Magazine("House and Garden"));
        rack.add (new Magazine("GQ"));

        System.out.println (rack);
    }
}
```

output

```
Time
Woodworking Today
Communications of the ACM
House and Garden
GQ
```

Another operation that would be helpful in the list ADT would be a `delete` method to remove a particular node. Recall from our discussion in Chapter 5 that by removing all references to an object, it becomes a candidate for garbage collection. Figure 12.3 shows how references would be updated to delete a node from a list. Care must be taken to accomplish the modifications to the references in the proper order to ensure that other nodes are not lost and that references continue to refer to valid, appropriate nodes in the list.

listing
    12.2

```java
//********************************************************************
//  MagazineList.java        Author: Lewis/Loftus
//
//  Represents a collection of magazines.
//********************************************************************

public class MagazineList
{
   private MagazineNode list;

   //-----------------------------------------------------------------
   //  Sets up an initially empty list of magazines.
   //-----------------------------------------------------------------
   public MagazineList()
   {
      list = null;
   }

   //-----------------------------------------------------------------
   //  Creates a new MagazineNode object and adds it to the end of
   //  the linked list.
   //-----------------------------------------------------------------
   public void add (Magazine mag)
   {

      MagazineNode node = new MagazineNode (mag);
      MagazineNode current;

      if (list == null)
         list = node;
      else
      {
         current = list;
         while (current.next != null)
            current = current.next;
         current.next = node;
      }
   }
```

listing
12.2   continued

```java
//-----------------------------------------------------------------
//  Returns this list of magazines as a string.
//-----------------------------------------------------------------
public String toString ()
{
   String result = "";

   MagazineNode current = list;

   while (current != null)
   {
      result += current.magazine + "\n";
      current = current.next;
   }

   return result;
}

//*****************************************************************
//  An inner class that represents a node in the magazine list.
//  The public variables are accessed by the MagazineList class.
//*****************************************************************
private class MagazineNode
{
   public Magazine magazine;
   public MagazineNode next;

   //-------------------------------------------------------------
   //  Sets up the node
   //-------------------------------------------------------------
   public MagazineNode (Magazine mag)
   {
      magazine = mag;
      next = null;
   }
}
}
```

listing
     12.3

```java
//********************************************************************
//  Magazine.java        Author: Lewis/Loftus
//
//  Represents a single magazine.
//********************************************************************

public class Magazine
{
   private String title;

   //-----------------------------------------------------------------
   //  Sets up the new magazine with its title.
   //-----------------------------------------------------------------
   public Magazine (String newTitle)
   {
      title = newTitle;
   }

   //-----------------------------------------------------------------
   //  Returns this magazine as a string.
   //-----------------------------------------------------------------
   public String toString ()
   {
      return title;
   }
}
```

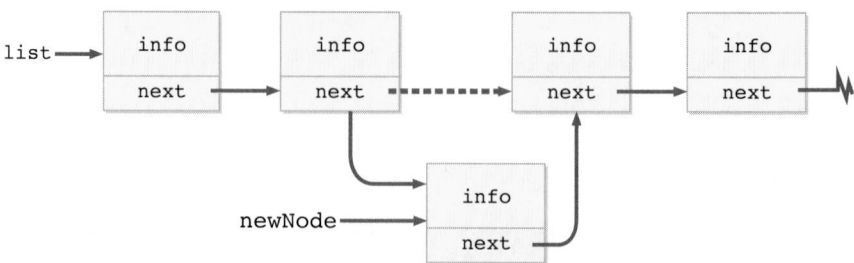

figure 12.2   Inserting a node into the middle of a list

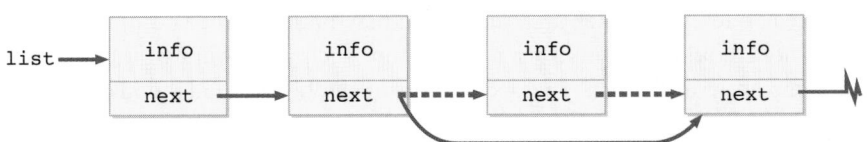

figure 12.3   Deleting a node from a list

other dynamic list representations

You can use different list implementations, depending on the specific needs of the program you are designing. For example, in some situations it may make processing easier to implement a *doubly linked list* in which each node has not only a reference to the next node in the list, but also another reference to the previous node in the list. Our generic Node class might be declared as follows:

```
class Node
{
    int info;
    Node next, prev;
}
```

Figure 12.4 shows a doubly linked list. Note that, like a single linked list, the next reference of the last node is null. Similarly, the previous node of the first node is null since there is no node that comes before the first one. This type of structure makes it easy to move back and forth between nodes in the list, but requires more effort to set up and modify.

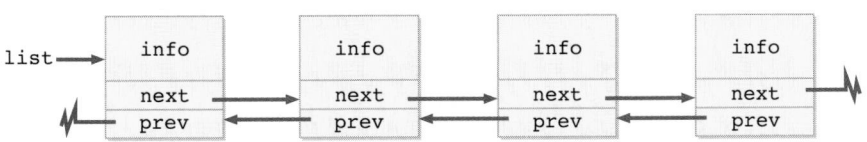

figure 12.4   A doubly linked list

Another implementation of a linked list could include a *header node* for the list that has a reference to the front of the list and another reference to the rear of the list. A rear reference makes it easier to add new nodes to the end of the list. The header node could contain other information, such as a count of the number of nodes currently in the list. The declaration of the header node would be similar to the following:

```
class ListHeader
{
    int count;
    Node front, rear;
}
```

Note that the header node is not of the same class as the Node class to which it refers. Figure 12.5 depicts a linked list that is implemented using a header node.

Still other linked list implementations can be created. For instance, the use of a header can be combined with a doubly linked list, or the list can be maintained in sorted order. The implementation should cater to the type of processing that is required. Some extra effort to maintain a more complex data structure may be worthwhile if it makes common operations on the structure more efficient.

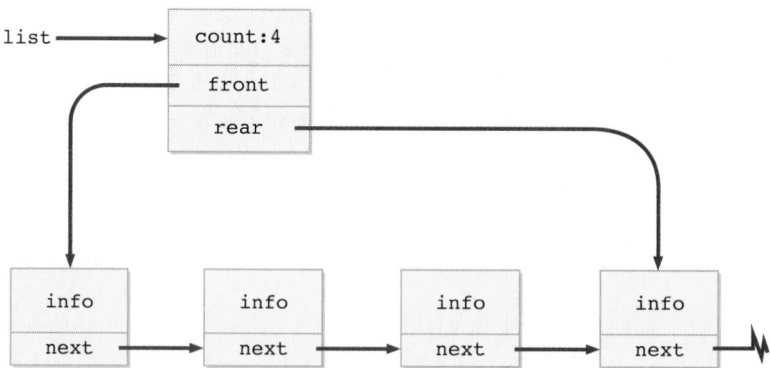

figure 12.5 A list with front and rear references

12.2 classic data structures

In addition to lists, some data structures have become classic in that they represent important generic situations that commonly occur in computing. They can be separated into two categories. Like lists, a queue and a stack are *linear data structures*, meaning that the data they represent is organized in a linear fashion. Trees and graphs, on the other hand, are *non-linear data structures* because their data is not organized linearly. Let's examine each of these data structures in more detail.

queues

A *queue* is similar to a list except that it has restrictions on the way you put items in and take items out. Specifically, a queue uses *first-in, first-out* (FIFO) processing. That is, the first item put in the list is the first item that comes out of the list. Figure 12.6 depicts the FIFO processing of a queue.

> **key concept**
> A queue is a linear data structure that manages data in a first-in, first-out manner.

Any waiting line is a queue. Think about a line of people waiting for a teller at a bank. A customer enters the queue at the back and moves forward as earlier customers are serviced. Eventually, each customer comes to the front of the queue to be processed.

Note that the processing of a queue is conceptual. We may speak in terms of people moving forward until they reach the front of the queue, but the reality might be that the front of the queue moves as elements come off. That is, we are not concerned at this point with whether the queue of customers moves toward the teller, or remains stationary as the teller moves when customers are serviced.

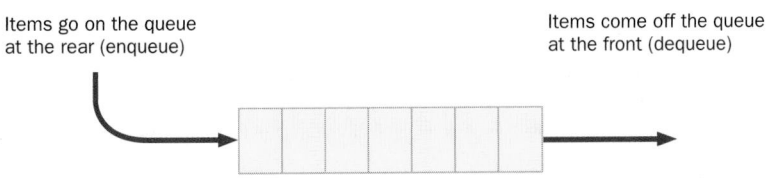

figure 12.6 A queue data structure

A queue data structure typically has the following operations:

▸ enqueue—adds an item to the rear of the queue

▸ dequeue—removes an item from the front of the queue

▸ empty—returns true if the queue is empty

stacks

A *stack* is similar to a queue except that its elements go on and come off at the same end. The last item to go on a stack is the first item to come off, like a stack of plates in the cupboard or a stack of hay bales in the barn. A stack, therefore, processes information in a *last-in, first-out* (LIFO) manner, as shown in Fig. 12.7.

A typical stack ADT contains the following operations:

▸ push—pushes an item onto the top of the stack

▸ pop—removes an item from the top of the stack

▸ peek—retrieves information from the top item of the stack without removing it

▸ empty—returns true if the stack is empty

The `java.util` package of the API contains a class called `Stack` that implements a stack data structure. It contains methods that correspond to the standard stack operations, plus a method that searches for a particular object in the stack.

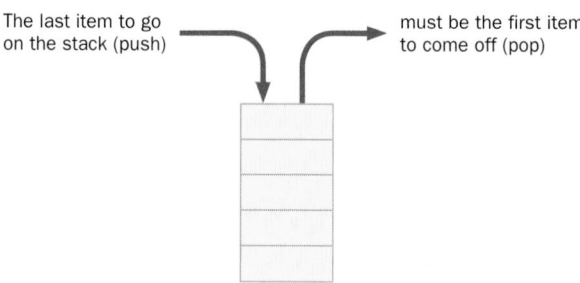

The last item to go on the stack (push)   must be the first item to come off (pop)

figure 12.7   A stack data structure

The `Stack` class has a `search` method that returns an integer corresponding to the position in the stack of the particular object. This type of searching is not usually considered to be part of the classic stack ADT.

Like `ArrayList` operations, the `Stack` operations operate on `Object` references. Because all objects are derived from the `Object` class, any object can be pushed onto a stack. If primitive types are to be stored, they must be treated as objects using the corresponding wrapper class. Unlike the `Stack` class, no class implementing a queue is defined in the Java API.

Let's look at an example that uses a stack to solve a problem. The program in Listing 12.4 accepts a string of characters that represents a secret message. The program decodes and prints the message.

listing
12.4

```java
//********************************************************************
//  Decode.java        Author: Lewis/Loftus
//
//  Demonstrates the use of the Stack class.
//********************************************************************

import java.util.Stack;
import cs1.Keyboard;

public class Decode
{
   //-----------------------------------------------------------------
   //  Decodes a message by reversing each word in a string.
   //-----------------------------------------------------------------
   public static void main (String[] args)
   {
      Stack word = new Stack();
      String message;
      int index = 0;

      System.out.println ("Enter the coded message:");
      message = Keyboard.readString();
      System.out.println ("The decoded message is:");

      while (index < message.length())
      {
         // Push word onto stack
```

listing
12.4   **continued**

```
        while (index < message.length() && message.charAt(index) != ' ')
        {
            word.push (new Character(message.charAt(index)));
            index++;
        }

        // Print word in reverse
        while (!word.empty())
            System.out.print (((Character)word.pop()).charValue());
        System.out.print (" ");
        index++;
    }

    System.out.println();
  }
}
```

output

```
Enter the coded message:
artxE eseehc esaelp
The decoded message is:
Extra cheese please
```

A message that has been encoded has each individual word in the message reversed. Words in the message are separated by a single space. The program uses the `Stack` class to push the characters of each word on the stack. When an entire word has been read, each character appears in reverse order as it is popped off the stack and printed.

trees and binary trees

A *tree* is a non-linear data structure that consists of a *root node* and potentially many levels of additional nodes that form a hierarchy. All nodes other than the root and leaf nodes are called *internal nodes*. Nodes that have no children are called *leaf nodes*. Figure 12.8 depicts a tree. Note that we draw a tree "upside down," with the root at the top and the leaves at the bottom.

> **key concept**
>
> A tree is a non-linear data structure that organizes data into a hierarchy.

In a general tree like the one in Fig. 12.8, each node could have many child nodes. As we mentioned in Chapter 7, the inheritance relationships among classes can be depicted using a general tree structure.

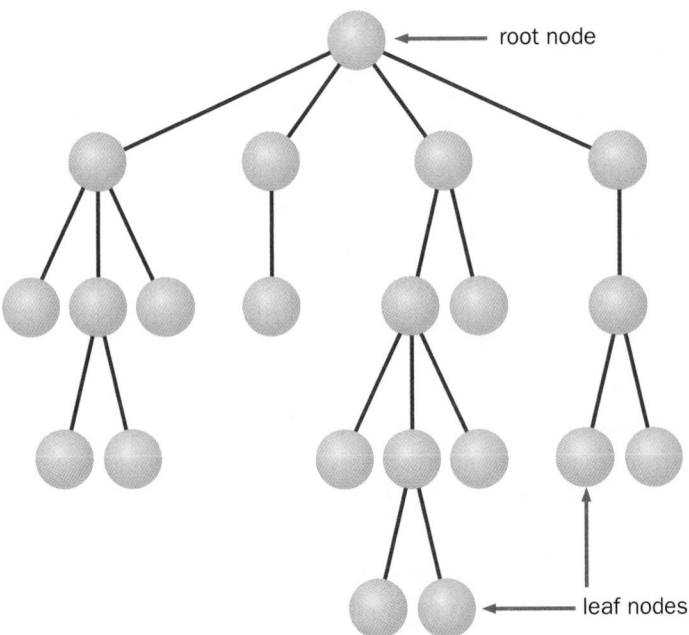

root node

leaf nodes

figure 12.8   A tree data structure

In a *binary tree*, each node can have no more than two child nodes. Binary trees are useful in various programming situations and usually are easier to implement than general trees. Technically, binary trees are a subset of general trees, but they are so important in the computing world that they usually are thought of as their own data structure.

The operations on trees and binary trees vary, but minimally include adding and removing nodes from the tree or binary tree. Because of their non-linear nature, trees and binary trees are implemented nicely using references as dynamic links. However, it is possible to implement a tree data structure using a fixed representation such as an array.

graphs and digraphs

Like a tree, a *graph* is a non-linear data structure. Unlike a tree, a graph does not have a primary entry point like the tree's root node. In a graph, a node is linked to another node by a connection called an *edge*.

Generally there are no restrictions on the number of edges that can be made between nodes in a graph. Figure 12.9 presents a graph data structure.

Graphs are useful when representing relationships for which linear paths and strict hierarchies do not suffice. For instance, the highway system connecting cities on a map and airline connections between airports are better represented as graphs than by any other data structure discussed so far.

In a general graph, the edges are bi-directional, meaning that the edge connecting nodes A and B can be followed from A to B and also from B to A. In a *directed graph*, or *digraph*, each edge has a specific direction. Figure 12.10 shows a digraph, in which each edge indicates the direction using an arrowhead.

A digraph might be used, for instance, to represent airline flights between airports. Unlike highway systems, which are in almost all cases bi-directional, having a flight from one city to another does not necessarily mean there is a corresponding flight going the other way. Or, if there is, we may want to associate different information with it, such as cost.

Like trees, graphs often are implemented using dynamic links, although they can be implemented using arrays as well.

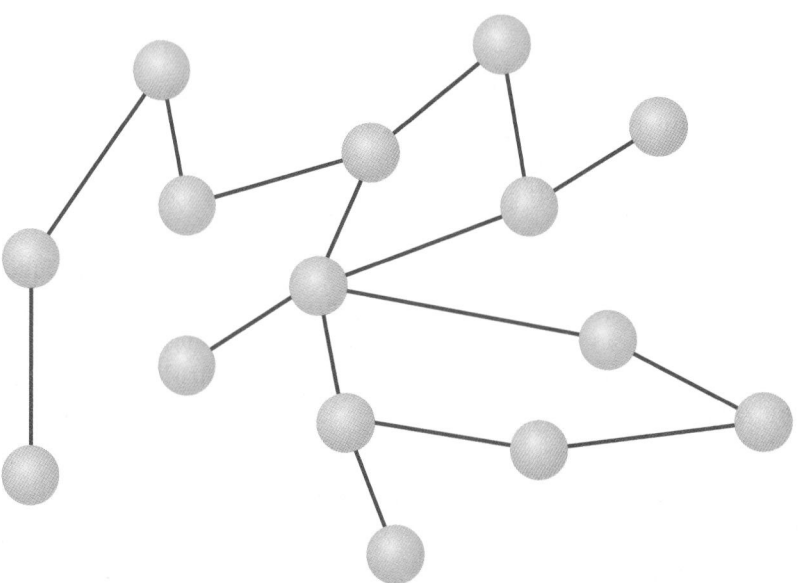

figure 12.9   A graph data structure

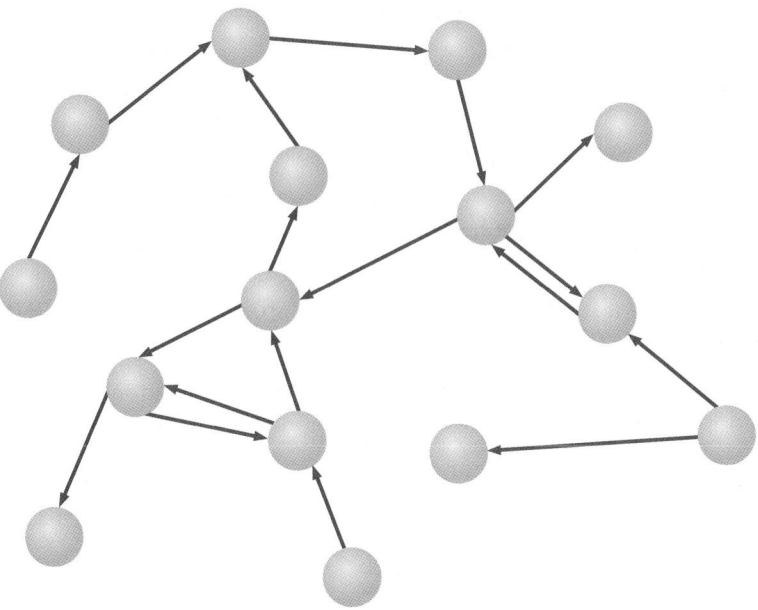

figure 12.10   A directed graph

12.3 java API collection classes

The Java standard class library contains several classes that represent collections of various types. These are often referred to as the *Java Collections API* (Application Programmer Interface).

The names of the classes in this set generally indicate both the collection type and the underlying implementation. One example is the `ArrayList` class. In addition, a `LinkedList` class represents a list collection with a dynamically linked internal implementation. The `Vector` class and the `Stack` classes are carried over from earlier Java incarnations.

Several interfaces are used to define the collection operations themselves. Theses interfaces include `List`, `Set`, `SortedSet`, `Map`, and `SortedMap`. A `Set` is consistent with its normal interpretation as a collection of elements without duplicates. A `Map` is a group of elements that can be referenced by a key value.

The details of these classes go beyond the scope of this book and so are not explored further here.

summary of
key concepts

▸ An abstract data type (ADT) hides the implementation of a data structure behind a well-defined interface. This characteristic makes objects a perfect way to define ADTs.

▸ A fixed data structure has a specific size for the duration of its existence, whereas a dynamic data structure grows and shrinks as needed.

▸ A dynamically linked list is managed by storing and updating references to objects.

▸ A versatile list ADT contains insert and delete operations, which can be implemented by carefully manipulating object references.

▸ Many variations on the implementation of dynamic linked lists exist.

▸ A queue is a linear data structure that manages data in a first-in, first-out manner.

▸ A stack is a linear data structure that manages data in a last-in, first-out manner.

▸ A tree is a non-linear data structure that organizes data into a hierarchy.

▸ A graph is a non-linear data structure that connects nodes using generic edges.

▸ The Java Collections API contains a class infrastructure that supports the organization and management of data.

self-review questions

12.1 What is a collection?

12.2 Why are objects particularly well suited for implementing abstract data types?

12.3 What is a dynamic data structure?

12.4 What is a doubly linked list?

12.5 What is a header node for a linked list?

12.6 How is a queue different from a list?

12.7 What is a stack?

12.8 What is the `Stack` class?

12.9   What do trees and graphs have in common?

12.10 What is the Java Collections API?

exercises

12.1   Suppose current is a reference to a Node object and that it currently refers to a specific node in a linked list. Show, in pseudocode, the steps that would delete the node following current from the list. Carefully consider the cases in which current is referring to the first and last nodes in the list.

12.2   Modify your answer to Exercise 12.1 assuming that the list was set up as a doubly linked list, with both next and prev references.

12.3   Suppose current and newNode are references to Node objects. Assume current currently refers to a specific node in a linked list and newNode refers to an unattached Node object. Show, in pseudocode, the steps that would insert newNode behind current in the list. Carefully consider the cases in which current is referring to the first and last nodes in the list.

12.4   Modify your answer to Exercise 12.3 assuming that the list was set up as a doubly linked list, with both next and prev references.

12.5   Would the front and rear references in the header node of a linked list ever refer to the same node? Would they ever both be null? Would one ever be null if the other was not? Explain your answers using examples.

12.6   Show the contents of a queue after the following operations are performed. Assume the queue is initially empty.

▸ enqueue (45);

▸ enqueue (12);

▸ enqueue (28);

▸ dequeue();

▸ dequeue();

▸ enqueue (69);

▸ enqueue (27);

▸ enqueue (99);

▸ dequeue();

- ▶ enqueue (24);
- ▶ enqueue (85);
- ▶ enqueue (16);
- ▶ dequeue();

12.7 In terms of the final state of a queue, does it matter how dequeue operations are intermixed with enqueue operations? Does it matter how the enqueue operations are intermixed among themselves? Explain using examples.

12.8 Show the contents of a stack after the following operations are performed. Assume the stack is initially empty.

- ▶ push (45);
- ▶ push (12);
- ▶ push (28);
- ▶ pop();
- ▶ pop();
- ▶ push (69);
- ▶ push (27);
- ▶ push (99);
- ▶ pop();
- ▶ push (24);
- ▶ push (85);
- ▶ push (16);
- ▶ pop();

12.9 In terms of the final state of a stack, does it matter how the pop operations are intermixed with the push operations? Does it matter how the push operations are intermixed among themselves? Explain using examples.

12.10 Would a tree data structure be a good choice to represent a family tree that shows lineage? Why or why not? Would a binary tree be a better choice? Why or why not?

12.11 What data structure would be a good choice to represent the links between various Web sites? Give an example.

programming projects

12.1 Consistent with the example from Chapter 6, design and implement an application that maintains a collection of compact discs using a linked list. In the main method of the a driver class, add various CDs to the collection and print the list when complete.

12.2 Modify the MagazineRack program presented in this chapter by adding delete and insert operations into the MagazineList class. Have the Magazine class implement the Comparable interface, and base the processing of the insert method on calls to the compareTo method in the Magazine class that determines whether one Magazine title comes before another lexicographically. In the driver, exercise various insertion and deletion operations. Print the list of magazines when complete.

12.3 Design and implement a version of selection sort (from Chapter 6) that operates on a linked list of nodes that each contain an integer.

12.4 Design and implement a version of insertion sort (from Chapter 6) that operates on a linked list of nodes that each contain an integer.

12.5 Design and implement an application that simulates the customers waiting in line at a bank. Use a queue data structure to represent the line. As customers arrive at the bank, customer objects are put in the rear of the queue with an enqueue operation. When the teller is ready to service another customer, the customer object is removed from the front of the queue with a dequeue operation. Randomly determine when new customers arrive at the bank and when current customers are finished at the teller window. Print a message each time an operation occurs during the simulation.

12.6 Modify the solution to the Programming Project 12.5 so that it represents eight tellers and therefore eight customer queues. Have new customers go to the shortest queue. Determine which queue had the shortest waiting time per customer on average.

12.7 Design and implement an application that evaluates a postfix expression that operates on integer operands using the arithmetic operators +, –, *, /, and %. We are already familiar with *infix expressions*, in which an operator is positioned between its two operands. A *postfix expression* puts the operators after its operands. Keep in mind that an operand could be the result of another operation. This eliminates the need for parentheses to force precedence. For example, the following infix expression:

(5 + 2) * (8 − 5)

is equivalent to the following postfix expression.

5 2 + 8 5 − *

The evaluation of a postfix expression is facilitated by using a stack. As you process a postfix expression from left to right, you encounter operands and operators. If you encounter an operand, push it on the stack. If you encounter an operator, pop two operands off the stack, perform the operation, and push the result back on the stack. When you have processed the entire expression, there will be one value on the stack, which is the result of the entire expression.

You may want to use a `StringTokenizer` object to assist in the parsing of the expression. You can assume the expression will be in valid postfix form.

answers to self-review questions

12.1   A collection is an object whose purpose is to store and organize primitive data or other objects. Some collections represent classic data structures that are helpful in particular problem solving situations.

12.2   An abstract data type (ADT) is a collection of data and the operations that can be performed on that data. An object is essentially the same thing in that we encapsulate related variables and methods in an object. The object hides the underlying implementation of the ADT, separating the interface from the underlying implementation, permitting the implementation to be changed without affecting the interface.

12.3   A dynamic data structure is constructed using references to link various objects together into a particular organization. It is dynamic in that it can grow and shrink as needed. New objects can be added to the structure and obsolete objects can be removed from the structure at runtime by adjusting references between objects in the structure.

12.4   Each node in a doubly linked list has references to both the node that comes before it in the list and the node that comes after it in the list. This organization allows for easy movement forward and backward in the list, and simplifies some operations.

12.5   A header node for a linked list is a special node that holds information about the list, such as references to the front and rear of the list and an integer to keep track of how many nodes are currently in the list.

12.6   A queue is a linear data structure like a list but it has more constraints on its use. A general list can be modified by inserting or deleting nodes anywhere in the list, but a queue only adds nodes to one end (enqueue) and takes them off of the other (dequeue). Thus a queue uses a first-in, first-out (FIFO) approach.

12.7   A stack is a linear data structure that adds (pushes) and removes (pops) nodes from one end. It manages information using a last-in, first-out (LIFO) approach.

12.8   The `Stack` class is defined in the `java.util` package of the Java standard class library. It implements a generic stack ADT. The `Stack` class stores `Object` references, so the stack can be used to store any kind of object.

12.9   Trees and graphs are both non-linear data structures, meaning that the data they store is not organized in a linear fashion. Trees create a hierarchy of nodes. The nodes in a graph are connected using general edges.

12.10   The Java Collections API is a set of classes in the Java standard class library that represents collections of various types, such as `ArrayList` and `LinkedList`.

abstract—A Java reserved word that serves as a modifier for classes, interfaces, and methods. An `abstract` class cannot be instantiated and is used to specify bodiless abstract methods that are given definitions by derived classes. Interfaces are inherently `abstract`.

abstract class—*See* abstract.

abstract data type (ADT)—A collection of data and the operations that are defined on that data. An abstract data type might be implemented in a variety of ways, but the interface operations are consistent.

abstract method—*See* abstract.

Abstract Windowing Toolkit (AWT)—The package in the Java API (`java.awt`) that contains classes related to graphics and graphical user interfaces. *See also* Swing.

abstraction—The concept of hiding details. If the right details are hidden at the right times, abstraction can significantly help control complexity and focus attention on appropriate issues.

access—The ability to reference a variable or invoke a method from outside the class in which it is declared. Controlled by the visibility modifier used to declare the variable or method. Also called the level of encapsulation. *See also* visibility modifier.

access modifier—*See* visibility modifier.

actual parameter—The value passed to a method as a parameter. *See also* formal parameter.

adaptor class—*See* listener adaptor class.

address—(1) A numeric value that uniquely identifies a particular memory location in a computer's main memory. (2) A designation that uniquely identifies a computer among all others on a network.

ADT—*See* abstract data type.

aggregate object—An object that contains variables that are references to other objects. *See also* has-a relationship.

aggregation—Something that is composed, at least in part, of other things. *See also* aggregate object.

algorithm—A step-by-step process for solving a problem. A program is based on one or more algorithms.

alias—A reference to an object that is currently also referred to by another reference. Each reference is an alias of the other.

analog—A representation that is in direct proportion to the source of the information. *See also* digital.

animation—A series of images or drawings that give the appearance of movement when displayed in order at a particular speed.

API—*See* Application Programming Interface.

applet—A Java program that is linked into an HTML document, then retrieved and executed using a Web browser, as opposed to a standalone Java application.

appletviewer—A software tool that interprets and displays Java applets through links in HTML documents. Part of the Java Development Kit.

application—(1) A generic term for any program. (2) A Java program that can be run without the use of a Web browser, as opposed to a Java applet.

Application Programming Interface (API)—A set of classes that defines services for a programmer. Not part of the language itself, but often relied on to perform even basic tasks. *See also* class library.

arc angle—When defining an arc, the radial distance that defines the arc's length. *See also* start angle.

architectural design—A high-level design that identifies the large portions of a software system and key data structures. *See also* detailed design.

architecture—*See* computer architecture.

architecture neutral—Not specific to any particular hardware platform. Java code is considered architecture neutral because it is compiled into bytecode and then interpreted on any machine with a Java interpreter.

arithmetic operator—An operator that performs a basic arithmetic computation, such as addition or multiplication.

arithmetic promotion—The act of promoting the type of a numeric operand to be consistent with the other operand.

array—A programming language construct used to store an ordered list of primitive values or objects. Each element in the array is referenced using a numerical index from 0 to $N-1$, where N is the size of the array.

array element—A value or object that is stored in an array.

array element type—The type of the values or objects that are stored in an array.

ASCII—A popular character set used by many programming languages. ASCII stands for American Standard Code for Information Interchange. It is a subset of the Unicode character set, which is used by Java.

assembly language—A low-level language that uses mnemonics to represent program commands.

assignment conversion—Some data types can be converted to another in an assignment statement. *See* widening conversion.

assignment operator—An operator that results in an assignment to a variable. The = operator performs basic assignment. Many other assignment operators perform additional operations prior to the assignment, such as the *= operator.

association—A relationship between two classes in which one uses the other or relates to it in some way. *See also* operator association, use relationship.

AWT—*See* Abstract Windowing Toolkit.

background color—(1) The color of the background of a graphical user interface component. (2) The color of the background of an HTML page. *See also* foreground color.

base—The numerical value on which a particular number system is based. It determines the number of digits available in that number system and the place value of each digit in a number. *See also* binary, decimal, hexadecimal, octal, place value.

base 2—*See* binary.

base 8—*See* octal.

base 10—*See* decimal.

base 16—*See* hexadecimal.

base case—The situation that terminates recursive processing, allowing the active recursive methods to begin returning to their point of invocation.

base class—*See* superclass.

behavior—The functional characteristics of an object, defined by its methods. *See also* identity, state.

binary—The base-2 number system. Modern computer systems store information as strings of binary digits (bits).

binary operator—An operator that uses two operands.

binary search—A searching algorithm that requires that the list be sorted. It repetitively compares the "middle" element of the list to the target value, narrowing the scope of the search each time. *See also* linear search.

binary string—A series of binary digits (bits).

binary tree—A tree data structure in which each node can have no more than two child nodes.

binding—The process of associating an identifier with the construct that it represents. For example, the process of binding a method name to the specific definition that it invokes.

bit—A binary digit, either 0 or 1.

bit shifting—The act of shifting the bits of a data value to the left or right, losing bits on one end and inserting bits on the other.

bits per second (bps)—A measurement rate for data transfer devices.

bitwise operator—An operator that manipulates individual bits of a value, either by calculation or by shifting.

black-box testing—Producing and evaluating test cases based on the input and expected output of a software component. The test cases focus on covering the equivalence categories and boundary values of the input. *See also* white-box testing.

block—A group of programming statements and declarations delimited by braces ({}).

boolean—A Java reserved word representing a logical primitive data type that can only take the values `true` or `false`.

boolean expression—An expression that evaluates to a true or false result, primarily used as conditions in selection and repetition statements.

boolean operator—Any of the bitwise operators AND (`&`), OR (`|`), or XOR (`^`) when applied to `boolean` operands. The results are equivalent to their logical counterparts, except that boolean operators are not short-circuited.

border—A graphical edge around a graphical user interface component to enhance its appearance or to group components visually. An empty border creates a buffer of space around a component.

bounding rectangle—A rectangle that delineates a region in which an oval or arc is defined.

boundary values—The input values corresponding to the edges of equivalence categories. Used in black-box testing.

bounds checking—The process of determining whether an array index is in bounds, given the size of the array. Java performs automatic bounds checking.

bps—*See* bits per second.

break—A Java reserved word used to interrupt the flow of control by breaking out of the current loop or `switch` statement.

browser—Software that retrieves HTML documents across network connections and formats them for viewing. A browser is the primary vehicle for accessing the World Wide Web. *See also* Netscape Navigator.

bug—A slang term for a defect or error in a computer program.

build-and-fix approach—An approach to software development in which a program is created without any significant planning or design, then modified until it reaches some level of acceptance. It is a prevalent, but unwise, approach.

bus—A group of wires in the computer that carry data between components such as the CPU and main memory.

button—A graphical user interface component that allows the user to initiate an action, set a condition, or choose an option with a mouse click. There are several kinds of GUI buttons. *See also* check box, push button, radio button

byte—(1) A unit of binary storage equal to eight bits. (2) A Java reserved word that represents a primitive integer type, stored using eight bits in two's complement format.

byte stream—An I/O stream that manages 8-bit bytes of raw binary data. *See also* character stream.

bytecode—The low-level format into which the Java compiler translates Java source code. The bytecodes are interpreted and executed by the Java interpreter, perhaps after transportation over the Internet.

capacity—*See* storage capacity.

case—(1) A Java reserved word that is used to identify each unique option in a `switch` statement. (2) The orientation of an alphabetic character (uppercase or lowercase).

case sensitive—Differentiating between the uppercase and lowercase versions of an alphabetic letter. Java is case sensitive; therefore the identifier `total` and the identifier `Total` are considered to be different identifiers.

cast—A Java operation expressed using a type or class name in parentheses to explicitly convert and return a value of one data type into another.

catch—A Java reserved word that is used to specify an exception handler, defined after a `try` block.

CD-Recordable (CD-R)—A compact disc on which information can be stored once using a home computer with an appropriate drive. *See also* CD-Rewritable, CD-ROM.

CD-Rewritable (CD-RW)—A compact disc on which information can be stored and rewritten multiple times using a home computer with an appropriate drive. *See also* CD-Recordable, CD-ROM.

CD-ROM—An optical secondary memory medium that stores binary information in a manner similar to a musical compact disc.

central processing unit (CPU)—The hardware component that controls the main activity of a computer, including the flow of information and the execution of commands.

char—A Java reserved word that represents the primitive character type. All Java characters are members of the Unicode character set and are stored using 16 bits.

character font—A specification that defines the distinct look of a character when it is printed or drawn.

character set—An ordered list of characters, such as the ASCII or Unicode character sets. Each character corresponds to a specific, unique numeric value within a given character set. A programming language adopts a particular character set to use for character representation and management.

character stream—An I/O stream that manages 16-bit Unicode characters. *See also* byte stream.

character string—A series of ordered characters. Represented in Java using the `String` class and string literals such as `"hello"`.

check box—A graphical user interface component that allows the user to set a boolean condition with a mouse click. A check box can be used alone or independently among other check boxes. *See also* radio button.

checked exception—A Java exception that must be either caught or explicitly thrown to the calling method. *See also* unchecked exception.

child class—*See* subclass.

class—(1) A Java reserved word used to define a class. (2) The blueprint of an object—the model that defines the variables and methods an object will contain when instantiated.

class diagram—A diagram that shows the relationships between classes, including inheritance and use relationships. *See also* Unified Modeling Language.

class hierarchy—A tree-like structure created when classes are derived from other classes through inheritance. *See also* interface hierarchy.

class library—A set of classes that define useful services for a programmer. *See also* Application Programming Interface.

class method—A method that can be invoked using only the class name. An instantiated object is not required as it is with instance methods. Defined in a Java program by using the `static` reserved word.

CLASSPATH—An operating system setting that determines where the Java interpreter searches for class files.

class variable—A variable that is shared among all objects of a class. It can also be referenced through the class name, without instantiating any object of that class. Defined in a Java program by using the `static` reserved word.

client-server model—A manner in which to construct a software design based on objects (clients) making use of the services provided by other objects (servers).

coding guidelines—A series of conventions that describe how programs should be constructed. They make programs easier to read, exchange, and integrate. Sometimes referred to as coding standards, especially when they are enforced.

coding standard—*See* coding guidelines.

cohesion—The strength of the relationship among the parts within a software component. *See also* coupling.

collision—The process of two hash values producing the same hash code. *See also* hash code, hashing.

color chooser—A graphical user interface component, often displayed as a dialog box, that allows the user to select or specify a color.

combo box—A graphical user interface component that allows the user to select one of several options. A combo box displays the most recent selection. *See also* list.

command-line arguments—The values that follow the program name on the command line. Accessed within a Java program through the `String` array parameter to the `main` method.

comment—A programming language construct that allows a programmer to embed human-readable annotations into the source code. *See also* documentation.

compiler—A program that translates code from one language to equivalent code in another language. The Java compiler translates Java source code into Java bytecode. *See also* interpreter.

compile-time error—Any error that occurs during the compilation process, often indicating that a program does not conform to the language syntax or that an operation was attempted on an inappropriate data type. *See also* logical error, run-time error, syntax error.

component—Any portion of a software system that performs a specific task, transforming input to output. *See also* GUI component.

computer architecture—The structure and interaction of the hardware components of a computer.

concatenation—*See* string concatenation.

condition—A `boolean` expression used to determine whether the body of a selection or repetition statement should be executed.

conditional coverage—A strategy used in white-box testing in which all conditions in a program are executed, producing both `true` and `false` results. *See also* statement coverage.

conditional operator—A Java ternary operator that evaluates one of two expressions based on a condition.

conditional statement—*See* selection statement.

const—A Java reserved word that is not currently used.

constant—An identifier that contains a value that cannot be modified. Used to make code more readable and to facilitate changes. Defined in Java using the `final` modifier.

constructor—A special method in a class that is invoked when an object is instantiated from the class. Used to initialize the object.

container—A Java graphical user interface component that can hold other components. *See also* containment hierarchy.

containment hierarchy—The relationships among graphical components of a user interface. *See also* container.

content pane—The part of a top-level container to which components are added.

control characters—*See* nonprintable characters.

controller—Hardware devices that control the interaction between a computer system and a particular kind of peripheral.

coupling—The strength of the relationship between two software components. *See also* cohesion.

CPU—*See* central processing unit.

data stream—An I/O stream that represents a particular source or destination for data, such as a file. *See also* processing stream.

data structure—Any programming construct, either defined in the language or by a programmer, used to organize data into a format to facilitate access and processing. Arrays, linked lists, and stacks can all be considered data structures.

data type—A designation that specifies a set of values (which may be infinite). For example, each variable has a data type that specifies the kinds of values that can be stored in it.

data transfer device—A hardware component that allows information to be sent between computers, such as a modem.

debugger—A software tool that allows a programmer to step through an executing program and examine the value of variables at any point. *See also* jdb.

decimal—The base-10 number system, which humans use in everyday life. *See also* binary.

default—A Java reserved word that is used to indicate the default case of a `switch` statement, used if no other cases match.

default visibility—The level of access designated when no explicit visibility modifier is used to declare a class, interface, method, or variable. Sometimes referred to as package visibility. Classes and interfaces declared with default visibility can be used within their package. A method or variable declared with default visibility is inherited and accessible by all subclasses in the same package.

defect testing—Testing designed to uncover errors in a program.

defined—Existing for use in a derived class, even if it can only be accessed indirectly. *See also* inheritance.

delimiter—Any symbol or word used to set the boundaries of a programming language construct, such as the braces ({}) used to define a Java block.

deprecated—Something, such as a particular method, that is considered old-fashioned and should not be used.

derived class—*See* subclass.

design—(1) The plan for implementing a program, which includes a specification of the classes and objects used and an expression of the important program algorithms. (2) The process of creating a program design.

desk check—A type of review in which a developer carefully examines a design or program to find errors.

detailed design—(1) The low-level algorithmic steps of a method. (2) The development stage at which low-level algorithmic steps are determined.

development stage—The software life-cycle stage in which a software system is first created, preceding use, maintenance, and eventual retirement.

dialog box—A graphical window that pops up to allow brief, specific user interaction.

digital—A representation that breaks information down into pieces, which are in turn represented as numbers. All modern computer systems are digital.

digitize—The act of converting an analog representation into a digital one by breaking it down into pieces.

digraph—A graph data structure in which each edge has a specific direction.

dimension—The number of index levels of a particular array.

direct recursion—The process of a method invoking itself. *See also* indirect recursion.

disable—Make a graphical user interface component inactive so that it cannot be used. A disabled component is grayed to indicate its disabled status. *See also* enable.

DNS—*See* Domain Name System.

do—A Java reserved word that represents a repetition construct. A do statement is executed one or more times. *See also* for, while.

documentation—Supplemental information about a program, including comments in a program's source code and printed reports such as a user's guide.

domain name—The portion of an Internet address that specifies the organization to which the computer belongs.

Domain Name System (DNS)—Software that translates an Internet address into an IP address using a domain server.

domain server—A file server that maintains a list of Internet addresses and their corresponding IP addresses.

double—A Java reserved word that represents a primitive floating point numeric type, stored using 64 bits in IEEE 754 format.

doubly linked list—A linked list with two references in each node: one that refers to the next node in the list and one that refers to the previous node in the list.

dynamic binding—The process of associating an identifier with its definition during run time. *See also* binding.

dynamic data structure—A set of objects that are linked using references, which can be modified as needed during program execution.

editor—A software tool that allows the user to enter and store a file of characters on a computer. Often used by programmers to enter the source code of a program.

efficiency—The characteristic of an algorithm that specifies the required number of a particular operation in order to complete its task. For example, the efficiency of a sort can be measured by the number of comparisons required to sort a list. *See also* order.

element—A value or object stored in another object such as an array.

element type—*See* array element type.

else—A Java reserved word that designates the portion of code in an `if` statement that will be executed if the condition is false.

enable—Make a graphical user interface component active so that it can be used. *See also* disable.

encapsulation—The characteristic of an object that limits access to the variables and methods contained in it. All interaction with an object occurs through a well-defined interface that supports a modular design.

equality operator—One of two Java operators that returns a boolean result based on whether two values are equal (`==`) or not equal (`!=`).

equivalence category—A range of functionally equivalent input values as specified by the requirements of the software component. Used when developing black-box test cases.

error—(1) Any defect in a design or program. (2) An object that can be thrown and processed by special `catch` blocks, though usually errors should not be caught. *See also* compile-time error, exception, logical error, run-time error, syntax error.

escape sequence—In Java, a sequence of characters beginning with the backslash character (`\`), used to indicate a special situation when printing values. For example, the escape sequence `\t` specifies that a horizontal tab should be printed.

exception—(1) A situation that arises during program execution that is erroneous or out of the ordinary. (2) An object that can be thrown and processed by special `catch` blocks. *See also* error.

exception handler—The code in a `catch` clause of a `try` statement, executed when a particular type of exception is thrown.

exception propagation—The process that occurs when an exception is thrown: control returns to each calling method in the stack trace until the exception is caught and handled or until the exception is thrown from the `main` method, terminating the program.

exponent—The portion of a floating point value's internal representation that specifies how far the decimal point is shifted. *See also* mantissa.

expression—A combination of operators and operands that produce a result.

extends—A Java reserved word used to specify the parent class in the definition of a child class.

event—(1) A user action, such as a mouse click or key press. (2) An object that represents a user action, to which the program can respond. *See also* event-driven programming.

event-driven programming—An approach to software development in which the program is designed to acknowledge that an event has occurred and to act accordingly. *See also* event.

false—A Java reserved word that serves as one of the two boolean literals (`true` and `false`).

fetch-decode-execute—The cycle through which the CPU continually obtains instructions from main memory and executes them.

FIFO—*See* first-in, first-out.

file—A named collection of data stored on a secondary storage device such as a disk. *See also* text file.

file chooser—A graphical user interface component, usually displayed as a dialog box, that allows the user to select a file from a storage device.

file server—A computer in a network, usually with a large secondary storage capacity, that is dedicated to storing software needed by many network users.

filtering stream—*See* processing stream.

final—A Java reserved word that serves as a modifier for classes, methods, and variables. A `final` class cannot be used to derive a new class. A `final` method cannot be overridden. A `final` variable is a constant.

finalize—A Java method defined in the `Object` class that can be overridden in any other class. It is called after the object becomes a candidate for garbage collection and before it is destroyed. It can be used to perform "clean-up" activity that is not performed automatically by the garbage collector.

finalizer method—A Java method, called `finalize`, that is called before an object is destroyed. *See also* finalize.

finally—A Java reserved word that designates a block of code to be executed when an exception is thrown, after any appropriate catch handler is processed.

first-in, first-out (FIFO)—A data management technique in which the first value that is stored in a data structure is the first value that comes out. *See also* last-in, first-out; queue.

float—A Java reserved word that represents a primitive floating point numeric type, stored using 32 bits in IEEE 754 format.

flushing—The process of forcing the contents of the output buffer to be displayed on the output device.

font—*See* character font.

for—A Java reserved word that represents a repetition construct. A for statement is executed zero or more times and is usually used when a precise number of iterations is known.

foreground color—The color in which any current drawing will be rendered. *See also* background color.

formal parameter—An identifier that serves as a parameter name in a method. It receives its initial value from the actual parameter passed to it. *See also* actual parameter.

fourth-generation language—A high-level language that provides built-in functionality such as automatic report generation or database management, beyond that of traditional high-level languages.

function—A named group of declarations and programming statements that can be invoked (executed) when needed. A function that is part of a class is called a method. Java has no functions because all code is part of a class.

garbage—(1) An unspecified or uninitialized value in a memory location. (2) An object that cannot be accessed anymore because all references to it have been lost.

garbage collection—The process of reclaiming unneeded, dynamically allocated memory. Java performs automatic garbage collection of objects that no longer have any valid references to them.

gigabyte (GB)—A unit of binary storage, equal to 2^{30} (approximately 1 billion) bytes.

goto—(1) A Java reserved word that is not currently used. (2) An unconditional branch.

grammar—A representation of language syntax that specifies how reserved words, symbols, and identifiers can be combined into valid programs.

graph—A non-linear data structure made up of nodes and edges that connect the nodes. *See also* digraph.

graphical user interface (GUI)—Software that provides the means to interact with a program or operating system by making use of graphical images and point-and-click mechanisms such as buttons and text fields.

graphics context—The drawing surface and related coordinate system on which a drawing is rendered or graphical user interface components are placed.

GUI component—A visual element, such as a button or text field, that is used to make up a graphical user interface (GUI).

hardware—The tangible components of a computer system, such as the keyboard, monitor, and circuit boards.

has-a relationship—The relationship between two objects in which one is composed, at least in part, of one or more of the other. *See also* aggregate object, is-a relationship.

hash code—An integer value calculated from any given data value or object, used to determine where a value should be stored in a hash table. Also called a hash value. *See also* hashing.

hash method—A method that calculates a hash code from a data value or object. The same data value or object will always produce the same hash code. Also called a hash function. *See also* hashing.

hash table—A data structure in which values are stored for efficient retrieval. *See also* hashing.

hashing—A technique for storing items so that they can be found efficiently. Items are stored in a hash table at a position specified by a calculated hash code. *See also* hash method.

hexadecimal—The base-16 number system, often used as an abbreviated representation of binary strings.

hierarchy—An organizational technique in which items are layered or grouped to reduce complexity.

high-level language—A programming language in which each statement represents many machine-level instructions.

HTML—*See* HyperText Markup Language.

hybrid object-oriented language—A programming language that can be used to implement a program in a procedural manner or an object-oriented manner, at the programmer's discretion. *See also* pure object-oriented language.

hypermedia—The concept of hypertext extended to include other media types such as graphics, audio, video, and programs.

hypertext—A document representation that allows a user to easily navigate through it in other than a linear fashion. Links to other parts of the document are embedded at the appropriate places to allow the user to jump from one part of the document to another. *See also* hypermedia.

HyperText Markup Language (HTML)—The notation used to define Web pages. *See also* browser, World Wide Web.

icon—A small, fixed-sized picture, often used to decorate a graphical interface. *See also* image.

identifier—Any name that a programmer makes up to use in a program, such as a class name or variable name.

identity—The designation of an object, which, in Java, is an object's reference name. *See also* state, behavior.

IEEE 754—A standard for representing floating point values. Used by Java to represent `float` and `double` data types.

if—A Java reserved word that specifies a simple conditional construct. *See also* else.

image—A picture, often specified using a GIF or JPEG format. *See also* icon.

immutable—The characteristic of something that does not change. For example, the contents of a Java character string are immutable once the string has been defined.

implementation—(1) The process of translating a design into source code. (2) The source code that defines a method, class, abstract data type, or other programming entity.

implements—A Java reserved word that is used in a class declaration to specify that the class implements the methods specified in a particular interface.

import—A Java reserved word that is used to specify the packages and classes that are used in a particular Java source code file.

index—The integer value used to specify a particular element in an array.

index operator—The brackets ([ ]) in which an array index is specified.

indirect recursion—The process of a method invoking another method, which eventually results in the original method being invoked again. *See also* direct recursion.

infinite loop—A loop that does not terminate because the condition controlling the loop never becomes false.

infinite recursion—A recursive series of invocations that does not terminate because the base case is never reached.

infix expression—An expression in which the operators are positioned between the operands on which they work. *See also* postfix expression.

inheritance—The ability to derive a new class from an existing one. Inherited variables and methods of the original (parent) class are available in the new (child) class as if they were declared locally.

initialize—To give an initial value to a variable.

initializer list—A comma-separated list of values, delimited by braces ({}), used to initialize and specify the size of an array.

inline documentation—Comments that are included in the source code of a program.

inner class—A nonstatic, nested class.

input/output buffer—A storage location for data on its way from the user to the computer (input buffer) or from the computer to the user (output buffer).

input/output devices—Hardware components that allow the human user to interact with the computer, such as a keyboard, mouse, and monitor.

input/output stream—A sequence of bytes that represents a source of data (input stream) or a destination for data (output stream).

insertion sort—A sorting algorithm in which each value, one at a time, is inserted into a sorted subset of the entire list. *See also* selection sort.

inspection—*See* walkthrough.

instance—An object created from a class. Multiple objects can be instantiated from a single class.

instance method—A method that must be invoked through a particular instance of a class, as opposed to a class method.

instance variable—A variable that must be referenced through a particular instance of a class, as opposed to a class variable.

instanceof—A Java reserved word that is also an operator, used to determine the class or type of a variable.

instantiation—The act of creating an object from a class.

int—A Java reserved word that represents a primitive integer type, stored using 32 bits in two's complement format.

integration test—The process of testing software components that are made up of other interacting components. Stresses the communication between components rather than the functionality of individual components.

interface—(1) A Java reserved word that is used to define a set of abstract methods that will be implemented by particular classes. (2) The set of messages to which an object responds, defined by the methods that can be invoked from outside of the object. (3) The techniques through which a human user interacts with a program, often graphically. *See also* graphical user interface.

interface hierarchy—A tree-like structure created when interfaces are derived from other interfaces through inheritance. *See also* class hierarchy.

interpreter—A program that translates and executes code on a particular machine. The Java interpreter translates and executes Java bytecode. *See also* compiler.

Internet—The most pervasive wide-area network in the world; it has become the primary vehicle for computer-to-computer communication.

Internet address—A designation that uniquely identifies a particular computer or device on the Internet.

Internet Naming Authority—The governing body that approves all Internet addresses.

invisible component—A graphical user interface component that can be added to a container to provide buffering space between other components.

invocation—*See* method invocation.

I/O devices—*See* input/output devices.

IP address—A series of several integer values, separated by periods (.), that uniquely identifies a particular computer or device on the Internet. Each Internet address has a corresponding IP address.

is-a relationship—The relationship created through properly derived classes via inheritance. The subclass *is-a* more specific version of the superclass. *See also* has-a relationship.

ISO-Latin-1—A 128-character extension to the ASCII character set defined by the International Standards Organization (ISO). The characters correspond to the numeric values 128 through 255 in both ASCII and Unicode.

iteration—(1) One execution of the body of a repetition statement. (2) One pass through a cyclic process, such as an iterative development process.

iteration statement—*See* repetition statement.

iterative development process—A step-by-step approach for creating software, which contains a series of stages that are performed repetitively.

Java Virtual Machine (JVM)—The conceptual device, implemented in software, on which Java bytecode is executed. Bytecode, which is architecture neutral, does not run on a particular hardware platform; instead, it runs on the JVM.

java—The Java command-line interpreter, which translates and executes Java bytecode. Part of the Java Development Kit.

Java—The programming language used throughout this text to demonstrate software development concepts. Described by its developers as object oriented, robust, secure, architecture neutral, portable, high-performance, interpreted, threaded, and dynamic.

Java API—*See* Application Programming Interface.

Java Development Kit (JDK)—A collection of software tools available free from Sun Microsystems, the creators of the Java programming language. *See also* Software Development Kit.

javac—The Java command-line compiler, which translates Java source code into Java bytecode. Part of the Java Development Kit.

javadoc—A software tool that creates external documentation in HTML format about the contents and structure of a Java software system. Part of the Java Development Kit.

javah—A software tool that generates C header and source files, used for implementing `native` methods. Part of the Java Development Kit.

javap—A software tool that disassembles a Java class file, containing unreadable bytecode, into a human-readable version. Part of the Java Development Kit.

jdb—The Java command-line debugger. Part of the Java Development Kit.

JDK—*See* Java Development Kit.

JVM—*See* Java Virtual Machine.

kilobit (Kb)—A unit of binary storage, equal to 2^{10}, or 1024 bits.

kilobyte (K or KB)—A unit of binary storage, equal to 2^{10}, or 1024 bytes.

label—(1) A graphical user interface component that displays text, an image, or both. (2) An identifier in Java used to specify a particular line of code. The `break` and `continue` statements can jump to a specific, labeled line in the program.

LAN—*See* local-area network.

last-in, first-out (LIFO)—A data management technique in which the last value that is stored in a data structure is the first value that comes out. *See also* first-in, first-out; stack.

layout manager—An object that specifies the presentation of graphical user interface components. Each container is governed by a particular layout manager.

lexicographic ordering—The ordering of characters and strings based on a particular character set such as Unicode.

life cycle—The stages through which a software product is developed and used.

LIFO—*See* last-in, first-out.

linear search—A search algorithm in which each item in the list is compared to the target value until the target is found or the list is exhausted. *See also* binary search.

link—(1) A designation in a hypertext document that "jumps" to a new document (or to a new part of the same document) when followed. (2) A connection between two items in a dynamically linked structure, represented as an object reference.

linked list—A dynamic data structure in which objects are linked using references.

list—A graphical user interface component that presents a list of items from which the user can choose. The current selection is highlighted in the list. *See also* combo box.

listener—An object that is set up to respond to an event when it occurs.

listener adaptor class—A class defined with empty methods corresponding to the methods invoked when particular events occur. A listener object can be derived from an adaptor class. *See also* listener interface.

listener interface—A Java interface that defines the methods invoked when particular events occur. A listener object can be created by implementing a listener interface. *See also* listener adaptor class.

literal—A primitive value used explicitly in a program, such as the numeric literal 147 or the string literal "hello".

local-area network (LAN)—A computer network designed to span short distances and connect a relatively small number of computers. *See also* wide-area network.

local variable—A variable defined within a method, which does not exist except during the execution of the method.

logical error—A problem stemming from inappropriate processing in the code. It does not cause an abnormal termination of the program, but it produces incorrect results. *See also* compile-time error, run-time error, syntax error.

logical line of code—A logical programming statement in a source code program, which may extend over multiple physical lines. *See also* physical line of code.

logical operator—One of the operators that perform a logical NOT (!), AND (&&), or OR (||), returning a boolean result. The logical operators are short-circuited, meaning that if their left operand is sufficient to determine the result, the right operand is not evaluated.

long—A Java reserved word that represents a primitive integer type, stored using 64 bits in two's complement format.

loop—*See* repetition statement.

loop control variable—A variable whose value specifically determines how many times a loop body is executed.

low-level language—Either machine language or assembly language, which are not as convenient to construct software in as high-level languages are.

machine language—The native language of a particular CPU. Any software that runs on a particular CPU must be translated into its machine language.

main memory—The volatile hardware storage device where programs and data are held when they are actively needed by the CPU. *See also* secondary memory.

maintenance—(1) The process of fixing errors in or making enhancements to a released software product. (2) The software life-cycle phase in which the software is in use and changes are made to it as needed.

mantissa—The portion of a floating point value's internal representation that specifies the magnitude of the number. *See also* exponent.

megabyte (MB)—A unit of binary storage, equal to 2^{20} (approximately 1 million) bytes.

member—A variable or method in an object or class.

memory—Hardware devices that store programs and data. *See also* main memory, secondary memory.

memory location—An individual, addressable cell inside main memory into which data can be stored.

memory management—The process of controlling dynamically allocated portions of main memory, especially the act of returning allocated memory when it is no longer required. *See also* garbage collection.

method—A named group of declarations and programming statements that can be invoked (executed) when needed. A method is part of a class.

method call conversion—The automatic widening conversion that can occur when a value of one type is passed to a formal parameter of another type.

method definition—The specification of the code that gets executed when the method is invoked. The definition includes declarations of local variables and formal parameters.

method invocation—A line of code that causes a method to be executed. It specifies any values that are passed to the method as parameters.

method overloading—*See* overloading.

mnemonic—(1) A word or identifier that specifies a command or data value in an assembly language. (2) A keyboard character used as a alternative means to activate a graphical user interface component such as a button.

modal—Having multiple modes (such as a dialog box).

modem—A data transfer device that allows information to be sent along a telephone line.

modifier—A designation used in a Java declaration that specifies particular characteristics to the construct being declared.

monitor—The screen in the computer system that serves as an output device.

multidimensional array—An array that uses more than one index to specify a value stored in it.

multiple inheritance—Deriving a class from more than one parent, inheriting methods and variables from each. Multiple inheritance is not supported in Java.

multiplicity—The numeric relationship between two objects, often shown in class diagrams.

NaN—An abbreviation that stands for "not a number," which is the designation for an inappropriate or undefined numeric value.

narrowing conversion—A conversion between two values of different but compatible data types. Narrowing conversions could lose information because the converted type usually has an internal representation smaller than the original storage space. *See also* widening conversion.

native—A Java reserved word that serves as a modifier for methods. A native method is implemented in another programming language.

natural language—A language that humans use to communicate, such as English or French.

negative infinity—A special floating point value that represents the "lowest possible" value. *See also* positive infinity.

nested class—A class declared within another class in order to facilitate implementation and restrict access.

nested if statement—An `if` statement that has as its body another `if` statement.

Netscape Navigator—A popular World Wide Web browser.

network—Two or more computers connected together so that they can exchange data and share resources.

network address—*See* address.

new—A Java reserved word that is also an operator, used to instantiate an object from a class.

newline character—A nonprintable character that indicates the end of a line.

nonprintable characters—Any character, such as escape or newline, that does not have a symbolic representation that can be displayed on a monitor or printed by a printer. *See also* printable characters.

nonvolatile—The characteristic of a memory device that retains its stored information even after the power supply is turned off. Secondary memory devices are nonvolatile. *See also* volatile.

null—A Java reserved word that is a reference literal, used to indicate that a reference does not currently refer to any object.

number system—A set of values and operations defined by a particular base value that determines the number of digits available and the place value of each digit.

object—(1) The primary software construct in the object-oriented paradigm. (2) An encapsulated collection of data variables and methods. (3) An instance of a class.

object diagram—A visual representation of the objects in a program at a given point in time, often showing the status of instance data.

object-oriented programming—An approach to software design and implementation that is centered around objects and classes. *See also* procedural programming.

octal—The base-8 number system, sometimes used to abbreviate binary strings. *See also* binary, hexadecimal.

off-by-one error—An error caused by a calculation or condition being off by one, such as when a loop is set up to access one too many array elements.

operand—A value on which an operator performs its function. For example, in the expression 5 + 2, the values 5 and 2 are operands.

operating system—The collection of programs that provide the primary user interface to a computer and manage its resources, such as memory and the CPU.

operator—A symbol that represents a particular operation in a programming language, such as the addition operator (+).

operator association—The order in which operators within the same precedence level are evaluated, either right to left or left to right. *See also* operator precedence.

operator overloading—Assigning additional meaning to an operator. Operator overloading is not supported in Java, though method overloading is.

operator precedence—The order in which operators are evaluated in an expression as specified by a well-defined hierarchy.

order—The dominant term in an equation that specifies the efficiency of an algorithm. For example, selection sort is of order n^2.

overflow—A problem that occurs when a data value grows too large for its storage size, which can result in inaccurate arithmetic processing. *See also* underflow.

overloading—Assigning additional meaning to a programming language construct, such as a method or operator. Method overloading is supported by Java but operator overloading is not.

overriding—The process of modifying the definition of an inherited method to suit the purposes of the subclass. *See also* shadowing variables.

package—A Java reserved word that is used to specify a group of related classes.

package visibility—*See* default visibility.

panel—A graphical user interface (GUI) container that holds and organizes other GUI components.

parameter—(1) A value passed from a method invocation to its definition. (2) The identifier in a method definition that accepts the value passed to it when the method is invoked. *See also* actual parameter, formal parameter.

parameter list—The list of actual or formal parameters to a method.

parent class—*See* superclass.

pass by reference—The process of passing a reference to a value into a method as the parameter. In Java, all objects are managed using references, so an object's formal parameter is an alias to the original. *See also* pass by value.

pass by value—The process of making a copy of a value and passing the copy into a method. Therefore any change made to the value inside the method is not reflected in the original value. All Java primitive types are passed by value.

PDL—*See* Program Design Language.

peripheral—Any hardware device other than the CPU or main memory.

persistence—The ability of an object to stay in existence after the executing program that creates it terminates. *See also* serialize.

physical line of code—A line in a source code file, terminated by a newline or similar character. *See also* logical line of code.

pixel—A picture element. A digitized picture is made up of many pixels.

place value—The value of each digit position in a number, which determines the overall contribution of that digit to the value. *See also* number system.

pointer—A variable that can hold a memory address. Instead of pointers, Java uses references, which provide essentially the same functionality as pointers but without the complications.

point-to-point connection—The link between two networked devices that are connected directly by a wire.

polyline—A shape made up of a series of connected line segments. A polyline is similar to a polygon, but the shape is not closed.

polymorphism—An object-oriented technique by which a reference that is used to invoke a method can result in different methods being invoked at different times. All Java method invocations are potentially polymorphic in that they invoke the method of the object type, not the reference type.

portability—The ability of a program to be moved from one hardware platform to another without having to change it. Because Java bytecode is not related to any particular hardware environment, Java programs are considered portable. *See also* architecture neutral.

positive infinity—A special floating point value that represents the "highest possible" value. *See also* negative infinity.

postfix expression—An expression in which an operator is positioned after the operands on which it works. *See also* infix expression.

postfix operator—In Java, an operator that is positioned behind its single operand, whose evaluation yields the value prior to the operation being performed. Both the increment (++) and decrement (−−) operators can be applied postfix. *See also* prefix operator.

precedence—*See* operator precedence.

prefix operator—In Java, an operator that is positioned in front of its single operand, whose evaluation yields the value after the operation has been performed. Both the increment (++) and decrement (−−) operators can be applied prefix. *See also* postfix operator.

primitive data type—A data type that is predefined in a programming language.

printable characters—Any character that has a symbolic representation that can be displayed on a monitor or printed by a printer. *See also* nonprintable characters.

private—A Java reserved word that serves as a visibility modifier for methods and variables. Private methods and variables are not inherited by subclasses, and can only be accessed in the class in which they are declared.

procedural programming—An approach to software design and implementation that is centered around procedures (or functions) and their interaction. *See also* object-oriented programming.

processing stream—An I/O stream that performs some type of manipulation on the data in the stream. Sometimes called a filtering stream. *See also* data stream.

program—A series of instructions executed by hardware, one after another.

Program Design Language (PDL)—A language in which a program's design and algorithms are expressed. *See also* pseudocode.

programming language—A specification of the syntax and semantics of the statements used to create a program.

programming language statement—An individual instruction in a given programming language.

prompt—A message or symbol used to request information from the user.

propagation—*See* exception propagation.

protected—A Java reserved word that serves as a visibility modifier for methods and variables. Protected methods and variables are inherited by all subclasses and are accessible from all classes in the same package.

prototype—A program used to explore an idea or prove the feasibility of a particular approach.

pseudocode—Structured and abbreviated natural language used to express the algorithmic steps of a program. *See also* Program Design Language.

pseudo–random number—A value generated by software that performs extensive calculations based on an initial seed value. The result is not truly random because it is based on a calculation, but it is usually random enough for most purposes.

public—A Java reserved word that serves as a visibility modifier for classes, interfaces, methods, and variables. A public class or interface can be used anywhere. A public method or variable is inherited by all subclasses and is accessible anywhere.

pure object-oriented language—A programming language that enforces, to some degree, software development using an object-oriented approach. *See also* hybrid object-oriented language.

push button—A graphical user interface component that allows the user to initiate an action with a mouse click. *See also* check box, radio button.

queue—An abstract data type that manages information in a first-in, first-out manner.

radio button—A graphical user interface component that allows the user choose one of a set of options with a mouse click. A radio button is useful only as part of a group of other radio buttons. *See also* check box.

RAM—*See* random access memory.

random access device—A memory device whose information can be directly accessed. *See also* random access memory, sequential access device.

random access memory (RAM)—A term basically interchangeable with main memory. Should probably be called read-write memory, to distinguish it from read-only memory.

random number generator—Software that produces a pseudo–random number, generated by calculations based on a seed value.

read-only memory (ROM)—Any memory device whose stored information is stored permanently when the device is created. It can be read from, but not written to.

recursion—The process of a method invoking itself, either directly or indirectly. Recursive algorithms sometimes provide elegant, though perhaps inefficient, solutions to a problem.

reference—A variable that holds the address of an object. In Java, a reference can be used to interact with an object, but its address cannot be accessed, set, or operated on directly.

refinement—One iteration of a evolutionary development cycle in which a particular aspect of the system, such as the user interface or a particular algorithm, is addressed.

refinement scope—The specific issues that are addressed in a particular refinement during evolutionary software development.

register—A small area of storage in the CPU of the computer.

relational operator—One of several operators that determine the ordering relationship between two values: less than (<), less than or equal to (<=), greater than (>), and greater than or equal to (>=). *See also* equality operator.

release—A version of a software product that is made available to the customer.

repetition statement—A programming construct that allows a set of statements to be executed repetitively as long as a particular condition is true. The body of the repetition statement should eventually make the condition false. Also called an iteration statement or loop. *See also* do, for, while.

requirements—(1) The specification of what a program must and must not do. (2) An early phase of the software development process in which the program requirements are established.

reserved word—A word that has special meaning in a programming language and cannot be used for any other purpose.

retirement—The phase of a program's life cycle in which the program is taken out of active use.

return—A Java reserved word that causes the flow of program execution to return from a method to the point of invocation.

return type—The type of value returned from a method, specified before the method name in the method declaration. Could be `void`, which indicates that no value is returned.

reuse—Using existing software components to create new ones.

review—The process of critically examining a design or program to discover errors. There are many types of reviews. *See also* desk check, walkthrough.

RGB value—A collection of three values that define a color. Each value represents the contribution of the primary colors red, green, and blue.

ROM—*See* read-only memory.

run-time error—A problem that occurs during program execution that causes the program to terminate abnormally. *See also* compile-time error, logical error, syntax error.

scope—The areas within a program in which an identifier, such as a variable, can be referenced. *See also* access.

scroll pane—A graphical user interface container that offers a limited view of a component and provides horizontal and/or vertical scrollbars to change that view.

SDK—*See* Software Development Kit.

searching—The process of determining the existence or location of a target value within a list of values. *See also* binary search, linear search.

secondary memory—Hardware storage devices, such as magnetic disks or tapes, which store information in a relatively permanent manner. *See also* main memory.

seed value—A value used by a random number generator as a base for the calculations that produce a pseudo-random number.

selection sort—A sorting algorithm in which each value, one at a time, is placed in its final, sorted position. *See also* insertion sort.

selection statement—A programming construct that allows a set of statements to be executed if a particular condition is true. *See also* if, switch.

semantics—The interpretation of a program or programming construct.

sentinel value—A specific value used to indicate a special condition, such as the end of input.

serialize—The process of converting an object into a linear series of bytes so it can be saved to a file or sent across a network. *See also* persistence.

service methods—Methods in an object that are declared with public visibility and define a service that the object's client can invoke.

shadowing variables—The process of defining a variable in a subclass that supersedes an inherited version.

short—A Java reserved word that represents a primitive integer type, stored using 16 bits in two's complement format.

sibling—Two items in a tree or hierarchy, such as a class inheritance hierarchy, that have the same parent.

sign bit—A bit in a numeric value that represents the sign (positive or negative) of that value.

signed numeric value—A value that stores a sign (positive or negative). All Java numeric values are signed. A Java character is stored as an unsigned value.

signature—The number, types, and order of the parameters of a method. Overloaded methods must each have a unique signature.

slider—A graphical user interface component that allows the user to specify a numeric value within a bounded range by moving a knob to the appropriate place in the range.

software—(1) Programs and data. (2) The intangible components of a computer system.

software component—*See* component.

Software Development Kit (SDK)—A collection of software tools that assist in the development of software. The Java Software Development Kit is another name for the Java Development Kit.

software engineering—The discipline within computer science that addresses the process of developing high-quality software within practical constraints.

sorting—The process of putting a list of values into a well-defined order. *See also* insertion sort, selection sort.

split pane—A graphical user interface container that displays two components, either side by side or one on top of the other, separated by a moveable divider bar.

stack—An abstract data type that manages data in a last-in, first-out manner.

stack trace—The series of methods called to reach a certain point in a program. The stack trace can be analyzed when an exception is thrown to assist the programmer in tracking down the problem.

standard I/O stream—One of three common I/O streams representing standard input (usually the keyboard), standard output (usually the monitor screen), and standard error (also usually the monitor). *See also* stream.

start angle—When defining an arc, the angle at which the arc begins. *See also* arc angle.

state—The state of being of an object, defined by the values of its data. *See also* behavior, identity.

statement—*See* programming language statement.

statement coverage—A strategy used in white-box testing in which all statements in a program are executed. *See also* condition coverage.

static—A Java reserved word that serves as a modifier for methods and variables. A static method is also called a class method and can be referenced without an instance of the class. A static variable is also called a class variable and is common to all instances of the class.

static data structure—A data structure that has a fixed size and cannot grow and shrink as needed. *See also* dynamic data structure.

storage capacity—The total number of bytes that can be stored in a particular memory device.

stream—A source of input or a destination for output.

strictfp—A Java reserved word that is used to control certain aspects of floating point arithmetic.

string—*See* character string.

string concatenation—The process of attaching the beginning of one character string to the end of another, resulting in one longer string.

strongly typed language—A programming language in which each variable is associated with a particular data type for the duration of its existence. Variables are not allowed to take on values or be used in operations that are inconsistent with their type.

structured programming—An approach to program development in which each software component has one entry and exit point and in which the flow of control does not cross unnecessarily.

stub—A method that simulates the functionality of a particular software component. Often used during unit testing.

subclass—A class derived from another class via inheritance. Also called a derived class or child class. *See also* superclass.

subscript—*See* index.

super—A Java reserved word that is a reference to the parent class of the object making the reference. Often used to invoke a parent's constructor.

super reference—*See* super.

superclass—The class from which another class is derived via inheritance. Also called a base class or parent class. *See also* subclass.

support methods—Methods in an object that are not intended for use outside the class. They provide support functionality for service methods. As such, they are usually not declared with public visibility.

swapping—The process of exchanging the values of two variables.

swing—The package in the Java API (javax.swing) that contains classes related to graphical user interfaces. Swing provides alternative components than the Abstract Windowing Toolkit package, but does not replace it.

switch—A Java reserved word that specifies a compound conditional construct.

synchronization—The process of ensuring that data shared among multiple threads cannot be accessed by more than one thread at a time. *See also* synchronized.

synchronized—A Java reserved word that serves as a modifier for methods. Separate threads of a process can execute concurrently in a method, unless the method is synchronized, making it a mutually exclusive resource. Methods that access shared data should be synchronized.

syntax rules—The set of specifications that govern how the elements of a programming language can be put together to form valid statements.

syntax error—An error produced by the compiler because a program did not conform to the syntax of the programming language. Syntax errors are a subset of compile-time errors. *See also* compile-time error, logical error, run-time error, syntax rules.

tabbed pane—A graphical user interface (GUI) container that presents a set of cards from which the user can choose. Each card contains its own GUI components.

target value—The value that is sought when performing a search on a collection of data.

TCP/IP—Software that controls the movement of messages across the Internet. The acronym stands for Transmission Control Protocol/Internet Protocol.

terabyte (TB)—A unit of binary storage, equal to 2^{40} (approximately 1 trillion) bytes.

termination—The point at which a program stops executing.

ternary operator—An operator that uses three operands.

test case—A set of input values and user actions, along with a specification of the expected output, used to find errors in a system.

testing—(1) The process of running a program with various test cases in order to discover problems. (2) The process of critically evaluating a design or program.

text area—A graphical user interface component that displays, or allows the user to enter, multiple lines of data.

text field—A graphical user interface component that displays, or allows the user to enter, a single line of data.

text file—A file that contains data formatted as ASCII or Unicode characters.

this—A Java reserved word that is a reference to the object executing the code making the reference.

thread—An independent process executing within a program. A Java program can have multiple threads running in a program at one time.

throw—A Java reserved word that is used to start an exception propagation.

throws—A Java reserved word that specifies that a method may throw a particular type of exception.

timer—An object that generates an event at regular intervals.

token—A portion of a string defined by a set of delimiters.

tool tip—A short line of text that appears when the mouse pointer is allowed to rest on top of a particular component. Usually, tool tips are used to inform the user of the component's purpose.

top-level domain—The last part of a network domain name, such as edu or com.

transient—A Java reserved word that serves as a modifier for variables. A transient variable does not contribute to the object's persistent state, and therefore does not need to be saved. *See also* serialize.

tree—A non-linear data structure that forms a hierarchy stemming from a single root node.

true—A Java reserved word that serves as one of the two boolean literals (`true` and `false`).

truth table—A complete enumeration of all permutations of values involved in a boolean expression, as well as the computed result.

try—A Java reserved word that is used to define the context in which certain exceptions will be handled if they are thrown.

two-dimensional array—An array that uses two indices to specify the location of an element. The two dimensions are often thought of as the rows and columns of a table. *See also* multidimensional array.

two's complement—A technique for representing numeric binary data. Used by all Java integer primitive types (`byte`, `short`, `int`, `long`).

type—*See* data type.

UML—*See* Unified Modeling Language.

unary operator—An operator that uses only one operand.

unchecked exception—A Java exception that does not need to be caught or dealt with if the programmer so chooses.

underflow—A problem that occurs when a floating point value becomes too small for its storage size, which can result in inaccurate arithmetic processing. *See also* overflow.

Unicode—The international character set used to define valid Java characters. Each character is represented using a 16-bit unsigned numeric value.

Unified Modeling Language (UML)—A graphical notation for visualizing relationships among classes and objects. Abbreviated UML. There are many types of UML diagrams. *See also* class diagrams.

uniform resource locator (URL)—A designation for a resource that can be located through a World Wide Web browser.

unit test—The process of testing an individual software component. May require the creation of stub modules to simulate other system components.

unsigned numeric value—A value that does not store a sign (positive or negative). The bit usually reserved to represent the sign is included in the value, doubling the magnitude of the number that can be stored. Java characters are stored as unsigned numeric values, but there are no primitive numeric types that are unsigned.

URL—*See* uniform resource locator.

use relationship—A relationship between two classes, often shown in a class diagram, that establishes that one class uses another in some way, such as relying on its services. *See also* association.

user interface—The manner in which the user interacts with a software system, which is often graphical. *See also* graphical user interface.

variable—An identifier in a program that represents a memory location in which a data value is stored.

visibility modifier—A Java modifier that defines the scope in which a construct can be accessed. The Java visibility modifiers are `public`, `protected`, `private`, and `default` (no modifier used).

void—A Java reserved word that can be used as a return value for a method, indicating that no value is returned.

volatile—(1) A Java reserved word that serves as a modifier for variables. A volatile variable might be changed asynchronously and therefore indicates that the compiler should not attempt optimizations on it. (2) The characteristic of a memory device that loses stored information when the power supply is interrupted. Main memory is a volatile storage device. *See also* nonvolatile.

von Neumann architecture—The computer architecture named after John von Neumann, in which programs and data are stored together in the same memory devices.

walkthrough—A form of review in which a group of developers, managers, and quality assurance personnel examine a design or program in order to find errors. Sometimes referred to as an inspection. *See also* desk check.

WAN—*See* wide-area network.

waterfall model—One of the earliest software development process models. It defines a basically linear interaction between the requirements, design, implementation, and testing stages.

Web—*See* World Wide Web.

while—A Java reserved word that represents a repetition construct. A `while` statement is executed zero or more times. *See also* do, for.

white-box testing—Producing and evaluating test cases based on the interior logic of a software component. The test cases focus on stressing decision points and ensuring coverage. *See also* black-box testing, condition coverage, statement coverage.

white space—Spaces, tabs, and blank lines that are used to set off sections of source code to make programs more readable.

wide-area network (WAN)—A computer network that connects two or more local area networks, usually across long geographic distances. *See also* local-area network.

widening conversion—A conversion between two values of different but compatible data types. Widening conversions usually leave the data value intact because the converted type has an internal representation equal to or larger than the original storage space. *See also* narrowing conversion.

word—A unit of binary storage. The size of a word varies by computer, and is usually two, four, or eight bytes. The word size indicates the amount of information that can be moved through the machine at one time.

World Wide Web (WWW or Web)—Software that makes the exchange of information across a network easier by providing a common user interface for multiple types of information. Web browsers are used to retrieve and format HTML documents.

wrapper class—A class designed to store a primitive type in an object. Usually used when an object reference is needed and a primitive type would not suffice.

WWW—*See* World Wide Web.

This appendix contains a detailed introduction to number systems and their underlying characteristics. The particular focus is on the binary number system, its use with computers, and its similarities to other number systems. This introduction also covers conversions between bases.

In our everyday lives, we use the *decimal number system* to represent values, to count, and to perform arithmetic. The decimal system is also referred to as the *base-10 number system*. We use 10 digits (0 through 9) to represent values in the decimal system.

Computers use the *binary number system* to store and manage information. The binary system, also called the *base-2 number system*, has only two digits (0 and 1). Each 0 and 1 is called a *bit*, short for binary digit. A series of bits is called a *binary string*.

There is nothing particularly special about either the binary or decimal systems. Long ago, humans adopted the decimal number system probably because we have 10 fingers on our hands. If humans had 12 fingers, we would probably be using a base-12 number system regularly and find it as easy to deal with as we do the decimal system now. It all depends on what you get used to. As you explore the binary system, it will become more familiar and natural.

Binary is used for computer processing because the devices used to manage and store information are less expensive and more reliable if they have to represent only two possible values. Computers have been made that use the decimal system, but they are not as convenient.

There are an infinite number of number systems, and they all follow the same basic rules. You already know how the binary number system works, but you just might not be aware that you do. It all goes back to the basic rules of arithmetic.

place value

In decimal, we represent the values of 0 through 9 using only one digit. To represent any value higher than 9, we must use more than one digit. The position of each digit has a *place value* that indicates the amount it contributes to the overall value. In decimal, we refer to the one's column, the ten's column, the hundred's column, and so on forever.

Each place value is determined by the *base* of the number system, raised to increasing powers as we move from right to left. In the decimal number system, the place value of the digit furthest to the right is 10^0, or 1. The place value of the next digit is 10^1, or 10. The place value of the third digit from the right is 10^2, or 100, and so on. Figure B.1 shows how each digit in a decimal number contributes to the value.

The binary system works the same way except that we exhaust the available digits much sooner. We can represent 0 and 1 with a single bit, but to represent any value higher than 1, we must use multiple bits.

The place values in binary are determined by increasing powers of the base as we move right to left, just as they are in the decimal system. However, in binary, the base value is 2. Therefore the place value of the bit furthest to the right is 2^0, or 1. The place value of the next bit is 2^1, or 2. The place value of the third bit from the right is 2^2, or 4, and so on. Figure B.2 shows a binary number and its place values.

The number 1101 is a valid binary number, but it is also a valid decimal number as well. Sometimes to make it clear which number system is being used, the base value is appended as a subscript to the end of a number. Therefore you can distinguish between 1101_2, which is equivalent to 13 in decimal, and 1101_{10} (one thousand, one hundred and one), which in binary is represented as 10001001101_2.

A number system with base N has N digits (0 through $N–1$). As we have seen, the decimal system has 10 digits (0 through 9), and the binary system has two digits (0 and 1). They all work the same way. For instance, the base-5 number system has five digits (0 to 4).

Note that, in any number system, the place value of the digit furthest to the right is 1, since any base raised to the zero power is 1. Also notice that the value 10, which we refer to as "ten" in the decimal system, always represents the base value in any number system. In base 10, 10 is one 10 and zero 1's. In base 2, 10 is one 2 and zero 1's. In base 5, 10 is one 5 and zero 1's.

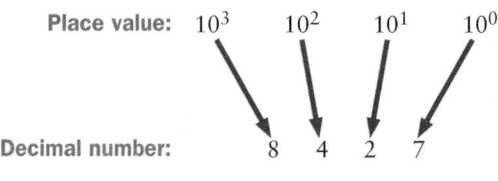

Place value: 10^3 10^2 10^1 10^0

Decimal number: 8   4   2   7

Decimal number: 8 * 10^3 +   4 * 10^2 +   2 * 10^1 +   7 * 10^0 =

   8 * 1000   +   4 * 100   +   2 * 10   +   7 * 1   =   8427

figure B.1   Place values in the decimal system

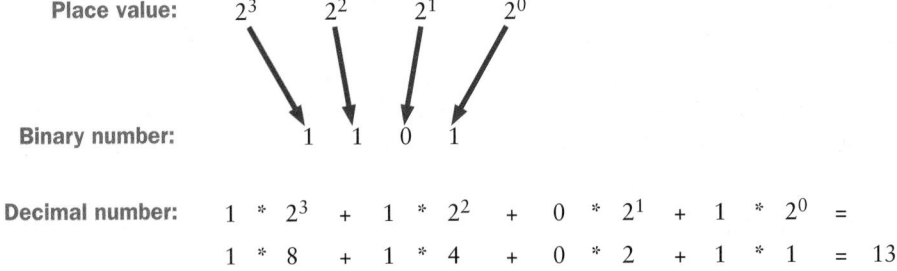

figure B.2   Place values in the binary system

bases higher than 10

Since all number systems with base N have N digits, then base 16 has 16 digits. But what are they? We are used to the digits 0 through 9, but in bases higher than 10, we need a single digit, a single symbol, that represents the decimal value 10. In fact, in *base 16*, which is also called *hexadecimal*, we need digits that represent the decimal values 10 through 15.

For number systems higher than 10, we use alphabetic characters as single digits for values greater than 9. The hexadecimal digits are 0 through F, where 0 through 9 represent the first 10 digits, and A represents the decimal value 10, B represents 11, C represents 12, D represents 13, E represents 14, and F represents 15.

Therefore the number 2A8E is a valid hexadecimal number. The place values are determined as they are for decimal and binary, using increasing powers of the base. So in hexadecimal, the place values are powers of 16. Figure B.3 shows how the place values of the hexadecimal number 2A8E contribute to the overall value.

All number systems with bases greater than 10 use letters as digits. For example, base 12 has the digits 0 through B and base 19 has the digits 0 through I. However, beyond having a different set of digits and a different base, the rules governing each number system are the same.

Keep in mind that when we change number systems, we are simply changing the way we represent values, not the values themselves. If you have 18_{10} pencils, it may be written as 10010 in binary or as 12 in hexadecimal, but it is still the same number of pencils.

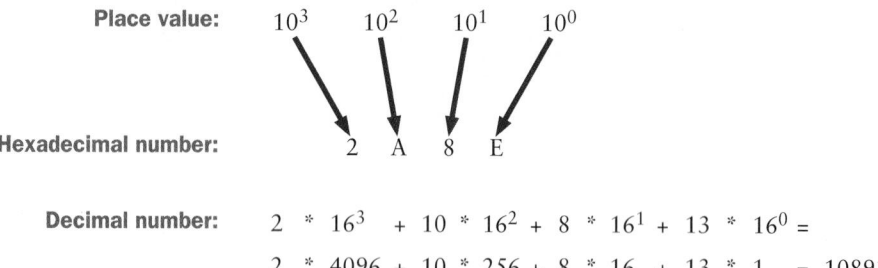

Place value: 10^3 10^2 10^1 10^0

Hexadecimal number: 2 A 8 E

Decimal number: $2 * 16^3 + 10 * 16^2 + 8 * 16^1 + 13 * 16^0 =$
$2 * 4096 + 10 * 256 + 8 * 16 + 13 * 1 = 10893$

figure B.3   Place values in the hexadecimal system

Figure B.4 shows the representations of the decimal values 0 through 20 in several bases, including *base 8*, which is also called *octal*. Note that the larger the base, the higher the value that can be represented in a single digit.

conversions

We've already seen how a number in another base is converted to decimal by determining the place value of each digit and computing the result. This process can be used to convert any number in any base to its equivalent value in base 10.

Now let's reverse the process, converting a base-10 value to another base. First, find the highest place value in the new number system that is less than or equal to the original value. Then divide the original number by that place value to determine the digit that belongs in that position. The remainder is the value that must be represented in the remaining digit positions. Continue this process, position by position, until the entire value is represented.

For example, Fig. B.5 shows the process of converting the decimal value 180 into binary. The highest place value in binary that is less than or equal to 180 is 128 (or 2^7), which is the eighth bit position from the right. Dividing 180 by 128 yields 1 with 52 remaining. Therefore the first bit is 1, and the decimal value 52 must be represented in the remaining seven bits. Dividing 52 by 64, which is the next place value (2^6), yields 0 with 52 remaining. So the second bit is 0. Dividing 52 by 32 yields 1 with 20 remaining. So the third bit is 1 and the remaining five bits must represent the value 20. Dividing 20 by 16 yields 1 with 4 remaining. Dividing 4 by 8 yields 0 with 4 remaining. Dividing 4 by 4 yields 0 with 0 remaining.

Binary (base 2)	Octal (base 8)	Decimal (base 10)	Hexadecimal (base 16)
0	0	0	0
1	1	1	1
10	2	2	2
11	3	3	3
100	4	4	4
101	5	5	5
110	6	6	6
111	7	7	7
1000	10	8	8
1001	11	9	9
1010	12	10	A
1011	13	11	B
1100	14	12	C
1101	15	13	D
1110	16	14	E
1111	17	15	F
10000	20	16	10
10001	21	17	11
10010	22	18	12
10011	23	19	13
10100	24	20	14

figure B.4 Counting in various number systems

Since the number has been completely represented, the rest of the bits are zero. Therefore 180_{10} is equivalent to 10110100 in binary. This can be confirmed by converting the new binary number back to decimal to make sure we get the original value.

This process works to convert any decimal value to any target base. For each target base, the place values and possible digits change. If you start with the correct place value, each division operation will yield a valid digit in the new base.

Place value	Number	Digit
128	180	1
64	52	0
32	52	1
16	20	1
8	4	0
4	4	1
2	0	0
1	0	0

$$180_{10} = 10110100_2$$

figure B.5   Converting a decimal value into binary

In the example in Fig. B.5, the only digits that could have resulted from each division operation would have been 1 or 0, since we were converting to binary. However, when we are converting to other bases, any valid digit in the new base could result. For example, Fig. B.6 shows the process of converting the decimal value 1967 into hexadecimal.

The place value of 256, which is 16^2, is the highest place value less than or equal to the original number, since the next highest place value is 16^3 or 4096. Dividing 1976 by 256 yields 7 with 175 remaining. Dividing 175 by 16 yields 10 with 15 remaining. Remember that 10 in decimal can be represented as the sin-

Place value	Number	Digit
256	1967	7
16	175	A
1	15	F

$$1967_{10} = 7AF_{16}$$

figure B.6   Converting a decimal value into hexadecimal

gle digit A in hexadecimal. The 15 remaining can be represented as the digit F. Therefore 1967_{10} is equivalent to 7AF in hexadecimal.

shortcut conversions

We have established techniques for converting any value in any base to its equivalent representation in base 10, and from base 10 to any other base. Therefore you can now convert a number in any base to any other base by going through base 10. However, an interesting relationship exists between the bases that are powers of 2, such as binary, octal, and hexadecimal, which allows very quick conversions between them.

To convert from binary to hexadecimal, for instance, you can simply group the bits of the original value into groups of four, starting from the right, then convert each group of four into a single hexadecimal digit. The example in Fig. B.7 demonstrates this process.

To go from hexadecimal to binary, we reverse this process, expanding each hexadecimal digit into four binary digits. Note that you may have to add leading zeros to the binary version of each expanded hexadecimal digit if necessary to make four binary digits. Figure B.8 shows the conversion of the hexadecimal value 40C6 to binary.

Why do we section the bits into groups of four when converting from binary to hexadecimal? The shortcut conversions work between binary and any base

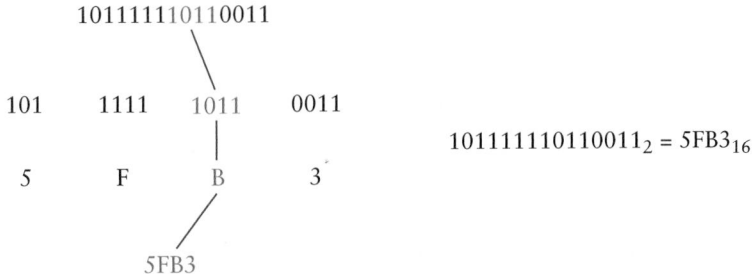

figure B.7   Shortcut conversion from binary to hexadecimal

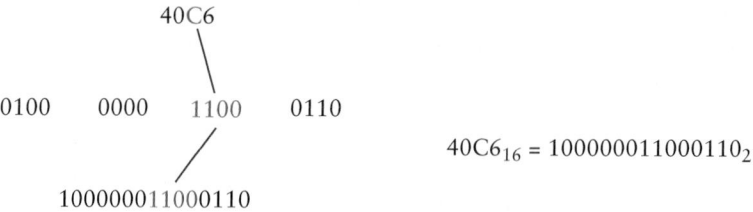

figure B.8   Shortcut conversion from hexadecimal to binary

that is a power of 2. We section the bits into groups of that power. Since $2^4 = 16$, we section the bits in groups of four.

Converting from binary to octal is the same process except that the bits are sectioned into groups of three, since $2^3 = 8$. Likewise, when converting from octal to binary, we expand each octal digit into three bits.

To convert between, say, hexadecimal and octal is now a process of doing two shortcut conversions. First convert from hexadecimal to binary, then take that result and perform a shortcut conversion from binary to octal.

By the way, these types of shortcut conversions can be performed between any base B and any base that is a power of B. For example, conversions between base 3 and base 9 can be accomplished using the shortcut grouping technique, sectioning or expanding digits into groups of two, since $3^2 = 9$.

The Java programming language uses the Unicode character set for managing text. A *character set* is simply an ordered list of characters, each corresponding to a particular numeric value. Unicode is an international character set that contains letters, symbols, and ideograms for languages all over the world. Each character is represented as a 16-bit unsigned numeric value. Unicode, therefore, can support over 65,000 unique characters. Only about half of those values have characters assigned to them at this point. The Unicode character set continues to be refined as characters from various languages are included.

Many programming languages still use the ASCII character set. ASCII stands for the American Standard Code for Information Interchange. The 8-bit extended ASCII set is quite small, so the developers of Java opted to use Unicode in order to support international users. However, ASCII is essentially a subset of Unicode, including corresponding numeric values, so programmers used to ASCII should have no problems with Unicode.

Figure C.1 shows a list of commonly used characters and their Unicode numeric values. These characters also happen to be ASCII characters. All of the characters in Fig. C.1 are called *printable characters* because they have a symbolic representation that can be displayed on a monitor or printed by a printer. Other characters are called *nonprintable characters* because they have no such symbolic representation. Note that the space character (numeric value 32) is considered a printable character, even though no symbol is printed when it is displayed. Nonprintable characters are sometimes called *control characters* because many of them can be generated by holding down the control key on a keyboard and pressing another key.

The Unicode characters with numeric values 0 through 31 are nonprintable characters. Also, the delete character, with numeric value 127, is a nonprintable character. All of these characters are ASCII characters as well. Many of them have fairly common and well-defined uses, while others are more general. The table in Fig. C.2 lists a small sample of the nonprintable characters.

Nonprintable characters are used in many situations to represent special conditions. For example, certain nonprintable characters can be stored in a text document to indicate, among other things, the beginning of a new line. An editor will process these characters by starting the text that follows it on a new line, instead of printing a symbol to the screen. Various types of computer systems use different nonprintable characters to represent particular conditions.

Except for having no visible representation, nonprintable characters are essentially equivalent to printable characters. They can be stored in a Java character variable and be part of a character string. They are stored using 16 bits, can be converted to their numeric value, and can be compared using relational operators.

Value	Char	Value	Char	Value	Char	Value	Char	Value	Char
32	space	51	3	70	F	89	Y	108	l
33	!	52	4	71	G	90	Z	109	m
34	"	53	5	72	H	91	[	110	n
35	#	54	6	73	I	92	\	111	o
36	$	55	7	74	J	93	]	112	p
37	%	56	8	75	K	94	^	113	q
38	&	57	9	76	L	95	_	114	r
39	'	58	:	77	M	96	'	115	s
40	(	59	;	78	N	97	a	116	t
41	)	60	<	79	O	98	b	117	u
42	*	61	=	80	P	99	c	118	v
43	+	62	>	81	Q	100	d	119	w
44	'	63	?	82	R	101	e	120	x
45	–	64	@	83	S	102	f	121	y
46	.	65	A	84	T	103	g	122	z
47	/	66	B	85	U	104	h	123	{
48	0	67	C	86	V	105	i	124		
49	1	68	D	87	W	106	j	125	}
50	2	69	E	88	X	107	k	126	~

figure C.1   A small portion of the Unicode character set

The first 128 characters of the Unicode character set correspond to the common ASCII character set. The first 256 characters correspond to the ISO-Latin-1 extended ASCII character set. Many operating systems and Web browsers will handle these characters, but they may not be able to print the other Unicode characters.

Value	Character
0	*null*
7	*bell*
8	*backspace*
9	*tab*
10	*line feed*
12	*form feed*
13	*carriage return*
27	*escape*
127	*delete*

figure C.2   Some nonprintable characters in the Unicode character set

Java operators are evaluated according to the precedence hierarchy shown in Fig. D.1. Operators at low precedence levels are evaluated before operators at higher levels. Operators within the same precedence level are evaluated according to the specified association, either right to left (R to L) or left to right (L to R). Operators in the same precedence level are not listed in any particular order.

Precedence Level	Operator	Operation	Associates
1	[ ] . (*parameters*) ++ --	array indexing object member reference parameter evaluation and method invocation postfix increment postfix decrement	L to R
2	++ -- + − ~ !	prefix increment prefix decrement unary plus unary minus bitwise NOT logical NOT	R to L
3	new (*type*)	object instantiation cast	R to L
4	* / %	multiplication division remainder	L to R
5	+ + −	addition string concatenation subtraction	L to R
6	<< >> >>>	left shift right shift with sign right shift with zero	
7	< <= > >= instanceof	less than less than or equal greater than greater than or equal type comparison	L to R
8	== !=	equal not equal	L to R

figure D.1   Java operator precedence

Precedence Level	Operator	Operation	Associates
9	&	bitwise AND	L to R
	&	boolean AND	
10	^	bitwise XOR	L to R
	^	boolean XOR	
11	|	bitwise OR	L to R
	|	boolean OR	
12	&&	logical AND	L to R
13	||	logical OR	L to R
14	?:	conditional operator	R to L
15	=	assignment	R to L
	+=	addition, then assignment	
	+=	string concatenation, then assignment	
	-=	subtraction, then assignment	
	*=	multiplication, then assignment	
	/=	division, then assignment	
	%=	remainder, then assignment	
	<<=	left shift, then assignment	
	>>=	right shift (sign), then assignment	
	>>>=	right shift (zero), then assignment	
	&=	bitwise AND, then assignment	
	&=	boolean AND, then assignment	
	^=	bitwise XOR, then assignment	
	^=	boolean XOR, then assignment	
	|=	bitwise OR, the assignment	
	|=	boolean OR, the assignment	

figure D.1   Java operator precedence, continued

The order of operator evaluation can always be forced by the use of parentheses. It is often a good idea to use parentheses even when they are not required to make it explicitly clear to a human reader how an expression is evaluated.

For some operators, the operand types determine which operation is carried out. For instance, if the + operator is used on two strings, string concatenation is performed, but if it is applied to two numeric types, they are added in the arithmetic sense. If only one of the operands is a string, the other is converted to a string, and string concatenation is performed. Similarly, the operators &, ^, and | perform bitwise operations on numeric operands but boolean operations on boolean operands. Appendix E describes the bitwise and boolean operators in more detail.

The boolean operators & and | differ from the logical operators && and || in a subtle way. The logical operators are "short-circuited" in that if the result of an expression can be determined by evaluating only the left operand, the right operand is not evaluated. The boolean versions always evaluate both sides of the expression. There is no logical operator that performs an exclusive OR (XOR) operation.

This appendix discusses the Java *bitwise operators*, which operate on individual bits within a primitive value. They are defined only for integers and characters. They are unique among all Java operators because they let us work at the lowest level of binary storage. Figure E.1 lists the Java bitwise operators.

Three of the bitwise operators are similar to the logical operators !, &&, and ||. The bitwise NOT, AND, and OR operations work basically the same way as their logical counterparts, except they work on individual bits of a value. The rules are essentially the same. Figure E.2 shows the results of bitwise operators on all combinations of two bits. Compare this chart to the truth tables for the logical operators in Chapter 3 to see the similarities.

The bitwise operators include the XOR operator, which stands for *exclusive OR*. The logical || operator is an *inclusive OR* operation, which means it returns true if both operands are true. The | bitwise operator is also inclusive and yields a 1 if both corresponding bits are 1. However, the exclusive OR operator (^) yields a 0 if both operands are 1. There is no logical exclusive OR operator in Java.

When the bitwise operators are applied to integer values, the operation is performed individually on each bit in the value. For example, suppose the integer variable number is declared to be of type byte and currently holds the value 45. Stored as an 8-bit byte, it is represented in binary as 00101101. When the bitwise complement operator (~) is applied to number, each bit in the value is inverted,

Operator	Description
~	bitwise NOT
&	bitwise AND
|	bitwise OR
^	bitwise XOR
<<	left shift
>>	right shift with sign
>>>	right shift with zero fill

figure E.1 Java bitwise operators

a	b	~ a	a & b	a | b	a ^ b
0	0	1	0	0	0
0	1	1	0	1	1
1	0	0	0	1	1
1	1	0	1	1	0

figure E.2   Bitwise operations on individual bits

yielding `11010010`. Since integers are stored using two's complement representation, the value represented is now negative, specifically –46.

Similarly, for all bitwise operators, the operations are applied bit by bit, which is where the term "bitwise" comes from. For binary operators (with two operands), the operations are applied to corresponding bits in each operand. For example, assume `num1` and `num2` are `byte` integers, and `num1` holds the value 45, and `num2` holds the value 14. Figure E.3 shows the results of several bitwise operations.

The operators `&`, `|`, and `^` can also be applied to boolean values, and they have basically the same meaning as their logical counterparts. When used with boolean values, they are called *boolean operators*. However, unlike the operators `&&` and `||`, which are "short-circuited," the boolean operators are not short-circuited. Both sides of the expression are evaluated every time.

Like the other bitwise operators, the three bitwise shift operators manipulate the individual bits of an integer value. They all take two operands. The left operand is the value whose bits are shifted; the right operand specifies how many positions they should move. Prior to performing a shift, `byte` and `short` values

num1 & num2	num1 | num2	num1 ^ num2
00101101	00101101	00101101
& 00001110	| 00001110	^ 00001110
= 00001100	= 00101111	= 00100011

figure E.3   Bitwise operations on bytes

are promoted to `int` for all shift operators. Furthermore, if either of the operands is `long`, the other operand is promoted to `long`. For readability, we use only 16 bits in the examples in this section, but the concepts are the same when carried out to 32- or 64-bit strings.

When bits are shifted, some bits are lost off one end, and others need to be filled in on the other. The *left shift* operator (<<) shifts bits to the left, filling the right bits with zeros. For example, if the integer variable `number` currently has the value 13, then the statement

```
number = number << 2;
```

stores the value 52 into `number`. Initially, `number` contains the bit string 0000000000001101. When shifted to the left, the value becomes 0000000000110100, or 52. Notice that for each position shifted to the left, the original value is multiplied by 2.

The sign bit of a number is shifted along with all of the others. Therefore the sign of the value could change if enough bits are shifted to change the sign bit. For example, the value −8 is stored in binary two's complement form as 1111111111111000. When shifted left two positions, it becomes 1111111111100000, which is −32. However, if enough positions are shifted, a negative number can become positive and vice versa.

There are two forms of the right shift operator: one that preserves the sign of the original value (>>) and one that fills the leftmost bits with zeros (>>>).

Let's examine two examples of the *right-shift-with-sign-fill* operator. If the `int` variable `number` currently has the value 39, the expression (`number >> 2`) results in the value 9. The original bit string stored in `number` is 0000000000100111, and the result of a right shift two positions is 0000000000001001. The leftmost sign bit, which in this case is a zero, is used to fill from the left.

If `number` has an original value of −16, or 1111111111110000, the right shift (with sign fill) expression (`number >> 3`) results in the binary string 1111111111111110, or −2. The leftmost sign bit is a 1 in this case and is used to fill in the new left bits, maintaining the sign.

If maintaining the sign is not desirable, the *right-shift-with-zero-fill* operator (>>>) can be used. It operates similarly to the >> operator but fills with zero no matter what the sign of the original value is.

This appendix summarizes the modifiers that give particular characteristics to Java classes, interfaces, methods, and variables. For discussion purposes, the set of all Java modifiers is divided into two groups: visibility modifiers and all others.

java visibility modifiers

The table in Fig. F.1 describes the effect of Java visibility modifiers on various constructs. Some relationships are not applicable (N/A). For instance, a class cannot be declared with protected visibility. Note that each visibility modifier operates in the same way on classes and interfaces and in the same way on methods and variables.

Default visibility means that no visibility modifier was explicitly used. Default visibility is sometimes called *package visibility*, but you cannot use the reserved word `package` as a modifier. Classes and interfaces can have default or public visibility; this visibility determines whether a class or interface can be referenced outside of its package. Only an inner class can have private visibility, in which case only the enclosing class may access it.

When applied to methods and variables, the visibility modifiers dictate two specific characteristics:

- *Inheritance,* which determines whether a method or variable can be referenced in a subclass as if it were declared locally.

- *Access,* or the degree of encapsulation, which determines the scope in which a method or variable can be directly referenced. All methods and variables are accessible in the class in which they are declared.

Modifier	Classes and interfaces	Methods and variables
default (no modifier)	Visible in its package.	Inherited by any subclass in the same package as its class. Accessible by any class in the same package as its class.
public	Visible anywhere.	Inherited by all subclasses of its class. Accessible anywhere.
protected	N/A	Inherited by all subclasses of its class. Accessible by any class in the same package as its class.
private	Visible to the enclosing class only	Not inherited by any subclass. Not accessible by any other class.

figure F.1   Java visibility modifiers

Public methods and variables are inherited by all subclasses and can be accessed by anyone. *Private* methods and variables are not inherited by any subclasses and can only be accessed inside the class in which they are declared.

Protected visibility and default visibility (no modifier) vary in subtle ways. Note that a subclass of a parent may or may not be in the same package as the parent, and that not all classes in a package are related by inheritance.

Protected methods and variables are inherited by all subclasses, whether they are in the same package as the parent or not. Access to protected methods and variables is given to any class in the same package as the class in which they are declared. Therefore a subclass in a different package will inherit the protected methods and variables, but the subclass cannot directly reference them in an instance of the parent. Furthermore, a class can directly access a protected method or variable that is declared in another class in the same package, whether the two classes are related by inheritance or not.

A method or variable with *default visibility* is inherited only by subclasses that are in the same package as the class in which the method or variable is declared. A method or variable with default visibility can be accessed by any class in the same package, whether they are related by inheritance or not.

All methods and variables declared in a parent class exist for all subclasses but are not necessarily inherited by them. For example, when a child class is instantiated, memory space is reserved for a private variable of the parent class. However, that child class cannot refer to that variable by name since the variable was not inherited. The child class can, however, call an inherited method that references that variable. Similarly, an inherited method can invoke a method that the child class cannot call explicitly. For this reason, inheritance is carefully defined using the words "as if it were declared locally." Noninherited methods and variables can still be referenced indirectly.

a visibility example

Consider the situation depicted in the Fig. F.2. Class `P` is the parent class that is used to derive child classes `C1` and `C2`. Class `C1` is in the same package as `P`, but `C2` is not. Class `P` contains four methods, each with different visibility modifiers. One object has been instantiated from each of these classes.

The `public` method `a()` has been inherited by `C1` and `C2`, and any code with access to object `x` can invoke `x.a()`. The `private` method `d()` is not inherited by `C1` or `C2`, so objects `y` and `z` have no such method available to them. Furthermore, `d()` is fully encapsulated and can only be invoked from within object `x`.

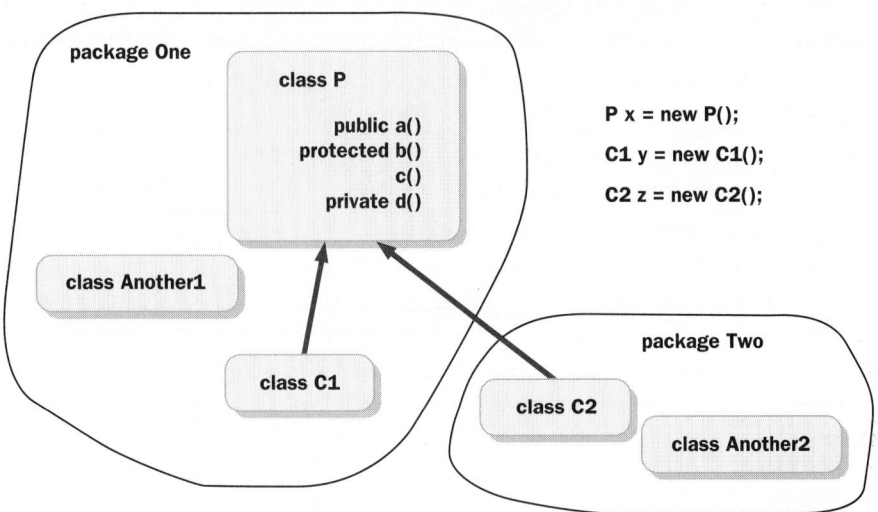

figure F.2 A situation demonstrating Java visibility modifiers

The `protected` method `b()` is inherited by both `C1` and `C2`. A method in `y` could invoke `x.b()`, but a method in `z` could not. Furthermore, an object of any class in package `One` could invoke `x.b()`, even those that are not related to class `P` by inheritance, such as an object created from class `Another1`.

Method `c()` has `default` visibility, since no visibility modifier was used to declare it. Class `C1` inherits `c()`, but `C2` does not. Therefore object `y` can refer to the method `c()` as if it were declared locally, but object `z` cannot. Object `y` can invoke `x.c()`, as can an object instantiated from any class in package `One`, such as `Another1`. Object `z` cannot invoke `x.c()`.

These rules generalize in the same way for variables. The visibility rules may appear complicated initially, but they can be mastered with a little effort.

other java modifiers

Figure F.3 summarizes the rest of the Java modifiers, which address a variety of issues. Furthermore, any given modifier has a different effect on classes, interfaces, methods, and variables. Some modifiers cannot be used with certain constructs and therefore are listed as not applicable (N/A).

Modifier	Class	Interface	Method	Variable
abstract	The class may contain abstract methods. It cannot be instantiated.	All interfaces are inherently abstract. The modifier is optional.	No method body is defined. The method requires implementation when inherited.	N/A
final	The class cannot be used to drive new classes.	N/A	The method cannot be overridden.	The variable is a constant, whose value cannot be changed once initially set.
native	N/A	N/A	No method body is necessary since implementation is in another language.	N/A
static	N/A	N/A	Defines a class method. It does not require an instantiated object to be invoked. It cannot reference non-static methods or variables. It is implicitly final.	Defines a class variable. It does not require an instantiated object to be referenced. It is shared (common memory space) among all instances of the class.
synchro-nized	N/A	N/A	The execution of the method is mutually exclusive among all threads.	N/A
transient	N/A	N/A	N/A	The variable will not be serialized.
volatile	N/A	N/A	N/A	The variable is changed asynchronously. The compiler should not perform optimizations on it.

figure F.3   The rest of the Java modifiers

The `transient` modifier is used to indicate data that need not be stored in a persistent (serialized) object. That is, when an object is written to a serialized stream, the object representation will include all data that is not specified as transient. See Chapter 8 for a more detailed description.

This appendix contains a series of guidelines that describe how to organize and format Java source code. They are designed to make programs easier to read and maintain. Some guidelines can be attributed to personal preferences and could be modified. However, it is important to have some standard set of practices that make sense and to follow them carefully. The guidelines presented here are followed in the example code throughout the text and are consistent with the Java naming conventions.

Consistency is half the battle. If you follow the same rules throughout a program, and follow them from one program to another, you make the effort of reading and understanding your code easier for yourself and others. It is not unusual for a programmer to develop software that seems straightforward at the time, only to revisit it months later and have difficulty remembering how it works. If you follow consistent development guidelines, you reduce this problem considerably.

When an organization adopts a coding standard, it is easier for people to work together. A software product is often created by a team of cooperating developers, each responsible for a piece of the system. If they all follow the same development guidelines, they facilitate the process of integrating the separate pieces into one cohesive entity.

You may have to make tradeoffs between some guidelines. For example, you may be asked to make all of your identifiers easy to read yet keep them to a reasonably short length. Use common sense on a case-by-case basis to embrace the spirit of all guidelines as much as possible.

You may choose, or be asked, to follow this set of guidelines as presented. If changes or additions are made, make sure they are clear and that they represent a conscious effort to use good programming practices. Most of these issues are discussed further in appropriate areas of the text but are presented succinctly here, without elaboration.

design guidelines

A. Design Preparation

1. The ultimate guideline is to develop a clean design. Think before you start coding. A working program is not necessarily a good program.

2. Express and document your design with consistent, clear notation.

B. Structured Programming

 1. Do not use the `continue` statement.

 2. Only use the `break` statement to terminate cases of a `switch` statement.

 3. Have only one `return` statement in a method, as the last line, unless it unnecessarily complicates the method.

C. Classes and Packages

 1. Do not have additional methods in the class that contains the `main` method.

 2. Define the class that contains the `main` method at the top of the file it is in, followed by other classes if appropriate.

 3. If only one class is used from an imported package, import that class by name. If two or more are imported, use the `*` symbol.

D. Modifiers

 1. Do not declare variables with `public` visibility.

 2. Do not use modifiers inside an interface.

 3. Always use the most appropriate modifiers for each situation. For example, if a variable is used as a constant, explicitly declare it as a constant using the `final` modifier.

E. Exceptions

 1. Use exception handling only for truly exceptional conditions, such as terminating errors, or for significantly unusual or important situations.

 2. Do not use exceptions to disguise or hide inappropriate processing.

 3. Handle each exception at the appropriate level of design.

F. Miscellaneous

 1. Use constants instead of literals in almost all situations.

 2. Design methods so that they perform one logical function. As such, the length of a method will tend to be no longer than 50 lines of code, and usually much shorter.

 3. Keep the physical lines of a source code file to less than 80 characters in length.

 4. Extend a logical line of code over two or more physical lines only when necessary. Divide the line at a logical place.

style guidelines

A. Identifier Naming

1. Give identifiers semantic meaning. For example, do not use single letter names such as `a` or `i` unless the single letter has semantic meaning.

2. Make identifiers easy to read. For example, use `currentValue` instead of `curval`.

3. Keep identifiers to a reasonably short length.

4. Use the underscore character to separate words of a constant.

B. Identifier Case

1. Use UPPERCASE for constants.

2. Use Title Case for class, package, and interface names.

3. Use lowercase for variable and method names, except for the first letter of each word other than the first word. For example, `minTaxRate`. Note that all reserved words must be lowercase.

C. Indentation

1. Indent the code in any block by three spaces.

2. If the body of a loop, `if` statement, or `else` clause is a single statement (not a block), indent the statement three spaces on its own line.

3. Put the left brace (`{`) starting each new block on a new line. Line up the terminating right brace (`}`) with the opening left brace. For example:

```
while (value < 25)
{
   value += 5;
   System.out.println ("The value is " + value);
}
```

4. In a `switch` statement, indent each `case` label three spaces. Indent all code associated with a `case` three additional spaces.

D. Spacing

1. Carefully use white space to draw attention to appropriate features of a program.

2. Put one space after each comma in a parameter list.

3. Put one space on either side of a binary operator.

4. Do not put spaces immediately after a left parenthesis or before a right parenthesis.

5. Do not put spaces before a semicolon.

6. Put one space before a left parenthesis, except before an empty parameter list.

7. When declaring arrays, associate the brackets with the element type, as opposed to the array name, so that it applies to all variables on that line. For example:

```
int[30] list1, list2;
```

8. When referring to the type of an array, do not put any spaces between the element type and the square brackets, such as `int[ ]`.

E. Messages and Prompts

1. Do not condescend.

2. Do not attempt to be humorous.

3. Be informative, but succinct.

4. Define specific input options in prompts when appropriate.

5. Specify default selections in prompts when appropriate.

F. Output

1. Label all output clearly.

2. Present information to the user in a consistent manner.

documentation guidelines

A. The Reader

1. Write all documentation as if the reader is computer literate and basically familiar with the Java language.

2. Assume the reader knows almost nothing about what the program is supposed to do.

3. Remember that a section of code that seems intuitive to you when you write it might not seem so to another reader or to yourself later. Document accordingly.

B. Content

1. Make sure comments are accurate.

2. Keep comments updated as changes are made to the code.

3. Be concise but thorough.

C. Header Blocks

1. Every source code file should contain a header block of documentation providing basic information about the contents and the author.

2. Each class and interface, and each method in a class, should have a small header block that describes its role.

3. Each header block of documentation should have a distinct delimiter on the top and bottom so that the reader can visually scan from one construct to the next easily. For example:

```
//****************************************
//              header block
//****************************************
```

D. In-Line Comments

1. Use in-line documentation as appropriate to clearly describe interesting processing.

2. Put a comment on the same line with code only if the comment applies to one line of code and can fit conveniently on that line. Otherwise, put the comment on a separate line above the line or section of code to which it applies.

E. Miscellaneous

1. Avoid the use of the `/* */` style of comment except to conform to the javadoc (`/** */`) commenting convention.

2. Don't wait until a program is finished to insert documentation. As pieces of your system are completed, comment them appropriately.

This appendix contains a checklist of issues that should be addressed during a design or code review. A *review* is a careful critique of the design or code after it has been completed. A review can take many forms. In a *desk check*, a programmer reviews his or her own work. In a *walkthrough* or *inspection*, a group of people meet to examine and discuss the product. No matter what form a review takes, using a checklist ensures that particular issues important to creating high-quality software are not overlooked.

Reviews involve reading through a program or design to check that objects and classes are well designed, that algorithms are implemented correctly, that code is commented properly, and that other quality attributes of the software are ensured. When a review is conducted as a walkthrough, the participants usually include the author of the code, the designer (if a separate person), one or more additional software engineers, and a person that understands the system requirements. Other people that might attend a walkthrough include managers and quality control personnel.

During a walkthrough, many problems usually come to light. Errors in implementation and misunderstandings about requirements are discovered. Careful notes must be taken so that these issues can be addressed. The goal is not necessarily to solve the problems in the meeting, but at least to note them for later consideration. Many walkthroughs have been sidetracked by participants following tangents concerning one particular problem.

Walkthroughs on large software projects are an absolute necessity. Unfortunately, on small software projects, walkthroughs are often overlooked or dismissed as nonessential. The same benefits that occur in reviews of large software projects also occur on smaller projects. They should never be considered unnecessary. Considerable evidence shows that as much as 70 percent of the errors in a program can be identified during a careful walkthrough.

Before a walkthrough can begin, the people involved must be prepared. The software or design must be complete and ready for review. The relevant documentation, such as design documents and requirements, must be gathered. The appropriate people to attend the walkthrough must be identified and given the documentation. By the time the meeting takes place, the participants should have reviewed all of the provided materials and prepared constructive comments and suggestions. An unsuccessful walkthrough is usually the result of a lack of preparation.

During the walkthrough, the author often presents a brief overview of the software or design. The author may ask the others in the meeting to concentrate on particular areas of concern. A specific person is usually designated as a recorder to capture the major questions or problems that come up. The author and reviewers then step through the code or design in detail, bringing up concerns and identifying problems at the appropriate time. After a walkthrough, the problems and corrective actions noted during the meeting should be summarized and presented to the author of the code or design so that they can be addressed.

The following checklist contains specific issues that should be covered in a review, whether conducted by yourself or in a meeting. A checklist makes the review process systematic and prevents important issues from being overlooked. Depending on your knowledge of software development and Java constructs, some of the checklist issues may not be clear. Focus on those issues that you understand and incorporate others as they become familiar.

This checklist can be augmented with other issues. Don't hesitate to add particular topics that address your own common programming and design challenges.

review checklist

General Issues

❑ Is the design or code complete?

❑ Can any algorithms be simplified?

❑ Does the program work for all valid input?

❑ Does the program handle invalid input appropriately?

❑ Does the program do everything it is supposed to?

❑ Does the program operate under all constraints that were established?

❑ Is the API being used to its fullest extent?

❑ Have resources (such as books and the Web) been checked for published sources of required algorithms?

Design Issues

❑ Are classes designed to encapsulate specific implementation decisions?

❑ Are classes designed to maximize reuse?

❑ Is the design modular, facilitating the inclusion of new algorithms or components?

❑ Does each inheritance derivation represent an appropriate *"is-a"* relationship?

❑ Is the class hierarchy appropriate for the problem being solved?

❑ Are abstract classes used to enhance the design of the class hierarchy?

❑ Are interfaces used properly in the design to maximize consistency among classes?

❑ Are classes grouped appropriately into packages?

❑ Are exceptions used only for handling erroneous conditions or truly unusual processing?

❑ Are threads used appropriately to minimize user response time?

Implementation Issues

❑ Are all coding standards followed?

❑ Are all comments complete and accurate?

❑ Are all variables initialized before they are used?

❑ Are constants used to make the code more readable and facilitate modifications?

❑ Are all identifiers named so that their role is clear?

❑ Do all loops terminate?

❑ Do all array indexes stay within bounds?

❑ Do all method arguments match their parameters appropriately?

❑ Are modifications to parameters in methods consistent with how those parameters are passed?

❑ Do all overriding methods have the same signature as the parent's method?

❑ Are all appropriate "clean-up" activities performed, such as files being closed?

❑ Is the implementation consistent with the design?

The designers of Java based much of its syntax on the programming languages C and C++ so that developers who know those languages would feel comfortable using Java. However, Java should not be thought of as a revision of C++. There are many critical differences between the two.

In fact, Java has integrated the best characteristics of several programming languages. At the heart of Java are important tenets of program design and implementation that are fundamentally distinct from the approach of C++. However, because of the similar syntax and the popularity of C++, comparisons between these two languages are inevitable.

This appendix compares and contrasts Java and C++. It is a focused summary of the primary similarities and differences, and is intended for developers with experience using C++.

primitive types

There are several important differences between Java and C++ concerning primitive data types and their use. Figure I.1 summarizes these differences.

Each variable in a Java program is either associated with a primitive type (`boolean`, `char`, `byte`, `short`, `int`, `long`, `float`, or `double`) or is a reference to an object. C++ has various primitive types, plus structs, unions, enums, arrays, and pointers. C++ pointers might or might not refer to objects.

C++ structs are subsumed by Java objects. Java does not currently have an enumerated type. Java designers thought the concept of unions to save memory space was unnecessary. All Java primitives are signed and have a consistent size no matter what platform is used, enhancing portability.

Java	C++
Two type categories.	Various type categories.
All nonprimitive types are objects.	Separate types for structs, unions, enums, and arrays.
All numeric types are signed.	Signed and unsigned numeric types.
All primitive types are a fixed size for all platforms.	Primitive type size varies by platform.
16-bit Unicode characters.	8-bit ASCII characters.
Boolean data type primitive.	No explicit boolean data type.
Conditions must be boolean expressions.	Integer results are interpreted as boolean conditions.
Variables are automatically initialized.	No automatic initialization of variables.

figure I.1 Java versus C++: Primitive types

All Java implementations are based on the international Unicode character set, whereas most C++ implementations use ASCII (American Standard Code for Information Interchange). However, since ASCII is essentially a subset of Unicode, this distinction is transparent for programmers used to using ASCII. Unicode characters can be used in identifiers and literals in a Java program.

The `boolean` type in Java cannot be cast to any other type, and vice versa. Java integers cannot be used as logical conditions. In C++, there is no built-in boolean type, and integers are used for decision making.

No Java variables can contain garbage since they are set to a default value if not initialized when created. However, Java compilers may warn against the use of variables before their value has been explicitly set, whether intentional or not.

pointers and data structures

The absence of pointers in Java is a key difference between the two languages. Figure I.2 summarizes the differences concerning the use of pointers, references, and basic data structures.

Java uses references that provide the functionality and versatility of pointers without their involved syntax and dangerous characteristics. Linked data structures are accomplished with references as you would with pointers in C++, but in Java it is impossible to get a segmentation fault since a reference can only refer to an object, not an arbitrary memory location.

Java	C++
References, with no explicit pointer manipulation and no pointer arithmetic.	Pointers, with dereferencing (* or ->) and address (&) operators.
Array references are not translated to pointer arithmetic.	Array references translate to pointer arithmetic.
Arrays automatically check index limits.	No automatic array bounds checking.
Array lengths in multidimensional arrays can vary from one element to the next within one dimension.	Array lengths in multidimensional arrays are all the same size in a given dimension, fixed by the declaration.
Strings are objects.	Strings are null-terminated character arrays.
Built-in string concatenation operator (+).	String concatenation through a library function.
Use string concatenation operator for long string literals.	Use line continuation (\) for long string literals.
No `typedef`.	`typedef` to define types.

figure I.2   Java versus C++: Pointers, references, and basic data structures

Arrays and character strings are objects in Java, with appropriate support methods. String concatenation is a built-in operation in the Java language, and array bounds checking is automatic.

Multidimensional arrays in Java are actually arrays of arrays, in which each array is a distinct object. Therefore, for example, each row in a two-dimensional array can have a different number of elements. The length of each array is determined when each array object is instantiated, not when the initial declaration is made.

Defining explicit type names is not necessary in either Java or C++ since the declaration of larger structures, such as classes, implicitly defines a type name. C++ includes the `typedef` operation for compatibility with C.

object-oriented programming

Both languages are object oriented but have significantly different philosophies and techniques, as summarized in Fig. I.3.

C++ supports the object-oriented approach, but it doesn't enforce it. Since C++ is essentially a superset of C, which is a procedural language, a program written in C++ could be a *hybrid* mix of procedural and object-oriented techniques. Java is a *pure* object-oriented language since it enforces the object-oriented approach. As such, all functions in Java are methods, defined inside a class.

Several constructs and techniques that are a part of C++ are not included in Java, mainly to keep the complexity of the language down. These include multiple inheritance, parameterized types, and operator overloading. However, Java

Java	C++
Pure object-oriented language.	Hybrid between procedural and object-oriented.
All functions (methods) are part of a class.	Can have stand-alone functions.
No multiple inheritance.	Multiple inheritance.
Formal interface specifications.	No formal interface specifications.
No parameterized type.	Templates as a parameterized type.
No operator overloading.	Operator overloading.
All methods (except final methods) are dynamically bound.	Virtual functions are dynamically bound.

figure I.3 Java versus C++: Object-oriented programming

has the ability to define a formal interface specification, which gives the most important characteristics of multiple inheritance to Java programs. Both languages support method overloading.

In C++, a method must be explicitly declared as virtual in order to allow runtime dynamic binding of a method invocation to the appropriate definition. In Java, all methods are handled consistently and are dynamically bound, except for methods that are defined with the `final` modifier.

special characteristics

Some of the most highly promoted aspects of Java concern its relationship to the Web and other special characteristics that distinguish it from C++. Figure I.4 summarizes these differences.

Links to Java applets can be embedded in HTML documents, then retrieved and executed using Web browsers. The Java API has specific support for network communication.

A C++ programmer must perform explicit dynamic memory management, releasing objects and other dynamically allocated data space when it is no longer needed. In Java, garbage collection is automatic. An object in a Java program is marked as a candidate for garbage collection after the last reference to it is removed. Therefore Java does not support destructors, though there is the ability to define a `finalize` method for other cleanup activity.

Java source code is compiled into bytecode, a low-level representation that is not tied to any particular processor. The bytecode can then be executed on any platform that has a Java interpreter. Java is therefore considered architecture neutral.

Java	C++
Specifically attuned to network and Web processing.	No relationship to networks or the Web.
Automatic garbage collection.	No automatic garbage collection.
Combination of compiled and interpreted.	Compiled.
Slower execution when interpreted.	Fast execution.
Architecture neutral.	Architecture specific.
Supports multithreading.	No multithreading.
Automatic generation of documentation in HTML format.	No automatic documentation generation.

figure I.4   Java versus C++: Special characteristics

When interpreted, Java programs have a slower execution speed; however, because they are already compiled to a low-level representation, the interpretation overhead is not problematic for many applications. C++ compilers are specific to each type of processor.

The Java language supports multiple threads of execution, with synchronization mechanisms. It also has a special comment syntax, which can be used to generate external documentation in HTML format about the contents and structure of a Java system.

general programming issues

Several specific differences between Java and C++ affect basic programming practices. Figure I.5 summarizes these differences.

Java does not support variable-length parameter lists for methods. It also does not allow parameters to be given a default value, which essentially makes them optional during invocation.

Java	C++
Method bodies must be defined inside the class to which they belong.	Method bodies must be defined inside the class to which they belong.
No forward referencing required.	Explicit forward referencing required.
No preprocessor.	Heavy reliance on preprocessor.
No comma operator.	Comma operator.
No variable-length parameter lists.	Variable-length parameter lists.
No optional method parameters.	Optional function parameters.
No const reference parameters.	const reference parameters.
No goto statement.	goto statement.
Labels on break and continue.	No labels on break and continue.
Command-line arguments do not include the program name.	Command-line arguments do not include the program name.
Main method cannot return a value.	Main function can return a value.
No global variables.	Global variables.
Character escape sequences can appear in a program.	Character escape sequences must appear in a string or character literal.
Cannot mask identifiers through scope.	Can mask identifiers through scope.

figure I.5   Java versus C++: General programming issues

Java has no comma operator, though its `for` loop syntactically allows multiple initializations and increments using the comma symbol. Java does not allow variables to be declared with global scope. In C++, you must use an explicit forward reference (function prototype) to inform the compiler that a function will be used prior to its definition, but in Java no such forward referencing is needed.

Java does not rely on a preprocessor. Most of the functionality that is provided by the C++ preprocessor is defined in the Java language itself.

There is no `goto` statement in Java, though `goto` is included in the Java reserved words. Java allows statements to be labeled, and the `break` and `continue` statements can jump to specific labeled points in the code.

Finally, in Java, an identifier name cannot be masked by another declaration and scope, as it can in C++. For example, the following code segment is valid in C++ but causes a compile-time error in Java:

```
{
int x = 12;
    {
        int x = 25;   // same variable name with
                      // distinct memory space
    }
}
```

This appendix contains a brief tutorial covering the HyperText Markup Language (HTML) and the creation of basic Web pages. HTML files contain instructions that describe how text, images, and multimedia are displayed by Web browsing software. Two of the more popular Web browsers are Microsoft's Internet Explorer and Netscape's Navigator.

HTML files can be created using a simple text editor. The files contain the text to be displayed and *tags* that describe the layout, style, and other features of a document. Tags suggest how the browser program should display the document, but each browser interprets the meaning of a tag in its own way. Furthermore, although all browsers recognize a common set of tags, a particular browser may also recognize additional tags that others do not. Therefore what you see when you view a particular HTML document with one browser might be different from what you see when viewed with another.

In this appendix, we describe the most popular HTML tags. If you plan to create advanced Web pages, you may want to use additional sources covering all aspects of HTML. Many Web sites contain detailed information on specific HTML constructs. In fact, one of the best ways to learn HTML is to find interesting Web pages and use your Web browser to view the HTML source for that document.

basic HTML documents

Every HTML file has two basic sections. The first section is the head of the document, which contains a description of the document, including its title. The second section is the body of the document, which contains the information to be displayed, such as text, images, and links to other documents. The following is an example of a basic HTML document for a local student activities group:

```
<HTML>
    <HEAD>
        <TITLE>Students in Action</TITLE>
    </HEAD>
    <BODY>
        Students in Action is dedicated to helping our local
        community by using the volunteer effort of college
        students.  This semester, our planned actions are
        to help a local food drive for flood victims in
        the Midwest, to visit local adult care centers, and to
        teach Java to grade-school students.
        Our group is active, energetic, and always in need of
        donations of equipment, effort, and money.  We are
```

```
        always willing to help staff and plan community
        events.
        As always, our president (at x222) is eager and
        willing to answer questions and hear suggestions on
        how we can be more active in our community.
    </BODY>
</HTML>
```

The words such as HEAD, TITLE, and BODY are called elements. Tags are specified using an element enclosed in angle brackets (<>). Tags are often used in pairs, called a start tag and an end tag. These tags delimit, or mark, a particular region of text. Generally, the start tag uses the element name, such as <HEAD>, and the end tag uses a slash (/) followed by the element name, such as </HEAD>.

Everything between <HEAD> and </HEAD> is considered the introduction of the document. In this case, it contains one line that defines the title of the document.

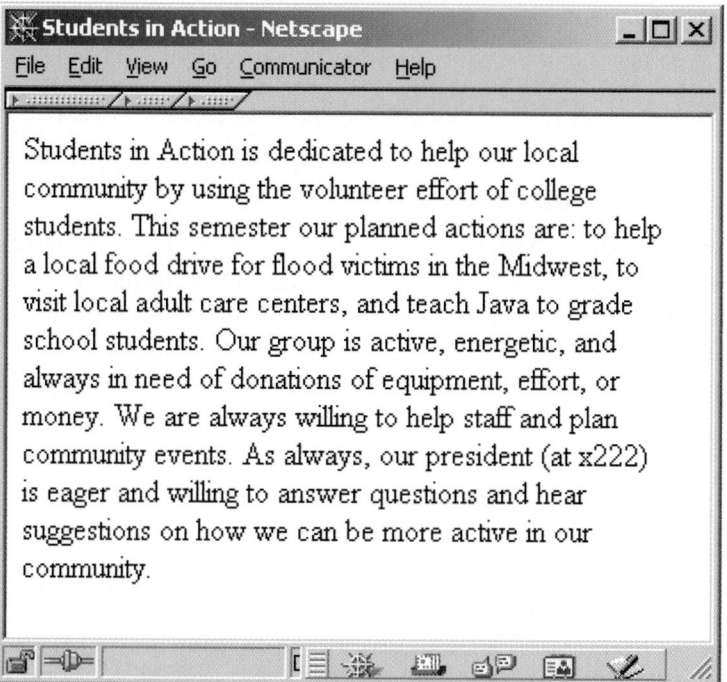

figure J.1   The initial Students in Action Web page

The text between <TITLE> and </TITLE> appears in the title bar of the Web browser when the document is displayed.

Everything between <BODY> and </BODY> is considered the body of the document. In this case, the body contains several paragraphs of text that will be displayed in the browser window. The text in an HTML document can be in any form convenient for its author. Browsers only pay attention to tags. Therefore it does not matter how white space is used to separate words or lines between tags. Browsers will reformat the text to be displayed appropriately for the width and height of the browser window, independent of how the document is written. Figure J.1 shows this Web page as displayed in a browser. Figure J.2 shows the same Web page but in a different-sized browser window. Notice how the text is reformatted because of the browser's width and height.

formatting text

Many tags can be used to aid browsers with formatting text. Notice in Figs J.1 and J.2 that the blank spaces in the paragraphs were ignored when the text was displayed. For browsers to understand how to format text, each part of the text must be marked with tags. To indicate to the browser what paragraphs are in the text, the P element should be used. The following is a marked-up version of the Students in Action Web page, including paragraph tags.

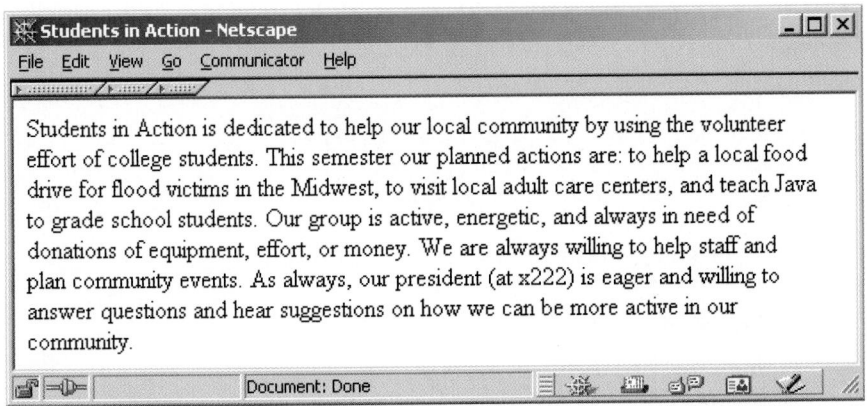

figure J.2   The Web page in a different-sized browser window

```
<HTML>
  <HEAD>
    <TITLE>Students in Action</TITLE>
  </HEAD>
  <BODY>
    <P>Students in Action is dedicated to helping our
    local community by using the volunteer effort of
    college students.  This semester, our planned actions
    are to help a local food drive for flood victims
    in the Midwest, to visit local adult care centers,
    and to teach Java to grade-school students.</P>
    <P>Our group is active, energetic, and always in
    need of donations of equipment, effort, and money.
    We are always willing to help staff and plan
    community events.</P>
    <P>As always, our president (at x222) is eager and
    willing to answer questions and hear suggestions on
    how we can be more active in our community.</P>
  </BODY>
</HTML>
```

Figure J.3 is a snapshot showing the effects of the <P> tag used in the text. Notice the <P> is not displayed by the browser, but instead a single blank line has been inserted.

In addition to the P element, many other elements can be used to change the format of the text. The table in Fig. J.4 shows some elements and their effect on the text associated with a tag.

B, I, and U are popular elements that control the style of the font presented. They work similarly to how a word processor allows text to be bold, italic, or underlined. For example, the following HTML lines:

```
<P><B>I'd buy that for a dollar</B></P>
<P><I>May the force be with you</I></P>
<P><I><B>I'll be back</B></I></P>
```

would be displayed by a browser as:

I'd buy that for a dollar
May the force be with you
I'll be back

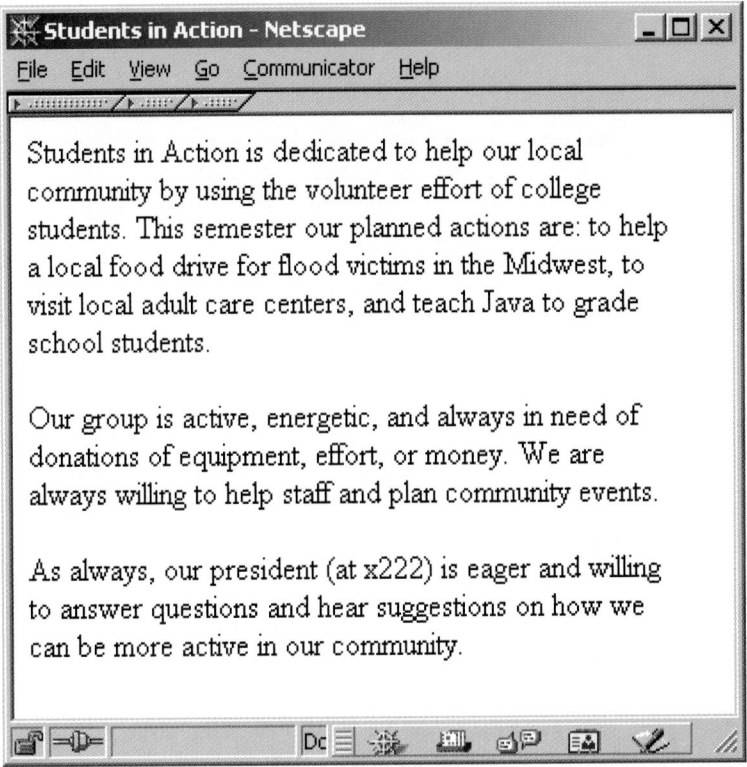

figure J.3   The Students in Action Web page with paragraph formatting

Many elements can be nested to produce a combination of effects. Notice the use of I and B on the last line of the previous example. Usually, it is considered good practice to unnest tags in the same order as they were nested. This practice makes it easier to modify the HTML later. The rest of the elements described in Fig. J.4 also change characteristics of the font displayed by the browser.

Several other elements can be used to change the layout of the text. The <CENTER> and </CENTER> tags indicate that the browser should center the text associated with the tag. The <BR> tag forces a line break in the text. The <HR> tag tells the browser to include a horizontal rule in the document. The horizontal rule is often used to separate sections of a document visually. Note that the HR and BR elements do not have associated ending tags because they do not affect text directly. The <NOBR> and </NOBR> tags indicate that the browser should not insert line breaks anywhere when displaying the text associated with the tags. The

Element	Effect or Purpose
U	Underline
B	Boldface
I	Italics
STRONG	Strong type, often rendered using boldface
EM	Emphasis, often rendered using italics
STRIKE	A line drawn through the text
TT	typewriter typeface
CODE	Code listings
KBD	Keyboard input
VAR	Variables or arguments to commands
BIG	A larger point size than the current font
SMALL	A smaller point size than the current font
SUB	Subscript
SUP	Superscript
CITE	Citation of reference documents
BLINK	Blinks on and off

figure J.4   Some HTML text elements

<Q> tag is used within a line of text to quote a few words. Text associated with the Q element is displayed within single quotes. The <BQ> tag can be used to quote a block of text, such as a paragraph.

In addition to marking up portions of the document to be displayed in a particular way, HTML header tags can provide an overall hierarchical structure to the document. Headers are used to indicate different sections of a document. HTML provides six heading levels: <H1>, <H2>, <H3>, <H4>, <H5>, and <H6>. The <H1> heading tag is the highest heading level, and <H6> is the lowest. An H1 element can be thought of as marking a chapter of a book. An H2 element can be thought of as marking a section of a chapter. An H3 element is associated with a subsection, and the other headers follow suit. Generally, headings are displayed by most browsers as bold text and usually are larger in size (compared to the rest of the "normal" text in the document). For example, consider the following HTML document:

```
<HTML>
    <HEAD>
        <TITLE>Header Example</TITLE>
    </HEAD>
    <BODY>
        <H1> 1. Heading One
        <H2> 2. Heading Two
        <H3> 3. Heading Three
        <H4> 4. Heading Four
        <H5> 5. Heading Five
        <H6> 6. Heading Six
    </BODY>
</HTML>
```

Figure J.5 shows the display of this page.

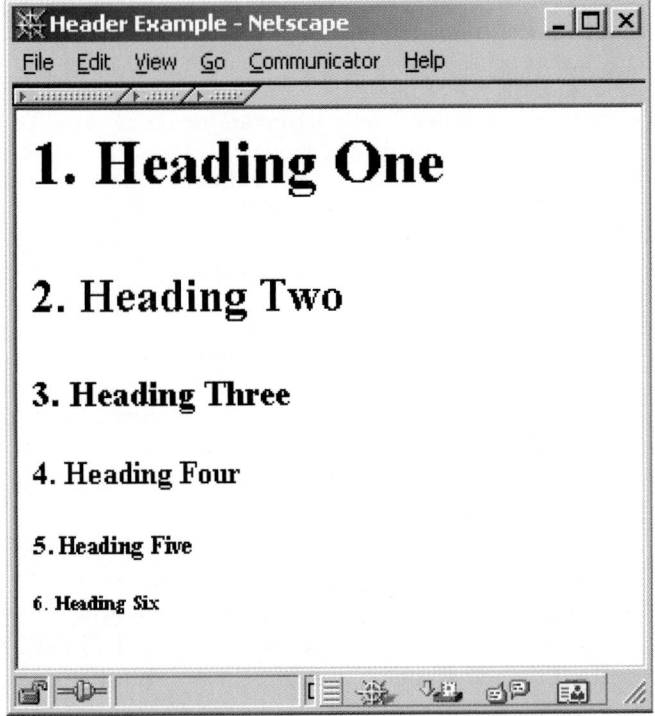

figure J.5   Header example

There are several reasons to use headers in your Web pages. The first is that headers make a document easier to read. They provide a visual cue to a reader of the different sections of your text. These cues enable a reader to easily identify and skip to the appropriate section of a Web page. The second reason is that Web search engines often catalog the text associated with headers in a document. Therefore using a good heading for a section of a document may help others find your page on the Internet. Generally, documents should contain no more than three levels of headings.

The following HTML is the Students in Action Web page marked up with a header and some font styles.

```
<HTML>
    <HEAD>
        <TITLE>Students in Action</TITLE>
    </HEAD>
    <BODY>
        <CENTER><H1>Students in Action</H1></CENTER>
        <CENTER><I>Dedicated to helping our local community
        by using the volunteer effort of college
        students.</I></CENTER>
        <P>This semester, our planned actions are to help a
        local food drive for flood victims in the Midwest,
        to visit local adult care centers, and to teach Java
        to grade-school students.</P>
        <P>Our group is active, energetic, and always in
        need of donations of equipment, effort, and money.
        We are always willing to help staff and plan
        community events.</P>
        <P>As always, our president (at x222) is eager and
        willing to answer questions and hear suggestions on
        how we can be more active in our community.</P>
    </BODY>
</HTML>
```

Figure J.6 shows the display of this page.

You can use several other elements, including frames, tables, and lists to structure a Web document. Frames and tables are more complicated than the tags we have seen so far and are beyond the scope of this tutorial. HTML has two types of lists: an ordered list and an unordered list. Creating a list requires two parts to be identified using tags. The first is the entire list. For an ordered list, place the <OL> tag at the start of the list, and </OL> at the end of the list, and then surround each item in the list with <LI> and </LI>. For example, the following HTML defines one list with three items:

```
<OL>
    <LI>I'd buy that for a dollar</LI>
    <LI>May the force be with you</LI>
    <LI>I'll be back</LI>
</OL>
```

This text will be formatted in browsers as:

> 1. I'd buy that for a dollar
> 2. May the force be with you
> 3. I'll be back

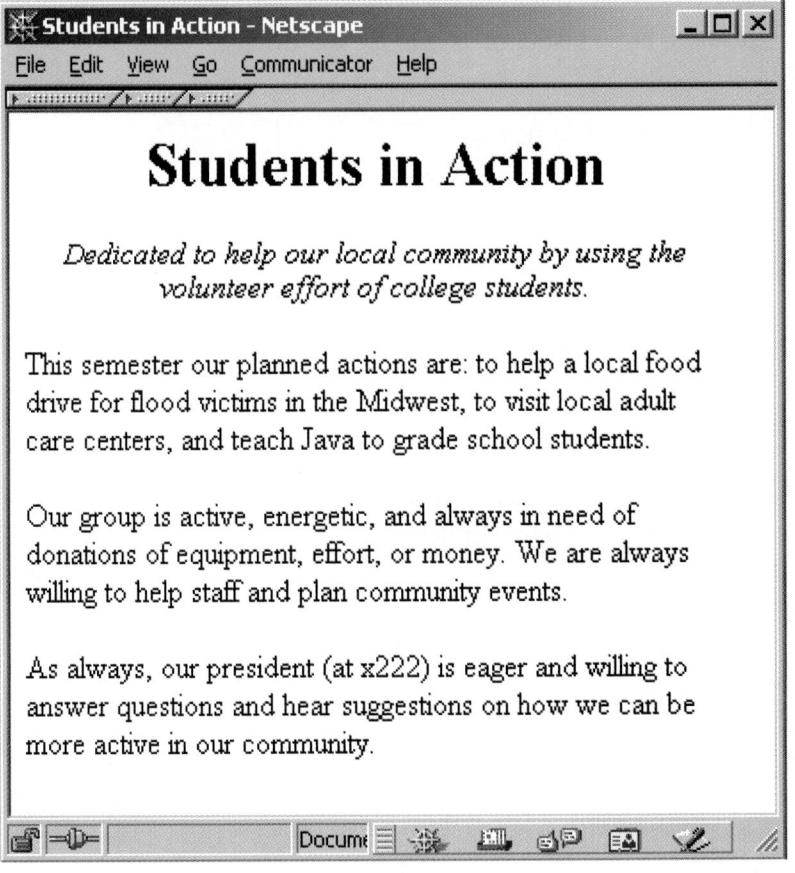

figure J.6   Header, centering, and font changes for the
Students in Action Web page

Notice that the browser will automatically count and sequence the items in the list. Lists can also be nested within lists. Consider the following HTML code:

```
<OL>
    <LI>First Item in first list</LI>
    <OL>
        <LI>First Item in first sublist</LI>
        <LI>Second Item in first sublist</LI>
    </OL>
    <LI>Second Item in first list</LI>
    <OL>
        <LI>First Item in second sublist</LI>
        <LI>Second Item in second sublist</LI>
    <OL>
</OL>
```

This text will be formatted similar to the following:

1. First Item in first list
   1. First Item in first sublist
   2. Second Item in first sublist
2. Second Item in first list
   1. First Item in second sublist
   2. Second Item in second sublist

An unordered list is very similar to an ordered list. Unordered lists use the UL element instead of the OL element. Unordered lists are usually displayed with a bullet symbol to the left of the list item. Some browsers may use a different symbol, and there are tag attributes you can specify that will let you use images as the list item symbol.

The following uses an unordered list to represent the various activities that the Students in Action have planned for this semester. In addition, we added horizontal rules to offset the H1 element in the document.

```
<HTML>
    <HEAD>
        <TITLE>Students in Action</TITLE>
    </HEAD>
    <BODY>
        <HR>
```

```
<CENTER><H1>Students in Action</H1></CENTER>

<HR>

<CENTER><I>Dedicated to helping our local community
by using the volunteer effort of college
students.</I></CENTER>

<HR>

<P>This semester, our planned actions are:</P>

<UL>
    <LI> to help a local food drive for flood
    victims in the Midwest</LI>
    <LI> to visit local adult care centers</LI>
    <LI> to teach Java to grade-school students</LI>
</UL>

<P>Our group is active, energetic, and always in
need of donations of equipment, effort, and money.
We are always willing to help staff and plan
community events.</P>

<P>As always, our president (at x222) is eager and
willing to answer questions and hear suggestions on
how we can be more active in our community.</P>

    </BODY>
</HTML>
```

Figure J.7 shows the display of this document. As you can see from Fig. J.7, although the content of the Web page has not changed since Fig. J.1, the presentation has changed dramatically.

links

The World Wide Web would not be a "web" without links between documents. A link connects one document to another. The destination of the link can be a local file or a remote file hosted on another computer. Links are displayed in a number of different ways, but the most popular and recognizable is underlined blue text. In most browsers, when you move your pointing device (a mouse or other device) over a link in a graphical browser, the destination of the link is displayed somewhere on the screen. The most popular browsers display the destination link on the bottom of the display window.

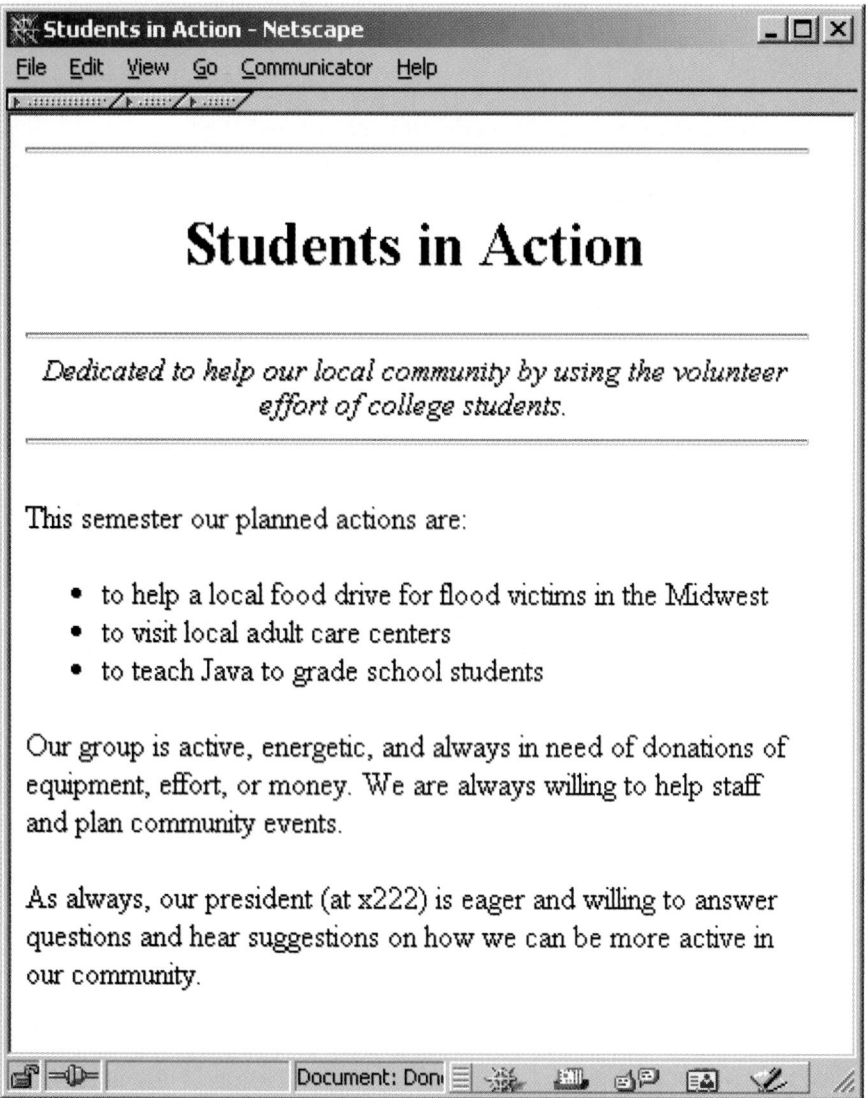

figure J.7   Lists and lines added to the Web page

The link tag, `<A>`, takes one attribute that defines its destination. Inside the link tags (also known as anchor tags), the URL of a new document is specified. For example, the following HTML creates two links:

```
<A HREF="http://duke.csc.villanova.edu/lewis">Dr. Lewis' Home
Page Link</A>
<A HREF="http://www.yahoo.com">Yahoo Internet Search Link</A>
```

The text associated with the `<A>` and `</A>` tags is what the browser will usually display as underlined blue text. No checking is done on the validity of the destination until the user selects (or clicks on) the link. Therefore when one writes a Web page, all links should be tested (that is, clicked on or exercised). Following the selection of a link by a user, the browser will attempt to load the contents of the destination. When a successful connection is made to the destination link (either as a remote computer or another file on your own computer), the browser will display the contents of the destination page.

Links are very useful for breaking up a document based on content. Links have been the driving force behind the popularity of HTML and the Web because they allow users to read documents located on computers throughout the world. The following HTML has five example links in it. The first three represent links to local documents that describe the Students in Action projects and are located on the same server. The fourth link represents an absolute URL, which can refer to any document in the Web. The fifth link is a mailto link. This is a special type of link that allows users to send mail by clicking on the link. In the following case, the mail would be sent to `president@breakaway.com`.

```
<HTML>
    <HEAD>
        <TITLE>Students in Action</TITLE>
    </HEAD>
    <BODY>
        <HR>

        <CENTER><H1>Students in Action</H1></CENTER>

        <HR>

        <CENTER><I>Dedicated to helping our local community
        by using the volunteer effort of college
        students.</I></CENTER>

        <HR>

        <P>This semester, our planned actions are:</P>

        <UL>
            <LI> to <A HREF="food.html">help a local food drive</A>
                for flood victims in the Midwest</LI>
            <LI> to <A HREF="adult.html">visit local adult care
                centers</A></LI>
```

```
    <LI> to <A HREF="grade.html">teach Java to grade-
        school students</A></LI>
</UL>

<P>Our group is active, energetic, and always in
need of donations of equipment, effort, and money.
We are always willing to help staff and plan
community events.</P>

<P>As always, our <A HREF="mailto:president@breakaway.com">
president</A> (at x222) is eager and willing to answer
questions and hear suggestions on how we can be more
active in our community.</P>

<P>Visit our <A HREF="http://www.vill.edu">University Home
Page</A>.</P>

    </BODY>
</HTML>
```

Figure J.8 shows how a browser would display this page.

color and images

Some of the most popular browsers (Netscape Navigator and Microsoft Internet Explorer) have introduced common extension attributes to the <BODY> tag to allow a background color or images for the document to be specified. Background images or color can dramatically improve the aesthetic appearance on a color-capable display.

The first attribute is the BGCOLOR attribute. This attribute is used to set the background color of the entire document. For example, the following will set the background color to red in an HTML document:

```
<BODY BGCOLOR=RED>
```

There are two basic methods for defining a color in HTML. The first, as seen in the previous example, uses a standard color name. Note that the display of HTML code is solely under the control of a browser; therefore these names are not truly standard but are common color names that most browsers support. Be sure to check all browsers your users may have to see what specific color names are accepted before choosing an appropriate color. A few de facto standard names for colors that are accepted by both Netscape's and Microsoft's browsers are black, blue, gray, green, navy, purple, red, yellow, and white. The second method of choosing a color is to change the color name to an RGB value. An RGB value is a sequence of three numbers that represents the amount of red, green, and blue

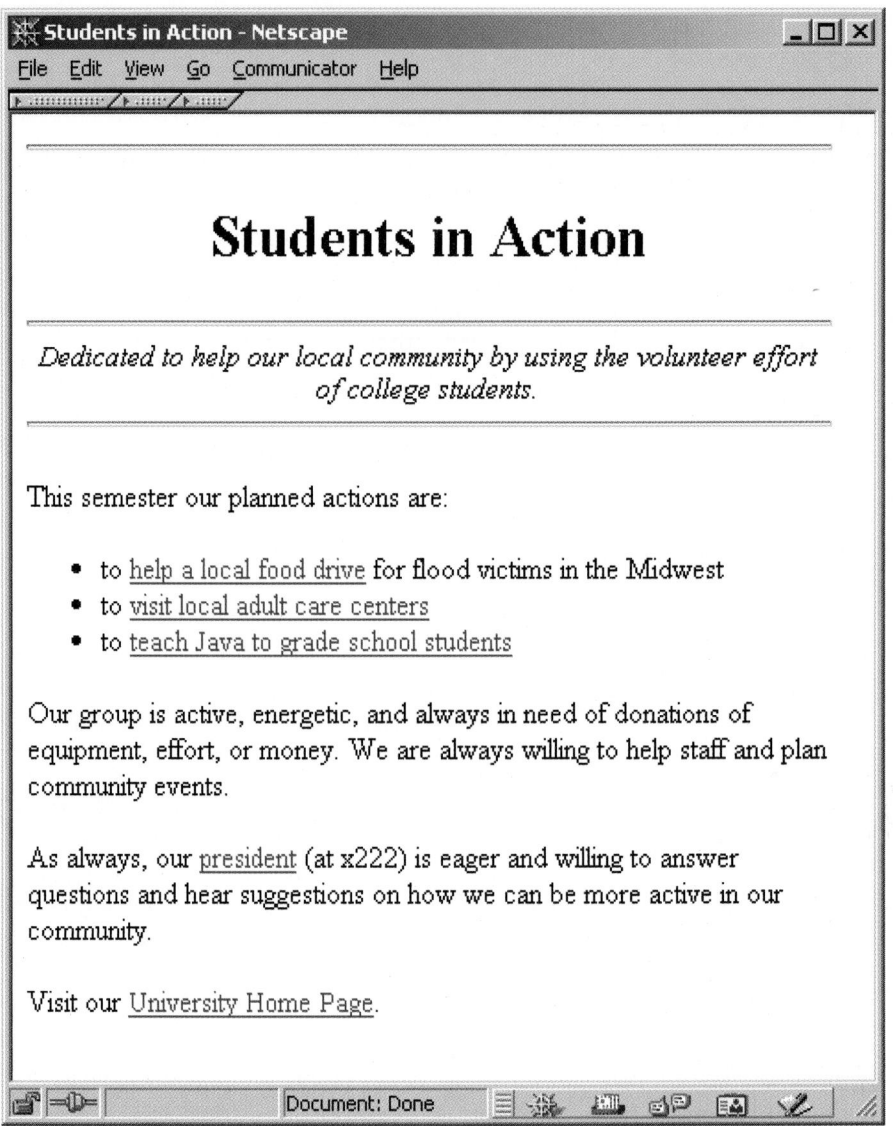

figure J.8   Links added to the Students in Action Web page

that will be used to create the color. The numbers represent the various strength of the colors involved (0=off, 255=full on). The combination of three values produce a specific color. The RGB values are represented as three pairs of hex characters preceded by a number sign (#) and surrounded by double quotes. For example, to represent the color in which red is 50, green is 150, and blue is 255, the <BODY> tag would look like the following:

```
<BODY BGCOLOR="#3296FF">
```

There are many good shareware programs available on the Internet that will help you determine the RGB values for a particular color.

In addition to setting the background to a single color, it is also possible to tile the background with a particular image. Most graphical browsers have implemented an extension to the <BODY> tag that will take a GIF or JPEG image and repeat it both horizontally and vertically (that is, tile it) to create a background pattern. Some images can be fairly simple, such as a single-color image. Others can be more complex, representing a repeating pattern such as bathroom tiles or a stone mosaic. To use an image as a background, use the BACKGROUND attribute in the <BODY> tag and follow it with the name of the image file in quotes. For example, the following piece of HTML code uses the STONE.GIF image as a tiling background image:

```
<BODY BACKGROUND="STONE.GIF">
```

Care should be given to the type of image and strength of its colors. Many times, using an interesting image can make the document's text difficult to read. Many pages on the Web have free images that you can copy and use as backgrounds.

Graphic images can be included in an HTML document in other ways as well. Most popular browsers can show both GIF and JPEG image formats. To include an image, use the <IMG> tag. The SRC attribute of the <IMG> tag can be used to describe the URL of the graphic image file. For example, the following HTML fragment will include an image called new.gif:

```
<IMG SRC="new.gif">
```

The following HTML code is the Students in Action Web page modified to use an image as a banner that introduces the organization, and a new image to draw attention to a portion of the page that may have changed recently.

```
<HTML>
   <HEAD>
      <TITLE>Students in Action</TITLE>
   </HEAD>
   <BODY>
      <HR>

      <CENTER><IMG SRC="SIA.gif"></CENTER>

      <HR>

      <CENTER><I>Dedicated to helping our local community
      by using the volunteer effort of college
      students.</I></CENTER>

      <HR>

      <P>This semester, our planned actions are:</P>

      <UL>
         <LI> to <A HREF="food.html">help a local food drive</A>
              for flood victims in the Midwest</LI>
         <LI> to <A HREF="adult.html">visit local adult care
              centers</A></LI>
         <LI> to <A HREF="grade.html">teach Java to grade-
              school students</A> <IMG SRC="new.gif"></LI>
      </UL>

      <P>Our group is active, energetic, and always in
      need of donations of equipment, effort, and money.
      We are always willing to help staff and plan
      community events.</P>

      <P>As always, our <A HREF="mailto:president@wpllabs.com">
      president</A> (at x222) is eager and willing to answer
      questions and hear suggestions on how we can be more
      active in our community.</P>

      <P>Visit our <A HREF="http://www.vill.edu">University Home
      Page</A>.</P>

   </BODY>
</HTML>
```

Figure J.9 shows how a browser would display this page.

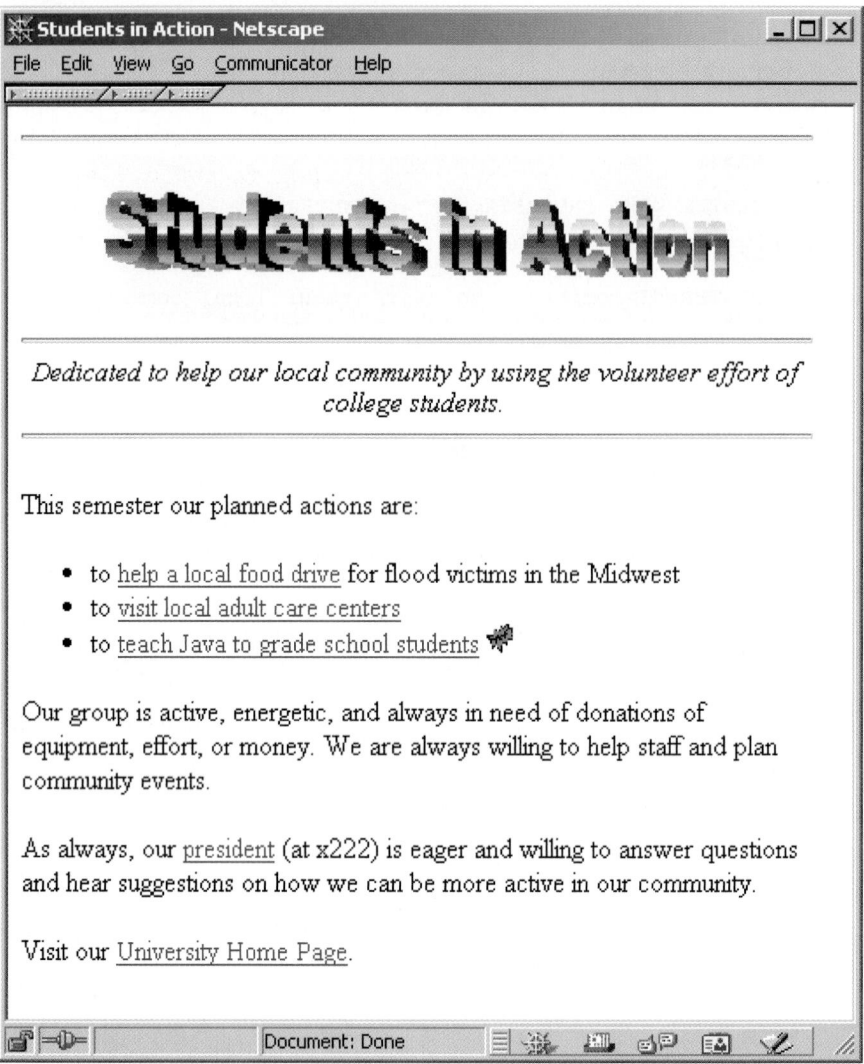

figure J.9   Images added to the Students in Action Web page

applets

The `<APPLET>` tag is used to execute an applet in a document. The `<APPLET>` tag has many possible attributes; however, its only required attribute is the `CODE` attribute. The `CODE` attribute names the class file of the applet that should execute in the document. The browser will load that applet's class file from the same URL as the document that contains the `<APPLET>` tag. For example, to execute the `Marquee` applet, the following HTML fragment is used:

```
<APPLET code=Marquee>
</APPLET>
```

A browser displaying this HTML code will load the `Marquee.class` file into the browser and execute it. Other attributes for the `<APPLET>` tag include:

▸ `HEIGHT`—used to define the space in pixels reserved for the display height of the applet

▸ `WIDTH`—used to define the space in pixels reserved for the display width of the applet

▸ `CODEBASE`—used to define an alternate URL for the location of the class file

In this example, we will reserve 50 pixels for the height and 100 pixels for the width. In the following code fragment, we also reset the location of the class code to another site:

```
<APPLET CODE=Marquee WIDTH=100 HEIGHT=50
    CODEBASE="http://www.javasite.com/applets2use">
</APPLET>
```

When inserted between the `<APPLET>` and `</APPLET>` tags, the `<PARAM>` tag allows you to pass parameters to the Java applet at run time. The `<PARAM>` tag has two required attributes that allow it to pass information to the applet program. The attributes are `NAME` and `VALUE`. By defining a `NAME` and `VALUE` pair, the applet can use and decipher the information it is passed at run time. The following example sends two parameters, a state and city, to the `Map` applet:

```
<APPLET CODE=Map WIDTH=100 HEIGHT=5
    CODEBASE="http://www.javasite.com/applets2use">
    <PARAM NAME="state" VALUE="pennsylvania">
    <PARAM NAME="city" VALUE="philadelphia">

</APPLET>
```

The following HTML code is the Students in Action Web page with an added applet that scrolls a message across the document as the page is browsed:

```
<HTML>
   <HEAD>
      <TITLE>Students in Action</TITLE>
   </HEAD>
   <BODY BGCOLOR="WHITE" TEXT="BLACK">
      <HR>

      <CENTER><IMG SRC="SIA.gif"></CENTER>

      <HR>

      <CENTER><I>Dedicated to helping our local community
      by using the volunteer effort of college
      students.</I></CENTER>

      <HR>

      <P>This semester, our planned actions are:</P>

      <UL>
         <LI> to <A HREF="food.html">help a local food drive</A>
              for flood victims in the Midwest</LI>
         <LI> to <A HREF="adult.html">visit local adult care
              centers</A></LI>
         <LI> to <A HREF="grade.html">teach Java to grade-
              school students</A> <IMG SRC="new.gif"></LI>
      </UL>

      <P>Our group is active, energetic, and always in
      need of donations of equipment, effort, and money.
      We are always willing to help staff and plan
      community events.</P>

      <P>As always, our <A HREF="mailto:loftus@wpllabs.com">
      president</A> (at x222) is eager and willing to answer
      questions and hear suggestions on how we can be more
      active in our community.</P>

      <APPLET CODE="Marquee.class" WIDTH=500 HEIGHT=50>
         <PARAM NAME=text
            VALUE="Join us for our Spring picnic in April!">
         <PARAM NAME=delay       VALUE="100">
         <PARAM NAME=bgcolor     VALUE="255255255">
         <PARAM NAME=fgcolor     VALUE="000000128">
      </APPLET>

      <P>Visit our <A HREF="http://www.vill.edu">University Home
      Page</A>.</P>

   </BODY>
</HTML>
```

This appendix contains a list of run-time *exceptions* and *errors* produced by the Java language and the classes of the Java standard class library. It is not an exhaustive list, but it does contain most of the exceptions and errors that arise in programs within the scope of this text.

Both exceptions and errors indicate that a problem has occurred while a program was executing. Exceptions can be caught and handled under programmer control using the Java `try` statement. Errors represent more serious problems and generally should not be caught. Some exceptions and errors indicate the same type of problem, such as `NoSuchMethodException` and `NoSuchMethodError`. In these cases, the particular situation in which the problem arises determines whether an exception or an error is thrown.

exceptions

`AccessControlException (java.security)`
Requested access to a critical system resource is denied.

`ArithmeticException (java.lang)`
An illegal arithmetic operation was attempted, such as dividing by zero.

`ArrayIndexOutOfBoundsException (java.lang)`
An index into an array object is out of range.

`ArrayStoreException (java.lang)`
An attempt was made to assign a value to an array element of an incompatible type.

`AWTException (java.awt)`
A general exception indicating that some problem has occurred in a class of the java.awt package.

`BindException (java.net)`
A socket could not be bound to a local address and port.

`ClassCastException (java.lang)`
An attempt was made to cast an object reference to an incompatible type.

`ClassNotFoundException (java.lang)`
A specific class or interface could not be found.

`CloneNotSupportedException (java.lang)`
An attempt was made to clone an object instantiated from a class that does not implement the `Cloneable` interface.

`EmptyStackException (java.util)`
An attempt was made to reference an element from an empty stack.

`EOFException (java.io)`
The end of file has been encountered before normal completion of an input operation.

`Exception (java.lang)`
The root of the exception hierarchy.

`FileNotFoundException (java.io)`
A specified file name could not be found.

`GeneralSecurityException (java.security)`
The root of all security exceptions.

`IllegalAccessException (java.lang)`
The currently executing method does not have access to the definition of a class that it is attempting to load.

`IllegalArgumentException (java.lang)`
An invalid or inappropriate argument was passed to a method.

`IllegalComponentStateException (java.awt)`
An operation was attempted on a component that was in an inappropriate state.

`IllegalMonitorStateException (java.lang)`
A thread attempted to notify or wait on another thread that is waiting on an object that it has not locked.

`IllegalStateException (java.lang)`
A method was invoked from an improper state.

`IllegalThreadStateException (java.lang)`
An operation was attempted on a thread that was not in an appropriate state for that operation to succeed.

`IndexOutOfBoundsException (java.lang)`
An index into an object such as an array, string, or vector was out of range. The invalid index could be part of a subrange, specified by a start and end point or a start point and a length.

`InstantiationException (java.lang)`
A class could not be instantiated using the `newInstance` method of class `Class` because it is abstract, an array, or an interface.

InterruptedException (java.lang)
While one thread was waiting, another thread interrupted it using the interrupt method of the Thread class.

InterruptedIOException (java.io)
While one thread was waiting for the completion of an I/O operation, another thread interrupted it using the interrupt method of the Thread class.

InvalidClassException (java.io)
The serialization run time has detected a problem with a class.

InvalidParameterException (java.security)
An invalid parameter has been passed to a method.

IOException (java.io)
A requested I/O operation could not be completed normally.

JarException (java.util.jar)
A problem occurred while reading from or writing to a JAR file.

MalformedURLException (java.net)
A specified URL does not have an appropriate format or used an unknown protocol.

NegativeArraySizeException (java.lang)
An attempt was made to instantiate an array that has a negative length.

NoRouteToHostException (java.net)
A path could not be found when attempting to connect a socket to a remote address and port.

NoSuchElementException (java.util)
An attempt was made to access an element of an empty vector.

NoSuchFieldException (java.lang)
An attempt was made to access a nonexistent field.

NoSuchMethodException (java.lang)
A specified method could not be found.

NullPointerException (java.lang)
A null reference was used where an object reference was needed.

NumberFormatException (java.lang)
An operation was attempted using a number in an illegal format.

ParseException (java.text)
A string could not be parsed according to the specified format.

`ProtocolException (java.net)`
Some aspect of a network communication protocol was not executed correctly.

`RuntimeException (java.lang)`
The superclass of all unchecked runtime exceptions.

`SecurityException (java.lang)`
An operation that violates some kind of security measure was attempted.

`SocketException (java.net)`
An operation using a socket could not be completed normally.

`StringIndexOutOfBoundsException (java.lang)`
An index into a `String` or `StringBuffer` object is out of range.

`TooManyListenersException (java.util)`
An event source has registered too many listeners.

`UTFDataFormatException (java.io)`
An attempt was made to convert a string to or from UTF-8 format, but the string was too long or the data were not in valid UTF-8 format.

`UnknownHostException (java.net)`
A specified network host name could not be resolved into a network address.

`UnknownServiceException (java.net)`
An attempt was made to request a service that the current network connection does not support.

errors

`AbstractMethodError (java.lang)`
An attempt was made to invoke an `abstract` method.

`AWTError (java.awt)`
A general error indicating that a serious problem has occurred in a class of the java.awt package.

`ClassCircularityError (java.lang)`
A circular dependency was found while performing class initialization.

`ClassFormatError (java.lang)`
The format of the bytecode in a class file is invalid.

`Error (java.lang)`
The root of the error hierarchy.

ExceptionInInitializerError (java.lang)
An exception has occurred in a static initializer.

IllegalAccessError (java.lang)
An attempt was made to reference a class, method, or variable that was not accessible.

IncompatibleClassChangeError (java.lang)
An illegal operation was attempted on a class.

InstantiationError (java.lang)
An attempt was made to instantiate an abstract class or an interface.

InternalError (java.lang)
An error occurred in the Java interpreter.

LinkageError (java.lang)
An error occurred while attempting to link classes or resolve dependencies between classes.

NoClassDefFoundError (java.lang)
The definition of a specified class could not be found.

NoSuchFieldError (java.lang)
A specified field could not be found.

NoSuchMethodError (java.lang)
A specified method could not be found.

OutOfMemoryError (java.lang)
The interpreter has run out of memory and cannot reclaim more through garbage collection.

StackOverflowError (java.lang)
A stack overflow has occurred in the Java interpreter.

ThreadDeath (java.lang)
The stop method of a thread has caused a thread (but not the interpreter) to terminate. No error message is printed.

UnknownError (java.lang)
An error has occurred in the Java Virtual Machine (JVM).

UnsatisfiedLinkError (java.lang)
All of the links in a loaded class could not be resolved.

VerifyError (java.lang)
A class failed the bytecode verification procedures.

VirtualMachineError (java.lang)
The superclass of several errors relating to the Java Virtual Machine (JVM).

This appendix contains syntax diagrams that collectively describe the way in which Java language elements can be constructed. Rectangles indicate something that is further defined in another syntax diagram, and ovals indicate a literal word or character.

Compilation Unit

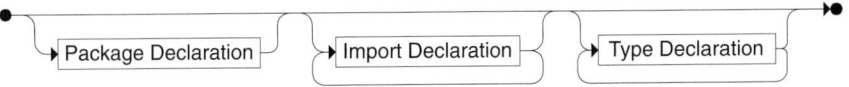

Package Declaration

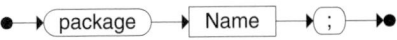

Import Declaration

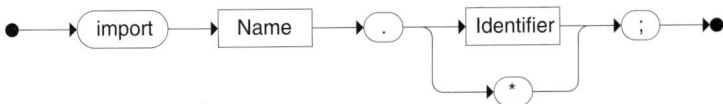

Type Declaration

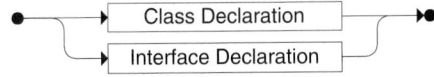

Class Declaration

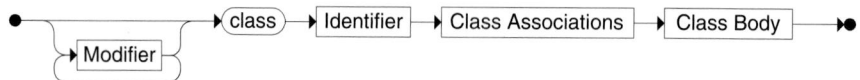

Class Associations

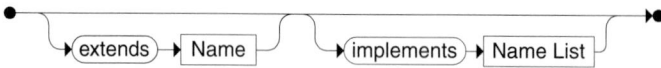

Class Body

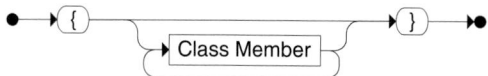

Class Member

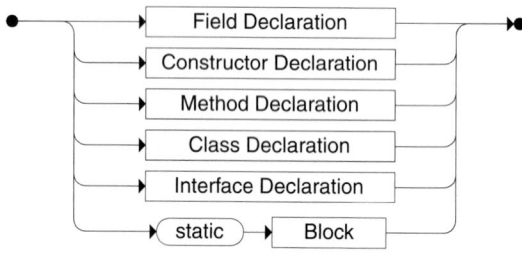

Interface Declaration

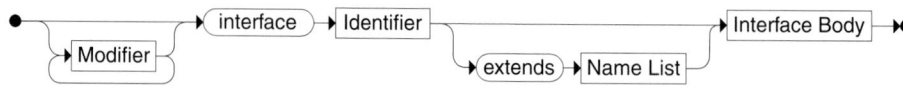

Interface Body

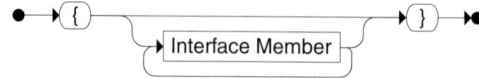

Interface Member

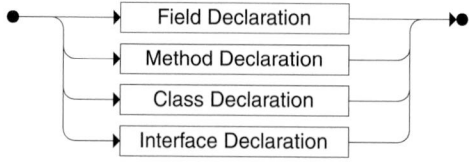

Field Declaration

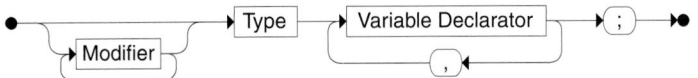

Variable Declarator

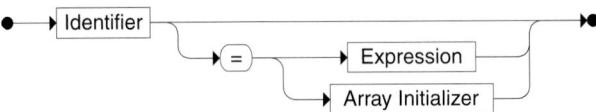

Type

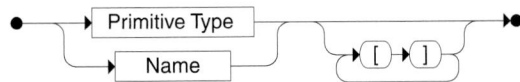

Modifier   **Primitive Type**

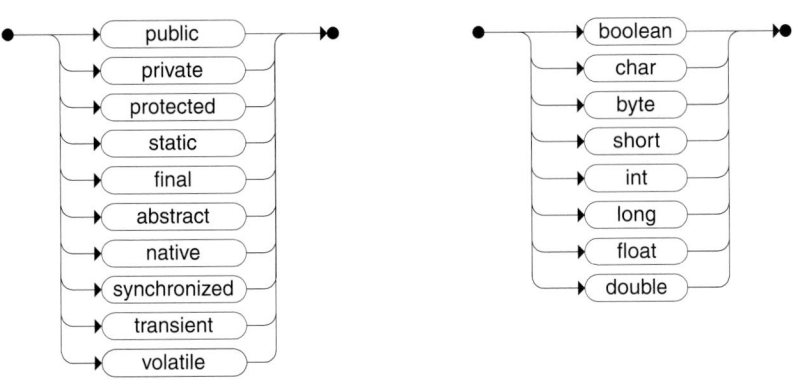

Array Initializer

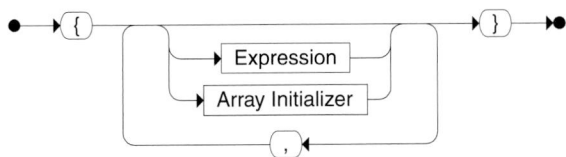

Name   **Name List**

Method Declaration

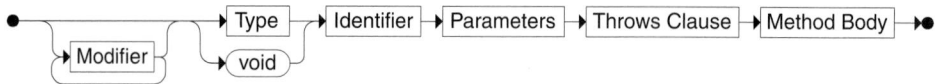

Parameters

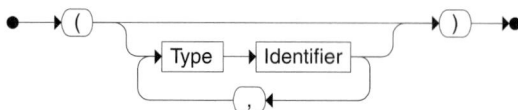

Throws Clause

Method Body

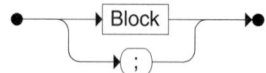

Constructor Declaration

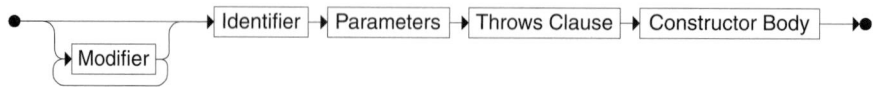

Constructor Body

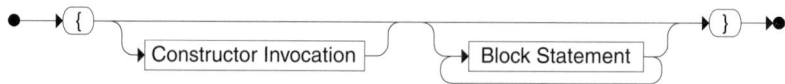

Constructor Invocation

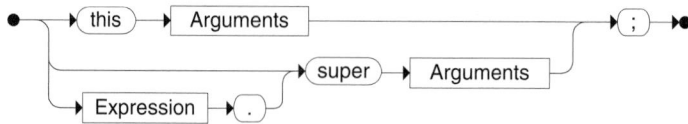

Block

Block Statement

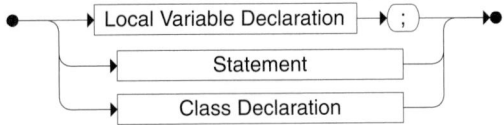

Local Variable Declaration

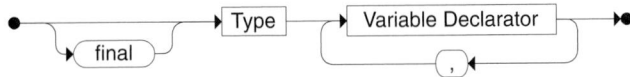

Statement

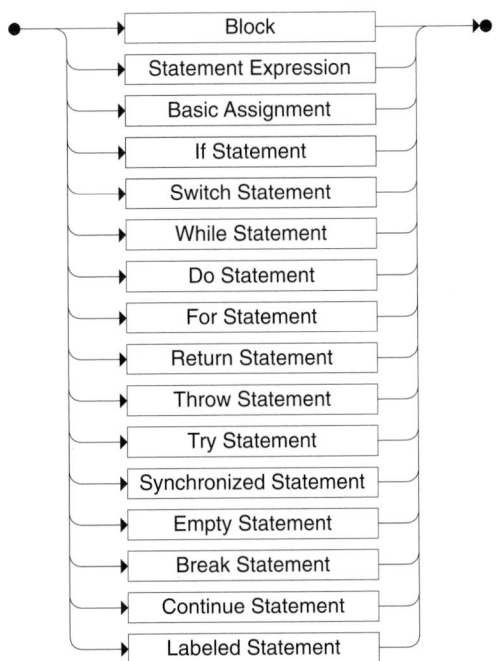

If Statement

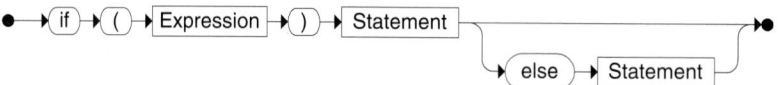

Switch Statement

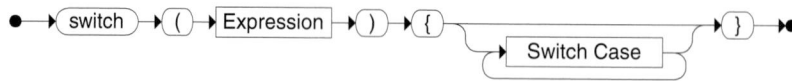

Switch Case

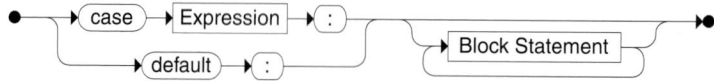

While Statement

Do Statement

For Statement

For Init

For Update

Basic Assignment

Return Statement

Throw Statement

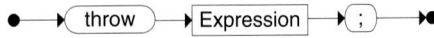

Try Statement

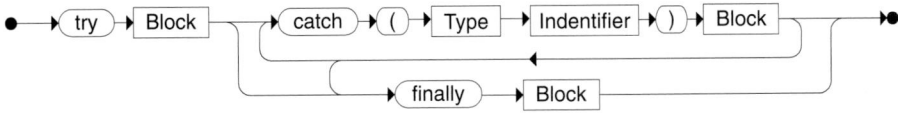

Synchronized Statement

Empty Statement

Break Statement

Continue Statement

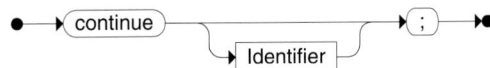

Labeled Statement

Expression

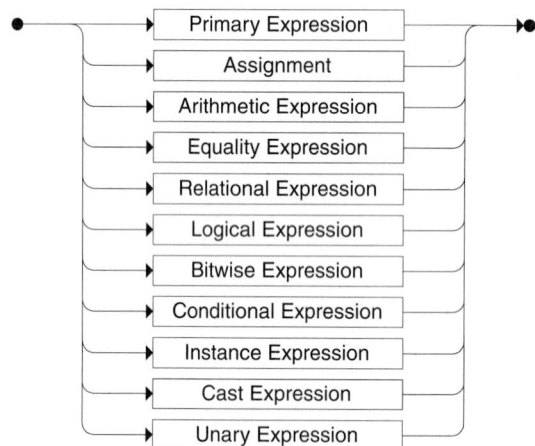

Primary Expression

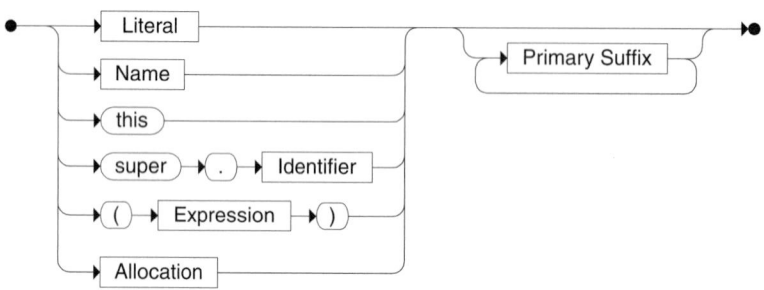

Primary Suffix

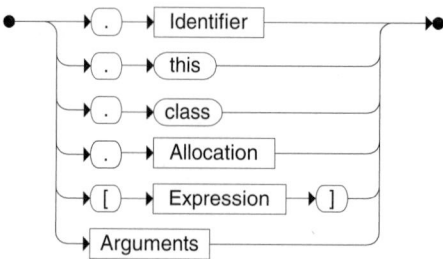

Arguments

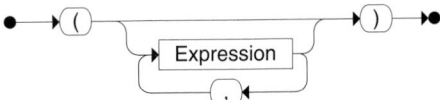

Allocation

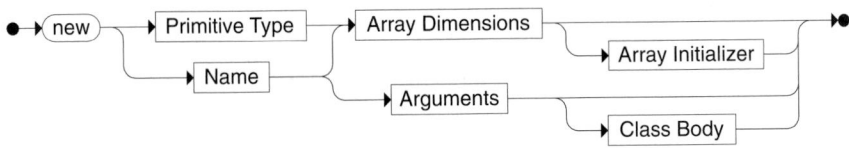

Array Dimensions

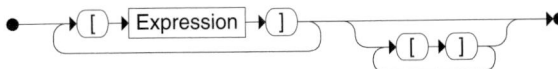

Statement Expression

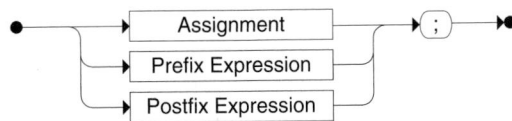

Assignment

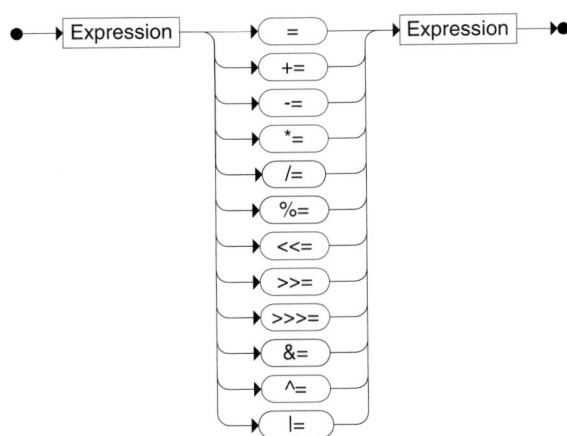

Arithmetic Expression

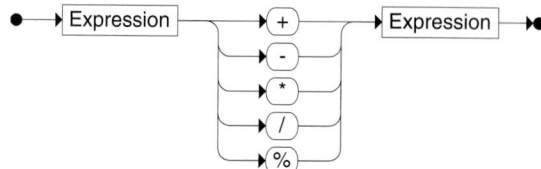

Equality Expression

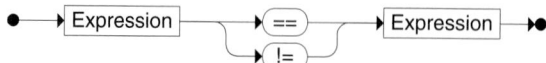

Relational Expression

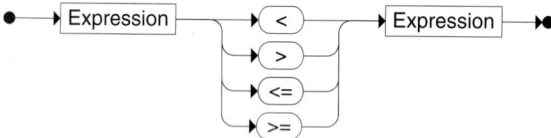

Logical Expression

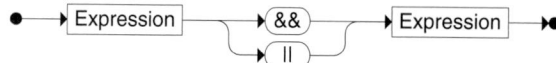

Bitwise Expression

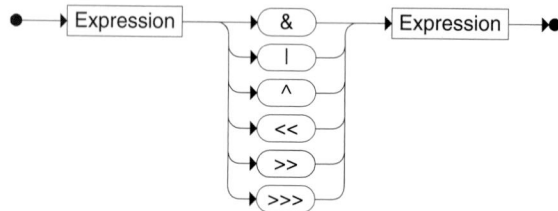

Conditional Expression

Instance Expression

Cast Expression

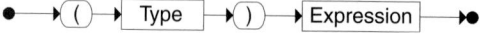

Unary Expression

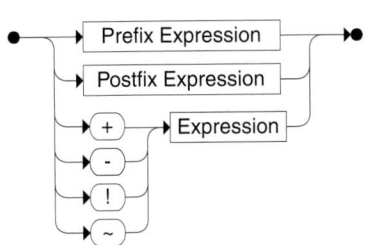

Prefix Expression

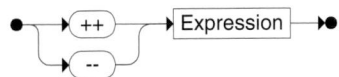

Postfix Expression

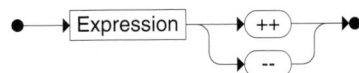

Literal

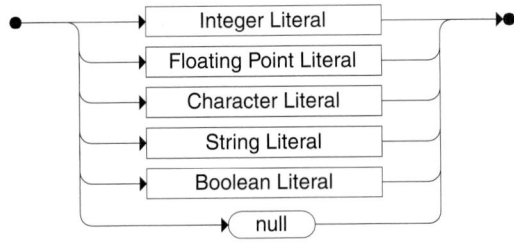

Integer Literal

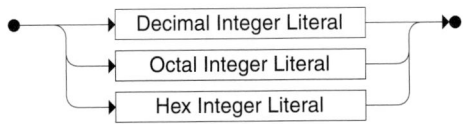

Decimal Integer Literal

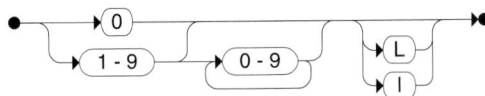

Octal Integer Literal   **Hex Digit**

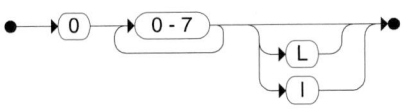   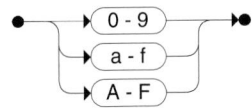

Hex Integer Literal

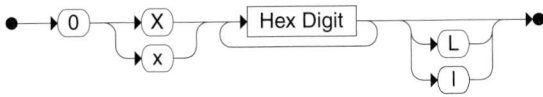

Floating Point Literal

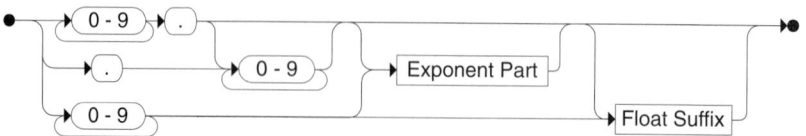

Exponent Part

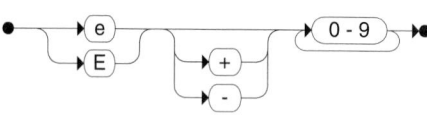

Float Suffix

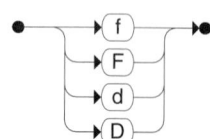

Character Literal

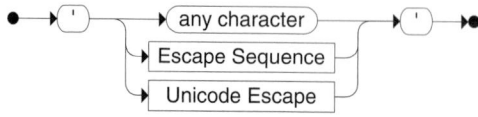

Boolean Literal

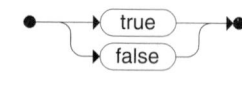

String Literal

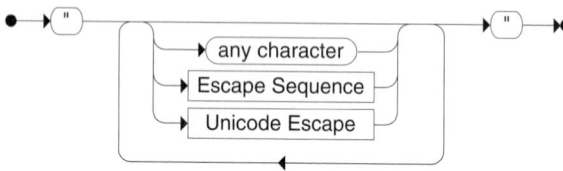

Escape Sequence

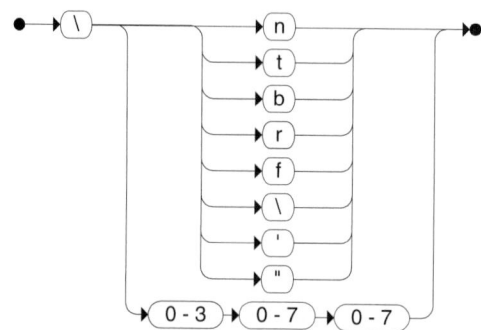

Identifier

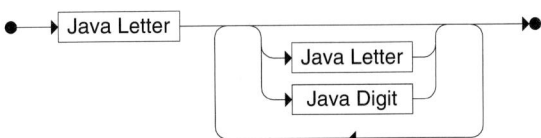

Java Letter

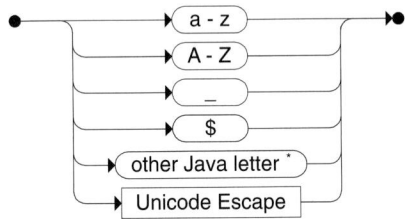

* The "other Java letter" category includes letters
from many languages other than English.

Java Digit

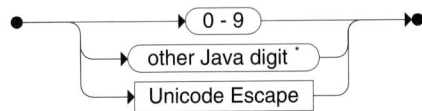

* The "other Java digit" category includes
additional digits defined in Unicode.

Unicode Escape*

* In some contexts, the character represented
by a Unicode Escape is restricted.

This appendix is a reference for many of the classes in the Java standard class library. We list the variables, constants, constructors, and methods of each class. Items within a class are grouped according to their purpose. The classes are listed in alphabetical order. The package each class is contained in is given in parentheses after the class name.

AbstractButton (javax.swing)

A public abstract class, derived from JComponent and implementing ItemSelectable and SwingConstants, that represents the common behaviors for buttons and menu items.

methods

```
public void addActionListener(ActionListener listener)
public void addChangeListener(ChangeListener listener)
public void addItemListener(ItemListener listener)
```
Adds a specific type of listener to this button.
```
public void doClick()
public void doClick(int pressTime)
```
Performs a button click programmatically (as if the user had used the mouse). The button stays visually "pressed" for pressTime milliseconds if specified.
```
public Icon getDisabledIcon()
public void setDisabledIcon(Icon disabeledIcon)
```
Gets or sets the icon used by this button when it is disabled.
```
public Icon getDisabledSelectedIcon()
public void setDisabledSelectedIcon(Icon disabledSelectedIcon)
```
Gets or sets the icon used by this button when it is disabled and selected.
```
public int getHorizontalAlignment()
public void setHorizontalAlignment(int alignment)
public int getVerticalAlignment()
public void setVerticalAlignment(int alignment)
```
Gets or sets the horizontal or vertical alignment of the icon and text.
```
public int getHorizontalTextPosition()
public void setHorizontalTextPosition(int position)
public int getVerticalTextPosition()
public void setVerticalTextPosition(int position)
```
Gets or sets the horizontal or vertical position of the text relative to the icon.
```
public Icon getIcon()
```

```
public void setIcon(Icon icon)
```
Gets or sets the default icon for this button.

```
public Insets getMargin()
public void setMargin(Insets insets)
```
Gets or sets the margin between this button's border and the label.

```
public int getMnemonic()
public void setMnemonic(int mnemonic)
```
Gets or sets this button's keyboard mnemonic.

```
public Icon getPressedIcon()
public void setPressedIcon(Icon icon)
```
Gets or sets the icon used by this button when it is pressed.

```
public Icon getRolloverIcon()
public void setRolloverIcon(Icon icon)
```
Gets or sets the icon used by this button when the mouse rolls over it.

```
public Icon getSelectedIcon()
public void setSelectedIcon(Icon icon)
```
Gets or sets the icon used by this button when it is selected.

```
public String getText()
public void setText(String text)
```
Gets or sets the text displayed on this button.

```
public void setEnabled(boolean flag)
```
Enables or disables this button.

```
public void setRolloverEnabled(boolean flag)
```
Enables or disables the rollover property for this button. Rollover effects will not occur if this property is disabled.

```
public isRolloverEnabled()
```
Returns true if this button currently has its rollover property enabled.

```
public void setSelected(boolean flag)
```
Selects or deselects ths button.

```
public boolean isSelected()
```
Returns true if this button is currently selected.

ActionEvent (java.awt.event)

A public class, derived from AWTEvent, that represents an AWT action event.

variables and constants

```
public static final int ALT_MASK
public static final int CTRL_MASK
public static final int META_MASK
public static final int SHIFT_MASK
```
Constant values which represent masks for the Alt, Control, Meta, and Shift keys being pressed during an action event.
```
public static final int ACTION_FIRST
public static final int ACTION_LAST
```
Constant values that represent the index of the first and last action event ids.
```
public static final int ACTION_PERFORMED
```
A constant value that represents an action performed AWT event type.

constructors

```
public ActionEvent(Object src, int type, String cmd)
public ActionEvent(Object src, int type, String cmd, int keys)
```
Creates a new instance of an `ActionEvent` from the specified source object, event type, and command string. Additionally, a mask value can be set that defines the types of keys depressed during the event.

methods

```
public String getActionCommand()
```
Returns the command string associated with this action.
```
public int getModifiers()
```
Returns the mask of the modifiers (special keys) depressed during this event.
```
public String paramString()
```
Returns a string containing the parameters of this ActionEvent.

AdjustmentEvent (java.awt.event)

A public class, derived from AWTEvent, that represents an AWT adjustment event.

variables and constructs

```
public static final int ADJUSTMENT_FIRST
public static final int ADJUSTMENT_LAST
```
Constant values that represent the index of the first and last adjustment event ids.

`public static final int ADJUSTMENT_VALUE_CHANGED`
A constant value that represents an adjustment value change event.
`public static final int BLOCK_DECREMENT`
`public static final int BLOCK_INCREMENT`
Constant values that represent block decrement and increment events.
`public static final int TRACK`
A constant value which represents an absolute tracking adjustment event.
`public static final int UNIT_DECREMENT`
`public static final int UNIT_INCREMENT`
Constant values which represent unit decrement and increment events.

constructors

`public AdjustmentEvent(Adjustable source, int id, int type, int val)`
Creates a new instance of an `AdjustmentEvent` from a specified `source` and having a specified `id`, `type`, and `value`.

methods

`public Adjustable getAdjustable()`
Returns the adjustable object that originated this AWT AdjustmentEvent.
`public int getAdjustmentType()`
Returns the type of adjustment for this event.
`public int getValue()`
Returns the current value of this `AdjustmentEvent`.
`public String paramString()`
Returns a string containing the parameters of this event.

Applet (java.applet)

A public class, derived from `Panel`, that is intended to be used as a program running inside a Web page.

constructors

`public Applet()`
Creates a new instance of an applet for inclusion on a Web page.

methods

`public void destroy()`
 Destroys the applet and all of its resources. This method contains no functionality and should be overridden by subclasses.

`public AppletContext getAppletContext()`
 Returns this applet's context (the environment in which it is running).

`public String getAppletInfo()`
 Returns a string representation of information regarding this applet. This method contains no functionality and should be overridden by subclasses.

`public AudioClip getAudioClip(URL audio)`

`public AudioClip getAudioClip(URL base, String filename)`
 Returns the AudioClip requested. The location of the audio clip can be given by the base URL and the filename relative to that base.

`public URL getCodeBase()`

`public URL getDocumentBase()`

`public Locale getLocale()`
 Returns the URL of this applet, the document that contains this applet, or the locale of this applet.

`public Image getImage(URL image)`

`public Image getImage(URL base, String filename)`
 Returns the image requested. The location of the image can be given by the base URL and the filename relative to that base.

`public String getParameter(String param)`

`public String[][] getParameterInfo()`
 Returns the value of the specified parameter for this applet. An array of string elements containing information about each parameter for this applet can also be obtained. Each element of the returned array should be comprised of three strings (parameter name, type, and description). This method contains no functionality and should be overridden by subclasses.

`public void init()`
 This method provides initialization functionality to the applet prior to the first time that the applet is started. It is automatically called by the browser or the appletviewer program. This method contains no functionality and should be overridden by subclasses.

`public boolean isActive()`
 Returns a true value if this applet is currently active. An applet is considered active just prior to execution of its start method and is no longer active just after execution of its stop method.

`public void play(URL source)`

`public void play(URL base, String filename)`
 Plays the audio clip located at source. The location of the audio clip can be given as a base URL and the filename relative to that base.

```
public void resize(Dimension dim)
public void resize(int w, int h)
```
Resizes this applet according to the specified dimension.
```
public final void setStub(AppletStub stub)
```
Sets the interface between this applet and the browser or appletviewer program.
```
public void showStatus(String message)
```
Prints the specified message in the browser's status window.
```
public void start()
```
This method generally contains functionality relevant to the starting of this applet. It is called after the applet has been initialized (with the init method) and every time the applet is reloaded in the browser or appletviewer program. This method contains no functionality and should be overridden by subclasses.
```
public void stop()
```
This method generally contains functionality relevant to the stopping of this applet. It is called by the browser (when the containing Web page is replaced) or appletviewer program. This method contains no functionality and should be overridden by subclasses.

ArrayList (java.util)

A public class, derived from `AbstractList`, that represents a resizable array implementation of a list. Similar to `Vector`, but unsynchronized.

constructors
```
public ArrayList()
public ArrayList(int initialCapacity)
```
Creates a new list with the specified initial capacity (ten by default).
```
public ArrayList(Collection col)
```
Creates a new list containing the elements of the specified collection.

methods
```
public void add(int index, Object element)
```
Inserts the specified element into this list at the specified index.
```
public boolean add(Object obj)
```
Appends the specified element to the end of this list.
```
public boolean addAll(Collection col)
public boolean addAll(int index, Collection col)
```
Inserts all of the elements in the specified collection into the list at the specified index, or appends them to the end of the list if no index is specified.

```
public void clear()
```
Removes all of the elements from this list.

```
public boolean contains(Object obj)
```
Returns true if this list contians the specified object.

```
public void ensureCapacity(int minimumCapacity)
```
Increases the capacity of this list to the specified value if necessary.

```
public Object get(int index)
```
Returns the element at the specified index. Throws IndexOutOfBoundsException if the index is out of range.

```
public int indexOf(Object obj)
```
Returns the index of the first occurrence of the specified object (based on the equals method) or –1 if it is not found.

```
public boolean isEmpty()
```
Returns true if this list contains no elements.

```
public int lastIndexOf(Object obj)
```
Returns the index of the last occurrence of the specified object (based on the equals method) or –1 if it is not found.

```
public Object remove(int index)
```
Removes and returns the object at the specified index in this list. Throws IndexOutOfBoundsException if the index is out of range.

```
protected void removeRange(int fromIndex, int toIndex)
```
Removes the elements at the indexes in the specified range, exclusive.

```
public Object set(int index, Object obj)
```
Replaces the element at the specified index with the specified object

```
public int size()
```
Returns the number of elements in this list.

```
public Object[] toArray()
```
Returns an array containing the elements in this list.

```
public void trimToSize()
```
Trims the capacity of this list to the current size.

AWTEvent (java.awt)

A public class, derived from EventObject, that is the root class for all of the AWT event classes.

variables and constants

```
public final static long ACTION_EVENT_MASK
public final static long ADJUSTMENT_EVENT_MASK
```

```
public final static long COMPONENT_EVENT_MASK
public final static long CONTAINER_EVENT_MASK
public final static long FOCUS_EVENT_MASK
public final static long ITEM_EVENT_MASK
public final static long KEY_EVENT_MASK
public final static long MOUSE_EVENT_MASK
public final static long MOUSE_MOTION_EVENT_MASK
public final static long TEXT_EVENT_MASK
public final static long WINDOW_EVENT_MASK
```
Constant values representing the AWT event masks for various events.

```
protected boolean consumed
```
A variable representing the state of the event. A true value means that it has not been sent to the appropriate peer, false indicates that it has.

```
protected int id
```
The numeric identification for this event.

constructors

```
public AWTEvent(Event evt)
```
Creates a new AWTEvent from the specified event.

```
public AWTEvent(Object src, int type)
```
Creates a new AWTEvent from a specified source, and having a defined type.

methods

```
protected void consume()
```
Targets this AWTEvent to be sent to the appropriate peer.

```
public int getID()
```
Returns this event's type.

```
protected boolean isConsumed()
```
Returns a true value if this AWTEvent has been sent to the appropriate peer.

```
public String paramString()
```
Returns the parameter string for this AWTEvent.

```
public String toString()
```
Returns a string representation of this AWTEvent.

BigDecimal (java.math)

A public class, derived from Number, which can be used to represent a decimal number with a definable precision.

variables and constants

ROUND_CEILING

A constant that represents a rounding mode in which the value of the `BigDecimal` is rounded up (away from zero) if the number is positive, and down (closer to zero) if the number is negative.

ROUND_DOWN

A constant that represents a rounding mode in which the value of the `BigDecimal` is rounded closer to zero (decreasing a positive number and increasing a negative number).

ROUND_FLOOR

A constant that represents a rounding mode in which the value of the BigDecimal is rounded down (closer to zero) if the number is positive, and up (away from zero) if the number is negative.

ROUND_HALF_DOWN

A constant that represents a rounding mode in which the value of the BigDecimal is rounded as in ROUND_UP if the fraction of the number is greater than 0.5 and as ROUND_DOWN in all other cases.

ROUND_HALF_EVEN

A constant that represents a rounding mode in which the value of the BigDecimal is rounded as in ROUND_HALF_UP if the number to the left of the decimal is odd and as ROUND_HALF_DOWN when the number is even.

ROUND_HALF_UP

A constant that represents a rounding mode in which the value of the BigDecimal is rounded as in ROUND_UP if the fraction of the number is greater than or equal to 0.5 and as in ROUND_DOWN in all other cases.

ROUND_UNNECESSARY

A constant that represents a rounding mode in which the value of the BigDecimal is not rounded (if possible) and an exact result be returned.

ROUND_UP

A constant that represents a rounding mode in which the value of the BigDecimal is rounded away from zero (increasing a positive number, and decreasing a negative number).

constructors

```
public BigDecimal(BigInteger arg)
public BigDecimal(BigInteger arg, int scale) throws NumberFormatException
public BigDecimal(double arg) throws NumberFormatException
public BigDecimal(String arg) throws NumberFormatException
```
Creates an instance of a BigDecimal from arg. The string argument may contain a preceding minus sign indicating a negative number. The resulting BigDecimal's scale will be the number of integers to the right of the decimal point in the string, a specified value, or 0 (zero) if none are present.

methods

```
public double doubleValue()
public float floatValue()
public int intValue()
public long longValue()
public BigInteger toBigInteger()
public String toString()
```
Converts this BigDecimal to either a Java primitive type or a BigInteger.

```
public BigDecimal abs()
```
Returns the absolute value of this BigDecimal with the same scale as this BigDecimal.

```
public BigDecimal add(BigDecimal arg)
public BigDecimal subtract(BigDecimal arg)
```
Returns the result of arg added to or subtracted from this BigDecimal, with the resulting scale equal to the larger of the two BigDecimal's scales.

```
public int compareTo(BigDecimal arg)
```
This method compares this BigDecimal to arg and will return a –1 if this BigDecimal is less than arg, 0 if equal to arg or a 1 if greater than arg. If the values of the two BigDecimals are identical and the scales are different, they are considered equal.

```
public BigDecimal divide(BigDecimal arg, int mode) throws ArithmeticException,
IllegalArgumentException
public BigDecimal divide(BigDecimal arg, int scale, int mode) throws
ArithmeticException, IllegalArgumentException
```
Returns the result of this BigDecimal divided by arg. If required the rounding mode is used. The resulting BigDecimal's scale is identical to this BigDecimal's scale or a specified value.

```
public boolean equals(Object arg)
```
Returns a true value if this BigDecimal's value and scale are equal to arg's value and scale.

```
public int hashCode()
```
Returns the hash code of this BigDecimal.

```
public BigDecimal max(BigDecimal arg)
public BigDecimal min(BigDecimal arg)
```
Returns the greater or lesser of this BigDecimal and arg.

```
public BigDecimal movePointLeft(int num)
public BigDecimal movePointRight(int num)
```
Returns this BigDecimal with the decimal point moved num positions.

```
public BigDecimal multiply(BigDecimal arg)
```
Returns the result of this BigDecimal multiplied with the value of arg. The scale of the resulting Big-Decimal is the result of the addition of the two BigDecimal's scales.

`public BigDecimal negate()`
Returns the negation of this BigDecimal's value with the same scale.

`public int scale()`
Returns the scale of this BigDecimal.

`public BigDecimal setScale(int val) throws ArithmeticException,`
`IllegalArgumentException`

`public BigDecimal setScale(int val, int mode) throws ArithmeticException,`
`IllegalArgumentException`
Returns a BigDecimal whose value is the same as this BigDecimal's and has a new scale specified by val. If rounding is necessary, a rounding mode can be specified.

`public int signum()`
Returns a –1 if this BigDecimal is negative, 0 if zero, and 1 if positive.

`public static BigDecimal valueOf(long value)`

`public static BigDecimal valueOf(long value, int scale) throws`
`NumberFormatException`
Returns a BigDecimal with a defined value. The scale of the returned number is specified or it defaults to 0 (zero).

BigInteger (`java.math`)

A public class, derived from `Number`, that can be used to represent an integer in a two's complement format of any precision.

constructors

`public BigInteger(byte[] arg) throws NumberFormatException`

`public BigInteger(int signum, byte[] magnitude) throws NumberFormatException`
Creates an instance of a BigInteger from the specified byte array. The sign of the number can be placed in signum (where –1 is negative, 0 is zero, and 1 is positive).

`public BigInteger(String arg) throws NumberFormatException`

`public BigInteger(String arg, int radix) throws NumberFormatException`
Creates an instance of a BigInteger from the string arg, which can contain decimal numbers preceded by an optional minus sign. The argument radix specifies the base of the arg value.

`public BigInteger(int size, Random rand) throws IllegalArgumentException`

`public BigInteger(int size, int prob, Random rand)`
Creates a (generally) prime instance of a BigInteger from a random integer, rand, of a specified length, size. The certainty parameter (prob) represents the amount of probability that the generated number is a prime.

methods

```
public double doubleValue()
public float floatValue()
public int intValue()
public long longValue()
public String toString()
public String toString(int base)
```
Converts this BigDecimal to either a Java primitive type or a BigInteger. The base can specify the radix of the number value returned.

```
public BigInteger abs()
```
Returns the absolute value of this BigInteger.

```
public BigInteger add(BigInteger arg) throws ArithmeticException
public BigInteger subtract(BigInteger arg)
```
Adds the argument to, or subtracts arg from this BigInteger and returns the result.

```
public BigInteger and(BigInteger arg)
public BigInteger andNot(BigInteger arg)
public BigInteger not()
public BigInteger or(BigInteger arg)
public BigInteger xor(BigInteger arg)
```
Returns the result of a logical operation of this BigInteger and the value of arg. The not method returns the logical not of this BigInteger.

```
public int bitCount()
```
Returns the number of bits from this BigInteger that are different from the sign bit.

```
public int bitLength()
```
Returns the number of bits from this BigInteger, excluding the sign bit.

```
public BigInteger clearBit(int index) throws ArithmeticException
```
Returns the modified representation of this BigInteger with the bit at position index cleared.

```
public int compareTo(BigInteger arg)
```
Compares this BigInteger to the parameter arg. If this BigInteger is less than arg, a -1 is returned, if equal to arg a 0 (zero) is returned, and if greater than arg, a 1 is returned.

```
public BigInteger divide(BigInteger arg) throws ArithmeticException
public BigInteger[] divideAndRemainder(BigInteger arg) throws ArithmeticException
```
Returns the result of this BigInteger divided by arg. The divideAndRemainder method returns as the first element ([0]) the quotient, and the second element ([1]) the remainder.

```
public boolean equals(Object arg)
```
Returns a true value if this BigInteger is equal to the parameter arg.

```
public BigInteger flipBit(int index) throws ArithmeticException
```
Returns the modified representation of this BigInteger with the bit at position index flipped.

```
public BigInteger gcd(BigInteger arg)
```
Returns the greatest common denominator of the absolute value of this `BigInteger` and the absolute value of the parameter `arg`.

```
public int getLowestSetBit()
```
Returns the index of the rightmost bit that is equal to one from this `BigInteger`.

```
public int hashCode()
```
Returns the hash code of this `BigInteger`.

```
public boolean isProbablePrime(int prob)
```
Returns a true value if this `BigInteger` is probably a prime number. The parameter prob represents the certainty of the decision.

```
public BigInteger max(BigInteger arg)
public BigInteger min(BigInteger arg)
```
Returns the larger or smaller of this `BigInteger` or arg.

```
public BigInteger mod(BigInteger arg)
public BigInteger modInverse(BigInteger arg) throws ArithmeticException
public BigInteger modPow(BigInteger exp, BigInteger arg)
```
Returns the result of this `BigInteger` mod arg. The modInverse returns the modular multiplicative inverse. modPow returns the result of this (BigInteger ** exp) mod arg.

```
public BigInteger multiply(BigInteger arg)
```
Returns the result of this `BigInteger` multiplied by arg.

```
public BigInteger negate()
```
Returns this `BigInteger` negated (this `BigInteger` * –1).

```
public BigInteger pow(int exp) throws ArithmeticException
```
Returns the result of this `BigInteger` ** exp.

```
public BigInteger remainder(BigInteger arg) throws ArithmeticException
```
Returns the result of this `BigInteger` mod arg.

```
public BigInteger setBit(int index) throws ArithmeticException
```
Returns the result of this BigInteger with the bit at the specified index set.

```
public BigInteger shiftLeft(int num)
public BigInteger shiftRight(int num)
```
Returns the result of this BigInteger shifted num bits.

```
public int signum()
```
Returns a –1 if the value of this BigInteger is negative, 0 if zero, and 1 if positive.

```
public boolean testBit(int index) throws ArithmeticException
```
Returns a true value if the bit at the specified index is set.

```
public byte[] toByteArray()
```
Returns the two's complement of this BigInteger in an array of bytes.

```
public static BigInteger valueOf(long arg)
```
Returns a `BigInteger` from the value of arg.

BitSet (java.util)

A public final class, derived from `Object` and implementing `Cloneable` and `Serializable`, that allows for the manipulation of a vectored array of bits.

constructors

```
public BitSet()
public BitSet(int size)
```
Creates a new instance of a bit sequence of `size` bits (the default is 64). Each of the initial bits are set to false.

methods

```
public void and(BitSet arg)
public void or(BitSet arg)
public void xor(BitSet arg)
```
Places all of the bits from both this BitSet AND/OR/XORed with the bits of `arg` into this `BitSet`.

```
public void clear(int index)
public void set(int index)
```
Clears or sets the bit (sets it to false) at location `index`.

```
public Object clone()
```
Returns a clone of this `BitSet`.

```
public boolean equals(Object arg)
```
Returns a true if `arg` is not null and all bits are equal to this `BitSet`.

```
public boolean get(int index)
```
Returns the boolean value of the bit at location `index`.

```
public int hashCode()
```
Returns the hash code of this `BitSet`.

```
public int size()
```
Returns the size of this `BitSet`.

```
public String toString()
```
Returns a string representation of this `BitSet` in set notation (i.e., {1, 2, 5})

Boolean (java.lang)

A public final class, derived from `Object` and implementing `Serializable`, that contains boolean logic operations, constants, and methods as a wrapper around the Java primitive type `boolean`.

variables and constructs

```
public final static Boolean TRUE
public final static Boolean FALSE
```
Boolean constant values of true or false.

```
public final static Class TYPE
```
The `Boolean` constant value of the boolean type class.

constructors

```
public Boolean(boolean arg)
public Boolean(String arg)
```
Creates an instance of the `Boolean` class from the parameter `arg`.

methods

```
public boolean booleanValue()
```
The boolean value of the current object.

```
public boolean equals(Object arg)
```
Returns the result of an equality comparison against `arg`. Here `arg` must be a boolean object with the same value as this `Boolean` for a resulting true value.

```
public static boolean getBoolean(String str)
```
Returns a `Boolean` representation of the system property named in `str`.

```
public int hashCode()
```
Returns the hash code for this object.

```
public String toString()
```
Returns the string representation of the state of the current object (i.e., "true" or "false").

```
public static Boolean valueOf(String str)
```
Returns a new Boolean initialized to the value of `str`.

BorderFactory (javax.swing)

A public class, derived from `Object`, that represents a factory for creating GUI borders.

methods

```
public static Border createBevelBorder(int type)
public static Border createBevelBorder(int type, Color highlight, Color shadow)
```

```
public static Border createBevelBorder(int type, Color outerHighlight, Color
innerHighlight, Color outerShadow, Color innerShadow)
```
Returns a bevel border with the specified type (BevelBorder.LOWERED or BevelBorder.RAISED) and shading.

```
public static CompoudBorder createCompoundBorder(Border outside, Border inside)
```
Returns a border composed of the two other specified borders.

```
public static Border createEmptyBorder()
```

```
public static Border createEmptyBorder(int top, int left, int bottom, int right)
```
Returns an empty (invisible) border with the specified dimensions, which default to 0.

```
public static Border createEtchedBorder()
```

```
public static Border createEtchedBorder(Color highlight, Color shadow)
```

```
public static Border createEtchedBorder(int type)
```

```
public static Border createEtchedBorder(int type, Color highlight, Color shadow)
```
Returns an etched border with the specified type (EtchedBorder.RAISED or EtchedBorder.LOWERED) and shading.

```
public static Border createLineBorder(Color color)
```

```
public static Border createLineBorder(Color color, int thickness)
```
Returns a line border with the specified color and thickness. If unspecified, the thickness defaults to one pixel.

```
public static Border createLoweredBevelBorder()
```

```
public static Border createRaisedBevelBorder()
```
Returns a border with a lowered or raised beveled edge.

```
public static MatteBorder createMatteBorder(int top, int left, int bottom, int
right, Color color)
```

```
public static MatteBorder createMatteBorder(int top, int left, int bottom, int
right, Icon icon)
```
Returns a matte border with the specified edge sizes. The border is made up either of the specified color or the specified icon.

```
public static TitledBorder createTitledBorder(Border border)
```

```
public static TitledBorder createTitledBorder(String title)
```

```
public static TitledBorder createTitledBorder(Border border, String title)
```

```
public static TitledBorder createTitledBorder(Border border, String title, int
justification, int position)
```

```
public static TitledBorder createTitledBorder(Border border, String title, int
justification, int position, Font font)
```

```
public static TitledBorder createTitledBorder(Border border, String title, int
justification, int position, Font font, Color color)
```
Returns a titled border with the specified border and the specified title text, justification, posiition, font, and color. Justification and position are defined by constants in the TitledBorder class.

Justification can be: LEFT, CENTER, RIGHT, LEADING, or TRAILING (default is LEADING). Position specifies the title's vertical position in relation to the border and can be: TOP, BELOW_TOP, ABOVE_BOTTOM, BOTTOM, or BELOW_BOTTOM (default is TOP).

BorderLayout (java.awt)

A public class, derived from `Object` and implementing `LayoutManager2` and `Serializable`, that lays out a container using five distinct areas (North, South, East, West, and Center).

variables and constructs

```
public final static String CENTER
public final static String EAST
public final static String NORTH
public final static String SOUTH
public final static String WEST
```
Constant values indicating areas of the border layout manager.

constructors

```
public BorderLayout()
public BorderLayout(int hgap, int vgap)
```
Creates a new instance of a `BorderLayout`. If no initial horizontal and vertical gaps are specified, they default to zero.

methods

```
public void addLayoutComponent(Component item, Object constraints)
public void removeLayoutComponent(Component item)
```
Adds or removes a component to this layout manager. When adding a component, it is possible to restrict the component to the specified constraints.

```
public int getHgap()
public int getVgap()
```
Returns the horizontal or vertical gap of components laid out by this layout manager.

```
public float getLayoutAlignmentX(Container cont)
public float getLayoutAlignmentY(Container cont)
```
Returns the horizontal or vertical alignment value of the specified container.

```
public void invalidateLayout(Container cont)
```
Forces this layout manager to discard any cached layout information about the specified container.

```
public void layoutContainer(Container cont)
```
Lays out the specified container with this layout manager.
```
public Dimension maximumLayoutSize(Container cont)
```
```
public Dimension minimumLayoutSize(Container cont)
```
```
public Dimension preferredLayoutSize(Container cont)
```
Returns the maximum, minimum or preferred size of the specified container when laid out by this layout manager.
```
public void setHgap(int hgap)
```
```
public void setVgap(int vgap)
```
Sets the horizontal or vertical gap in pixels of components laid out by this layout manager.

Box (javax.swing)

A public class, derived from `JComponent` and implementing `Accessible`, that represents a lightweight container that uses a box layout.

constructors

```
public Box(int axis)
```
Creates a box that displays its components along the specified axis (BoxLayout. X_AXIS or BoxLayout.Y_AXIS).

methods

```
public static Box createHorizontalBox()
```
```
public static Box createVerticalBox()
```
Returns a box that displays its components horizontally (from left to right) or vertically (from top to bottom).
```
public static Component createGlue()
```
```
public static Component createHorizontalGlue()
```
```
public static Component createVerticalGlue()
```
Returns an invisible glue component that expands as much as necessary to fill the space between neighboring components.
```
public static Component createRigidArea(Dimension dim)
```
Returns an invisible component with the specified size.
```
public static Component createHorizontalStrut(int width)
```
```
public static Component createVerticalStrut(int height)
```
Returns an invisible component with a fixed width or height.

BoxLayout (javax.swing)

A public class, derived from `Object` and implementing `LayoutManager2` and `Serializable`, that lays out components either vertically or horizontally.

variables and constructs

```
public static final int X_AXIS
public static final int Y_AXIS
```
Specifies that components should be laid out left to right or top to bottom.

constructors

```
public BoxLayout(Container target, int axis)
```
Creates a box layout for the specified target container along the specified axis.

methods

```
public float getLayoutAlignmentX(Container cont)
public float getLayoutAlignmentY(Container cont)
```
Returns the horizontal or vertical alignment value of the specified container.

```
public void invalidateLayout(Container cont)
```
Forces this layout manager to discard any cached layout information about the specified container.

```
public void layoutContainer(Container cont)
```
Lays out the specified container with this layout manager.

```
public Dimension maximumLayoutSize(Container cont)
public Dimension minimumLayoutSize(Container cont)
public Dimension preferredLayoutSize(Container cont)
```
Returns the maximum, minimum or preferred size of the specified container when laid out by this layout manager.

BufferedReader (java.io)

A public class, derived from `Reader`, that provides a buffered stream of character-based input.

constructors

```
public BufferedReader(Reader rdr)
public BufferedReader(Reader rdr, int size)
```
Creates a `BufferedReader` from the specified `Reader`, by using a specified size (in characters). The default size is 8192 characters.

methods

`public void close() throws IOException`
Closes this BufferedReader.

`public void mark(int readAheadLimit) throws IOException`
Sets a mark in the stream where attempts to reset this BufferedReader will return to. The readAheadLimit determines how far ahead the stream can be read before the mark expires.

`public boolean markSupported()`
An overridden method from Reader that determines if this stream supports the setting of a mark.

`public int read() throws IOException`

`public String readLine() throws IOException`
Reads a single character or an entire line from this BufferedReader stream. The character is returned as an int, the line as a string. A line of text is considered to be a series of characters ending in a carriage return (\r), a line feed (\n), or a carriage return followed by a line (\r\n).

`public int read(char[] dest, int offset, int size) throws IOException`
Reads size characters from this BufferedReader stream. Reading will skip offset characters into the current location in the stream, and place them in the destination array. This method will return the number of characters read from the stream or a -1 if the end of the stream was reached.

`public boolean ready() throws IOException`
Returns a true value if this BufferedReader is capable of being read from. This state can only be true if the buffer is not empty.

`public void reset() throws IOException`
Resets this BufferedReader to the last mark.

`public long skip(long num) throws IOException`
Skips forward num characters in the stream and returns the actual number of characters skipped.

BufferedWriter (java.io)

A public class, derived from Writer, that represents a character output stream that buffers characters for efficiency.

constructors

`public BufferedWriter(Writer out)`

`public BufferedWriter(Writer out, int size)`
Creates a buffered output stream using the specified Writer stream and a buffer of the specified size.

methods

`public void close()`
 Closes this stream

`public void flush()`
 Flushes this stream

`public void newLine()`
 Writes a line separator to this stream.

`public void write(int ch)`

`public void write(String str)`

`public void write(String str, int offset, int length)`

`public void write(char[] buffer)`

`public void write(char[] buffer, int offset, int length)`
 Writes a single character, string, or character array to this stream. A portion of the string or character array can be specified.

ButtonGroup (javax.swing)

A public class, derived from `Object` and implementing `Serializable`, that represents a set of mutually exclusive buttons.

constructors

`public ButtonGroup()`
 Creates an empty button group.

methods

`public void add(AbstractButton button)`

`public void remove(AbstractButton button)`
 Adds or removes the specified button to this group.

`public int getButtonCount()`
 Returns the number of buttons in this group.

Byte (java.lang)

A public final class, derived from `Number`, that contains byte logic operations, constants, and methods as a wrapper around the Java primitive type `byte`.

variables and constructs

```
public final static byte MAX_VALUE
public final static byte MIN_VALUE
```
   A constant value that holds the maximum (127) and minimum (−128) values a byte can contain.
```
public final static Class TYPE
```
   The Byte constant value of the byte type class.

constructors

```
public Byte(byte arg)
public Byte(String arg) throws NumberFormatException
```
   Creates a new instance of a Byte from arg.

methods

```
public byte byteValue()
public double doubleValue()
public float floatValue()
public int intValue()
public long longValue()
public short shortValue()
```
   Returns the value of this Byte as a Java primitive type.
```
public static Byte decode(String str) throws NumberFormatException
```
   Returns the given string (str) as a Byte. The parameter string may be encoded as an octal, hexadecimal, or binary number.
```
public boolean equals(Object arg)
```
   Returns a true value if this Byte is equal to the parameter object arg.
```
public int hashCode()
```
   Returns the hash code of this Byte.
```
public static byte parseByte(String str) throws NumberFormatException
public static byte parseByte(String str, int base) throws NumberFormatException
```
   Returns the value of the parsed string (str) as a byte. The radix of the string can be specified in base.
```
public String toString()
public static String toString(byte prim)
```
   Returns a string representation of this Byte or the specified primitive byte (prim), whose radix is assumed to be 10.
```
public static Byte valueOf(String str) throws NumberFormatException
```

public static Byte valueOf(String str, int base) throws NumberFormatException
   Returns a Byte object whose initial value is the result of the parsed parameter (str). The parameter is assumed to be the text representation of a byte and its radix 10 (unless specified in base).

Calendar (java.util)

A public abstract class, derived from Object and implementing Cloneable and Serializable, that allows for the manipulation of a Date object.

variables and constructs

public static final int AM
public static final int PM
   Constant values that represent ante and post meridian.
public static final int ERA
public static final int YEAR
public static final int MONTH
public static final int WEEK_OF_YEAR
public static final int WEEK_OF_MONTH
public static final int DATE
public static final int DAY_OF_MONTH
public static final int DAY_OF_YEAR
public static final int DAY_OF_WEEK
public static final int DAY_OF_WEEK_IN_MONTH
public static final int AM_PM
public static final int HOUR
public static final int HOUR_OF_DAY
public static final int MINUTE
public static final int SECOND
public static final int MILLISECOND
public static final int ZONE_OFFSET
public static final int DST_OFFSET
   Constant values that represent the index to the field where particular data is stored representing an instance of time (to millisecond precision). The combination of all of these fields yields a full representation of a moment of time with respect to a particular calendar (i.e., GregorianCalendar).
public static final int JANUARY
public static final int FEBRUARY
public static final int MARCH

```
public static final int APRIL
public static final int MAY
public static final int JUNE
public static final int JULY
public static final int AUGUST
public static final int SEPTEMBER
public static final int OCTOBER
public static final int NOVEMBER
public static final int DECEMBER
public static final int UNDECIMBER
```
Constant values representing various calendar months. UNDECIMBER represents the 13th month of a Gregorian calendar (lunar month).

```
public static final int SUNDAY
public static final int MONDAY
public static final int TUESDAY
public static final int WEDNESDAY
public static final int THURSDAY
public static final int FRIDAY
public static final int SATURDAY
```
Constant values representing the days of a week.

```
protected boolean areFieldsSet
```
A boolean flag that indicates if the time fields have been set for this Calendar.

```
public static final int FIELD_COUNT
```
A constant value that represents the number of date/time fields stored by a Calendar.

```
protected int fields[]
```
The integer array that contains the values that make up the information about this Calendar.

```
protected boolean isSet[]
```
The boolean array that contains status values used to indicate if a corresponding time field has been set.

```
protected boolean isTimeSet
```
A boolean flag field that is used to indicate if the time is set for this Calendar.

```
protected long time
```
A long int field that contains the time set for this Calendar.

methods

```
public abstract void add(int field, int val)
```
Adds (or subtracts in the case of a negative val) an amount of days or time from the specified field.

`public abstract boolean after(Object arg)`

`public abstract boolean before(Object arg)`

Returns a true value if this `Calendar` date is after or before the date specified by `arg`.

`public final void clear()`

`public final void clear(int field)`

Clears the value from the specified time `field` from this `Calendar`. The `clear` method will clear all of the values from this `Calendar`.

`public Object clone()`

Returns a clone of this `Calendar`.

`protected void complete()`

Attempts to complete any empty date/time fields by calling the `completeTime()` and `completeFields()` methods of this `Calendar`.

`protected abstract void computeFields()`

`protected abstract void computeTime()`

Computes the values of the time fields based on the currently set time (`computeFields()`) or computes the time based on the currently set time fields (`computeTime()`) for this `Calendar`.

`public abstract boolean equals(Object arg)`

Returns a true value if this `Calendar` is equal to the value of `arg`.

`public final int get(int fld)`

Returns the value of the specified time field from this `Calendar`.

`public static synchronized Locale[] getAvailableLocales()`

Returns the list of locales that are available.

`public int getFirstDayOfWeek()`

`public void setFirstDayOfWeek(int val)`

Returns or sets the first day of the week to `val` for this `Calendar`.

`public abstract int getGreatestMinimum(int fld)`

Returns the largest allowable minimum value for the specified field.

`public static synchronized Calendar getInstance()`

`public static synchronized Calendar getInstance(Locale locale)`

`public static synchronized Calendar getInstance(TimeZone tz)`

`public static synchronized Calendar getInstance(TimeZone tz, Locale locale)`

Returns an instance of a `Calendar` based on the default time zone and locale, or from a specified time zone and/or locale.

`public abstract int getLeastMaximum(int fld)`

Returns the smallest allowable maximum value for the specified field.

`public abstract int getMaximum(int fld)`

`public abstract int getMinimum(int fld)`

Returns the largest or smallest allowable value for the specified field.

```
public int getMinimalDaysInFirstWeek()
public void setMinimalDaysInFirstWeek(int val)
```
Returns or sets the smallest allowable number of days in the first week of the year, based on the locale.
```
public final Date getTime()
public final void setTime(Date dt)
```
Returns or sets the time for this Calendar.
```
protected long getTimeInMillis()
protected void setTimeInMillis(long ms)
```
Returns or sets the time in milliseconds for this Calendar.
```
public TimeZone getTimeZone()
public void setTimeZone(TimeZone val)
```
Returns or sets the time zone for this Calendar.
```
protected final int internalGet(int fld)
```
An internal method used to obtain field values to be used by subclasses of Calendar.
```
public boolean isLenient()
public void setLenient(boolean flag)
```
Returns or sets the flag indicating leniency for date/time input.
```
public final boolean isSet(int fld)
```
Returns a true value if a value is set for the specified field.
```
public abstract void roll(int fld, boolean direction)
```
Adds one single unit of time to the specified date/time field. A true value specified for direction increases the field's value, false decreases it.
```
public final void set(int fld, int val)
```
Sets a single specified field to a value.
```
public final void set(int year, int month, int date)
public final void set(int year, int month, int date, int hour, int min)
public final void set(int year, int month, int date, int hour, int min, int sec)
```
Sets the year, month, date, hour, minute, and seconds of the time fields for this Calendar.

CardLayout (java.awt)

A public class, derived from Object and implementing LayoutManager2 and Serializable, that lays out components in a series of separate cards, only one of which is visible at any time. The visibility of the cards can be changed, essentially providing the ability to sequence through the cards.

constructors

`public CardLayout()`

`public CardLayout(int hg, int vg)`
  Creates a new instance of a card layout with a specified horizontal and vertical gap (or no gap in the case of the first constructor).

methods

`public void addLayoutComponent(Component item, Object constr)`

`public void removeLayoutComponent(Component item)`
  Adds or removes a component to this layout manager. While adding, it is possible to restrict the component to the specified constraints (`constr`).

`public void first(Container cont)`

`public void last(Container cont)`
  Moves to the first or last card in the layout. `cont` is the container that is laid out by this layout manager.

`public int getHgap()`

`public int getVgap()`
  Returns the horizontal or vertical gap between the components laid out by this layout manager.

`public float getLayoutAlignmentX(Container parent)`

`public float getLayoutAlignmentY(Container parent)`
  Returns the horizontal or vertical alignment value of the specified container.

`public void invalidateLayout(Container cont)`
  Forces this layout manager to discard any cached layout information about the specified container.

`public void layoutContainer(Container cont)`
  Lays out the specified container with this layout manager.

`public Dimension maximumLayoutSize(Container cont)`

`public Dimension minimumLayoutSize(Container cont)`

`public Dimension preferredLayoutSize(Container cont)`
  Returns the maximum, minimum or preferred size of the specified container when laid out by this layout manager.

`public void next(Container cont)`

`public void previous(Container cont)`
  Cycles to the next or previous card. `cont` is container that is laid out by this layout manager.

`public void setHgap(int hg)`

`public void setVgap(int vg)`
  Sets the horizontal or vertical gap in pixels of components laid out by this layout manager.

```
public void show(Container cont, String str)
```
Cycles to the card the contains the component with the name str. When found, the specified container is laid out with this layout manager.
```
public String toString()
```
Returns a string representation of this layout manager.

Character (java.lang)

A public class, derived from Object and implementing Serializable, that contains character constants and methods to convert and identify characters.

variables and constructs

```
public final static byte COMBINING_SPACING_MARK
public final static byte CONNECTOR_PUNCTUATION
public final static byte CONTROL
public final static byte CURRENCY_SYMBOL
public final static byte DASH_PUNCTUATION
public final static byte DECIMAL_DIGIT_NUMBER
public final static byte ENCLOSING_MARK
public final static byte END_PUNCTUATION
public final static byte FORMAT
public final static byte LETTER_NUMBER
public final static byte LINE_SEPARATOR
public final static byte LOWERCASE_LETTER
public final static byte MATH_SYMBOL
public final static byte MODIFIER_LETTER
public final static byte MODIFIER_SYMBOL
public final static byte NON_SPACING_MARK
public final static byte OTHER_LETTER
public final static byte OTHER_NUMBER
public final static byte OTHER_PUNCTUATION
public final static byte OTHER_SYMBOL
public final static byte PARAGRAPH_SEPARATOR
public final static byte PRIVATE_USE
public final static byte SPACE_SEPARATOR
public final static byte START_PUNCTUATION
```

```
public final static byte SURROGATE
public final static byte TITLECASE_LETTER
public final static byte UNASSIGNED
public final static byte UPPERCASE_LETTER
```
Constant values representing various character symbols and types.
```
public final static int MAX_RADIX
```
A constant value that represents the largest possible value of a radix (base).
```
public final static char MAX_VALUE
```
A constant value that represents the largest possible value of a character in Java = \uffff'.
```
public final static int MIN_RADIX
```
A constant value that represents that smallest possible value of a radix (base).
```
public final static char MIN_VALUE
```
A constant value that represents the smallest possible value of a character in Java = \u0000'.
```
public final static Class TYPE
```
The Character constant value of the character type class.

constructors
```
public Character(char prim)
```
Creates an instance of the Character class from the primitive parameter prim.

methods
```
public char charValue()
```
Returns the value of this Character as a primitive character.
```
public static int digit(char c, int base)
public static char forDigit(int c, int base)
```
Returns the numeric value or the character depiction of the parameter c in radix base.
```
public boolean equals(Object arg)
```
Returns a true value if this Character is equal to the parameter arg.
```
public static int getNumericValue(char c)
```
Returns the Unicode representation of the character parameter (c) as a nonnegative integer. If the character has no numeric representation, a -1 is returned. If the character cannot be represented as a nonnegative number, –2 will be returned.
```
public static int getType(char c)
```
Returns an integer value that represents the type of character the parameter c is.
```
public int hashCode()
```
Returns a hash code for this Character.
```
public static boolean isDefined(char c)
```

```
public static boolean isISOControl(char c)
```
Returns a true value if the parameter c has a defined meaning in Unicode or is an ISO control character.

```
public static boolean isIdentifierIgnorable(char c)
```
Returns a true value if the parameter c is a character that can be ignored in a Java identifier (such as control characters).

```
public static boolean isJavaIdentifierPart(char c)
```
```
public static boolean isJavaIdentifierStart(char c)
```
Returns a true value if the parameter c can be used in a valid Java identifier in any but the leading character. `isJavaIdentifierStart` returns a true value if the parameter c can be used as the leading character in a valid Java identifier.

```
public static boolean isDigit(char c)
```
```
public static boolean isLetter(char c)
```
```
public static boolean isLetterOrDigit(char c)
```
```
public static boolean isLowerCase(char c)
```
```
public static boolean isSpaceChar(char c)
```
```
public static boolean isTitleCase(char c)
```
```
public static boolean isUnicodeIdentifierPart(char c)
```
```
public static boolean isWhitespace(char c)
```
```
public static boolean isUnicodeIdentifierStart(char c)
```
```
public static boolean isUpperCase(char c)
```
Returns a true value if the parameter c is a digit; letter; letter or a digit; lowercase character; space character; titlecase character; can be used in a valid Unicode identifier in any but the leading character; a white space character; can be used as the leading character in a valid Unicode identifier or an uppercase character (respectively).

```
public static char toLowerCase(char c)
```
```
public String toString()
```
```
public static char toTitleCase(char c)
```
```
public static char toUpperCase(char c)
```
Returns a lowercase character, string representation, titlecase, or uppercase character of the parameter c.

Class (java.lang)

A public final class, derived from `Object` and implementing `Serializable`, that describes both interfaces and classes in the currently running Java program.

methods

```
public static Class forName(String class) throws ClassNotFoundException
```
Returns a `Class` object that corresponds with the named `class`. The name of the specified class must be a fully qualified class name (as in `java.io.Reader`).

```
public Class[] getClasses()
```

```
public Class[] getDeclaredClasses() throws SecurityException
```
Returns an array of `Classes` that contains all of the interfaces and classes that are members of this `Class` (excluding superclasses). `getClasses` returns only the list of public interfaces and classes.

```
public ClassLoader getClassLoader()
```
Returns the `ClassLoader` for this `Class`.

```
public Class getComponentType()
```
Returns the `Component` type of the array that is represented by this `Class`.

```
public Constructor getConstructor(Class[] types) throws NoSuchMethodException,
SecurityException
```

```
public Constructor[] getConstructors() throws SecurityException
```
Returns the `Constructor` object or an array containing the public constructors for this class. The signature of the public constructor that is returned must match exactly the types and sequence of the parameters specified by the `types` array.

```
public Constructor getDeclaredConstructor(Class[] types) throws
NoSuchMethodException, SecurityException
```

```
public Constructor[] getDeclaredConstructors() throws SecurityException
```
Returns the `Constructor` object or an array containing the constructors for this class. The signature of the public constructor that is returned must match exactly the types and sequence of the parameters specified by the `types` array parameter.

```
public Field getDeclaredField(String field) throws NoSuchFieldException,
SecurityException
```

```
public Field[] getDeclaredFields() throws SecurityException
```
Returns the `Field` object or an array containing all of the fields for the specified matching `field` name for this `Class`.

```
public Method getDeclaredMethod(String method, Class[] types) throws
NoSuchMethodException, SecurityException
```

```
public Method[] getDeclaredMethods() throws SecurityException
```
Returns a `Method` object or an array containing all of the methods for the specified `method` of this `Class`. The requested method's parameter list must match identically the types and sequence of the elements of the `types` array.

```
public Class getDeclaringClass()
```
Returns the declaring class of this `Class`, provided that this `Class` is a member of another class.

```
public Field getField(String field) throws NoSuchFieldException,
SecurityException
```

```
public Field[] getFields() throws SecurityException
```
Returns a `Field` object or an array containing all of the fields of a specified matching `field` name for this `Class`.

```
public Class[] getInterfaces()
```
Returns an array containing all of the interfaces of this `Class`.

```
public Method getMethod(String method, Class[] types) throws
NoSuchMethodException, SecurityException
```

```
public Method[] getMethods() throws SecurityException
```
Returns a `Method` object or an array containing all of the public methods for the specified public method of this `Class`. The requested method's parameter list must match identically the types and sequence of the elements of the `types` array.

```
public int getModifiers()
```
Returns the encoded integer visibility modifiers for this `Class`. The values can be decoded using the `Modifier` class.

```
public String getName()
```
Returns the string representation of the name of the type that this `Class` represents.

```
public URL getResource(String arg)
```
Returns a URL representing the system resource for the class loader of this `Class`.

```
public InputStream getResourceAsStream(String arg)
```
Returns an input stream representing the named system resource from the class loader of this `Class`.

```
public Object[] getSigners()
```
Returns an array of `Object`s that contains the signers of this `Class`.

```
public Class getSuperclass()
```
Returns the superclass of this `Class`, or null if this `Class` is an interface or of type `Object`.

```
public boolean isArray()
```
Returns a true value if this `Class` represents an array type.

```
public boolean isAssignableFrom(Class other)
```
Returns a true value if this `Class` is the same as a superclass or superinterface of the `other` class.

```
public boolean isInstance(Object target)
```
Returns a true value if the specified `target` object is an instance of this `Class`.

```
public boolean isInterface()
```

```
public boolean isPrimitive()
```
Returns a true value if this `Class` represents an interface class or a primitive type in Java.

```
public Object newInstance() throws InstantiationException, IllegalAccessException
```
Creates a new instance of this `Class`.

```
public String toString()
```
Returns a string representation of this `Class` in the form of the word class or interface, followed by the fully qualified name of this `Class`.

Color (java.awt)

A public final class, derived from Object and implementing Serializable, that is used to represent colors. A color is defined by three components, red, blue, and green, that each have a value ranging from 0 to 255.

variables and constructs

```
public final static Color black
public final static Color blue
public final static Color cyan
public final static Color darkGray
public final static Color gray
public final static Color green
public final static Color lightGray
public final static Color magenta
public final static Color orange
public final static Color pink
public final static Color red
public final static Color white
public final static Color yellow
```
A constant value that describes the colors black (0, 0, 0), blue (0, 0, 255), cyan (0, 255, 255), darkGray (64, 64, 64), gray (128, 128, 128), green (0, 255, 0), lightGray (192, 192, 192), magenta (255, 0, 255), orange (255, 200, 0), pink (255, 175, 175), red (255, 0, 0), white (255, 255, 255) and yellow (255, 255, 0) as a set of RGB values.

constructors

```
public Color(float r, float g, float b)
public Color(int rgb)
public Color(int r, int g, int b)
```
Creates a new instance of the color described by the rgb value. When passed as a single integer value, the red component is represented in bits 16 to 23, green in 15 to 8, and blue in 0 to 7.

methods

```
public Color brighter()
public Color darker()
```
Returns a brighter or darker version of this color.
```
public static Color decode(String str) throws NumberFormatException
```
Returns the color specified by str.

`public boolean equals(Object arg)`
 Returns a true value if this color is equal to `arg`.
`public int getBlue()`
`public int getGreen()`
`public int getRed()`
 Returns the blue, green, or red component value for this color.
`public static Color getColor(String str)`
`public static Color getColor(String str, Color default)`
`public static Color getColor(String str, int default)`
 Returns the color represented in the string `str` (where its value is an integer). If the value is not determined, the color `default` is returned.
`public static Color getHSBColor(float h, float s, float b)`
 Returns a color specified by the Hue-Saturation-Brightness model for colors, where h is the hue, s is the saturation, and b is the brightness of the desired color.
`public int getRGB()`
 Returns an integer representation of the RGB value for this color.
`public int hashCode()`
 Returns the hash code for this color.
`public static int HSBtoRGB(float hue, float saturation, float brightness)`
 Converts a hue, saturation, and brightness representation of a color to a RGB value.
`public static float[] RGBtoHSB(int r, int g, int b, float[] hsbvals)`
 Converts a RGB representation of a color to a HSB value, placing the converted values into the hsbvals array. The RGB value is represented via a red (r), green (g), and blue (b) value.
`public String toString()`
 Returns a string representation of this color.

Component (java.awt)

A public abstract class, derived from `Object` and implementing `ImageObserver`, `MenuContainer`, and `Serializable`, that is the superclass to every AWT item that is represented on screen with a specific size and position.

variables and constructs

`public final static float BOTTOM_ALIGNMENT`
`public final static float LEFT_ALIGNMENT`
`public final static float RIGHT_ALIGNMENT`

`public final static float TOP_ALIGNMENT`
   Constant values that represent specified alignments within the component.

`protected Locale locale`
   Holds the locale for this component.

constructors

`protected Component()`
   Creates a new instance of a component.

methods

`public synchronized void add(PopupMenu popmenu)`

`public synchronized void remove(MenuComponent popmenu)`
   Adds or removes the specified popup menu to this component.

`public synchronized void addComponentListener(ComponentListener listener)`

`public synchronized void addFocusListener(FocusListener listener)`

`public synchronized void addKeyListener(KeyListener listener)`

`public synchronized void addMouseListener(MouseListener listener)`

`public synchronized void addMouseMotionListener(MouseMotionListener listener)`

`public synchronized void removeComponentListener(ComponentListener listener)`

`public synchronized void removeFocusListener(FocusListener listener)`

`public synchronized void removeKeyListener(KeyListener listener)`

`public synchronized void removeMouseListener(MouseListener listener)`

`public synchronized void removeMouseMotionListener(MouseMotionListener listener)`
   Adds or removes the specified `listener` to this component.

`public void addNotify()`

`public void removeNotify()`
   Notifies the component that a peer must be created or destroyed.

`public int checkImage(Image img, ImageObserver obs)`

`public int checkImage(Image img, int width, int height, ImageObserver obs)`
   Returns the status of the construction of a scaled image img. The image created can be scaled to a width and height. The image obs will be informed of the status of the image.

`public boolean contains(int x, int y)`

`public boolean contains(Point pt)`
   Returns a true value if this component contains the specified position.

`public Image createImage(ImageProducer prod)`

`public Image createImage(int width, int height)`
   Returns a new image created from prod. The second method creates another image which is generally offscreen (having width and height), used for double-buffering drawings.

```
protected final void disableEvents(long mask)
protected final void enableEvents(long mask)
```
  Disables or enables all events specified by the mask for this component.
```
public final void dispatchEvent(AWTEvent event)
```
  Dispatches an AWTEvent to this component or one of its subcomponents.
```
public void doLayout()
```
  Lays out this component.
```
public float getAlignmentX()
public float getAlignmentY()
```
  Returns the horizontal or vertical alignment for this component.
```
public Color getBackground()
public Color getForeground()
public void setBackground(Color clr)
public void setForeground(Color clr)
```
  Returns or sets the background or foreground color for this component.
```
public Rectangle getBounds()
public void setBounds(int x, int y, int width, int height)
```
  Returns or sets the bounds of this component. Setting the bounds resizes and reshapes this component to the bounding box of <x, y> to <x+width, y+height>.
```
public ColorModel getColorModel()
```
  Returns the color model of this component.
```
public Component getComponentAt(int x, int y)
public Component getComponentAt(Point pt)
```
  Returns the component located at the specified point.
```
public Cursor getCursor()
public synchronized void setCursor(Cursor csr)
```
  Returns or sets the cursor set for this component.
```
public Font getFont()
public void setFont(Font ft)
```
  Returns or sets the font of this component.
```
public FontMetrics getFontMetrics(Font ft)
```
  Returns the font metrics of the specified font.
```
public Graphics getGraphics()
```
  Returns the graphics context for this component.
```
public Locale getLocale()
public void setLocale(Locale locale)
```
  Returns or sets the locale for this component.
```
public Point getLocation()
```

```
public Point getLocationOnScreen()
```
Returns the location of this component relative to the containing or screen space.
```
public Dimension getMaximumSize()
public Dimension getMinimumSize()
public Dimension getPreferredSize()
```
Returns the maximum, minimum or preferred size of this component.
```
public String getName()
public void setName(String str)
```
Returns or sets the name of this component.
```
public Container getParent()
```
Returns the parent container of this component.
```
public Dimension getSize()
public void setSize(Dimension dim)
public void setSize(int width, int height)
```
Returns the size of or resizes this component to the specified dimension(s).
```
public Toolkit getToolkit()
```
Returns the toolkit of this component.
```
public final Object getTreeLock()
```
Returns the AWT object that is used as the base of the component tree and layout operations for this component.
```
public boolean imageUpdate(Image src, int flags, int x, int y, int width, int height)
```
Draws more of an image (src) as its information becomes available. The exact value of the x, y, width, and height variables is dependent on the value of the flags variable.
```
public void invalidate()
```
Forces this component to be laid out again by making it "invalid."
```
public boolean isEnabled()
public void setEnabled(boolean toggle)
```
Returns or sets the enabled state of this component.
```
public boolean isFocusTraversable()
```
Returns a true value if this component can be traversed using Tab or Shift-Tab sequences.
```
public boolean isShowing()
public boolean isValid()
```
Returns a true value if this component is visible on screen or does not need to be laid out (valid).
```
public boolean isVisible()
public void setVisible(boolean toggle)
```
Returns or sets the state of this component's visibility.
```
public void list()
```

```
public void list(PrintStream outstrm)
public void list(PrintStream outstrm, int spc)
public void list(PrintWriter outstrm)
public void list(PrintWriter outstrm, int spc)
```
Prints a listing of this component's parameters to the print writer stream outstrm (default of System.out), indenting spc spaces (default of 0).
```
public void paint(Graphics gc)
public void print(Graphics gc)
```
Paints or prints this component with the graphics context gc.
```
public void paintAll(Graphics gc)
public void printAll(Graphics gc)
```
Paints or prints this component and all of its subcomponents with the graphics context gc.
```
protected String paramString()
```
Returns a string describing the parameters of this component.
```
public boolean prepareImage(Image src, ImageObserver obs)
public prepareImage(Image src, int width, int height, ImageObserver obs)
```
Downloads the src for display. The image can be scaled to a width and height. The obs is informed of the status of the image.
```
protected void processComponentEvent(ComponentEvent event)
protected void processFocusEvent(FocusEvent event)
protected void processKeyEvent(KeyEvent event)
protected void processMouseEvent(MouseEvent event)
protected void processMouseMotionEvent(MouseEvent event)
```
Processes the specified event for this component, sending the event to a registered event listener.
```
protected void processEvent(AWTEvent event)
```
Processes an AWT event for this component, sending it to the appropriate processing routine (i.e., processComponentEvent method) for further handling.
```
public void repaint()
public void repaint(int x, int y, int width, int height)
```
Repaints a rectangular portion of this component from <x, y> to <x+width, y+height>.
```
public void repaint(long msec)
public void repaint(long msec, int x, int y, int width, int height)
```
Repaints a rectangular portion of this component from <x, y> to <x+width, y+height> after a delay of msec milliseconds.
```
public void requestFocus()
```
Requests that this component get the input focus.
```
public void setLocation(int x, int y)
```

```
public void setLocation(Point pt)
```
Moves this component to the specified point in the containing space.

```
public String toString()
```
Returns a string representation of this component.

```
public void transferFocus()
```
Transfers focus from this component to the next component.

```
public void update(Graphics gc)
```
Updates this component using graphics context gc.

```
public void validate()
```
Validates this component if needed.

ComponentAdapter (java.awt.event)

A public abstract class, derived from Object and implementing ComponentListener, that permits a derived class to override the predefined no-op component events.

constructors

```
public ComponentAdapter()
```
Creates a new instance of a ComponentAdapter.

methods

```
public void componentHidden(ComponentEvent event)
public void componentMoved(ComponentEvent event)
public void componentResized(ComponentEvent event)
public void componentShown(ComponentEvent event)
```
Empty methods that should be overridden in order to implement event handling for AWT components.

ComponentEvent (java.awt.event)

A public class, derived from AWTEvent, that represents an AWT component event.

variables and constructs

```
public static final int COMPONENT_FIRST
public static final int COMPONENT_LAST
```
Constant values that represent the index of the first and last component event ids.

```
public static final int COMPONENT_MOVED
public static final int COMPONENT_RESIZED
public static final int COMPONENT_SHOWN
public static final int COMPONENT_HIDDEN
```
   Constant values that represent AWT component event ids.

constructors

```
public ComponentEvent(Component src, int type)
```
   Creates a new instance of a ComponentEvent from the specified source and of a specific type.

methods

```
public Component getComponent()
```
   Returns the AWT component that triggered this event.

```
public String paramString()
```
   Returns a string containing the parameters of this event.

Container (java.awt)

A public abstract class, derived from Component, that is the superclass to any AWT component that can contain one or more AWT components.

constructors

```
protected Container()
```
   Creates a new instance of a container.

methods

```
public Component add(Component item)
public Component add(Component item, int idx)
public void add(Component item, Object constr)
public void add(Component item, Object constr, int idx)
public Component add(String str, Component item)
```
   Adds component item to this container at index idx (or to the end by default). The new item can have constraints (constr) applied to it. A string name can be associated with the added component in the case of the last constructor.

```
public void addContainerListener(ContainerListener listener)
public void removeContainerListener(ContainerListener listener)
```
   Adds or removes the specified listener to this container.

```
protected void addImpl(Component item, Object constr, int idx)
```
Adds component item to this container at index idx, and passes the constraints for the new item (constr) to the layout manager for this container.

```
public void addNotify()
public void removeNotify()
```
Creates or destroys this container's peer.

```
public void doLayout()
```
Lays out the components of this container.

```
public float getAlignmentX()
public float getAlignmentY()
```
Returns the horizontal or vertical alignment value of this container.

```
public Component getComponent(int idx) throws ArrayIndexOutOfBoundsException
public Component getComponentAt(int x, int y)
public Component getComponentAt(Point pt)
```
Returns the component that is located at the specified point or index.

```
public int getComponentCount()
```
Returns the number of components in this container.

```
public Component[] getComponents()
```
Returns an array of all of the components in this container.

```
public Insets getInsets()
```
Returns the insets of this container.

```
public LayoutManager getLayout()
public void setLayout(LayoutManager layout)
```
Returns or sets the layout manager of this container.

```
public Dimension getMaximumSize()
public Dimension getMinimumSize()
public Dimension getPreferredSize()
```
Returns the maximum, minimum, or preferred size of this container.

```
public void invalidate()
```
Marks the layout of this container as invalid, forcing the need to lay out the components again.

```
public boolean isAncestorOf(Component comp)
```
Returns a true value if the specified component (comp) is contained in the component hierarchy of this container.

```
public void list(PrintStream outstream, int spaces)
public void list(PrintWriter outstream, int spaces)
```
Prints a listing of all of the components of this container to print stream outstream, indented a specified number of spaces (default of 0).

```
public void paint(Graphics gwin)
```

```
public void print(Graphics gwin)
```
Paints or prints this container with graphics context gwin.

```
public void paintComponents(Graphics gwin)
public void printComponents(Graphics gwin)
```
Repaints or prints all of the components in this container with graphics context gwin.

```
protected String paramString()
```
Returns a string representation of this container's parameters.

```
protected void processContainerEvent(ContainerEvent event)
```
Processes any container event, passing the event to a registered container listener.

```
protected void processEvent(AWTEvent event)
```
Handles any AWTEvent, invoking processContainerEvent for container events, and passing the event to the superclass' processEvent otherwise.

```
public void remove(Component comp)
public void remove(int idx)
```
Removes the specified component (or the component at the specified index) from this container.

```
public void removeAll()
```
Removes all components from this container.

```
public void validate()
```
Validates this container and all of the subcomponents in it.

```
protected void validateTree()
```
Validates this container and all subcontainers in it.

ContainerAdapter (java.awt.event)

A public abstract class, derived from Object and implementing ContainerListener, that permits a derived class to override the predefined no-op container events.

constructors

```
public ContainerAdapter()
```
Creates a new instance of a ContainerAdapter.

methods

```
public void componentAdded(ContainerEvent event)
public void componentRemoved(ContainerEvent event)
```
Empty methods that should be overridden in order to implement event handling for AWT containers.

ContainerEvent (java.awt.event)

A public class, derived from ComponentEvent, that describes a particular AWT container event.

variables and constructs

```
public static final int COMPONENT_ADDED
public static final int COMPONENT_REMOVED
```
Constant values that represent various container events (a component being added or removed to this container).
```
public static final int CONTAINER_FIRST
public static final int CONTAINER_LAST
```
Constant values that represent the index of the first and last component event ids.

constructors

```
public ContainerEvent(Component src, int type, Component comp)
```
Creates a new instance of a ContainerEvent with a specified source component, event type and a defined component (which is being added or removed).

methods

```
public Component getChild()
```
Returns the child component that was added or removed, triggering this event.
```
public Container getContainer()
```
Returns the container in which this event was triggered.
```
public String paramString()
```
Returns a string containing the parameters of this ComponentEvent.

Cursor (java.awt)

A public class, derived from Object and implementing Serializable, that represents the different states and images of the mouse cursor in a graphical application or applet.

variables and constructs

```
public final static int CROSSHAIR_CURSOR
public final static int DEFAULT_CURSOR
public final static int E_RESIZE_CURSOR
public final static int HAND_CURSOR
public final static int MOVE_CURSOR
```

```
public final static int N_RESIZE_CURSOR
public final static int NE_RESIZE_CURSOR
public final static int NW_RESIZE_CURSOR
public final static int S_RESIZE_CURSOR
public final static int SE_RESIZE_CURSOR
public final static int SW_RESIZE_CURSOR
public final static int TEXT_CURSOR
public final static int W_RESIZE_CURSOR
public final static int WAIT_CURSOR
```
   Constant values that represent various cursors.
```
protected static Cursor predefined[]
```
   An array used to hold the cursors as they are defined and implemented.

constructors
```
public Cursor(int cursortype)
```
   Creates a new instance of a cursor of the specified type (cursortype).

methods
```
public static Cursor getDefaultCursor()
```
   Returns the default cursor.
```
public static Cursor getPredefinedCursor(int cursortype)
```
   Returns the cursor of the specified type (cursortype).
```
public int getType()
```
   Returns the type of this cursor.

Date (java.util)

A public class, derived from Object and implementing Serializable and Cloneable, that creates and manipulates a single moment of time.

constructors
```
public Date()
public Date(long date)
```
   Creates a new instance of a Date from a specified date (time in milliseconds since midnight, January 1, 1970 GMT) or by using the current time.

methods

`public boolean after(Date arg)`

`public boolean before(Date arg)`

Returns a true value if this `Date` is after/before the date specified in `arg`.

`public boolean equals(Object arg)`

Returns a true value if this `Date` is equal to `arg`.

`public long getTime()`

`public void setTime(long tm)`

Returns or sets the time specified by this `Date`. The time is represented as a long integer equal to the number of seconds since midnight, January 1, 1970 UTC.

`public int hashCode()`

Returns the hash code for this `Date`.

`public String toString()`

Returns a string representation of this `Date`.

DateFormat (java.text)

A public abstract class, derived from `Cloneable`, that is used to convert date/time objects to locale-specific strings, and vice versa.

variables and constructs

`public static final int DEFAULT`

`public static final int FULL`

`public static final int LONG`

`public static final int MEDIUM`

`public static final int SHORT`

Constant values that represent formatting styles.

`public static final int AM_PM_FIELD`

`public static final int DATE_FIELD`

`public static final int DAY_OF_WEEK_FIELD`

`public static final int DAY_OF_WEEK_IN_MONTH_FIELD`

`public static final int DAY_OF_YEAR_FIELD`

`public static final int ERA_FIELD`

`public static final int HOUR0_FIELD`

`public static final int HOUR1_FIELD`

```
public static final int HOUR_OF_DAY0_FIELD
public static final int HOUR_OF_DAY1_FIELD
public static final int MILLISECOND_FIELD
public static final int MINUTE_FIELD
public static final int MONTH_FIELD
public static final int SECOND_FIELD
public static final int TIMEZONE_FIELD
public static final int WEEK_OF_MONTH_FIELD
public static final int WEEK_OF_YEAR_FIELD
public static final int YEAR_FIELD
```
Constant values that represent various fields for date/time formatting.

```
protected Calendar calendar
```
Holds the calendar that this DateFormat uses to produce its date/time formatting.

```
protected NumberFormat numberFormat
```
Holds the number format that this DateFormat uses to produce its number formatting.

constructors

```
protected DateFormat()
```
Creates a new instance of a DateFormat.

methods

```
public Object clone()
```
Returns a copy of this DateFormat.

```
public boolean equals(Object arg)
```
Returns a true value is this DateFormat is equal to arg.

```
public final String format(Date src)
```
Formats the specified Date object into a string.

```
public abstract StringBuffer format(Date src, StringBuffer dest, FieldPosition
pos)
```

```
public final StringBuffer format(Object src, StringBuffer dest, FieldPosition
pos)
```
Formats the source object into the specified destination, starting at field pos. This method returns the same value as the destination buffer.

```
public static Locale[] getAvailableLocales()
```
Returns the set of available locales for this DateFormat.

```
public Calendar getCalendar()
```

```
public void setCalendar(Calendar cal)
```
Returns or sets the calendar associated with this DateFormat.

```
public static final DateFormat getDateInstance()
```

```
public static final DateFormat getDateInstance(int style)
```

```
public static final DateFormat getDateInstance(int style, Locale locale)
```
Returns the DateFormat for the specified or default locale (using the default or specified date formatting style).

```
public static final DateFormat getDateTimeInstance()
```

```
public static final DateFormat getDateTimeInstance(int dstyle, int tstyle)
```

```
public static final DateFormat getDateTimeInstance(int dstyle, int tstyle,
Locale locale)
```
Returns the DateFormat for the specified or default locale (using the default or specified date and time formatting styles).

```
public static final DateFormat getInstance()
```
Returns the DateFormat for the default locale using the short formatting style.

```
public NumberFormat getNumberFormat()
```

```
public void setNumberFormat(NumberFormat format)
```
Returns or sets the NumberFormat for this DateFormat.

```
public static final DateFormat getTimeInstance()
```

```
public static final DateFormat getTimeInstance(int style)
```

```
public static final DateFormat getTimeInstance(int style, Locale locale)
```
Returns the DateFormat for the specified or default locale (using the default or specified time formatting style).

```
public TimeZone getTimeZone()
```

```
public void setTimeZone(TimeZone tz)
```
Returns or sets the time zone for this DateFormat.

```
public int hashCode()
```
Returns the hash code for this DateFormat.

```
public boolean isLenient()
```

```
public void setLenient(boolean lenient)
```
Returns or sets the state of the leniency for this DateFormat.

```
public Date parse(String src) throws ParseException
```
Parses the specified source to a Date object.

```
public abstract Date parse(String src, ParsePosition pos)
```

```
public Object parseObject(String src, ParsePosition pos)
```
Parses the specified source string to a Date or Object, starting at the specified position.

DateFormatSymbols (java.text)

A public class, derived from Object and implementing Serializable and Cloneable, that contains functionality for formatting both date and time values. This class is usually utilized as part of a DateFormat class (or subclass).

constructors

```
public DateFormatSymbols()
public DateFormatSymbols(Locale locale)
```
Creates a new instance of DateFormatSymbols using the specified or default locale.

methods

```
public Object clone()
```
Returns a clone of this DateFormatSymbols.

```
public boolean equals(Object arg)
```
Returns a true value if this DateFormatSymbols is equal to arg.

```
public String[] getAmPmStrings()
public void setAmPmStrings(String[] newstr)
```
Returns or sets the AM/PM strings for this set of symbols.

```
public String[] getEras()
public void setEras(String[] newstr)
```
Returns or sets the eras for this set of symbols.

```
public String getLocalPatternChars()
public void setLocalPatternChars(String newchars)
```
Returns or sets the local pattern characters for date and time for this set of symbols.

```
public String[] getMonths()
public void setMonths(String[] newmon)
```
Returns or sets the full names of months for this set of symbols.

```
public String[] getShortMonths()
public void setShortMonths(String[] newmon)
```
Returns or sets the short names of months for this set of symbols.

```
public String[] getShortWeekdays()
public void setShortWeekdays(String[] newdays)
```
Returns or sets the short names of weekdays for this set of symbols.

```
public String[] getWeekdays()
public void setWeekdays(String[] newdays)
```
Returns or sets the full names of weekdays for this set of symbols.

```
public String[][] getZoneStrings()
```

```
public void setZoneStrings(String[][] newzone)
```
Returns or sets the time zone strings for this set of symbols.

```
public int hashCode()
```
Returns the hash code for this set of symbols.

DecimalFormat (java.text)

A public class, derived from `NumberFormat`, that is used to format decimal numbers to locale-based strings, and vice versa.

constructors

```
public DecimalFormat()
```
```
public DecimalFormat(String str)
```
```
public DecimalFormat(String str, DecimalFormatSymbols sym)
```
Creates a new instance of a `DecimalFormat` from the specified or default pattern, specified or default symbols and using the default locale.

methods

```
public void applyLocalizedPattern(String str)
```
```
public String toLocalizedPattern()
```
Sets or returns the pattern of this `DecimalFormat`. The specified pattern is in a locale-specific format.

```
public void applyPattern(String str)
```
```
public String toPattern()
```
Sets or returns the pattern of this `DecimalFormat`.

```
public Object clone()
```
Returns a copy of this `DecimalFormat`.

```
public boolean equals(Object arg)
```
Returns a true value if this `DecimalFormat` is equal to arg.

```
public StringBuffer format(double num, StringBuffer dest, FieldPosition pos)
```
```
public StringBuffer format(long num, StringBuffer dest, FieldPosition pos)
```
Formats the specified Java primitive type starting at pos, according to this `DecimalFormat`, placing the resulting string in the specified destination buffer. This method returns the value of the string buffer.

```
public DecimalFormatSymbols getDecimalFormatSymbols()
```
```
public void setDecimalFormatSymbols(DecimalFormatSymbols symbols)
```
Returns or sets the decimal number format symbols for this `DecimalFormat`.

```
public int getGroupingSize()
```

```
public void setGroupingSize(int val)
```
Returns or sets the size of groupings for this `DecimalFormat`.
```
public int getMultiplier()
public void setMultiplier(int val)
```
Returns or sets the value of the multiplier for use in percent calculations.
```
public String getNegativePrefix()
public void setNegativePrefix(String val)
```
Returns or sets the prefix for negative numbers for this `DecimalFormat`.
```
public String getNegativeSuffix()
public void setNegativeSuffix(String val)
```
Returns or sets the suffix for negative numbers for this `DecimalFormat`.
```
public String getPositivePrefix()
public void setPositivePrefix(String val)
```
Returns or sets the prefix for positive numbers for this `DecimalFormat`.
```
public String getPositiveSuffix()
public void setPositiveSuffix(String val)
```
Returns or sets the suffix for positive numbers for this `DecimalFormat`.
```
public int hashCode()
```
Returns the hash code for this `DecimalFormat`.
```
public boolean isDecimalSeparatorAlwaysShown()
public void setDecimalSeparatorAlwaysShown(boolean toggle)
```
Returns or sets the state value that allows/prevents the display of the decimal point when formatting integers.
```
public Number parse(String src, ParsePosition pos)
```
Parses the specified string as a long (if possible) or double, starting a position pos, and returns a `Number`.

DecimalFormatSymbols (java.text)

A public class, derived from `Object` and implementing `Serializable` and `Cloneable`, that contains functionality for formatting decimal values. This class is usually utilized as part of a `DecimalFormat` class (or subclass).

constructors
```
public DecimalFormatSymbols()
public DecimalFormatSymbols(Locale locale)
```
Creates a new instance of `DecimalFormatSymbols` using the specified or default locale.

methods

```
public Object clone()
```
Returns a clone of this DecimalFormatSymbols.

```
public boolean equals(Object arg)
```
Returns a true value if this DecimalFormatSymbols is equal to arg.

```
public char getDecimalSeparator()
public void setDecimalSeparator(char separator)
```
Returns or sets the character used to separate decimal numbers in this set of symbols.

```
public char getDigit()
public void setDigit(char num)
```
Returns or sets the character used as a digit placeholder in a pattern for this set of symbols.

```
public char getGroupingSeparator()
public void setGroupingSeparator(char separator)
```
Returns or sets the character used to separate groups of thousands for this set of symbols.

```
public String getInfinity()
public void setInfinity(String str)
```
Returns or sets the string used to represent the value of infinity for this set of symbols.

```
public char getMinusSign()
public void setMinusSign(char minus)
```
Returns or sets the character used to represent the minus sign for this set of symbols.

```
public String getNaN()
public void setNaN(String str)
```
Returns or sets the character used to represent a NAN value for this set of symbols.

```
public char getPatternSeparator()
public void setPatternSeparator(char separator)
```
Returns or sets the character used to separate positive and negative numbers in a pattern from this set of symbols.

```
public char getPercent()
public void setPercent(char percent)
```
Returns or sets the character used as a percent sign for this set of symbols.

```
public char getPerMill()
public void setPerMill(char perMill)
```
Returns or sets the character used as a mille percent sign for this set of symbols.

```
public char getZeroDigit()
public void setZeroDigit(char zero)
```
Returns or sets the character used to represent zero for this set of symbols.

```
public int hashCode()
```
Returns the hash code for this set of symbols.

Dimension (`java.awt`)

A public class, derived from `Object` and implementing `Serializable`, that is used to encapsulate an object's dimensions (height and width).

variables and constructs

```
public int height
public int width
```
Variables which contain the height and width of an object.

constructors

```
public Dimension()
public Dimension(Dimension dim)
public Dimension(int width, int height)
```
Creates a new instance of a dimension from specified dimensions (or 0 width and 0 height by default).

methods

```
public boolean equals(Object arg)
```
Returns a true value if this dimension is equal to `arg`.
```
public Dimension getSize()
public void setSize(Dimension dim)
public void setSize(int width, int height)
```
Returns or sets the size of this dimension.
```
public String toString()
```
Returns the string representation of this dimension.

Double (`java.lang`)

A public final class, derived from `Number`, that contains floating point math operations, constants, methods to compute minimum and maximum numbers, and string manipulation routines related to the `double` primitive type.

variables and constructs

```
public final static double MAX_VALUE
public final static double MIN_VALUE
```
Constant values that contain the maximum (1.79769313486231570e+308d) and minimum (4.94065645841246544e2324d) possible values of an integer in Java.

`public final static double NaN`
A constant value that contains the representation of the Not-A-Number double (0.0d).

`public final static double NEGATIVE_INFINITY`

`public final static double POSITIVE_INFINITY`
Constant values that contain the negative (−1.0d / 0.0d) and positive (1.0d / 0.0d) infinity double.

`public final static Class TYPE`
A constant value of the `Double` type class.

constructors

`public Double(double arg)`

`public Double(String arg) throws NumberFormatException`
Creates an instance of the `Double` class from the parameter `arg`.

methods

`public byte byteValue()`

`public double doubleValue()`

`public float floatValue()`

`public int intValue()`

`public long longValue()`

`public short shortValue()`
Returns the value of the current object as a Java primitive type.

`public static long doubleToLongBits(double num)`

`public static double longBitsToDouble(long num)`
Returns a long bit stream or a double representation of parameter num. Bit 63 of the returned `long` is the sign bit, bits 52 to 62 are the exponent, and bits 0 to 51 are the mantissa.

`public boolean equals(Object param)`
Returns a true value if this `Double` is equal to the specified parameter (`param`).

`public int hashCode()`
Returns a hash code for this `Double`.

`public boolean isInfinite()`

`public static boolean isInfinite(double num)`
Returns true if the current object or num is positive or negative infinity, false in all other cases.

`public boolean isNaN()`

`public static boolean isNaN(double num)`
Returns true if the current object or num is Not-A-Number, false in all other cases.

`public static double parseDouble(String str) throws NumberFormatException`
Returns the double value represented by `str`.

`public String toString()`

```
public static String toString(double num)
```
Returns the string representation of the current object or num in base 10 (decimal).
```
public static Double valueOf(String str) throws NumberFormatException
```
Returns a Double initialized to the value of str.

Error (java.lang)

A public class, derived from Throwable, that is used to signify program-terminating errors that should not be caught.

constructors

```
public Error()
```
```
public Error(String str)
```
Creates a new instance of an error. A message can be provided via str.

Event (java.awt)

A public class, derived from Object, that represents event obtained from a graphical user interface.

variables and constructs

```
public final static int ACTION_EVENT
```
A constant that represents the user desires an action.
```
public final static int ALT_MASK
```
```
public final static int CTRL_MASK
```
```
public final static int META_MASK
```
```
public final static int SHIFT_MASK
```
Constant values which represent the mask for Alt, Control, Meta, and Shift keys modifying events.
```
public Object arg
```
An optional argument used by some events.
```
public final static int BACK_SPACE
```
```
public final static int CAPS_LOCK
```
```
public final static int DELETE
```
```
public final static int DOWN
```
```
public final static int END
```
```
public final static int ENTER
```
```
public final static int ESCAPE
```
```
public final static int F1
```

```
public final static int F2
public final static int F3
public final static int F4
public final static int F5
public final static int F6
public final static int F7
public final static int F8
public final static int F9
public final static int F10
public final static int F11
public final static int F12
public final static int HOME
public final static int INSERT
public final static int LEFT
public final static int NUM_LOCK
public final static int PAUSE
public final static int PGDN
public final static int PGUP
public final static int PRINT_SCREEN
public final static int RIGHT
public final static int SCROLL_LOCK
public final static int TAB
public final static int UP
```
Constant values that represent keyboard keys.

```
public int clickCount
```
The number of consecutive clicks during a MOUSE_DOWN event.

```
public Event evt
```
The next event to take place, as in a linked list.

```
public final static int GOT_FOCUS
```
An id field constant that represents when an AWT component gets the focus.

```
public int id
```
The numeric identification for this event.

```
public int key
```
The keyboard key that was pressed during this event.

```
public final static int KEY_ACTION
public final static int KEY_ACTION_RELEASE
```
Constant values that represent when the user presses or releases a function key.

```
public final static int KEY_PRESS
```

```
public final static int KEY_RELEASE
```
Constant values that represent when the user presses or releases a keyboard key.
```
public final static int LIST_DESELECT
```
```
public final static int LIST_SELECT
```
Constant values that represent when the user deselects or selects a list item.
```
public final static int LOAD_FILE
```
```
public final static int SAVE_FILE
```
Constant values that represent when a file load or save event occurs.
```
public final static int LOST_FOCUS
```
An id field constant that represents when an AWT component loses the focus.
```
public int modifiers
```
Value of any key modifiers for this event.
```
public final static int MOUSE_DOWN
```
```
public final static int MOUSE_DRAG
```
```
public final static int MOUSE_ENTER
```
```
public final static int MOUSE_EXIT
```
```
public final static int MOUSE_MOVE
```
```
public final static int MOUSE_UP
```
Constant values that represent mouse events.
```
public final static int SCROLL_ABSOLUTE
```
An id field constant that represents when the user has moved the bubble in a scrollbar.
```
public final static int SCROLL_BEGIN
```
```
public final static int SCROLL_END
```
Constant values that represent the scroll begin or ending event.
```
public final static int SCROLL_LINE_DOWN
```
```
public final static int SCROLL_LINE_UP
```
Constant values that represent when the user has clicked in the line down or up area of the scroll-bar.
```
public final static int SCROLL_PAGE_DOWN
```
```
public final static int SCROLL_PAGE_UP
```
Constant values that represent when the user has clicked in the page down or up area of the scroll-bar.
```
public Object target
```
The object that this event was created from or took place over.
```
public long when
```
The time stamp of this event. Represented as the number of milliseconds since midnight, January 1, 1970 UTC.
```
public final static int WINDOW_DEICONIFY
```

```
public final static int WINDOW_DESTROY
public final static int WINDOW_EXPOSE
public final static int WINDOW_ICONIFY
public final static int WINDOW_MOVED
```
Constant values that represent various window events.
```
public int x
public int y
```
The horizontal or vertical coordinate location of this event.

constructors

```
public Event(Object obj, int id, Object arg)
public Event(Object obj, long ts, int id, int x, int y, int key, int state)
public Event(Object obj, long ts, int id, int x, int y, int key, int state,
Object arg)
```
Creates a new instance of an event with an initial target Object (obj), id, x location, y location, key, modifier state, time stamp (ts), and argument (arg).

methods

```
public boolean controlDown()
public boolean metaDown()
public boolean shiftDown()
```
Returns a true value if the Control, Meta, or Shift key is down for this event.
```
protected String paramString()
```
Returns the parameter string for this event.
```
public String toString()
```
Returns a string representation of this event.
```
public void translate(int xval, int yval)
```
Translates this event, modifying the x and y coordinates for this event by adjusting the x location by xval and the y location by yval.

Exception (java.lang)

A public class, derived from Throwable, that catches conditions that are thrown by methods.

constructors

```
public Exception()
public Exception(String str)
```
Creates a new instance of an exception. A message can be provided via str.

Float `(java.lang)`

A public final class, derived from `Number`, that contains floating point math operations, constants, methods to compute minimum and maximum numbers, and string manipulation routines related to the primitive `float` type.

variables and constructs

```
public final static float MAX_VALUE
public final static float MIN_VALUE
```
Constant values that contain the maximum possible value (3.40282346638528860e+38f) or the minimum possible value (1.40129846432481707e245f) of a float in Java.

```
public final static float NaN
```
A constant value that contains the representation of the Not-A-Number float (0.0f).

```
public final static float NEGATIVE_INFINITY
public final static float POSITIVE_INFINITY
```
Constant values that contain the representation of the negative (–1.0f / 0.0f) or positive (1.0f / 0.0f) infinity float.

```
public final static Class TYPE
```
The `Float` constant value of the float type class.

constructors

```
public Float(double arg)
public Float(float arg) throws NumberFormatException
public Float(String arg)
```
Creates an instance of the Float class from the parameter `arg`.

methods

```
public byte byteValue()
public float floatValue()
public double doubleValue()
public int intValue()
public long longValue()
public short shortValue()
```
Returns the value of the current object as a Java primitive type.

```
public boolean equals(Object arg)
```
Returns the result of an equality comparison against `arg`.

```
public static int floatToIntBits(float num)
public static float intBitsToFloat(int num)
```
Returns the bit stream or float equivalent of the parameter num as an int. Bit 31 of the int returned value is the sign bit, bits 23 to 30 are the exponent, while bits 0 to 22 are the mantissa.
```
public int hashCode()
```
Returns a hash code for this object.
```
public boolean isInfinite()
public static boolean isInfinite(float num)
```
Returns true if the current object or num is positive or negative infinity, false in all other cases.
```
public boolean isNaN()
public static boolean isNaN(float num)
```
Returns true if the current object or num is Not-A-Number, false in all other cases.
```
public static float parseFloat(String str) throws NumberFormatException
```
Returns the float value represented by str.
```
public String toString()
public static String toString(float num)
```
Returns the string representation of the current object or num.
```
public static Float valueOf(String str) throws NumberFormatException
```
Returns a Float initialized to the value of str.

FlowLayout (java.awt)

A public class, derived from Object implementing LayoutManager and Serializable, that lays out components in a sequential horizontal order using their preferred size.

variables and constructs

```
public final static int CENTER
public final static int LEFT
public final static int RIGHT
```
Constant values indicating areas of the flow layout manager.

constructors

```
public FlowLayout()
public FlowLayout(int al)
public FlowLayout(int al, int hg, int vg)
```
Creates a new instance of a flow layout and gives it al alignment (default of centered) with a vg vertical and hg horizontal gap (default of 0).

methods

```
public void addLayoutComponent(String str, Component cpnt)
public void removeLayoutComponent(Component cpnt)
```
Adds or removes a component to/from this layout manager. When adding a component, a name may be specified.
```
public int getAlignment()
public void setAlignment(int alg)
```
Returns or sets the alignment value for this layout manager.
```
public int getHgap()
public int getVgap()
```
Returns the value of the horizontal or vertical gap between components laid out by this layout manager.
```
public void layoutContainer(Container cont)
```
Lays out the specified container with this layout manager.
```
public Dimension minimumLayoutSize(Container cont)
public Dimension preferredLayoutSize(Container cont)
```
Returns the minimum or preferred size of the specified container when laid out by this layout manager.
```
public void setHgap(int hg)
public void setVgap(int vg)
```
Sets the horizontal or vertical gap for this layout manager.
```
public String toString()
```
Returns a string representation of this layout manager.

FocusAdapter (java.awt.event)

A public abstract class, derived from Object and implementing FocusListener, that permits derived classes to override the predefined no-op focus events.

constructors

```
public FocusAdapter()
```
Creates a new instance of a FocusAdapter.

methods

```
public void focusGained(FocusEvent event)
```

```
public void focusLost(FocusEvent event)
```
Empty methods that should be overridden in order to implement event handling for AWT focus-based events.

FocusEvent (java.awt.event)

A public class, derived from `ComponentEvent`, that describes a particular AWT focus event.

variables and constructs

```
public static final int FOCUS_FIRST
public static final int FOCUS_LAST
```
Constant values that represent the index of the first and last focus event ids.
```
public static final int FOCUS_GAINED
public static final int FOCUS_LOST
```
Constant values that represent the gain and loss of focus events.

constructors

```
public FocusEvent(Component src, int type)
public FocusEvent(Component src, int type, boolean toggle)
```
Creates a new instance of a `FocusEvent` from the specified source, having a defined event type and toggling this event as a temporary change of focus (false by default).

methods

```
public boolean isTemporary()
```
Returns the status value of the temporary focus toggle.
```
public String paramString()
```
Returns a string containing the parameters of this `FocusEvent`.

Font (java.awt)

A public class, derived from `Object` and implementing `Serializable`, that represents a GUI font.

variables and constructs

```
public final static int BOLD
public final static int ITALIC
public final static int PLAIN
```
Constant values that indicate the style of the font.

`protected String name`
  The name of the font.
`protected int size`
  The size of the font in pixels.
`protected int style`
  The style of the font.

constructors

`public Font(String str, int st, int sz)`
  Creates a new font with an initial name (`str`), style (`st`), and size (`sz`).

methods

`public static Font decode(String arg)`
  Returns the requested font from a specified string.
`public boolean equals(Object obj)`
  Returns a true value if this font is equal to `obj`.
`public String getFamily()`
  Returns the name of the family this font belongs to.
`public static Font getFont(String str)`
`public static Font getFont(String str, Font ft)`
  Returns the font named `str`. If the font cannot be located, the second method returns `ft` as the default.
`public String getName()`
  Returns the name of this font.
`public FontPeer getPeer()`
  Returns the peer of this font.
`public int getSize()`
`public int getStyle()`
  Returns the size or style of this font.
`public int hashCode()`
  Returns the hash code for this font.
`public boolean isBold()`
`public boolean isItalic()`
`public boolean isPlain()`
  Returns a true value if this font is bolded, italicized, or plain.
`public String toString()`
  Returns a string representation of this font.

FontMetrics (java.awt)

A public class, derived from `Object` and implementing `Serializable`, that provides detailed information about a particular font.

variables and constructs

`protected Font font`
    The font upon which the metrics are generated.

constructors

`protected FontMetrics(Font f)`
    Creates a new instance of metrics from a given font `f`.

methods

`public int bytesWidth(byte[] src, int offset, int size)`
`public int charsWidth(char[] src, int offset, int size)`
    Returns the advance width for displaying the subarray of `src`, starting at index `offset`, and having a length of `size`.

`public int charWidth(char c)`
`public int charWidth(int c)`
    Returns the advance width of the character `c` for the font in this font metric.

`public int getAscent()`
`public int getDescent()`
    Returns the amount of ascent or descent for the font in this font metric.

`public Font getFont()`
    Returns the font in this font metric.

`public int getHeight()`
    Returns the standard height of the font in this font metric.

`public int getLeading()`
    Returns the standard leading of the font in this font metric.

`public int getMaxAdvance()`
    Returns the maximum amount of advance for the font in this font metric.

`public int getMaxAscent()`
`public int getMaxDescent()`
    Returns the maximum amount of ascent or descent for the font in this font metric.

`public int[] getWidths()`
    Returns an `int` array containing the advance widths of the first 256 characters of the font.

`public int stringWidth(String str)`
 Returns the advance width of the string `str` as represented by the font in this font metric.

`public String toString()`
 Returns a string representation of the font metrics.

Format (java.text)

A public abstract class, derived from `Object` and implementing `Cloneable` and `Serializable`, which is used to format locale-based values into Strings, and vice versa.

constructors

`public Format()`
 Creates a new instance of a `Format`.

methods

`public Object clone()`
 Returns a copy of this `Format`.

`public final String format(Object arg)`
 Returns a formatted string from `arg`.

`public abstract StringBuffer format(Object arg, StringBuffer dest, FieldPosition pos)`
 Formats the specified argument (starting at field pos) into a string, and appends it to the specified `StringBuffer`. This method returns the same value as the destination buffer.

`public Object parseObject(String src) throws ParseException`
 Parses the specified source string into a formatted object.

`public abstract Object parseObject(String src, ParsePosition pos)`
 Parses the specified source string into a formatted object starting at the specified `ParsePosition`.

Graphics (java.awt)

A public abstract class, derived from `Object`, that provides many useful drawing methods and tools for the manipulation of graphics. A `Graphics` object defines a context in which the user draws.

constructors

`protected Graphics()`
 Creates a new `Graphics` instance. This constructor cannot be called directly.

methods

`public abstract void clearRect(int x, int y, int width, int height)`
Draws a rectangle (with no fill pattern) in the current background color at position <x, y>, and having a width and height.

`public abstract void clipRect(int x, int y, int width, int height)`
Sets a clipping rectangle at position <x, y> and having a width and height.

`public abstract void copyArea(int x, int y, int width, int height, int xoffset, int yoffset)`
Copies a graphic rectangular area at position <x, y> and having a width and height, to position newx and newy.

`public abstract Graphics create()`

`public Graphics create(int x, int y, int width, int height)`
Returns a copy of this graphics context from position <x, y>, and having a width and height. In the case of the first method, the entire area is copied.

`public abstract void dispose()`
Disposes this graphics context.

`public void draw3DRect(int x, int y, int width, int height, boolean toggle)`
Draws a 3D rectangle at position <x, y> and having a width and height. If toggle is true, the rectangle will appear raised; otherwise, it will appear indented.

`public abstract void drawArc(int x, int y, int width, int height, int sAngle, int aAngle)`
Draws an arc with a starting position <x, y> and having a width and height. The start angle (sAngle) and arc angle (aAngle) are both measured in degrees and describe the starting and ending angle of the arc.

`public void drawBytes(byte[] src, int index, int ln, int x, int y)`

`public void drawChars(char[] src, int index, int ln, int x, int y)`
Draw ln bytes or characters of array src (starting at the offset index) at position <x, y>.

`public abstract boolean drawImage(Image src, int x, int y, Color bgc, ImageObserver obsv)`

`public abstract boolean drawImage(Image src, int x, int y, ImageObserver obsv)`
Draws a graphic image (src) at position <x, y>. Any transparent color pixels are drawn as bgc, and the obsv monitors the progress of the image.

`public abstract boolean drawImage(Image src, int x, int y, int width, int height, Color bgc, ImageObserver obsv)`

`public abstract boolean drawImage(Image src, int x, int y, int width, int height, ImageObserver obsv)`
Draws a graphic image (src) at position <x, y> and having a width and height. Any transparent color pixels are drawn as bgc, and the obsv monitors the progress of the image.

```
public abstract boolean drawImage(Image src, int xsrc1, int ysrc1, int xsrc1, int
ysrc2, int xdest1, int ydest1, int xdest1, int ydest2, Color bgc, ImageObserver
obsv)
public abstract boolean drawImage(Image src, int xsrc1, int ysrc1, int xsrc1, int
ysrc2, int xdest1, int ydest1, int xdest1, int ydest2, ImageObserver obsv)
```
Draws a graphic image (src) from the area defined by the bounding rectangle <xsrc1, ysrc1> to <xsrc2, ysrc2> in the area defined by the bounding rectangle <xdest1, ydest1> to <xdest2, ydest2>. Any transparent color pixels are drawn as bgc, and the obsv monitors the progress of the image.

```
public abstract void drawLine(int xsrc, int ysrc, int xdest, int ydest)
```
Draws a line from position <xsrc, ysrc> to <xdest, ydest>.

```
public abstract void drawOval(int xsrc, int ysrc, int width, int height)
```
Draws an oval starting at position <xsrc, ysrc> and having a width and height.

```
public abstract void drawPolygon(int[] x, int[] y, int num)
public void drawPolygon(Polygon poly)
```
Draws a polygon constructed from poly or an array of x points, y points and a number of points in the polygon (num).

```
public void drawRect(int xsrc, int ysrc, int width, int height)
public abstract void drawRoundRect(int xsrc, int ysrc, int width, int height, int
awd, int aht)
```
Draws a rectangle with or without rounded corners at position <xsrc, ysrc> and having a width and height. The shape of the rounded corners are determined by the width of the arc (awd) and the height of the arc (aht).

```
public abstract void drawString(String str, int x, int y)
```
Draws the string str at position <x, y> in this Graphic's current font and color.

```
public void fill3DRect(int x, int y, int width, int height, boolean toggle)
```
Draws a filled 3D rectangle at position <x, y> and having a width and height. The rectangle is filled with this Graphic's current color, and if toggle is true, the rectangle is drawn raised. (Otherwise it is drawn indented.)

```
public abstract void fillArc(int x, int y, int width, int height, int sAngle, int
aAngle)
```
Draws a filled arc at position <x, y> and having a width and height. The arc has a starting angle of sAngle and an ending angle of aAngle.

```
public abstract void fillOval(int x, int y, int width, int height)
```
Draws a filled oval at position <x, y> and having a width and height.

```
public abstract void fillPolygon(int[] x, int[] y, int num)
public void fillPolygon(Polygon poly)
```
Draws a filled polygon defined by poly or the arrays x, y and the number of points in the polygon, num.

```
public abstract void fillRect(int x, int y, int width, int height)
```

```
public abstract void fillRoundRect(int x, int y, int width, int height, int
aWidth, int aHeight)
```
Draws a filled rectangle with or without rounded corners at position <x, y> and having a width and height. The shape of the rounded corners are determined by the width of the arc (aWidth) and the height of the arc (aHeight).

```
public void finalize()
```
Disposes of the current graphics context.

```
public abstract Shape getClip()
```
Returns a shape object of the current clipping area for this graphics context.

```
public abstract Rectangle getClipBounds()
```
Returns a rectangle describing the bounds of the current clipping area for this graphics context.

```
public abstract Color getColor()
public abstract void setColor(Color clr)
```
Returns or sets the current color for this graphics context.

```
public abstract Font getFont()
public abstract void setFont(Font ft)
```
Returns or sets the current font of this graphics context.

```
public FontMetrics getFontMetrics()
public abstract FontMetrics getFontMetrics(Font fn)
```
Returns the font metrics associated with this graphics context or font fn.

```
public abstract void setClip(int x, int y, int width, int height)
public abstract void setClip(Shape shp)
```
Sets the clipping area for this graphics context to be at position <x, y> and having a width and height or to be of a specified shape (shp).

```
public abstract void setPaintMode()
```
Sets the current graphics context's paint mode to overwrite any subsequent destinations with the current color.

```
public abstract void setXORMode(Color clr)
```
Sets the current graphics context's paint mode to overwrite any subsequent destinations with the alternating current color and clr color.

```
public String toString()
```
Returns a string representation of this graphics context.

```
public abstract void translate(int x, int y)
```
Modifies the origin of this graphics context to be relocated to <x, y>.

GregorianCalendar (java.util)

A public class, derived from Calendar, that represents the standard world Gregorian calendar.

variables and constructs

AD

BC

Constant values representing periods of an era.

constructors

```
public GregorianCalendar()
public GregorianCalendar(Locale locale)
public GregorianCalendar(TimeZone zone)
public GregorianCalendar(TimeZone zone, Locale locale)
```

Creates a new GregorianCalendar from the current time in the specified time zone (or the default) and the specified locale (or the default).

```
public GregorianCalendar(int year, int month, int date)
public GregorianCalendar(int year, int month, int date, int hour, int min)
public GregorianCalendar(int year, int month, int date, int hour, int min, int sec)
```

Creates a new GregorianCalendar, setting the year, month, date, hour, minute, and seconds of the time fields.

methods

```
public void add(int field, int val)
```

Adds (or subtracts in the case of a negative val) an amount of days or time from the specified field.

```
public boolean after(Object arg)
public boolean before(Object arg)
```

Returns a true value if this GregorianCalendar date is after or before the date specified by arg.

```
public Object clone()
```

Returns a clone of this GregorianCalendar.

```
protected void computeFields()
protected void computeTime()
```

Computes the values of the time fields based on the currently set time (computeFields()) or computes the time based on the currently set time fields (computeTime()) for this GregorianCalendar.

```
public boolean equals(Object arg)
```

Returns a true value if this GregorianCalendar is equal to the value of arg.

```
public int getGreatestMinimum(int fld)
```

```
public int getLeastMaximum(int fld)
```
Returns the largest allowable minimum or smallest allowable maximum value for the specified field.

```
public final Date getGregorianChange()
```
```
public void setGregorianChange(Date dt)
```
Returns or sets the date of the change from Julian to Gregorian calendars for this calendar. The default value is October 15, 1582 (midnight local time).

```
public int getMaximum(int fld)
```
```
public int getMinimum(int fld)
```
Returns the largest or smallest allowable value for the specified field.

```
public synchronized int hashCode()
```
Returns the hash code for this GregorianCalendar.

```
public boolean isLeapYear(int year)
```
Returns a true value if the specified year is a leap year.

```
public void roll(int fld, boolean direction)
```
Adds one single unit of time to the specified date/time field. A true value specified for direction increases the field's value, false decreases it.

GridBagConstraints (java.awt)

A public class, derived from Object and implementing Cloneable, that specifies the layout constraints for each component laid out with a GridBagLayout.

variables and constructs

```
public int anchor
```
Determines where to place a component that is smaller in size than its display area in the gridbag.
```
public final static int BOTH
```
```
public final static int HORIZONTAL
```
```
public final static int NONE
```
```
public final static int VERTICAL
```
Constant values that indicate the direction(s) that the component should grow.
```
public final static int CENTER
```
```
public final static int EAST
```
```
public final static int NORTH
```
```
public final static int NORTHEAST
```
```
public final static int NORTHWEST
```
```
public final static int SOUTH
```

```
public final static int SOUTHEAST
public final static int SOUTHWEST
public final static int WEST
```
Constant values that indicate where the component should be placed in its display area.

```
public int fill
```
Determines how to resize a component that is smaller than its display area in the gridbag.

```
public int gridheight
public int gridwidth
```
Specifies the number of vertical and horizontal cells the component shall occupy.

```
public int gridx
public int gridy
```
Describes horizontal and vertical cell locations (indices) in the gridbag, where `gridx=0` is the leftmost cell and `gridy=0` is the topmost cell.

```
public Insets insets
```
Defines the amount of space (in pixels) around the component in its display area.

```
public int ipadx
public int ipady
```
Defines the amount of space (in pixels) to add to the minimum horizontal and vertical size of the component.

```
public final static int RELATIVE
```
A constant that specifies that this component is the next to last item in its gridbag row or that it should be placed next to the last item added to the gridbag.

```
public final static int REMAINDER
```
A constant that specifies that this component is the last item in its gridbag row.

```
public double weightx
public double weighty
```
Specifies the weight of horizontal and vertical growth of this component relative to other components during a resizing event. A larger value indicates a higher percentage of growth for this component.

constructors

```
public GridBagConstraints()
```
Creates a new instance of `GridBagConstraints`.

methods

```
public Object clone()
```
Creates a copy of these gridbag constraints.

GridBagLayout (java.awt)

A public class, derived from Object and implementing Serializable and LayoutManager, that creates a gridlike area for component layout. Unlike GridLayout, GridBagLayout does not force the components to be the same size or to be constrained to one cell.

variables and constructs

`public double columnWeights[ ]`

`public int columnWidths[ ]`

 Holds the weights and widths of each column of this GridBagLayout.

`protected Hashtable comptable`

 A hashtable of the components managed by this layout manager.

`protected GridBagConstraints defaultConstraints`

 Holds the default constraints for any component laid out by this layout manager.

`protected GridBagLayoutInfo layoutInfo`

 Holds specific layout information (such as the list of components or the constraints of this manager) for this GridBagLayout.

`protected final static int MAXGRIDSIZE`

 A constant value that contains the maximum (512) number of grid cells that can be laid out by this GridBagLayout.

`protected final static int MINSIZE`

 A constant value that contains the minimum (1) number of cells contained within this GridBagLayout.

`protected final static int PREFERREDSIZE`

 A constant value that contains the preferred (2) number of cells contained within this GridBagLayout.

`public int rowHeights[ ]`

`public double rowWeights[ ]`

 Holds the heights and weights of each row of this GridBagLayout.

constructors

`public GridBagLayout()`

 Creates a new instance of a GridBagLayout.

methods

`public void addLayoutComponent(Component item, Object constraints)`

 Adds the component item to this layout manager using the specified constraints on the item.

`public void addLayoutComponent(String str, Component item)`
Adds the component item to this layout manager and names it str.

`protected void AdjustForGravity(GridBagConstraints constraints, Rectangle rect)`
Sets the characteristics of rect based on the specified constraints.

`protected void ArrangeGrid(Container parent)`
Arranges the entire grid on the parent.

`public GridBagConstraints getConstraints(Component item)`
Returns a copy of the constraints for the item component.

`public float getLayoutAlignmentX(Container parent)`

`public float getLayoutAlignmentY(Container parent)`
Returns the horizontal and vertical alignment values for the specified container.

`public int[][] getLayoutDimensions()`
Returns a two-dimensional array in which the zero index of the first dimension holds the minimum width of each column and the one index of the first dimension holds the minimum height of each column.

`protected GridBagLayoutInfo GetLayoutInfo(Container parent, int sizeflag)`
Computes and returns a GridBagLayoutInfo object for components associated with the specified parent container.

`public Point getLayoutOrigin()`
Returns this layout's point of origin.

`public double[][] getLayoutWeights()`
Returns a two-dimensional array in which the zero index of the first dimension holds the weight in the x direction of each column and the one index of the first dimension holds the weight in the y direction of each column.

`protected Dimension GetMinSize(Container parent, GridBagLayoutInfo info)`
Returns the minimum size for the specified parent container based on laying out the container using the specified GridBagLayoutInfo.

`public void invalidateLayout(Container cont)`
Forces this layout manager to discard any cached layout information about the specified container.

`public void layoutContainer(Container cont)`
Lays out the specified container with this layout manager.

`public Point location(int x, int y)`
Returns the upper right corner of the cell in this GridBagLayout with dimensions greater than the specified <x, y> coordinate.

`protected GridBagConstraints lookupConstraints(Component item)`
Returns the actual constraints for the specified component.

`public Dimension maximumLayoutSize(Container cont)`

`public Dimension minimumLayoutSize(Container cont)`

```
public Dimension preferredLayoutSize(Container cont)
```
Returns the maximum, minimum, or preferred size of the specified container when laid out by this layout manager.

```
public void removeLayoutComponent(Component comp)
```
Removes the specified component from this layout manager.

```
public void setConstraints(Component item, GridBagConstraints constraints)
```
Sets the `constraints` for the `item` component in this layout manager.

GridLayout (java.awt)

A public class, derived from `Object` and implementing `Serializable` and `LayoutManager`, that creates a grid area of equal sized rectangles to lay out components in.

constructors

```
public GridLayout()
```
```
public GridLayout(int r, int c)
```
Creates a new instance of a `GridLayout` with a dimension of r rows and c columns (default of 1 by any).

```
public GridLayout(int r, int c, int hg, int vg)
```
Creates a new instance of a `GridLayout` with a dimension of r rows and c columns. The grid cells have a hg pixel horizontal gap and a vg pixel vertical gap.

methods

```
public void addLayoutComponent(String str, Component comp)
```
```
public void removeLayoutComponent(Component comp)
```
Adds or removes the specified component. When adding, the component can be given a name (`str`).

```
public int getColumns()
```
```
public void setColumns(int val)
```
Returns or sets the number of columns of this layout manager.

```
public int getHgap()
```
```
public int getVgap()
```
Returns the value of the horizontal or vertical gap for this layout manager.

```
public int getRows()
```
```
public void setRows(int val)
```
Returns or sets the number of rows of this layout manager.

```
public void layoutContainer(Container cont)
```
Lays out the specified container with this layout manager.

```
public Dimension minimumLayoutSize(Container cont)
public Dimension preferredLayoutSize(Container cont)
```
Returns the minimum or preferred size of the specified container when laid out with this layout manager.

```
public void setHgap(int val)
public void setVgap(int val)
```
Sets the horizontal or vertical gap for this layout manager to val.

Hashtable (java.util)

A public class, derived from Dictionary and implementing Serializable and Cloneable, that allows for the storing of objects that have a relationship with a key. You can then use this key to access the object stored.

constructors

```
public Hashtable()
public Hashtable(int size)
public Hashtable(int size, float load) throws IllegalArgumentException
```
Creates a new instance of a hashtable, setting the initial capacity (or using the default size of 101) and a load factor (default of 0.75). The initial capacity sets the number of objects the table can store, and the load factor value is the percentage filled the table may become before being resized.

methods

```
public void clear()
```
Removes all keys and elements from this Hashtable.

```
public Object clone()
```
Returns a clone of this Hashtable (the keys and values are not cloned).

```
public boolean contains(Object arg) throws NullPointerException
```
Returns a true value if this Hashtable contains a key that is related to the element arg.

```
public boolean containsKey(Object obj)
```
Returns a true value if this Hashtable contains an entry for the key at obj.

```
public Enumeration elements()
public Enumeration keys()
```
Returns an enumerated list of all of the elements or keys of this Hashtable.

```
public Object get(Object obj)
public Object put(Object obj, Object arg) throws NullPointerException
public Object remove(Object obj)
```
Returns, inserts or removes the element arg that corresponds to the key obj.

```
public boolean isEmpty()
```
Returns a true value if the Hashtable is empty.
```
protected void rehash()
```
Resizes this Hashtable. The method is invoked automatically when the number of keys exceeds the capacity and load factor.
```
public int size()
```
Returns the number of elements in this Hashtable.
```
public String toString()
```
Returns a string representation of this Hashtable's key-element pairings.

Image (java.awt)

A public abstract class, derived from Object, that is used to manage graphic images.

variables and constructs

```
public final static int SCALE_AREA_AVERAGING
public final static int SCALE_DEFAULT
public final static int SCALE_FAST
public final static int SCALE_REPLICATE
public final static int SCALE_SMOOTH
```
Constant values used to indicate specific scaling algorithms.
```
public final static Object UndefinedProperty
```
A constant value that is returned whenever an undefined property for an image is attempted to be obtained.

constructors

```
public Image()
```
Creates a new instance of an image.

methods

```
public abstract void flush()
```
Frees the cache memory containing this image.
```
public abstract Graphics getGraphics()
```
Returns a newly created graphics context for drawing off-screen images.
```
public abstract int getHeight(ImageObserver obs)
public abstract int getWidth(ImageObserver obs)
```
Returns the height or width of this image. If the height is not known, a –1 is returned and the obs is informed later.

```
public abstract Object getProperty(String property, ImageObserver obs)
```
Returns the value of the property for this image. If the value is not known, a null is returned and obs is informed later.

```
public Image getScaledInstance(int width, int height, int algo)
```
Returns a scaled version of this image. The new image is scaled to `width` pixels by `height` pixels using the specified scaling algorithm (`algo`). If either of the new width or height values are –1, then the new image will maintain the aspect ratios of the old image.

```
public abstract ImageProducer getSource()
```
Returns the source image producer for this image.

ImageIcon (javax.swing)

A public class, derived from `Object` and implementing `Accessible`, `Icon`, and `Serializable`, that represents an icon based on an image.

constructors

```
public ImageIcon()
public ImageIcon(byte[] imageData)
public ImageIcon(byte[] imageData, String description)
public ImageIcon(Image image)
public ImageIcon(Image image, String description)
public ImageIcon(String filename)
public ImageIcon(String filename, String description)
public ImageIcon(URL location)
public ImageIcon(URL location, String description)
```
Creates an icon using an image described by raw image data (in a supported format such as GIF or JPEG), and `Image` object, a file, or a URL. An optional description can be specified as well.

methods

```
public String getDescription()
```
Returns the description of this image icon.

```
public int getIconHeight()
public int getIconWidth()
```
Returns this icon's height or width.

```
public Image getImage()
```
Returns this icon's image.

```
public void paintIcon(Component observer, Graphics page, int x, int y)
```
Paints this icon on the specified graphics context at the specified location using the specified image observer.

```
public setDescription(String description)
```

```
public setImage(Image image)
```
Sets the description or the image for this icon.

InputEvent (java.awt.event)

A public abstract class, derived from ComponentEvent, that describes a particular AWT input event.

variables and constructs

```
public static final int ALT_MASK
```

```
public static final int BUTTON1_MASK
```

```
public static final int BUTTON2_MASK
```

```
public static final int BUTTON3_MASK
```

```
public static final int CTRL_MASK
```

```
public static final int META_MASK
```

```
public static final int SHIFT_MASK
```
Constant values which represent various keyboard and mouse masks.

methods

```
public void consume()
```
Consumes this event, preventing it from being passed to its peer component.

```
public int getModifiers()
```
Returns the modifiers for this event.

```
public long getWhen()
```
Returns the timestamp of this event.

```
public boolean isConsumed()
```
Returns a true value if this event is consumed.

```
public boolean isAltDown()
```

```
public boolean isControlDown()
```

```
public boolean isMetaDown()
```

```
public boolean isShiftDown()
```
Returns a true value if the Alt, Control, Meta, or Shift key is depressed during this event.

InputStream (java.io)

A public abstract class, derived from `Object`, that is the parent class of any type of input stream that reads bytes.

constructors

```
public InputStream()
```
  Generally called only by subclasses, this constructor creates a new instance of an `InputStream`.

methods

```
public int available() throws IOException
```
  Returns the number of available bytes that can be read. This method returns a 0 (zero) value and should be overridden by a subclass implementation.

```
public void close() throws IOException
```
  Closes the input stream. This method has no functionality and should be overridden by a subclass implementation.

```
public void mark(int size)
```
  Sets a mark in the input stream, allowing a rereading of the stream data to occur if the reset method is invoked. The `size` parameter indicates how many bytes may be read following the mark being set, before the mark is considered invalid.

```
public boolean markSupported()
```
  Returns a true value if this `InputStream` object supports the mark and reset methods. This method always returns a false value and should be overridden by a subclass implementation.

```
public abstract int read() throws IOException
```
  Reads the next byte of data from this `InputStream` and returns it as an `int`. This method has no functionality and should be implemented in a subclass. Execution of this method will block until data is available to be read, the end of the input stream occurs, or an exception is thrown.

```
public int read(byte[] dest) throws IOException
public int read(byte[] dest, int offset, int size) throws IOException
```
  Reads from this InputStream into the array `dest`, and returns the number of bytes read. `size` specifies the maximum number of bytes read from this InputStream into the array `dest[ ]` starting at index `offset`. This method returns the actual number of bytes read or –1, indicating that the end of the stream was reached. To read `size` bytes and throw them away, call this method with `dest[ ]` set to null.

```
public synchronized void reset() throws IOException
```
  Resets the read point of this `InputStream` to the location of the last mark set.

```
public long skip(long offset) throws IOException
```
  Skips over `offset` bytes from this `InputStream`. Returns the actual number of bytes skipped, as it is possible to skip over less than `offset` bytes.

InputStreamReader (java.io)

A public class, derived from Reader, that is an input stream of characters.

constructors

```
public InputStreamReader(InputStream input)
public InputStreamReader(InputStream input, String encoding) throws
UnsupportedEncodingException
```
Creates an instance of InputStreamReader from the InputStream input with a specified encoding.

methods

```
public void close() throws IOException
```
Closes this InputStreamReader.

```
public String getEncoding()
```
Returns the string representation of this InputStreamReader's encoding.

```
public int read() throws IOException
```
Reads a single character from this InputStreamReader. The character read is returned as an int, or a −1 is returned if the end of this InputStreamReader was encountered.

```
public int read(char[] dest, int offset, int size) throws IOException
```
Reads no more than size bytes from this InputStreamReader into the array dest[] starting at index offset. This method returns the actual number of bytes read or −1, indicating that the end of the stream was reached. To read size bytes and throw them away, call this method with dest[] set to null.

```
public boolean ready() throws IOException
```
Returns a true value if this InputStreamReader is capable of being read from. This state can only be true if the buffer is not empty.

Insets (java.awt)

A public class, derived from Object and implementing Serializable and Cloneable, that specify the margins of a container.

variables and constructs

```
public int bottom
public int left
public int right
```

`public int top`
  Contains the value of the inset for a particular margin.

constructors

`public Insets(int t, int l, int b, int r)`
  Creates an instance of insets with initial top (t), bottom (b), left (l) and right (r) inset values.

methods

`public Object clone()`
  Creates a copy of this group of inset values.

`public boolean equals(Object arg)`
  Returns a true value if this inset is equal to the object arg.

`public String toString()`
  Returns a string representation of this group of inset values.

Integer (java.lang)

A public final class, derived from Number, that contains integer math operations, constants, methods to compute minimum and maximum numbers, and string manipulation routines related to the primitive int type.

variables and constructs

`public final static int MAX_VALUE`
`public final static int MIN_VALUE`
  Constant values that contain the maximum possible value (2147483647) or minimum possible value (22174783648) of an integer in Java.

`public final static Class TYPE`
  The Integer constant value of the integer type class.

constructors

`public Integer(int num)`
`public Integer(String num) throws NumberFormatException`
  Creates an instance of the Integer class from the parameter num.

methods

`public byte byteValue()`
`public double doubleValue()`
`public float floatValue()`

```
public int intValue()
public long longValue()
public short shortValue()
```
Returns the value of this integer as a Java primitive type.
```
public static Integer decode(String str) throws NumberFormatException
```
Decodes the given string (`str`) and returns it as an `Integer`. The decode method can handle octal, hexadecimal, and decimal input values.
```
public boolean equals(Object num)
```
Returns the result of an equality comparison against num.
```
public static Integer getInteger(String str)
public static Integer getInteger(String str, int num)
public static Integer getInteger(String str, Integer num)
```
Returns an `Integer` representation of the system property named in `str`. If there is no property corresponding to num, or the format of its value is incorrect, then the default num is returned as an `Integer` object.
```
public int hashCode()
```
Returns a hash code for this object.
```
public static int parseInt(String str) throws NumberFormatException
public static int parseInt(String str, int base) throws NumberFormatException
```
Evaluates the string `str` and returns the `int` equivalent in radix base.
```
public static String toBinaryString(int num)
public static String toHexString(int num)
public static String toOctalString(int num)
```
Returns the string representation of parameter num in base 2 (binary), 8 (octal), or 16 (hexadecimal).
```
public String toString()
public static String toString(int num)
public static String toString(int num, int base)
```
Returns the string representation of this integer or num. The radix of num can be specified in base.
```
public static Integer valueOf(String str) throws NumberFormatException
public static Integer valueOf(String str, int base) throws NumberFormatException
```
Returns an `Integer` initialized to the value of str in radix base.

ItemEvent (java.awt.event)

A public class, derived from `AWTEvent`, that represents an AWT item event (from a component such as a `Checkbox`, `CheckboxMenuItem`, `Choice`, or `List`).

variables and constructs

```
public static final int DESELECTED
public static final int SELECTED
```
Constant values representing the deselection or selection of an AWT item component.
```
public static final int ITEM_FIRST
public static final int ITEM_LAST
```
Constant values that represent the index of the first and last item event ids.
```
public static final int ITEM_STATE_CHANGED
```
A constant value that represents the event of the change of state for an AWT item.

constructors

```
public ItemEvent(ItemSelectable src, int type, Object obj, int change)
```
Creates a new instance of an `ItemEvent` from the specified source, having a specific `type`, item object, and state change.

methods

```
public Object getItem()
```
Returns the specific item that triggered this event.
```
public ItemSelectable getItemSelectable()
```
Returns the `ItemSelectable` object that triggered this event.
```
public int getStateChange()
```
Returns the state change type (deselection or selection) that triggered this event.
```
public String paramString()
```
Returns a parameter string containing the values of the parameters for this event.

JApplet (javax.swing)

A public class, derived from `Applet` and implementing `Accessible` and `RootPaneContainer`, that represents a primary applet container.

constructors

```
public JApplet()
```
Creates an applet container.

methods

```
public Container getContentPane()
public Component getGlassPane()
```

```
public JLayeredPane getLayeredPane()
public JRootPane getRootPane()
```
Returns the content pane, glass pane, layered pane, or root pane for this applet.
```
public void setContentPane(Container contenetPane)
public void setGlassPane(Component glassPane)
public void setLayeredPane(JLayeredPane layeredPane)
public void setRootPane(JRootPane rootPane)
```
Sets the content pane, glass pane, layered pane, or root pane for this applet.
```
public void remove(Component comp)
```
Removes the specified component from this applet.
```
public JMenuBar getJMenuBar()
public void setJMenuBar setJMenuBar(JMenuBar menuBar)
```
Gets or sets the menu bar for this applet.

JButton (javax.swing)

A public class, derived from `AbstractButton` and implementing `Accessible`, that represents a GUI push button.

constructors
```
public JButton()
public JButton(Icon icon)
public JButton(String text)
public JButton(String text, Icon icon)
```
Creates a button with the specified text and icon.

methods
```
public boolean isDefaultButton()
```
Returns true if this button is the current default button for its root pane.
```
public boolean isDefaultCapable()
public void setDefaultCapable(boolean capable)
```
Gets or sets the property that determines if this button can be the default button for its root pane.

JCheckBox (javax.swing)

A public class, derived from `JToggleButton` and implementing `Accessible`, that represents a GUI component that can be selected or deselected (displaying its state to the user).

constructors

```
public JCheckBox()
public JCheckBox(Icon icon)
public JCheckBox(Icon icon, boolean selected)
public JCheckBox(String text)
public JCheckBox(String text, boolean selected)
public JCheckBox(String text, Icon icon)
public JCheckBox(String text, Icon icon, boolean selected)
```
Creates a check box with the specified text, icon, and selected state (which defaults to unselected).

JCheckBoxMenuItem (javax.swing)

A public class, derived from JMenuItem and implementing Accessible and SwingConstants, that represents a menu item that can be selected or deselected.

constructors

```
public JCheckBoxMenuItem()
public JCheckBoxMenuItem(Icon icon)
public JCheckBoxMenuItem(String text)
public JCheckBoxMenuItem(String text, boolean selected)
public JCheckBoxMenuItem(String text, Icon icon)
public JCheckBoxMenuItem(String text, Icon icon, boolean selected)
```
Creates a menu check box with the specified text, icon, and selected state (which defaults to unselected).

JColorChooser (javax.swing)

A public class, derived from JComponent and implementing Accessible, that represents a pane of controls that allows a user to define and select a color. A color chooser can be displayed as a dialog box or within any container.

constructors

```
public JColorChooser()
public JColorChooser(Color initialColor)
```
Creates a color chooser with the specified initial color (white by default).

methods

```
public Color getColor()
public void setColor(Color color)
public void setColor(int color)
public void setColor(int red, int green, int blue)
```
Gets or sets the current color for this color chooser.

```
public static Color showDialog(Component parent, String title, Color
initialColor)
```
Shows a color chooser dialog box, returning the selected color when the user presses the OK button.

JComboBox (javax.swing)

A public class, derived from JComponent and implementing ItemSelectable, ListDataListener, ActionListener, and Accessible, that represents a GUI component that combines a button (or editable field) and a drop down list.

constructors

```
public JComboBox()
public JComboBox(Object[] items)
public JComboBox(Vector items)
```
Creates a combo box containing the specified items.

methods

```
public addActionListener(ActionListener listener)
public addItemListener(ItemListener listener)
```
Adds a secific type of listener to this combo box.

```
public void addItem(Object item)
public insertItemAt(Object item, int index)
```
Adds the specified item to the end of the item list or inserts it at the specified index.

```
public Object getItemAt(int index)
```
Returns the item at the specified index.

```
public int getItemCount()
```
Returns the number of items in the list.

```
public Object getSelectedItem()
```
Returns the currently selected item.

```
public void setEditable(boolean flag)
```
Sets whether this combo box is editable.

```
public boolean isEditable()
```
Returns true if this combo box is editable.

```
public void setEnabled(boolean flag)
```
Enables or disables this combo box. When disabled, items cannot be selected.

```
public void removeAllItems()
```
```
public void removeItem(Object item)
```
```
public void removeItemAt(int index)
```
Removes all items, a specific item, or the item at a specific index, from the list.

JComponent (javax.swing)

A public abstract class, derived from Component and implementing Serializable, that represents the base class for all Swing components (except top-level containers).

methods

```
public float getAlignmentX()
```
```
public void setAlignmentX(float alignment)
```
```
public float getAlignmentY()
```
```
public void setAlignmentY(float alignment)
```
Gets or sets the horizontal or vertical alignment for this component.

```
public Border getBorder()
```
```
public void setBorder(Border border)
```
Gets or sets the border for this component.

```
public Graphics getGraphics()
```
Returns the graphics context for this component.

```
public int getHeight()
```
```
public int getWidth()
```
Returns the height or width of this component.

```
public Dimension getMaximumSize()
```
```
public void setMaximumSize(Dimension size)
```
```
public Dimension getMinimumSize()
```
```
public void setMinimumSize(Dimension size)
```
```
public Dimension getPreferredSize()
```
```
public void setPreferredSize(Dimension size)
```
Gets or sets the maximum, minimum, or preferred size for this component.

```
public JRootPane getRootPane()
```
Returns the root pane ancestor for this component.
```
public String getToolTipText()
public void setToolTipText(String text)
```
Gets or sets the text for this component's tool tip.
```
public int getX()
public int getY()
```
Returns the x or y coordinate of this component.
```
public void setEnabled(boolean enabled)
```
Enables or disables this component.
```
public void setFont(Font font)
```
Sets the font for this component.
```
public void setBackground(Color color)
public void setForeground(Color color)
```
Sets the background or foreground color for this component.
```
public setVisible(boolean flag)
```
Makes this component visible or invisible.

JFileChooser (javax.swing)

A public class, derived from JComponent and implementing Accessible, that represents a GUI component that allows the user to select a file from a file system.

variables and constructs
```
public static final int APPROVE_OPTION
```
Return value if approval (Yes, Ok) is chosen.
```
public static final int CANCEL_OPTION
```
Return value if Cancel is chosen.
```
public static final int ERROR_OPTION
```
Return value if an error occured.

constructors
```
public JFileChooser()
public JFileChooser(File directory)
public JFileChooser(FileSystemView view)
public JFileChooser(String path)
```

```
public JFileChooser(File directory, FileSystemView view)
public JFileChooser(String path, FileSystemView view)
```
Creates a file chooser with the specified directory or path and optional file system view.

methods

```
public File getCurrentDirectory()
public void setCurrentDirectory(File directory)
```
Gets or sets the current directory for this file chooser.

```
public String getDescription(File file)
public String getName(File file)
```
Returns the description or name of the specified file.

```
public boolen getDraggedEnabled()
public void setDraggedEnabled(boolean flag)
```
Gets or sets the property that determines whether the user can drag to select files.

```
public File getSelectedFile()
public File[] getSelectedFiles()
```
Gets the currently selected file or files.

```
public boolean isMultiSelectionEnabled()
```
Returns true if multiple files can be selected.

```
public void setDialogTitle(String title)
```
Sets the title of the dialog box.

```
public void setFileFilter(FileFilter filter)
```
Sets the current file filter.

```
public void setSelectedFile(File file)
public void setSelectedFiles(File[] files)
```
Sets the selected file or files.

```
public int showDialog(Component parent, String approveButtonText)
```
Displays a custom file chooser dialog with the specified approve button text.

```
public int showOpenDialog(Component parent)
```
Displays an "open file" file chooser dialog.

```
public int showSaveDialog(Component parent)
```
Displays a "save file" file chooser dialog.

JFrame (javax.swing)

A public class, derived from `Frame` and implementing `WindowConstants`, `Accessible`, and `RootPaneContainer`, that represents a primary GUI window.

variables and constructs

`public static final int EXIT_ON_CLOSE`
Represents the exit application default window close operation.

constructors

`public JFrame()`
`public JFrame(String title)`
Creates a frame with the specified title.

methods

`public Container getContentPane()`
`public Component getGlassPane()`
`public JLayeredPane getLayeredPane()`
`public JRootPane getRootPane()`
Returns the content pane, glass pane, layered pane, or root pane for this frame.
`public void setContentPane(Container contenetPane)`
`public void setGlassPane(Component glassPane)`
`public void setLayeredPane(JLayeredPane layeredPane)`
`public void setRootPane(JRootPane rootPane)`
Sets the content pane, glass pane, layered pane, or root pane for this frame.
`public void remove(Component comp)`
Removes the specified component from this frame.
`public JMenuBar getJMenuBar()`
`public void setJMenuBar setJMenuBar(JMenuBar menuBar)`
Gets or sets the menu bar for this frame.
`public void setDefaultCloseOperation(int operation)`
Sets the default operation when the user closes this frame.

JLabel (javax.swing)

A public class, derived from `JComponent` and implementing `Accessible` and `SwingConstants`, that represents a GUI display area for a string, and image, or both.

constructors

`public JLabel()`
`public JLabel(String text)`
`public JLabel(Icon icon)`

```
public JLabel(String text, int horizontalAlignment)
public JLabel(Icon icon, int horizontalAlignment)
public JLabel(String text, Icon icon, int horizontalAlignment)
```
Creates a label containing the specified icon and string, and using the specified horizontal alignment.

methods

```
public int getHorizontalAlignment()
public void setHorizontalAlignment(int alignment)
public int getVerticalAlignment()
public void setVerticalAlignment(int alignment)
```
Gets or sets the horizontal or vertical alignment of the icon and text.

```
public int getHorizontalTextPosition()
public void setHorizontalTextPosition(int position)
public int getVerticalTextPosition()
public void setVerticalTextPosition(int position)
```
Gets or sets the horizontal or vertical position of the text relative to the icon.

```
public Icon getIcon()
public void setIcon(Icon icon)
```
Gets or sets the default icon for this button.

```
public String getText()
public void setText(String text)
```
Gets or sets the text displayed on this button.

```
public Component getLabelFor()
public void setLabelFor(Component comp)
```
Gets or sets the component that this label describes.

JList (javax.swing)

A public class, derived from JComponent and implementing Accessible and Scrollable, that represents a GUI component that allows the user to select one or more objects from a list.

variables and constructs

```
public static final int HORIZONTAL_WRAP
```
Indicates that cells flow horizontally, then vertically.

```
public static final int VERTICAL
```
Indicates one column of cells (the default).

```
public static final int VERTICAL_WRAP
```
Indicates that cells flow vertically, then horizontally.

constructors

```
public JList()
public JList(Object[] items)
public JList(Vector items)
```
Creates a list that displays the specified items.

methods

```
public void addListSelectionListener(ListSelectionListener listener)
```
Adds the specified listener to this list.
```
public void clearSelection()
```
Clears the selection (no items will be selected).
```
public void ensureIndexIsVisible(int index)
```
Scrolls the list to make the specified item visible.
```
public int getLastVisibleIndex()
```
Returns the index of the last visible cell.
```
public int getLayoutOrientation()
public void setLayoutOrientation(int orientation)
```
Gets or sets the layout orientation for this list.
```
public int getMaxSelectionIndex()
public int getMinSelectionIndex()
```
Returns the largest or smallest selected cell index.
```
public int getSelectedIndex()
public void setSelectedIndex(int index)
public int[] getSelectedIndices()
public void setSelectedIndex(int[] indices)
```
Gets or sets the selected index or indices.
```
public void setSelectionInterval(int from, int to)
```
Selects the specified index interval.
```
public Object getSelectedValue()
public Object[] getSelectedValues()
```
Returns the currently selected value or values.
```
public Color getSelectionBackground()
public void setSelectionBackground(Color color)
public Color getSelectionForeground()
```

```
public void setSelectionForeground(Color color)
```
Gets or sets the background or foreground color of the selection.
```
public boolean isSelectedIndex(int index)
```
Returns true if the specified index is selected.
```
public boolean isSelectionEmpty()
```
Returns true if no item is currently selected.
```
public void setDragEnabled(boolean flag)
```
Enables or disables the property allowing the user to select multiple items by dragging the mouse.
```
public void setListData(Object[] items)
public void setListData(Vector items)
```
Sets the contents of the list to the specified items.
```
public void setSelectionMode(int selectionMode)
```
Sets the selection mode for this list using ListSelectionModel constants.

JOptionPane (javax.swing)

A public class, derived from JComponent and implementing Accessible, that provides methods for creating standard dialog boxes.

variables and constructs

```
public static final int CANCEL_OPTION
public static final int OK_OPTION
public static final int YES_OPTION
```
Return value if a specific button option is chosen.
```
public static final int CLOSED_OPTION
```
Return value if the user closes the window without selecting anything.
```
public static final int DEFAULT_OPTION
public static final int YES_NO_OPTION
public static final int YES_NO_CANCEL_OPTION
public static final int OK_CANCEL_OPTION
```
Specifies the types of buttons to use in the dialog.
```
public static final int ERROR_MESSAGE
public static final int INFORMATION_MESSAGE
public static final int WARNING_MESSAGE
public static final int QUESTION_MESSAGE
public static final int PLAIN_MESSAGE
```
Specifies a message style.

methods

```
public static void showConfirmDialog(Component parent, Object message)
public static void showConfirmDialog(Component parent, Object message, String
title, int buttonSet)
public static void showConfirmDialog(Component parent, Object message, String
title, int buttonSet, int messageStyle)
public static void showConfirmDialog(Component parent, Object message, String
title, int buttonSet, int messageStyle, Icon icon)
```
Displays a dialog box allowing the user to confirm an option. Uses the specified message, title, button set, message style, and icon.

```
public static void showInputDialog(Component parent, Object message)
public static void showInputDialog(Component parent, Object message, Object
initialSelectionValue)
public static void showInputDialog(Component parent, Object message, String
title, int messageStyle)
public static void showInputDialog(Object message)
public static void showInputDialog(Object message, Object initialSelectionValue)
public static void showInputDialog(Component parent, Object message, String
title, int messageStyle, Icon icon, Object[] selectionValues, Object
initialSelectionValue)
```
Displays a dialog box allowing the user to enter input. Uses the specified message, title, and message style. An initial selection and options can also be specified.

```
public static void showMessageDialog(Component parent, Object message)
public static void showMessageDialog(Component parent, Object message, String
title, int messageStyle)
public static void showMessageDialog(Component parent, Object message, String
title, int buttonSet, int messageStyle, Icon icon)
```
Displays a dialog box presenting a message. Uses the specified message, title, message style, and icon.

```
public static void showOptionDialog(Component parent, Object message, String
title, int buttonSet, int messageStyle, Icon icon, Object[] options, Object
initialValue)
```
Displays a dialog box allowing the user to make a general choice. Uses the specified message, title, button set, message style, and icon. An initial selection and options can also be specified.

JPanel (javax.swing)

A public class, derived from JComponent and implementing Accessible, that represents a light-weight GUI container used to organize other components.

constructors

```
public JPanel()
public JPanel(LayoutManager manager)
```
Creates a panel with the specified layout manager, which defaults to a flow layout.

JPasswordField (javax.swing)

A public class, derived from JTextField, that represents a GUI text field into which the user can type a password. The password itself is not displayed as it is typed, but a visual indication that characters are being typed is shown.

constructors

```
public JPasswordField()
public JPasswordField(int columns)
public JPasswordField(String text)
public JPasswordField(String text, int columns)
```
Creates a password field with the specified number of columns, initialized to the specified text.

methods

```
public char[] getPassword()
```
Returns the text contained in this password field.
```
public char getEchoChar()
public void setEchoChar(char ch)
```
Gets or sets the character that is displayed as the user types into this field.

JRadioButton (javax.swing)

A public class, derived from JToggleButton and implementing Accessible, that represents a radio button, used as part of a button group (ButtonGroup), to present a set of mutually exclusive options.

constructors

```
public JRadioButton()
public JRadioButton(String text)
public JRadioButton(Icon icon)
public JRadioButton(String text, boolean selected)
public JRadioButton(Icon icon, boolean selected)
```

```
public JRadioButton(String text, Icon icon)
public JRadioButton(String text, Icon icon, boolean selected)
```
Creates a radio button with the specified text, icon, and initial selection status (unselected by default).

JScrollPane (javax.swing)

A public class, derived from JComponent and implementing Accessible and ScrollPaneConstants, that represents a lightweight GUI container with a scrollable view.

constructors

```
public JScrollPane()
public JScrollPane(Component comp)
public JScrollPane(int verticalPolicy, int horizontalPolicy)
public JScrollPane(Component comp, int verticalPolicy, int horizontalPolicy)
```
Creates a scroll pane displaying the specified component and using the specified horizontal and vertical scrollbar policies.

methods

```
public int getHorizontalScrollBarPolicy()
public void setHorizontalScrollBarPolicy(int policy)
public int getHorizontalScrollBarPolicy()
public void setHorizontalScrollBarPolicy(int policy)
```
Gets or sets the horizontal or vertical scrollbar policy for this scroll pane.

JSlider (javax.swing)

A public class, derived from JComponent, that represents a GUI component that allows the user to select a numeric value by sliding a knob within a bounded interval.

constructors

```
public JSlider()
public JSlider(int orientation)
public JSlider(int min, int max)
public JSlider(int min, int max, int initialValue)
```

`public JSlider(int orientation, int min, int max, int initialValue)`
 Creates a new slider with the specified orientation, minimum value, maximum value, and initial value. The default orientation is horizontal, the default minimum value is 0, the default maximum value is 100, and the default initial value is the range midpoint.

methods

`public void addChangeListener(ChangeListener listener)`
 Adds a ChangeListener to this slider.

`public int getExtent()`
 Returns the range of values covered by the knob.

`public int getMajorTickSpacing()`

`public int getMinorTickSpacing()`
 Returns the major or minor tick spacing of this slider.

`public int getMinimum()`

`public int getMaximum()`
 Returns the minimum or maximum value of this slider.

`public int getOrientation()`
 Returns this slider's orientation.

`public boolean getPaintLabels()`

`public boolean getPaintTicks()`

`public boolean getPaintTrack()`
 Returns true if this slider's labels, tick marks, or track are to be painted.

`public boolean getSnapToTicks()`
 Returns true if this slider's knob snaps to the closest tick mark when the user moves the knob.

`public int getValue()`
 Returns this slider's values.

`public boolean getValueIsAdjusting()`
 Returns true if the slider knob is being dragged.

`public void setExtent(int extent)`
 Sets the size of the range covered by this slider's knob.

`public void setMajorTickSpacing(int value)`

`public void setMinorTickSpacing(int value)`
 Sets the major or minor tick spacing for this slider.

`public void setMinimum(int minimumValue)`

`public void setMaximum(int maximumValue)`
 Sets the minimum or maximum value for this slider.

`public void setOrientation(int orientation)`
 Sets the orientation for this slider.

`public void setPaintLabels(boolean flag)`

```
public void setPaintTicks(boolean flag)
```
```
public void setPaintTrack(boolean flag)
```
Determines whether this slider's labels, tick marks, or track are to be painted.

```
public void setSnapToTicks(boolean flag)
```
Determines whether the knob (and value) snaps to the closest tick mark when the user moves the knob.

```
public void setValue(int value)
```
Sets this slider's current value.

JTabbedPane (javax.swing)

A public class, derived from JComponent and implementing Accessible, Serializable, and SwingConstants, that represents a GUI container that allows the user to switch between a group of components by clicking on a tab.

variables and constructs

```
public static final int SCROLL_TAB_LAYOUT
```
Specifies a tab layout that provides a scrollable region of tabs when all tabs won't fit in a single run.

```
public static final int WRAP_TAB_LAYOUT
```
Specifies a tab layout that wraps tabs in multiple rows when all tabs won't fit in a single run.

constructors

```
public JTabbedPane()
```
```
public JTabbedPane(int tabPlacement)
```
```
public JTabbedPane(int tabPlacement, int tabLayoutPolicy)
```
Creates a tabbed pane with the specified tab placement and tab layout policy. The tab placement is specified using SwingConstants.

methods

```
public Component add(String title, Component comp)
```
Adds the specified component to a tab with the specified title.

```
public int getTabCount()
```
Returns the number of tabs in this tabbed pane.

```
public Color getBackgroundAt(int index)
```
```
public void setBackgroundAt(int index, Color color)
```
```
public Color getForegroundAt(int index)
```
```
public void setForegroundAt(int index, Color color)
```
Gets or sets the background or foreground color of the tab at the specified index.

```
public JToggleButton(String text, Icon icon)
public JToggleButton(String text, Icon icon, boolean selected)
```
Creates a toggle button with the specified string, icon, and selection state.

JToolTip (javax.swing)

A public class, derived from JComponent and implementing Accessible, that represents a text tip that is displayed when the mouse cursor rests momentarily over a GUI component.

constructors

```
public JToolTip()
```
Creates a tool tip.

methods

```
public JComponent getComponent()
public void setComponent(JComponent comp)
```
Gets or sets the component to which this tool tip applies.
```
public String getTipText()
public void setTipText(String text)
```
Gets or sets the text shown when this tool tip is displayed.

KeyAdapter (java.awt.event)

A public abstract class, derived from Object and implementing KeyListener, that permits derived classes to override the predefined no-op keyboard events.

constructors

```
public KeyAdapter()
```
Creates a new instance of a KeyAdapter.

methods

```
public void keyPressed(KeyEvent event)
public void keyReleased(KeyEvent event)
public void keyTyped(KeyEvent event)
```
Empty methods that should be overridden in order to implement event handling for keyboard events.

KeyEvent (java.awt.event)

A public class, derived from InputEvent, that represents an AWT keyboard event.

variables and constructs

```
public static final int VK_0
public static final int VK_1
public static final int VK_2
public static final int VK_3
public static final int VK_4
public static final int VK_5
public static final int VK_6
public static final int VK_7
public static final int VK_8
public static final int VK_9
```
Constant values that represent the keyboard keys 0–9.
```
public static final int KEY_FIRST
public static final int KEY_LAST
```
Constant values that represent the index of the first and last key event ids.
```
public static final int KEY_PRESSED
public static final int KEY_RELEASED
public static final int KEY_TYPED
```
Constant values that represent the ids of a key being pressed, released, or typed.
```
public static final char CHAR_UNDEFINED
```
A constant value that represents an event of a key press or release that does not correspond to a Unicode character.
```
public static final int VK_LEFT
public static final int VK_RIGHT
public static final int VK_UP
public static final int VK_DOWN
public static final int VK_HOME
public static final int VK_END
public static final int VK_PAGE_UP
public static final int VK_PAGE_DOWN
```
Constant values that represent various keyboard directional keys.
```
public static final int VK_INSERT
public static final int VK_DELETE
```
Constant values that represent various keyboard editing control keys.

```
public static final int VK_NUMPAD0
public static final int VK_NUMPAD1
public static final int VK_NUMPAD2
public static final int VK_NUMPAD3
public static final int VK_NUMPAD4
public static final int VK_NUMPAD5
public static final int VK_NUMPAD6
public static final int VK_NUMPAD7
public static final int VK_NUMPAD8
public static final int VK_NUMPAD9
public static final int VK_ADD
public static final int VK_SUBTRACT
public static final int VK_MULTIPLY
public static final int VK_DIVIDE
public static final int VK_ENTER
public static final int VK_DECIMAL
```
Constant values that represent various keyboard number pad keys.
```
public static final int VK_PERIOD
public static final int VK_EQUALS
public static final int VK_OPEN_BRACKET
public static final int VK_CLOSE_BRACKET
public static final int VK_BACK_SLASH
public static final int VK_SLASH
public static final int VK_COMMA
public static final int VK_SEMICOLON
public static final int VK_SPACE
public static final int VK_BACK_SPACE
public static final int VK_QUOTE
public static final int VK_BACK_QUOTE
public static final int VK_TAB
public static final int VK_SLASH
```
Constant values that represent various keyboard character keys.
```
public static final int VK_PAUSE
public static final int VK_PRINTSCREEN
public static final int VK_SHIFT
public static final int VK_HELP
public static final int VK_CONTROL
```

```
public static final int VK_ALT
public static final int VK_ESCAPE
public static final int VK_META
public static final int VK_ACCEPT
public static final int VK_CANCEL
public static final int VK_CLEAR
public static final int VK_CONVERT
public static final int VK_NONCONVERT
public static final int VK_MODECHANGE
public static final int VK_SEPARATER
public static final int VK_KANA
public static final int VK_KANJI
public static final int VK_FINAL
```
Constant values that represent various keyboard command and control keys.
```
public static final int VK_UNDEFINED
```
A constant value for KEY_TYPED events for which there is no defined key value.
```
public static final int VK_F1
public static final int VK_F2
public static final int VK_F3
public static final int VK_F4
public static final int VK_F5
public static final int VK_F6
public static final int VK_F7
public static final int VK_F8
public static final int VK_F9
public static final int VK_F10
public static final int VK_F11
public static final int VK_F12
```
Constant values that represent the keyboard keys F1–F12.
```
public static final int VK_CAPS_LOCK
public static final int VK_NUM_LOCK
public static final int VK_SCROLL_LOCK
```
Constant values that represent various keyboard control keys.
```
public static final int VK_A
public static final int VK_B
public static final int VK_C
public static final int VK_D
```

```
public static final int VK_E
public static final int VK_F
public static final int VK_G
public static final int VK_H
public static final int VK_I
public static final int VK_J
public static final int VK_K
public static final int VK_L
public static final int VK_M
public static final int VK_N
public static final int VK_O
public static final int VK_P
public static final int VK_Q
public static final int VK_R
public static final int VK_S
public static final int VK_T
public static final int VK_U
public static final int VK_V
public static final int VK_W
public static final int VK_X
public static final int VK_Y
public static final int VK_Z
```
Constant values that represent the keyboard keys A–Z.

constructors

```
public KeyEvent(Component src, int id, long when, int modifiers, int keyCode)
public KeyEvent(Component src, int id, long when, int modifiers, int keyCode,
char keyChar)
```
Creates a new instance of a KeyEvent from the specified source, having a specific type (id), time stamp, modifiers, key code, and/or key character.

methods

```
public char getKeyChar()
public void setKeyChar(char character)
```
Returns or sets the character associated with this KeyEvent. For events that have no corresponding character, a CHAR_UNDEFINED is returned.

```
public int getKeyCode()
```

```
public void setKeyCode(int code)
```
Returns or sets the code associated with this `KeyEvent`. For events that have no corresponding code, a `VK_UNDEFINED` is returned.

```
public static String getKeyModifiersText(int mods)
```
```
public static String getKeyText(int keyCode)
```
Returns a string representation of the `KeyEvent` modifiers key code (i.e., "Meta+Shift" or "F1").

```
public boolean isActionKey()
```
Returns a true value if this event is from an action key.

```
public String paramString()
```
Returns a string representation of the parameters of this event.

```
public void setModifiers(int mods)
```
Sets the key event modifiers for this event.

Locale (java.util)

A public class, derived from `Object` and implementing `Serializable` and `Cloneable`, that represents geographic-specific or political-specific information.

variables and constructs

```
public static final Locale CANADA
```
```
public static final Locale CANADA_FRENCH
```
```
public static final Locale CHINA
```
```
public static final Locale FRANCE
```
```
public static final Locale GERMANY
```
```
public static final Locale ITALY
```
```
public static final Locale JAPAN
```
```
public static final Locale KOREA
```
```
public static final Locale PRC
```
```
public static final Locale TAIWAN
```
```
public static final Locale UK
```
```
public static final Locale US
```
Constant values that represent locales based on countries.

```
public static final Locale CHINESE
```
```
public static final Locale ENGLISH
```
```
public static final Locale FRENCH
```
```
public static final Locale GERMAN
```
```
public static final Locale ITALIAN
```

```
public static final Locale JAPANESE
public static final Locale KOREAN
public static final Locale SIMPLIFIED_CHINESE
public static final Locale TRADITIONAL_CHINESE
```
Constant values that represent locales based on languages.

constructors

```
public Locale(String lang, String country)
public Locale(String lang, String country, String var)
```
Creates a new locale from the specified two character ISO codes for a language and country. A computer and browser variant of a locale can also be included. These usually take the form of WIN for Windows or MAC for Macintosh.

methods

```
public Object clone()
```
Returns a copy of this locale.

```
public boolean equals(Object arg)
```
Returns a true value if this locale is equal to arg.

```
public String getCountry()
public String getLanguage()
public String getVariant()
```
Returns the character code for the name of this locale's country, language or variant.

```
public static synchronized Locale getDefault()
public static synchronized void setDefault(Locale locale)
```
Returns or sets the default locale.

```
public final String getDisplayCountry()
public String getDisplayCountry(Locale displaylocale)
```
Returns the display version of the country name for this locale in either the specified or default locales.

```
public final String getDisplayLanguage()
public String getDisplayLanguage(Locale displaylocale)
```
Returns the display version of the language name for this locale in either the specified or default locales.

```
public final String getDisplayName()
public String getDisplayName(Locale displaylocale)
```
Returns the display version of the name for this locale in either the specified or default locales.

```
public final String getDisplayVariant()
```

public String getDisplayVariant(Locale displaylocale)
   Returns the display version of the variant for this locale in either the specified or default locales.

public String getISO3Country() throws MissingResourceException

public String getISO3Language() throws MissingResourceException
   Returns the three-character ISO abbreviation for the country or language for this locale.

hashCode()
   Returns the hash code for this locale.

toString()
   Returns a string representation of this locale.

Long (java.lang)

A public final class, derived from Number, that contains long integer math operations, constants, methods to compute minimum and maximum numbers, and string manipulation routines related to the primitive long type.

variables and constructs

public final static long MAX_VALUE

public final static long MIN_VALUE
   Constant values that contain the maximum possible value (9223372036854775807L) or minimum possible value (29223372036854775808L) of a long in Java.

public final static Class TYPE
   The Integer constant value of the integer type class.

constructors

public Long(long num)

public Long(String num) throws NumberFormatException
   Creates an instance of the Long class from the parameter num.

methods

public byte byteValue()

public double doubleValue()

public float floatValue()

public int intValue()

public long longValue()

public short shortValue()
   Returns the value of this Long as a Java primitive type.

```
public boolean equals(Object arg)
```
  Returns the result of the equality comparison between this Long and the parameter arg.
```
public static Long getLong(String prop)
public static Long getLong(String prop, long num)
public static Long getLong(String prop, long num)
```
  Returns a Long representation of the system property named in prop. If there is no property corresponding to prop, or the format of its value is incorrect, then the default num is returned.
```
public int hashCode()
```
  Returns a hash code for this Long.
```
public static long parseLong(String str) throws NumberFormatException
public static long parseLong(String str, int base) throws NumberFormatException
```
  Evaluates the string str and returns the long equivalent in radix base.
```
public static String toBinaryString(long num)
public static String toHexString(long num)
public static String toOctalString(long num)
```
  Returns the string representation of parameter num in base 2 (binary), 8 (octal), or 16 (hexadecimal).
```
public String toString()
public static String toString(long num)
public static String toString(long num, int base)
```
  Returns the string representation of this long or num in base 10 (decimal). The radix of the returned number can also be specified in base.
```
public static Long valueOf(String str) throws NumberFormatException
public static Long valueOf(String str, int base) throws NumberFormatException
```
  Returns a Long initialized to the value of str in radix base.

Math (java.lang)

A public final class, derived from Object, that contains integer and floating point constants, and methods to perform various math operations, compute minimum and maximum numbers, and generate random numbers.

variables and constructs

```
public final static double E
public final static double PI
```
  Constant values that contain the natural base of logarithms (2.7182818284590452354) and the ratio of the circumference of a circle to its diameter (3.14159265358979323846).

methods

```
public static double abs(double num)
public static float abs(float num)
public static int abs(int num)
public static long abs(long num)
```
Returns the absolute value of the specified parameter.

```
public static double acos(double num)
public static double asin(double num)
public static double atan(double num)
```
Returns the arc cosine, arc sine, or arc tangent of parameter num as a double.

```
public static double atan2(double x, double y)
```
Returns the component *e* of the polar coordinate {r,*e*} that corresponds to the cartesian coordinate <x, y>.

```
public static double ceil(double num)
```
Returns the smallest integer value that is not less than the argument num.

```
public static double cos(double angle)
public static double sin(double angle)
public static double tan(double angle)
```
Returns the cosine, sine, or tangent of parameter angle measured in radians.

```
public static double exp(double num)
```
Returns *e* to the num, where *e* is the base of natural logarithms.

```
public static double floor(double num)
```
Returns a double that is the largest integer value that is not greater than the parameter num.

```
public static double IEEEremainder(double arg1, double arg2)
```
Returns the mathematical remainder between arg1 and arg2 as defined by IEEE 754.

```
public static double log(double num) throws ArithmeticException
```
Returns the natural logarithm of parameter num.

```
public static double max(double num1, double num2)
public static float max(float num1, float num2)
public static int max(int num1, int num2)
public static long max(long num1, long num2)
```
Returns the larger of parameters num1 and num2.

```
public static double min(double num1, double num2)
public static float min(float num1, float num2)
public static int min(int num1, int num2)
public static long min(long num1, long num2)
```
Returns the minimum value of parameters num1 and num2.

```
public static double pow(double num1, double num2) throws ArithmeticException
```
Returns the result of num1 to num2.
```
public static double random()
```
Returns a random number between 0.0 and 1.0.
```
public static double rint(double num)
```
Returns the closest integer to parameter num.
```
public static long round(double num)
public static int round(float num)
```
Returns the closest long or int to parameter num.
```
public static double sqrt(double num) throws ArithmeticException
```
Returns the square root of parameter num.

MessageFormat (java.text)

A public class, derived from Format, that is used to build formatted message strings.

constructors
```
public MessageFormat(String str)
```
Creates a new instance of a MessageFormat from the specified string pattern.

methods
```
public void applyPattern(String str)
public String toPattern()
```
Sets and returns the pattern for this MessageFormat.
```
public Object clone()
```
Returns a copy of this MessageFormat.
```
public boolean equals(Object arg)
```
Returns a true value if this MessageFormat is equal to arg.
```
public final StringBuffer format(Object src, StringBuffer dest, FieldPosition
ignore)
public final StringBuffer format(Object[] src, StringBuffer dest, FieldPosition
ignore)
```
Formats the specified source object with this MessageFormat, placing the result in dest. This method returns the value of the destination buffer.
```
public static String format(String str, Object[] args)
```
Formats the given string applying specified arguments. This method allows for message formatting with the creation of a MessageFormat.
```
public Format[] getFormats()
```

```
public void setFormats(Format[] newFormats)
```
Returns and sets the formats for this `MessageFormat`.
```
public Locale getLocale()
public void setLocale(Locale locale)
```
Returns and sets the locale for this `MessageFormat`.
```
public int hashCode()
```
Returns the hash code for this `MessageFormat`.
```
public Object[] parse(String src) throws ParseException
public Object[] parse(String src, ParsePosition pos)
```
Parses the string source (starting at position pos, or 0 by default), returning its objects.
```
public Object parseObject(String src, ParsePosition pos)
```
Parses the string source (starting at position pos, or 0 by default), returning one object.
```
public void setFormat(int var, Format fmt)
```
Sets an individual format at index var.

MouseAdapter (java.awt.event)

A public abstract class, derived from `Object` and implementing `MouseListener`, that permits derived classes to override the predefined no-op mouse events.

constructors

```
public MouseAdapter()
```
Creates a new instance of a `MouseAdapter`.

methods

```
public void mouseClicked(MouseEvent event)
public void mouseEntered(MouseEvent event)
public void mouseExited(MouseEvent event)
public void mousePressed(MouseEvent event)
public void mouseReleased(MouseEvent event)
```
Empty methods which should be overridden in order to implement event handling for mouse events.

MouseEvent (java.awt.event)

A public class, derived from `InputEvent`, that represents events triggered by the mouse.

variables and constructs

```
public static final int MOUSE_CLICKED
public static final int MOUSE_DRAGGED
public static final int MOUSE_ENTERED
public static final int MOUSE_EXITED
public static final int MOUSE_MOVED
public static final int MOUSE_PRESSED
public static final int MOUSE_RELEASED
```
Constant values that represent a variety of mouse events.
```
public static final int MOUSE_FIRST
public static final int MOUSE_LAST
```
Constant values that represent the index of the first and last mouse event ids.

constructors

```
public MouseEvent(Component src, int type, long timestamp, int mods, int x, int
y, int clickCount, boolean popupTrigger)
```
Creates a new instance of a MouseEvent from a given source, with a specified type, timestamp, keyboard modifiers, x and y locations, number of clicks and a state value, if this event triggers a popup menu.

methods

```
public int getClickCount()
```
Returns the number of mouse clicks in this event.
```
public Point getPoint()
```
Returns the point location of this event, relative to the source component's space.
```
public int getX()
public int getY()
```
Returns the x or y location of this event, relative to the source component's space.
```
public boolean isPopupTrigger()
```
Returns a true value if this event is a trigger for popup-menus.
```
public String paramString()
```
Returns a string representation of the parameters of this MouseEvent.
```
public synchronized void translatePoint(int xoffset, int yoffset)
```
Offsets the x and y locations of this event by the specified amounts.

MouseMotionAdapter (java.awt.event)

A public abstract class, derived from Object and implementing MouseMotionListener, that permits a derived class to override the predefined no-op mouse motion events.

constructors

```
public MouseMotionAdapter()
```
Creates a new instance of a MouseMotionAdapter.

methods

```
public void mouseDragged(MouseEvent event)
public void mouseMoved(MouseEvent event)
```
Empty methods that should be overridden in order to implement event handling for mouse motion events.

Number (java.lang)

A public abstract class, derived from Object and implementing Serializable, that is the parent class to the wrapper classes Byte, Double, Integer, Float, Long and Short.

constructors

```
public Number()
```
Creates a new instance of a Number.

methods

```
public byte byteValue()
public abstract double doubleValue()
public abstract float floatValue()
public abstract int intValue()
public abstract long longValue()
public short shortValue()
```
Returns the value of this Number as a Java primitive type.

NumberFormat (java.text)

A public abstract class, derived from Format and implementing Cloneable, that is used to convert number objects to locale-specific strings, and vice versa.

variables and constructs

```
public static final int FRACTION_FIELD
public static final int INTEGER_FIELD
```
Constant values that indicate field locations in a NumberFormat.

constructors

```
public NumberFormat()
```
Creates a new instance of a NumberFormat.

methods

```
public Object clone()
```
Returns a copy of this NumberFormat.

```
public boolean equals(Object arg)
```
Returns a true value if this NumberFormat is equal to arg.

```
public final String format(double num)
public final String format(long num)
```
Formats the specified Java primitive type according to this NumberFormat, returning a string.

```
public abstract StringBuffer format(double num, StringBuffer dest,FieldPosition
pos)
public abstract StringBuffer format(long num, StringBuffer dest, FieldPosition
pos)
public final StringBuffer format(Object num, StringBuffer dest, FieldPosition
pos)
```
Formats the specified Java primitive type (or object) starting at pos, according to this NumberFormat, placing the resulting string in the specified destination buffer. This method returns the value of the string buffer.

```
public static Locale[] getAvailableLocales()
```
Returns the available locales.

```
public static final NumberFormat getCurrencyInstance()
public static NumberFormat getCurrencyInstance(Locale locale)
```
Returns the NumberFormat for currency for the default or specified locale.

```
public static final NumberFormat getInstance()
public static NumberFormat getInstance(Locale locale)
```
Returns the default number format for the default or specified locale.

```
public int getMaximumFractionDigits()
public void setMaximumFractionDigits(int val)
```
Returns or sets the maximum number of fractional digits allowed in this NumberFormat.

```
public int getMaximumIntegerDigits()
```

```
public void setMaximumIntegerDigits(int val)
```
Returns or sets the maximum number of integer digits allowed in this NumberFormat.
```
public int getMinimumFractionDigits()
public void setMinimumFractionDigits(int val)
```
Returns or sets the minimum number of fractional digits allowed in this NumberFormat.
```
public int getMinimumIntegerDigits()
public void setMinimumIntegerDigits(int val)
```
Returns or sets the minimum number of integer digits allowed in this NumberFormat.
```
public static final NumberFormat getNumberInstance()
public static NumberFormat getNumberInstance(Locale locale)
```
Returns the NumberFormat for numbers for the default or specified locale.
```
public static final NumberFormat getPercentInstance()
public static NumberFormat getPercentInstance(Locale locale)
```
Returns the NumberFormat for percentages for the default or specified locale.
```
public int hashCode()
```
Returns the hash code for this NumberFormat.
```
public boolean isGroupingUsed()
public void setGroupingUsed(boolean toggle)
```
Returns or sets the toggle flag for the use of the grouping indicator by this NumberFormat.
```
public boolean isParseIntegerOnly()
public void setParseIntegerOnly(boolean toggle)
```
Returns or sets the toggle flag for the use of parsing numbers as integers only by this NumberFormat.
```
public Number parse(String str) throws ParseException
```
Parses the specified string as a number.
```
public abstract Number parse(String str, ParsePosition pos)
public final Object parseObject(String str, ParsePosition pos)
```
Parses the specified string as a long (if possible) or double, starting a position pos. Returns a number or an object.

Object (java.lang)

A public class that is the root of the hierarchy tree for all classes in Java.

constructors

```
public Object()
```
Creates a new instance of the object class.

constructors

```
public SimpleDateFormat()
public SimpleDateFormat(String str)
public SimpleDateFormat(String str, Locale locale)
```
Creates a new instance of a `SimpleDateFormat` using the specified or default pattern and the specified or default locale.
```
public SimpleDateFormat(String str, DateFormatSymbols format)
```
Creates a new instance of a `SimpleDateFormat` using the specified pattern and format data.

methods

```
public void applyLocalizedPattern(String str)
public String toLocalizedPattern()
```
Sets or returns the locale-based string that describes this `SimpleDateFormat`.
```
public void applyPattern(String str)
public String toPattern()
```
Sets or returns the non-locale-based string that describes this `SimpleDateFormat`.
```
public Object clone()
```
Returns a copy of this `SimpleDateFormat`.
```
public boolean equals(Object arg)
```
Returns a true value if this `SimpleDateFormat` is equal to `arg`.
```
public StringBuffer format(Date date, StringBuffer dest, FieldPosition pos)
```
Formats the specified string, starting at field `pos`, placing the result in the specified destination buffer. This method returns the value of the buffer.
```
public DateFormatSymbols getDateFormatSymbols()
public void setDateFormatSymbols(DateFormatSymbols symbols)
```
Returns or sets the date/time formatting symbols for this `SimpleDateFormat`.
```
public int hashCode()
```
Returns the hash code for this `SimpleDateFormat`.
```
public Date parse(String str, ParsePosition pos)
```
Parses the specified string, starting at position `pos`, and returns a `Date` object.

SimpleTimeZone (java.util)

A public class, derived from `TimeZone`, that represents a time zone in a Gregorian calendar.

constructors

```
public SimpleTimeZone(int offset, String id)
```

```
public SimpleTimeZone(int offset, String id, int stMonth, int
stNthDayWeekInMonth, int stDayOfWeek, int stTime, int endMonth, int
endNthDayWeekInMonth, int endDayOfWeek, int endTime)
```
Creates a new `SimpleTimeZone` from an offset from GMT and a time zone id. ID should be obtained from the `TimeZone.getAvailableIDs` method. You can also define the starting and ending times for daylight savings time. Each period has a starting and ending month (`stMonth`, `endMonth`), day of the week in a month (`stNthDayWeekInMonth`, `endNthDayWeekInMonth`), day of the week (`stDayOfWeek`, `endDayOfWeek`), and time (`stTime`, `endTime`).

methods

```
public Object clone()
```
Returns a copy of this `SimpleTimeZone`.

```
public boolean equals(Object arg)
```
Returns a true value if this `SimpleTimeZone` is equal to arg.

```
public int getOffset(int era, int year, int month, int day, int dayOfWeek, int
millisec)
```
Returns the offset from the Greenwich Mean Time (GMT), taking into account daylight savings time.

```
public int getRawOffset()
```
```
public void setRawOffset(int millisec)
```
Returns or sets the offset from Greenwich Mean Time (GMT) for this `SimpleTimeZone`. These methods do not take daylight savings time into account.

```
public synchronized int hashCode()
```
Returns the hash code for this `SimpleTimeZone`.

```
public boolean inDaylightTime(Date dt)
```
Returns a true value if the specified date falls within Daylight Savings Time.

```
public void setEndRule(int month, int dyWkInMo, int dyWk, int tm)
```
```
public void setStartRule(int month, int dyWkInMo, int dyWk, int tm)
```
Sets the starting and ending times for Daylight Savings Time for this `SimpleTimeZone` to a specified month, day of a week in a month, day of a week, and time (in milliseconds).

```
public void setStartYear(int year)
```
Sets the Daylight Savings starting year for this `SimpleTimeZone`.

```
public boolean useDaylightTime()
```
Returns a true value if this `SimpleTimeZone` uses Daylight Savings Time.

Stack (java.util)

A public class, derived from `Vector`, that represents a last-in-first-out stack.

constructors

```
public Stack()
```
   Creates a new instance of an empty stack.

methods

```
public boolean empty()
```
   Returns a true value if this stack contains no elements.
```
public Object peek() throws EmptyStackException
```
   Returns the item on the top of the stack, but does not remove it.
```
public Object pop() throws EmptyStackException
public Object push(Object obj)
```
   Returns and removes the item on the top of the stack (pop) or pushes a new item onto the stack (push).
```
public int search(Object obj)
```
   Returns the relative position of item obj from the top of the stack, or −1 if the item is not in this stack.

String (java.lang)

A public final class, derived from Object and implementing Serializable, that contains methods for creating and parsing strings. Because the contents of a string cannot be modified, many of the methods return a new string.

constructors

```
public String()
public String(byte[] arg)
public String(byte[] arg, int index, int count)
public String(byte[] arg, String code) throws UnsupportedEncodingException
public String(byte[] arg, int index, int count, String code) throws
UnsupportedEncodingException
```
   Creates a new instance of the String class from the array arg. The parameter index indicates which element of arg is the first character of the resulting string, and the parameter count is the number of characters to add to the new string. The String() method creates a new string of no characters. The characters are converted using code encoding format.
```
public String(char[] chars)
```

```
public String(char[] chars, int index, int count) throws
StringIndexOutOfBoundsException
```
Creates an instance of the String class from the array chars. The parameter index indicates which element of chars is the first character of the resulting string, and the parameter count is the number of characters to add to the new string.

```
public String(String str)
```

```
public String(StringBuffer str)
```
Creates an instance of the String class from the parameter str.

methods

```
public char charAt(int idx) throws StringIndexOutOfBoundsException
```
Returns the character at index idx in the current object. The first character of the source string is at index 0.

```
public int compareTo(String str)
```
Compares the current object to str. If both strings are equal, 0 (zero) is returned. If the current string is lexicographically less than the argument, an int less than zero is returned. If the current string is lexicographically greater than the argument, an int greater than zero is returned.

```
public String concat(String source)
```
Returns the product of the concatenation of argument source to the end of the current object.

```
public static String copyValueOf(char[] arg)
```

```
public static String copyValueOf(char[] arg, int index, int count)
```
Returns a new String that contains the characters of arg, beginning at index index, and of length count.

```
public boolean endsWith(String suff)
```
Returns true if the current object ends with the specified suffix.

```
public boolean equals(Object arg)
```

```
public boolean equalsIgnoreCase(String arg)
```
Returns true if the current object is equal to arg. arg must not be null, and must be of exact length and content as the current object. equalsIgnoreCase disregards the case of the characters.

```
public byte[] getBytes()
```

```
public byte[] getBytes(String enc) throws UnsupportedEncodingException
```
Returns the contents of the current object in an array of bytes decoded with enc. When a decoding format is not present, the platform default it used.

```
public void getChars(int start, int end, char[] dest, int destStart)
```
Copies the contents of the current object starting at index start and ending at end into the character array dest starting at index destStart.

```
public int hashCode()
```
Returns the hash code of the current object.

```
public int indexOf(char c)
public int indexOf(char c, int index)
```
Returns the index of the first occurrence of the character c in the current object not less than index (default of 0). Returns a –1 if there is no such occurrence.

```
public int indexOf(String str)
public int indexOf(String str, int index)
```
Returns the index of the first occurrence of the string str in the current object not less than index (default of 0). Returns a –1 if there is no such occurrence.

```
public String intern()
```
Creates a new canonical string with identical content to this string.

```
public int lastIndexOf(char c)
public int lastIndexOf(char c, int index)
```
Returns the index of the last occurrence of the character c in the current object not less than index (default of 0). Returns a –1 if there is no such occurrence.

```
public int lastIndexOf(String str)
public int lastIndexOf(String str, int index)
```
Returns the index of the last occurrence of the string str in the current object not less than index (default of 0). Returns a –1 if there is no such occurrence.

```
public int length()
```
Returns the integer length of the current object.

```
public boolean regionMatches(boolean case, int cindex, String str, int strindex,
int size)
public boolean regionMatches(int cindex, String str, int strindex, int size)
```
Returns a true result if the subregion of parameter str starting at index strindex and having length size, is identical to a substring of the current object starting at index cindex and having the same length. If case is true, then character case is ignored during the comparisons.

```
public String replace(char oldC, char newC)
```
Returns a new string with all occurrences of the oldC replaced with the newC.

```
public boolean startsWith(String str)
public boolean startsWith(String str, int index)
```
Returns a true if the current object starts with the string str at location index (default of 0).

```
public String substring(int startindex) throws StringIndexOutOfBoundsException
public String substring(int startindex, int lastindex) throws
StringIndexOutOfBoundsException
```
Returns the substring of the current object starting with startindex and ending with lastindex-1 (or the last index of the string in the case of the first method).

```
public char[] toCharArray()
```

`public String toString()`
   Returns the current object as an array of characters or a string. Is present due to the automatic use of the `toString` method in output routines.

`public String toLowerCase()`

`public String toLowerCase(Locale loc)`
   Returns the current object with each character in lower case, taking into account variations of the specified locale (`loc`).

`public String toUpperCase()`

`public String toUpperCase(Locale loc)`
   Returns the current object with each character in uppercase, taking into account variations of the specified locale (`loc`).

`public String trim()`
   Returns the current object with leading and trailing white space removed.

`public static String valueOf(boolean arg)`

`public static String valueOf(char arg)`

`public static String valueOf(char[] arg)`

`public static String valueOf(char[] arg, int index, int size)`

`public static String valueOf(double arg)`

`public static String valueOf(float arg)`

`public static String valueOf(int arg)`

`public static String valueOf(long arg)`

`public static String valueOf(Object arg)`
   Returns a string representation of the parameter `arg`. A starting `index` and specified `size` are permitted.

StringBuffer (java.lang)

A public class, derived from `Object` and implementing `Serializable`, that contains methods for creating, parsing and modifying string buffers. Unlike a `String`, the content and length of a `StringBuffer` can be changed dynamically.

constructors

`public StringBuffer()`

`public StringBuffer(int size) throws NegativeArraySizeException`
   Creates an instance of the `StringBuffer` class that is empty but has an initial capacity of `size` characters (16 by default).

`public StringBuffer(String arg)`
   Creates an instance of the `StringBuffer` class from the string `arg`.

methods

```
public StringBuffer append(boolean arg)
public StringBuffer append(char arg)
public StringBuffer append(char[] arg)
public StringBuffer append(char[] arg, int index, int size)
public StringBuffer append(double arg)
public StringBuffer append(float arg)
public StringBuffer append(int arg)
public StringBuffer append(long arg)
public StringBuffer append(Object arg)
public StringBuffer append(String arg)
```
Returns the current object with the String parameter arg appended to the end. A substring of a character array can be appended by specifying an index and size.

```
public int capacity()
```
Returns the capacity of this StringBuffer.

```
public char charAt(int idx) throws StringIndexOutOfBoundsException
```
Returns the character at the specified index of this StringBuffer.

```
public void ensureCapacity(int min)
```
Sets the minimum capacity of this StringBuffer to be no less than min. The new capacity set by this method may actually be greater than min.

```
public void getChars(int start, int end, char[] dest, int destindex) throws
StringIndexOutOfBoundsException
```
Copies the characters at index start to end from this StringBuffer to dest, starting at index destindex.

```
public StringBuffer insert(int index, boolean arg) throws
StringIndexOutOfBoundsException
public StringBuffer insert(int index, char arg) throws
StringIndexOutOfBoundsException
public StringBuffer insert(int index, char[] arg) throws
StringIndexOutOfBoundsException
public StringBuffer insert(int index, double arg) throws
StringIndexOutOfBoundsException
public StringBuffer insert(int index, float arg) throws
StringIndexOutOfBoundsException
public StringBuffer insert(int index, int arg) throws
StringIndexOutOfBoundsException
public StringBuffer insert(int index, long arg) throws
StringIndexOutOfBoundsException
```

```
public StringBuffer insert(int index, Object arg) throws
StringIndexOutOfBoundsException
public StringBuffer insert(int index, String arg) throws
StringIndexOutOfBoundsException
```
Inserts the string representation of parameter arg into this StringBuffer at index index. Characters to the right of the specified index of this StringBuffer are shifted to the right.

```
public int length()
```
Returns the length of this StringBuffer.

```
public StringBuffer reverse()
```
Returns the value of this StringBuffer with the order of the characters reversed.

```
public void setCharAt(int idx, char c)
```
Sets the character at the specified index to c.

```
public void setLength(int size) throws StringIndexOutOfBoundsException
```
Truncates this StringBuffer, if needed, to the new length of size.

```
public String toString()
```
Returns the String representation of this StringBuffer.

StringTokenizer (java.util)

A public class, derived from Object and implementing Enumeration, that manipulates string values into tokens separated by delimiter characters.

constructors

```
public StringTokenizer(String arg)
public StringTokenizer(String arg, String delims)
public StringTokenizer(String arg, String delims, boolean tokens)
```
Creates a new instance of a StringTokenizer with the string initialized to arg, and utilizing the specified delimiters or the defaults (" \t\n\r": a space, tab, newline, and carriage return). If tokens is true, the delimiters are treated as words within the string and are subject to being returned as tokens.

methods

```
public int countTokens()
```
Returns the number of tokens present in this string tokenizer.

```
public boolean hasMoreElements()
```

```
public boolean hasMoreTokens()
```
Returns a true value if there are more tokens to be returned by this string tokenizer. `hasMoreElements()` is identical to `hasMoreTokens()` and is implemented to complete the implementation of the `Enumerated` interface.
```
public Object nextElement() throws NoSuchElementException
public String nextToken() throws NoSuchElementException
public String nextToken(String delims) throws NoSuchElementException
```
Returns the next token in the string. `nextElement()` is identical to `nextToken()` and is implemented to complete the implementation of the `Enumerated` interface. New delimiters can be specified in the last method, and stay in effect until changed.

System (java.lang)

A public final class, derived from `Object`, that contains the standard input, output, and error streams, as well as various system related methods.

variables and constructs

```
public static PrintStream err
public static InputStream in
public static PrintStream out
```
Constant values that are the standard error output stream (stderr), standard input stream (stdin), and the standard output stream (stdout).

methods

```
public static void arraycopy(Object source, int srcindex, Object dest, int
destindex, int size) throws ArrayIndexOutOfBoundsException, ArrayStoreException
```
Copies a subarray of `size` objects from `source`, starting at index `srcindex`, to `dest` starting at `destindex`.
```
public static long currentTimeMillis()
```
Returns the current system in milliseconds from midnight, January 1st, 1970 UTC.
```
public static void exit(int num) throws SecurityException
```
Exits the program with the status code of num.
```
public static void gc()
```
Executes the `gc` method of the `Runtime` class, which attempts to garbage collect any unused objects, freeing system memory.
```
public static Properties getProperties() throws SecurityException
```

```
public static void setProperties(Properties newprops) throws SecurityException
```
   Returns or sets the current system properties.
```
public static String getProperty(String name) throws SecurityException
public static String getProperty(String name, String default) throws
SecurityException
```
   Returns the system property for name, or returns the value default as a default result if no such
   name exists.
```
public static SecurityManager getSecurityManager()
public static void setSecurityManager(SecurityManager mgr) throws
SecurityException
```
   Returns or sets the security manager for the current application. If no security manager has been
   initialized, then a null value is returned by the get method.
```
public static int identityHashCode(Object arg)
```
   Returns the hash code for the specified object. This will return the default hash code, in the event
   that the object's hashCode method has been overridden.
```
public static void load(String name) throws UnsatisfiedLinkError,
SecurityException
```
   Loads name as a dynamic library.
```
public static void loadLibrary(String name) throws UnsatisfiedLinkError,
SecurityException
```
   Loads name as a system library.
```
public static void runFinalization()
```
   Requests that the Java Virtual Machine execute the finalize method on any outstanding objects.
```
public static void runFinalizersOnExit(boolean toggle)
```
   Allows the execution of the finalizer methods for all objects, when toggle is true.
```
public static void setErr(PrintStream strm)
public static void setIn(InputStream strm)
public static void setOut(PrintStream strm)
```
   Reassigns the error stream, input stream, or output stream to strm.

SystemColor (java.awt)

A public final class, derived from Color and implementing Serializable, that represents the current
window system color for the current system. If the user changes the window system colors for this system and the window system can update the new color selection, these color values will change as well.

variables and constructs

```
public final static int ACTIVE_CAPTION
```
   Constant index to the active caption color in the system color array.

```
public final static int ACTIVE_CAPTION_BORDER
public final static int ACTIVE_CAPTION_TEXT
```
Constant indices to the active caption border and text colors in the system color array.
```
public final static int CONTROL
```
Constant index to the control color in the system color array.
```
public final static int CONTROL_DK_SHADOW
public final static int CONTROL_SHADOW
```
Constant indices to the control shadow and control dark shadow colors in the system color array.
```
public final static int CONTROL_HIGHLIGHT
public final static int CONTROL_LT_HIGHLIGHT
```
Constant indices to the control highlight and light highlight colors in the system color array.
```
public final static int CONTROL_TEXT
```
Constant index to the control text color in the system color array.
```
public final static int DESKTOP
```
Constant index to the desktop color in the system color array.
```
public final static int INACTIVE_CAPTION
```
Constant index to the inactive caption color in the system color array.
```
public final static int INACTIVE_CAPTION_BORDER
public final static int INACTIVE_CAPTION_TEXT
```
Constant indices to the inactive caption border and text colors in the system color array.
```
public final static int INFO
```
Constant index to the information (help) text background color in the system color array.
```
public final static int INFO_TEXT
public final static int MENU_TEXT
```
Constant indices to the information (help) and menu text colors in the system color array.
```
public final static int NUM_COLORS
```
Constant value that holds the number of colors in the system color array.
```
public final static int SCROLLBAR
```
Constant index to the scrollbar background color in the system color array.
```
public final static int TEXT
```
Constant index to the background color of text components in the system color array.
```
public final static int TEXT_HIGHLIGHT
public final static int TEXT_HIGHLIGHT_TEXT
```
Constant indices to the background and text colors for highlighted text in the system color array.
```
public final static int TEXT_INACTIVE_TEXT
```
Constant index to the inactive text color in the system color array.
```
public final static int TEXT_TEXT
```
Constant index to the color of text components in the system color array.

```
public final static int WINDOW
```
Constant index to the background color of windows in the system color array.
```
public final static int WINDOW_BORDER
public final static int WINDOW_TEXT
```
Constant indices to the border and text colors of windows in the system color array.
```
public final static SystemColor activeCaption
```
The system's background color for window border captions.
```
public final static SystemColor activeCaptionBorder
public final static SystemColor activeCaptionText
```
The system's border and text colors for window border captions.
```
public final static SystemColor control
```
The system's color for window control objects.
```
public final static SystemColor controlDkShadow
public final static SystemColor controlShadow
```
The system's dark shadow and regular shadow colors for control objects.
```
public final static SystemColor controlHighlight
public final static SystemColor controlLtHighlight
```
The system's highlight and light highlight colors for control objects.
```
public final static SystemColor controlText
```
The system's text color for control objects.
```
public final static SystemColor desktop
```
The system's color of the desktop background.
```
public final static SystemColor inactiveCaption
```
The system's background color for inactive caption areas of window borders.
```
public final static SystemColor inactiveCaptionBorder
public final static SystemColor inactiveCaptionText
```
The system's border and text colors for inactive caption areas of window borders.
```
public final static SystemColor info
```
The system's background color for information (help) text.
```
public final static SystemColor infoText
```
The system's text color for information (help) text.
```
public final static SystemColor menu
```
The system's background color for menus.
```
public final static SystemColor menuText
```
The system's text color for menus.
```
public final static SystemColor scrollbar
```
The system's background color for scrollbars.

`public final static SystemColor text`
The system's color for text components.

`public final static SystemColor textHighlight`
The system's background color for highlighted text.

`public final static SystemColor textHighlightText`
`public final static SystemColor textInactiveText`
The system's text color for highlighted and inactive text.

`public final static SystemColor textText`
The system's text color for text components.

`public final static SystemColor window`
The system's background color for windows.

`public final static SystemColor windowBorder`
`public final static SystemColor windowText`
The system's border and text colors for windows.

methods

`public int getRGB()`
Returns the RGB values of this `SystemColor`'s symbolic color.

`public String toString()`
Returns a string representation of this `SystemColor`'s values.

Thread (java.lang)

A public class, derived from `Object` and implementing `Runnable`, that handles the implementation and management of Java execution threads.

variables and constructs

`public final static int MAX_PRIORITY`
`public final static int MIN_PRIORITY`
`public final static int NORM_PRIORITY`
Constant values that contain the maximum (10), minimum (1), and normal (6) priority values a thread can have.

constructors

`public Thread()`
Creates a new instance of a thread.

```
public Thread(Runnable arg)
```
Creates a new instance of a thread. `arg` specifies which object's run method is invoked to start the thread.

```
public Thread(String str)
```

```
public Thread(Runnable arg, String str)
```
Creates a new instance of a thread, named `str`. `arg` specifies which object's run method is invoked to start the thread.

```
public Thread(ThreadGroup tgrp, String str) throws SecurityException
```

```
public Thread(ThreadGroup tgrp, Runnable arg) throws SecurityException
```

```
public Thread(ThreadGroup tgrp, Runnable arg, String str) throws
SecurityException
```
Creates a new instance of a thread, named `str` and belonging to thread group `tgrp`. The `arg` parameter specifies which object's run method is invoked to start the thread.

methods

```
public static int activeCount()
```
Returns the number of active threads in this thread's group.

```
public void checkAccess() throws SecurityException
```
Validates that the current executing thread has permission to modify this thread.

```
public static Thread currentThread()
```
Returns the currently executing thread.

```
public void destroy()
```
Destroys this thread.

```
public static void dumpStack()
```
Dumps a trace of the stack for the current thread.

```
public static int enumerate(Thread[] dest)
```
Copies each of the members of this thread's group into the thread array `dest`.

```
public final String getName()
```

```
public final int getPriority()
```

```
public final ThreadGroup getThreadGroup()
```
Returns the name, priority, or thread group of this thread.

```
public void interrupt()
```
Interrupts this thread's execution.

```
public static boolean interrupted()
```
Returns a true value if the current thread's execution has been interrupted.

```
public final boolean isAlive()
```

```
public boolean isInterrupted()
```
Returns a true value if this thread's execution is alive or has been interrupted.

```
public final boolean isDaemon()
```
Returns a true value if this thread is a daemon thread.
```
public final void join() throws InterruptedException
public final void join(long msec) throws InterruptedException
public final void join(long msec, int nsec) throws InterruptedException
```
Waits up to msec milliseconds and nsec nanoseconds for this thread to die. The join() method waits forever for this thread to die.
```
public void run()
```
Method containing the main body of the executing thread code. Run methods can run concurrently with other thread run methods.
```
public final void setDaemon(boolean flag) throws IllegalThreadStateException
```
Sets this thread as a daemon thread, if flag is true.
```
public final void setName(String str) throws SecurityException
public final void setPriority(int val) throws SecurityException
```
Sets the name of this thread to str or the priority to val.
```
public static void sleep(long msec) throws InterruptedException
public static void sleep(long msec, int nsec) throws InterruptedException
```
Causes the current thread to sleep for msec milliseconds and nsec nanoseconds.
```
public void start() throws IllegalThreadStateException
```
Start this thread's execution, calling this thread's run method.
```
public String toString()
```
Returns a string representation of this thread.
```
public static void yield()
```
Causes the currently executing thread to pause in execution, allowing other threads to run.

Throwable (java.lang)

A public class, derived from Object and implementing Serializable, that is the superclass of all of the errors and exceptions thrown.

constructors
```
public Throwable()
public Throwable(String str)
```
Creates a new instance of a throwable object with the specified message (str) or none present.

methods
```
public Throwable fillInStackTrace()
```
Fills in the executable stack trace for this throwable object.

```
public String getLocalizedMessage()
```
Returns a locale specific description of this object. Locale specific messages should override this method; otherwise, the same message that the `getMessage` method produces will be returned.
```
public String getMessage()
```
Returns the detail message for this throwable.
```
public void printStackTrace()
```
```
public void printStackTrace(PrintStream stream)
```
```
public void printStackTrace(PrintWriter stream)
```
Prints the stack trace for this throwable to the standard error stream or to the specified `stream`.
```
public String toString()
```
Returns a string representation of this throwable object.

Timer (`javax.swing`)

A public class, derived from `Object` and implementing `Serializable`, that fires an action event after a specified delay. Often used to control animations.

constructors
```
public Timer(int delay, ActionListener listener)
```
Creates a timer that notifies the specified action listener every `delay` milliseconds.

methods
```
public void addActionListener(ActionListener listener)
```
Adds the specified action listener to this timer.
```
public int getDelay()
```
```
public void setDelay(int delay)
```
Gets or sets this timer's delay (in milliseconds).
```
public void start()
```
```
public void stop()
```
Starts or stops this timer.
```
public boolean isRunning()
```
Returns true if this timer is currently running.

TimeZone (`java.util`)

A public abstract class, derived from `Object` and implementing `Serializable` and `Cloneable`, that represents an amount of time offset from GMT that results in local time. Functionality is provided to allow for Daylight Savings Time within a time zone.

methods

`clone()`
   Returns a copy of this `TimeZone`.

`public static synchronized String[] getAvailableIDs()`

`public static synchronized String[] getAvailableIDs(int offset)`
   Returns a list of all of the supported time zone ids, or only those for a specified time zone offset.

`public static synchronized TimeZone getDefault()`

`public static synchronized void setDefault(TimeZone tz)`
   Returns or sets the default time zone.

`public String getID()`
   Returns the id of this time zone.

`public abstract int getOffset(int era, int year, int month, int day, int dayOfWeek, int milliseconds)`
   Returns the offset from the Greenwich Mean Time (GMT), taking into account daylight savings time.

`public abstract int getRawOffset()`

`public abstract void setRawOffset(int millisec)`
   Returns or sets the offset from Greenwich Mean Time (GMT) for this `SimpleTimeZone`. These methods do not take daylight savings time into account.

`public static synchronized TimeZone getTimeZone(String id)`
   Returns the time zone corresponding to the specified id value.

`public abstract boolean inDaylightTime(Date dt)`
   Returns a true result if the specified date falls within the Daylight Savings Time for this `TimeZone`.

`public void setID(String id)`
   Sets the id value of this `TimeZone`.

`public abstract boolean useDaylightTime()`
   Returns a true value if this `TimeZone` uses Daylight Savings Time.

URL (java.net)

A public final class, derived from `Object` and implementing `Serializable`, that represents a Web Uniform Resource Locator (URL).

constructors

`public URL(String arg) throws MalformedURLException`

`public URL(URL url, String type) throws MalformedURLException`
   Creates a URL instance from a string argument, or by parsing a `type` (http, gopher, ftp) and the remaining base.

`public URL(String proto, String source, int num, String doc) throws MalformedURLException`

`public URL(String proto, String source, String doc) throws MalformedURLException`
 Creates a URL instance using a defined protocol (proto), source system, destination port num, and document (doc).

methods

`public boolean equals(Object obj)`
 Returns a true value if this URL is equal in all respects (protocol, source, port, and document) to obj.

`public final Object getContent() throws IOException`
 Returns the retrieved contents as an Object.

`public String getFile()`

`public String getRef()`
 Returns the name of the file (document) or its anchor this URL will attempt to retrieve.

`public String getHost()`

`public int getPort()`
 Returns the name of the host (source) or the port this URL will attempt to connect to.

`public String getProtocol()`
 Returns the protocol this URL will use in retrieving the data.

`public int hashCode()`
 Returns the hash code for this URL.

`public URLConnection openConnection() throws IOException`

`public final InputStream openStream() throws IOException`
 Returns a connection to this URL and returns the connection or a stream.

`public boolean sameFile(URL arg)`
 Returns a true value if this URL retrieves the same file as the arg URL.

`protected void set(String proto, String source, int num, String doc, String anchor)`
 Sets the protocol (proto), source, port num, file (doc) and reference (anchor) for this URL.

`public static void setURLStreamHandlerFactory(URLStreamHandlerFactory fac) throws Error`
 Sets the URL StreamHandlerFactory for this application to fac.

`public String toExternalForm()`

`public String toString()`
 Returns a string representation of this URL.

Vector (java.util)

A public class, derived from Object and implementing Serializable and Cloneable, that manages an array of objects. Elements can be added or removed from this list and the size of the list can change dynamically.

variables and constructs

`protected int capacityIncrement`
The amount of element spaces to be added to the vector each time that an increase must occur. A capacityIncrement of 0 indicates that the list will double in size at every resizing.

`protected int elementCount`

`protected Object elementData[ ]`
The number of elements and the array containing the elements currently in this Vector.

constructors

`public Vector( )`

`public Vector(int size)`

`public Vector(int size, int incr)`
Creates a new instance of a vector with an initial size of size (or using the default of 10). An initial capacityIncrement can also be specified.

methods

`public final void addElement(Object arg)`

`public final void insertElementAt(Object arg, int index) throws ArrayIndexOutOfBoundsException`
Adds element arg to the end of this Vector or at a specific index. The capacity of the vector is adjusted if needed.

`public final int capacity( )`

`public final void ensureCapacity(int size)`
Returns the current capacity of this Vector, or ensures that it can contain at least size elements

`public Object clone( )`
Returns the clone of this Vector.

`public final boolean contains(Object arg)`
Returns a true value if this Vector contains object arg.

`public final void copyInto(Object[ ] dest)`
Copies each of the elements of this Vector into the array dest.

`public final Object elementAt(int index) throws ArrayIndexOutOfBoundsException`
Returns the element at location index from this Vector.

```
public final Enumeration elements()
```
Returns an Enumeration of the elements in this Vector.
```
public final Object firstElement() throws NoSuchElementException
public final Object lastElement() throws NoSuchElementException
```
Returns the first or last element in this Vector.
```
public final int indexOf(Object arg)
public final int indexOf(Object arg, int index)
```
Returns the index of the first occurrence of element arg, starting at index. A −1 value is returned if the element is not found.
```
public final boolean isEmpty()
```
Returns a true value if this Vector contains no elements.
```
public final int lastIndexOf(Object arg)
public final int lastIndexOf(Object arg, int index)
```
Returns the first index that object arg occurs at in this Vector, starting a backwards search at the specified index. If the object is not located, a −1 is returned.
```
public final void removeAllElements()
public final boolean removeElement(Object arg)
public final void removeElementAt(int index) throws
ArrayIndexOutOfBoundsException
```
Removes element arg and returns a true value. If the object requested is not located, a false value is returned. An element can also be removed at a specific index value, or all elements can be removed.
```
public final void setElementAt(Object arg, int index) throws
ArrayIndexOutOfBoundsException
```
Sets the element at the specified index equal to object arg.
```
public final void setSize(int size)
```
Sets the size of this Vector to size.
```
public final int size()
```
Returns the number of elements in this Vector.
```
public final String toString()
```
Returns a string representation of this Vector.
```
public final void trimToSize()
```
Reduces the size of this Vector to contain all of the elements present.

Void (java.lang)

An uninstantiable class that acts as a placeholder for the primitive void type in the Class object.

variables and constructs

```
public final static Class TYPE
```
The Void constant value of the void type class.

Window (java.awt)

A public class, derived from Container, that creates a graphical area that has no borders or menus and can be used to contain AWT components.

constructors

```
public Window(Frame frm)
```
Creates a new instance of a window that has a parent frame (frm). The window is initially not visible.

methods

```
public void addNotify()
```
Creates this window's peer.

```
public synchronized void addWindowListener(WindowListener listener)
public synchronized void removeWindowListener(WindowListener listener)
```
Removes or adds the specified window listener (listener) for this window.

```
public void dispose()
```
Removes this window and deletes any resources used by this window.

```
public Component getFocusOwner()
```
Returns the component from this active window that currently has the focus.

```
public Locale getLocale()
```
Returns the locale for this window.

```
public Toolkit getToolkit()
```
Returns the toolkit for this window.

```
public final String getWarningString()
```
Returns the warning string for this window.

```
public boolean isShowing()
```
Returns a true value if this window is currently visible on the screen.

```
public void pack()
```
Causes all of the components of this window to be laid out according to their preferred size.

```
protected void processEvent(AWTEvent event)
```
Processes the specified event for this window. If the event is a WindowEvent, then this method calls the process WindowEvent method of this window, otherwise it will call the parent class' processEvent method.

```
protected void processWindowEvent(WindowEvent event)
```
Handles any WindowEvent (event) generated on this window, and passes them to a registered listener for that event.
```
public void show()
```
Makes this window visible to the user and brings it to the front (on top of other windows).
```
public void toBack()
void toFront()
```
Sends this window to the back or front of other windows currently displayed on the screen.

WindowAdapter (java.awt.event)

A public abstract class, derived from Object and implementing WindowListener, that permits a derived class to override the predefined no-op AWT window events.

constructors

```
public WindowAdapter()
```
Creates a new instance of a WindowAdapter.

methods

```
public void windowActivated(WindowEvent event)
public void windowClosed(WindowEvent event)
public void windowClosing(WindowEvent event)
public void windowDeactivated(WindowEvent event)
public void windowDeiconified(WindowEvent event)
public void windowIconified(WindowEvent event)
public void windowOpened(WindowEvent event)
```
Empty methods that should be overridden in order to implement event handling for window events.

WindowEvent (java.awt.event)

A public class, derived from ComponentEvent, that describes a particular AWT window-based event.

variables and constructs

```
public static final int WINDOW_ACTIVATED
public static final int WINDOW_CLOSED
public static final int WINDOW_CLOSING
public static final int WINDOW_DEACTIVATED
```

```
public static final int WINDOW_DEICONIFIED
public static final int WINDOW_FIRST
public static final int WINDOW_ICONIFIED
public static final int WINDOW_LAST
public static final int WINDOW_OPENED
```
Constant values which represent a variety of window event types.

constructors

```
public WindowEvent(Window src, int type)
```
Creates a new instance of a `WindowEvent` from a specified source window and having a specific event type.

methods

```
public Window getWindow()
```
Returns the source window that this event was triggered in.

```
public String paramString()
```
Returns a string containing the parameters for this `WindowEvent`.

symbols

f

g

h

Terms and conditions of the license & export for Java^{TM} 2 SDK, Standard Edition 1.4.0

Sun Microsystems, Inc.

Binary Code License Agreement

READ THE TERMS OF THIS AGREEMENT AND ANY PROVIDED SUP-PLEMENTAL LICENSE TERMS (COLLECTIVELY "AGREEMENT") CARE-FULLY BEFORE OPENING THE SOFTWARE MEDIA PACKAGE. BY OPEN-ING THE SOFTWARE MEDIA PACKAGE, YOU AGREE TO THE TERMS OF THIS AGREEMENT. IF YOU ARE ACCESSING THE SOFTWARE ELEC-TRONICALLY, INDICATE YOUR ACCEPTANCE OF THESE TERMS BY SELECTING THE "ACCEPT" BUTTON AT THE END OF THIS AGREE-MENT. IF YOU DO NOT AGREE TO ALL THESE TERMS, PROMPTLY RETURN THE UNUSED SOFTWARE TO YOUR PLACE OF PURCHASE FOR A REFUND OR, IF THE SOFTWARE IS ACCESSED ELECTRONICALLY, SELECT THE "DECLINE" BUTTON AT THE END OF THIS AGREEMENT.

1. LICENSE TO USE. Sun grants you a non-exclusive and non-transferable license for the internal use only of the accompanying software and documentation and any error corrections provided by Sun (collectively "Software"), by the number of users and the class of computer hardware for which the corresponding fee has been paid.

2. RESTRICTIONS. Software is confidential and copyrighted. Title to Software and all associated intellectual property rights is retained by Sun and/or its licensors. Except as specifically authorized in any Supplemental License Terms, you may not make copies of Software, other than a single copy of Software for archival purposes. Unless enforcement is prohibited by applicable law, you may not modify, decompile, or reverse engineer Software. You acknowledge that Software is not designed, licensed or intended for use in the design, construction, operation or maintenance of any nuclear facility. Sun disclaims any express or implied warranty of fitness for such uses. No right, title or interest in or to any trademark, service mark, logo or trade name of Sun or its licensors is granted under this Agreement.

3. LIMITED WARRANTY. Sun warrants to you that for a period of ninety (90) days from the date of purchase, as evidenced by a copy of the receipt, the media on which Software is furnished (if any) will be free of defects in materials and workmanship under normal use. Except for the foregoing, Software is provided "AS IS." Your exclusive remedy and Sun's entire liability under this limited warranty will be at Sun's option to replace Software media or refund the fee paid for Software.

4. DISCLAIMER OF WARRANTY. UNLESS SPECIFIED IN THIS AGREE-MENT, ALL EXPRESS OR IMPLIED CONDITIONS, REPRESENTATIONS AND WARRANTIES, INCLUDING ANY IMPLIED WARRANTY OF MER-CHANTABILITY, FITNESS FOR A PARTICULAR PURPOSE OR NON-INFRINGEMENT ARE DISCLAIMED, EXCEPT TO THE EXTENT THAT THESE DISCLAIMERS ARE HELD TO BE LEGALLY INVALID.

5. LIMITATION OF LIABILITY. TO THE EXTENT NOT PROHIBITED BY LAW, IN NO EVENT WILL SUN OR ITS LICENSORS BE LIABLE FOR ANY LOST REVENUE, PROFIT OR DATA, OR FOR SPECIAL, INDIRECT, CON-SEQUENTIAL, INCIDENTAL OR PUNITIVE DAMAGES, HOWEVER CAUSED REGARDLESS OF THE THEORY OF LIABILITY, ARISING OUT OF OR RELATED TO THE USE OF OR INABILITY TO USE SOFTWARE, EVEN IF SUN HAS BEEN ADVISED OF THE POSSIBILITY OF SUCH DAMAGES. In no event will Sun's liability to you, whether in contract, tort (including negligence), or otherwise, exceed the amount paid by you for Software under this Agreement. The foregoing limitations will apply even if the above stated warranty fails of its essential purpose.

6. Termination. This Agreement is effective until terminated. You may terminate this Agreement at any time by destroying all copies of Software. This Agreement will terminate immediately without notice from Sun if you fail to comply with any provision of this Agreement. Upon Termination, you must destroy all copies of Software.

7. Export Regulations. All Software and technical data delivered under this Agreement are subject to US export control laws and may be subject to export or import regulations in other countries. You agree to comply strictly with all such laws and regulations and acknowledge that you have the responsibility to obtain such licenses to export, re-export, or import as may be required after delivery to you.

8. U.S. Government Restricted Rights. If Software is being acquired by or on behalf of the U.S. Government or by a U.S. Government prime contractor or sub-contractor (at any tier), then the Government's rights in Software and accompanying documentation will be only as set forth in this Agreement; this is in accordance with 48 CFR 227.7201 through 227.7202-4 (for Department of Defense (DOD) acquisitions) and with 48 CFR 2.101 and 12.212 (for non-DOD acquisitions).

9. Governing Law. Any action related to this Agreement will be governed by California law and controlling U.S. federal law. No choice of law rules of any jurisdiction will apply.

10. Severability. If any provision of this Agreement is held to be unenforceable, this Agreement will remain in effect with the provision omitted, unless omission would frustrate the intent of the parties, in which case this Agreement will immediately terminate.

11. Integration. This Agreement is the entire agreement between you and Sun relating to its subject matter. It supersedes all prior or contemporaneous oral or written communications, proposals, representations and warranties and prevails over any conflicting or additional terms of any quote, order, acknowledgment, or other communication between the parties relating to its subject matter during the term of this Agreement. No modification of this Agreement will be binding, unless in writing and signed by an authorized representative of each party.

JAVA™ 2 SOFTWARE DEVELOPMENT KIT (J2SDK), STANDARD EDITION, VERSION 1.4.X

SUPPLEMENTAL LICENSE TERMS

These supplemental license terms ("Supplemental Terms") add to or modify the terms of the Binary Code License Agreement (collectively, the "Agreement"). Capitalized terms not defined in these Supplemental Terms shall have the same meanings ascribed to them in the Agreement. These Supplemental Terms shall supersede any inconsistent or conflicting terms in the Agreement, or in any license contained within the Software.

1. Software Internal Use and Development License Grant. Subject to the terms and conditions of this Agreement, including, but not limited to Section 4 (Java Technology Restrictions) of these Supplemental Terms, Sun grants you a non-exclusive, non-transferable, limited license to reproduce internally and use internally the binary form of the Software complete and unmodified for the sole purpose of designing, developing and testing your Java applets and applications intended to run on the Java platform ("Programs").

2. License to Distribute Software. Subject to the terms and conditions of this Agreement, including, but not limited to Section 4 (Java Technology Restrictions) of these Supplemental Terms, Sun grants you a non-exclusive, non-transferable, limited license to reproduce and distribute the Software, provided that (i) you distribute the Software complete and unmodified (unless otherwise specified in the applicable README file) and only bundled as part of, and for the sole purpose of running, your Programs, (ii) the Programs add significant and primary functionality to the Software, (iii) you do not distribute additional software intended to replace any component(s) of the Software (unless otherwise specified in the applicable README file), (iv) you do not remove or alter any proprietary legends or notices contained in the Software, (v) you only distribute the Software

subject to a license agreement that protects Sun's interests consistent with the terms contained in this Agreement, and (vi) you agree to defend and indemnify Sun and its licensors from and against any damages, costs, liabilities, settlement amounts and/or expenses (including attorneys' fees) incurred in connection with any claim, lawsuit or action by any third party that arises or results from the use or distribution of any and all Programs and/or Software. (vi) include the following statement as part of product documentation (whether hard copy or electronic), as a part of a copyright page or proprietary rights notice page, in an "About" box or in any other form reasonably designed to make the statement visible to users of the Software: "This product includes code licensed from RSA Security, Inc.", and (vii) include the statement, "Some portions licensed from IBM are available at http://oss.software.ibm.com/icu4j/".

3. License to Distribute Redistributables. Subject to the terms and conditions of this Agreement, including but not limited to Section 4 (Java Technology Restrictions) of these Supplemental Terms, Sun grants you a non-exclusive, nontransferable, limited license to reproduce and distribute those files specifically identified as redistributable in the Software "README" file ("Redistributables") provided that: (i) you distribute the Redistributables complete and unmodified (unless otherwise specified in the applicable README file), and only bundled as part of Programs, (ii) you do not distribute additional software intended to supersede any component(s) of the Redistributables (unless otherwise specified in the applicable README file), (iii) you do not remove or alter any proprietary legends or notices contained in or on the Redistributables, (iv) you only distribute the Redistributables pursuant to a license agreement that protects Sun's interests consistent with the terms contained in the Agreement, (v) you agree to defend and indemnify Sun and its licensors from and against any damages, costs, liabilities, settlement amounts and/or expenses (including attorneys' fees) incurred in connection with any claim, lawsuit or action by any third party that arises or results from the use or distribution of any and all Programs and/or Software, (vi) include the following statement as part of product documentation (whether hard copy or electronic), as a part of a copyright page or proprietary rights notice page, in an "About" box or in any other form reasonably designed to make the statement visible to users of the Software: "This product includes code licensed from RSA Security, Inc.", and (vii) include the statement, "Some portions licensed from IBM are available at http://oss.software.ibm.com/icu4j/".

4. Java Technology Restrictions. You may not modify the Java Platform Interface ("JPI", identified as classes contained within the "java" package or any subpackages of the "java" package), by creating additional classes within the JPI or otherwise causing the addition to or modification of the classes in the JPI. In the

event that you create an additional class and associated API(s) which (i) extends the functionality of the Java platform, and (ii) is exposed to third party software developers for the purpose of developing additional software which invokes such additional API, you must promptly publish broadly an accurate specification for such API for free use by all developers. You may not create, or authorize your licensees to create, additional classes, interfaces, or subpackages that are in any way identified as "java," "javax," "sun" or similar convention as specified by Sun in any naming convention designation.

5. Notice of Automatic Software Updates from Sun. You acknowledge that the Software may automatically download, install, and execute applets, applications, software extensions, and updated versions of the Software from Sun ("Software Updates"), which may require you to accept updated terms and conditions for installation. If additional terms and conditions are not presented on installation, the Software Updates will be considered part of the Software and subject to the terms and conditions of the Agreement.

6. Notice of Automatic Downloads. You acknowledge that, by your use of the Software and/or by requesting services that require use of the Software, the Software may automatically download, install, and execute software applications from sources other than Sun ("Other Software"). Sun makes no representations of a relationship of any kind to licensors of Other Software. TO THE EXTENT NOT PROHIBITED BY LAW, IN NO EVENT WILL SUN OR ITS LICENSORS BE LIABLE FOR ANY LOST REVENUE, PROFIT OR DATA, OR FOR SPECIAL, INDIRECT, CONSEQUENTIAL, INCIDENTAL OR PUNITIVE DAMAGES, HOWEVER CAUSED REGARDLESS OF THE THEORY OF LIABILITY, ARISING OUT OF OR RELATED TO THE USE OF OR INABILITY TO USE OTHER SOFTWARE, EVEN IF SUN HAS BEEN ADVISED OF THE POSSIBILITY OF SUCH DAMAGES.

7. Trademarks and Logos. You acknowledge and agree as between you and Sun that Sun owns the SUN, SOLARIS, JAVA, JINI, FORTE, and iPLANET trademarks and all SUN, SOLARIS, JAVA, JINI, FORTE, and iPLANET-related trademarks, service marks, logos and other brand designations ("Sun Marks"), and you agree to comply with the Sun Trademark and Logo Usage Requirements currently located at http://www.sun.com/policies/trademarks. Any use you make of the Sun Marks inures to Sun's benefit.

8. Source Code. Software may contain source code that is provided solely for reference purposes pursuant to the terms of this Agreement. Source code may not be redistributed unless expressly provided for in this Agreement.

9. Termination for Infringement. Either party may terminate this Agreement immediately should any Software become, or in either party's opinion be likely to become, the subject of a claim of infringement of any intellectual property right.

For inquiries please contact: Sun Microsystems, Inc. 901 San Antonio Road, Palo Alto, California 94303

(LFI#109998/Form ID#011801)